Ubuntu® Linux®
Bible

Ubuntu® Linux®
BIBLE

David Clinton

Christopher Negus

WILEY

Published by

John Wiley & Sons, Inc.
10475 Crosspoint Boulevard
Indianapolis, IN 46256
www.wiley.com

Copyright © 2021 by John Wiley & Sons, Inc., Indianapolis, Indiana

Published simultaneously in Canada

ISBN: 978-1-119-72233-5

ISBN: 978-1-119-72234-2 (ebk)

ISBN: 978-1-119-72235-9 (ebk)

Manufactured in the United States of America

For general information on our other products and services please contact our Customer Care Department within the United States at (877) 762-2974, outside the United States at (317) 572-3993 or fax (317) 572-4002.

Wiley publishes in a variety of print and electronic formats and by print-on-demand. Some material included with standard print versions of this book may not be included in e-books or in print-on-demand. If this book refers to media such as a CD or DVD that is not included in the version you purchased, you may download this material at booksupport.wiley.com. For more information about Wiley products, visit www.wiley.com.

Library of Congress Control Number: 2020945959

SKY10021644_100920

About the Authors

David Clinton is a Linux server admin and AWS Solutions Architect who has worked with IT infrastructure in both academic and enterprise environments. He's administrated physical systems, containers, and networks using many Ubuntu flavors for more than a dozen years. He has authored technology books—including *AWS Certified Solutions Architect Study Guide: Associate SAA-C01 Exam* (Sybex, 2020)—and created tens of video courses for Pluralsight teaching Amazon Web Services and Linux administration, server virtualization, and IT security.

In a previous life, David spent 20 years as a high school teacher. He currently lives in Toronto, Canada, with his wife and family and can be reached through his website: www.bootstrap-it.com.

Chris Negus is a principal technical writer for Red Hat, Inc. In his decades of working with Linux and UNIX, Chris has taught hundreds of IT professionals to become certified Linux engineers, and he has written scores of documents on everything from Linux to virtualization to cloud computing and containerization.

Chris has also written and contributed to dozens of books on Linux and UNIX, including the *Linux Bible* (all editions), *Linux Troubleshooting Bible*, *Red Hat Linux Bible* (all editions), *Docker Containers*, *CentOS Bible*, *Fedora Bible*, *Linux Toys*, and *Linux Toys II*. Chris also co-authored several books for the Linux Toolbox series for power users: *Ubuntu Linux Toolbox*, *Fedora Linux Toolbox*, *SUSE Linux Toolbox*, *Mac OS X Toolbox*, and *BSD UNIX Toolbox*.

Before becoming an author and educator, Chris worked for eight years with the organization at AT&T that developed the UNIX operating system before moving to Utah to help contribute to Novell's UnixWare project in the early 1990s. When not writing about Linux, Chris enjoys playing soccer, hanging out with his wife, Sheree, and spending what time he can with his sons, Seth and Caleb.

About the Technical Editor

Jason W. Eckert is an experienced technical trainer, consultant, and best-selling author in the technology industry. With 45 industry certifications, over 30 years of technology and programming experience, 4 published apps, and 25 published textbooks covering topics such as UNIX, Linux, Security, Windows Server, Microsoft Exchange Server, PowerShell, BlackBerry Enterprise Server, and Video Game Development, Mr. Eckert brings his expertise to every class that he teaches at triOS College. He was also named 2019 Outstanding Train-the-Trainer from the Computing Technology Industry Association (CompTIA). For more information about Mr. Eckert, visit www.jasoneckert.net.

Acknowledgments

Looking through the chapters of this book forces me to wonder at the size and ambition of the world of open source software. And that makes me think about all the thousands of developers, admins, architects, and—yes—writers who make this vast universe possible. This book is a testament to the hard work and community spirit of those individuals.

I would like to thank my wife for all her help and support through the long and demanding process of writing these books. And, once again, I'm indebted to all the great people at Wiley who helped me turn a plain old manuscript into a great teaching tool.

—David Clinton

When I was hired at Red Hat about a dozen years ago, I didn't know that the organization would grow to about seven times its size, be bought by IBM for $34 billion, and (so far) still maintain the spirit of openness and excitement that it had when I first signed on. Every day when I come to work, I interact with many of the greatest Linux and cloud developers, testers, instructors, and support professionals in the world.

While I can't thank everyone individually, there are a few people that I want to acknowledge in particular. I have the good fortune to take on so many cool and challenging projects because of the freedom that I receive from the people to whom I report at work. They include Michelle Bearer, Dawn Eisner, and Sam Knuth. Sam in particular has had my back and encouraged my work for more than a decade.

In my daily work, I want to give a shout out to my incredibly talented colleagues Scott McCarty, Ben Breard, Laurie Friedman, Dave Darrah, Micah Abbott, Steve Milner, Ian McLeod, Tom McKay, Joey Schorr, Bill Dettelback, Richa Marwaha, and Dirk Herrmann. Finally, a special thank you to Vikram Goyal, who luckily lives in Australia, so he is always available to bail me out when I blow up git in the middle of the night.

When it comes to support for writing this book, I have had the luxury of an excellent technical editor: Jason Eckert. He also worked on my most recent edition of *The Linux Bible*, and his broad experience with Linux systems has helped immensely. As for Devon Lewis, Kelly Talbot, and the people at Wiley, thanks for letting me continue to develop and improve this book over the years. Thanks also to Margot Maley Hutchison from Waterside Productions for contracting the book for me with Wiley and always looking out for my best interests.

Finally, thanks to my wife, Sheree, for sharing her life with me and doing such a great job raising Seth and Caleb.

—Christopher Negus

Contents at a Glance

Contents

Contents

Part II: Becoming a Linux Power User   43

Contents

Contents

Contents

Contents

Introduction

You can't learn Ubuntu without using it. But if you're ready for some serious hands-on research and experimentation, you can go a long way with this book. The *Ubuntu Linux Bible* is based on the 10th edition of *Linux Bible*, but has been refocused to ensure everything will work specifically on Ubuntu "right out of the box."

Ubuntu may be the world's most popular all-purpose Linux distribution. Canonical, the company that stands behind Ubuntu, reports that "Ubuntu powers millions of PCs worldwide." It describes it as "the world's most popular operating system across public clouds and OpenStack clouds" and "the #1 OS for containers." In fact, as of this writing, of the more than a million virtual server instances currently running on the Amazon Web Services cloud, more than 32 percent are standalone Ubuntu installations (the total number, when you include Bitnami stacks, is probably closer to 60 percent). Compare that to Microsoft Windows share of 6 percent and the 2 percent attributed to Red Hat Enterprise Linux (see www.thecloudmarket .com/stats).

Ubuntu has become such an industry standard that when Microsoft released its Windows Subsystem for Linux feature back in 2016, Ubuntu was the only Linux distribution initially available.

Most of the skills we'll learn here will transfer well to other Linux distributions—and especially to distros like Debian, Mint, and Kali Linux that share upstream sources with Ubuntu. So if you're looking to get in on the action, stick around for the whole thing.

> **Beginner to certified professional:** As long as you have used a computer, mouse, and keyboard, you can reach good places using this book. We'll show you how to get and install Ubuntu, quickly put it to productive use, use it to solve critical problems and build powerful server environments, and ultimately excel at administering and securing it.

> **System administrator focused:** When you're finished with this book, you will know how to use, modify, and maintain Ubuntu. Almost all of the topics needed to achieve one or more Linux administration certifications are covered in this book. That said, many software developers and hobbyists will also enjoy it as they work to improve their skills.

> **Emphasis on command-line tools:** Although point-and-click graphic interfaces are as good or better as anything else these days, many advanced features can only be utilized by entering commands and editing configuration files manually. We'll mostly focus on mastering the Linux command-line shell.

Many, many demos and exercises: Instead of just telling you what Ubuntu does, we actually show you what it does. Then, to make sure that you've nailed it, you'll have the opportunity to try it yourself. Every procedure and exercise has been tested to work in Ubuntu.

Ubuntu Linux Bible includes in-depth discussions covering server virtualization, infrastructure orchestration, and managing cloud and containerized applications (individually or at scale):

Cockpit administration web UI: Since the dawn of the Linux age, people have struggled to develop simple graphical or browser-based interfaces for managing Linux systems. Cockpit may well have finally delivered a way to manage the basic Linux features through its web UI. Throughout this book, Cockpit will be our graphic tool of choice. With Cockpit, you can now add users, manage storage, monitor activities, and do many other administrative tasks through a single interface.

Cloud technologies: Our coverage will include setting up your own Linux host for running virtual machines and running Linux in a cloud environment, such as Amazon Web Services. Linux is at the heart of most technological advances in cloud computing today. That means you need a solid understanding of Linux to work effectively in tomorrow's data centers. The first chapters will cover all the Linux basics, which you'll use through our various cutting-edge virtualization, networking, and storage administration exercises.

Ansible: Automating tasks for managing systems is now an unavoidable part of modern digital administration. Using Ansible, you can create playbooks that define the state of a Linux system. This includes things like setting which packages are installed, which services are running, and how features are configured. A playbook can configure one system or a thousand systems, be combined to form a set of system services, and be run again to return a system to a defined state. We'll get introduced to Ansible, create our first Ansible playbook, and run ad-hoc Ansible commands.

Containers: Packaging and running applications in containers is becoming the preferred method for deploying, managing, and updating small, scalable software services and features. You'll learn how to pull container images, run them, stop them, and even build your own container images using LXD and Docker.

Kubernetes: While containers are nice on their own, to be able to deploy, manage, and upgrade containers in a large enterprise, you need an orchestration platform. The Kubernetes project provides a powerful platform for just that purpose.

How This Book Is Organized

The book is organized to enable you to start off at the very beginning with Linux and grow to become a professional Ubuntu system administrator and power user.

Part I, "Getting Started," includes two chapters designed to help you understand what Linux is and get you started with an Ubuntu desktop:

- Chapter 1, "Starting with Linux," covers topics such as what the Linux operating system is, where Ubuntu fits in, and how to get started using it.
- Chapter 2, "Creating the Perfect Linux Desktop," provides information on how you can create a desktop system and use some of the most popular desktop features.

Part II, "Becoming a Linux Power User," provides in-depth details on how to use the Linux shell, work with filesystems, manipulate text files, manage processes, and use shell scripts:

- Chapter 3, "Using the Shell," includes information on how to access a shell, run commands, recall commands (using history), and do tab completion. The chapter also describes how to use variables, aliases, and man pages (traditional Linux command reference pages).
- Chapter 4, "Moving Around the Filesystem," includes commands for listing, creating, copying, and moving files and directories. More advanced topics in this chapter include filesystem security, such as file ownership, permissions, and access control lists.
- Chapter 5, "Working with Text Files," includes everything from basic text editors to tools for finding files and searching for text within files.
- Chapter 6, "Managing Running Processes," describes how to see what processes are running on your system and change them. Ways of changing processes include killing, pausing, and sending other types of signals.
- Chapter 7, "Writing Simple Shell Scripts," includes shell commands and functions that you can gather together into a file to run as a command itself.

In Part III, "Becoming a Linux System Administrator," you learn how to administer Ubuntu systems:

- Chapter 8, "Learning System Administration," provides information on basic graphical tools, commands, and configuration files for administering Ubuntu systems. It introduces the Cockpit web UI for simplified, centralized administration.
- Chapter 9, "Installing Linux," covers common installation tasks, such as disk partitioning and initial software package selection, as well as more advanced installation tools.
- Chapter 10, "Getting and Managing Software," provides an understanding of how software packages work and how to get and manage software packages.
- Chapter 11, "Managing User Accounts," discusses tools for adding and deleting users and groups as well as how to centralize user account management.
- Chapter 12, "Managing Disks and Filesystems," provides information on adding partitions, creating filesystems, and mounting filesystems, as well as working with logical volume management.

In Part IV, "Becoming a Linux Server Administrator," you learn to create powerful network servers and the tools needed to manage them:

- Chapter 13, "Understanding Server Administration," covers remote logging, monitoring tools, and the Linux boot process.
- Chapter 14, "Administering Networking," discusses how to configure networking.
- Chapter 15, "Starting and Stopping Services," provides information on process management tools—especially systemd.
- Chapter 16, "Configuring a Print Server," describes how to configure printers to use locally on your Ubuntu system or over the network from other computers.
- Chapter 17, "Configuring a Web Server," describes how to configure an Apache web server.
- Chapter 18, "Configuring an FTP Server," covers procedures for setting up a vsftpd FTP server that can be used by others to download files from your Ubuntu system over the network.
- Chapter 19, "Configuring a Windows File Sharing (Samba) Server," covers Windows file server configuration with Samba.
- Chapter 20, "Configuring an NFS File Server," describes how to use Network File System features to share folders of files among systems over a network.
- Chapter 21, "Troubleshooting Linux," covers popular tools for troubleshooting your Ubuntu system.

In Part V, "Learning Linux Security Techniques," you learn how to secure your Linux systems and services:

- Chapter 22, "Understanding Basic Linux Security," covers basic security concepts and techniques.
- Chapter 23, "Understanding Advanced Linux Security," provides information on using Pluggable Authentication Modules (PAM) and cryptology tools to tighten system security and authentication.
- Chapter 24, "Enhancing Linux Security with AppArmor," shows you how AppArmor can be configured to secure system services.
- Chapter 25, "Securing Linux on a Network," covers network security features, such as the Uncomplicated Firewall (UFW) and iptables firewalls, to secure system services.

In Part VI," Engaging with Cloud Computing," the book pivots from a single-system focus toward containerization, cloud computing, and automation:

- Chapter 26, "Shifting to Clouds and Containers," describes how to pull, push, start, stop, tag, and build container images.
- Chapter 27, "Deploying Linux to the Cloud," describes how to deploy Ubuntu images to different cloud environments, including OpenStack, Amazon EC2, or a local Ubuntu system configured for virtualization.

- Chapter 28, "Automating Apps and Infrastructure with Ansible," tells you how to create Ansible playbooks and run ad-hoc Ansible commands to automate the configuration of Ubuntu systems and other devices.
- Chapter 29, "Deploying Applications as Containers with Kubernetes," describes the Kubernetes project and how it is used to orchestrate container images, with the potential to massively scale up for large data centers.

Part VII contains an appendix with Exercise Answers, providing sample solutions to the exercises included in Chapters 2 through 29.

Conventions Used in This Book

Throughout the book, special typography indicates code and commands. Commands and code are shown in a monospaced font:

```
This is how code looks.
```

In the event that an example includes both input and output, the monospaced font is still used, but input is presented in bold type to distinguish the two. Here's an example:

```
$ ftp ftp.handsonhistory.com
Name (home:jake): jake
Password: ******
```

Commands that must be run using administrator permissions (often through sudo) will display a # command-line prompt, like this:

```
# nano /etc/group
```

All other commands will use the $ character, like this:

```
$ cat /etc/group
```

As for styles in the text:

- New terms and important words appear in *italic* when introduced.
- Keyboard strokes appear like this: Ctrl+A. This convention indicates to hold the Ctrl key as you also press the "a" key.
- Filenames, URLs, and code within the text appear as follows: persistence .properties.

The following items call your attention to points that are particularly important.

> **NOTE**
> A Note box provides extra information to which you need to pay special attention.

> **TIP**
> A Tip box shows a special way of performing a particular task.

> **CAUTION**
>
> A Caution box alerts you to take special care when executing a procedure or damage to your computer hardware or software could result.

Jumping into Linux

If you are new to Linux, you might have vague ideas about what it is and where it came from. You may have heard something about it being free (as in cost) or free (as in freedom to use it as you please). Before you start putting your hands on Linux (which we'll do soon enough), Chapter 1 seeks to answer some of your questions about the origins and features of Linux and, in particular, Ubuntu.

Take your time and work through this book to get up to speed on Linux and how you can make it work to meet your needs. This is your invitation to jump in and take the first step toward becoming a Linux expert!

Visit the Ubuntu Linux Bible website

To find links to various Linux distributions, tips on gaining Linux certification, and corrections to the book as they become available, go to www.wiley.com/go/ubuntulinuxbible.

How to Contact Wiley or the Authors

If you believe you've found a mistake in this book, please bring it to our attention. At John Wiley & Sons, we understand how important it is to provide our customers with accurate content, but even with our best efforts an error may occur.

In order to submit your possible errata, please email it to our Customer Service Team at wileysupport@wiley.com with the subject line "Possible Book Errata Submission".

You can contact Christopher Negus at striker57@gmail.com and David Clinton at info@bootstrap-it.com.

Part I

Getting Started

Starting with Linux

The operating systems war is over, and Linux has won. Proprietary operating systems simply cannot keep up with the pace of improvements and quality that Linux can achieve with its culture of sharing and innovation. Even Microsoft, whose former CEO Steve Ballmer once referred to Linux as "a cancer," now says that Linux's use on Microsoft's Azure cloud computing service has surpassed the use of Windows.

Linux is one of the most important technological advancements of the twenty-first century. Beyond its impact on the growth of the Internet and its place as an enabling technology for a range of computer-driven devices, Linux development has become a model for how collaborative projects can surpass what single individuals and companies can do alone.

Google runs thousands upon thousands of Linux servers to power its search technology. Its Android phones are based on Linux. Likewise, when you download and run Google's Chrome OS, you get a browser that is backed by a Linux operating system.

Facebook builds and deploys its site using what is referred to as a *LAMP stack* (Linux, Apache web server, MySQL database, and PHP web scripting language)—all open source projects. In fact, Facebook itself uses an open source development model, making source code for the applications and tools that drive Facebook available to the public. This model has helped Facebook shake out bugs quickly, get contributions from around the world, and fuel its exponential growth.

Financial organizations that have trillions of dollars riding on the speed and security of their operating systems also rely heavily on Linux. These include the New York Stock Exchange, Chicago Mercantile Exchange, and the Tokyo Stock Exchange.

As *cloud* continues to be one of the hottest buzzwords today, one part of the cloud that isn't hype is that Linux and other open source technologies continue to be the foundation on which today's greatest cloud innovations are being built. Every software component that you need to build a private or public cloud (such as hypervisors, cloud controllers, network storage, virtual networking, and authentication) is freely available from within the open source world.

The widespread adoption of Linux around the world has created huge demand for Linux expertise. This chapter starts you down a path to becoming a Linux—and Ubuntu—expert by helping you understand what Linux is, where it came from, and what your opportunities are for becoming proficient in it. The rest of this book provides you with hands-on activities to help you gain that expertise. The book's final part will show you how to apply that expertise to cloud technologies, including automation tools and container orchestration technologies.

Understanding What Linux Is

Linux is a computer operating system. An operating system consists of the software that manages your computer and lets you run applications on it. The features that make up Linux and similar computer operating systems include the following:

- **Detecting and preparing hardware**: When the Linux system boots up (when you turn on your computer), it looks at the components on your computer (CPU, hard drive, network cards, and so on) and loads the software (drivers and modules) needed to access those particular hardware devices.

- **Managing processes**: The operating system must keep track of multiple processes running at the same time and decide which have access to the CPU and when. The system also must offer ways of starting, stopping, and changing the status of processes.

- **Managing memory**: RAM and swap space (extended memory) must be allocated to applications as they need memory. The operating system decides how requests for memory are handled.

- **Providing user interfaces**: An operating system must provide ways of accessing the system. The first Linux systems were accessed from a command-line interpreter called a *shell*. Today, graphical desktop interfaces are commonly available as well.

- **Controlling filesystems**: Filesystem structures are built into the operating system (or loaded as modules). The operating system controls ownership and access to the files and directories (folders) that the filesystems contain.

- **Providing user access and authentication**: Creating user accounts and allowing boundaries to be set between users is a basic feature of Linux. Separate user and group accounts enable users to control their own files and processes.

- **Offering administrative utilities**: In Linux, hundreds (perhaps thousands) of commands and graphical windows are available to do such things as add users, manage disks, monitor the network, install software, and generally secure and manage your computer. Web UI tools, such as Cockpit, have lowered the bar for doing complex administrative tasks.

Starting up services: To use printers, handle log messages, and provide a variety of system and network services, processes called *daemon processes* run in the background, waiting for requests to come in. Many types of services run in Linux. Linux provides different ways of starting and stopping these services. In other words, while Linux includes web browsers to view web pages, it can also be the computer that serves up web pages to others. Popular server features include web, mail, database, printer, file, DNS, and DHCP servers.

Programming tools: A wide variety of programming utilities for creating applications and libraries for implementing specialty interfaces are available with Linux.

As someone managing Linux systems, you need to learn how to work with these features. While many of them can be managed using graphical interfaces, an understanding of the shell command line is critical for someone administering Linux systems.

Modern Linux systems now go way beyond what the first UNIX systems (on which Linux was based) could do. Advanced features in Linux, often used in large enterprises, include the following:

Clustering: Linux can be configured to work in clusters so that multiple systems can appear as one system to the outside world. Services can be configured to pass back and forth between cluster nodes while appearing to those using the services that they are running without interruption.

Virtualization: To manage computing resources more efficiently, Linux can run as a virtualization host. On that host, you could run other Linux systems, Microsoft Windows, BSD, or other operating systems as virtual guests. To the outside world, each of those virtual guests appears as a separate computer. KVM and Xen are two technologies in Linux for creating virtual hosts.

Cloud computing: To manage large-scale virtualization environments, you can use full-blown cloud computing platforms based on Linux. Projects such as OpenStack and Red Hat Virtualization (and its upstream oVirt project) can simultaneously manage many virtualization hosts, virtual networks, user and system authentication, virtual guests, and networked storage. Projects such as Kubernetes can manage containerized applications across massive data centers.

Real-time computing: Linux can be configured for real-time computing, where high-priority processes can expect fast, predictable attention.

Specialized storage: Instead of just storing data on the computer's hard disk, you can store it on many specialized local and networked storage interfaces that are available in Linux. Shared storage devices available in Linux include iSCSI, Fibre Channel, and Infiniband. Entire open source storage platforms include projects such as Ceph (www.ceph.io) and GlusterFS (www.gluster.org).

Some of these advanced topics are not covered in this book. However, the features covered here for using the shell, working with disks, starting and stopping services, and configuring a variety of servers should serve as a foundation for working with those advanced features.

Understanding How Linux Differs from Other Operating Systems

If you are new to Linux, chances are good that you have used a Microsoft Windows or macOS operating system. Although macOS had its roots in a free software operating system, referred to as the Berkeley Software Distribution (more on that later), operating systems from both Microsoft and Apple are considered proprietary operating systems. What that means is the following:

- You cannot see the code used to create the operating system, and therefore, you cannot change the operating system at its most basic level if it doesn't suit your needs, and you can't use the operating system to build your own operating system from source code.
- You cannot check the code to find bugs, explore security vulnerabilities, or simply learn what that code is doing.
- You may not be able to plug your own software easily into the operating system if the creators of that system don't want to expose the programming interfaces you need to the outside world.

You might look at those statements about proprietary software and say, "What do I care? I'm not a software developer. I don't want to see or change how my operating system is built."

That may be true. However, the fact that others can take free and open source software and use it as they please has driven the explosive growth of the Internet (think Google), mobile phones (think Android), special computing devices (think TiVo), and hundreds of technology companies. Free software has driven down computing costs and allowed for an explosion of innovation.

Maybe you don't want to use Linux—as Google, Facebook, and other companies have done—to build the foundation for a multibillion-dollar company. Nonetheless, those companies and others who now rely on Linux to drive their computer infrastructures need more and more people with the skills to run those systems.

You may wonder how a computer system that is so powerful and flexible has come to be free as well. To understand how that could be, you need to see where Linux came from. Thus the next sections of this chapter describe the strange and winding path of the free software movement that led to Linux.

Exploring Linux History

Some histories of Linux begin with the following message, titled "What would you like to see most in minix?" posted by Linus Torvalds to the `comp.os.minix` newsgroup on August 25, 1991, at

`groups.google.com/forum/#!msg/comp.os.minix/dlNtH7RRrGA/SwRavCzVE7gJ`

> Linus Benedict Torvalds
>
> Hello everybody out there using minix -
>
> I'm doing a (free) operating system (just a hobby, won't be big and professional like gnu) for 386(486) AT clones. This has been brewing since april, and is starting to get ready. I'd like any feedback on things people like/dislike in minix, as my OS resembles it somewhat (same physical layout of the file-system (due to practical reasons, among other things). . .Any suggestions are welcome, but I won't promise I'll implement them :-)
>
> Linus (`torvalds@kruuna.helsinki.fi`)
>
> PS. Yes—it's free of any minix code, and it has a multi-threaded fs. It is NOT protable[sic] (uses 386 task switching etc), and it probably never will support anything other than AT-harddisks, as that's all I have :-(.

Minix was a UNIX-like operating system that ran on PCs in the early 1990s. Like Minix, Linux was also a clone of the UNIX operating system. With few exceptions, such as Microsoft Windows, most modern computer systems (including macOS and Linux itself) were derived from UNIX operating systems, created originally by AT&T.

To truly appreciate how a free operating system could have been modeled after a proprietary system from AT&T Bell Laboratories, it helps to understand the culture in which UNIX was created and the chain of events that made the essence of UNIX possible to reproduce freely.

> **NOTE**
>
> To learn more about how Linux was created, pick up the book *Just for Fun: The Story of an Accidental Revolutionary* by Linus Torvalds (Harper Collins Publishing, 2001).

Free-flowing UNIX culture at Bell Labs

The UNIX operating system was created and, from the very beginning, nurtured in a communal environment. Its creation was not driven by market needs but by a desire to overcome impediments to producing programs. AT&T, which owned the UNIX trademark originally, eventually made UNIX into a commercial product. By that time, however, many of the concepts (and even much of the early code) that made UNIX special had fallen into the public domain.

If you are not old enough to remember when AT&T split up in 1984, you may not remember a time when AT&T was *the* phone company. Up until the early 1980s, AT&T didn't have to think much about competition because if you wanted a phone in the United States, you had to go to AT&T. It had the luxury of funding pure research projects. The mecca for such projects was the Bell Laboratories site in Murray Hill, New Jersey.

After a project called Multics failed around 1969, Bell Labs employees Ken Thompson and Dennis Ritchie set off on their own to create an operating system that would offer an improved environment for developing software. Up to that time, most programs were written on paper punch cards that had to be fed in batches to mainframe computers. In a 1980 lecture on "The Evolution of the UNIX Time-Sharing System," Dennis Ritchie summed up the spirit that started UNIX:

> What we wanted to preserve was not just a good environment in which to do programming, but a system around which a fellowship could form. We knew from experience that the essence of communal computing as supplied by remote-access, time-shared machines is not just to type programs into a terminal instead of a keypunch, but to encourage close communication.

The simplicity and power of the UNIX design began breaking down barriers that, until this point, had impeded software developers. The foundation of UNIX was set with several key elements:

The UNIX filesystem: Because it included a structure that allowed levels of subdirectories (which, for today's desktop users, look like folders inside of folders), UNIX could be used to organize the files and directories in intuitive ways. Furthermore, complex methods of accessing disks, tapes, and other devices were greatly simplified by representing those devices as individual device files that you could also access as items in a directory.

Input/output redirection: Early UNIX systems also included input redirection and pipes. From a command line, UNIX users could direct the output of a command to a file using a right-arrow key (>). Later, the concept of pipes (|) was added where the output of one command could be directed to the input of another command. For example, the following command line concatenates (cat) file1 and file2, sorts (sort) the lines in those files alphabetically, paginates the sorted text for printing (pr), and directs the output to the computer's default printer (lp):

```
$ cat file1 file2 | sort | pr | lp
```

This method of directing input and output enabled developers to create their own specialized utilities that could be joined with existing utilities. This modularity made it possible for lots of code to be developed by lots of different people. A user could just put together the pieces they needed.

Portability: Simplifying the experience of using UNIX also led to it becoming extraordinarily portable to run on different computer hardware. By having device drivers (represented by files in the filesystem tree), UNIX could present an interface to applications in such a way that the programs didn't have to know about the details of the underlying hardware. To port UNIX later to another system, developers had only to change the drivers. The application programs didn't have to change for different hardware!

To make portability a reality, however, a high-level programming language was needed to implement the software. To that end, Brian Kernighan and Dennis Ritchie created the C programming language. In 1973, UNIX was rewritten in C. Today, C is still the primary language used to create the UNIX (and Linux) operating system kernels.

As Ritchie went on to say in a 1979 lecture (www.bell-labs.com/usr/dmr/www/hist.html):

> Today, the only important UNIX program still written in assembler is the assembler itself; virtually all the utility programs are in C, and so are most of the application's programs, although there are sites with many in Fortran, Pascal, and Algol 68 as well. It seems certain that much of the success of UNIX follows from the readability, modifiability, and portability of its software that in turn follows from its expression in high-level languages.

If you are a Linux enthusiast and are interested in what features from the early days of Linux have survived, an interesting read is Dennis Ritchie's reprint of the first UNIX programmer's manual (dated November 3, 1971). You can find it at Dennis Ritchie's website: www.bell-labs.com/usr/dmr/www/1stEdman.html. The form of this documentation is UNIX man pages, which is still the primary format for documenting UNIX and Linux operating system commands and programming tools today.

What's clear as you read through the early documentation and accounts of the UNIX system is that the development was a free-flowing process, lacked ego, and was dedicated to making UNIX excellent. This process led to a sharing of code (both inside and outside of Bell Labs), which allowed rapid development of a high-quality UNIX operating system. It also led to an operating system that AT&T would find difficult to reel back in later.

Commercial UNIX

Before the AT&T divestiture in 1984, when it was split up into AT&T and seven "Baby Bell" companies, AT&T was forbidden to sell computer systems with software. Companies that would later become Verizon, Qwest, Nokia, and Alcatel-Lucent were all part of AT&T. As a result of AT&T's monopoly of the telephone system, the US government was concerned that an unrestricted AT&T might dominate the fledgling computer industry.

Because AT&T was restricted from selling computers directly to customers before its divestiture, UNIX source code was licensed to universities for a nominal fee. This allowed UNIX installations to grow in size and mindshare among top universities. However, there was still no UNIX operating system for sale from AT&T that you didn't have to compile yourself.

Berkeley Software Distribution arrives

In 1975, UNIX V6 became the first version of UNIX available for widespread use outside of Bell Laboratories. From this early UNIX source code, the first major variant of UNIX was created at University of California, Berkeley. It was named the Berkeley Software Distribution (BSD).

For most of the next decade, the BSD and Bell Labs versions of UNIX headed off in separate directions. BSD continued forward in the free-flowing, share-the-code manner that was the hallmark of the early Bell Labs UNIX, whereas AT&T started steering UNIX toward commercialization. With the formation of a separate UNIX Laboratory, which moved out of Murray Hill and down the road to Summit, New Jersey, AT&T began its attempts to commercialize UNIX. By 1984, divestiture was behind AT&T, and it was really ready to start selling UNIX.

UNIX Laboratory and commercialization

The UNIX Laboratory was considered a jewel that couldn't quite find a home or a way to make a profit. As it moved between Bell Laboratories and other areas of AT&T, its name changed several times. It is probably best remembered by the name it had as it began its spin-off from AT&T: UNIX System Laboratories (USL).

The UNIX source code that came out of USL, the legacy of which was sold in part to Santa Cruz Operation (SCO), was used for a time as the basis for ever-dwindling lawsuits by SCO against major Linux vendors (such as IBM and Red Hat, Inc.). Because of that, it's possible that the efforts from USL that have contributed to the success of Linux are lost on most people.

During the 1980s, of course, many computer companies were afraid that a newly divested AT&T would pose more of a threat to controlling the computer industry than would an upstart company in Redmond, Washington. To calm the fears of IBM, Intel, Digital Equipment Corporation, and other computer companies, the UNIX Lab made the following commitments to ensure a level playing field:

Source code only: Instead of producing its own boxed set of UNIX, AT&T continued to sell source code only and to make it available equally to all licensees. Each company would then port UNIX to its own equipment. It wasn't until about 1992, when the lab was spun off as a joint venture with Novell (called Univel), and then eventually sold to Novell, that a commercial boxed set of UNIX (called UnixWare) was produced directly from that source code.

Published interfaces: To create an environment of fairness and community for its OEMs (original equipment manufacturers), AT&T began standardizing what different versions of UNIX had to be able to do to still be called UNIX. To that end, Portable Operating System Interface (POSIX) standards and the AT&T UNIX System V Interface Definition (SVID) were specifications UNIX vendors could use to create compliant UNIX systems. Those same documents also served as road maps for the creation of Linux.

> **NOTE**
>
> In an early email newsgroup post, Linus Torvalds made a request for a copy, preferably online, of the POSIX standard. I think that no one from AT&T expected someone to actually be able to write their own clone of UNIX from those interfaces without using any of its UNIX source code.

Technical approach: Again, until the very end of USL, most decisions on the direction of UNIX were made based on technical considerations. Management was promoted up through the technical ranks, and there didn't seem to have been any talk of writing software to break other companies' software or otherwise restrict the success of USL's partners.

When USL eventually started taking on marketing experts and creating a desktop UNIX product for end users, Microsoft Windows already had a firm grasp on the desktop market. Also, because the direction of UNIX had always been toward source-code licensing destined for large computing systems, USL had pricing difficulties for its products. For example, on software that was included with UNIX, USL found itself having to pay out per-computer licensing fees that were based on $100,000 mainframes instead of $2,000 PCs. Add to that the fact that no application programs were available with UnixWare and you can see why the endeavor failed.

Successful marketing of UNIX systems at the time, however, was happening with other computer companies. SCO had found a niche market, primarily selling PC versions of UNIX running dumb terminals in small offices. Sun Microsystems was selling lots of UNIX work-stations (originally based on BSD but merged with UNIX in SVR4) for programmers and high-end technology applications (such as stock trading).

Other commercial UNIX systems were also emerging by the 1980s. This new ownership assertion of UNIX was beginning to take its toll on the spirit of open contributions. Law-suits were launched to protect UNIX source code and trademarks. In 1984, this new, restrictive UNIX gave rise to an organization that eventually led the path to Linux: the Free Software Foundation.

GNU transitions UNIX to freedom

In 1984, Richard M. Stallman started the GNU project (gnu.org), recursively known by the phrase *GNU is Not UNIX*. As a project of the Free Software Foundation (FSF), GNU was intended to become a recoding of the entire UNIX operating system that could be freely distributed.

The GNU Project page (gnu.org/gnu/thegnuproject.html) tells the story of how the project came about in Stallman's own words. It also lays out the problems that proprietary soft-ware companies were imposing on those software developers who wanted to share, create, and innovate.

Although rewriting millions of lines of code might seem daunting for one or two people, spreading the effort across dozens or even hundreds of programmers made the project pos-sible. Remember that UNIX was designed to be built in separate pieces that could be piped together. Because they were reproducing commands and utilities with well-known, pub-lished interfaces, that effort could easily be split among many developers.

It turned out that not only could the same results be gained by all new code, but in some cases that code was better than the original UNIX versions. Because everyone could see the code being produced for the project, poorly written code could be corrected quickly or replaced over time.

If you are familiar with UNIX, try searching the hundreds of GNU software packages, which contain thousands of commands, for your favorite UNIX command from the Free Software Directory (directory.fsf.org/wiki/GNU). Chances are good that you will find it there, along with many, many other available software projects.

Over time, the term *free software* has been mostly replaced by the term *open source software*. The term *free software* is preferred by the Free Software Foundation, while *open source software* is promoted by the Open Source Initiative (opensource.org).

To accommodate both camps, some people use the term *Free and Open Source Software (FOSS)* instead. An underlying principle of FOSS, however, is that although you are free to use the software as you like, you have some responsibility to make the improvements that you make to the code available to others. This way, everyone in the community can benefit from your work, as you have benefited from the work of others.

To define clearly how open source software should be handled, the GNU software project created the GNU Public License, or GPL. Although many other software licenses cover slightly different approaches to protecting free software, the GPL is the most well-known—and it's the one that covers the Linux kernel itself. The GNU Public License includes the following basic features:

Author rights: The original author retains the rights to their software.

Free distribution: People can use the GNU software in their own software, changing and redistributing it as they please. They do, however, have to include the source code with their distribution (or make it easily available).

Copyright maintained: Even if you were to repackage and resell the software, the original GNU agreement must be maintained with the software, which means that all future recipients of the software have the opportunity to change the source code, just as you did.

There is no warranty on GNU software. If something goes wrong, the original developer of the software has no obligation to fix the problem. However, many organizations, large and small, offer paid support (often in subscription form) for the software when it is included in their Linux or other open source software distribution. (See the section "OSI open source definition" later in this chapter for a more detailed definition of open source software.)

Despite its success in producing thousands of UNIX utilities, the GNU project itself failed to produce one critical piece of code: the kernel. Its attempts to build an open source kernel with the GNU Hurd project (gnu.org/software/hurd/) were unsuccessful at first, so it failed to become the premier open source kernel.

BSD loses some steam

The one software project that had a chance of beating out Linux to be the premier open source kernel was the venerable BSD project. By the late 1980s, BSD developers at University of California (UC) Berkeley realized that they had already rewritten most of the UNIX source code they had received a decade earlier.

In 1989, UC Berkeley distributed its own UNIX-like code as Net/1 and later (in 1991) as Net/2. Just as UC Berkeley was preparing a complete, UNIX-like operating system that was free from all AT&T code, AT&T hit them with a lawsuit in 1992. The suit claimed that the software was written using trade secrets taken from AT&T's UNIX system.

It's important to note here that BSD developers had completely rewritten the copyright-protected code from AT&T. Copyright was the primary means AT&T used to protect its rights to the UNIX code. Some believe that if AT&T had patented the concepts covered in that code, there might not be a Linux (or any UNIX clone) operating system today.

The lawsuit was dropped when Novell bought UNIX System Laboratories from AT&T in 1994. Nevertheless, during that critical period there was enough fear and doubt about the legality of the BSD code that the momentum that BSD had gained to that point in the fledgling open source community was lost. Many people started looking for another open source alternative. The time was ripe for a college student from Finland who was working on his own kernel.

NOTE

Today, BSD versions are available from three major projects: FreeBSD, NetBSD, and OpenBSD. People generally characterize FreeBSD as the easiest to use, NetBSD as available on the most computer hardware platforms, and OpenBSD as fanatically secure. Many security-minded individuals still prefer BSD to Linux. Also, because of its licensing, BSD code can be used by proprietary software vendors, such as Microsoft and Apple, who don't want to share their operating system code with others. macOS is built on a BSD derivative.

Linus builds the missing piece

Linus Torvalds started work on Linux in 1991, while he was a student at the University of Helsinki, Finland. He wanted to create a UNIX-like kernel so that he could use the same kind of operating system on his home PC that he used at school. At the time, Linus was using Minix, but he wanted to go beyond what the Minix standards permitted.

As noted earlier, Linus announced the first public version of the Linux kernel to the `comp.os.minix` newsgroup on August 25, 1991, although Torvalds guesses that the first version didn't actually come out until mid-September of that year.

Although Torvalds stated that Linux was written for the 386 processor and probably wasn't portable, others persisted in encouraging (and contributing to) a more portable approach in the early versions of Linux. By October 5, 1991, Linux 0.02 was released with much of the original assembly code rewritten in the C programming language, which made it possible to start porting it to other machines.

The Linux kernel was the last—and the most important—piece of code that was needed to complete a whole UNIX-like operating system under the GPL. So when people started putting together distributions, the name Linux, not GNU, is what stuck. Some distributions, such as Debian, however, refer to themselves as GNU/Linux distributions. (Not including GNU in the title or subtitle of a Linux operating system is also a matter of much public grumbling by some members of the GNU project. See gnu.org.)

Today, Linux can be described as an open source UNIX-like operating system that reflects a combination of SVID, POSIX, and BSD compliance. Linux continues to aim toward compliance with POSIX as well as with standards set by the owner of the UNIX trademark, The Open Group (opengroup.org).

The nonprofit Open Source Development Labs, renamed the Linux Foundation after merging with the Free Standards Group (linuxfoundation.org) and which employs Linus Torvalds, manages the direction of Linux development efforts. Its sponsors list is like a Who's Who of commercial Linux system and application vendors, including IBM, Red Hat, SUSE, Oracle, HP, Dell, Computer Associates, Intel, Cisco Systems, and hundreds of others. The Linux Foundation's primary charter is to protect and accelerate the growth of Linux by providing legal protection and software development standards for Linux developers.

Although much of the thrust of corporate Linux efforts is on enterprise computing, huge improvements are continuing in the desktop arena as well. The KDE and GNOME desktop environments continuously improve the Linux experience for casual users. Newer lightweight desktop environments such as Chrome OS, Xfce, and LXDE now offer efficient alternatives that bring Linux to thousands of netbook owners.

Linus Torvalds continues to maintain and improve the Linux kernel.

> **NOTE**
> For a more detailed history of Linux, see the book *Open Sources*: *Voices from the Open Source Revolution* (O'Reilly, 1999). The entire first edition is available online at
> oreilly.com/openbook/opensources/book/

OSI open source definition

Linux provides a platform that lets software developers change the operating system as they like and get a wide range of help creating the applications they need. One of the watchdogs of the open source movement is the *Open Source Initiative*, or *OSI* (opensource.org).

Although the primary goal of open source software is to make source code available, other goals of open source software are defined by OSI in its open source definition. Most of the following rules for acceptable open source licenses serve to protect the freedom and integrity of the open source code:

Free distribution: An open source license can't require a fee from anyone who resells the software.

Source code: The source code must be included with the software, and there can be no restrictions on redistribution.

Derived works: The license must allow modification and redistribution of the code under the same terms.

Integrity of the author's source code: The license may require that those who use the source code remove the original project's name or version if they change the source code.

No discrimination against persons or groups: The license must allow all people to be equally eligible to use the source code.

No discrimination against fields of endeavor: The license can't restrict a project from using the source code because it is commercial or because it is associated with a field of endeavor that the software provider doesn't like.

Distribution of license: No additional license should be needed to use and redistribute the software.

License must not be specific to a product: The license can't restrict the source code to a particular software distribution.

License must not restrict other software: The license can't prevent someone from including the open source software on the same medium as non–open source software.

License must be technology neutral: The license can't restrict methods in which the source code can be redistributed.

Open source licenses used by software development projects must meet these criteria to be accepted as open source software by OSI. About 70 different licenses are accepted by OSI to be used to label software as "OSI Certified Open Source Software." In addition to the GPL, other popular OSI-approved licenses include the following:

LGPL: The GNU Lesser General Public License (LGPL) is often used for distributing libraries that other application programs depend upon.

BSD: The Berkeley Software Distribution License allows redistribution of source code, with the requirement that the source code keep the BSD copyright notice and not use the names of contributors to endorse or promote derived software without written permission. A major difference from GPL, however, is that BSD does not require people modifying the code to pass those changes on to the community. As a result, proprietary software vendors such as Apple and Microsoft have used BSD code in their own operating systems.

MIT: The MIT license is like the BSD license, except that it doesn't include the endorsement and promotion requirement.

Mozilla: The Mozilla license covers the use and redistribution of source code associated with the Firefox web browser and other software related to the Mozilla project (www.mozilla.org/en-US/). It is a much longer license than the others because it contains more definitions of how contributors and those reusing the source code should behave. This entails including a file of changes when submitting modifications and that those making their own additions to the code for redistribution should be aware of patent issues or other restrictions associated with their code.

The end result of open source code is software that has more flexibility to grow and fewer boundaries in how it can be used. Many believe that the fact that numerous people look over the source code for a project results in higher-quality software for everyone. As open source advocate Eric S. Raymond says in an often-quoted line, "Given enough eyeballs, all bugs are shallow."

Understanding How Linux Distributions Emerged

Having bundles of source code floating around the Internet that could be compiled and packaged into a Linux system worked well for geeks. More casual Linux users, however, needed a simpler way to put together a Linux system. To respond to that need, some of the best geeks began building their own Linux distributions.

A *Linux distribution* (often called a *distro*) consists of the components needed to create a working Linux system and the procedures needed to get those components installed and running. Technically, Linux is really just what is referred to as the *kernel*. Before the kernel can be useful, you must have other software, such as basic commands (GNU utilities), services that you want to offer (such as remote login or web servers), and possibly a desktop interface and graphical applications. Then you must be able to gather all that together and install it on your computer's hard disk.

Slackware (www.slackware.com) is one of the oldest Linux distributions still supported today. It made Linux friendly for less technical users by distributing software already compiled and grouped into packages. (Those packages of software components were in a format called *Tarballs*.) Then you would use basic Linux commands to do things like format your disk, enable swap, and create user accounts.

Before long, many other Linux distributions were created. Some Linux distributions were created to meet special needs, such as KNOPPIX (a live CD Linux), Gentoo (a cool customizable Linux), and Mandrake (later called Mandriva, which was one of several desktop Linux distributions). But two major distributions rose to become the foundation for many other distributions: Red Hat Linux and Debian.

Understanding Red Hat

Arguably, the first widely popular and deeply functional distro was Red Hat Linux. Red Hat simplified the initial installation process and included a software management tool that provided updates, life cycle management, package information, and documentation. Graphical tools and a desktop environment were also available.

Over time, Red Hat Linux was divided into three distinct and independent distros, all based on the same code base:

- **Red Hat Enterprise Linux (RHEL).** RHEL is a commercial product focused on enterprise workloads. When customers purchase an RHEL subscription, they get engineering support, hardware compatibility guarantees, and access to the full range of RHEL tools spanning orchestration, cloud, and virtualization environments. Red Hat has been a huge commercial success. In 2019, it was purchased by IBM for an eye-popping 34 billion dollars.
- **Fedora.** The Fedora distro is sponsored by Red Hat and represents a more experimental, cutting-edge version of the code base. Fedora is freely available.
- **CentOS.** CentOS is a community-supported distro that's closely linked to the current active version of RHEL. As free software (that's also supported by Red Hat), CentOS is an excellent way to simulate the RHEL experience without the cost.

Those three distros—along with a few others—can be thought of as a distribution family. They all share common command sets, filesystem conventions, and, significantly, a single package management system (the Red Hat Package Manager, RPM).

The Red Hat family is one of two dominant Linux ecosystems. The other is Debian.

Understanding Ubuntu and other Debian distributions

Like Red Hat Linux, the Debian GNU/Linux distribution was an early Linux distribution that excelled at packaging and managing software. Debian uses the deb packaging format and tools to manage all of the software packages on its systems. Debian also has a reputation for stability.

Many Linux distributions can trace their roots back to Debian. According to DistroWatch (distrowatch.com), more than 130 active Linux distributions can be traced back to Debian. Popular Debian-based distributions include Linux Mint, elementary OS, Zorin OS, LXLE, Kali Linux, and many others. However, the Debian derivative that has achieved the most success is Ubuntu (ubuntu.com).

By relying on stable Debian software development and packaging, the Ubuntu Linux distribution (sponsored by Canonical Ltd.) was able to come along and add those features that Debian lacked. In pursuit of bringing new users to Linux, the Ubuntu project added a simple graphical installer and easy-to-use graphical tools. It also focused on full-featured desktop systems while still offering popular server packages.

Ubuntu was also an innovator in creating new ways to run Linux. Using live CDs or live USB drives offered by Ubuntu, you could have Ubuntu up and running in just a few minutes. Often included on live CDs were open source applications, such as web browsers and word processors, that actually ran in Windows. This made the transition to Linux from Windows easier for some people.

This book, as I'm sure you've already noticed, will focus on the Ubuntu universe. Nearly everything you'll learn here will, one way or another, be possible on any other Linux distro, but our plan is to use our time here to fully enjoy Ubuntu's many pleasures.

> **NOTE**
> Ubuntu is pronounced "Oobuntu" (as in "oops") and not "Youbuntu."

Finding Professional Opportunities with Linux Today

If you want to develop a concept for a computer-related research project or technology company, where do you begin? You begin with an idea. After that, you look for the tools that you need to explore and eventually create your vision. Then you look for others to help you during that creation process.

Today, the hard costs of starting a company like Google or Facebook include just a computer, a connection to the Internet, and enough caffeinated beverage of your choice to keep you up all night writing code. If you have your own world-changing idea, Linux and thousands of software packages are available to help you build your dreams. The open source world also comes with communities of developers, administrators, and users who are available to help you.

If you want to get involved with an existing open source project, projects are always looking for people to write code, test software, or write documentation. In those projects, you will find people who use the software, work on that software, and are usually willing to share their expertise to help you as well.

Whether you seek to develop the next great open source software project, or you simply want to gain the skills needed to compete for the thousands of well-paying Linux administrator or development jobs, it will help you to know how to install, secure, and maintain Linux systems.

So, what are the prospects for Linux careers? "The 2018 Open Source Jobs Report" from the Linux Foundation (linuxfoundation.org/publications/2019/07/open-source-jobs-report-2018-2/) found the following:

> **Linux talent is a high priority:** Hiring people with Linux expertise is a priority for 83 percent of hiring managers. That is up from 76 percent in 2017.
>
> **Linux in demand:** Linux is the most in-demand skill category.
>
> **Demand for container skills is growing:** The demand for skills with containers is growing quickly, with 57 percent of hiring managers looking for container skills. That is up from 27 percent over the previous year.

The message to take from this survey is that Linux continues to grow and create demands for Linux expertise. Companies that have begun using Linux have continued to move forward with it. Those using Linux continue to expand its use and find that cost savings, security, and the flexibility it offers continue to make Linux a good investment.

Understanding how companies make money with Linux

Open source enthusiasts believe that better software can result from an open source software development model than from proprietary development models. So, in theory, any company creating software for its own use can save money by adding its software contributions to those of others to gain a much better end product for themselves.

Companies that want to make money by selling software need to be more creative than they were in the old days. Although you can sell the software you create, which includes GPL software, you must pass the source code of that software forward. Of course, others can then recompile that product, basically using and even reselling your product without charge. Here are a few ways that companies are dealing with that issue:

Software subscriptions: Red Hat, Inc., sells its Red Hat Enterprise Linux products on a subscription basis. For a certain amount of money per year, you get binary code to run Linux (so you don't have to compile it yourself), guaranteed support, tools for tracking the hardware and software on your computer, access to the company's knowledge base, and other assets.

Enterprise services: Canonical, the company that stands behind Ubuntu, is one of the leading providers of Linux-based server and professional support solutions. Many of those solutions are built on various flavors of Ubuntu, along with other open source software stacks. Canonical's service business model is what allows it to provide as much support for Ubuntu as it does.

Training and certification: With Linux system use growing in government and big business, professionals are needed to support those systems. There's a wide range of training courses and certifications to help system administrators demonstrate their proficiency managing complex systems.

Certification programs are offered by the Linux Professional Institute (www.lpi.org), CompTIA (www.comptia.org/certifications/linux), and Red Hat (www.redhat.com/en/services/training-and-certification).

Bounties: Software bounties are a fascinating way for open source software companies to make money. Suppose that you are using the XYZ software package and you need a new feature right away. By paying a software bounty to the project itself, or to other software developers, you can have your required improvements moved to the head of the queue. The software you pay for will remain covered by its open source license, but you will have the features you need—probably at a fraction of the cost of building the project from scratch.

Donations: Many open source projects accept donations from individuals or open source companies that use code from their projects. Amazingly, many open source projects support one or two developers and run exclusively on donations.

Boxed sets, mugs, and T-shirts: Some open source projects have online stores where you can buy boxed sets (some people still like physical DVDs and hard copies of documentation) and a variety of mugs, T-shirts, mouse pads, and other items. If you really love a project, for goodness sake, buy a T-shirt!

This is in no way an exhaustive list, because more creative ways are being invented every day to support those who create open source software. Remember that many people have become contributors to and maintainers of open source software because they needed or wanted the software themselves. The contributions they make for free are worth the return they get from others who do the same.

Summary

Linux is an operating system that is built by a community of software developers around the world, and Linus Torvalds still leads the development of the Linux kernel. It is derived originally from the UNIX operating system but has grown beyond UNIX in popularity and power over the years.

The history of the Linux operating system can be tracked from early UNIX systems that were distributed free to colleges and improved upon by initiatives such as the Berkeley Software Distribution (BSD). The Free Software Foundation helped make many of the components needed to create a fully free UNIX-like operating system. The Linux kernel itself was the last major component needed to complete the job.

Most Linux software projects are protected by one of a set of licenses that fall under the Open Source Initiative umbrella. The most prominent of these is the GNU Public License (GPL). Standards such as the Linux Standard Base and world-class Linux organizations and companies (such as Canonical Ltd. and Red Hat, Inc.) make it possible for Linux to continue to be a stable, productive operating system into the future.

Learning the basics of how to use and administer a Linux system will serve you well in any aspect of working with Linux. The remaining chapters provide a series of exercises with which you can test your understanding. That's why, for the rest of the book, you will learn best with a Linux system in front of you so that you can work through the examples in each chapter and complete the exercises successfully.

The next chapter explains how to get started with Linux by describing how to get and use a Linux desktop system.

Creating the Perfect Linux Desktop

IN THIS CHAPTER

Understanding the X Window System and desktop environments

Running Linux from a Live DVD image

Navigating the GNOME 3 desktop

Adding extensions to GNOME 3

Using Nautilus to manage files in GNOME 3

Working with the GNOME and the Unity graphical shell

Working with Metacity

U sing Linux as your everyday desktop system is becoming easier to do all the time. As with everything in Linux, you have choices. There are fully featured GNOME or KDE desktop environments or lightweight desktops such as LXDE or Xfce. There are even simpler standalone window managers.

After you have chosen a desktop, you will find that almost every major type of desktop application on a Windows or Mac system has equivalent applications in Linux. For applications that are not available in Linux, you can often run a Windows application in Linux using Windows compatibility software.

The goal of this chapter is to familiarize you with the concepts related to Linux desktop systems and to give you tips for working with a Linux desktop. In this chapter you do the following:

- Step through the desktop features and technologies that are available in Linux
- Tour the major features of the GNOME desktop environment
- Learn tips and tricks for getting the most out of your GNOME desktop experience

To use the descriptions in this chapter, I recommend that you have an Ubuntu system running in front of you. You can get Ubuntu in lots of ways, including the following:

Running Ubuntu from a live medium

You can download and burn an Ubuntu Live image to a DVD or USB drive so that you can boot it live to use with this chapter.

Installing Ubuntu permanently

Install Ubuntu to your hard disk and boot it from there (as described in Chapter 9, "Installing Linux").

The current release of Ubuntu uses the GNOME 3 interface by default.

> **NOTE**
> Ubuntu switched to GNOME 3 from its own Unity graphical shell (that was built to run on the GNOME desktop) with release 17.10. Unity is still available for newer releases but only from the unsupported, community-maintained *Universe* repository.

Understanding Linux Desktop Technology

Modern computer desktop systems offer graphical windows, icons, and menus that are operated from a mouse and keyboard. If you are under 40 years old, you might think that there's nothing special about that. However, the first Linux systems did not have graphical interfaces available. Also, many Linux servers today that are built for specialized tasks (for example, functioning as a web server or file server) don't have desktop software installed.

Nearly every major Linux distribution that offers desktop interfaces is based on the X Window System from the X.Org Foundation (www.x.org). The X Window System provides a framework on which different types of desktop environments or simple window managers can be built. A replacement for x.org called Wayland (wayland.freedesktop.org) is being developed. Although Wayland has been used as the default X server for some Ubuntu releases, stability and compatibility issues have meant that its full deployment has not yet occurred. For now, x.org is still widely used.

The X Window System (sometimes simply called *X*) was created before Linux existed, and it even predates Microsoft Windows. It was built to be a lightweight, networked desktop framework.

X works in sort of a backward client/server model. The X server runs on the local system, providing an interface to your screen, mouse, and keyboard. X clients (such as word processors, music players, and image viewers) can be launched from the local system or from any system on your network to which the X server gives permission to do so.

X was created in a time when graphical terminals (thin clients) simply managed the keyboard, mouse, and display. Applications, disk storage, and processing power were all on larger centralized computers. So, applications ran on larger machines but were displayed and managed over the network on the thin client. Later, thin clients were replaced by desktop personal computers. Most client applications on PCs ran locally using local processing power, disk space, memory, and other hardware features, while applications that didn't start from the local system were blocked.

X itself provides a plain gray background and a simple "X" mouse cursor. There are no menus, panels, or icons on a plain X screen. If you were to launch an X client (such as a terminal window or word processor), it would appear on the X display with no border around it to move, minimize, or close the window. Those features are added by a window manager.

A *window manager* adds the capability to manage the windows on your desktop and often provides menus for launching applications and otherwise working with the desktop. A full-blown desktop environment includes a window manager, but it also adds menus, panels, and usually an application programming interface that is used to create applications that play well together.

So how does an understanding of how desktop interfaces work in Linux help you when it comes to using Linux? Here are some of the ways:

- Because Linux desktop environments are not required to run a Linux system, a Linux system may have been installed without a desktop. It might offer only a plain-text, command-line interface. You can choose to add a desktop later. After it is installed, you can choose whether to start up the desktop when your computer boots or start it as needed.
- For a very lightweight Linux system, such as one meant to run on less powerful computers, you can choose an efficient, though less feature-rich, window manager (such as `twm` or `fluxbox`) or a lightweight desktop environment (such as LXDE or Xfce).
- For more robust computers, you can choose more powerful desktop environments (such as GNOME and KDE) that can do things such as watch for events to happen (such as inserting a USB flash drive) and respond to those events (such as opening a window to view the contents of the drive).
- You can have multiple desktop environments installed and you can choose which one to launch when you log in. This way, different users on the same computer can use different desktop environments.

Many different desktop environments are available to choose from in Linux. Here are some examples:

GNOE 3

GNOME 3 is currently the default desktop environment for Ubuntu, Fedora, Red Hat Enterprise Linux, and many others. Think of it as a professional desktop environment focusing on stability more than fancy effects.

K Desktop Environment

KDE is probably the second most popular desktop environment for Linux. It has more bells and whistles than GNOME and offers more integrated applications. KDE is also available with Ubuntu and many other Linux systems.

Xfce

The Xfce desktop was one of the first lightweight desktop environments. It is good to use on older or less powerful computers. It is available for Ubuntu and other Linux distributions.

LXDE

The Lightweight X11 Desktop Environment (LXDE) was designed to be a fast-performing, energy-saving desktop environment. Often, LXDE is used on less-expensive devices (such as netbook computers) and on live media (such as a live CD or live USB stick). It is the default desktop for the KNOPPIX live CD distribution but, again, is available for Ubuntu.

Starting with the GNOME 3 Desktop Live Image

A live Linux ISO image is the quickest way to get a Linux system up and running so that you can begin trying it out. Depending on its size, the image can be burned to a CD, DVD, or USB drive and booted on your computer. With a Linux live image, you can have Linux take over the operation of your computer temporarily without harming the contents of your hard drive.

If you have Windows installed, Linux just ignores it and temporarily takes control over your computer. When you're finished with the Linux live image, you can remove the USB or DVD media, reboot the computer, and go back to running whatever operating system was installed on the hard disk.

To try out a GNOME desktop along with the descriptions in this section, I suggest that you build yourself an Ubuntu installation device. Because a live USB does all its work from the USB and in system memory, it runs slower than an installed Linux system. Also, although you can change files, add software, and otherwise configure your system, by default, the work you do disappears when you reboot unless you explicitly save that data to your hard drive or external storage.

The fact that changes you make to the live environment go away on reboot is very good for trying out Linux but not that great if you want an ongoing desktop or server system. For that reason, I recommend that if you have a spare computer, you install Linux permanently on that computer's hard disk to use with the rest of this book (as described in Chapter 9).

After you have a live USB in hand, do the following to get started:

1. **Get a computer**. If you have a standard PC with a USB port, at least 4GB of memory (RAM), and at least a 2GHz processor, you are ready to start. Running a live Ubuntu session using a weaker system will probably work, but those are the current recommended minimums for a desktop session.

2. **Start the live session**. Insert the live drive into your computer and reboot. Depending on your computer's configured boot order, the Linux drive might start up automatically or you might need to manually select it. Hitting a designated "boot order" key during the boot early stages—F12 will work on many systems—may be necessary.

3. **Start Ubuntu.** If the selected drive is able to boot, you'll soon see a screen asking you to select a language and offering you two choices: Try Ubuntu and Install Ubuntu. For this demo, select Try Ubuntu.

4. **Begin using the desktop.** After a minute or two, you'll find yourself facing a fully functioning Ubuntu desktop session. Enjoy yourself.

You can now proceed to the next section, "Using the GNOME 3 Desktop."

Using the GNOME 3 Desktop

The GNOME 3 desktop offers a radical departure from the now-deprecated Unity graphical interface (which, to cover you in case you ever find yourself servicing older installations, we'll discuss later in the chapter). The older GNOME 2.x tools were serviceable, but GNOME 3 is elegant. With GNOME 3, a Linux desktop now appears more like the graphical interfaces on mobile devices, with less focus on multiple mouse buttons and key combinations and more on mouse movement and one-click operations.

Instead of feeling structured and rigid, the GNOME 3 desktop seems to expand as you need it to. As a new application is run, its icon is added to the vertical Dock that, by default, lives on the left side of your desktop.

After the computer boots up

If you booted up a live image, when you reach the desktop, you are assigned as the Live System User for your username. For an installed system, you see the login screen, with user accounts on the system ready for you to select and enter a password. Log in with the username and password that you have defined for your system.

Figure 2.1 is an example of an Ubuntu GNOME 3 desktop screen. Press the Windows key (or click the mouse cursor at the upper-left corner of the desktop) to toggle between a blank desktop and the Activities screen.

There is very little on the GNOME 3 desktop when you start out. The top bar has the word "Activities" on the left, a clock in the middle, and some icons on the right for such things as adjusting audio volume, checking your network connection, and viewing the name of the current user. The Activities screen is where you can select applications to open, switch between active windows, or open multiple workspaces.

Navigating with the mouse

To get started, try navigating the GNOME 3 desktop with your mouse:

1. **Toggle activities and windows.** Click your mouse cursor at the upper-left corner of the screen near the Activities button. Each time you click, your screen changes between showing you the windows that you are actively using and a set of available Activities. (This has the same effect as pressing the Windows key.)

FIGURE 2.1

Starting with the GNOME 3 desktop in Ubuntu

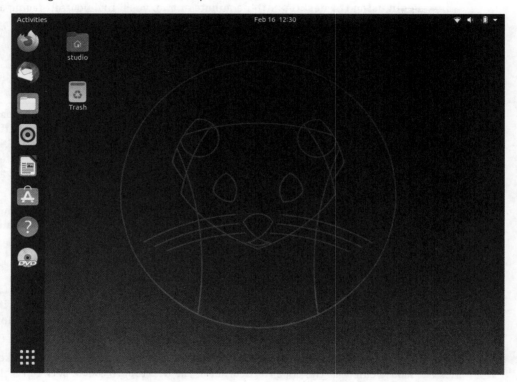

2. **Open windows from the Applications bar.** Open one or two applications by clicking their icons in the Dock on the left (Firefox, LibreOffice, etc.). Move the mouse to the upper-left corner again, and toggle between showing all active windows minimized (Activities screen) and showing them overlapping (full-sized). Figure 2.2 shows an example of the Activities windows view.

3. **Open applications from the Applications list.** Select the Application button from the bottom of the Dock (the button has nine dots in a box). The view changes to a set of icons representing some of the applications installed on your system, as shown in Figure 2.3.

4. **View additional applications.** From the Applications screen, you can change the view of your applications in several ways, as well as launch them in different ways:

   a. **Page through.** To see icons representing applications that are not onscreen, use the mouse to click the dots on the right to page through applications. If you have a wheel mouse, you can use that to scroll the icons.

FIGURE 2.2

Show all windows on the desktop minimized.

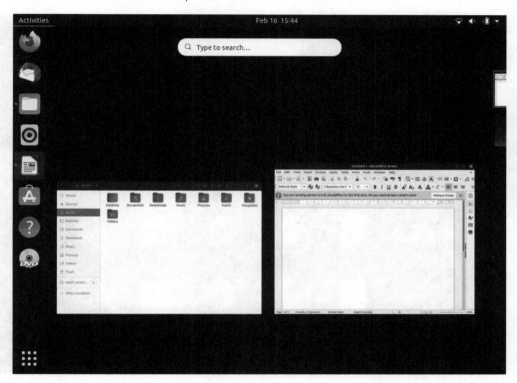

b. **Frequent**. Select the Frequent button on the bottom of the screen to see often-run applications or the All button to see all applications again.

c. **Launching an application**. To start the application you want, left-click its icon to open the application in the current workspace. Right-click to open a menu that lets you choose to open a new window, add or remove the application from Favorites (so the application's icon permanently appears on the Dock), or show details about the application. Figure 2.4 shows an example of the menu.

5. **Open additional applications**. Start up additional applications. Notice that as you open a new application, an icon representing that application appears in the Dock bar on the left. Here are other ways to start applications:

a. **Application icon**. Click any application icon to open that application.

b. **Drop Dock icons on the workspace**. From the Windows view, you can drag any application icon from the Dock by pressing and holding the left mouse button on it and dragging that icon to any of the miniature workspaces on the right.

FIGURE 2.3

Show the list of available applications.

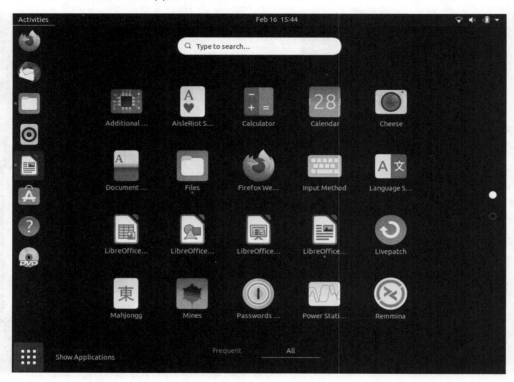

6. **Use multiple workspaces**. Move the mouse to the upper-left corner again to show a minimized view of all windows. Notice all of the applications on the right jammed into a small representation of one workspace while an additional workspace is empty. Drag and drop a few of the windows to an empty desktop space. Figure 2.5 shows what the small workspaces look like. Notice that an additional empty workspace is created each time the last empty one is used. You can drag and drop the miniature windows to any workspace and then select the workspace to view it.

7. **Use the window menu**. Move the mouse to the upper-left corner of the screen to return to the active workspace (large window view). Right-click the title bar on a window to view the window menu. Try these actions from that menu:

   a. **Minimize**. Remove the window temporarily from view.

   b. **Maximize**. Expand the window to maximum size.

FIGURE 2.4

Click the right mouse button to display an application's selection menu.

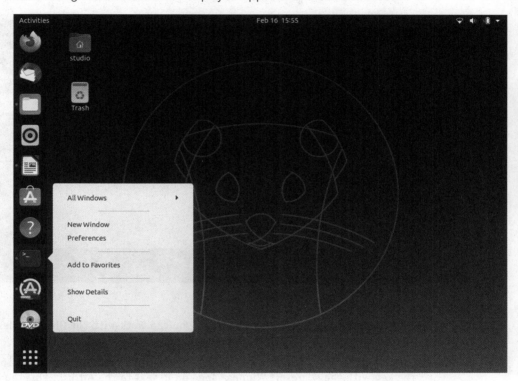

c. **Move**. Change the window to moving mode. Moving your mouse moves the window. Click to fix the window to a spot.

d. **Resize**. Change the window to resize mode. Moving your mouse resizes the window. Click to keep the size.

e. **Workspace selections**. Several selections let you use workspaces in different ways. Select Always on Top to make the current window always on top of other windows in the workspace. Select Always on Visible Workspace to always show the window on the workspace that is visible, or select Move to Workspace Up or Move to Workspace Down to move the window to the workspace above or below, respectively.

If you don't feel comfortable navigating GNOME 3 with your mouse, or if you don't have a mouse, the next section helps you navigate the desktop from the keyboard.

FIGURE 2.5

As new desktops are used, additional ones appear on the right.

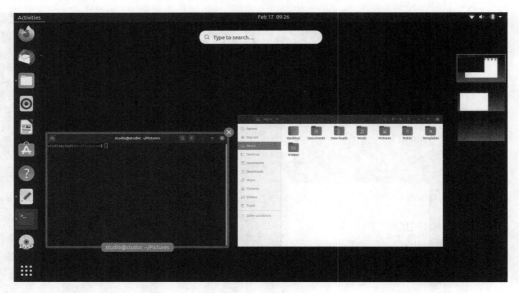

Navigating with the keyboard

If you prefer to keep your hands on the keyboard, you can work with the GNOME 3 desktop directly from the keyboard in a number of ways, including the following:

Windows key. Press the Windows key on the keyboard. On most PC keyboards, this is the key with the Microsoft Windows logo on it next to the Alt key. This toggles the mini-window (Activities) and active-window (current workspace) views. Many people use this key often.

Select an active window. Return to any of your workspaces (press the Windows key if you are not already on an active workspace). Press Alt+Tab to see a list of all active windows. Continue to hold the Alt key as you press the Tab key (or right or left arrow keys) to highlight the application that you want from the list of active desktop application windows. If an application has multiple windows open, press Alt+` (back-tick, located above the Tab key) to choose among those sub-windows. Release the Alt key to select it.

Launch a command or application. From any active workspace, you can launch a Linux command or a graphical application. Here are some examples:

Applications. From the Activities screen, press Ctrl+Alt+Tab and continue to press Tab until the Applications icon is highlighted; then release Ctrl+Alt. The Applications view appears, with the first icon highlighted. Use the Tab key or arrow keys (up, down, right, and left) to highlight the application icon you want, and press Enter.

Command box. If you know the name (or part of a name) of a command that you want to run, press Alt+F2 to display a command box. Type the name of the command that you want to run into the box (try `gnome-terminal` to open a terminal session, for example).

Search box. From the Activities screen, press Ctrl+Alt+Tab and continue to press Tab until the magnifying glass (Search) icon is highlighted; then release Ctrl+Alt. In the search box now highlighted, type a few letters of an application's name or description (type **scr** to see what you get). Keep typing until the application you want is highlighted (in this case, Screenshot), and press Enter to launch it.

Escape. When you are stuck in an action that you don't want to complete, try pressing the Esc key. For example, after pressing Alt+F2 (to enter a command), opening an icon from the top bar, or going to an overview page, pressing Esc returns you to the active window on the active desktop.

I hope you now feel comfortable navigating the GNOME 3 desktop. Next, you can try running some useful and fun desktop applications from GNOME 3.

Setting up the GNOME 3 desktop

Much of what you need GNOME 3 to do for you is set up automatically. However, you need to make a few tweaks to get the desktop the way you want. Most of these setup activities are available from the System Settings window (see Figure 2.6). Open the Settings icon from the Applications list.

Here are some suggestions for configuring a GNOME 3 desktop:

Configure networking. A wired network connection is often configured automatically when you boot up your system. For wireless, you probably have to select your wireless network and add a password when prompted. An icon in the top bar lets you do any wired or wireless network configuration that you need to do. Refer to Chapter 14, "Administering Networking," for further information on configuring networking.

Bluetooth. If your computer has Bluetooth hardware, you can enable that device to communicate with other Bluetooth devices (such as a Bluetooth headset or printer).

Devices. From the Devices screen, you can configure your keyboard, mouse and touchpad, printers, removable media, and other settings.

Sound. Click the Sound settings button to adjust sound input and output devices on your system.

Extending the GNOME 3 desktop

If the GNOME 3 shell doesn't do everything you'd like, don't despair. You can add extensions to provide additional functionality. Also, a tool called GNOME Tweaks lets you change advanced settings in GNOME 3.

FIGURE 2.6

The System Settings window

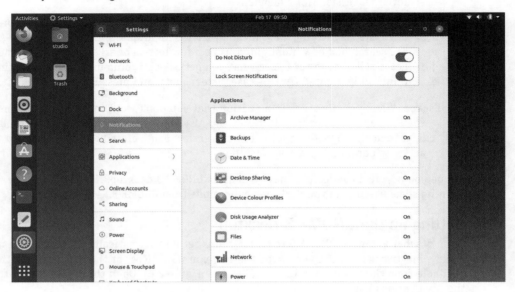

Using GNOME shell extensions

GNOME shell extensions are available to change the way your GNOME desktop looks and behaves. Visit the GNOME Shell Extensions site (extensions.gnome.org) from the browser on your GNOME 3 desktop. That site tells you what extensions you have installed and which ones are available to install. To manage extensions through your browser, you'll need to install the browser extension by following the link you're shown on the Gnome.org page and then installing the native host connector using:

```
sudo apt install chrome-gnome-shell
```

Because the extensions page knows what extensions you have and the version of GNOME 3 that you are running, it will present only those extensions that are compatible with your system. Many of the extensions help you add features from GNOME 2, including the following:

Applications Menu. Adds an Applications menu to the top panel, just as it did in GNOME 2.

Places Status Indicator. Adds a systems status menu, similar to the Places menu in GNOME 2, to let you navigate quickly to useful folders on your system.

Window list. Adds a list of active windows to the top panel, similar to the Window list that appeared on the bottom panel in GNOME 2.

To install an extension, simply select the ON button next to the name. Or, you can click the extension name from the list to see the extension's page and click the button on that page from OFF to ON. Click Install when you are asked if you want to download and install the extension. The extension is then added to your desktop.

More than 100 GNOME shell extensions are available now, and more are being added all the time. Other popular extensions include Notifications Alert (which alerts you of unread messages), Presentation Mode (which prevents the screensaver from executing when you're giving a presentation), and Music Integration (which integrates popular music players into GNOME 3, so that you are alerted about songs being played).

Because the Extensions site can keep track of your extensions, you can click the Installed extensions button at the top of the page and see every extension that is installed. You can turn the extensions off and on from there and even delete them permanently.

Using the GNOME Tweak Tool

If you don't like the way some of the built-in features of GNOME 3 behave, you can change many of them with the GNOME Tweak Tool. This tool is not installed by default, but you can add it by installing the gnome-tweaks package. After installation, the GNOME Tweak Tool is available by launching the Advanced Settings icon from your Applications screen. Start with the Desktop category to consider what you might want to change in GNOME 3. Figure 2.7 shows the Tweak Tool displaying Appearance settings.

If fonts are too small for you, select the Fonts category and click the plus sign next to the Scaling Factor box to increase the font size, or change fonts individually for documents, window titles, or monospace fonts.

Under Top Bar settings, you can change how clock information is displayed in the top bar or set whether to show the week number in the calendar. To change the look of the desktop, select the Appearance category and change, for example, the Icons theme to fit your needs.

Starting with desktop applications

Live sessions come with some cool applications that you can start using immediately. To use GNOME 3 as your everyday desktop, you should install Ubuntu permanently to your computer's hard disk and add the applications you need (a word processor, image editor, drawing application, and so on). If you are just getting started, the following sections list some useful applications to try out.

Managing files and folders with Nautilus

To move, copy, delete, rename, and otherwise organize files and folders in GNOME 3, you can use the Nautilus file manager. Nautilus comes with the GNOME desktop and works like other file managers that you may use in Windows or Mac.

To open Nautilus, click the Files icon from the Dock or Applications list. Your user account starts with a set of folders designed to hold the most common types of content: music, pictures, videos, and the like. These are all stored in what is referred to as your Home directory.

FIGURE 2.7

Change desktop settings using the GNOME Tweak Tool (Appearance settings).

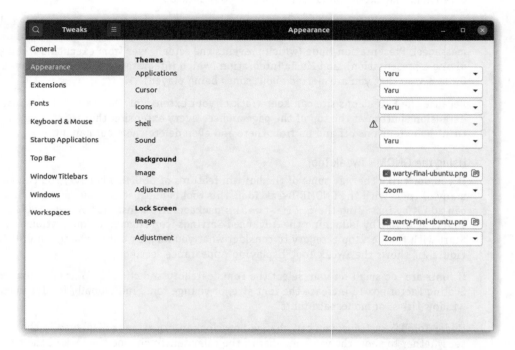

When you want to save files that you downloaded from the Internet or created with a word processor, you can organize them into these folders. You can create new folders as needed, drag and drop files and folders to copy and move them, and delete them.

Because Nautilus is not much different from most file managers that you have used on other computer systems, this chapter does not go into detail about how to use drag-and-drop and navigate through folders to find your content. However, I do want to make a few observations that may not be obvious about how to use Nautilus:

Home folder

You have complete control over the files and folders that you create in your Home folder. However, most other parts of the filesystem are not accessible to you as a regular user.

Filesystem organization

Although it appears under the name Home, your Home folder is actually located in the filesystem under the /home folder in a folder named after your username: for example, /home/ubuntu or /home/chris. In the next few chapters, you learn how the filesystem is organized (especially in relation to the Linux command shell).

Working with files and folders

Right-click a file or folder icon to see how you can act on it. For example, you can copy, cut, move to trash (delete), or open any file or folder icon.

Creating folders

To create a new folder, right-click in a folder window and select New Folder. Type the new folder name over the highlighted Untitled Folder, and press Enter to name the folder.

Accessing remote content

Nautilus can display content from remote servers as well as the local filesystem. In Nautilus, select Other Locations from the file menu. From the Connect to Server box that appears at the bottom, you can connect to a remote server via SSH (secure shell), FTP with login, Public FTP, Windows share, WebDav (HTTP), or Secure WebDav (HTTPS). Add appropriate user and password information as needed, and the content of the remote server appears in the Nautilus window. Figure 2.8 shows an example of a Nautilus window prompting you for a password to log in to a remote server over SSH protocol (ssh://192.168.1.3).

FIGURE 2.8

Access remote folders using the Nautilus Connect to Server feature.

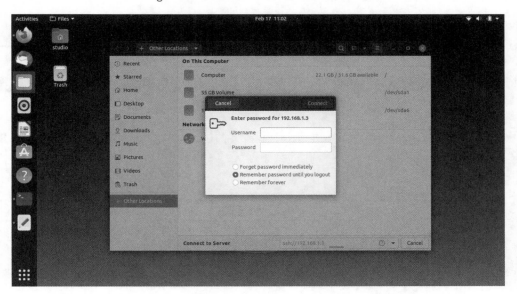

Installing and managing additional software

The Ubuntu Desktop comes with a web browser (Firefox), a file manager (Nautilus), and a few other common applications. However, there are many other useful applications that, because of their size, just wouldn't fit on the live installation media. When you install Ubuntu to your hard disk (as described in Chapter 9), you will almost certainly want to add some more software.

When Ubuntu is installed, it's automatically configured to connect your system to the huge Debian-based software repository over the Internet. As long as you have an Internet connection, you can run the Add/Remove software tool to download and install any of thousands of software packages.

Although the facility for managing software in Ubuntu (using apt and dpkg) is described in detail in Chapter 10, "Getting and Managing Software," you can start installing some software packages without knowing much about how the feature works. Begin by going to the applications screen and opening the Ubuntu Software window (via the Dock icon).

With the Software window open, you can select the applications that you want to install by browsing by category or hitting Ctrl+F and searching by name. Figure 2.9 shows an example of the Software window.

FIGURE 2.9

Download and install software from the Ubuntu repository.

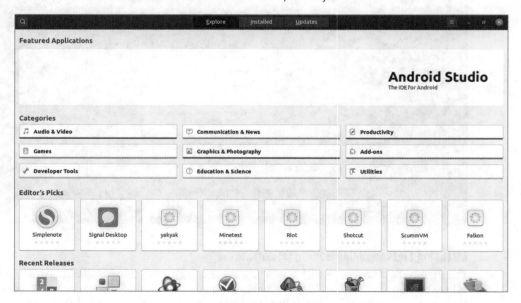

By searching for and installing some common desktop applications, you should be able to start using your desktop effectively. Refer to Chapter 10 for details on how to administrate your software repositories more effectively and efficiently.

Playing music with Rhythmbox

Rhythmbox is the music player that comes with your Ubuntu Desktop. You can launch Rhythmbox from the GNOME 3 Dock and immediately play music CDs, podcasts, or Internet radio shows. You can import audio files in WAV and Ogg Vorbis formats or add plug-ins for MP3 or other audio formats.

Here are a few ways that you can get started with Rhythmbox:

Radio

Double-click the Radio selection under Library and choose a radio station from the list that appears to the right.

Podcasts

Search for podcasts on the Internet and find the URL for one that interests you. Right-click the Podcasts entry and select New Podcast Feed. Paste or type the URL of the podcast and click Add. A list of podcasts from the site that you selected appears to the right. Double-click the one to which you want to listen.

Audio CDs

Insert an audio CD and press Play when it appears in the Rhythmbox window. Rhythmbox also lets you rip and burn audio CDs.

Audio files

Rhythmbox can play WAV and Ogg Vorbis files. By adding plug-ins, you can play many other audio formats, including MP3. Because there are patent issues related to the MP3 format, you'll need to download and install unfree software codecs to play MP3s. Ubuntu makes it easy to select that option during the standard installation process. In Chapter 10, I describe how to get software that you need that is not in your Ubuntu repository.

Plug-ins are available for Rhythmbox to get cover art, show information about artists and songs, add support for music services (such as Last.fm and Magnatune), and fetch song lyrics.

Stopping the GNOME 3 desktop

When you are finished with your GNOME 3 session, select the down arrow button in the upper-right corner of the top bar. From there, you can choose the On/Off button, which allows you to log out or switch to a different user account without logging out.

Using the Unity Graphical Shell with the GNOME Desktop

From version 10.10 (released in October—the tenth month—of 2010), Ubuntu moved to a user interface stack that included the GNOME desktop and the Unity graphical shell. By the time version 18.04 (released in April—the fourth month—of 2018) came out, Ubuntu's use of Unity was ended, in favor of adoption of a standard implementation of GNOME 3.

Because, from time to time, you may still come across Ubuntu systems running Unity, we're going to explore how some of the more critical features from those days worked. You should become familiar with the following components:

Metacity (window manager)

The default window manager was Metacity. Metacity configuration options let you control such things as themes, window borders, and controls used on your desktop.

Compiz (window manager)

You can enable this window manager to provide 3D desktop effects.

Panels (application/task launcher)

These panels, which line the top and bottom of the desktop, were designed to make it convenient for you to launch the applications you use, manage running applications, and work with multiple virtual desktops. By default, the top panel contained menu buttons (Applications, Places, and System), desktop application launchers (Evolution email and Firefox web browser), a workspace switcher (for managing four virtual desktops), and a clock. Icons appeared in the panel with alerts: when you needed software updates, for instance. The bottom panel had a Show Desktop button, window lists, a trash can, and workspace switcher.

Desktop area

The windows and icons you use were arranged on the desktop area, which supports drag-and-drop between applications, a desktop menu (right-click to see it), and icons for launching applications. A Computer icon consolidates CD drives, floppy drives, the filesystem, and shared network resources in one place.

There was also a set of Preferences windows that enabled you to configure different aspects of your desktop. You could change backgrounds, colors, fonts, keyboard shortcuts, and other features related to the look and behavior of the desktop.

Using the Metacity window manager

The Metacity window manager seems to have been chosen as the default window manager because of its simplicity. The creator of Metacity refers to it as a "boring window manager for the adult in you" and then goes on to compare other window managers to colorful, sugary cereal, whereas Metacity is characterized as Cheerios.

NOTE

To use 3D effects, your best solution is to use the Compiz window manager. You can't do much with Metacity (except get your work done efficiently). You assign new themes to Metacity and change colors and window decorations through the preferences (described later).

You can use other keyboard shortcuts with the window manager as well. Select System ⇨ Preferences ⇨ Keyboard Shortcuts to see a list of shortcuts, such as the following:

Run Dialog

To run a command to launch an application from the desktop by command name, press Alt+F2. From the dialog box that appears, type the command and press Enter. For example, type `gedit` to run a simple graphical text editor.

Lock Screen

If you want to step away from your screen and lock it, press Ctrl+Alt+L. You need to type your user password to open the screen again. Note: to lock your screen in GNOME 3, press Windows+L.

Show Main Menu

To open an application from the Applications, Places, or System menu, press Alt+F1. Then use the up and down arrow keys to select from the current menu or use the right and left arrow keys to select from other menus.

Another Metacity feature of interest is the Workspace Switcher. Four virtual workspaces appear in the workspace switcher on the panel. You can do the following with the workspace switcher:

Choose current workspace

Four virtual workspaces appear in the workspace switcher. Click any of the four virtual workspaces to make it your current workspace.

Move windows to other workspaces

Click any window, each represented by a tiny rectangle in a workspace, to drag and drop it to another workspace. Likewise, you can drag an application from the Window list to move that application to another workspace.

Add more workspaces

Right-click the workspace switcher and select Preferences. You can add workspaces (up to 32).

Name workspaces

Right-click the workspace switcher and select Preferences. Click in the Workspaces pane to change names of workspaces to any names you choose.

You can view and change information about Metacity controls and settings using the gconf-editor window (type `gconf-editor` from a Terminal window). As the window says, it is not the recommended way to change preferences, so when possible, you should change the desktop through preferences. However, gconf-editor is a good way to see descriptions of each Metacity feature.

From the gconf-editor window, select Apps ⇨ Metacity, and choose from general, global_keybindings, keybindings_commands, window_keybindings, and workspace_names. Click each key to see its value, along with short and long descriptions of the key.

Changing GNOME's appearance

You can change the general look of your GNOME desktop by selecting System ⇨ Preferences ⇨ Appearance. From the Appearance Preferences window, select from three tabs:

Theme

Entire themes are available for the desktop that change the colors, icons, fonts, and other aspects of the desktop. Several different themes come with the desktop, which you can simply select from this tab to use. Or click "Get more themes online" to choose from a variety of available themes.

Background

To change your desktop background, select from a list of backgrounds on this tab to have the one you choose immediately take effect. To add a different background, put the background you want on your system (select "Get more backgrounds online" and download it to your Pictures folder). Then click Add and select the image from your Pictures folder.

Fonts

Different fonts can be selected to use by default with your applications, documents, desktop, window title bar, and for fixed width.

Using the panels

The panels are placed on the top and bottom of the desktop. From those panels, you can start applications (from buttons or menus), see what programs are active, and monitor how your system is running. You can also change the top and bottom panels in many ways—by adding applications or monitors or by changing the placement or behavior of the panel, for example.

Right-click any open space on either panel to see the Panel menu.

From the Panel menu, you can choose from a variety of functions, including these:

Use the menus.

- The Applications menu displays most of the applications and system tools that you will use from the desktop.
- The Places menu lets you select places to go, such as the Desktop folder, Home folder, removable media, or network locations.
- The System menu lets you change preferences and system settings as well as get other information about your system.

Add to Panel. Add an applet, menu, launcher, drawer, or button.

Properties. Change the panel's position, size, and background properties.

Delete This Panel. Delete the current panel.

New Panel. Add panels to your desktop in different styles and locations.

You can also work with items on a panel. For example, you can do the following:

Move items. To move an item on a panel, right-click it, select Move, and drag and drop it to a new position.

Resize items. You can resize some elements, such as the Window list, by clicking an edge and dragging it to the new size.

Use the Window list. Tasks running on the desktop appear in the Window list area. Click a task to minimize or maximize it.

The following sections describe some things that you can do with the Panel.

Adding a drawer

A *drawer* is an icon that you can click to display other icons representing menus, applets, and launchers; it behaves just like a panel. Essentially, any item that you can add to a panel you can add to a drawer. By adding a drawer to your GNOME panel, you can include several applets and launchers that together take up the space of only one icon. Click the drawer to show the applets and launchers as if they were being pulled out of a drawer icon on the panel.

To add a drawer to your panel, right-click the panel and select Add to Panel ➪ Drawer. A drawer appears on the panel. Right-click it and add applets or launchers to it as you would to a panel. Click the icon again to retract the drawer.

Changing panel properties

You can change the orientation, size, hiding policy, and background properties of your desktop panels. To open the Panel Properties window that applies to a specific panel, right-click an open space on the panel and choose Properties. The Panel Properties window that appears includes the following values:

Orientation

Move the panel to a different location on the screen by clicking a new position.

Size

Select the size of your panel by choosing its height in pixels (48 pixels by default).

Expand

Select this check box to have the panel expand to fill the entire side or clear the check box to make the panel only as wide as the applets it contains.

AutoHide

Select whether a panel is automatically hidden (appearing only when the mouse pointer is in the area).

Show Hide buttons

Choose whether the Hide/Unhide buttons (with pixmap arrows on them) appear on the edges of the panel.

Arrows on Hide buttons

If you select Show Hide buttons, you can choose to have arrows on those buttons.

Background

From the Background tab, you can assign a color to the background of the panel, assign a pixmap image, or just leave the default (which is based on the current system theme). Click the Background Image check box if you want to select an image for the background, and then select an image, such as a tile from `/usr/share/backgrounds/tiles` or another directory.

Summary

The GNOME desktop environment has become the default desktop environment for many Linux systems, including Ubuntu. The GNOME 3 desktop is a modern, elegant desktop, designed to match the types of interfaces available on many of today's mobile devices. The Unity graphical shell running on GNOME was, until the release of Ubuntu 18.04, the default graphical environment for Ubuntu.

Besides GNOME desktops, you can try out other popular and useful desktop environments. The K Desktop Environment (KDE) offers many more bells and whistles than GNOME and works with Ubuntu. Ubuntu can also use lightweight desktops such as LXDE or Xfce desktops.

Now that you have a grasp of how to get and use a Linux desktop, it's time to start digging into the more professional administrative interfaces. Chapter 3, "Using the Shell," introduces you to the Linux command-line shell interface.

Exercises

Use these exercises to test your skill in using a GNOME desktop. If you are stuck, solutions to the tasks are shown in Appendix A.

1. Obtain an Ubuntu system with a graphic desktop. Start the system and log in.

2. Launch the Firefox web browser and go to the GNOME home page (www.gnome.org).

3. Pick a background you like from the GNOME art site (www.gnome-look.org), download it to your Pictures folder, and select it as your current background.

4. Start a Nautilus File Manager window and move it to the second workspace on your desktop.

5. Find the image that you downloaded to use as your desktop background and open it in any image viewer.

6. Move back and forth between the workspace with Firefox on it and the one with the Nautilus file manager.

7. Open a list of applications installed on your system and select an image viewer to open from that list. Use as few clicks or keystrokes as possible.

8. Change the view of the windows on your current workspace to smaller views you can step through. Select any window you'd like to make it your current window.

9. From your desktop, using only the keyboard, launch a music player.

Part II

Becoming a Linux Power User

IN THIS PART

Using the Shell

IN THIS CHAPTER

Before icons and windows took over computer screens, you typed commands to interact with most computers. On UNIX systems, from which Linux was derived, the program used to interpret and manage commands was referred to as the *shell*.

No matter which Linux distribution you are using, you can always count on the fact that the shell is still available to you, and Ubuntu is no exception. It provides a way to create executable script files, run programs, work with filesystems, compile computer code, and manage the computer. Although the shell is less intuitive than common graphical user interfaces (GUIs), most Linux experts consider the shell to be much more powerful than GUIs. Shells have been around a long time, and many advanced features that aren't available from the desktop can be accessed by running shell commands.

The Linux shell illustrated in this chapter is called the *Bash shell*, which stands for Bourne Again Shell. The name is derived from the fact that Bash is compatible with one of the earliest UNIX shells: the Bourne shell (named after its creator, Stephen Bourne, and represented by the sh command).

Although Bash is included with Ubuntu and considered a standard, other shells are available, including the C shell (csh), which is popular among BSD UNIX users, and the Korn shell (ksh), which is popular among UNIX System V users. Ubuntu uses the dash shell by default at boot time, which is designed to perform faster than the Bash shell. Linux also has a tcsh shell (an improved C shell) and an ash shell (another Bourne shell look-alike).

Ubuntu has more than one shell available for your use. This chapter, however, focuses primarily on the Bash shell. That is because Ubuntu uses the Bash shell by default when you open a Terminal window.

The following are a few major reasons to learn how to use the shell:

- *You will learn to get around any Linux or other UNIX-like system*. For example, with strong shell skills, you can be equally productive in just about any Linux server, home router, or even a Mac computer. You can even log in and run commands on your Android phone. They're all running Linux or similar systems on the inside.

- *Special shell features enable you to gather data input and direct data output between commands and Linux filesystems*. To save on typing, you can find, edit, and repeat commands from your shell history. Many power users hardly touch a graphical interface, doing most of their work from a shell.

- *You can gather commands into a file using programming constructs such as conditional tests, loops, and case statements to quickly perform complex operations, which would be difficult to retype over and over*. Programs consisting of commands that are stored and run from a file are referred to as *shell scripts*. Many Linux system administrators use shell scripts to automate tasks such as backing up data, monitoring log files, or checking system health.

The shell is a command language interpreter. If you have used Microsoft operating systems, you'll see that using a shell in Linux is similar to, but generally much more powerful than, the PowerShell interpreter used to run commands. You can happily use Linux from a graphical desktop interface, but as you grow into Linux you will surely need to use the shell at some point to track down a problem or administer some features.

How to use the shell isn't obvious at first, but with the right help you can quickly learn many of the most important shell features. This chapter is your guide to working with the Linux system commands, processes, and filesystem from the shell. It describes the shell environment and helps you tailor it to your needs.

About Shells and Terminal Windows

There are several ways to get to a shell interface in Linux. Three of the most common are the shell prompt, Terminal window, and virtual console, which you learn more about in the following sections.

To start, boot up your Linux system. On your screen, you should see either a graphical login screen or a plain-text login prompt similar to the following:

```
Ubuntu 18.04.3 LTS ubuntu tty1
ubuntu login:
```

In either case, you should log in with a regular user account. If you have a plain-text login prompt, continue to the next section, "Using the shell prompt." If you log in through a graphical screen, go to the section "Using a Terminal window" to see how to access a shell from the desktop. In either case, you can access more shells as described in the section "Using virtual consoles," which appears shortly in this chapter.

Using the shell prompt

If your Linux system has no graphical user interface (or one that isn't working at the moment), you will most likely see a shell prompt after you log in. Typing commands from the shell will probably be your primary means of using the Linux system.

The default prompt for a regular user is simply a dollar sign:

```
$
```

The default prompt for the root user is a pound sign (also called a *number sign* or a *hash tag*):

```
#
```

In most Linux systems, the $ and # prompts are preceded by your username, system name, and current directory name. For example, a login prompt for the user named jake on a computer named pine with /usr/share/ as the current working directory would appear as follows:

```
[jake@pine share]$
```

You can change the prompt to display any characters you like and even read in pieces of information about your system. For example, you can use the current working directory, the date, the local computer name, or any string of characters as your prompt. To configure your prompt, see the section "Setting your prompt" later in this chapter.

Although a tremendous number of features are available with the shell, it's easy to begin by just entering a few commands. Try some of the commands shown in the remaining sections to become familiar with your current shell environment.

In the examples that follow, the dollar ($) and pound (#) symbols indicate a prompt. A $ indicates that the command can be run by any user, but a # typically means that you should run the command as the root user; that is, many administrative tools require root permission to be able to run them. The prompt is followed by the command that you type (and then press Enter). The lines that follow show the output resulting from the command.

> **NOTE**
>
> Although we use # to indicate that a command should be run as the root user, you do not need to log in as the root user to run a command as root. In fact, the most common way to run a command as a root user is to use the `sudo` command. See Chapter 8, "Learning System Administration," for further information about the `sudo` command.

Using a Terminal window

With the desktop GUI running, you can open a terminal emulator program (sometimes referred to as a Terminal window) to start a shell. Ubuntu makes it easy for you to get to a shell from the GUI. Here are some common ways to launch a Terminal window from the desktop:

Right-click the desktop In the context menu that appears, you should see Open Terminal or something similar. Select it to start a Terminal window.

Select Terminal from the Applications screen You can search for "terminal" within the GNOME 3 Applications page.

Press Ctrl+Alt+T Ubuntu systems will respond to the Ctrl+Alt+T combination by opening a new terminal shell.

Press Alt+F2 Alt+F2 will open a command prompt into which you can type `gnome-terminal`.

The GNOME Terminal supports many features beyond the basic shell. For example, you can cut and paste text to or from a GNOME Terminal window, change fonts, set a title, choose colors or images to use as background, and set how much text to save when text scrolls off the screen.

To try some GNOME Terminal features, open a new terminal and then follow this procedure:

1. Select Edit ⇨ Preferences.
2. On the General tab or current profile (depending on your version of GNOME), check the "Custom font" box.
3. With the Text tab selected and Custom font selected, try a different font and size. The new font appears in the Terminal window.
4. Return to the Preferences menu and unselect the "Custom font" box. This will restore the original font.
5. On the Colors tab, clear the "Use colors from system theme" check box. From here, you can try some different font and background colors.
6. Re-select the "Use colors from system theme" box to go back to the default colors.
7. Go to your Profile window. There are other features with which you may want to experiment, such as setting how much scrolled data is kept.
8. Close the Profile window when you are finished. You are now ready to use your Terminal window.

If you are using Linux from a graphical desktop, you will probably most often access the shell from a Terminal window.

Using virtual consoles

Most Linux systems that include a desktop interface start multiple virtual consoles running on the computer. Virtual consoles are a way to have multiple shell sessions open at once in addition to the graphical interface you are using.

You can switch between virtual consoles by holding the Ctrl and Alt keys and pressing a function key between F2 and F6. For example, pressing Ctrl+Alt+F2 will open a new virtual console session. You can return to your initial GUI session by pressing Ctrl+Alt+F1.

Try it right now. Hold down the Ctrl+Alt keys and press F3 (invoking the F keys might require additional actions on some laptop keyboards). You should see a plain-text login prompt. Log in using your username and password. Try a few commands. When you are finished, type **exit** to exit the shell and then press Ctrl+Alt+F1 to return to your graphical desktop interface. You can go back and forth between these consoles as much as you like.

Choosing Your Shell

In most Linux systems, your default shell is the Bash shell. To find out your default login shell, enter the following commands:

```
$ whoami
chris
$ grep chris /etc/passwd
chris:x:1000:1000:Chris,,,:/home/chris:/bin/bash
```

Notice that the command-line examples shown here and throughout the book show the command followed by output from that command. When the command completes, you are presented with the command prompt again.

The whoami command shows your username, and the grep command (replacing chris with your username) shows the definition of your user account in the /etc/passwd file. The last field in that entry shows that the Bash shell (/bin/bash) is your default shell (the one that starts up when you log in or open a Terminal window).

It's possible, although not likely, that you might have a different default shell set. To try a different shell, simply type the name of that shell (like **dash** and others, assuming that they're installed). You can try a few commands in that shell and type **exit** when you are finished to return to the Bash shell.

You might choose to use different shells for the following reasons:

- You are used to using UNIX System V systems (often ksh by default) or Sun Microsystems and other Berkeley UNIX-based distributions (frequently csh by default), and you are more comfortable using default shells from those environments.
- You want to run shell scripts that were created for a particular shell environment, and you need to run the shell for which they were made so that you can test or use those scripts from your current shell.

3

- You simply prefer features in one shell over those in another. For example, some prefer `ksh` over Bash because they don't like the way aliases are used with Bash.

Although most Linux users have a preference for one shell or another, when you know how to use one shell, you can quickly learn any of the others by occasionally referring to the shell's man page (for example, type **man Bash**). The man pages (described later in the section "Getting Information about Commands") provide documentation for commands, file formats, and other components in Linux. Most people use Bash just because they don't have a particular reason for using a different shell.

Bash includes features originally developed for `sh` and `ksh` shells in early UNIX systems, as well as some `csh` features. Expect Bash to be the default login shell in most Linux systems that you are using, with the exception of some specialized Linux systems (such as some that run on embedded devices) that may require a smaller shell that needs less memory and requires fewer features. Most of the examples in this chapter are based on the Bash shell.

> **TIP**
>
> The Bash shell is worth knowing not only because it is the default in most installations, but because it is the one you will use with most Linux certification exams.

Running Commands

The simplest way to run a command is just to type the name of the command from a shell. From your desktop, open a Terminal window. Then enter the following command:

```
$ date
Thu Jun 29 08:14:53 EDT 2019
```

Entering the `date` command, with no options or arguments, causes the current day, month, date, time, time zone, and year to be displayed as just shown.

Here are a few other commands you can try:

```
$ pwd
/home/chris
$ hostname
mydesktop
$ ls
Desktop    Downloads  Pictures  Templates
Documents  Music      Public    Videos
```

The `pwd` command shows your current working directory. Entering `hostname` shows your computer's hostname. The `ls` command lists the files and directories in your current directory. Although many commands can be run by just entering command names, it's more common to type other characters after the command to modify its behavior. The characters and words that you can type after a command are called *options* and *arguments*.

Understanding command syntax

Most commands have one or more *options* that you can add to change the command's behavior. Options typically consist of a single letter preceded by a hyphen. However, you can group single-letter options together or precede each with a hyphen to use more than one option at a time. For example, the following two uses of options for the `ls` command are the same:

```
$ ls -l -a -t
$ ls -lat
```

In both cases, the `ls` command is run with the -l (long listing), -a (show hidden dot files), and -t options (list by age).

Some commands include options that are represented by a whole word. To tell a command to use a whole word as an option, you typically precede it with a double hyphen (--). For example, to use the help option on many commands, you enter `--help` on the command line. Without the double hyphen, the letters h, e, l, and p would be interpreted as separate options. There are some commands that don't follow the double hyphen convention, using a single hyphen before a word, but most commands use double hyphens for word options.

> **NOTE**
>
> You can use the `--help` option with most commands to see the options and arguments that they support. For example, try typing `hostname --help`.

Many commands also accept arguments after certain options are entered or at the end of the entire command line. An *argument* is an extra piece of information, such as a filename, directory, username, device, or other item, that tells the command what to act on. For example, `cat /etc/passwd` displays the contents of the /etc/passwd file on your screen. In this case, /etc/passwd is the argument. Usually, you can have as many arguments as you want on the command line, limited only by the total number of characters allowed on a command line. Sometimes, an argument is associated with an option. In that case, the argument must immediately follow the option. With single-letter options, the argument typically follows after a space. For full-word options, the argument often follows an equal sign (=). Here are some examples:

```
$ ls --hide=Desktop
Documents   Music      Public      Videos
Downloads   Pictures   Templates
```

In the previous example, the `--hide` option tells the `ls` command not to display the file or directory named `Desktop` when listing the contents of the directory. Notice that the equal sign immediately follows the option (no space) and then the argument (again, no space).

Here's an example of a single-letter option that is followed by an argument:

```
$ tar -cvf backup.tar /home/chris
```

3

In the `tar` example just shown, the options say to create (c) a file (f) named `backup.tar` that includes all of the contents of the `/home/chris` directory and its subdirectories and show verbose messages as the backup is created (v). Because `backup.tar` is an argument to the `f` option, `backup.tar` must immediately follow the option. As it turns out, you don't actually need the hyphen to introduce your options (`cvf`) for the `tar` command, although it doesn't do any harm.

Here are a few commands that you can try out. See how they behave differently with different options:

```
$ ls
Desktop  Documents  Downloads  Music  Pictures  Public  Templates  Videos
$ ls -a
.                 Desktop      .gnome2_private  .lesshst       Public
..                Documents    .gnote           .local         Templates
.bash_history     Downloads    .gnupg           .mozilla       Videos
.bash_logout      .emacs       .gstreamer-0.10  Music          .xsession-errors
.bash_profile     .esd_auth    .gtk-bookmarks   Pictures       .zshrc
.bashrc           .fsync.log   .gvfs            Pictures
$ uname
Linux
$ uname -a
Linux workstation 5.3.0-28-generic #30~18.04.1-Ubuntu SMP Fri Jan 17
06:14:09 UTC 2020
x86_64 x86_64 x86_64 GNU/Linux
$ date
Thu Jun 29 08:14:53 EDT 2019
$ date +'%d/%m/%y'
06/29/19
$ date +'%A, %B %d, %Y'
Thursday, June 29, 2019
```

The `ls` command, by itself, shows all regular files and directories in the current directory. By adding the `-a`, you can also see the hidden files in the directory (those beginning with a dot). The `uname` command shows the type of system you are running (Linux). When you add `-a`, you also can see the hostname, kernel release, and kernel version.

The `date` command has some special types of options. By itself, `date` simply prints the current day, date, and time as shown in the preceding code. But the `date` command supports a special + format option, which lets you display the date in different formats. Enter **date --help** to see different format indicators you can use.

Try the `id` and `who` commands to get a feel for your current Linux environment, as described in the following paragraphs.

When you log in to a Linux system, Linux views you as having a particular identity, which includes your username, group name, user ID, and group ID. Linux also keeps track of your login session: It knows when you logged in, how long you have been idle, and where you logged in from.

To find out information about your identity, use the id command as follows:

```
$ id
uid=1000(chris) gid=1000(chris) groups=1005(sales), 7(lp)
```

In this example, the username is chris, which is represented by the numeric user ID (uid) 1000. The primary group for chris also is called chris, which has a group ID (gid) of 1000. It is normal for Ubuntu users to have the same primary group name as their username. The user chris also belongs to other groups called sales (gid 1005) and lp (gid 7). These names and numbers represent the permissions that chris has to access computer resources.

You can see information about your current login session by using the who command. In the following example, the -u option says to add information about idle time and the process ID and -H asks that a header be printed:

```
$ who -uH
NAME      LINE     TIME          IDLE     PID        COMMENT
chris     tty1     2020-02-17    18:53    00:38      10782
```

The output from this who command shows that the user chris is logged in on tty1 (which is the first virtual console on the monitor connected to the computer) and his login session began at 18:53 on February 17. The IDLE time shows how long the shell has been open without any command being typed. PID shows the process ID of the user's login shell. COMMENT would show the name of the remote computer from which the user had logged in, if that user had logged in from another computer on the network, or the name of the local X display if that user were using a Terminal window (such as :0.0).

Locating commands

Now that you have typed a few commands, you may wonder where those commands are located and how the shell finds the commands you type. To find commands you type, the shell looks in what is referred to as your *path*. For commands that are not in your path, you can type the complete identity of the location of the command.

If you know the directory that contains the command that you want to run, one way to run it is to type the full, or absolute, path to that command. For example, you run the date command from the /bin directory by entering the following:

```
$ /bin/date
```

Of course, this can be inconvenient, especially if the command resides in a directory with a long pathname. The better way is to have commands stored in well-known directories and then add those directories to your shell's PATH environment variable. The path consists of a list of directories that are checked sequentially for the commands you enter. To see your current path, enter the following:

```
$ echo $PATH
/usr/local/bin:/usr/bin:/bin:/usr/local/sbin:/usr/sbin:/sbin:↵
/home/chris/bin
```

The results show a common default path for a regular Linux user. Directories in the path list are separated by colons. Most user commands that come with Linux are stored in the /bin, /usr/bin, or /usr/local/bin directory. The /sbin and /usr/sbin directories contain administrative commands (some Linux systems don't put those directories in regular users' paths). The last directory shown is the bin directory in the user's home directory (/home/chris/bin).

> **TIP**
>
> If you want to add your own commands or shell scripts, place them in the bin directory in your home directory (such as /home/chris/bin for the user named chris). This directory is automatically added to your path in some Linux systems, although you may need to create that directory or add it to your PATH on other Linux systems. So, as long as you add the command to your bin with execute permission, you can begin using it by simply typing the command name at your shell prompt. To make commands available to all users, add them to /usr/local/bin.

Unlike some other operating systems, Linux does not, by default, check the current directory for an executable before searching the path. It immediately begins searching the path, and executables in the current directory are run only if they are in the PATH variable or you give their absolute (such as /home/chris/scriptx.sh) or relative (for example, ./scriptx.sh) location.

The path directory order is important. Directories are checked from left to right. So, in this example, if there is a command called foo located in both the /usr/bin and /bin directories, the one in /usr/bin is executed. To have the other foo command run, you either type the full path to the command or change your PATH variable. (Changing your PATH and adding directories to it are described later in this chapter.)

Not all of the commands you run are located in directories in your PATH variable. Some commands are built into the shell. Other commands can be overridden by creating aliases that define any commands and options that you want the command to run. There are also ways of defining a function that consists of a stored series of commands. Here is the order in which the shell checks for the commands you type:

1. **Aliases.** These are names set by the alias command that represent a particular command and a set of options. Type **alias** to see what aliases are set. Often, aliases enable you to define a short name for a long, complicated command. (I describe how to create your own aliases later in this chapter.)

2. **Shell reserved word.** These are words reserved by the shell for special use. Many of these are words that you would use in programming-type functions, such as do, while, case, and else. (I cover some of these reserved words in Chapter 7, "Writing Simple Shell Scripts.")

3. **Function.** This is a set of commands that are executed together within the current shell.

4. **Built-in command.** This is a command built into the shell. As a result, there is no representation of the command in the filesystem. Some of the most common commands that you will use are shell built-in commands, such as cd (to change directories), echo (to output text to the screen), exit (to exit from a shell), fg (to

bring a command running in the background to the foreground), `history` (to see a list of commands that were previously run), `pwd` (to list the present working directory), `set` (to set shell options), and `type` (to show the location of a command).

5. **Filesystem command.** This command is stored in and executed from the computer's filesystem. (These are the commands that are indicated by the value of the `PATH` variable.)

To determine the location of a particular command, you can use the `type` command. (If you are using a shell other than Bash, use the `which` command instead.) For example, to find out where the Bash shell command is located, enter the following:

```
$ type bash
bash is /bin/bash
```

Try these few words with the `type` command to see other locations of commands: `which`, `case`, and `return`. If a command resides in several locations, you can add the `-a` option to have all of the known locations of the command printed. For example, the command `type -a ls` should show an aliased and filesystem location for the `ls` command.

> **TIP**
>
> Sometimes, you run a command and receive an error message that the command was not found or that permission to run the command was denied. If the command was not found, check that you spelled the command correctly and that it is located in your `PATH` variable. If permission to run the command was denied, the command may be in the `PATH` variable but may not be executable. Also remember that case is important, so typing CAT or Cat will not find the `cat` command.

If a command is not in your `PATH` variable, you can use the `locate` command to try to find it. Using `locate`, you can search any part of the system that is accessible to you. (Some files are only accessible to the root user.) For example, if you wanted to find the location of the `chage` command, you could enter the following:

```
$ locate chage
/snap/core/8268/usr/bin/chage
/snap/core/8268/usr/share/bash-completion/completions/chage
/snap/core/8592/usr/bin/chage
/snap/core/8592/usr/share/bash-completion/completions/chage
/snap/core18/1650/usr/bin/chage
/snap/core18/1668/usr/bin/chage
/usr/bin/chage
/usr/share/bash-completion/completions/chage
/usr/share/man/de/man1/chage.1.gz
/usr/share/man/fr/man1/chage.1.gz
/usr/share/man/it/man1/chage.1.gz
/usr/share/man/ja/man1/chage.1.gz
/usr/share/man/man1/chage.1.gz
/usr/share/man/pl/man1/chage.1.gz
```

Continues

Continued

```
/usr/share/man/ru/man1/chage.1.gz
/usr/share/man/sv/man1/chage.1.gz
/usr/share/man/tr/man1/chage.1.gz
/usr/share/man/zh_CN/man1/chage.1.gz
/var/lib/app-info/icons/ubuntu-bionic-universe/64x64/patchage_
patchage.png
```

Notice that `locate` not only found the `chage` command, it also found a variety of man pages associated with `chage` for different languages. The `locate` command looks all over your filesystem, not just in directories that contain commands. (If `locate` does not find files recently added to your system, run `updatedb` as root to update the locate database.)

In the coming chapters, you'll learn to use these and additional commands. But for now, I want you to become more familiar with how the shell itself works. So next I discuss features for recalling commands, completing commands, using variables, and creating aliases.

Recalling Commands Using Command History

Being able to repeat a command you ran earlier in a shell session can be convenient. Recalling a long and complex command line that you mistyped can save you some trouble. Fortunately, some shell features enable you to recall previous command lines, edit those lines, or complete a partially typed command line.

The *shell history* is a list of the commands that you have entered before. Using the `history` command in a Bash shell, you can view your previous commands. Then using various shell features, you can recall individual command lines from that list and change them however you please.

The rest of this section describes how to do command-line editing, how to complete parts of command lines, and how to recall and work with the history list.

Command-line editing

If you type something wrong on a command line, the Bash shell ensures that you don't have to delete the entire line and start over. Likewise, you can recall a previous command line and change the elements to make a new command.

By default, the Bash shell uses command-line editing that is based on the emacs text editor. (Type **man emacs** to read about it, if you care to do so.) If you are familiar with emacs, you probably already know most of the keystrokes described here.

> **TIP**
>
> If you prefer the `vi` command for editing shell command lines, you can easily make that happen. Add the following line to the `.bashrc` file in your home directory:
>
> ```
> set -o vi
> ```
>
> The next time you open a shell, you can use `vi` commands to edit your command lines.

To do the editing, you can use a combination of control keys, Meta keys, and arrow keys. For example, Ctrl+F means to hold down the Ctrl key, and type **f**. Alt+F means to hold down the Alt key, and type **f**. (Instead of the Alt key, your keyboard may use a Meta key or the Esc key. On a Windows keyboard, you can use the Windows key.)

To try out a bit of command-line editing, enter the following:

```
$ ls /usr/bin | sort -f | less
```

This command lists the contents of the /usr/bin directory, sorts the contents in alphabetical order (regardless of case), and pipes the output to less. The less command displays the first page of output, after which you can go through the rest of the output a line (press Enter) or a page (press spacebar) at a time. Simply press **q** when you are finished. Now, suppose that you want to change /usr/bin to /bin. You can use the following steps to change the command:

1. **Press the up arrow (↑) key.** This displays the most recent command from your shell history.
2. **Press Ctrl+A.** This moves the cursor to the beginning of the command line.
3. **Press Ctrl+F or the right arrow (→) key.** Repeat this command a few times to position the cursor under the first slash (/).
4. **Press Ctrl+D.** Type this command four times to delete /usr from the line.
5. **Press Enter.** This executes the command line.

As you edit a command line, at any point you can type regular characters to add those characters to the command line. The characters appear at the location of your text cursor. You can use right (→) and left (←) arrows to move the cursor from one end to the other on the command line. You can also press the up (↑) and down (↓) arrow keys to step through previous commands in the history list to select a command line for editing. (See the section "Command-line recall" for details on how to recall commands from the history list.) You can use many keystrokes to edit your command lines. Table 3.1 lists the keystrokes that you can use to move around the command line.

TABLE 3.1 Keystrokes for Navigating Command Lines

keystroke	Full Name	Meaning
Ctrl+F	Character forward	Go forward one character.
Ctrl+B	Character backward	Go backward one character.
Alt+F	Word forward	Go forward one word.
Alt+B	Word backward	Go backward one word.
Ctrl+A	Beginning of line	Go to the beginning of the current line.
Ctrl+E	End of line	Go to the end of the line.
Ctrl+L	Clear screen	Clear screen and leave line at the top of the screen.

The keystrokes in Table 3.2 can be used to edit command lines.

TABLE 3.2   Keystrokes for Editing Command Lines

KEYSTROKE	FULL NAME	MEANING	
Ctrl+D	Delete current	Delete the current character.	
Back-space	Delete previous	Delete the previous character.	
Ctrl+T	Transpose character	Switch positions of current and previous characters.	
Alt+T	Transpose words	Switch positions of current and previous words.	
Alt+U	Uppercase word	Change the current word to uppercase.	
Alt+L	Lowercase word	Change the current word to lowercase.	
Alt+C	Capitalize word	Change the current word to an initial capital.	
Ctrl+V	Insert special character	Add a special character. For example, to add a Tab character, press Ctrl+V+Tab.	

Use the keystrokes in Table 3.3 to cut and paste text on a command line.

TABLE 3.3   Keystrokes for Cutting and Pasting Text from within Command Lines

KEYSTROKE	FULL NAME	MEANING	
Ctrl+K	Cut end of line	Cut text to the end of the line.	
Ctrl+U	Cut beginning of line	Cut text to the beginning of the line.	
Ctrl+W	Cut previous word	Cut the word located behind the cursor.	
Alt+D	Cut next word	Cut the word following the cursor.	
Ctrl+Y	Paste recent text	Paste most recently cut text.	
Alt+Y	Paste earlier text	Rotate back to previously cut text and paste it.	
Ctrl+C	Delete whole line	Delete the entire line.	

Command-line completion

To save you a few keystrokes, the Bash shell offers several different ways of completing partially typed values. To attempt to complete a value, type the first few characters and press Tab. Here are some of the values you can type partially from a Bash shell:

Command, alias, or function If the text you type begins with regular characters, the shell tries to complete the text with a command, alias, or function name.

Variable If the text you type begins with a dollar sign ($), the shell completes the text with a variable from the current shell.

Username If the text you type begins with a tilde (~), the shell completes the text with a username. As a result, *~username* indicates the home directory of the named user.

Hostname If the text you type begins with the at symbol (@), the shell completes the text with a hostname taken from the /etc/hosts file.

TIP

To add hostnames from an additional file, you can set the HOSTFILE variable to the name of that file. The file must be in the same format as /etc/hosts.

Here are a few examples of command completion. (When you see *<Tab>*, it means to press the Tab key on your keyboard.) Enter the following:

```
$ echo $OS<Tab>
$ cd ~ro<Tab>
$ userm<Tab>
```

The first example causes $OS to expand to the $OSTYPE variable. In the next example, ~ro expands to the root user's home directory (~root/). Next, userm expands to the usermod command.

Pressing Tab twice offers some wonderful possibilities. Sometimes, several possible completions for the string of characters you have entered are available. In those cases, you can check the possible ways that text can be expanded by pressing Tab twice at the point where you want to do completion.

The following shows the result you would get if you checked for possible completions on $P:

```
$ echo $P<Tab><Tab>
$PATH $PPID $PS1 $PS2 $PS4 $PWD
$ echo $P
```

In this case, there are six possible variables that begin with $P. After possibilities are displayed, the original command line returns, ready for you to complete it as you choose. For example, if you typed another P and hit Tab again, the command line would be completed with $PPID (the only unique possibility).

Command-line recall

After you type a command, the entire command line is saved in your shell's history list. The list is stored in the current shell until you exit the shell. After that, it is written to a history file, from which any command can be recalled to be run again in your next session. After a command is recalled, you can modify the command line, as described earlier.

To view your history list, use the `history` command. Enter the command without options or followed by a number to list that many of the most recent commands. For example:

```
$ history 8
 382 date
 383 ls /usr/bin | sort -a | more
 384 man sort
 385 cd /usr/local/bin
 386 man more

 387 passwd chris
 388 history 7
```

A number precedes each command line in the list. You can recall one of those commands using an exclamation point (!). Keep in mind that when an exclamation point is used, the command runs blind without presenting an opportunity to confirm the command you're referencing. There are several ways to run a command immediately from this list, including the following:

!*n*   *Run command number.* Replace the *n* with the number of the command line and that line is run. For example, here's how to repeat the `date` command shown as command number 382 in the preceding history listing:

```
$ !382
date
Fri Jun 29 15:47:57 EDT 2019
```

!!—!!   *Run previous command.* Runs the previous command line. Here's how you would immediately run that same `date` command:

```
$ !!
date
Fri Jun 29 15:53:27 EDT 2019
```

!?*string*—? *Run command containing string.* This runs the most recent command that contains a particular string of characters. For example, you can run the `date` command again by just searching for part of that command line as follows:

```
$ !?dat?
date
Fri Jun 29 16:04:18 EDT 2019
```

Instead of just running a `history` command line immediately, you can recall a particular line and edit it. You can use the following keys or key combinations to do that, as shown in Table 3.4.

Another way to work with your history list is to use the `fc` command. Type **fc** followed by a history line number, and that command line is opened in your default text editor. Make the changes that you want. When you exit the editor, the command runs. You can also give a range of line numbers (for example, `fc 100 105`). All of the commands open in your text editor and then run one after the other when you exit the editor.

TABLE 3.4 **Keystrokes for Using Command History**

Key(s)	Function Name	Description
Arrow keys (↑ and ↓)	Step	Press the up and down arrow keys to step through each command line in your history list to arrive at the one you want. (Ctrl+P and Ctrl+N do the same functions, respectively.)
Ctrl+R	Reverse incremental search	After you press these keys, you enter a search string to do a reverse search. As you type the string, a matching command line appears that you can run or edit.
Ctrl+S	Forward incremental search	This is the same as the preceding function but for forward search. (It may not work in all instances.)
Alt+P	Reverse search	After you press these keys, you enter a string to do a reverse search. Type a string and press Enter to see the most recent command line that includes that string.
Alt+N	Forward search	This is the same as the preceding function but for forward search. (It may not work in all instances.)

After you close your shell, the history list is stored in the `.bash _ history` file in your home directory. Up to 1,000 history commands are stored for you by default.

> **NOTE**
>
> Some people disable the history feature for the root user by setting the `HISTFILE` shell variable to `/dev/null` or simply leaving `HISTSIZE` blank. This prevents information about the root user's activities from potentially being exploited. If you are an administrative user with root privileges, you may want to consider emptying your file upon exiting as well for the same reasons. Also, because shell history is stored permanently when the shell exits properly, you can prevent storing a shell's history by killing a shell. For example, to kill a shell with process ID 1234, type `kill -9 1234` from any shell.

Connecting and Expanding Commands

A truly powerful feature of the shell is the capability to redirect the input and output of commands to and from other commands and files. To allow commands to be strung together, the shell uses metacharacters. A *metacharacter* is a typed character that has special meaning to the shell for connecting commands or requesting expansion.

Metacharacters include the pipe character (|), ampersand (&), semicolon (;), right parenthesis ( )), left parenthesis (( ), less than sign (<), and greater than sign (>). The next sections describe how to use metacharacters on the command line to change how commands behave.

Piping between commands

The pipe (|) metacharacter connects the output from one command to the input of another command. This lets you have one command work on some data and then have the next command deal with the results. Here is an example of a command line that includes pipes:

```
$ cat /etc/passwd | sort | less
```

This command lists the contents of the /etc/passwd file and pipes the output to the sort command. The sort command takes the usernames that begin each line of the /etc/passwd file, sorts them alphabetically, and pipes the output to the less command (to page through the output).

Pipes are an excellent illustration of how UNIX, the predecessor of Linux, was created as an operating system made up of building blocks. A standard practice in UNIX was to connect utilities in different ways to get different jobs done. For example, before the days of graphical word processors, users created plain-text files that included macros to indicate formatting. To see how the document really appeared, they would use a command such as the following:

```
$ gunzip < /usr/share/man/man1/grep.1.gz | nroff -c -man | less
```

In this example, the contents of the grep man page (grep.1.gz) are directed to the gunzip command to be unzipped. The output from gunzip is piped to the nroff command to format the man page using the manual macro (-man). The output is piped to the less command to be displayed. Because the file being displayed is in plain text, you could have substituted any number of options to work with the text before displaying it. You could sort the contents, change or delete some of the content, or bring in text from other documents. The key is that, instead of all of those features being in one program, you get results from piping and redirecting input and output between multiple commands.

Sequential commands

Sometimes, you may want a sequence of commands to run, with one command completing before the next command begins. You can do this by typing several commands on the same command line and separating them with semicolons (;):

```
$ date ; troff -me verylargedocument | lp ; date
```

In this example, I was formatting a huge document and wanted to know how long it would take. The first command (date) showed the date and time before the formatting started. The troff command formatted the document and then piped the output to the printer. When the formatting was finished, the date and time were printed again (so I knew how long the troff command took to complete).

Another useful command to add to the end of a long command line is mail. You could add the following to the end of a command line:

```
; mail -s "Finished the long command" chris@example.com
```

Then, for example, a mail message is sent to the user you choose after the command completes.

Background commands

Some commands can take a while to complete. Sometimes, you may not want to tie up your shell waiting for a command to finish. In those cases, you can have the commands run in the background by using the ampersand (&).

Text formatting commands (such as nroff and troff, described earlier) are examples of commands that can be run in the background to format a large document. You also might want to create your own shell scripts that run in the background to check continuously for certain events to occur, such as the hard disk filling up or particular users logging in.

The following is an example of a command being run in the background:

```
$ troff -me verylargedocument | lp &
```

Don't close the shell until the process is completed or that kills the process. Other ways to manage background and foreground processes are described in Chapter 6, "Managing Running Processes."

Expanding commands

With command substitution, you can have the output of a command interpreted by the shell instead of by the command itself. In this way, you can have the standard output of a command become an argument for another command. The two forms of command substitution are $(command) and `command` (backticks, not single quotes).

The command in this case can include options, metacharacters, and arguments. The following is an example of using command substitution:

```
$ nano $(find /home | grep xyzzy)
```

In this example, the command substitution is done before the nano command is run. First, the find command starts at the /home directory and prints out all of the files and directories below that point in the filesystem. The output is piped to the grep command, which filters out all files except for those that include the string xyzzy in the filename. Finally, the nano command opens all filenames for editing (one at a time) that include xyzzy.

This particular example is useful if you want to edit a file for which you know the name but not the location. As long as the string is uncommon, you can find and open every instance of a filename existing beneath a point you choose in the filesystem. (In other words, don't use grep from the root filesystem or you'll match and try to edit several thousand files.)

Expanding arithmetic expressions

Sometimes, you want to pass arithmetic results to a command using *$[expression]*. The following is an example:

```
$ echo "I am $[2019 - 1957] years old."
I am 62 years old.
```

The shell interprets the arithmetic expression first [2019 - 1957] and then passes that information to the echo command. The echo command displays the text with the results of the arithmetic (58) inserted.

Here's an example of another way to do this:

```
$ echo "There are $(ls | wc -w) files in this directory."
There are 14 files in this directory.
```

This lists the contents of the current directory (ls) and runs the word count command to count the number of files found (wc -w). The resulting number (14, in this case) is echoed back with the rest of the sentence shown.

Expanding variables

Variables that store information within the shell can be expanded using the dollar sign ($) metacharacter. When you expand an environment variable on a command line, the value of the variable is printed instead of the variable name itself, as follows:

```
$ ls -l $BASH
-rwxr-xr-x. 1 root root 1219248 Oct 12 17:59 /usr/bin/bash
```

Using $BASH as an argument to ls -l causes a long listing of the Bash command to be printed.

Using Shell Variables

The shell itself stores information that may be useful to the user's shell session in what are called *variables*. Examples of variables include $SHELL (which identifies the shell you are using), $PS1 (which defines your shell prompt), and $MAIL (which identifies the location of your user's mailbox).

You can see all variables set for your current shell by typing the set command. A subset of your local variables is referred to as *environment variables*. Environment variables are variables that are exported to any new shells opened from the current shell. Type **env** to see environment variables.

You can type **echo $VALUE**, where **VALUE** is replaced by the name of a particular environment variable you want to list. And because there are always multiple ways to do anything in Linux, you can also type **declare** to get a list of the current environment variables and their values along with a list of shell functions.

Besides those that you set yourself, system files set variables that store things such as locations of configuration files, mailboxes, and path directories. They can also store values for your shell prompts, the size of your history list, and type of operating system. You can refer to the value of any of those variables by preceding it with a dollar sign ($) and placing it anywhere on a command line. For example:

```
$ echo $USER
chris
```

This command prints the value of the USER variable, which holds your username (chris). Substitute any other value for USER to print its value instead.

When you start a shell (by logging in via a virtual console or opening a Terminal window), many environment variables are already set. Table 3.5 shows some variables that are either set when you use a Bash shell or that can be set by you to use with different features.

TABLE 3.5 Common Shell Environment Variables

VARIABLE	DESCRIPTION
BASH	This contains the full pathname of the bash command. This is usually /bin/bash.
BASH _ VERSION	This is a number representing the current version of the bash command.
EUID	This is the effective user ID number of the current user. It is assigned when the shell starts, based on the user's entry in the /etc/passwd file.
FCEDIT	If set, this variable indicates the text editor used by the fc command to edit history commands. If this variable isn't set, the default browser is used.
HISTFILE	This is the location of your history file. It is typically located at $HOME/. bash _ history.
HISTFILESIZE	This is the number of history entries that can be stored. After this number is reached, the oldest commands are discarded. The default value is 1,000.
HISTCMD	This returns the number of the current command in the history list.
HOME	This is your home directory. It is your current working directory each time you log in or type the cd command with any options.
HOSTTYPE	This is a value that describes the computer architecture on which the Linux system is running. For most modern PCs, the value is x86 _ 64.
MAIL	This is the location of your mailbox file. The file is typically your username in the /var/spool/mail directory.
OLDPWD	This is the directory that was the working directory before you changed to the current working directory.
OSTYPE	This name identifies the current operating system. For Ubuntu, the OSTYPE value is either linux or linux-gnu, depending on the type of shell you are using. (Bash can run on other operating systems as well.)
PATH	This is the colon-separated list of directories used to find commands that you type. The default value for regular users varies for different distributions but typically includes the following: /bin:/usr/bin:/usr/local/bin:/usr/bin/X11:/usr/X11R6/bin:~/bin. You need to type the full path or a relative path to a command that you want to run which is not in your PATH. For the root user, the value also includes /sbin, /usr/sbin, and /usr/local/sbin.
PPID	This is the process ID of the command that started the current shell (for example, the Terminal window containing the shell).
PROMPT _ COMMAND	This can be set to a command name that is run each time before your shell prompt is displayed. Setting PROMPT_COMMAND=date lists the current date/time before the prompt appears.

Continues

TABLE 3.5   *(continued)*

VARIABLE	DESCRIPTION
PS1	This sets the value of your shell prompt. There are many items that you can read into your prompt (date, time, username, hostname, and so on). Sometimes a command requires additional prompts, which you can set with the variables PS2, PS3, and so on.
PWD	This is the directory that is assigned as your current directory. This value changes each time you change directories using the cd command.
RANDOM	Accessing this variable causes a random number to be generated. The number is between 0 and 99999.
SECONDS	This is the number of seconds since the time the shell was started.
SHLVL	This is the number of shell levels associated with the current shell session. When you log in to the shell, the SHLVL is 1. Each time you start a new Bash command (by, for example, using su to become a new user, or by simply typing bash), this number is incremented.
TMOUT	This can be set to a number representing the number of seconds the shell can be idle without receiving input. After the number of seconds is reached, the shell exits. This security feature makes it less likely for unattended shells to be accessed by unauthorized people. (This must be set in the login shell for it actually to cause the shell to log out the user.)

Creating and using aliases

Using the alias command, you can effectively create a shortcut to any command and options that you want to run later. You can add and list aliases with the alias command. Consider the following examples of using alias from a Bash shell:

```
$ alias p='pwd ; ls -CF'
$ alias rm='rm -i'
```

In the first example, the letter p is assigned to run the command pwd and then to run ls -CF to print the current working directory and list its contents in column form. The second example runs the rm command with the -i option each time you type rm. (This is an alias that is often set automatically for the root user. Instead of just removing files, you are prompted for each individual file removal. This prevents you from automatically removing all of the files in a directory by mistakenly typing something such as rm *.)

While you are in the shell, you can check which aliases are set by typing the alias command. If you want to remove an alias, use **unalias.** (Remember that if the alias is set in a configuration file, it will be set again when you open another shell.)

Exiting the shell

To exit the shell when you are finished, type **exit** or press Ctrl+D. If you go to the shell from a Terminal window and you are using the original shell from that window, exiting causes the Terminal window to close. If you are at a virtual console, the shell exits and returns you to a login prompt.

If you have multiple shells open from the same shell session, exiting a shell simply returns you to the shell that launched the current shell. For example, the su command opens a shell as a new user. Exiting from that shell simply returns you to the original shell.

Creating Your Shell Environment

You can tune your shell to help you work more efficiently. You can set aliases to create shortcuts to your favorite command lines and environment variables to store bits of information. By adding those settings to shell configuration files, you can have the settings available every time you open a shell.

Configuring your shell

Several configuration files support how your shell behaves. Some of the files are executed for every user and every shell, whereas others are specific to the user who creates the configuration file. Table 3.6 shows the files that are of interest to anyone using the Bash shell in Linux. (Notice the use of ~ in the filenames to indicate that the file is located in each user's home directory.)

TABLE 3.6   Bash Configuration Files

FILE	DESCRIPTION
/etc/profile	This sets up user environment information for every user. It is executed when you first log in. This file provides values for your path in addition to setting environment variables for such things as the location of your mailbox and the size of your history files. Finally, /etc/profile gathers shell settings from configuration files in the /etc/profile.d directory.
/etc/bash.bashrc	This executes for every user who runs the Bash shell each time a Bash shell is opened. It sets the default prompt and may add one or more aliases. Values in this file can be overridden by information in each user's ~/.bashrc file.
~/.profile	This is used by each user to enter information that is specific to his or her use of the shell. It is executed only once—when the user logs in. By default, it sets a few environment variables and executes the user's .bashrc file. This is a good place to add environment variables because, once set, they are inherited by future shells. This file will be overruled if a ~/.bash _ profile file exists.
~/.bashrc	This contains the information that is specific to your Bash shells. It is read when you log in and also each time you open a new Bash shell. This is the best location to add aliases so that your shell picks them up.
~/.bash _ logout	This executes each time you log out (exit the last Bash shell).

To change the /etc/profile or /etc/bashrc files, you must be the root user. It is better to create a /etc/profile.d/custom.sh file to add system-wide settings instead of editing those files directly, however. Users can change the information in the $HOME/.bash _ profile, $HOME/.bashrc, and $HOME/.bash_logout files in their own home directories.

Until you learn to use the vi editor, described in Chapter 5, "Working with Text Files," you can use a simple editor called nano to edit plain-text files. For example, enter the following to edit and add stuff to your $HOME/.bashrc file:

```
$ nano $HOME/.bashrc
```

With the file open in nano, move the cursor down to the bottom of the file (using the down arrow key). Type the line you want (for example, you could type **alias d='date +%D'**). To save the file, press Ctrl+O (the letter *O*); to quit, press Ctrl+X. The next time you log in or open a new shell, you can use the new alias (in this case, just type **d**). To make the new information you just added to the file available from the current shell right away, type the following:

```
$ source $HOME/.bashrc
$ d
06/29/19
```

The following sections provide ideas about items to add to your shell configuration files. In most cases, you add these values to the .bashrc file in your home directory. However, if you administer a system, you may want to set some of these values as defaults for all your Ubuntu system's users.

Setting your prompt

Your prompt consists of a set of characters that appear each time the shell is ready to accept a command. The PS1 environment variable sets what the prompt contains and is what you will interact with most of the time. If your shell requires additional input, it uses the values of PS2, PS3, and PS4.

When your Ubuntu system is installed, your prompt is set to include the following information: your username, your hostname, and the base name of your current working directory. That information is followed by a dollar sign (for regular users) or a pound sign (for the root user). The following is an example of that prompt:

```
chris@workstation:~/myfiles$
```

If you change directories, the myfiles name would change to the name of the new directory. Likewise, if you were to log in as a different user or to a different host, that information would change.

You can use several special characters (indicated by adding a backslash to a variety of letters) to include different information in your prompt. Special characters can be used to output your terminal number, the date, and the time as well as other pieces of information. Table 3.7 provides some examples (you can find more on the Bash man page).

TIP

If you are setting your prompt temporarily by typing at the shell, you should put the value of PS1 in quotes. For example, you could type `export PS1="[\t \w]\$ "` to see a prompt that looks like this:

`[20:26:32 /var/spool]$.`

TABLE 3.7 Characters to Add Information to *bash* Prompt

SPECIAL CHARACTER	DESCRIPTION
\!	This shows the current command history number. This includes all previous commands stored for your username.
\#	This shows the command number of the current command. This includes only the commands for the active shell.
\$	This shows the user prompt ($) or root prompt (#), depending on which type of user you are.
\W	This shows only the current working directory base name. For example, if the current working directory was /var/spool/mail, this value simply appears as mail.
\[	This precedes a sequence of nonprinting characters. This can be used to add a terminal control sequence into the prompt for such things as changing colors, adding blink effects, or making characters bold. (Your terminal determines the exact sequences available.)
\]	This follows a sequence of nonprinting characters.
\\	This shows a backslash.
\d	This displays the day name, month, and day number of the current date, for example, Sat Jan 23.
\h	This shows the hostname of the computer running the shell.
\n	This causes a new line to occur.
\nnn	This shows the character that relates to the octal number replacing *nnn*.
\s	This displays the current shell name. For the Bash shell, the value would be bash.
\t	This prints the current time in hours, minutes, and seconds, for example, 10:14:39.
\u	This prints your current username.
\w	This displays the full path to the current working directory.

To make a change to your prompt permanent, add the value of PS1 to your .bashrc file in your home directory (assuming that you are using the Bash shell). There may already be a PS1 value in that file, which you can modify. Refer to the Bash Prompt HOWTO (www.tldp.org/HOWTO/Bash-Prompt-HOWTO) for information on changing colors, commands, and other features of your Bash shell prompt.

Adding environment variables

You might want to consider adding a few environment variables to your .bashrc file. These can help make working with the shell more efficient and effective:

TMOUT This sets how long the shell can be inactive before Bash automatically exits. The value is the number of seconds for which the shell has not received input. This can be a nice security feature, in case you leave your desk while you are still logged in to Linux. To prevent being logged off while you are working, you may want to set the value to something like TMOUT=1800 (to allow 30 minutes of idle time). You can use any terminal session to close the current shell after a set number of seconds, for example, TMOUT=30.

PATH As described earlier, the PATH variable sets the directories that are searched for the commands that you use. If you often use directories of commands that are not in your path, you can permanently add them. To do this, add a PATH variable to your .bashrc file. For example, to add a directory called /getstuff/bin, add the following:

```
PATH=$PATH:/getstuff/bin ; export PATH
```

This example first reads all of the current path directories into the new PATH ($PATH), adds the /getstuff/bin directory, and then exports the new PATH.

CAUTION

Some people add the current directory to their PATH by adding a directory identified simply as a dot (.), as follows:

```
PATH=.:$PATH ; export PATH
```

This enables you to run commands in your current directory before evaluating any other command in the path (which people may be used to if they have used DOS). However, the security risk with this procedure is that you could be in a directory that contains a command that you don't intend to run from that directory. For example, a malicious person could put an ls command in a directory that, instead of listing the content of your directory, does something devious. Because of this, the practice of adding the dot to your path is highly discouraged.

Custom environment variables You can create your own environment variables to provide shortcuts in your work. Choose any name that is not being used and assign a useful value to it. For example, if you do lots of work with files in the /work/time/ files/info/memos directory, you could set the following variable:

```
M=/work/time/files/info/memos ; export M
```

You could make that your current directory by typing **cd $M**. You could run a program from that directory called hotdog by typing **$M/hotdog**. You could edit a file from there called bun by typing **vi $M/bun**.

Getting Information about Commands

When you first start using the shell, it can be intimidating. All that you see is a prompt. How do you know which commands are available, which options they use, or how to use advanced features? Fortunately, lots of help is available. Here are some places that you can look to supplement what you learn in this chapter:

- **Check the PATH.** Type `echo $PATH`. You see a list of the directories containing commands that are immediately accessible to you. Listing the contents of those directories displays most standard Linux commands. For example:

```
$ ls /bin
bash              fuser            networkctl        static-sh
brltty            fusermount       nisdomainname     stty
bunzip2           getfacl          ntfs-3g           su
busybox           grep             ntfs-3g.probe     sync
bzcat             gunzip           ntfscat           systemctl
bzcmp             gzexe            ntfscluster       systemd
bzdiff            gzip             ntfscmp           systemd-ask-password
bzegrep           hciconfig        ntfsfallocate     systemd-escape
bzexe             hostname         ntfsfix           systemd-hwdb
bzfgrep           ip               ntfsinfo          systemd-inhibit
bzgrep            journalctl       ntfsls            systemd-machine-id-setup
bzip2             kbd_mode         ntfsmove          systemd-notify
bzip2recover      kill             ntfsrecover       systemd-sysusers
bzless            kmod             ntfssecaudit      systemd-tmpfiles
bzmore            less             ntfstruncate      systemd-tty-ask-password-agent
cat               lessecho         ntfsusermap       tar
chacl             lessfile         ntfswipe          tempfile
chgrp             lesskey          open              touch
chmod             lesspipe         openvt            true
chown             ln               pidof             udevadm
chvt              loadkeys         ping              ulockmgr_server
cp                login            ping4             umount
cpio              loginctl         ping6             uname
dash              lowntfs-3g       plymouth          uncompress
date              ls               ps                unicode_start
dd                lsblk            pwd               vdir
df                lsmod            rbash             wdctl
dir               mkdir            readlink          which
dmesg             mknod            red               whiptail
dnsdomainname     mktemp           rm                ypdomainname
domainname        more             rmdir             zcat
dumpkeys          mount            rnano             zcmp
echo              mountpoint       run-parts         zdiff
ed                mt               sed               zegrep
efibootdump       mt-gnu           setfacl           zfgrep
efibootmgr        mv               setfont           zforce
```

3

```
egrep          nano           setupcon       zgrep
false          nc             sh             zless
fgconsole      nc.openbsd     sh.distrib     zmore
fgrep          netcat         sleep          znew
findmnt        netstat        ss
```

- **Use the `help` command.** Some commands are built into the shell, so they do not appear in a directory. The `help` command lists those commands and shows options available with each of them. (Enter **help | less** to page through the list.) For help with a particular built-in command, enter **help *command***, replacing ***command*** with the name that interests you. The `help` command works with the Bash shell only.

- **Use `--help` with the command.** Many commands include a `--help` option that you can use to get information about how the command is used. For example, if you enter **date --help | less**, the output shows not only options, but also time formats that you can use with the `date` command. Other commands simply use a –h option, like `fdisk -h`.

- **Use the `info` command.** The `info` command is another tool for displaying information about commands from the shell. The `info` command can move among a hierarchy of nodes to find information about commands and other items. Not all commands have information available in the info database, but sometimes more information can be found there than on a man page.

- **Use the `man` command.** To learn more about a particular command, enter **man *command***. (Replace ***command*** with the command name you want.) A description of the command and its options appears on the screen.

Man pages are the most common means of getting information about commands as well as other basic components of a Linux system. Each man page falls into one of the categories listed in Table 3.8. As a regular user, you will be most interested in the man pages in section 1. As a system administrator, you will also be interested in sections 5 and 8, and occasionally section 4. Programmers will be interested in section 2 and 3 man pages.

Options to the `man` command enable you to search the man page database or display man pages on the screen. Here are some examples of man commands and options:

```
$ man -k passwd
...
passwd              (1)  - update user's authentication tokens
passwd              (5)  - password file
$ man passwd
$ man 5 passwd
```

Using the –k option, you can search the name and summary sections of all man pages installed on the system. There are about a dozen man pages that include "passwd" in the name or description of a command.

TABLE 3.8 **Manual Page Sections**

Section Number	Section Name	Description
1	User Commands	Commands that can be run from the shell by a regular user (typically no administrative privilege is needed)
2	System Calls	Programming functions used within an application to make calls to the kernel
3	C Library Functions	Programming functions that provide interfaces to specific programming libraries (such as those for certain graphical interfaces or other libraries that operate in user space)
4	Devices and Special Files	Filesystem nodes that represent hardware devices (such as terminals or CD drives) or software devices (such as random number generators)
5	File Formats and Conventions	Types of files (such as a graphics or word processing file) or specific configuration files (such as the passwd or group file)
6	Games	Games available on the system
7	Miscellaneous	Overviews of topics such as protocols, filesystems, character set standards, and so on
8	System Administration Tools and Daemons	Commands that require root or other administrative privileges to use

NOTE

If man -k displays no output, it may be that the man page database has not been initialized. Type mandb as root to initialize the man page database.

Let's say that the two man pages in which I am interested are the passwd command (in section 1 of the man pages) and the passwd file (in section 5) man pages. Because just typing man passwd displays the section 1 page, I need to request explicitly the section 5 man page if I want to see that instead (man 5 passwd).

While you are displaying a man page, you can view different parts of the file using Page Down and Page Up keys (to move a page at a time). Use the Enter key or up and down arrows to move a line at a time. Type a forward slash (/) and type a term to search the document for that term. Type n to repeat the search forward or N to repeat the search backward. To quit the man page, type q.

Summary

To become an expert Linux user, you must be able to use the shell to type commands. This chapter focuses on the Bash shell, which is the one that is most commonly used with Linux systems. You learned how commands are structured and how many special features, such as variables, command completion, and aliases, are used.

The next chapter describes how to move around the Linux filesystem from the shell command line.

Exercises

Use these exercises to test your knowledge of using the shell. If you are stuck, solutions to the tasks are shown in Appendix A (although in Linux, there are often multiple ways to complete a task).

1. From your desktop, switch to the third virtual console and log in to your user account. Run a few commands. Then exit the shell and return to the desktop.

2. Open a Terminal window and change the font color to red and the background to yellow.

3. Find the location of the mount command and the tracepath man page.

4. Type the following three commands, and then recall and change those commands as described:

```
$ cat /etc/passwd
$ ls $HOME
$ date
```

   a. Use the command-line recall feature to recall the cat command and change /etc/passwd to /etc/group.

   b. Recall the ls command, determine how to list files by time (using the man page), and add that option to the ls $HOME command line.

   c. Add format indicators to the date command to display the date output as *month/day/year*.

5. Run the following command, typing as few characters as possible (using tab completion):

```
basename /usr/share/doc/
```

6. Use the cat command to list the contents of the /etc/services file and pipe those contents to the less command so that you can page through it (type q to quit when you are finished).

7. Run the date command in such a way that the output from that command produces the current day, month, date, and year. Have that read into another command line, resulting in text that appears like the following (your date, of course, will be different): Today is Thursday, December 19, 2019.

8. Using variables, find out what your hostname, username, shell, and home directories are currently set to.

9. Create an alias called mypass that displays the contents of the /etc/passwd file on your screen in such a way that it is available every time you log in or open a new shell from your user account.

10. Display the man page for the mount system call.

3

Moving Around the Filesystem

IN THIS CHAPTER

Learning about the Linux filesystem

Listing file and directory attributes

Making files and directories

Listing and changing permission and ownership

Making copies and moving files

The Linux filesystem is the structure in which all of the information on your computer is stored. In fact, one of the defining properties of the UNIX systems on which Linux is based is that nearly everything you need to identify on your system (data, commands, symbolic links, devices, and directories) is represented by items in the filesystems. Knowing where things are and understanding how to get around the filesystem from the shell are critical skills in Linux.

In Linux, files are organized within a hierarchy of directories. Each directory can contain files as well as other directories. You can refer to any file or directory using either a full path (for example, /home/joe/myfile.txt) or a relative path (for example, if /home/joe were your current directory, you could simply refer to the file as myfile.txt).

If you were to map out the files and directories in Linux, it would look like an upside-down tree. At the top is the *root* directory (not to be confused with the root user), which is represented by a single slash (/). Below that is a set of common directories in the Linux system, such as bin, dev, home, lib, and mnt. Each of those directories, as well as directories added to the root directory, can contain subdirectories.

Figure 4.1 illustrates how the Linux filesystem is organized as a hierarchy. To demonstrate how directories are connected, Figure 4.1 shows a /home directory that contains a subdirectory for the user joe. Within the joe directory are Desktop, Documents, and other subdirectories. To refer to a file called memo1.doc in the memos directory, you can type the full path of /home/joe/Documents/memos/memo1.doc. If your current directory is /home/joe/, refer to the file as Documents/memos/memo1.doc.

FIGURE 4.1

The Linux filesystem is organized as a hierarchy of directories.

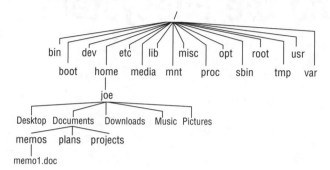

Some of these Linux directories may interest you:

/bin Contains common Linux user commands, such as ls, sort, date, and chmod.

/boot Has the bootable Linux kernel, initial RAM disk, and bootloader configuration files (GRUB).

/dev Contains files representing access points to devices on your systems. These include terminal devices (tty*), hard disks (hd* or sd*), RAM (ram*), and CD-ROMs (cd*). Users can access these devices directly through these device files; however, applications often hide the actual device names to end users.

/etc Contains administrative configuration files. Most of these files are plain text files that, given the user has proper permission, can be edited with any text editor.

/home Contains directories assigned to each regular user with a login account. (The root user is an exception, using /root as its home directory.)

/media Provides a standard location for automounting devices (removable media in particular). If the medium has a volume name, that name is typically used as the mount point. For example, a USB drive with a volume name of myusb would be mounted on /media/myusb.

/lib Contains shared libraries needed by applications in /bin and /sbin to boot the system.

/mnt A common mount point for many devices before it was supplanted by the standard /media directory. Some bootable Linux systems still use this directory to mount hard disk partitions and remote filesystems. Many people still use this directory to temporarily mount local or remote filesystems, which are not mounted permanently.

/opt   Directory structure available to store add-on application software.

/proc   Contains information about system resources.

/root   Represents the root user's home directory. The home directory for root does not reside beneath /home for security reasons.

/sbin   Contains administrative commands and daemon processes.

/snap   The home directory for filesystems used by the snapd package management system.

/sys   Contains parameters for such things as tuning block storage and managing cgroups.

/tmp   Contains temporary files used by applications.

/usr   Contains user documentation, games, graphical files (X11), libraries (lib), and a variety of other commands and files that are not needed during the boot process. The /usr directory is meant for files that don't change after installation (in theory, /usr could be mounted read-only).

/var   Contains directories of data used by various applications. In particular, this is where you would place files that you share as an FTP server (/var/ftp) or a web server (/var/www). It also contains all system log files (/var/log) and spool files in /var/spool (such as mail, cups, and news). The /var directory contains directories and files that are meant to change often. On server computers, it is common to create the /var directory as a separate filesystem, using a filesystem type that can be easily expanded. Previous Ubuntu versions might have kept some shared files in /srv.

The filesystems in the DOS or Microsoft Windows operating systems differ from Linux's file structure, as the sidebar "Linux Filesystems versus Windows-Based Filesystems" explains.

Linux Filesystems versus Windows-Based Filesystems

Although similar in many ways, the Linux filesystem has some striking differences when compared to filesystems used in MS-DOS and Windows operating systems. Here are a few of these differences:

- In MS-DOS and Windows filesystems, drive letters represent different storage devices. In Linux, all storage devices are connected to the filesystem hierarchy. So, the fact that all of /usr may be on a separate hard disk or that /mnt/remote1 is a filesystem from another computer is invisible to the user.

- Slashes (also known as forward slashes), rather than backslashes, are used to separate directory names in Linux. So C:\home\joe in a Microsoft system is /home/joe in a Linux system.

4

- Filenames almost always have suffixes in DOS (such as .txt for text files or .docx for word-processing files). Although at times you can use that convention in Linux, three-character suffixes have no required meaning in Linux. They can be useful for visually identifying a file type. Many Linux applications and desktop environments use file suffixes to determine the contents of a file. In Linux, however, DOS command extensions such as .com, .exe, and .bat don't necessarily signify an executable. (Permission flags make Linux files executable.)

- Every file and directory in a Linux system has permissions and ownership associated with it. Security varies among Microsoft systems. Because DOS and Microsoft Windows began as single-user systems, file ownership was not built into those systems when they were designed. Later releases added features such as file and folder attributes to address this problem.

Using Basic Filesystem Commands

Let's explore a few simple commands for moving around the filesystem. If you want to follow along, log in and open a shell. When you open a Linux shell, you are placed in your home directory. As a Linux user, most of the files you save and work with will probably be in that directory or in subdirectories that you create. Table 4.1 shows commands to create and use files and directories.

TABLE 4.1   Commands to Create and Use Files

Command	Result
cd	Changes to another directory
pwd	Prints the name of the current (or present) working directory
mkdir	Creates a directory
chmod	Changes the permission on a file or directory
ls	Lists the contents of a directory

One of the most basic commands that you use from the shell is cd. The cd command can be used with no options (to take you to your home directory) or with full or relative paths. Consider the following commands:

```
$ cd /usr/share/
$ pwd
/usr/share
$ cd doc
$ pwd
/usr/share/doc
$ cd
$ pwd
/home/chris
```

The /usr/share option represents the *absolute path* to a directory on the system. Because it begins with a slash (/), this path tells the shell to start at the root of the filesystem and take you to the share directory that exists in the usr directory. The doc option to the cd command looks for a directory called doc that is relative to the current directory. So that command made /usr/share/doc your current directory.

After that, by typing cd alone, you are returned to your home directory. If you ever wonder where you are in the filesystem, the pwd command can help you. Here are a few other interesting cd command options:

```
$ cd ~
$ pwd
/home/chris
$ cd ~/Music
$ pwd
/home/chris/Music
$ cd ../../../usr
$ pwd
/usr
```

The tilde (~) represents your home directory. So cd ~ takes you there. You can use the tilde to refer to directories relative to your home directory as well, such as /home/chris/Music with ~/Music. Typing a name as an option takes you to a directory below the current directory, but you can use two dots (..) to go to a directory above the current directory. The example shown takes you up three directory levels (to /), and then takes you into the /usr directory.

The following steps lead you through the process of creating directories within your home directory, moving among your directories, and setting appropriate file permissions:

1. Go to your home directory. To do this, simply type **cd** in a shell and press Enter. (For other ways of referring to your home directory, see the sidebar "Identifying Directories" on page 88.)

2. To make sure that you're in your home directory, type **pwd**. When I do this, I get the following response (yours will reflect your home directory):

   ```
   $ pwd
   /home/joe
   ```

3. Create a new directory called test in your home directory, as follows:

   ```
   $ mkdir test
   ```

4. Check the directory's permissions:

   ```
   $ ls -ld test
   drwxr-xr-x 2 joe joe 4096 Feb 19 09:48 test
   ```

   This listing shows that test is a directory (d). The d is followed by the permissions (rwxr-xr-x), which are explained later in the section "Understanding File Permissions and Ownership." The rest of the information indicates the owner (joe), the group (joe), and the date that the files in the directory were most recently modified (Feb 19 at 9:48 a.m.).

NOTE

When you add a new user in Ubuntu, the user is assigned to a group of the same name by default. For example, in the preceding text, the user joe would be assigned to the group joe. This approach to assigning groups is referred to as the *user private group scheme*.

For now, enter the following:

```
$ chmod 700 test
```

This step changes the permissions of the directory to give you complete access and everyone else no access at all. (The new permissions should read rwx------.)

5. Make the test directory your current directory as follows:

```
$ cd test
$ pwd
/home/joe/test
```

If you followed along, at this point a subdirectory of your home directory called test is your current working directory. You can create files and directories in the test directory along with the descriptions in the rest of this chapter.

Using Metacharacters and Operators

Whether you are listing, moving, copying, removing, or otherwise acting on files in your Linux system, certain special characters, referred to as metacharacters and operators, help you to work with files more efficiently. Metacharacters can help you match one or more files without completely typing each filename. Operators enable you to direct information from one command or file to another command or file.

Using file-matching metacharacters

To save you some keystrokes and enable you to refer easily to a group of files, the Bash shell lets you use metacharacters. Any time you need to refer to a file or directory, such as to list, open, or remove it, you can use metacharacters to match the files you want. Here are some useful metacharacters for matching filenames:

* * Matches any number of characters.

* ? Matches any one character.

[...] Matches any one of the characters between the brackets, which can include a hyphen-separated range of letters or numbers.

Try out some of these file-matching metacharacters by first going to an empty directory (such as the `test` directory described in the previous section) and creating some empty files:

```
$ touch apple banana grape grapefruit watermelon
```

The `touch` command updates the modification time stamp of an existing file or, if no file of that name currently exists, will create an empty file. The commands that follow show you how to use shell metacharacters with the `ls` command to match filenames. Try the following commands to see whether you get the same responses:

```
$ ls a*
apple
$ ls g*
grape grapefruit
$ ls g*t
grapefruit
$ ls *e*
apple grape grapefruit watermelon
$ ls *n*
banana watermelon
```

The first example matches any file that begins with a (apple). The next example matches any files that begin with g (grape, grapefruit). Next, files beginning with g and ending in t are matched (grapefruit). Next, any file that contains e in the name is matched (apple, grape, grapefruit, watermelon). Finally, any file that contains n is matched (banana, watermelon).

Here are a few examples of pattern matching with the question mark (?):

```
$ ls ????e
apple grape
$ ls g???e*
grape grapefruit
```

The first example matches any five-character file that ends in e (apple, grape). The second matches any file that begins with g and has e as its fifth character (grape, grapefruit).

The following examples use braces to do pattern matching:

```
$ ls [abw]*
apple banana watermelon
$ ls [agw]*[ne]
apple grape watermelon
```

In the first example, any file beginning with a, b, or w is matched. In the second, any file that begins with a, g, or w and also ends with either n or e is matched. You can also include ranges within brackets. For example:

```
$ ls [a-g]*
apple banana grape grapefruit
```

Here, any filenames beginning with a letter from a through g are matched.

Using file-redirection metacharacters

Commands receive data from standard input and send it to standard output. Using pipes (described earlier), you can direct standard output from one command to the standard input of another. With files, you can use less than (<) and greater than (>) signs to direct data to and from files. Here are the file-redirection characters:

- **<** Directs the contents of a file to the command. In most cases, this is the default action expected by the command and the use of the character is optional; using `less bigfile` is the same as `less < bigfile`.

- **>** Directs the standard output of a command to a file. If the file exists, the content of that file is overwritten.

- **2>** Directs standard error (error messages) to the file.

- **&>** Directs both standard output and standard error to the file.

- **>>** Directs the output of a command to a file, adding the output to the end of the existing file.

The following are some examples of command lines where information is directed to and from files:

```
$ mail root < ~/.bashrc
$ man chmod | col -b > /tmp/chmod
$ echo "I finished the project on $(date)" >> ~/projects
```

In the first example, the content of the .bashrc file in the home directory is sent in a mail message to the computer's root user. (This example assumes that you've installed email server software—like mailutils—on your system.) The second command line formats the chmod man page (using the man command), removes extra back spaces (col -b), and sends the output to the file /tmp/chmod (overwriting the contents of the previous /tmp/chmod file, if it exists). The final command results in the following text being added to the user's project file:

```
I finished the project on Sat Jun 15 13:46:49 EDT 2019
```

Another type of redirection, referred to as *here text* (also called *here document*), enables you to type text that can be used as standard input for a command. Here, documents involve entering two less-than characters (<<) after a command, followed by a word. All typing following that word is taken as user input until the word is repeated on a line by itself. Here is an example:

```
$ mail root cnegus rjones bdecker << thetext
> I want to tell everyone that there will be a 10 a.m.
> meeting in conference room B. Everyone should attend.
>
> -- James
> thetext
$
```

This example sends a mail message to the root, cnegus, rjones, and bdecker usernames. The text entered between <<thetext and thetext becomes the content of the message. A common use of here text is to use it with a text editor to create or add to a file from within a script:

```
/bin/ed /etc/resolv.conf <<resendit
a
nameserver 100.100.100.100
.
w
q
resendit
```

With these lines added to a script run by the root user, the ed text editor adds the IP address of a DNS server to the /etc/resolv.conf file. If, by the way, you take a moment to read the current contents of /etc/resolv.conf, you'll see that it's no longer used to manually configure your DNS settings. It seems that change happens even to software tools that have been running successfully for 30 years.

Using brace expansion characters

By using curly braces ({}), you can expand out a set of characters across filenames, directory names, or other arguments to which you give commands. For example, if you want to create a set of files such as memo1 through memo5, you can do that as follows:

```
$ touch memo{1,2,3,4,5}
$ ls
memo1 memo2 memo3 memo4 memo5
```

The items that are expanded don't have to be numbers or even single digits. For example, you could use ranges of numbers or digits. You could also use any string of characters, as long as you separate them with commas. Here are some examples:

```
$ touch {John,Bill,Sally}-{Breakfast,Lunch,Dinner}
$ ls
Bill-Breakfast Bill-Lunch John-Dinner Sally-Breakfast Sally-Lunch
Bill-Dinner John-Breakfast John-Lunch Sally-Dinner
```

Continues

4

Continued

```
$ rm {John,Bill,Sally}-{Breakfast,Lunch,Dinner}
$ touch {a..f}{1..5}
$ ls
a1 a3 a5 b2 b4 c1 c3 c5 d2 d4 e1 e3 e5 f2 f4
a2 a4 b1 b3 b5 c2 c4 d1 d3 d5 e2 e4 f1 f3 f5
```

In the first example, the use of two sets of braces means John, Bill, and Sally each have filenames associated with Breakfast, Lunch, and Dinner. If I had made a mistake, I could easily recall the command and change touch to rm to delete all of the files. In the next example, the use of two dots between letters a and f and numbers 1 and 5 specifies the ranges to be used. Note the files that were created from those few characters.

Listing Files and Directories

The ls command is the most common command used to list information about files and directories. Many options available with the ls command allow you to gather different sets of files and directories as well as to view different kinds of information about them.

By default, when you type the ls command, the output shows you all non-hidden files and directories contained in the current directory. When you type ls, however, many Linux systems assign an alias ls to add options. To see if ls is aliased, enter the following:

```
$ alias ls
alias ls='ls --color=auto'
```

The --color=auto option causes different types of files and directories to be displayed in different colors. So, return to the $HOME/test directory created earlier in the chapter, add a couple of different types of files, and then see what they look like with the ls command:

```
$ cd $HOME/test
$ touch scriptx.sh apple
$ chmod 755 scriptx.sh
$ mkdir Stuff
$ ln -s apple pointer_to_apple
$ ls
apple pointer_to_apple scriptx.sh Stuff
```

Although you can't see it in the preceding code example, the directory Stuff shows up in blue, pointer _ to _ apple (a symbolic link) appears as aqua, and scriptx.sh (which is an executable file) appears in green. All other regular files show up in black. Typing ls -1 to see a long listing of those files can make these different types of files clearer still:

```
$ ls -l
total 4
-rw-rw-r--. 1 joe joe 0 Dec 18 13:38 apple
lrwxrwxrwx. 1 joe joe 5 Dec 18 13:46 pointer_to_apple -> apple
```

```
-rwxr-xr-x. 1 joe joe 0 Dec 18 13:37 scriptx.sh
drwxrwxr-x. 2 joe joe 4096 Dec 18 13:38 Stuff
```

As you look at the long listing, notice that the first character of each line shows the type of file. A hyphen (-) indicates a regular file, d indicates a directory, and l (lower-case *L*) indicates a symbolic link. An executable file (a script or binary file that runs as a command) has execute bits turned on (*x*). See more on execute bits in the upcoming section "Understanding File Permissions and Ownership."

You should become familiar with the contents of your home directory next. Use the -l and -a options to ls:

```
$ ls -la /home/frank
total 32
drwxr-xr-x 3      frank frank 4096    Feb 19 17:09 .
drwxr-xr-x 5      root  root  4096    May 30 2019  ..
-rw------- 1      frank frank 311     May  5 2019  .bash_history
-rw-r--r-- 1      frank frank 220     May  5 2019  .bash_logout
-rw-r--r-- 1      frank frank 3771    May  5 2019  .bashrc
drwx------ 3      frank frank 4096    May  5 2019  .gnupg
-rw------- 1      frank frank 34      May  5 2019  .lesshst
-rw-r--r-- 1      frank frank 807     May  5 2019  .profile
-rw-rw-r-- 1      frank frank 0       May  5 2019  letter
^                 ^     ^     ^       ^            ^

col 1   col 2 col 3 col 4 col 5 col  6            col 7
```

Displaying a long list (-l option) of the contents of your home directory shows you more about file sizes and directories. The `total` line shows the total amount of disk space used by the files in the list (32 kilobytes in this example). Adding the all files option (-a) displays files that begin with a dot (.). Directories such as the current directory (.) and the parent directory (..)—the directory above the current directory—are noted as directories by the letter d at the beginning of each entry. Each directory begins with a d and each file begins with a dash (-).

The file and directory names are shown in column 7. In this example, a dot (.) represents /home/frank and two dots (..) represent /home—the parent directory of /frank. Most of the files in this example are dot (.) files that are used to store shell properties (.bash files). The only non-dot file in this list is the one named `letter`. Column 3 shows the directory or file owner. The /home directory is owned by root, and everything else is owned by the user frank, who belongs to the frank group (groups are listed in column 4).

In addition to the d or -, column 1 on each line contains the permissions set for that file or directory. Other information in the listing includes the number of hard links to the item (column 2), the size of each file in bytes (column 5), and the date and time each file was most recently modified (column 6).

4

Here are a few other facts about file and directory listings:

- The number of characters shown for a directory (4096 bytes in these examples) reflects the size of the file containing information about the directory. Although this number can grow above 4096 bytes for a directory that contains lots of files, this number doesn't reflect the size of files contained in that directory.

- On occasion, instead of seeing the execute bit (x) set on an executable file, you may see an s in that spot instead. With an s appearing within either the owner (-rwsr-xr-x) or group (-rwxr-sr-x) permissions, or both (-rwsr-sr-x), the application can be run by any user, but ownership of the running process is assigned to the application's user/group instead of that of the user launching the command. This is referred to as a *set UID* or *set GID* program, respectively. For example, the mount command (/bin/mount) has permissions set as -rwsr-xr-x. This allows any user to run mount to list mounted filesystems (although you still have to be root to use mount to actually mount filesystems from the command line, in most cases).

- If a t appears at the end of a directory, it indicates that the *sticky bit* is set for that directory (for example, drwxrwxr-t). By setting the sticky bit on a directory, the directory's owner can allow other users and groups to add files to the directory but prevent users from deleting each other's files in that directory. With a set GID assigned to a directory, any files created in that directory are assigned the same group as the directory's group. (If you see a capital S or T instead of the execute bits on a directory, it means that the set GID or sticky bit permission, respectively, was set, but for some reason the execute bit was not also turned on.)

Identifying Directories

When you need to identify your home directory on a shell command line, you can use the following:

- **$HOME** This environment variable stores your home directory name.

- **~** The tilde (~) represents your home directory on the command line. You can also use the tilde to identify someone else's home directory. For example, ~joe would be expanded to the joe home directory (probably /home/joe). So, if I wanted to go to the directory/home/joe/test, I could enter cd ~joe/test to get there.

Other special ways of identifying directories in the shell include the following:

- **.** A single dot (.) refers to the current directory.

- **..** Two dots (..) refer to a directory directly above the current directory.

- **$PWD** This environment variable refers to the current working directory.

- **$OLDPWD** This environment variable refers to the previous working directory before you changed to the current one. (Entering cd – returns you to the directory represented by $OLDPWD.)

As I mentioned earlier, there are many useful options for the `ls` command. Return to the `$HOME/test` directory in which you've been working. Here are some examples of `ls` options. Don't worry if the output doesn't exactly match what is in your directory at this point.

Any file or directory beginning with a dot (.) is considered hidden and is not displayed by default with `ls`. These dot files are typically configuration files or directories that need to be in your home directory but don't need to be seen in your daily work. The `-a` lets you see those files.

The `-t` option displays files in the order in which they were most recently modified. With the `-F` option, a slash (/) appears at the end of directory names, an asterisk (*) is added to executable files, and an at sign (@) is shown next to symbolic links.

To show hidden and non-hidden files:

```
$ ls -a
.  apple docs grapefruit pointer_to_apple .stuff watermelon
.. banana grape .hiddendir script.sh .tmpfile
```

To list all files by time most recently modified:

```
$ ls -at
.tmpfile .hiddendir .. docs watermelon banana script.sh
.  .stuff pointer_to_apple grapefruit apple grape
```

To list files and append file-type indicators:

```
$ ls -F
apple banana docs/ grape grapefruit pointer_to_apple@ script.sh*
watermelon
```

To avoid displaying certain files or directories when you use `ls`, use the `--hide=` option. In the next set of examples, any file beginning with g does not appear in the output. Using a `-d` option on a directory shows information about that directory instead of showing the files and directories the directory contains. The `-R` option lists all files in the current directory as well as any files or directories that are associated with the original directory. The `-S` option lists files by size.

To exclude any files beginning with the letter g in the list:

```
$ ls --hide=g*
apple banana docs pointer_to_apple script.sh watermelon
```

To list info about a directory instead of the files it contains:

```
$ ls -ld $HOME/test/
drwxrwxr-x. 4 joe joe 4096 Dec 18 22:00 /home/joe/test/
```

To create multiple directory layers (-p is needed):

```
$ mkdir -p $HOME/test/documents/memos/
```

4

To list all files and directories recursively from the current directory down:

```
$ ls -R
...
```

To list files by size from the current directory down:

```
$ ls -S
...
```

Understanding File Permissions and Ownership

After you've worked with Linux for a while, you are almost sure to get a `Permission denied` message. Permissions associated with files and directories in Linux were designed to keep users from accessing other users' private files and to protect important system files.

The nine bits assigned to each file for permissions define the access that you and others have to your file. Permission bits for a regular file appear as `-rwxrwxrwx`. Those bits are used to define who can read, write, or execute the file.

> **NOTE**
>
> For a regular file, a dash appears in front of the nine-bit permissions indicator. Instead of a dash, you might see a `d` (for a directory), `l` (for a symbolic link), `b` (for a block device), `c` (for a character device), `s` (for a socket), or `p` (for a named pipe).

Of the nine-bit permissions, the first three bits apply to the owner's permission, the next three apply to the group assigned to the file, and the last three apply to all others. The `r` stands for read, the `w` stands for write, and the `x` stands for execute permissions. If a dash appears instead of the letter, it means that permission is turned off for that associated read, write, or execute bit.

Because files and directories are different types of elements, read, write, and execute permissions on files and directories mean different things. Table 4.2 explains what you can do with each of them.

TABLE 4.2 Setting Read, Write, and Execute Permissions

PERMISSION	FILE	DIRECTORY
Read	View what's in the file.	See what files and subdirectories it contains.
Write	Change the file's content, rename it, or delete it.	Add files or subdirectories to the directory. Remove files or directories from the directory.
Execute	Run the file as a program.	Change to the directory as the current directory, search through the directory, or execute a program from the directory. Access file metadata (file size, time stamps, and so on) of files in that directory.

As noted earlier, you can see the permission for any file or directory by typing the `ls -ld` command. The named file or directory appears as those shown in this example:

```
$ ls -ld ch3 test
-rw-rw-r-- 1 joe sales 4983 Jan 18 22:13 ch3
drwxr-xr-x 2 joe sales 1024 Jan 24 13:47 test
```

The first line shows that the ch3 file has read and write permission for the owner and the group. All other users have read permission, which means that they can view the file but cannot change its contents or remove it. The second line shows the test directory (indicated by the letter d before the permission bits). The owner has read, write, and execute permissions while the group and other users have only read and execute permissions. As a result, the owner can add, change, or delete files in that directory, and everyone else can only read the contents, change to that directory, and list the contents of the directory. (If you had not used the -d options to ls, you would have listed files in the test directory instead of permissions of that directory.)

Changing permissions with chmod (numbers)

If you own a file, you can use the chmod command to change the permission on it. In one method of doing this, each permission (read, write, and execute) is assigned a number— r=4, w=2, and x=1—and you use each set's total number to establish the permission. For example, to make permissions wide open for yourself as owner, you would set the first number to 7 (4+2+1), and then you would give the group and others read-only permission by setting both the second and third numbers to 4 (4+0+0), so that the final number is 744. Any combination of permissions can result from 0 (no permission) through 7 (full permission).

Here are some examples of how to change permission on a file (named file) and what the resulting permission would be. The following chmod command results in this permission: rwxrwxrwx

```
# chmod 777 file
```

The following chmod command results in this permission: rwxr-xr-x

```
# chmod 755 file
```

The following chmod command results in this permission: rw-r--r--

```
# chmod 644 file
```

The following chmod command results in this permission: ---------

```
# chmod 000 file
```

The chmod command also can be used recursively. For example, suppose that you wanted to give an entire directory structure 755 permissions (rwxr-xr-x), starting at the $HOME/ myapps directory. To do that, you could use the -R option, as follows:

```
$ chmod -R 755 $HOME/myapps
```

4

All files and directories below, and including, the myapps directory in your home directory will have 755 permissions set.

Changing permissions with chmod (letters)

You can also turn file permissions on and off using plus (+) and minus (–) signs, respectively, along with letters to indicate what changes and for whom. Using letters, for each file you can change permissions for the user (u), group (g), other (o), and all users (a). What you would change includes the read (r), write (w), and execute (x) bits. For example, start with a file that has all permissions open (rwxrwxrwx). Run the following chmod commands using minus sign options. The resulting permissions are shown to the right of each command.

The following chmod command results in this permission: r-xr-xr-x

```
$ chmod a-w file
```

The following chmod command results in this permission: rwxrwxrw-

```
$ chmod o-x file
```

The following chmod command results in this permission: rwx------

```
$ chmod go-rwx file
```

Likewise, the following examples start with all permissions closed (---------). The plus sign is used with chmod to turn permissions on.

The following chmod command results in this permission: rw-------

```
$ chmod u+rw files
```

The following chmod command results in this permission: --x--x--x

```
$ chmod a+x files
```

The following chmod command results in this permission: r-xr-x---

```
$ chmod ug+rx files
```

Using letters to change permission recursively with chmod generally works better than using numbers because you can change bits selectively instead of changing all permission bits at once. For example, suppose that you want to remove write permission for "other" without changing any other permission bits on a set of files and directories. You could do the following:

```
$ chmod -R o-w $HOME/myapps
```

This example recursively removes write permissions for "other" on any files and directories below the myapps directory. If you had used numbers such as 644, execute permission would be turned off for directories; using 755, execute permission would be turned on for regular files. Using o-w, only one bit is turned off and all other bits are left alone.

Setting default file permission with umask

When you create a file as a regular user, it's given permission `rw-rw-r--` by default. A directory is given the permission `rwxrwxr-x`. For the root user, file and directory permission are `rw-r--r--` and `rwxr-xr-x`, respectively. These default values are determined by the value of umask. Enter **umask** to see what your umask value is. For example:

```
$ umask
0022
```

If you ignore the leading zero for the moment, the umask value masks what is considered to be fully opened permissions for a file 666 or a directory 777. The umask value of 002 results in permission for a directory of 775 (`rwxrwxr-x`). That same umask results in a file permission of 644 (`rw-rw-r--`). (Execute permissions are off by default for regular files.)

To change your umask value temporarily, run the umask command. Then try creating some files and directories to see how the umask value affects how permissions are set. For example:

```
$ umask 777 ; touch file01 ; mkdir dir01 ; ls -ld file01 dir01
d---------. 2 joe joe 6 Dec 19 11:03 dir01
----------. 1 joe joe 0 Dec 19 11:02 file01
$ umask 000 ; touch file02 ; mkdir dir02 ; ls -ld file02 dir02
drwxrwxrwx. 2 joe joe 6 Dec 19 11:00 dir02/
-rw-rw-rw-. 1 joe joe 0 Dec 19 10:59 file02
$ umask 022 ; touch file03 ; mkdir dir03 ; ls -ld file03 dir03
drwxr-xr-x. 2 joe joe 6 Dec 19 11:07 dir03
-rw-r--r--. 1 joe joe 0 Dec 19 11:07 file03
```

If you want to change your umask value permanently, add a umask command to the .bashrc file in your home directory (near the end of that file). The next time you open a shell, your umask is set to whatever value you chose.

Changing file ownership

As a regular user, you cannot change ownership of files or directories to have them belong to another user. You *can* change ownership as the root user. For example, suppose that you created a file called memo.txt in the user joe's home directory while you were root user. Here's how you could change it to be owned by joe:

```
# chown joe /home/joe/memo.txt
# ls -l /home/joe/memo.txt
-rw-r--r--. 1 joe root 0 Dec 19 11:23 /home/joe/memo.txt
```

Notice that the chown command changed the user to joe but left the group as root. To change both user and group to joe, you could enter the following instead:

```
# chown joe:joe /home/joe/memo.txt
# ls -l /home/joe/memo.txt
-rw-r--r--. 1 joe joe 0 Dec 19 11:23 /home/joe/memo.txt
```

The chown command can be use recursively as well. Using the recursive option (-R) is helpful if you need to change a whole directory structure to ownership by a particular user. For example, if you inserted a USB drive, which is mounted on the /media/myusb directory, and you wanted to give full ownership of the contents of that drive to the user joe, you could enter the following:

```
# chown -R joe:joe /media/myusb
```

Moving, Copying, and Removing Files

Commands for moving, copying, and deleting files are fairly straightforward. To change the location of a file, use the mv command. To copy a file from one location to another, use the cp command. To remove a file, use the rm command. These commands can be used to act on individual files and directories or recursively to act on many files and directories at once. Here are some examples:

```
$ mv abc def
$ mv ghi ~
$ mv /home/joe/mymemos/ /home/joe/Documents/
```

The first mv command moves the file abc to the file def in the same directory (essentially renaming it), whereas the second mv command moves the file ghi to your home directory (~). The next mv command moves the mymemos directory (and all its contents) to the /home/joe/Documents directory.

By default, the mv command overwrites any existing files in the target directory using the same names. However, many Linux systems alias the mv command so that it uses the -i option (which causes mv to prompt you before overwriting existing files). Here's how to check if that is true on your system:

```
$ alias mv
alias mv='mv -i'
```

Here are some examples of using the cp command to copy files from one location to another:

```
$ cp abc def
$ cp abc ~
$ cp -r /usr/share/doc/bash-completion* /tmp/a/
$ cp -ra /usr/share/doc/bash-completion* /tmp/b/
```

The first copy command (cp) copies abc to the new name def in the same directory, whereas the second copies abc to your home directory (~), keeping the name abc. The two recursive (-r) copies copy the bash-completion directory and all of the files it contains, first to new /tmp/a/ and /tmp/b/ directories. If you run ls -l on those two directories, you see that for the cp command run with the archive (-a) option, the date/time stamps and permissions are maintained by the copy. Without the -a, current date/time stamps are used, and permissions are determined by your umask.

The cp command may also be aliased with the -i option in order to prevent you from inadvertently overwriting files.

As with the cp and mv commands, rm is also sometimes aliased to include the -i option. This can prevent the damage that can come from an inadvertent recursive remove (-r) option. Here are some examples of the rm command:

```
$ rm abc
$ rm *
```

The first remove command deletes the abc file; the second removes all of the files in the current directory (except that it doesn't remove directories and/or any files that start with a dot). If you want to remove a directory, you need to use the recursive (-r) option to rm or, for an empty directory, you can use the rmdir command. Consider the following examples:

```
$ rmdir /home/joe/nothing/
$ rm -r /home/joe/bigdir/
$ rm -rf /home/joe/hugedir/
```

The rmdir command in the preceding code only removes the directory (nothing) if it is empty. The rm -r example removes the directory bigdir and all of its contents (files and multiple levels of subdirectories).

> **Caution**
>
> When you don't use the -i option on the mv, cp, and rm commands, you risk removing some (or lots) of files by mistake. Using wildcards (such as *) and no -i makes mistakes even more likely (and their consequences even more painful). That said, sometimes you don't want to be bothered to step through each file you delete. If you've set -i as the aliased default but want to bypass it for a particular operation, you have other options as follows:
>
> - You can force rm to delete without prompting by adding the -f argument. An alternative is to run rm, cp, or mv with a backslash in front of it (\rm bigdir). The backslash causes any command to run unaliased.
>
> - Another alternative with mv is to use the -b option. With -b, if a file of the same name exists at the destination, a backup copy of the old file is made before the new file is moved there.

4

Summary

Commands for moving around the filesystem, copying files, moving files, and removing files are among the most basic commands that you need to work from the shell. This chapter covers lots of commands for moving around and manipulating files as well as commands for changing ownership and permission.

The next chapter describes commands for editing and searching for files. These commands include the vim/vi text editors, the find command, and the grep command.

Exercises

Use these exercises to test your knowledge of efficient ways to get around the Linux file-system and work with files and directories. When possible, try to use shortcuts to type as little as possible to get the desired results. If you are stuck, solutions to the tasks are shown in Appendix A (although in Linux, there are often multiple ways to complete a task).

1. Create a directory in your home directory called projects. In the projects directory, create nine empty files that are named house1, house2, house3, and so on up to house9. Assuming that there are lots of other files in that directory, come up with a single argument to ls that would list just those nine files.

2. Make the $HOME/projects/houses/doors/ directory path. Create the following empty files within this directory path (try using absolute and relative paths from your home directory):

   ```
   $HOME/projects/houses/bungalow.txt
   $HOME/projects/houses/doors/bifold.txt
   $HOME/projects/outdoors/vegetation/landscape.txt
   ```

3. Copy the files house1 and house5 to the $HOME/projects/houses/ directory.

4. Recursively copy the /usr/share/doc/initscripts* directory to the $HOME/projects/ directory. Maintain the current date/time stamps and permissions.

5. Recursively list the contents of the $HOME/projects/ directory. Pipe the output to the less command so that you can page through the output.

6. Move house3 and house4 to the $HOME/projects/houses/doors directory.

7. Remove the $HOME/projects/houses/doors directory and its contents.

8. Change the permissions on the $HOME/projects/house2 file so that it can be read by and written to the user who owns the file, only read by the group, and have no permission for others.

9. Recursively change permissions of the $HOME/projects/ directory so that nobody has write permission to any files or directories beneath that point in the filesystem.

Working with Text Files

IN THIS CHAPTER

Using `vim` and `vi` to edit text files

Searching for files

Searching in files

When the UNIX system was created, on which Linux was based, most information was managed on the system in plain text files. Thus it was critical for users to know how to use tools for searching for and within plain text files and to be able to change and configure those files.

Today, configuration of Linux systems can still be done by editing plain text files. Whether you are modifying files in the `/etc` directory to configure a local service or editing Ansible inventory files to configure sets of host computers, plain text files are still commonly used for those tasks.

Before you can become a full-fledged system administrator, you need to be able to use a plain text editor. The fact that most professional Linux servers don't even have a graphical interface available makes the need for editing of plain text configuration files with a non-graphical text editor necessary.

After you know how to edit text files, you still might find it tough to figure out where the files are located. With commands such as `find`, you can search for files based on various attributes (filename, size, modification date, and ownership to name a few). With the `grep` command, you can search inside of text files to find specific search terms.

Editing Files with Vim and Vi

It's almost impossible to use Linux for any period of time and not need a text editor because, as noted earlier, most Linux configuration files are plain text files that you will almost certainly need to change manually at some point.

If you are using a GNOME desktop, you can run `gedit` from a terminal (or select Gedit from the Applications screen), which is fairly intuitive for editing text. You can also run a simple text editor called `nano` from within the shell. However, many Linux shell users use either the `vi` or `emacs` command to edit text files.

The advantage of `vi` or `emacs` over a graphical editor is that you can use the command from any shell, character terminal, or character-based connection over a network (using `telnet` or `ssh`, for example)—no graphical interface is required. They each also contain tons of features, so you can continue to grow with them.

The following sections provide a brief tutorial on the `vi` text editor, which you can use to manually edit a text file from any shell. It also describes an improved version of `vi` called `vim`. (If `vi` doesn't suit you, see the sidebar "Exploring Other Text Editors" for further options.)

The `vi` editor is difficult to learn at first, but after you know it you will never have to use a mouse or a function key—you can edit and move around quickly and efficiently within files just by using the keyboard.

Exploring Other Text Editors

Dozens of text editors are available for use with Linux. You can try them out if you find `vi` to be too taxing. Here are some of the options:

nano: This popular, streamlined text editor is used with many bootable Linux systems and other limited-space Linux environments. nano is included in nearly all Ubuntu images by default.

gedit: The GNOME text editor runs on the desktop.

jed: This screen-oriented editor was made for programmers. Using colors, jed can highlight code that you create so that you can easily read the code and spot syntax errors. Use the Alt key to select menus to manipulate your text.

joe: The joe editor is similar to many PC text editors. Use Ctrl and arrow keys to move around. Press Ctrl+C to exit with no save or Ctrl+X to save and exit.

kate: This nice-looking editor comes in the kdebase package. It has lots of bells and whistles, such as highlighting for different types of programming languages and controls for managing word wrap.

kedit: This GUI-based text editor comes with the KDE desktop.

nedit: This is an excellent programmer's editor. You need to install the optional nedit package to get this editor.

If you use ssh to log in to other Linux computers on your network, you can use any available text editor to edit files. If you use ssh -X to connect to the remote system, a GUI-based editor pops up on your local screen. When no GUI is available, you need a text editor that runs in the shell, such as vi, jed, or joe.

Starting with vi

Most often, you start `vi` to open a particular file. For example, to open a file called `/tmp/test`, enter the following command:

```
$ vi /tmp/test
```

If this is a new file, you should see something similar to the following:

```
☐
~
~
~
~
~
"/tmp/test" [New File]
```

A blinking box at the top represents where your cursor is located. The bottom line keeps you informed about what is going on with your editing (here, you just opened a new file). In between, there are tildes (~) as filler because there is no text in the file yet. Now here's the intimidating part: There are no hints, menus, or icons to tell you what to do. To make it worse, you can't just start typing. If you do, the computer is likely to beep at you. (And some people complain that Linux isn't friendly.)

First, you need to know the two main operating modes: command and input. The `vi` editor always starts in command mode. Before you can add or change text in the file, you have to type a command (one or two letters, sometimes preceded by an optional number) to tell `vi` what you want to do. Case is important, so use uppercase and lowercase exactly as shown in the examples!

> **NOTE**
>
> On many Ubuntu systems, the `vi` command will actually run `vim`. The first obvious difference between `vi` and `vim` is that any known text file type, such as HTML, C code, or a common configuration file will, assuming the syntax option is enabled, appear in color. The colors indicate the structure of the file. Other features of `vim` that are not in `vi` include features such as visual highlighting and split-screen mode. By default, the root user doesn't have `vi` aliased to `vim`. If `vim` is not on your system, try installing the `vim-enhanced` package.

Adding text

To get into input mode, type an input command letter. To begin, type any of the following letters. When you are finished inputting text, press the Esc key (sometimes twice) to return to command mode. Remember the Esc key!

- **a:** The *add* command. With this command, you can input text that starts to the *right* of the cursor.

- **A:** The *add at end* command. With this command, you can input text starting at the end of the current line.

5

i: The *insert* command. With this command, you can input text that starts to the *left* of the cursor.

I: The *insert at beginning* command. With this command, you can input text that starts at the beginning of the current line.

o: The *open below* command. This command opens a line below the current line and puts you in insert mode.

O: The *open above* command. This command opens a line above the current line and puts you in insert mode.

TIP

When you are in insert mode, -- INSERT -- appears at the bottom of the screen.

Type a few words, and press Enter. Repeat that a few times until you have a few lines of text. When you're finished typing, press Esc to return to command mode. Now that you have a file with some text in it, try moving around in your text with the keys or letters described in the next section.

TIP

Remember the Esc key! It always places you back into command mode. Remember that sometimes you must press Esc twice. For example, if you type a colon (:) to go into ex mode, you must press Esc twice to return to command mode.

Moving around in the text

To move around in the text, you can use the up, down, right, and left arrows. However, many of the keys for moving around are right under your fingertips when they are in typing position:

Arrow keys: Move the cursor up, down, left, or right in the file one character at a time. To move left and right, you can also use Backspace and the spacebar, respectively. If you prefer to keep your fingers on the keyboard, move the cursor with h (left), l (right), j (down), or k (up).

w: Moves the cursor to the beginning of the next word (delimited by spaces, tabs, or punctuation).

W: Moves the cursor to the beginning of the next word (delimited by spaces or tabs).

b: Moves the cursor to the beginning of the previous word (delimited by spaces, tabs, or punctuation).

B: Moves the cursor to the beginning of the previous word (delimited by spaces or tabs).

0 (zero): Moves the cursor to the beginning of the current line.

$: Moves the cursor to the end of the current line.

H: Moves the cursor to the upper-left corner of the screen (first line on the screen).

M: Moves the cursor to the first character of the middle line on the screen.

L: Moves the cursor to the lower-left corner of the screen (last line on the screen).

Deleting, copying, and changing text

The only other editing that you need to know is how to delete, copy, or change text. The x, d, y, and c commands can be used to delete and change text. These can be used along with movement keys (arrows, PgUp, PgDn, letters, and special keys) and numbers to indicate exactly what you are deleting, copying, or changing. Consider the following examples:

x: Deletes the character under the cursor.

X: Deletes the character directly before the cursor.

d<?>: Deletes some text.

c<?>: Changes some text.

y<?>: Yanks (copies) some text.

The <?> after each letter in the preceding list identifies the place where you can use a movement command to choose what you are deleting, changing, or yanking. For example:

dw: Deletes (d) a word (w) after the current cursor position.

db: Deletes (d) a word (b) before the current cursor position.

dd: Deletes (d) the entire current line (d).

**c$**: Changes (c) the characters (actually erases them) from the current character to the end of the current line ($) and goes into input mode.

c0: Changes (c) (again, erases) characters from the previous character to the beginning of the current line (0) and goes into input mode.

c1: Erases (c) the current letter (1) and goes into input mode.

cc: Erases (c) the line (c) and goes into input mode.

yy: Copies (y) the current line (y) into the buffer.

y): Copies (y) the current sentence ( )), to the right of the cursor, into the buffer.

y}: Copies (y) the current paragraph (}), to the right of the cursor, into the buffer.

Any of the commands just shown can be further modified using numbers, as you can see in the following examples:

3dd: Deletes (d) three (3) lines (d), beginning at the current line.

3dw: Deletes (d) the next three (3) words (w).

5c1: Changes (c) the next five (5) letters (1) (that is, removes the letters and enters input mode).

5

12j: Moves down (j) 12 lines (12).

5cw: Erases (c) the next five (5) words (w) and goes into input mode.

4y): Copies (y) the next four (4) sentences ( )).

Pasting (putting) text

After text has been copied to the buffer (by deleting, changing, or yanking it), you can place that text back in your file using the letter p or P. With both commands, the text most recently stored in the buffer is put into the file in different ways:

P: Puts the copied text to the left of the cursor if the text consists of letters or words; puts the copied text above the current line if the copied text contains lines of text.

p: Puts the buffered text to the right of the cursor if the text consists of letters or words; puts the buffered text below the current line if the buffered text contains lines of text.

Repeating commands

After you delete, change, or paste text, you can repeat that action by typing a period (.). For example, with the cursor on the beginning of the name Joe, you type cw and then type Jim to change Joe to Jim. You search for the next occurrence of Joe in the file, position the cursor at the beginning of that name, and press a period. The word changes to Jim, and you can search for the next occurrence. You can go through a file this way, pressing n to go to the next occurrence and period (.) to change the word.

Exiting vi

To wrap things up, use the following commands to save or quit the file:

ZZ: Saves the current changes to the file and exits from vi.

:w: Saves the current file but you can continue editing.

:wq: Works the same as ZZ.

:q: Quits the current file. This works only if you don't have any unsaved changes.

:q!: Quits the current file and *doesn't* save the changes you just made to the file.

TIP

If you've really trashed the file by mistake, the :q! command is the best way to exit and abandon your changes. The file reverts to the most recently changed version. So, if you just saved with :w, you are stuck with the changes up to that point. However, despite having saved the file, you can press u to back out of changes (all the way back to the beginning of the editing session if you like) and then save again.

You have learned a few vi editing commands. I describe more commands in the following sections. First, however, consider the following tips to smooth out your first trials with vi:

Esc: Remember that Esc gets you back to command mode. Esc followed by ZZ gets you out of command mode, saves the file, and exits.

u: Press u to undo the previous change you made. Continue to press u to undo the change before that and the one before that.

Ctrl+R: If you decide that you didn't want to undo the previous undo command, use Ctrl+R for Redo. Essentially, this command undoes your undo.

Caps Lock: Beware of hitting Caps Lock by mistake. Everything that you type in vi has a different meaning when the letters are capitalized. You don't get a warning that you are typing capitals; things just start acting weird.

:!command: You can run a shell command while you are in vi using :! followed by a shell command name. For example, type :!date to see the current date and time, type :!pwd to see what your current directory is, or type :!jobs to see whether you have any jobs running in the background. When the command completes, press Enter and you are back to editing the file. You could even use this technique to launch a shell (:!bash) from vi, run a few commands from that shell, and then type exit to return to vi. (I recommend doing a save before escaping to the shell, just in case you forget to go back to vi.)

Ctrl+g: If you forget what you are editing, pressing these keys displays the name of the file that you are editing and the current line that you are on at the bottom of the screen. It also displays the total number of lines in the file, the percentage of how far you are through the file, and the column number the cursor is on. This just helps you get your bearings after you've stopped for a cup of coffee at 3 a.m.

Skipping around in the file

Besides the few movement commands described earlier, there are other ways of moving around a vi file. To try these out, open a large file that you can't damage too much. (Try copying /var/log/syslog to /tmp and opening it in vi.) Here are some movement commands that you can use:

Ctrl+f: Pages ahead one page at a time.

Ctrl+b: Pages back one page at a time.

Ctrl+d: Pages ahead one-half page at a time.

Ctrl+u: Pages back one-half page at a time.

G: Goes to the last line of the file.

1G: Goes to the first line of the file.

35G: Goes to any line number (35, in this case).

Searching for text

To search for the next or previous occurrence of text in the file, use either the slash (/) or the question mark (?) character. Follow the slash or question mark with a pattern (string of

5

text) to search forward or backward, respectively, for that pattern. Within the search, you can also use metacharacters. Here are some examples:

/hello: Searches forward for the word hello.

?goodbye: Searches backward for the word goodbye.

/The.*foot: Searches forward for a line that has the word The in it and also, after that at some point, the word foot.

?[pP]rint: Searches backward for either print or Print. Remember that case matters in Linux, so make use of brackets to search for words that could have different capitalization.

After you have entered a search term, simply type **n** or **N** to search again in the same direction (n) or the opposite direction (N) for the term.

Using ex mode

The vi editor was originally based on the ex editor, which didn't let you work in full-screen mode. However, it did enable you to run commands that let you find and change text on one or more lines at a time. When you type a colon and the cursor goes to the bottom of the screen, you are essentially in ex mode. The following are examples of some of those ex commands for searching for and changing text. (I chose the words Local and Remote to search for, but you can use any appropriate word.)

:g/Local: Searches for the word Local and prints every occurrence of that line from the file. (If there is more than a screenful, the output is piped to the more command.)

:s/Local/Remote: Substitutes Remote for the first occurrence of the word Local on the current line.

:g/Local/s//Remote: Substitutes the first occurrence of the word Local on every line of the file with the word Remote.

:g/Local/s//Remote/g: Substitutes every occurrence of the word Local with the word Remote in the entire file.

:g/Local/s//Remote/gp: Substitutes every occurrence of the word Local with the word Remote in the entire file and then prints each line so that you can see the changes (piping it through less if output fills more than one page).

Learning more about vi and vim

To learn more about the vi editor, try typing **vimtutor**. The vimtutor command opens a tutorial in the vim editor that steps you through common commands and features you can use in vim. (You may need to install the vim-runtime package before you can load the document.)

Finding Files

Even a basic Linux installation can have thousands of files installed on it. To help you find files on your system, you can use commands such as locate (to find commands by name), find (to find files based on lots of different attributes), and grep (to search within text files to find lines in files that contain search text).

Using locate to find files by name

On most Linux systems, the updatedb command runs once per day to gather the names of files throughout your Linux system into a database. By running the locate command, you can search that database to find the location of files stored in it.

Here are a few things that you should know about searching for files using the locate command:

- There are advantages and disadvantages to using locate to find filenames instead of the find command. A locate command finds files much (much!) faster because it searches a database instead of having to search the whole filesystem live. A disadvantage is that the locate command cannot find any files added to the system since the previous time the database was updated.

- Not every file in your filesystem is stored in the database. The contents of the /etc/updatedb.conf file limit which filenames are collected by pruning out select mount types, filesystem types, file types, and mount points. For example, filenames are not gathered from remotely mounted filesystems (cifs, nfs, and so on) or locally mounted CDs or DVDs (iso9660). Paths containing temporary files (/tmp) and spool files (/var/spool/cups) are also pruned. You can add items to prune (or remove some items that you don't want pruned) the locate database to better fit your needs. In Ubuntu 18.04, the updatedb.conf file contains the following:

```
PRUNE_BIND_MOUNTS="yes"
# PRUNENAMES=".git .bzr .hg .svn"
PRUNEPATHS="/tmp /var/spool /media /var/lib/os-prober /var/lib/ceph
/home/.ecryptfs /var/lib/schroot"
PRUNEFS="NFS nfs nfs4 rpc_pipefs afs binfmt_misc proc smbfs autofs
iso9660 ncpfs coda devpts ftpfs devfs devtmpfs fuse.mfs shfs sysfs
cifs lustre tmpfs usbfs udf fuse.glusterfs fuse.sshfs curlftpfs
ceph fuse.ceph fuse.rozofs ecryptfs fusesmb"
```

- As a regular user, you can't see any files from the locate database that you can't see in the filesystem normally. For example, if you can't type ls to view files in the /root directory, you can't locate files stored in that directory.

5

- When you search for a string, the string can appear anywhere in a file's path. For example, if you search for passwd, you could turn up /etc/passwd, /usr/bin/passwd, /home/chris/passwd/pwdfiles.txt, and many other files with passwd in the path.
- If you add files to your system after updatedb runs, you can't locate those files until updatedb runs again (probably that night). To get the database to contain all files up to the current moment, you can simply run updatedb from the shell as root.

Here are some examples of using the locate command to search for files:

```
$ locate .bashrc
/etc/bash.bashrc
/etc/skel/.bashrc
/home/ubuntu/.bashrc
/snap/core/8268/etc/bash.bashrc
/snap/core/8268/etc/skel/.bashrc
/snap/core/8268/usr/share/base-files/dot.bashrc
/snap/core/8592/etc/bash.bashrc
/snap/core/8592/etc/skel/.bashrc
/snap/core/8592/usr/share/base-files/dot.bashrc
/usr/share/base-files/dot.bashrc
/usr/share/doc/adduser/examples/adduser.local.conf.examples/
bash.bashrc
/usr/share/doc/adduser/examples/adduser.local.conf.examples/skel/
dot.bashrc
# locate .bashrc
/etc/bash.bashrc
/etc/skel/.bashrc
/home/ubuntu/.bashrc
/root/.bashrc
/snap/core/8268/etc/bash.bashrc
/snap/core/8268/etc/skel/.bashrc
/snap/core/8268/root/.bashrc
/snap/core/8268/usr/share/base-files/dot.bashrc
/snap/core/8592/etc/bash.bashrc
/snap/core/8592/etc/skel/.bashrc
/snap/core/8592/root/.bashrc
/snap/core/8592/usr/share/base-files/dot.bashrc
/usr/share/base-files/dot.bashrc
/usr/share/doc/adduser/examples/adduser.local.conf.examples/
bash.bashrc
/usr/share/doc/adduser/examples/adduser.local.conf.examples/skel/
dot.bashrc
```

When run as a regular user, locate only finds .bashrc in /etc/skel and the user's own home directory. Run as root, the same command locates .bashrc files in the /root directory (along with that of any other user on the system).

```
$ locate dir_color
/usr/share/man/man5/dir_colors.5.gz
...
$ locate -i dir_color
/etc/DIR_COLORS
/etc/DIR_COLORS.256color
/etc/DIR_COLORS.lightbgcolor
/usr/share/man/man5/dir_colors.5.gz
```

Using `locate -i`, filenames are found regardless of case. In the previous example, DIR_COLORS was found with `-i` whereas it wasn't found without the `-i` option.

```
$ locate services
/etc/services
/etc/avahi/services
[...]
/usr/lib/libreoffice/program/services/pyuno.rdb
[...]
```

Unlike the `find` command, which uses the `-name` option to find filenames, the `locate` command locates the string you enter if it exists in any part of the file's path. In this example, searching for `services` using the `locate` command finds files and directories containing the "services" text string.

Searching for files with find

The `find` command is the best one for searching your filesystem when you need to filter your results by a variety of attributes. After files are found, you can act on those files as well (using the `-exec` or `-okay` option) by running any commands you want on them.

When you run `find`, it searches your filesystem live, which causes it to run slower than `locate`, but it gives you an up-to-the-moment view of the files on your Linux system. However, you can also tell `find` to start at a particular point in the filesystem so that the search can go faster by limiting the area of the filesystem being searched.

Nearly any file attribute that you can think of can be used as a search option. You can search for filenames, ownership, permission, size, modification times, and other attributes. You can even use combinations of attributes. Here are some basic examples of using the `find` command:

```
$ find
$ find /etc
# find /etc
$ find $HOME -ls
```

Run on a line by itself, the `find` command finds all files and directories below the current directory. If you want to search from a particular point in the directory tree, just add the name of the directory you want to search (such as /etc). As a regular user, `find` does not give you special permission to find files that have permissions that make them readable

5

only by the root user. So, find produces a bunch of error messages. Run as the root user, find /etc finds all files under /etc.

A special option to add to the find command is -ls. A long listing (ownership, permission, size, and so on) is printed with each file when you add -ls to the find command (similar to output of the ls -l command). This option will help you in later examples when you want to verify that you have found files that contain the ownership, size, modification times, or other attributes that you are trying to find.

> **NOTE**
>
> If, as a regular user, you are searching an area of the filesystem where you don't have full permission to access all of the files it contains (such as the /etc directory), you might receive lots of error messages when you search with find. To get rid of those messages, direct standard errors to /dev/null. To do that, add the following to the end of the command line: 2> /dev/null. The 2> redirects standard errors to the next option (in this case /dev/null, where the output is discarded).

Finding files by name

To find files by name, you can use the -name and -iname options. The search is done by base name of the file; the directory names are not searched by default. To make the search more flexible, you can use file-matching characters, such as asterisks (*) and question marks (?), as in the following examples:

```
# find /etc -name passwd
/etc/cron.daily/passwd
/etc/passwd
/etc/pam.d/passwd
# find /etc -iname &lsquo;*passwd*'
/etc/cron.daily/passwd
/etc/passwd
/etc/passwd-
/etc/pam.d/passwd
/etc/pam.d/chpasswd
/etc/security/opasswd
```

Using the -name option and no asterisks, the first example lists any files in the /etc directory that are named passwd exactly. By using -iname instead, you can match any combination of upper- and lowercase (meaning that the search will be case-insensitive). Using asterisks, you can match any filename that includes the word passwd.

Finding files by size

If your disk is filling up and you want to find out where your biggest files are located, you can search your system by file size. The -size option enables you to search for files that are exactly, smaller than, or larger than a selected size, as you can see in the following examples:

```
$ find /usr/share/ -size +10M
$ find /mostlybig -size -1M
$ find /bigdata -size +500M -size -5G -exec du -sh {} \;
4.1G    /bigdata/images/ubuntu-container.img
606M    /bigdata/Ubuntu20_04-16-i686-Desktop.iso
560M    /bigdata/dance2.avi
```

The first example in the preceding code finds files larger than 10 MB. The second finds files less than 1 MB. In the third example, we're searching for files that are between 500 MB and 5 GB. This includes an example of the -exec option (which we'll describe later) to run the du command on each file to see its size.

Finding files by user

You can search for a particular owner (-user) or group (-group) when you try to find files. By using -not and -or, you can refine your search for files associated with specific users and groups, as you can see in the following examples:

```
$ find /home -user chris -ls
131077      4 -rw-r--r--    1 chris    chris 379 Jun 29   2014 ./.bashrc
# find /home \( -user chris -or -user joe \) -ls
131077      4 -rw-r--r--    1 chris    chris 379 Jun 29   2014 ./.bashrc
181022      4 -rw-r--r--    1 joe      joe   379 Jun 15   2014 ./.bashrc
# find /etc -group root -ls
14155777     12 drwxr-xr-x 149 root       root       12288 Feb 19
08:23 /etc
# find /var/spool -not -user root -ls
262100      0 -rw-rw----    1 rpc      mail    0 Jan 27   2014 /var/
spool/mail/rpc
278504      0 -rw-rw----    1 joe      mail    0 Apr  3   2014 /var/
spool/mail/joe
261230      0 -rw-rw----    1 bill     mail    0 Dec 18 14:17 /var/
spool/mail/bill
277373 2848 -rw-rw----    1 chris    mail 8284 Mar 15   2014 /var/
spool/mail/chris
```

The first example outputs a long listing of all of the files under the /home directory that are owned by the user chris. The next lists files owned by chris or joe. The find command of /etc turns up all files that have root as their primary group assignment (although only one of the many results is actually included in this example). The last example shows all files under /var/spool that are not owned by root. You can see files owned by other users in the sample output.

Finding files by permission

Searching for files by permission is an excellent way to turn up security issues on your system or uncover access issues. Just as you changed permissions on files using numbers or letters (with the chmod command), you can likewise find files based on number or letter

5

permissions along with the -perm options. (Refer to Chapter 4, "Moving Around the File-system," to see how to use numbers and letters with chmod to reflect file permissions.)

If you use numbers for permissions as we will in the following examples, remember that the three numbers represent permissions for the *user*, *group*, and *other*. Each of those three numbers varies from no permission (0) to full read/write/execute permission (7) by adding read (4), write (2), and execute (1) bits together. With a hyphen (-) in front of the number, all three of the bits indicated must match; with a forward slash (/) in front of it, any of the numbers can match for the search to find a file. The full, exact numbers must match if neither a hyphen nor a forward slash is used.

Consider the following examples:

```
$ find /usr/bin -perm 755 -ls
788884    28 -rwxr-xr-x    1 root      root          28176 Mar 10
2014 /bin/echo
[...]

$ find /home/chris/ -perm -222 -type d -ls
144503     4 drwxrwxrwx    8 chris    chris 4096 Jun 23   2014 /home/
chris/OPENDIR
```

By searching for -perm 755, any files or directories with exactly rwxr-xr-x permission are matched. By using -perm -222, only files that have write permission for user, group, and other are matched. Notice that, in this case, the -type d is added to match only directories.

```
$ find /myreadonly -perm /222 -type f
685035     0 -rw-rw-r--    1 chris    chris       0 Dec 30 16:34 /
myreadonly/abc

$ find . -perm -002 -type f -ls
266230     0 -rw-rw-rw-    1 chris    chris       0 Dec 30 16:28 ./
LINUX_BIBLE/abc
```

Using -perm /222, you can find any file (-type f) that has write permission turned on for the user, group, or other. You might do that to make sure that all files are read-only in a particular part of the filesystem (in this case, beneath the /myreadonly directory). The last example, -perm /002, is very useful for finding files that have open write permission for "other," regardless of how the other permission bits are set.

Finding files by date and time

Date and timestamps are stored for each file when it is created, when it is accessed, when its content is modified, or when its metadata is changed. Metadata includes owner, group, time stamp, file size, permissions, and other information stored in the file's inode. You might want to search for file data or metadata changes for any of the following reasons:

- You just changed the contents of a configuration file, and you can't remember which one. So, you search /etc to see what has changed in the past 60 minutes:

  ```
  # find /etc/ -mmin -60
  ```

- You suspect that someone hacked your system three days ago. So, you search the system to see if any commands have had their ownership or permissions changed in the past three days:

  ```
  $ find /bin /usr/bin /sbin /usr/sbin -ctime -3
  ```

- You want to find files in your FTP server (/var/ftp) and web server (/var/www) that have not been accessed in more than 300 days so that you can see if any need to be deleted:

  ```
  # find /var/ftp /var/www -atime +300
  ```

As you can glean from the examples, you can search for content or metadata changes over a certain number of days or minutes. The time options (-atime, -ctime, and -mtime) enable you to search based on the number of days since each file was accessed, changed, or had its metadata changed. The min options (-amin, -cmin, and -mmin) do the same in minutes.

Numbers that you give as arguments to the min and time options are preceded by a hyphen (to indicate a time from the current time to that number of minutes or days ago) or a plus (to indicate time from the number of minutes or days ago and older). With no hyphen or plus, the exact number is matched.

Using "not" and "or" when finding files

With the -not and -or options, you can further refine your searches. There may be times when you want to find files owned by a particular user but not assigned to a particular group. You may want files larger than a certain size but smaller than another size. Or you might want to find files owned by any of several users. The -not and -or options can help you do that. Consider the following examples:

- There is a shared directory called /var/allusers. This command line enables you to find files that are owned by either joe or chris:

  ```
  $ find /var/allusers \( -user joe -o -user chris \) -ls
  679967    0 -rw-r--r-- 1 chris chris    0 Dec 31 12:57
      /var/allusers/myjoe
  ```

```
679977 1812 -rw-r--r-- 1 joe    joe    4379 Dec 31 13:09
   /var/allusers/dict.dat


679972    0 -rw-r--r-- 1 joe    sales    0 Dec 31 13:02
   /var/allusers/one
```

- This command line searches for files owned by the user joe, but only those that are not assigned to the group joe:

```
$ find /var/allusers/ -user joe -not -group joe -ls
679972 0 -rw-r--r-- 1 joe sales  0 Dec 31 13:02 /var/
allusers/one
```

- You can also add multiple requirements on your searches. Here, a file must be owned by the user joe and must also be more than 1MB in size:

```
$ find /var/allusers/ -user joe -and -size +1M -ls
679977 1812 -rw-r--r-- 1 joe root 1854379 Dec 31 13:09
   /var/allusers/dict.dat
```

Finding files and executing commands

One of the most powerful features of the find command is the capability to execute commands on any files that you find. With the -exec option, the command you use is executed on every file found, without stopping to ask if that's okay. The -ok option stops at each matched file and asks whether you want to run the command on it.

The advantage of using -ok is that, if you are doing something destructive, you can make sure that you okay each file individually before the command is run on it. The syntax for using -exec and -ok is the same:

```
$ find [options] -exec command {} \;
$ find [options] -ok command {} \;
```

With -exec or -ok, you run find with any options you like in order to find the files you are seeking. Then you enter the -exec or -ok option followed by the command you want to run on each file. The set of curly braces indicates where on the command line to read in each file that is found. Each file can be included in the command line multiple times. To end the line, you need to add a backslash and semicolon (\;). Here are some examples:

- This command finds any file named passwd under the /etc directory and includes that name in the output of an echo command:

```
$ find /etc -iname passwd -exec echo "I found {}" \;
I found /etc/cron.daily/passwd
I found /etc/pam.d/passwd
I found /etc/passwd
```

- The following command finds every file under the `/usr/share` directory that is more than 5MB in size. Then it lists the size of each file with the `du` command. The output of `find` is then sorted by size, from largest to smallest. With `-exec` entered, all entries found are processed, without prompting:

```
$ find /usr/share -size +5M -exec du {} \; | sort -nr

116932   /usr/share/icons/HighContrast/icon-theme.cache

69048    /usr/share/icons/gnome/icon-theme.cache

20564    /usr/share/fonts/cjkuni-uming/uming.ttc
```

- The `-ok` option enables you to choose, one at a time, whether each file found is acted upon by the command you enter. For example, you want to find all files that belong to `joe` in the `/var/allusers` directory (and its subdirectories) and move them to the `/tmp/joe` directory:

```
# find /var/allusers/ -user joe -ok mv {} /tmp/joe/ \;

< mv ... /var/allusers/dict.dat > ? y

< mv ... /var/allusers/five > ? y
```

Notice in the preceding code that you are prompted for each file that is found before it is moved to the `/tmp/joe` directory. You would simply type **y** and press Enter at each line to move the file, or just press Enter to skip it.

For more information on the `find` command, enter **man find**.

Searching in files with grep

If you want to search for files that contain a certain search term, you can use the `grep` command. With `grep`, you can search a single file or search a whole directory structure of files recursively.

When you search, you can have every line containing the term printed on your screen (standard output) or just list the names of the files that contain the search term. By default, `grep` searches text in a case-sensitive way, although you can do case-insensitive searches as well.

Instead of just searching files, you can also use `grep` to search standard output. So, if a command turns out lots of text and you want to find only lines that contain certain text, you can use `grep` to filter just what you want.

Here are some examples of `grep` command lines used to find text strings in one or more files:

```
$ grep network /etc/services
wipld            1300/tcp                        # Wipl network monitor
sane-port        6566/tcp         sane saned     # SANE network
scanner daemon
mandelspawn      9359/udp         mandelbrot     # network mandelbrot
```

Continues

Continued

```
$ grep -i network /etc/services
# Network services, Internet style
ntp             123/udp                         # Network Time Protocol
snpp            444/tcp                         # Simple Network
Paging Protocol
nqs             607/tcp                         # Network Queuing system
webster         765/tcp                         # Network dictionary
nfs             2049/tcp                        # Network File System
nfs             2049/udp                        # Network File System
nut             3493/tcp                        # Network UPS Tools
nbd             10809/tcp                       # Linux Network
Block Device
vnetd           13724/tcp                       # Veritas
Network Utility
wipld           1300/tcp                        # Wipl network monitor
sane-port       6566/tcp        sane saned      # SANE network
scanner daemon
mandelspawn     9359/udp        mandelbrot      # network mandelbrot
```

In the first example, a `grep` for the word `network` in the /etc/services file turned up three lines. Searching again, using the -i to be case-insensitive (as in the second example), there were 13 lines of text produced.

To search for lines that don't contain a selected text string, use the -v option. In the following example, all lines from the /etc/services file are displayed except those containing the text `tcp` (case-insensitive):

```
$ grep -vi tcp /etc/services
```

To do recursive searches, use the -r option and a directory as an argument. The following example includes the -l option, which just lists files that include the search text without showing the actual lines of text. That search turns up files that contain the text `peerdns` (case-insensitive).

```
$ grep -rli peerdns /usr/share/doc/
/usr/share/doc/dnsmasq-2.66/setup.html
/usr/share/doc/initscripts-9.49.17/sysconfig.txt
...
```

The next example recursively searches the /etc/sysconfig directory for the term `root`. It lists every line in every file beneath the directory that contains that text. To make it easier to have the term `root` stand out on each line, the --color option is added. By default, the matched term appears in red.

```
$ grep -ri --color root /etc/systemd/
```

To search the output of a command for a term, you can pipe the output to the `grep` command. In this example, I know that IP addresses are listed on output lines from the `ip` command that include the string `inet`, so I use `grep` to display just those lines:

```
$ ip addr show | grep inet
```

```
inet 127.0.0.1/8 scope host lo
inet 192.168.1.231/24 brd 192.168.1.255 scope global wlan0
```

Summary

Being able to work with plain text files is a critical skill for using Linux. Because so many configuration files and document files are in plain text format, you need to become proficient with a text editor to use Linux effectively. Finding filenames and content in files is also a critical skill. In this chapter, you learned to use the `locate` and `find` commands for finding files and `grep` for searching files.

The next chapter covers a variety of ways to work with processes. There, you learn how to see what processes are running, run processes in the foreground and background, and change processes (send signals).

Exercises

Use these exercises to test your knowledge of using the `vi` (or `vim`) text editor, commands for finding files (`locate` and `find`), and commands for searching files (`grep`). If you are stuck, solutions to the tasks are shown in Appendix A (although in Linux, there are often multiple ways to complete a task).

1. Copy the /etc/services file to the /tmp directory. Open the /tmp/services file in `vim`, and search for the term `WorldWideWeb`. Change that to read `World Wide Web`.

2. Find the following paragraph in your /tmp/services file (if it is not there, choose a different paragraph) and move it to the end of that file.

```
        # Note that it is presently the policy of IANA to assign a
single well-known
        # port number for both TCP and UDP; hence, most entries
here have two entries
        # even if the protocol doesn't support UDP operations.
        # Updated from RFC 1700, "Assigned Numbers" (October 1994).
Not all ports
        # are included, only the more common ones.
```

3. Using `ex` mode, search for every occurrence of the term `tcp` (case-sensitive) in your /tmp/services file and change it to `WHATEVER`.

4. As a regular user, search the /etc directory for every file named `passwd`. Redirect error messages from your search to /dev/null.

5. Create a directory in your home directory called `TEST`. Create files in that directory named `one`, `two`, and `three` that have full read/write/execute permissions for everyone (user, group, and other). Construct a `find` command to find those files and any other files that have write permission open to "others" from your home directory and below.

6. Find files under the /usr/share/doc directory that have not been modified in more than 300 days.

7. Create a /tmp/FILES directory. Find all files under the /usr/share directory that are more than 5 MB and less than 10 MB and copy them to the /tmp/FILES directory.

8. Find every file in the /tmp/FILES directory and make a backup copy of each file in the same directory. Use each file's existing name and just append .mybackup to create each backup file.

Managing Running Processes

IN THIS CHAPTER

Displaying processes

Running processes in the foreground and background

Killing and renicing processes

I n addition to being a multiuser operating system, Linux is a multitasking system. *Multitasking* means that many programs can be running at the same time. An instance of a running program is referred to as a *process*. Linux provides tools for listing running processes, monitoring system usage, and stopping (or killing) processes when necessary.

From a shell, you can launch processes and then pause, stop, or kill them. You can also put them in the background and bring them to the foreground. This chapter describes tools such as ps, top, kill, jobs, and other commands for listing and managing processes.

Understanding Processes

A process is a running instance of a command. For example, there may be one vi command on the system. But if vi is currently being run by 15 different users, that command is represented by 15 different running processes.

A process is identified on the system by what is referred to as a *process ID (PID)*. That PID is unique for the current system. In other words, no other process can use that number as its process ID while that first process is still running. However, after a process has ended, another process can reuse that number.

Along with a PID, other attributes are associated with a process. Each process, when it is run, is associated with a particular user account and group account. That account information helps determine what system resources the process can access. For example, a process run as the root user has much more access to system files and resources than a process running as a regular user.

The ability to manage processes on your system is critical for a Linux system administrator. Sometimes, runaway processes may be killing your system's performance. Finding and dealing with processes, based on attributes such as memory and CPU usage, are covered in this chapter.

> **NOTE**
>
> Commands that display information about running processes get most of that information from raw data stored in the /proc filesystem. Each process stores its information in a subdirectory of /proc, named after the process ID of that process. You can view some of that raw data by displaying the contents of files in one of those directories (using cat or less commands).

Listing Processes

From the command line, the ps command is the oldest and most common command for listing processes currently running on your system. The Linux version of ps contains a variety of options from old UNIX and BSD systems, some of which are conflicting and implemented in nonstandard ways. See the ps man page for descriptions of those different options.

The top command provides a more screen-oriented approach to listing processes, and it can also be used to change the status of processes. If you are using the GNOME desktop, you can use the System Monitor tool (gnome-system-monitor) to provide a graphical means of working with processes. These commands are described in the following sections.

Listing processes with ps

The most common utility for checking running processes is the ps command. Use it to see which programs are running, the resources they are using, and who is running them. The following is an example of the ps command:

```
$ ps u
USER    PID %CPU %MEM  VSZ    RSS    TTY    STAT  START  TIME   COMMAND
jake    2147 0.0  0.7  1836   1020   tty1   S+    14:50  0:00   -bash
jake    2310 0.0  0.7  2592   912    tty1   R+    18:22  0:00   ps u
```

In this example, the u option (equivalent to -u) asks that usernames be shown, as well as other information such as the time the process started and memory and CPU usage for processes associated with the current user. The processes shown are associated with the current terminal (tty1). The concept of a terminal comes from the old days when people worked exclusively from character terminals, so a terminal typically represented a single person at a single screen. Nowadays, you can have many "terminals" on one screen by opening multiple virtual terminals or Terminal windows on the desktop.

In this shell session, not much is happening. The first process shows that the user named jake opened a Bash shell after logging in. The next process shows that jake has run the ps u command. The terminal device tty1 is being used for the login session. The STAT column represents the state of the process, with R indicating a currently running process and S representing a sleeping process.

The USER column shows the name of the user who started the process. Each process is represented by a unique or PID. You can use the PID if you ever need to kill a runaway process or send another kind of signal to a process. The %CPU and %MEM columns show the percentages of your system's processor and random access memory, respectively, that the process is consuming.

VSZ (virtual set size) shows the size of the image process (in kilobytes), and *RSS (resident set size)* shows the size of the program in memory. The VSZ and RSS sizes may be different because VSZ is the amount of memory allocated for the process, whereas RSS is the amount that is actually being used. RSS memory represents physical memory that cannot be swapped.

START shows the time the process began running, and TIME shows the cumulative system time used. (Many commands consume very little CPU time, as reflected by 0:00 for processes that haven't yet used a full second of CPU time.)

Many processes running on a computer are not associated with a terminal. A normal Linux system has many processes running in the background. Background system processes perform such tasks as logging system activity or listening for data coming in from the network. They are often started when Linux boots up and run continuously until the system shuts down. Likewise, logging in to a Linux desktop causes many background processes to kick off, such as processes for managing audio, desktop panels, authentication, and other desktop features.

To page through all of the processes running on your Linux system for the current user, add the pipe (|) and the less command to ps ux:

```
$ ps ux | less
```

To page through all processes running for all users on your system, use the ps aux command as follows:

```
$ ps aux | less
```

A pipe (located above the backslash character on the keyboard) enables you to direct the output of one command to be the input of the next command. In this example, the output of the ps command (a list of processes) is directed to the less command, which enables you to page through that information. Use the spacebar to page through and type q to end the list. You can also use the arrow keys to move one line at a time through the output.

The ps command can be customized to display selected columns of information and to sort information by one of those columns. Using the -o option, you can use keywords to indicate the columns you want to list with ps. For example, the next example lists every running process (-e) and then follows the -o option with every column of information I want to display, including the process ID (pid), username (user), user ID (uid), group name (group), group ID (gid), virtual memory allocated (vsz), resident memory used (rss), and the full command line that was run (comm). By default, output is sorted by process ID number.

```
$ ps -eo pid,user,uid,group,gid,vsz,rss,comm | less
  PID USER       UID GROUP      GID    VSZ    RSS COMMAND
  1   root         0 root         0 187660  13296 systemd
  2   root         0 root         0      0      0 kthreadd
```

If you want to sort by a specific column, you can use the sort= option. For example, to see which processes are using the most memory, I sort by the vsz field. That sorts from lowest memory use to highest. Because I want to see the highest ones first, I put a hyphen in front of that option to sort (sort=-vsz).

```
$ ps -eo pid,user,group,gid,vsz,rss,comm --sort=-vsz | head
   PID USER      GROUP       GID     VSZ    RSS COMMAND
  2366 chris     chris      1000 3720060 317060 gnome-shell
  1580 gdm       gdm          42 3524304 205796 gnome-shell
  3030 chris     chris      1000 2456968 248340 firefox
  3233 chris     chris      1000 2314388 316252 Web Content
```

Refer to the ps man page for information on other columns of information by which you can display and sort.

Listing and changing processes with top

The top command provides a screen-oriented means of displaying processes running on your system. With top, the default is to display processes based on how much CPU time they are currently consuming. However, you can sort by other columns as well. After you identify a misbehaving process, you can also use top to kill (completely end) or renice (reprioritize) that process.

If you want to be able to kill or renice any processes, you need to run top as the root user. If you just want to display processes and possibly kill or change your own processes, you can do that as a regular user. Figure 6.1 shows an example of the top window.

General information about your system appears at the top of the top output, followed by information about each running process (or at least as many as will fit on your screen). At the top, you can see how long the system has been up, how many users are currently logged in to the system, and how much demand there has been on the system for the past 1, 5, and 10 minutes.

FIGURE 6.1

Displaying running processes with top

```
top - 14:59:56 up  1:02,  1 user,  load average: 0.44, 0.41, 0.31
Tasks: 254 total,   1 running, 253 sleeping,   0 stopped,   0 zombie
%Cpu(s):  3.7 us,  1.2 sy,  0.0 ni, 94.9 id,  0.0 wa,  0.2 hi,  0.2 si,  0.0 st
MiB Mem :   2336.0 total,    163.9 free,   1723.2 used,    448.9 buff/cache
MiB Swap:      0.0 total,      0.0 free,      0.0 used.    412.1 avail Mem

   PID USER       PR  NI    VIRT    RES    SHR S  %CPU  %MEM     TIME+ COMMAND
  2366 chris      20   0 3754664 360232  82412 S   4.3  15.1   5:04.14 gnome-shell
  3233 chris      20   0 2315412 323812 112896 S   2.3  13.5   1:55.87 Web Content
 15222 cockpit+   20   0  607588  13200  10212 S   0.7   0.6   0:06.82 cockpit-ws
 16924 chris      20   0  680312  49244  35320 S   0.7   2.1   0:22.68 gnome-system-mo
  1797 root       20   0   49132   2456   2084 S   0.3   0.1   0:00.83 spice-vdagentd
  3030 chris      20   0 2456968 252124 101972 S   0.3  10.5   0:48.93 firefox
 15246 root       20   0  887040  12060   7584 S   0.3   0.5   0:04.45 cockpit-bridge
     1 root       20   0  187660  13236   7884 S   0.0   0.6   0:04.81 systemd
     2 root       20   0       0      0      0 S   0.0   0.0   0:00.00 kthreadd
     3 root        0 -20       0      0      0 I   0.0   0.0   0:00.00 rcu_gp
     4 root        0 -20       0      0      0 I   0.0   0.0   0:00.00 rcu_par_gp
```

Other general information includes how many processes (tasks) are currently running, how much CPU is being used, and how much RAM and swap are available and being used. Following the general information are listings of each process, sorted by what percent of the CPU is being used by each process. All of this information is redisplayed every 5 seconds, by default.

The following list includes actions that you can do with top to display information in different ways and modify running processes:

- Press **h** to see help options, and then press any key to return to the top display.
- Press **M** to sort by memory usage instead of CPU, and then press **P** to return to sorting by CPU.
- Press the number **1** to toggle showing CPU usage of all your CPUs if you have more than one on your system.
- Press **R** to reverse sort your output.
- Press **u** and enter a username to display processes only for a particular user.

A common practice is to use top to find processes that are consuming too much memory or processing power and then act on those processes in some way. A process consuming too much CPU can be reniced to give it less priority to the processors. A process consuming too much memory can be killed. With top running, here's how to renice or kill a process:

Renicing a process

Note the process ID of the process you want to renice and press **r**. When the PID to renice: message appears, type the process ID of the process you want to renice. When prompted to Renice PID to value:, type in a number from **−20 to 19**. (See "Setting processor priority with nice and renice" later in this chapter for information on the meanings of different renice values.)

Killing a process

Note the process ID of the process you want to kill and press **k**. Type **15** to terminate cleanly or **9** to just kill the process outright. (See "Killing processes with kill and killall" later in this chapter for more information on using different signals you can send to processes.)

Listing processes with System Monitor

If you have GNOME desktop available on your Linux system, System Monitor (gnome-system-monitor) is available to provide a more graphical way of displaying processes on your system. You sort processes by clicking columns. You can right-click processes to stop, kill, or renice them.

To start System Monitor from the GNOME desktop, press the Windows key and then type **System Monitor** and press Enter. Then select the Processes tab. Figure 6.2 shows an example of the System Monitor window, displaying processes for the current user in order by memory use.

FIGURE 6.2

Use the System Monitor window to view and change running processes.

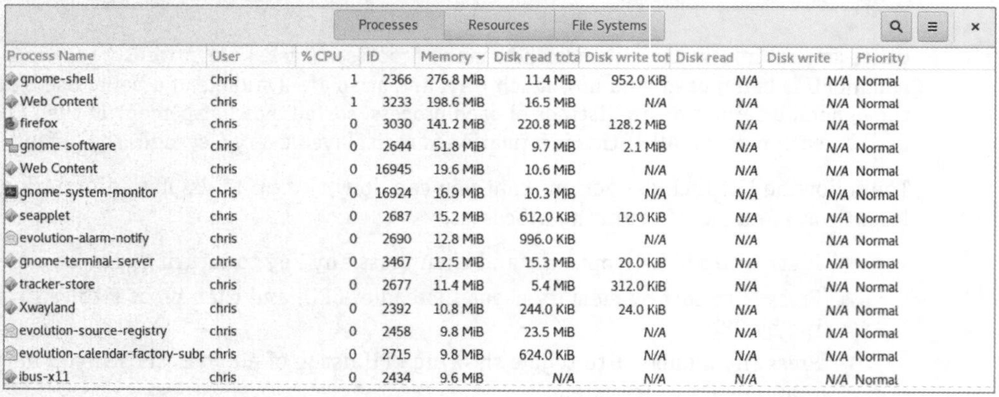

Process Name	User	% CPU	ID	Memory ▾	Disk read tota	Disk write tot	Disk read	Disk write	Priority
gnome-shell	chris	1	2366	276.8 MiB	11.4 MiB	952.0 KiB	N/A	N/A	Normal
Web Content	chris	1	3233	198.6 MiB	16.5 MiB	N/A	N/A	N/A	Normal
firefox	chris	0	3030	141.2 MiB	220.8 MiB	128.2 MiB	N/A	N/A	Normal
gnome-software	chris	0	2644	51.8 MiB	9.7 MiB	2.1 MiB	N/A	N/A	Normal
Web Content	chris	0	16945	19.6 MiB	10.6 MiB	N/A	N/A	N/A	Normal
gnome-system-monitor	chris	0	16924	16.9 MiB	10.3 MiB	N/A	N/A	N/A	Normal
seapplet	chris	0	2687	15.2 MiB	612.0 KiB	12.0 KiB	N/A	N/A	Normal
evolution-alarm-notify	chris	0	2690	12.8 MiB	996.0 KiB	N/A	N/A	N/A	Normal
gnome-terminal-server	chris	0	3467	12.5 MiB	15.3 MiB	20.0 KiB	N/A	N/A	Normal
tracker-store	chris	0	2677	11.4 MiB	5.4 MiB	312.0 KiB	N/A	N/A	Normal
Xwayland	chris	0	2392	10.8 MiB	244.0 KiB	24.0 KiB	N/A	N/A	Normal
evolution-source-registry	chris	0	2458	9.8 MiB	23.5 MiB	N/A	N/A	N/A	Normal
evolution-calendar-factory-subp	chris	0	2715	9.8 MiB	624.0 KiB	N/A	N/A	N/A	Normal
ibus-x11	chris	0	2434	9.6 MiB	N/A	N/A	N/A	N/A	Normal

By default, only running processes associated with your user account are displayed. Those processes are normally listed alphabetically. You can resort the processes by clicking any of the field headings (forward and reverse). For example, click the %CPU heading to see which processes are consuming the most processing power. Click the Memory heading to see which processes consume the most memory.

You can manage your processes in various ways by right-clicking a process name and selecting from the menu that appears (see Figure 6.3 for an example).

Here are some of the things you can do to a process from the menu you clicked:

Stop: Pauses the process so that no processing occurs until you select Continue Process. (This is the same as pressing Ctrl+Z on a process from the shell.)

Continue: Continues running a paused process.

End: Sends a Terminate signal (15) to a process. In most cases, this terminates the process cleanly.

Kill: Sends a Kill signal (9) to a process. This should kill a process immediately, regardless of whether it can be done cleanly.

Change Priority: Presents a list of priorities from Very Low to Very High. Select Custom to see a slider bar from which you can renice a process. Normal priority is 0. To get better processor priority, use a negative number from –1 to –20. To have a lower processor priority, use a positive number (0 to 19). Only the root user can assign negative priorities, so when prompted you need to provide the sudo password to set a negative nice value.

Memory Maps: Lets you view the system memory map to see which libraries and other components are being held in memory for the process.

Open Files: Lets you view which files are currently being held open by the process.

Properties: Lets you see other settings associated with the process (such as security context, memory usage, and CPU use percentages).

FIGURE 6.3

Renice, kill, or pause a process from the System Monitor window.

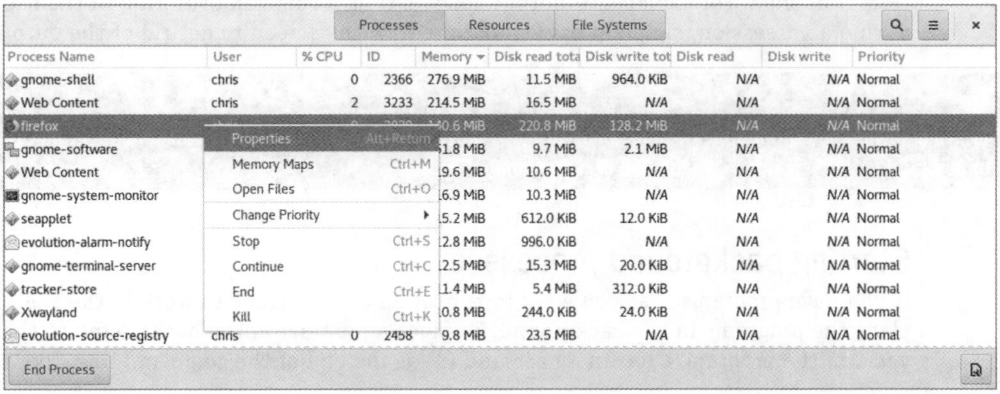

You can display running processes associated with users other than yourself. To do that, highlight any process in the display (just click it). Then, from the menu button (the button with three bars on it), select All Processes. You can modify processes you don't own only if you are the root user or if you can provide the root password when prompted after you try to change a process. Sometimes you won't have the luxury of working with a graphical interface. To change processes without a graphical interface, you can use a set of commands and keystrokes to change, pause, or kill running processes. Some of those are described next.

Managing Background and Foreground Processes

If you are using Linux over a network or from a *dumb terminal* (a monitor that allows only text input with no GUI support), your shell may be all that you have. You may be used to a graphical environment in which you have lots of programs active at the same time so that you can switch among them as needed. This shell thing can seem pretty limited.

Although the Bash shell doesn't include a GUI for running many programs at once, it does let you move active programs between the background and foreground. In this way, you can have lots of stuff running and selectively choose the one you want to deal with at the moment.

You can place an active program in the background in several ways. One is to add an ampersand (&) to the end of a command line when you first run the command. You can also use the at command to run commands in such a way that they are not connected to the shell.

To stop a running command and put it in the background, press Ctrl+Z. After the command is stopped, you can either bring it back into the foreground to run (the fg command) or start it running in the background (the bg command). Keep in mind that any command running in the background might spew output during commands that you run subsequently from that shell. For example, if output appears from a command running in the background during a vi session, simply press Ctrl+L to redraw the screen to get rid of the output.

> **TIP**
>
> To avoid having the output appear, you should have any process running in the background send its output to a file or to null (add 2> /dev/null to the end of the command line).

Starting background processes

If you have programs that you want to run while you continue to work in the shell, you can place the programs in the background. To place a program in the background at the time you run the program, type an ampersand (&) at the end of the command line, like this:

```
$ find /usr > /tmp/allusrfiles &
[3] 15971
```

This example command finds all files on your Linux system (starting from /usr), prints those filenames, and puts those names in the file /tmp/allusrfiles. The ampersand (&) runs that command line in the background. Notice that the job number, [3], and process ID number, 15971, are displayed when the command is launched. To check which commands you have running in the background, use the jobs command, as follows:

```
$ jobs
[1]   Stopped (tty output)  vi /tmp/myfile
[2]   Running               find /usr -print > /tmp/allusrfiles &
[3]   Running               nroff -man /usr/man2/* >/tmp/man2 &
[4]- Running                nroff -man /usr/man3/* >/tmp/man3 &
[5]+ Stopped                nroff -man /usr/man4/* >/tmp/man4
```

The first job shows a text-editing command (vi) that I placed in the background and stopped by pressing Ctrl+Z while I was editing. Job 2 shows the find command I just ran. Jobs 3 and 4 show nroff commands currently running in the background. Job 5 had been running in the shell (foreground) until I decided too many processes were running and pressed Ctrl+Z to stop job 5 until a few processes had completed.

The plus sign (+) next to number 5 shows that it was most recently placed in the background. The minus sign (–) next to number 4 shows that it was placed in the background just before the most recent background job. Because job 1 requires terminal input, it cannot run in the background. As a result, it is Stopped until it is brought to the foreground again.

> **TIP**
>
> To see the process ID for the background job, add a -l (the lowercase letter *L*) option to the jobs command. If you type ps, you can use the process ID to figure out which command is for a particular background job.

Using foreground and background commands

Continuing with the example, you can bring any of the commands on the jobs list to the foreground. For example, to edit myfile again, enter the following:

```
$ fg %1
```

As a result, the vi command opens again. All text is as it was when you stopped the vi job.

> **CAUTION**
>
> Before you put a text processor, word processor, or similar program in the background, make sure that you save your file. It's easy to forget that you have a program in the background, and you will lose your data if you log out or the computer reboots.

To refer to a background job (to cancel or bring it to the foreground), use a percent sign (%) followed by the job number. You can also use the following to refer to a background job:

%   Refers to the most recent command put into the background (indicated by the plus sign when you type the jobs command). This action brings the command to the foreground.

%string   Refers to a job where the command begins with a particular string of characters. The string must be unambiguous. (In other words, typing %vi when there are two vi commands in the background results in an error message.)

%?string   Refers to a job where the command line contains a string at any point. The string must be unambiguous or the match fails.

%--   Refers to the job stopped before the one most recently stopped.

If a command is stopped, you can start it running again in the background using the `bg` command. For example, take job 5 from the jobs list in the previous example:

```
[5]+ Stopped nroff -man /usr/man4/* >/tmp/man4
```

Enter the following:

```
$ bg %5
```

After that, the job runs in the background. Its `jobs` entry appears as follows:

```
[5] Running nroff -man /usr/man4/* >/tmp/man4 &
```

Killing and Renicing Processes

Just as you can change the behavior of a process using graphical tools such as System Monitor (described earlier in this chapter), you can also use command-line tools to kill a process or change its CPU priority. The `kill` command can send a kill signal to any process to end it, assuming you have permission to do so. It can also send different signals to a process to otherwise change its behavior. The `nice` and `renice` commands can be used to set or change the processor priority of a process.

Killing processes with kill and killall

Although usually used for ending a running process, the `kill` and `killall` commands can actually be used to send any valid signal to a running process. Besides telling a process to end, a signal might tell a process to reread configuration files, pause (stop), or continue after being paused, just to name a few possibilities.

Signals are represented by both numbers and names. Signals that you might send most commonly from a command include SIGKILL (9), SIGTERM (15), and SIGHUP (1). The default signal is SIGTERM, which tries to terminate a process cleanly. To kill a process immediately, you can use SIGKILL. The SIGHUP signal can, depending on the program, tell a process to restart and reread its configuration files. SIGSTOP (19) pauses a process, while SIGCONT (18) continues a stopped process.

Different processes respond to different signals. Processes cannot block SIGKILL and SIG-STOP signals, however. Table 6.1 shows examples of some signals (enter **man 7 signal** to read about other available signals).

Notice that there are multiple possible signal numbers for SIGCONT and SIGSTOP because different numbers are used in different computer architectures. For most _64 and POWER architectures, use the middle value. The first value usually works for Alpha and SPARC, while the last one is for MIPS architecture.

TABLE 6.1 **Signals Available in Linux**

SIGNAL	NUMBER	DESCRIPTION
SIGHUP	1	Hang-up detected on controlling terminal or death of controlling process.
SIGINT	2	Interrupt from keyboard.
SIGQUIT	3	Quit from keyboard.
SIGABRT	6	Abort signal from abort(3).
SIGKILL	9	Kill signal.
SIGTERM	15	Termination signal.
SIGCONT	19,18,25	Continue if stopped.
SIGSTOP	17,19,23	Stop process.

Using kill to signal processes by PID

Using commands such as ps and top, you can find processes to which you want to send a signal. Then you can use the process ID of that process as an option to the kill command, along with the signal you want to send.

For example, you run the top command and see that the bigcommand process is consuming most of your processing power:

```
  PID USER      PR  NI  VIRT  RES  SHR S %CPU %MEM    TIME+ COMMAND
10432 chris     20   0  471m 121m  18m S 99.9  3.2 77:01.76
bigcommand
```

Here, the bigcommand process is consuming 99.9 percent of the CPU. You decide that you want to kill it so that other processes have a shot at the CPU. If you use the process ID of the running bigcommand process, here are some examples of the kill command that you can use to kill that process:

```
$ kill 10432
$ kill -15 10432
$ kill -SIGKILL 10432
```

The default signal sent by kill is 15 (SIGTERM), so the first two examples have exactly the same results. On occasion, a SIGTERM doesn't kill a process, so you may need a SIGKILL to kill it. Instead of SIGKILL, you can use –9 to get the same result.

Another useful signal is SIGHUP. If, for example, something on your GNOME desktop were corrupted, you could send the gnome-shell a SIGHUP signal to reread its configuration files and restart the desktop. If the process ID for gnome-shell were 1833, here are two ways you could send it a SIGHUP signal:

```
# kill -1 1833
# kill -HUP 1833
```

Using killall to signal processes by name

With the `killall` command, you can signal processes by name instead of by process ID. The advantage is that you don't have to look up the process ID of the process that you want to kill. The potential downside is that you can kill more processes than you mean to if you are not careful. (For example, typing `killall bash` may kill a bunch of shells that you don't mean to kill.)

Like the `kill` command, `killall` uses SIGTERM (signal 15) if you don't explicitly enter a signal number. Also as with `kill`, you can send any signal you like to the process you name with `killall`. For example, if you see a process called `testme` running on your system and you want to kill it, you can simply enter the following:

```
$ killall -9 testme
```

The `killall` command can be particularly useful if you want to kill a bunch of commands of the same name. For that same reason, it's also potentially the most destructive command because it will also kill any other instances of that software running—even those of which you're unaware.

Setting processor priority with nice and renice

When the Linux kernel tries to decide which running processes get access to the CPUs on your system, one of the things it takes into account is the nice value set on the process. Every process running on your system has a nice value between –20 and 19. By default, the nice value is set to 0. Here are a few facts about nice values:

- The lower the nice value, the more access to the CPUs the process has. In other words, the *nicer* a process is, the less CPU attention it gets. So, a –20 nice value gets more attention than a process with a 19 nice value (which is very nice, indeed).
- A regular user can set nice values only from 0 to 19. No negative values are allowed. So a regular user can't ask for a value that gives a process more attention than most processes get by default.
- A regular user can set the nice value higher, not lower. So, for example, if a user sets the nice value on a process to 10 and then later wants to set it back to 5, that action will fail. Likewise, any attempt to set a negative value will fail.
- A regular user can set the nice value only on the user's own processes.
- The root user can set the nice value on any process to any valid value, up or down.

You can use the `nice` command to run a command with a particular nice value. When a process is running, you can change the nice value using the `renice` command, along with the process ID of the process, as in the example that follows:

```
# nice -n +5 updatedb &
```

The `updatedb` command is used to generate the locate database manually by gathering names of files throughout the filesystem. In this case, I just wanted `updatedb` to run in the background (&) and not interrupt work being done by other processes on the system. I ran the `top` command to make sure that the nice value was set properly:

```
PID USER          PR  NI  VIRT  RES  SHR S %CPU %MEM    TIME+  COMMAND
20284 root        25   5 98.7m  932  644 D  2.7  0.0   0:00.96 updatedb
```

Notice that under the `NI` column, the nice value is set to 5. Because the command was run as the root user, the root user can lower the nice value later by using the `renice` command. (Remember that a regular user can't reduce the nice value or ever set it to a negative number.) Here's how you would change the nice value for the `updatedb` command just run to –5:

```
# renice -n -5 20284
```

If you ran the `top` command again, you might notice that the `updatedb` command is now at or near the top of the list of processes consuming CPU time because you gave it priority to get more CPU attention.

Limiting Processes with cgroups

You can use a feature like "nice" to give a single process more or less access to CPU time. Setting the nice value for one process, however, doesn't apply to child processes that a process might start up or any other related processes that are part of a larger service. In other words, "nice" doesn't limit the total amount of resources a particular user or application can consume from a Linux system.

As cloud computing takes hold, many Linux systems will be used more as hypervisors than as general-purpose computers. Their memory, processing power, and access to storage will become commodities to be shared by many users. In that model, more needs to be done to control the amount of system resources to which a particular user, application, container, or virtual machine running on a Linux system has access.

That's where *cgroups* come in.

Cgroups can be used to identify a process as a task, belonging to a particular control group. Tasks can be set up in a hierarchy where, for example, there may be a task called daemons that sets default limitations for all daemon server processes, then subtasks that may set specific limits on a web server daemon (`apache2`) or FTP service daemon (`vsftpd`).

As a task launches a process, other processes that the initial process launches (called child processes) inherit the limitations set for the parent process. Those limitations might say that all the processes in a control group only have access to particular processors and certain sets of RAM. Or they may only allow access to up to 30 percent of the total processing power of a machine.

The types of resources that can be limited by cgroups include the following:

Storage (blkio): Limits total input and output access to storage devices (such as hard disks, USB drives, and so on).

Processor scheduling (cpu): Assigns the amount of access a cgroup has to be scheduled for processing power.

Process accounting (cpuacct): Reports on CPU usage. This information can be leveraged to charge clients for the amount of processing power they use.

CPU assignment (cpuset): On systems with multiple CPU cores, assigns a task to a particular set of processors and associated memory.

Device access (devices): Allows tasks in a cgroup to open or create (mknod) selected device types.

Suspend/resume (freezer): Suspends and resumes cgroup tasks.

Memory usage (memory): Limits memory usage by task. It also creates reports on memory resources used.

Network bandwidth (net_cls): Limits network access to selected cgroup tasks. This is done by tagging network packets to identify the cgroup task that originated the packet and having the Linux traffic controller monitor and restrict packets coming from each cgroup.

Network traffic (net_prio): Sets priorities of network traffic coming from selected cgroups and lets administrators change these priorities on the fly.

Name spaces (ns): Separates cgroups into namespaces, so processes in one cgroup can only see the namespaces associated with the cgroup. Namespaces can include separate process tables, mount tables, and network interfaces.

At its most basic level, creating and managing cgroups is generally not a job for new Linux system administrators. It can involve editing configuration files to create your own cgroups (/etc/cgconfig.conf) or setting up limits for particular users or groups (/etc/cgrules.conf). Or you can use the cgreate command to create cgroups, which results in those groups being added to the /sys/fs/cgroup hierarchy. Setting up cgroups can be tricky and, if done improperly, can make your system unbootable.

The reason we're talking about the concept of cgroups here is to help you understand some of the underlying features in Linux that can be used to limit and monitor resource usage. In the future, you will probably run into these features from controllers that manage your cloud infrastructure. You will be able to set rules like "Allow the Marketing department's virtual machines to consume up to 40 percent of the available memory" or "Pin the database application to a particular CPU and memory set."

Knowing how Linux can limit and contain the resource usage by the set of processes assigned to a task will ultimately help you manage your computing resources better.

Summary

Even on a Linux system where there isn't much activity, typically dozens or even hundreds of processes are running in the background. Using the tools described in this chapter, you can view and manage the processes running on your system.

Managing processes includes viewing processes in different ways, running them in the foreground or background, and killing or renicing them. More advanced features for limiting resource usage by selected processes are available using the cgroups feature.

In the next chapter, you learn how to combine commands and programming functions into files that can be run as shell scripts.

Exercises

Use these exercises to test your knowledge of viewing running processes and then changing them later by killing them or changing processor priority (nice value). If you are stuck, solutions to the tasks are shown in Appendix A (although in Linux, you can often use multiple ways to complete a task).

1. List all processes running on your system, showing a full set of columns. Pipe that output to the `less` command so that you can page through the list of processes.

2. List all processes running on the system and sort those processes by the name of the user running each process.

3. List all processes running on the system and display the following columns of information: process ID, username, group name, virtual memory size, resident memory size, and the command.

4. Run the `top` command to view processes running on your system. Go back and forth between sorting by CPU usage and memory consumption.

5. Start the `gedit` process from your desktop. Make sure that you run it as the user you are logged in as. Use the System Monitor window to kill that process.

6. Run the `gedit` process again. This time, using the `kill` command, send a signal to the `gedit` process that causes it to pause (stop). Try typing some text into the `gedit` window and make sure that no text appears yet.

7. Use the `killall` command to tell the `gedit` command that you paused in the previous exercise to continue working. Make sure that the text you type after `gedit` was paused now appears on the window.

8. As a regular user, run the `gedit` command so that it starts with a nice value of 5.

9. Using the `renice` command, change the nice value of the `gedit` command you just started to 7. Use any command you like to verify that the current nice value for the `gedit` command is now set to 7.

Writing Simple Shell Scripts

IN THIS CHAPTER

Working with shell scripts

Doing arithmetic in shell scripts

Running loops and cases in shell scripts

Creating simple shell scripts

You'd never get any work done if you typed every command that needs to be run on your Linux system when it starts. Likewise, you could work more efficiently if you grouped together sets of commands that you run all the time. Shell scripts can handle these tasks.

A *shell script* is a group of commands, functions, variables, or just about anything else you can use from a shell. These items are typed into a plain text file. That file can then be run as a command. Linux systems have traditionally used system initialization shell scripts during system startup to run commands needed to get services going. You can create your own shell scripts to automate the tasks that you need to do regularly.

For decades, building shell scripts was the primary skill needed to join sets of tasks in UNIX and Linux systems. As demands for configuring Linux systems grew beyond single-system setups to complex, automated cluster configurations, more structured methods have arisen. These methods include Ansible playbooks and Kubernetes YAML files, described later in cloud-related chapters. That said, writing shell scripts is still a hugely important tool for automating repeatable tasks in Linux systems.

This chapter provides a rudimentary overview of the inner workings of shell scripts and how they can be used. You'll learn how simple scripts can be harnessed for a scheduling facility (such as `cron` or `at`) to simplify administrative tasks or just run on demand as they are needed.

Understanding Shell Scripts

Have you ever had a task that you needed to do over and over that took lots of typing on the command line? Do you ever think to yourself, "Wow, I wish I could just type one command to do all this"? Maybe a shell script is what you're after.

Shell scripts are the equivalent of batch files in Windows and can contain long lists of commands, complex flow control, arithmetic evaluations, user-defined variables, user-defined functions, and sophisticated condition testing. Shell scripts are capable of handling everything from simple one-line commands to something as complex as starting up a Linux system. Although dozens of different shells are available in Linux, the default shell for most Linux systems is called Bash, the **B**ourne **A**gain **SH**ell.

Executing and debugging shell scripts

One of the primary advantages of shell scripts is that you can read the code by simply opening it in any text editor. A big disadvantage is that large or complex shell scripts often execute more slowly than compiled programs.

You can execute a shell script in two basic ways:

- The filename is used as an argument to the shell (as in `bash myscript`). In this method, the file does not need to be executable; it just contains a list of shell commands. The shell specified on the command line is used to interpret the commands in the script file. This is most common for quick, simple tasks.
- The shell script may also have the name of the interpreter placed in the first line of the script preceded by #! (as in `#!/bin/bash`) and have the execute bit of the file containing the script set (using `chmod +x filename`). You can then run your script just as you would any other program in your path simply by typing the name of the script on the command line.

When scripts are executed in either manner, options for the program may be specified on the command line. Anything following the name of the script is referred to as a *command-line argument*.

As with writing any software, there is no substitute for clear and thoughtful design and lots of comments. The pound sign (#) prefaces comments that can take up an entire line or exist on the same line after script code. It is best to implement more complex shell scripts in stages, making sure that the logic is sound at each step before continuing. Here are a few good, concise tips to make sure that things are working as expected during testing:

- In some cases, you can place an `echo` statement at the beginning of lines within the body of a loop and surround the command with quotes. That way, rather than executing the code, you can see what will be executed without making any permanent changes.
- To achieve the same goal, you can place dummy `echo` statements throughout the code. If these lines get printed, you know the correct logic branch is being taken.
- You can use `set -x` near the beginning of the script to display each command that is executed or launch your scripts using

```
$ bash -x myscript
```

- Because useful scripts have a tendency to grow over time, keeping your code readable as you go along is extremely important. Do what you can to keep the logic of your code clean and easy to follow.

Understanding shell variables

Often within a shell script, you want to reuse certain items of information. During the course of processing the shell script, the name or number representing this information may change. To store information used by a shell script in such a way that it can be easily reused, you can set *variables*. Variable names within shell scripts are case sensitive and can be defined in the following manner:

```
NAME=value
```

The first part of a variable is the variable name, and the second part is the value set for that name. Be sure that the NAME and value touch the equal sign, without any spaces. Variables can be assigned from constants, such as text, numbers, and underscores. This is useful for initializing values or saving lots of typing for long constants. The following examples show variables set to a string of characters (CITY) and a numeric value (PI):

```
CITY="Springfield"
PI=3.14159265
```

Variables can contain the output of a command or command sequence. You can accomplish this by preceding the command with a dollar sign and open parenthesis, following it with a closing parenthesis. For example, MYDATE=$(date) assigns the output from the date command to the MYDATE variable. Enclosing the command in back-ticks (`) can have the same effect. In this case, the date command is run when the variable is set and not each time the variable is read.

Escaping Special Shell Characters

Keep in mind that characters such as the dollar sign ($), back-tick (`), asterisk (*), exclamation point (!), and others have special meaning to the shell, which you will see as you proceed through this chapter. On some occasions, you want the shell to use these characters' special meaning and other times you don't. For example, if you typed echo $HOME, the shell would think that you meant to display the name of your home directory (stored in the $HOME variable) to the screen (such as /home/chris) because a $ indicates a variable name follows that character.

If you wanted literally to show $HOME, you would need to escape the $. Typing echo '$HOME' or echo \$HOME would show $HOME on the screen. So, if you want to have the shell interpret a single character literally, precede it with a backslash (\). To have a whole set of characters interpreted literally, surround those characters with single quotes (').

Using double quotes is a bit trickier. Surround a set of text with double quotes if you want all but a few characters used literally. For example, for text surrounded with double quotes, dollar signs ($), back-ticks (`), and exclamation points (!) are interpreted specially, but other characters (such as an asterisk) are not. Type these three lines to see the different output (shown on the right):

```
echo '$HOME * `date`'     $HOME * `date`
echo "$HOME * `date`"     /home/chris * Tue Jan 21 16:56:52 EDT 2020
echo $HOME * `date`       /home/chris file1 file2 Tue Jan 21
16:56:52 EDT 2020
```

Using variables is a great way to get information that can change from computer to computer or from day to day. The following example sets the output of the uname -n command to the MACHINE variable. Then I use parentheses to set NUM_FILES to the number of files in the current directory by piping (|) the output of the ls command to the word count command (wc -l):

```
MACHINE=`uname -n`
NUM_FILES=$(/bin/ls | wc -l)
```

Variables can also contain the value of other variables. This is useful when you have to preserve a value that will change so that you can use it later in the script. Here, BALANCE is set to the value of the CurBalance variable:

```
BALANCE="$CurBalance"
```

> **NOTE**
>
> When assigning variables, use only the variable name (for example, BALANCE). When you reference a variable, meaning that you want the *value* of the variable, precede it with a dollar sign (as in $CurBalance). The result of the latter is that you get the value of the variable, not the variable name itself.

Special shell positional parameters

There are special variables that the shell assigns for you. One set of commonly used variables is called *positional parameters* or *command-line arguments*, and it is referenced as $0, $1, $2, $3. . .${10}, ${11}, ${12}.... $0 is special, and it is assigned the name used to invoke your script; the others are assigned the values of the parameters passed on the command line in the order they appeared. For instance, let's say that you had a shell script named myscript that contained the following:

```
#!/bin/bash
# Script to echo out command-line arguments
echo "The first argument is $1, the second is $2."
echo "The command itself is called $0."
echo "There are $# parameters on your command line"
echo "Here are all the arguments: $@"
```

Assuming that the script is executable and located in a directory in your $PATH, the following shows what would happen if you ran that command with foo and bar as arguments:

```
$ chmod 755 /home/chris/bin/myscript
$ myscript foo bar
The first argument is foo, the second is bar.
The command itself is called /home/chris/bin/myscript.
There are 2 parameters on your command line
Here are all the arguments: foo bar
```

As you can see, the positional parameter $0 is the full path or relative path to myscript, $1 is foo, and $2 is bar.

Another variable, $#, tells you how many parameters your script was given. In the example, $# would be 2. The $@ variable holds all of the arguments entered at the command line. Another particularly useful special shell variable is $?, which receives the exit status of the last command executed. Typically, a value of zero means that the command exited successfully, and anything other than zero indicates an error of some kind. For a complete list of special shell variables, refer to the bash man page.

Reading in parameters

Using the read command, you can prompt the user for information and store that information to use later in your script. Here's an example of a script that uses the read command:

```
#!/bin/bash
read -p "Type in an adjective, noun and verb (past tense): " adj1
noun1 verb1
echo "He sighed and $verb1 to the elixir. Then he ate the
$adj1 $noun1."
```

This script, after prompting for an adjective, noun, and verb, expects the user to enter words that are then assigned to the adj1, noun1, and verb1 variables. Those three variables are then included in a silly sentence, which is displayed on the screen. If the script were called sillyscript, here's an example of how it might run:

```
$ chmod 755 /home/chris/bin/sillyscript
$ sillyscript
Type in an adjective, noun and verb (past tense): hairy football
danced
He sighed and danced to the elixir. Then he ate the hairy football.
```

Parameter expansion in Bash

As mentioned earlier, if you want the value of a variable, you precede it with a $ (for example, $CITY). This is really just shorthand for the notation ${CITY}; curly braces are used when the value of the parameter needs to be placed next to other text without a space. Bash has special rules that allow you to expand the value of a variable in different ways. Going into all of the rules is overkill for a quick introduction to shell scripts, but the following list presents some common constructs you're likely to see in Bash scripts that you find on your Linux system:

${var:-value}: If variable is unset or empty, expand this to *value*.

${var#pattern}: Chop the shortest match for *pattern* from the front of *var*'s value.

${var##pattern}: Chop the longest match for *pattern* from the front of *var*'s value.

${var%pattern}: Chop the shortest match for *pattern* from the end of *var*'s value.

${var%%pattern}: Chop the longest match for *pattern* from the end of *var*'s value.

Try typing the following commands from a shell to test how parameter expansion works:

```
$ THIS="Example"
$ THIS=${THIS:-"Not Set"}
$ THAT=${THAT:-"Not Set"}
$ echo $THIS
Example
$ echo $THAT
Not Set
```

In the examples here, the THIS variable is initially set to the word Example. In the next two lines, the THIS and THAT variables are set to their current values or to Not Set, if they are not currently set. Notice that because I just set THIS to the string Example, when I echo the value of THIS it appears as Example. However, because THAT was not set, it appears as Not Set.

> **NOTE**
>
> For the rest of this section, I show how variables and commands may appear in a shell script. To try out any of those examples, however, you can simply type them into a shell, as shown in the previous example.

In the following example, MYFILENAME is set to /home/digby/myfile.txt. Next, the FILE variable is set to myfile.txt and DIR is set to /home/digby. In the NAME variable, the filename is cut down simply to myfile; then, in the EXTENSION variable, the file extension is set to txt. (To try these out, you can type them at a shell prompt as in the previous example and echo the value of each variable to see how it is set.) Type the code on the left. The material on the right side describes the action.

MYFILENAME=/home/digby/myfile.txt: Sets the value of MYFILENAME

FILE=${MYFILENAME##*/}: FILE becomes myfile.txt

DIR=${MYFILENAME%/*}: DIR becomes /home/digby

NAME=${FILE%.*}: NAME becomes myfile

EXTENSION=${FILE##*.}: EXTENSION becomes txt

Performing arithmetic in shell scripts

Bash uses *untyped variables,* meaning that you are not required to specify whether a variable is text or numbers. It normally treats variables as strings or text, so unless you tell it otherwise with declare, your variables are just a bunch of letters to bash. However, when you start trying to do arithmetic with them, bash converts them to integers if it can. This makes it possible to do some fairly complex arithmetic in bash.

Integer arithmetic can be performed using the built-in let command or through the external expr or bc commands. After setting the variable BIGNUM value to 1024, the three commands that follow would all store the value 64 in the RESULT variable. The bc command is a calculator application that is available in most Linux distributions. The last command gets a random number and echoes the results back to you.

```
BIGNUM=1024
let RESULT=$BIGNUM/16
RESULT=`expr $BIGNUM / 16`
RESULT=`echo "$BIGNUM / 16" | bc`
let foo=$RANDOM; echo $foo
```

Another way to grow a variable incrementally is to use $(()) notation with ++I added to increment the value of I. Try typing the following:

```
$ I=0
$ echo "The value of I after increment is $((++I))"
The value of I after increment is 1

$ echo "The value of I before and after increment is $((I++)) and $I"
The value of I before and after increment is 1 and 2
```

Repeat either of those commands to continue to increment the value of $I.

NOTE

Although most elements of shell scripts are relatively freeform (where white space, such as spaces or tabs, is insignificant), both `let` and `expr` are particular about spacing. The `let` command insists on no spaces between each operand and the mathematical operator, whereas the syntax of the `expr` command requires white space between each operand and its operator. In contrast to those, `bc` isn't picky about spaces, but it can be trickier to use because it does floating-point arithmetic.

To see a complete list of the kinds of arithmetic that you can perform using the `let` command, type **help let** at the bash prompt.

Using programming constructs in shell scripts

One of the features that makes shell scripts so powerful is that their implementation of looping and conditional execution constructs is similar to those found in more complex scripting and programming languages. You can use several different types of loops, depending on your needs.

The "if. . .then" statements

The most commonly used programming construct is conditional execution, or the `if` statement. It is used to perform actions only under certain conditions. There are several variations of `if` statements for testing various types of conditions.

The first `if...then` example tests if `VARIABLE` is set to the number 1. If it is, then the `echo` command is used to say that it is set to 1. The `fi` statement then indicates that the `if` statement is complete, and processing can continue.

```
VARIABLE=1
if [ $VARIABLE -eq 1 ] ; then
echo "The variable is 1"
fi
```

Instead of using `-eq`, you can use the equal sign (=), as shown in the following example. The = works best for comparing string values, while `-eq` is often better for comparing numbers. Using the `else` statement, different words can be echoed if the criterion of the `if` statement isn't met ($STRING = "Friday"). Keep in mind that it's good practice to put strings in double quotes.

```
STRING="Friday"
if [ $STRING = "Friday" ] ; then
echo "WhooHoo.  Friday."
else
echo "Will Friday ever get here?"
fi
```

You can also reverse tests with an exclamation mark (!). In the following example, if `STRING` is not Monday, then "At least it's not Monday" is echoed.

```
STRING="FRIDAY"
if [ "$STRING" != "Monday" ] ; then
    echo "At least it's not Monday"
fi
```

In the following example, `elif` (which stands for "else if") is used to test for an additional condition (for example, whether `filename` is a file or a directory).

```
filename="$HOME"
if [ -f "$filename" ] ; then
    echo "$filename is a regular file"
elif [ -d "$filename" ] ; then
    echo "$filename is a directory"
else
    echo "I have no idea what $filename is"
fi
```

As you can see from the preceding examples, the condition you are testing is placed between square brackets [ ]. When a test expression is evaluated, it returns either a value of 0, meaning that it is true, or a 1, meaning that it is false. Notice that the `echo` lines are indented. The indentation is optional and done only to make the script more readable.

Table 7.1 is a handy reference list of the conditions that are testable. (If you're in a hurry, you can type **help test** on the command line to get the same information.)

TABLE 7.1 **Operators for Test Expressions**

OPERATOR	WHAT IS BEING TESTED?
-a *file*	Does the file exist? (same as -e)
-b *file*	Is the file a block special device?
-c *file*	Is the file character special (for example, a character device)? Used to identify serial lines and terminal devices.
-d *file*	Is the file a directory?
-e *file*	Does the file exist? (same as -a)
-f *file*	Does the file exist, and is it a regular file (for example, not a directory, socket, pipe, link, or device file)?
-g *file*	Does the file exist and have the set-group-id (SGID) bit set?
-h *file*	Is the file a symbolic link? (same as -L)
-k *file*	Does the file have the sticky bit set?
-L *file*	Is the file a symbolic link?
-n *string*	Is the length of the string greater than 0 bytes?
-O *file*	Do you own the file?
-p *file*	Is the file a named pipe?
-r *file*	Is the file readable by you?
-s *file*	Does the file exist, and is it larger than 0 bytes?
-S *file*	Does the file exist, and is it a socket?
-t *fd*	Is the file descriptor connected to a terminal?
-u *file*	Does the file have the set-user-id (SUID) bit set?
-w *file*	Is the file writable by you?
-x *file*	Is the file executable by you?
-z *string*	Is the length of the string 0 (zero) bytes?
expr1 -a *expr2*	Are both the first expression and the second expression true?
expr1 -o *expr2*	Is either of the two expressions true?
file1 -nt *file2*	Is the first file newer than the second file (using the modification time stamp)?
file1 -ot *file2*	Is the first file older than the second file (using the modification time stamp)?
file1 -ef *file2*	Are the two files associated by a link (a hard link or a symbolic link)?
var1 = *var2*	Is the first variable equal to the second variable?
var1 -eq *var2*	Is the first variable equal to the second variable?
var1 -ge *var2*	Is the first variable greater than or equal to the second variable?

(Continues)

TABLE 7.1 *(continued)*

OPERATOR	WHAT IS BEING TESTED?
var1 -gt var2	Is the first variable greater than the second variable?
var1 -le var2	Is the first variable less than or equal to the second variable?
var1 -lt var2	Is the first variable less than the second variable?
var1 != var2	Is the first variable not equal to the second variable?
var1 -ne var2	Is the first variable not equal to the second variable?

There is also a special shorthand method of performing tests that can be useful for simple *one-command actions*. In the following example, the two pipes (||) indicate that if the directory being tested for doesn't exist (-d dirname), then make the directory (mkdir $dirname):

```
# [ test ] || action
# Perform simple single command if test is false
dirname="/tmp/testdir"
[ -d "$dirname" ] || mkdir "$dirname"
```

Instead of pipes, you can use two ampersands to test if something is true. In the following example, a command is being tested to see if it includes at least three command-line arguments:

```
# [ test ] && {action}
# Perform simple single action if test is true
[ $# -ge 3 ] && echo "There are at least 3 command line arguments."
```

You can combine the && and || operators to make a quick, one-line if-then-else statement. The following example tests that the directory represented by $dirname already exists. If it does, a message says the directory already exists. If it doesn't, the statement creates the directory:

```
# dirname=mydirectory
[ -e $dirname ] && echo $dirname already exists || mkdir $dirname
```

The case command

Another frequently used construct is the case command. Similar to a switch statement in programming languages, this can take the place of several nested if statements. The following is the general form of the case statement:

```
case "VAR" in
   Result1)
       { body };;
```

```
    Result2)
        { body };;
    *)
        { body } ;;
esac
```

Among other things, you can use the `case` command to help with your backups. The following `case` statement tests for the first three letters of the current day (`case 'date +%a' in`). Then, depending on the day, a particular backup directory (`BACKUP`) and tape drive (`TAPE`) are set.

```
# Our VAR doesn't have to be a variable,
# it can be the output of a command as well
# Perform action based on day of week
case `date +%a` in
    "Mon")
            BACKUP=/home/myproject/data0
            TAPE=/dev/rft0
# Note the use of the double semi-colon to end each option
            ;;
# Note the use of the "|" to mean "or"
    "Tue" | "Thu")
            BACKUP=/home/myproject/data1
            TAPE=/dev/rft1
            ;;
    "Wed" | "Fri")
            BACKUP=/home/myproject/data2
            TAPE=/dev/rft2
            ;;
# Don't do backups on the weekend.
    *)

BACKUP="none"
            TAPE=/dev/null
            ;;
esac
```

The asterisk (*) is used as a catchall, similar to the `default` keyword in the C programming language. In this example, if none of the other entries are matched on the way down the loop, the asterisk is matched and the value of `BACKUP` becomes `none`. Note the use of `esac`, or `case` spelled backwards, to end the `case` statement.

The "for. . .do" loop

Loops are used to perform actions over and over again until a condition is met or until all data has been processed. One of the most commonly used loops is the `for...do` loop. It iterates through a list of values, executing the body of the loop for each element in the list. The syntax and a few examples are presented here:

```
for VAR in LIST
do
```

Continues

Continued

```
    { body }
done
```

The `for` loop assigns the values in *LIST* to *VAR* one at a time. Then, for each value, the *body* in braces between `do` and `done` is executed. `VAR` can be any variable name, and `LIST` can be composed of pretty much any list of values or anything that generates a list.

```
for NUMBER in 0 1 2 3 4 5 6 7 8 9
do
    echo The number is $NUMBER
done

for FILE in `/bin/ls`
do
    echo $FILE
done
```

You can also write it this way, which is somewhat cleaner:

```
for NAME in John Paul Ringo George ; do
    echo $NAME is my favorite Beatle
done
```

Each element in the `LIST` is separated from the next by white space. This can cause trouble if you're not careful because some commands, such as `ls -l`, output multiple fields per line, each separated by white space. The string `done` ends the `for` statement.

If you're a die-hard C programmer, bash allows you to use C syntax to control your loops:

```
LIMIT=10
# Double parentheses, and no $ on LIMIT even though it's a variable!
for ((a=1; a <= LIMIT ; a++)) ; do
    echo "$a"
done
```

The "while. . .do" and "until. . .do" loops

Two other possible looping constructs are the `while...do` loop and the `until...do` loop. The structure of each is presented here:

```
while condition          until condition
do                       do
    { body }                 { body }
done                     done
```

The `while` statement executes while the condition is true. The `until` statement executes until the condition is true—in other words, while the condition is false.

Here is an example of a `while` loop that outputs the number 0123456789:

```
N=0
while [ $N -lt 10 ] ; do
    echo -n $N
```

```
        let N=$N+1
    done
```

Another way to output the number 0123456789 is to use an `until` loop as follows:

```
N=0
until [ $N -eq 10 ] ; do
    echo -n $N
    let N=$N+1
done
```

Trying some useful text manipulation programs

Bash is great and has lots of built-in commands, but it usually needs some help to do anything really useful. Some of the most common useful programs you'll see used are `grep`, `cut`, `tr`, `awk`, and `sed`. As with all of the best UNIX tools, most of these programs are designed to work with standard input and output, so you can easily use them with pipes and shell scripts.

The global regular expression print

The name *global regular expression print* (`grep`) sounds intimidating, but `grep` is just a way to find patterns in files or text. Think of it as a useful search tool. Gaining expertise with regular expressions is quite a challenge, but after you master it, you can accomplish many useful things with just the simplest forms.

For example, you can display a list of all regular user accounts by using `grep` to search for all lines that contain the text `/home` in the `/etc/passwd` file as follows:

```
$ grep /home /etc/passwd
```

Or you could find all environment variables that begin with `HO` using the following command:

```
$ env | grep ^HO
```

> **NOTE**
>
> The ^ in the preceding code is the actual caret character, ^, not what you'll commonly see for a backspace, ^H. Type grep with ^, H, and O (the uppercase letter) to see what items start with the uppercase characters HO.

To find a list of options to use with the `grep` command, type **man grep**.

Remove sections of lines of text (cut)

The `cut` command can extract fields from a line of text or from files. It is very useful for parsing system configuration files into easy-to-digest chunks. You can specify the field separator you want to use and the fields you want, or you can break up a line based on bytes.

The following example lists all home directories of users on your system. This `grep` command line pipes a list of regular users from the `/etc/passwd` file and displays the sixth field (-f6) as delimited by a colon (-d':'). The hyphen at the end tells `cut` to read from standard input (from the pipe).

```
$ grep /home /etc/passwd | cut  -d':' -f6 -
/home/syslog
/home/chris
/home/joe
```

Translate or delete characters (tr)

The `tr` command is a character-based translator that can be used to replace one character or set of characters with another or to remove a character from a line of text.

The following example translates all uppercase letters to lowercase letters and displays the words `mixed upper and lower case` as a result:

```
$ FOO="Mixed UPpEr aNd LoWeR cAsE"
$ echo $FOO | tr [A-Z] [a-z]
mixed upper and lower case
```

In the next example, the `tr` command is used on a list of filenames to rename any files in that list so that any tabs or spaces (as indicated by the `[:blank:]` option) contained in a filename are translated into underscores. Try running the following code in a test directory:

```
for file in * ; do
    f=`echo $file | tr [:blank:] [_]`
    [ "$file" = "$f" ] || mv -i -- "$file" "$f"
done
```

The stream editor (sed)

The `sed` command is a simple scriptable editor, so it can only perform simple edits, such as removing lines that have text matching a certain pattern, replacing one pattern of characters with another, and so on. To get a better idea of how `sed` scripts work, there's no substitute for the online documentation, but here are some examples of common uses.

You can use the `sed` command essentially to do what I did earlier with the `grep` example: search the /etc/passwd file for the word `home`. Here the `sed` command searches the entire /etc/passwd file, searches for the word `home`, and prints any line containing the word `home`:

```
$ sed -n '/home/p' /etc/passwd
chris:x:1000:1000:Chris Negus:/home/chris:/bin/bash
joe:x:1001:1001:Joe Smith:/home/joe:/bin/bash
```

In this next example, sed searches the file `somefile.txt` and replaces every instance of the string `Mac` with `Linux`. Notice that the letter `g` (meaning "global") is needed at the end of the substitution command to cause every occurrence of `Mac` on each line to be changed to `Linux`. (Otherwise, only the first instance of `Mac` on each line is changed.) The output is then sent to the `fixed _ file.txt` file. The output from `sed` goes to `stdout`, so this command redirects the output to a file for safekeeping.

```
$ sed 's/Mac/Linux/g' somefile.txt > fixed_file.txt
```

You can get the same result using a pipe:

```
$ cat somefile.txt | sed 's/Mac/Linux/g' > fixed_file.txt
```

By searching for a pattern and replacing it with a null pattern, you delete the original pattern. This example searches the contents of the `somefile.txt` file and replaces extra blank spaces at the end of each line (s/ *$) with nothing (//). Results go to the `fixed _ file.txt` file.

```
$ cat somefile.txt | sed 's/ *$//' > fixed_file.txt
```

Using simple shell scripts

Sometimes, the simplest of scripts can be the most useful. If you type the same sequence of commands repetitively, it makes sense to store those commands (once!) in a file. The following sections offer a couple of simple, but useful, shell scripts.

Telephone list

This idea has been handed down from generation to generation of old UNIX hacks. It's really quite simple, but it employs several of the concepts just introduced.

```
#!/bin/bash
# (@)/ph
# A very simple telephone list
# Type "ph new name number" to add to the list, or
# just type "ph name" to get a phone number

PHONELIST=~/.phonelist.txt

# If no command line parameters ($#), there
# is a problem, so ask what they're talking about.
if [ $# -lt 1 ] ; then
  echo "Whose phone number did you want? "
    exit 1
fi

# Did you want to add a new phone number?
if [ $1 = "new" ] ; then
  shift
  echo $* >> $PHONELIST
  echo $* added to database
  exit 0
fi
```

Continues

Continued

```
# Nope. But does the file have anything in it yet?
# This might be our first time using it, after all.
if [ ! -s $PHONELIST ] ; then
  echo "No names in the phone list yet! "
  exit 1
else
  grep -i -q "$*" $PHONELIST      # Quietly search the file
  if [ $? -ne 0 ] ; then          # Did we find anything?
    echo "Sorry, that name was not found in the phone list"
    exit 1
  else
    grep -i "$*" $PHONELIST
  fi
fi
exit 0
```

So, if you created the telephone list file as ph in your current directory, you could type the following from the shell to try out your ph script:

```
$ chmod 755 ph
$ ./ph new "Mary Jones" 608-555-1212
Mary Jones 608-555-1212 added to database
$ ./ph Mary
Mary Jones 608-555-1212
```

The chmod command makes the ph script executable. The ./ph command runs the ph command from the current directory with the new option. This adds Mary Jones as the name and 608-555-1212 as the phone number to the database ($HOME/.phonelist.txt). The next ph command searches the database for the name Mary and displays the phone entry for Mary. If the script works, add it to a directory in your path (such as $HOME/bin).

Backup script

Because nothing works forever and mistakes happen, backups are just a fact of life when dealing with computer data. This simple script backs up all of the data in the home directories of all of the users on your system:

```
#!/bin/bash
# (@)/my_backup
# A very simple backup script
#

# Change the TAPE device to match your system.
# Check /var/log/messages to determine your tape device.

TAPE=/dev/rft0

# Rewind the tape device $TAPE
mt $TAPE rew
```

```
# Get a list of home directories
HOMES=`grep /home /etc/passwd | cut -f6 -d':'`
# Back up the data in those directories
tar cvf $TAPE $HOMES
# Rewind and eject the tape.
mt $TAPE rewoffl
```

Summary

Writing shell scripts gives you the opportunity to automate many of your most common system administration tasks. This chapter covered common commands and functions that you can use in scripting with the Bash shell. It also provided some concrete examples of scripts for doing backups and other procedures.

In the next chapter, you transition from learning about user features into examining system administration topics. Chapter 8, "Learning System Administration," covers how to become the root user, as well as how to use administrative commands, monitor log files, and work with configuration files.

Exercises

Use these exercises to test your knowledge of writing simple shell scripts. If you are stuck, solutions to the tasks are shown in Appendix A (although in Linux, there are often multiple ways to complete a task).

1. Create a script in your $HOME/bin directory called myownscript. When the script runs, it should output information that appears as follows:

   ```
   Today is Sat Jan 4 15:45:04 EST 2020.
   You are in /home/joe and your host is abc.example.com.
   ```

   Of course, you need to read in your current date/time, current working directory, and hostname. Also, include comments about what the script does and indicate that the script should run with the /bin/bash shell.

2. Create a script that reads in three positional parameters from the command line, assigns those parameters to variables named ONE, TWO, and THREE, respectively, and outputs that information in the following format:

   ```
   There are X parameters that include Y.
   The first is A, the second is B, the third is C.
   ```

   Replace X with the number of parameters and Y with all parameters entered. Then replace A with the contents of variable ONE, B with variable TWO, and C with variable THREE.

3. Create a script that prompts users for the name of the street and town where they grew up. Assign town and street to variables called `mytown` and `mystreet`, and output them with a sentence that reads as shown in the following example (of course, $mystreet and $mytown will appear with the actual town and street the user enters):

```
The street I grew up on was $mystreet and the town was $mytown
```

4. Create a script called `myos` that asks the user, "What is your favorite operating system?" Output an insulting sentence if the user types "Windows" or "Mac." Respond "Great choice!" if the user types "Linux." For anything else, say "Is *what is typed in* an operating system?"

5. Create a script that runs through the words *moose, cow, goose,* and *sow* through a `for` loop. Have each of those words appended to the end of the line "I have a. . .."

Part III

Becoming a Linux System Administrator

IN THIS PART

Learning System Administration

IN THIS CHAPTER

Doing graphical administration

Invoking administration privileges

Understanding administrative commands, config files, and log files

Working with devices and filesystems

L inux, like other UNIX-based systems, was intended for use by more than one person at a time. *Multiuser features* enable many people to have accounts on a single Linux system with their data kept secure from others. *Multitasking* enables many people to run many programs on the computer at the same time, with each person able to run more than one program. Sophisticated networking protocols and applications make it possible for a Linux system to extend its capabilities to network users and computers around the world. The person assigned to manage all of a Linux system's resources is called the *system administrator*.

Even if you are the only person using a Linux system, system administration is still set up to be separate from other computer use. To do most administrative tasks, you need to be logged in as the *root user* (also called the *superuser*) or to get root permission temporarily (usually using the sudo command). Regular users who don't have root permission cannot change, or in some cases cannot even see, some of the configuration information for a Linux system. Even the encrypted versions of stored passwords are protected from general view.

Because Linux system administration is such a huge topic, this chapter focuses on the general principles of Linux system administration. In particular, it examines some of the basic tools that you need to administer a Linux system for a personal desktop or on a small server. Beyond the basics, this chapter also teaches you how to work with filesystems and monitor the setup and performance of your Linux system.

Understanding System Administration

Separating the role of system administrator from that of other users has several effects. For a system that has many people using it, limiting who can manage it enables you to keep it more secure. A separate administrative role also prevents others from casually harming your system when they are just using it to write a document or browse the Internet.

If you are the system administrator of a Linux system, you generally log in using a regular user account and then invoke administrative privileges when you need them. This is often done with one of the following:

su command: Often, su is used to open a shell as root user. After the shell is open, the administrator can run multiple commands and then exit to return as a regular user.

sudo command: With sudo, a regular user is given root privileges, but only when that user runs the sudo command to run another command. After running that one command with sudo, the user is immediately returned to a shell and acts as the regular user again. Ubuntu by default assigns sudo privilege to the first user account created when the system is installed.

Cockpit browser-based administration: Like many newer releases of other Linux distributions, Ubuntu has committed to Cockpit as its primary browser-based system administration facility. With Cockpit enabled, you can monitor and change your system's general activities, storage, networking, accounts, services, and other features.

Tasks that can be done only by the root user tend to be those that affect the system as a whole or impact the security or health of the system. Following is a list of common features that a system administrator is expected to manage:

Filesystems: When you first install Linux, the directory structure is set up to make the system usable. However, if users later want to add extra storage or change the filesystem layout outside of their home directory, they need administrative privileges to do that. Also, the root user has permission to access files owned by any user. As a result, the root user can copy, move, or change any other user's files—a privilege needed to make backup copies of the filesystem for safekeeping.

Software installation: Because malicious software can harm your system or make it insecure, you need root privilege to install software using a primary software package manager (like APT or Snap) so that it's available to all users. Regular users can still install some software in their own directories and can list information about installed system software.

User accounts: Only the root user can add and remove user and group accounts.

Network interfaces: In the past, the root user had to configure and stop and start network interfaces. Now, many Linux desktops allow regular users to start and stop WiFi connections—something whose absence would make day-to-day life difficult for users of mobile devices.

Servers: Configuring web servers, file servers, domain name servers, mail servers, and dozens of other servers requires root privilege, as does starting and stopping those services. Content, such as web pages, can be added to servers by non-root users if you configure your system to allow that. Services are often run as special adminis-trative user accounts, such as apache (for the httpd service) and rpc (for the DNS server rpcbind service). This means that, even if someone breaks into one service, they can't get root privilege to other services or system resources.

Security features: Setting up security features, such as firewalls and user access lists, is usually done with root privilege. It's also up to the root user to monitor how the services are being used and to make sure that server resources are not exhausted or abused.

The easiest way to begin system administration is to use some graphical administra-tion tools.

Using Graphical Administration Tools

Most system administration for the first Linux systems was done from the command line. As Linux became more popular, however, both graphical and command-line interfaces began to be offered for most common Linux administrative tasks.

The following sections describe some of the point-and-click types of interfaces that are available for doing system administration in Linux.

Using Cockpit browser-based administration

Cockpit brings together a range of Linux administrative activities into one interface and taps into a diverse set of Linux APIs using cockpit-bridge. As someone doing Linux admin-istration, however, you just need to know that Cockpit is a consistent and stable way of administering your systems.

Getting started is as simple as enabling the cockpit socket and pointing a web browser at the Cockpit service. Because of Cockpit's plug-in design, there are new tools being created all the time that you can add to your system's Cockpit interface.

If you are starting with the latest Ubuntu system, performing the following procedure lets you enable and start using Cockpit on your system:

> **NOTE**
>
> No configuration is required to start this procedure. However, you can configure Cockpit to use your own OpenSSL certificate instead of the self-signed one used by default. This lets you avoid having to accept the unverified self-signed certificate when you open the Cockpit interface from your browser.

1. If Cockpit is not already installed, do the following:

```
# apt install cockpit
```

2. Open your web browser to port 9090 on the system where you just enabled Cockpit. You can use the server's hostname or IP address. You can run `ip addr` on the server to retrieve its IP address. Port 9090 is configured for https by default, although you can reconfigure that if you like to use http. Here are examples of addresses to type into your browser's address bar:

   ```
   https://host1.example.com:9090/
   https://192.168.122.114:9090/
   ```

3. Assuming you didn't replace the self-signed certificate for Cockpit, you are warned that the connection is not safe. To accept it anyway, and depending on your browser, you must select Advanced and agree to an exception to allow the browser to use the Cockpit service.

4. Enter your username and password. Log in as a user with `sudo` privileges if you expect to change your system configuration. A regular user can see but not change most settings. Figure 8.1 shows an example of the login window.

FIGURE 8.1

Logging in to Cockpit

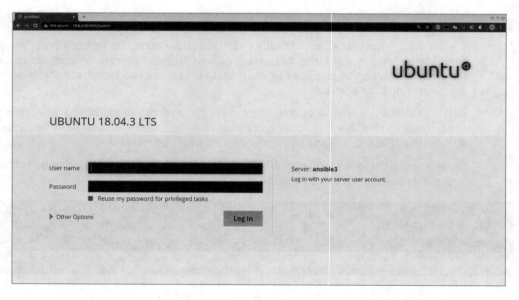

5. Begin using Cockpit. The Cockpit dashboard contains a good set of features by default (you can add more later). Figure 8.2 shows an example of the System area of the Cockpit dashboard.

FIGURE 8.2

View system activity and other topics from the Cockpit dashboard.

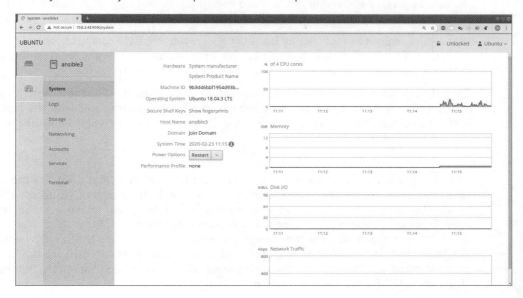

Immediately after logging in to Cockpit, you see system activity related to CPU usage, memory, disk input/output, and network traffic. Selections in the left navigation pane let you begin working with logs, storage, networking, user and group accounts, services, and many other features on your system.

As you proceed through the rest of this book, you will see descriptions of how to use the different features of Cockpit in the appropriate section. To dive deeper into any of the topics that you encounter with Cockpit, I recommend checking out the Cockpit project website: www.cockpit-project.org.

Using other browser-based admin tools

To simplify the management of many enterprise-quality open source projects, those projects have begun offering browser-based graphical management tools. In most cases, command-line tools are offered for managing these projects as well.

Kubernetic (www.kubernetic.com/), for instance, is a GUI tool for administrating Kubernetes container workloads. Webmin (www.webmin.com/) is a time-tested interface for managing complex web hosting operations. And many infrastructure deployment environments like OpenStack (www.ubuntu.com/openstack/install) come out of the box with their own browser GUIs. All of those will happily get along with Ubuntu operations.

Invoking Administration Privileges

The Ubuntu installation process prompts you to create a primary user account that will, by default, be given membership in the sudo user group. A root user exists, but it won't have a password and Ubuntu doesn't recommend you ever log in to that account.

When you become the root user by invoking sudo, you will have complete control of the operation of your Linux system. You'll be able to open any file, run any program, install software packages, and add accounts for other people who use the system.

Even though you won't normally log in as root, the root account will have its own home directory: /root. The home directory and other information associated with the root user account are located in the /etc/passwd file. Here's what the root entry looks like in the /etc/passwd file:

```
root:x:0:0:root:/root:/bin/bash
```

This shows that for the user named root, the user ID is set to 0 (root user), the group ID is set to 0 (root group), the home directory is /root, and the shell for that user is /bin/bash. (Linux uses the /etc/shadow file to store encrypted password data, so the password field here contains only a single x to represent the password. For root, of course, there normally is no password.) You can change the home directory or the shell used by editing the values in this file. A better way to change these values, however, is to use the usermod command (see the section "Modifying users with usermod" in Chapter 11, "Managing User Accounts," for further information).

When actually logged in as root (using, say, the sudo su command), any command that you run from your shell is run with root privilege. So be careful. You have much more power to change (and damage) the system than you did as a regular user. Type **exit** when you are finished to leave the root environment.

> **NOTE**
> It's good to be aware that other distributions like Red Hat Enterprise Linux (RHEL) expect that you will use the root account for active operations. In fact, the password you create when installing distros of the RHEL family will be meant for use with root.

Becoming root from the shell

Although you shouldn't normally spend a lot of time playing around in the root account, it can be done using sudo su. When prompted, you'll enter your user's password. This will only work if your user is a member in good standing of the sudo group.

```
david@workstation:~$ sudo su
[sudo] password for david:
root@workstation:/home/david#
```

After successfully entering your password, note that your prompt will now read "root" rather than your username. From this point until you exit the shell, you are the root user.

You can also use the su command (which, after all, stands for "switch user") to become a user other than root. This is useful for troubleshooting a problem that is being experienced by a particular user but not by others on the computer (such as an inability to access a particular system resource). For example, to have the permissions of a user named *jsmith*, you'd type the following:

```
$ su jsmith
```

Even if you were the root user when you typed this command, afterward you would have only the permissions to open files and run programs that are available to jsmith. As root user, however (if you had previously opened a shell using sudo su), after you type the su command to become another user, you won't need a password. If you type that command as a regular user, you must type the new user's password.

When you are finished using superuser permissions, return to the previous shell by exiting the current shell. Do this by pressing Ctrl+D or by typing **exit**. If you are the administrator for a computer that is accessible to multiple users, don't leave a root shell open on someone else's screen unless you want to give that person freedom to do anything he or she wants to the computer!

Gaining temporary admin access with sudo

Regular users can also be given administrative permissions for individual tasks by typing sudo followed by the command they want to run. The quick and simple way to provide this authority is by adding an existing user to the sudo group (other Linux distributions have a wheel group that services a similar function). Someone using an existing admin account can do that by running this usermod command:

```
# usermod -aG sudo joe
```

You could also edit the /etc/group and add the username to the sudo line. That line might look like this:

```
sudo:x:27:david,joe
```

Be careful not to leave any spaces between commas and names.

The thing about the quick and simple way is that the results are sometimes not quite as precise as you might prefer. Adding a user to the sudo group provides full admin access, while not adding the user provides no admin access at all. It's either all or nothing. If you want a user to get more nuanced access, you'll need to use the official method: editing the /etc/sudoers file. Using the sudoers system for any users or groups, you can do the following:

- Assign root privilege for any command they run with sudo.
- Assign root privilege for a select set of commands.

- Give users root privilege without telling them a root password, because they only have to provide their own user password to gain root privilege.
- Allow users, if you choose, to run sudo without entering a password at all.
- Track which users have run administrative commands on your system.

With the sudoers facility, giving full or limited root privileges to any user simply entails adding the user to /etc/sudoers and defining what privilege you want that user to have. Then the user can run any command they are privileged to use by preceding that command with the sudo command.

Here's an example of how to use the sudo facility to give the user *joe* full root privilege:

1. As the root user, edit the /etc/sudoers file by running the visudo command:

   # /usr/sbin/visudo

   By default, the file opens in vi, unless your EDITOR variable happens to be set to some other editor acceptable to visudo (for example, export EDITOR=gedit). The reason for using visudo is that the command locks the /etc/sudoers file and does some basic sanity checking of the file to ensure that it has been edited correctly.

NOTE

If you are stuck here, try running the vimtutor command for a quick tutorial on using vi and vim.

2. Add the following line to allow joe to have full root privileges on the computer:

   joe   ALL=(ALL)   ALL

   This line requires joe to provide a password (his own password, not a root password) in order to use administrative commands. To allow joe to have that privilege without using a password, type the following line instead:

   joe   ALL=(ALL)   NOPASSWD: ALL

3. Save the changes to the /etc/sudoers file (in vi, type **Esc** and then **:wq**).

Even after joe has entered the password to run a command, he must still use the sudo command to run subsequent administrative commands as root. Nevertheless, after entering his password successfully, he can enter as many sudo commands as he wants for the duration of the current shell. You can change the time-out value from five minutes to any length of time you want by setting the passwd_timeout value in the /etc/sudoers file.

The preceding example grants a simple all-or-nothing administrative privilege to joe. However, the /etc/sudoers file gives you an incredible amount of flexibility in permitting individual users and groups to use individual applications or groups of applications.

Refer to the `sudoers` and `sudo` man pages for information about how to tune your `sudo` facility.

Exploring Administrative Commands, Configuration Files, and Log Files

You can expect to find many commands, configuration files, and log files in the same places in the filesystem in Ubuntu as you would in other distributions. The following sections give you some pointers on where to look for these important elements.

> **NOTE**
>
> If GUI administrative tools for Linux have become so good, why do you need to know about administrative files? For one thing, while GUI tools differ among Linux versions, many underlying configuration files are the same. So if you learn to work with them, you can work with almost any Linux system. Also, if a feature is broken or you need to do something that's not supported by the GUI, when you ask for help, Linux experts almost always tell you how to run commands or change the configuration file directly.

Administrative commands

Only the root user is intended to use many administrative commands. When you're acting as root, your $PATH variable is set to include some directories that contain commands for the root user. In the past, these have included the following:

/sbin: Contains commands needed to boot your system, including commands for checking filesystems (`fsck`) and turning on swap devices (`swapon`).

/usr/sbin: Contains commands for such things as managing user accounts (such as `adduser`) and checking processes that are holding files open (such as `lsof`). Commands that run as daemon processes are also contained in this directory. *Daemon processes* are processes that run in the background, waiting for service requests such as those to access a printer or a web page. (Look for commands that end in d, such as `sshd`, `pppd`, and `cupsd`.)

Some administrative commands are contained in regular user directories (such as `/bin` and `/usr/bin`). This is especially true of commands that have some options available to everyone. An example is the `/bin/mount` command, which anyone can use to list mounted filesystems but only root can use to mount filesystems. (Some desktops, however, are configured to let regular users use `mount` to mount CDs, DVDs, or other removable media.)

> **NOTE**
>
> See the section "Mounting Filesystems" in Chapter 12, "Managing Disks and Filesystems," for instructions on how to mount a filesystem.

To find commands intended primarily for the system administrator, check out the section 8 man pages (usually in /usr/share/man/man8). They contain descriptions and options for most Linux administrative commands.

If you want to add commands to your system, consider adding them to directories such as /usr/local/bin or /usr/local/sbin. Ubuntu automatically adds those directories to your PATH, usually before your standard bin and sbin directories. In that way, commands installed to those directories are not only accessible, but can also override commands of the same name in other directories. Some third-party applications that are not included with your Ubuntu distribution are sometimes placed in the /usr/local/bin, /opt/bin or /usr/local/sbin directory.

Administrative configuration files

Configuration files are another mainstay of Linux administration. Almost everything that you set up for your particular computer—user accounts, network addresses, or GUI preferences—results in settings being stored in plain text files. This has advantages and disadvantages.

The advantage of plain text files is that it's easy to read and change them. Any text editor will do. The downside, however, is that as you edit configuration files, no error checking is done. You sometimes have to run the program that reads these files (such as a network daemon or the X desktop) to find out whether you set up the files correctly.

While some configuration files use standard structures, such as XML for storing information, many do not. So, you need to learn the specific structure rules for each configuration file. A comma or a quote in the wrong place can sometimes cause an entire interface to fail.

Some software packages offer a command to test the sanity of the configuration file tied to a package before you start a service. For example, the testparm command is used with Samba to check the sanity of your smb.conf file. Other times, the daemon process providing a service offers an option for checking your config file. For example, run apache2 -t to check your Apache web server configuration before starting your web server.

> **NOTE**
>
> Some text editors, such as the vim command (not vi), understand the structure of some types of configuration files. If you open such a configuration file in vim, notice that different elements of the file are shown in different colors. In particular, you can see comment lines in a different color than data.

Throughout this book, you'll find descriptions of the configuration files that you need to set up the different features that make up Linux systems. The two major locations of configuration files are your home directory (where your personal configuration files are kept) and the /etc directory (which holds system-wide configuration files).

Following are descriptions of directories (and subdirectories) that contain useful configuration files—assuming the underlying software is actually installed on your system. The descriptions are followed by some individual configuration files in /etc that are of particular interest. Viewing the contents of Linux configuration files can teach you a lot about administering Linux systems.

$HOME: In their home directories, all users store information that directs how their login accounts behave. Many configuration files are stored directly in each user's home directory (such as /home/joe) and begin with a dot (.), so they don't appear in a user's directory when you use a standard ls command (you need to type **ls -a** to see them). Likewise, dot files and directories won't show up in most file manager windows by default. There are dot files that define the behavior of each user's shell, the desktop look and feel, and options used with your text editor. There are even files such as those in each user's $HOME/.ssh directory that configure permissions for logging in to remote systems. (To see the name of your home directory, type **echo $HOME** from a shell.)

/etc: This directory contains most of the basic Linux system configuration files.

/etc/cron*: Directories in this set contain files that define how the crond utility runs applications on an hourly (cron.hourly), daily (cron.daily), weekly (cron.weekly), or monthly (cron.monthly) schedule.

/etc/cups: Contains files used to configure the CUPS printing service.

/etc/default: Contains files that set default values for various utilities. For example, the ufw file for the adduser contains default values for the Uncomplicated Firewall service.

/etc/apache2: Contains a variety of files used to configure the behavior of your Apache web server (specifically, the apache2 daemon process).

/etc/mail: Contains files used to configure your sendmail mail transport agent.

/etc/postfix: Contains configuration files for the postfix mail transport agent.

/etc/ppp: Contains several configuration files used to set up Point-to-Point Protocol (PPP) so that you can have your computer dial out to the Internet. (PPP was more commonly used when dial-up modems were popular.)

/etc/rc?.d: There is a separate rc?.d directory for each valid system state: rc0.d (shutdown state), rc1.d (single-user state), rc2.d (multiuser state), rc3.d (multiuser plus networking state), rc4.d (user-defined state), rc5.d (multiuser, networking, plus GUI login state), and rc6.d (reboot state). These directories are maintained for compatibility with old UNIX SystemV init services but, since the broad adoption of systemd process management, are rarely used.

/etc/security: Contains files that set a variety of default security conditions for your computer, basically defining how authentication is done. These files are part of the pam (Pluggable Authentication Modules) package.

/etc/skel: Any files contained in this directory are automatically copied to a user's home directory when that user is added to the system. By default, most of these files are dot (.) files, such as .kde (a directory for setting KDE desktop defaults) and .bashrc (for setting default values used with the Bash shell).

8

/etc/systemd: Contains files associated with the `systemd` facility, for managing the boot process and system services. In particular, when you run `systemctl` commands to enable and disable services, files that make that happen are stored in subdirectories of the `/etc/systemd system` directory.

The following are some interesting configuration files in `/etc`:

bash.bashrc: Sets system-wide defaults for Bash shell users.

crontab: Sets times for running automated tasks and variables associated with the `cron` facility (such as the `SHELL` and `PATH` associated with `cron`).

fstab: Identifies the devices for common storage media (hard disk, DVD, CD-ROM, and so on) and locations where they are mounted in the Linux system. This is used by the `mount` command to choose which filesystems to mount when the system first boots.

group: Identifies group names and group IDs (GIDs) that are defined on the system. Group permissions in Linux are defined by the second of three sets of `rwx` (read, write, execute) bits associated with each file and directory.

gshadow: Contains shadow passwords for groups.

host.conf: Used by older applications to set the locations in which domain names (for example, www.ubuntu.com) are searched for on TCP/IP networks (such as the Internet). By default, the local hosts file is searched and then any name server entries in `resolv.conf`.

hostname: Contains the hostname for the local system.

hosts: Contains IP addresses and hostnames that you can reach from your computer. (Usually this file is used just to store names of computers on your LAN or small private network.)

mtab: Contains a list of filesystems that are currently mounted.

mtools.conf: Contains settings used by DOS tools in Linux.

nsswitch.conf: Contains name service switch settings, for identifying where critical system information (user accounts, hostname-to-address mappings, and so on) comes from (local host or via network services).

ntp.conf: Includes information needed to run the Network Time Protocol (NTP).

passwd: Stores account information for all valid users on the local system. Also includes other information, such as the home directory and default shell. (Rarely includes the user passwords themselves, which are typically stored in the `/etc /shadow` file.)

printcap: Contains definitions for the printers configured for your computer. (The `printcap` file is actually automatically generated by the cupsd service based on the contents of the `/etc/cups/printers.conf` file.)

profile: Sets system-wide environment and startup programs for all users. This file is read when the user logs in.

protocols: Sets protocol numbers and names for a variety of Internet services.

rpc: Defines remote procedure call names and numbers.

services: Defines TCP/IP and UDP service names and their port assignments.

shadow: Contains encrypted passwords for users who are defined in the passwd file. (This is viewed as a more secure way to store passwords than the original encrypted password in the passwd file since, unlike the shadow file, the passwd file needs to be publicly readable.)

shells: Lists the shell command-line interpreters (bash, sh, csh, and so on) that are available on the system as well as their locations.

sudoers: Sets commands that can be run by users, who may not otherwise have permission to run the command, using the sudo command. In particular, this file is used to provide selected users with root permission.

rsyslog.conf: Defines what logging messages are gathered by the rsyslogd daemon and in which files they are stored. (Typically, log messages are stored in files contained in the /var/log directory.)

Another directory, /etc/X11, includes subdirectories that each contain system-wide configuration files used by X and different X window managers available for Linux.

Administrative log files and systemd journal

One of the things that Linux does well is keep track of itself. This is a good thing when you consider how much is going on in a complex operating system.

Sometimes you are trying to get a new facility to work, and it fails without giving you the foggiest reason why. Other times, you want to monitor your system to see whether people are trying to access your computer illegally. In any of those cases, you want to be able to refer to messages coming from the kernel and services running on the system.

For Linux systems that don't use the systemd facility, the main utility for logging error and debugging messages is the rsyslogd daemon. (Some older Linux systems use syslogd and syslogd daemons.) Although you can still use rsyslogd with systemd systems, systemd has its own method of gathering and displaying messages called the systemd journal and uses the journalctl command.

Using journalctl to view the systemd journal

The primary command for viewing messages from the systemd journal is the journalctl command. The boot process, the kernel, and all systemd-managed services direct their status and error messages to the systemd journal.

Using the `journalctl` command, you can display journal messages in many different ways. Here are some examples:

```
# journalctl
# journalctl --list-boots | head -3
-2 93bdb6164... Sat 2020-01-04 21:07:28 EST—Sat 2020-01-04
21:19:37 EST
-1 7336cb823... Sun 2020-01-05 10:38:27 EST—Mon 2020-01-06
09:29:09 EST
 0 eaebac25f... Sat 2020-01-18 14:11:41 EST—Sat 2020-01-18
16:03:37 EST
# journalctl -b 488e152a3e2b4f6bb86be366c55264e7
# journalctl -k
```

In these examples, the `journalctl` command with no options lets you page through all messages in the `systemd` journal. To list the boot IDs for each time the system was booted, use the `--list-boots` option. To view messages associated with a particular boot instance, use the `-b` option with one of the boot instance IDs. To see only kernel messages, use the `-k` option. Here are some more examples:

```
# journalctl _SYSTEMD_UNIT=ssh.service
# journalctl PRIORITY=0
# journalctl -a -f
```

Use the `_SYSTEMD_UNIT=` options to show messages for specific services (here, the `ssh` service) or for any other `systemd` unit file (such as other services or mounts). Specifying `PRIORITY=0` will return only messages associated with the particular syslog log level 0 (any value from 0 to 7 is available). In this case, only emergency (0) messages are shown. To follow messages as they come in, use the `-f` option; to show all fields, use the `-a` option.

Managing log messages with rsyslogd

The `rsyslogd` facility and its predecessor `syslogd` gather log messages and direct them to log files or remote log hosts. Logging is done according to information in the `/etc/rsyslog.conf` file. Messages are typically directed to log files that are usually in the `/var/log` directory, but they can also be directed to log hosts for additional security. Here are a few common log files:

boot.log: Contains boot messages about services as they start up.

syslog: Contains all log messages generated by the system except those categorized as "auth."

dpkg.log: Contains logs involving package managing events.

Refer to Chapter 13, "Understanding Server Administration," for information on configuring the `rsyslogd` facility.

Using Other Administrative Accounts

You don't hear much about logging in to administrative user accounts on Linux systems. It was a fairly common practice in UNIX systems to have several different administrative accounts that allowed administrative tasks to be split among several users. For example, people sitting near a shared printer could have lp permissions to move print jobs to another printer if they knew a printer wasn't working.

In any case, administrative accounts are available with Linux; however, logging in directly as those users is disabled by default. The accounts are maintained primarily to provide ownership for files and processes associated with particular services. When daemon processes are run under separate administrative logins, having one of those processes cracked does not give the cracker root permission and the ability to access other processes and files. Consider the following examples:

lp: User owns printing-related objects like the /etc/cups/cupsd.conf file.

www-data: User can manage content files and directories on an Apache web server. It is primarily used to run the web server processes (Apache2).

avahi: User runs the avahi daemon process to provide networking and DNS services on your network.

chrony: User runs the chronyd daemon, which is used to maintain accurate computer clocks.

postfix: User owns various mail server spool directories and files. The user runs the daemon processes used to provide the postfix service (master).

By default, the administrative logins in the preceding list are disabled. You would need to change the default shell from its current setting (usually /usr/sbin/nologin or /bin/false) to a real shell (typically /bin/bash) to be able to log in as these users. However, they are really not intended for interactive logins.

Checking and Configuring Hardware

In a perfect world, after installing and booting Linux, all of your hardware is detected and available for access. Although Linux systems have become quite good at detecting hardware, sometimes you must take special steps to get your computer hardware working. Also, the growing use of removable USB devices (including USB-based CDs and DVDs, flash drives, digital cameras, and removable hard drives) has made it important for Linux to do the following:

- Efficiently manage hardware that comes and goes.
- Look at the same piece of hardware in different ways (For example, it should be able to see a printer as a fax machine, scanner, and storage device as well as a printer.)

Linux kernel features added in the past few years have made it possible to drastically change the way that hardware devices are detected and managed. The Udev subsystem dynamically names and creates devices as hardware comes and goes.

If this sounds confusing, don't worry. It's designed to make your life as a Linux user much easier. The result of features built on the kernel is that device handling in Linux has become more automatic and more flexible:

More automatic

For most common hardware, when a hardware device is connected or disconnected, it is automatically detected and identified. Interfaces to access the hardware are added so it is accessible to Linux. Then the fact that the hardware is present (or removed) is passed to the user level, where applications listening for hardware changes are ready to mount the hardware and/or launch an application (such as an image viewer or music player).

More flexible

If you don't like what happens automatically when a hardware item is connected or disconnected, you can change it. For example, features built into GNOME and KDE desktops let you choose what happens when a music CD or data DVD is inserted or when a digital camera is connected. If you prefer that a different program be launched to handle it, you can easily make that change.

The following sections cover several issues related to getting your hardware working properly in Linux. First, it describes how to check information about the hardware components of your system. It then covers how to configure Linux to deal with removable media. Finally, it describes how to use tools for manually loading and working with drivers for hardware that is not detected and loaded properly.

Checking your hardware

When your system boots, the kernel detects your hardware and loads drivers that allow Linux to work with that hardware. Because messages about hardware detection scroll quickly off the screen when you boot, to view potential problem messages you have to redisplay those messages after the system comes up.

There are a few ways to view kernel boot messages after Linux comes up. Any user can run the dmesg command to see what hardware was detected and which drivers were loaded by the kernel at boot time. As new messages are generated by the kernel, those messages are also made available to the dmesg command.

A second way to see boot messages is the journalctl command to show the messages associated with a particular boot instance.

> **NOTE**
>
> After your system is running, many kernel messages are sent to the /var/log/syslog file. So, for example, if you want to see what happens when you plug in a USB drive, you can type tail -f /var/log/syslog and watch as devices and mount points are created. Likewise, you could use the journalctl -f command to follow messages as they come into the systemd journal.

The following is an example of some output from the dmesg command that was trimmed down to show some interesting information:

```
$ dmesg | less
[    0.000000] Linux version 5.3.0-40-generic (buildd@lcy01-
amd64-024) (gcc version 7.4.0 (Ubuntu 7.4.0-1ubuntu1~18.04.1))
#32~18.04.1-Ubuntu SMP Mon Feb 3 14:05:59 UTC 2020 (Ubuntu
5.3.0-40.32~18.04.1-generic 5.3.18)
[    0.000000] Command line: BOOT_IMAGE=/boot/vmlinuz-5.3.0-40-
generic root=UUID=c0e513f0-f840-4174-912d-241d30fd2e26 ro quiet
splash vt.handoff=1
[    0.000000] KERNEL supported cpus:
[    0.000000]   Intel GenuineIntel
[    0.000000]   AMD AuthenticAMD
[    0.000000]   Hygon HygonGenuine
[    0.000000]   Centaur CentaurHauls
[    0.000000]   zhaoxin   Shanghai
[    0.000000] x86/fpu: Supporting XSAVE feature 0x001: 'x87 floating
point registers'
[    0.000000] x86/fpu: Supporting XSAVE feature 0x002: 'SSE
registers'
[    0.000000] x86/fpu: Supporting XSAVE feature 0x004: 'AVX
registers'
[    0.000000] x86/fpu: xstate_offset[2]:   576, xstate_sizes[2]:   256
[    0.000000] x86/fpu: Enabled xstate features 0x7, context size is
832 bytes, using 'compacted' format.
[    0.000000] BIOS-provided physical RAM map:
[    0.000000] BIOS-e820: [mem 0x0000000000000000-
0x000000000009ffff] usable
[    0.000000] BIOS-e820: [mem 0x00000000000a0000-
0x00000000000fffff] reserved
```

From this output, you first see the Linux kernel version, followed by kernel command-line options.

If something goes wrong detecting your hardware or loading drivers, you can refer to this information to see the name and model number of hardware that's not working. Then you can search Linux forums or documentation to try to solve the problem. After your system is up and running, some other commands let you look at detailed information about your computer's hardware. The lspci command lists PCI buses on your computer and devices connected to them. Here's a snippet of output:

```
$ lspci
00:00.2 IOMMU: Advanced Micro Devices, Inc. [AMD] Device 15d1
00:01.1 PCI bridge: Advanced Micro Devices, Inc. [AMD] Device 15d3
00:14.0 SMBus: Advanced Micro Devices, Inc. [AMD] FCH SMBus
Controller (rev 61)
00:14.3 ISA bridge: Advanced Micro Devices, Inc. [AMD] FCH LPC
Bridge (rev 51)
```

Continues

Continued

```
00:18.0 Host bridge: Advanced Micro Devices, Inc. [AMD] Device 15e8
01:00.0 VGA compatible controller: NVIDIA Corporation GT218 [GeForce
210] (rev a2)
01:00.1 Audio device: NVIDIA Corporation High Definition Audio
Controller (rev a1)
02:00.0 USB controller: Advanced Micro Devices, Inc. [AMD] Device
43d5 (rev 01)
02:00.1 SATA controller: Advanced Micro Devices, Inc. [AMD] Device
43c8 (rev 01)
08:00.0 Ethernet controller: Realtek Semiconductor Co., Ltd.
RTL8111/8168/8411 PCI Express Gigabit Ethernet Controller (rev 15)
09:00.0 VGA compatible controller: Advanced Micro Devices, Inc.
[AMD/ATI] Raven Ridge [Radeon Vega Series / Radeon Vega Mobile
Series] (rev c8)
09:00.1 Audio device: Advanced Micro Devices, Inc. [AMD/ATI]
Device 15de
09:00.2 Encryption controller: Advanced Micro Devices, Inc. [AMD]
Device 15df
0a:00.0 SATA controller: Advanced Micro Devices, Inc. [AMD] FCH SATA
Controller [AHCI mode] (rev 61)
```

The host bridge connects the local bus to the other components on the PCI bridge. I cut down the output to show information about the different devices on the system that handle various features: sound (Audio device), flash drives and other USB devices (USB controller), the video display (VGA compatible controller), and wired network cards (Ethernet controller). If you are having trouble getting any of these devices to work, noting the model names and numbers gives you something to feed into your favorite search engine.

To get more verbose output from lspci, add one or more -v options. For example, using lspci -vvv, I received information about my Ethernet controller, including latency and capabilities of the controller.

If you are specifically interested in USB devices, try the lsusb command. By default, lsusb lists information about the computer's USB hubs along with any USB devices connected to the computer's USB ports:

```
$ lsusb
Bus 006 Device 001: ID 1d6b:0003 Linux Foundation 3.0 root hub
Bus 005 Device 006: ID 04f9:0249 Brother Industries, Ltd
Bus 005 Device 005: ID 093a:2510 Pixart Imaging, Inc. Optical Mouse
Bus 005 Device 004: ID 046d:c31c Logitech, Inc. Keyboard K120
Bus 005 Device 003: ID b58e:9e84 Blue Microphones Yeti Stereo
Microphone
Bus 005 Device 002: ID 1a40:0101 Terminus Technology Inc. Hub
Bus 005 Device 001: ID 1d6b:0002 Linux Foundation 2.0 root hub
Bus 004 Device 001: ID 1d6b:0003 Linux Foundation 3.0 root hub
Bus 003 Device 002: ID 046d:081a Logitech, Inc.
Bus 003 Device 001: ID 1d6b:0002 Linux Foundation 2.0 root hub
```

```
Bus 002 Device 001: ID 1d6b:0003 Linux Foundation 3.0 root hub
Bus 001 Device 002: ID 0cf3:9271 Atheros Communications, Inc.
AR9271 802.11n
Bus 001 Device 001: ID 1d6b:0002 Linux Foundation 2.0 root hub
```

From the preceding output, you can see the model of a keyboard (Logitech, Inc. Keyboard K120), mouse (Pixart Imaging, Inc. Optical Mouse), and printer (Brother Industries, Ltd) connected to the computer. As with lspci, you can add one or more -v options to see more details.

To see details about your processor, run the lscpu command. That command gives basic information about your computer's processors:

```
$ lscpu
Architecture:          x86_64
CPU op-mode(s):        32-bit, 64-bit
CPU(s):                4
On-line CPU(s) list:   0-3
Thread(s) per core:    1
Core(s) per socket:    4
...
```

From the sampling of output of lscpu, you can see that this is a 64-bit system (x86-64), it can operate in 32-bit or 64-bit modes, and there are four CPUs.

Managing removable hardware

Linux systems which support full GNOME desktop environments include simple graphical tools for configuring what happens when you attach popular removable devices to the computer. So, with a GNOME desktop running, you simply plug in a USB device or insert a CD or DVD and a window may pop up to deal with that device.

Although different desktop environments share many of the same underlying mechanisms (in particular, Udev) to detect and name removable hardware, they offer different tools for configuring how they are mounted or used. Udev (using the udevd daemon) creates and removes devices (/dev directory) as hardware is added and removed from the computer. Settings that are of interest to someone using a desktop Linux system, however, can be configured with easy-to-use desktop tools.

The Nautilus file manager used with the GNOME desktop lets you define what happens when you attach removable devices or insert removable media into the computer from the File Management Preferences window.

From the GNOME 3 desktop, select Activities and type **Removable Media**. You can also get there by opening the Settings dialog and clicking Devices.

The settings managed in this window relate to how removable media is handled when it is inserted or plugged in. You can control the default behavior when the system detects audio CDs, DVDs, data devices containing audio files, photos, or software. You'll be asked to choose between installed media playing software (like Rhythmbox for music or Shotwell for photos). There's also an Other Media button for devices—like e-book readers—that don't fit into the main categories.

Note that the settings described here are only for the user who is currently logged in. If multiple users have login accounts, each can have their own way of handling removable media.

> **NOTE**
>
> The Totem movie player does not play movie DVDs unless you add extra software to decrypt the DVD. You should look into legal issues and other movie player options (like the popular VLC software) if you want to easily play commercial DVD movies from Linux.

The options to connect regular USB flash drives or hard drives are not listed on this window. If you connect one of those drives to your computer, however, devices are automatically created when you plug them in (named /dev/sda, /dev/sdb, and so on). Any filesystems found on those devices are automatically mounted on /run/media/*username*, and you are prompted if you want to open a Nautilus window to view files on those devices. This is done automatically, so you don't have to do any special configuration to make this happen.

When you are finished with a USB drive, right-click the device's name in the Nautilus file manager window and select Safely Remove Drive. This action unmounts the drive and removes the mount point in the /media/*username* directory. After that, you can safely unplug the USB drive from your computer.

Working with loadable modules

If you have added hardware to your computer that isn't properly detected, you might need to load a module manually for that hardware. Linux comes with a set of commands for loading, unloading, and getting information about hardware modules.

Kernel modules are installed in /lib/modules/ subdirectories. The name of each subdirectory is based on the release number of the kernel. For example, if the kernel were 5.3.0-40, the /lib/modules/5.3.0-40 directory would contain drivers for that kernel. Modules in those directories can then be loaded and unloaded as they are needed.

Commands for listing, loading, unloading, and getting information about modules are available with Linux. The following sections describe how to use those commands.

Listing loaded modules

To see which modules are currently loaded into the running kernel on your computer, use the lsmod command. Consider the following partial example:

```
# lsmod
Module                  Size  Used by
```

```
nls_utf8              16384   0
isofs                 49152   0
uas                   24576   0
usb:storage           73728   1 uas
veth                  28672   0
ebtable_filter        16384   0
ebtables              36864   1 ebtable_filter
ip6table_nat          16384   0
ip6table_filter       16384   0
ip6_tables            32768   2 ip6table_filter,ip6table_nat
iptable_mangle        16384   1
iptable_filter        16384   1
uvcvideo              94208   0
ath9k_htc             77824   0
eeepc_wmi             16384   0
asus_wmi              32768   1 eeepc_wmi
```

This output shows a variety of modules that have been loaded on a Linux system, including one for a network interface card (ath9k_htc).

To find information about any of the loaded modules, use the modinfo command. For example, you can enter the following:

```
# /sbin/modinfo -d ath9k_htc
Atheros driver 802.11n HTC based wireless devices
```

Not all modules have descriptions available and, if nothing is available, no data are returned. In this case, however, the ath9k _ htc module is described as an Atheros driver 802.11n HTC based wireless device. You can also use the -a option to see the author of the module or -n to see the object file representing the module. The author information often has the email address of the driver's creator, so you can contact the author if you have problems or questions about it.

Loading modules

You can (as root user) load any module that has been compiled and installed (to a / lib/modules subdirectory) into your running kernel using the modprobe command. A common reason for loading a module is to use a feature temporarily (such as loading a module to support a special filesystem on some removable media you want to access). Another reason to load a module is to identify that module as one that will be used by a particular piece of hardware that could not be autodetected.

Here is an example of the modprobe command being used to load the parport module, which provides the core functions to share parallel ports with multiple devices:

```
# modprobe parport
```

After parport is loaded, you can load the parport_pc module to define the PC-style ports available through the interface. The parport_pc module lets you optionally define the addresses and IRQ numbers associated with each device sharing the parallel port, as in the following example:

```
# modprobe parport_pc io=0x3bc irq=auto
```

In this example, a device is identified as having an address of 0x3bc, and the IRQ for the device is autodetected.

The modprobe command loads modules temporarily—they disappear at the next reboot. To add the module to your system permanently, add the modprobe command line to one of the startup scripts run at boot time.

Removing modules

Use the rmmod command to remove a module from a running kernel. For example, to remove the module parport _ pc from the current kernel, type the following:

```
# rmmod parport_pc
```

If it's not currently busy, the parport_pc module is removed from the running kernel. If it is busy, try killing any process that might be using the device. Then run rmmod again. Sometimes, the module you are trying to remove depends on other modules that may be loaded. For instance, the usbcore module cannot be unloaded because it is a built-in module:

```
# rmmod usbcore
rmmod: ERROR: Module usbcore is builtin.
```

Instead of using rmmod to remove modules, you could use the modprobe -r command. With modprobe -r, instead of just removing the module you request, you can also remove dependent modules that are not being used by other modules.

Summary

Many features of Linux, especially those that can potentially damage the system or impact other users, require that you gain root privilege. This chapter describes different ways of obtaining root privilege using the sudo or sudo su commands. It also covers some of the key responsibilities of a system administrator and components (configuration files, browser-based tools, and so on) that are critical to a system administrator's work.

The next chapter describes how to install a Linux system. Approaches to installing Linux that are covered in that chapter include how to install from live media and from installation media.

Exercises

Use these exercises to test your knowledge of system administration and to explore information about your system hardware. If you are stuck, solutions to the tasks are shown in Appendix A (although in Linux, there are often multiple ways to complete a task).

1. From a shell as root user (or using `sudo`), enable Cockpit (`cockpit.socket`) using the `systemctl` command.

2. Open your web browser to the Cockpit interface (9090) on your system.

3. Find all files under the `/var/spool` directory that are owned by users other than root and display a long listing of them.

4. Become the root user using the `sudo su` command. To prove that you have root privilege, create an empty or plain text file named `/etc/test.txt`. Exit the shell when you are finished.

5. Log in as a regular user and become root using `sudo su`. Edit the `/etc/sudoers` file to allow a regular user account you've created to have full root privilege via the `sudo` command.

6. As the user to whom you just gave `sudoers` privilege, use the `sudo` command to create a file called `/etc/test2.txt`. Verify that the file is there and owned by the root user.

7. Run the `journalctl -f` command and plug a USB drive into a USB port on your computer. If it doesn't mount automatically, mount it on `/mnt/test`. In a second terminal, unmount the device and remove it, continuing to watch the output from `journalctl -f`.

8. Run a command to see what USB devices are connected to your computer.

9. Pretend that you added a TV card to your computer, but the module needed to use it (`bttv`) was not properly detected and loaded. Load the `bttv` module yourself, and then look to see that it was loaded. Were other modules loaded with it?

10. Remove the `bttv` module along with any other modules that were loaded with it. List your modules to make sure that this was done.

Installing Linux

IN THIS CHAPTER

Choosing an installation method

Installing a single- or multi-boot system

Performing a live media installation of Ubuntu

Understanding cloud-based installations

Partitioning the disk for installation

Understanding the GRUB boot loader

The basic installation process for Linux desktops has become a fairly easy thing to navigate—if you're starting with a computer that is up to spec (hard disk, RAM, CPU, and so on) and you don't mind totally erasing your hard drive. With cloud computing and virtualization, installation can be even simpler. It allows you to bypass traditional installation and spin a Linux system up or down within a few minutes by adding metadata to prebuilt images.

But peeking just a little bit below the surface will reveal vast layers of complexity for installing to alternative architectures like 32-bit or ARM chipsets, multi-boot configurations, or network-based installations. It wouldn't make sense to try to cover all the possible permutations and combinations here. The screen shot from Ubuntu's website displayed in Figure 9.1 shows just how many ways there are to consume the OS.

Instead, we'll start off with a simple desktop installation on a physical computer using removable media and then see how it works for a straightforward server installation. We'll then introduce, in more general terms, each of the installation options that can get you going for each category out of the vast Linux functionality spectrum.

In Chapters 27, "Deploying Linux to the Public Cloud," and 28, "Automating Apps and Infrastructure with Ansible," I'll also describe ways of installing or deploying a virtual machine on a Linux KVM host or in a cloud environment.

FIGURE 9.1

A list of the many architectures on which Ubuntu can be installed

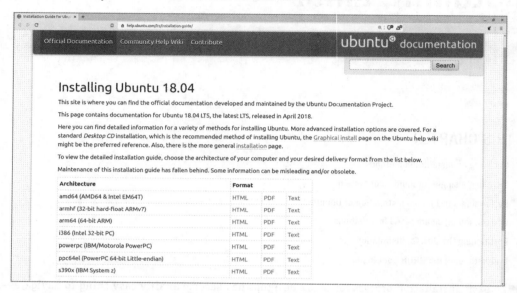

To try all this along with me, you should have a computer in front of you that you don't mind totally erasing. You could also create a virtual machine using software like Oracle's Virtual-Box. When prompted for a startup disk for your new VM, point VirtualBox to the Ubuntu ISO image you've downloaded. A third alternative would be to use a computer that has another operating system such as Windows already installed, as long as there is enough unused disk space available outside of that operating system. That method would, however, require you to accept the risk of losing all your existing data should the installation process go wrong. If you're successful with this third method, on the other hand, you'll find yourself with a machine that can boot to either Ubuntu or the original OS anytime you like.

Choosing a Computer

You can get a Linux distribution that runs on handheld devices or an old PC in your closet with as little as 24MB of RAM and a 486 processor. To have a good desktop PC experience with Linux, however, you should consider what you want to be able to do with Linux when you are choosing your computer.

Be sure to consider the basic specifications that you need for a PC-type computer to run Ubuntu.

A 2GHz dual-core processor is the minimum for a desktop installation. For older applications, a 32-bit processor is fine (x86). But to ensure compatibility in the modern application world—and make full use of systems with more than 3GB of RAM installed—you should look for 64-bit (X86_64) architectures.

> **NOTE**
>
> If you have a less powerful computer than the minimum described here, consider using a lightweight Linux distribution. Lightweight Ubuntu distributions include Peppermint OS (www.peppermintos.com/) and Lubuntu (www.lubuntu.net/).

RAM

Ubuntu recommends at least 4GB of RAM for desktop installations.

DVD or USB drive

You need to be able to boot up the installation process from a DVD or USB drive. If you can't boot from a DVD or USB drive, there are ways to start the installation from a hard disk or by using a PXE install. After the installation process is started, more software can sometimes be retrieved from different locations (over the network or from hard disk, for example).

> **NOTE**
>
> PXE (pronounced pixie) stands for Preboot eXecution Environment . You can boot a client computer from a Network Interface Card (NIC) that is PXE-enabled. If a PXE boot server is available on the network, it can provide everything a client computer needs to boot. What it boots can be an installer. So, with a PXE boot, it is possible to do a complete Linux installation without a CD, DVD, or any other physical medium.

Disk space

Ubuntu recommends at least 25GB of disk space for an average desktop installation, although installations can range (depending on which packages you choose to install) from 600MB (for a minimal server with no GUI install) to 7GB (to install all packages from the installation DVD). Consider the amount of data that you need to store. Although documents can consume very little space, videos can consume massive amounts of space.

If you're not sure about your computer hardware, there are a few ways to check what you have. If you are running Windows, the System Properties window can show you the processor you have as well as the amount of RAM that's installed. As an alternative, with a live session running, open a shell and type `dmesg | less` to see a listing of hardware as it is detected on your system.

With your hardware in place, you can now install Linux, as described in the following section.

Installing Ubuntu Desktop

Users of Ubuntu and many of its derivative distros have been able to enjoy a clear and intuitive installation process for some years now. The wizard—officially called Ubiquity—does a great job getting the basic configuration details out of the way quickly, so the actual installation can begin before you finish setting up your account and location details. Figure 9.2 shows how a live Ubuntu session presents the initial choice between trying and installing Ubuntu. Note how it includes the option of choosing the language with which you want to interact with your computer.

FIGURE 9.2

The initial dialog for starting your installation

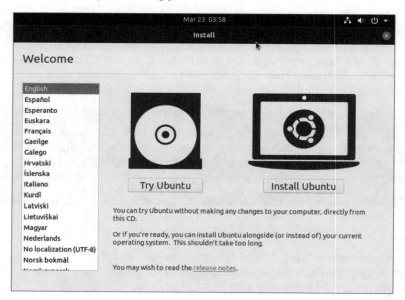

You'll then choose the keyboard layout you prefer. This setting, shown in Figure 9.3, will also determine some elements of system functionality, like the spell checkers used by office tools.

You'll then see the dialog shown in Figure 9.4 asking you how much software you'd like included in the initial installation process. If you're working with limited storage capacity and haven't any need for games and a full office suite (like LibreOffice), then you'll probably go with the Minimal installation. Checking "Download updates while installing Ubuntu" can save time later.

FIGURE 9.3

Select the keyboard layout you'll use.

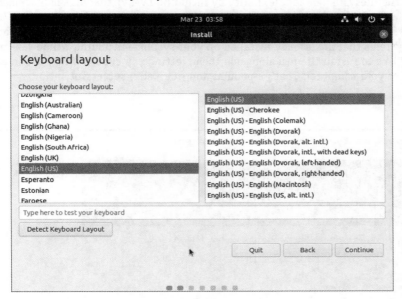

FIGURE 9.4

Choose the software you want installed.

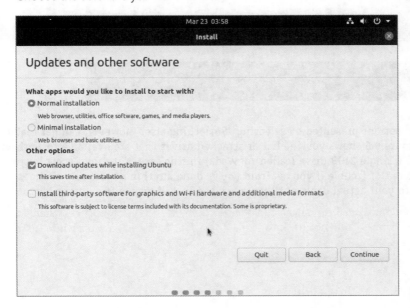

The "Installation type" page (shown in Figure 9.5) confronts you with some tough decisions. For a simple desktop environment on brand new hardware, you're safe going with "Erase disk and install Ubuntu." You can choose to enhance the security of your data by encrypting the filesystem or add flexibility by including LVM virtual disk management. You can, by the way, always change your mind and add encryption later, but applying LVM to an existing filesystem may not be possible. Ubuntu will often automatically detect other operating systems that are already installed on your system—including Windows—and ask you if you'd like to install Ubuntu alongside them, letting you choose which to run each time you boot your computer. That's a popular and (normally) successful option.

FIGURE 9.5

Choose how you want your storage drives configured.

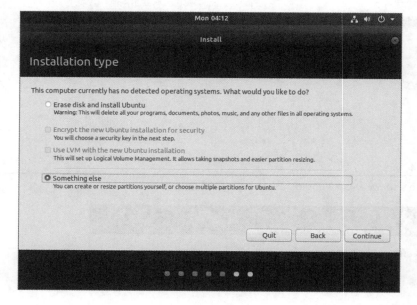

The manual options presented by selecting "Something else," however, can get really complicated. Figure 9.6 shows you the list of attached drives that are available to work with. There's only a single 21GB drive (called /dev/sda) in this case. Note the Revert button that can get you out of trouble if you're afraid you've done anything wrong. No changes will be written to your actual drive until you click the Install Now button at the bottom of the dialog.

FIGURE 9.6

The main dialog where you can manually edit your disks and partitions

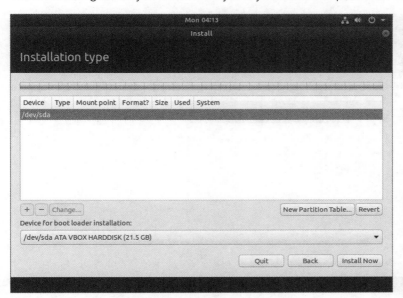

The New Partition Table button in the menu that'll appear if you go with "Something else" will let you edit your drive by dividing it into smaller partitions and assigning each partition a filesystem mount point and type. The example shown in Figure 9.7 will use the Ext4 type (a popular choice that's often used by default) and have the partition mounted at run time as the /boot directory. In the past, it was fairly common to keep /boot separate within its own partition, but larger disk sizes and, in particular, larger kernel images, have made this less attractive.

Figure 9.8 shows how a completed partition configuration may look. /boot is on a relatively small partition (1.5GB or so), while both the root (/) and /var partitions share the rest of the disk space evenly. If the applications you plan to use extensively are likely to generate a lot of data—saving it to directories within the /var hierarchy—then it can make sense to protect your root filesystem from being overwhelmed by disk bloat from /var by maintaining them in separate partitions.

Of course, in our age of cheap and available storage space, you're not likely to ever need to work with a 21GB drive, but this example does illustrate the principle. We'll talk a bit more about partitions later in this chapter. Note that Ubuntu will automatically create a system partition mounted to /boot/efi using the vfat filesystem to accommodate for UEFI firmware.

FIGURE 9.7

Creating a separate /boot partition

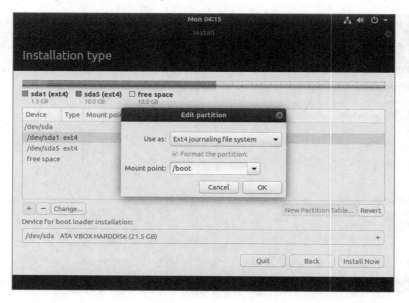

FIGURE 9.8

A complete manual partition configuration

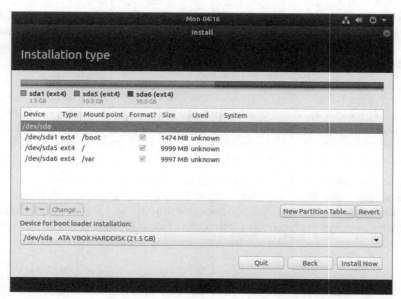

Once you pull the trigger on your partition setup, the installation will leap into life. The remaining account and location information Ubuntu needs will be entered within a couple of dialogs as all that happens. But you can trust me: the way things work these days is exponentially simpler and more relaxing than the typical desktop installation experience of a decade or more ago.

Installing Ubuntu Server

The biggest difference between the image used to install Ubuntu desktop and the one used for Ubuntu server is the GUI and GUI-based applications (like web browsers and LibreOffice): desktop comes with them and server does not. This makes the server image a great deal smaller and, consequently, allows it to get its work done much faster. But because server doesn't come with all those fancy graphic drivers, we won't have our familiar user interface to help us through the installation process.

Still, it'll be the differences between the configuration details used by server as opposed to desktop that'll interest us the most right now. For instance, as you can see in Figure 9.9, you'll often be asked to choose between a regular server installation and either one of two versions of the MaaS cloud infrastructure server.

FIGURE 9.9

Select a regular or MaaS server configuration.

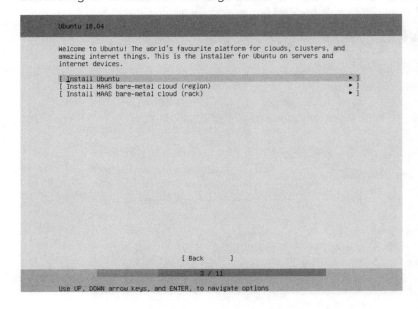

I can already hear you asking: "What's MaaS?" After all, at this point at least, it's not exactly a widely used acronym like IaaS (Infrastructure as a Service) or PaaS (Platform as a Service). So MaaS stands for Metal as a Service and, as Ubuntu's corporate sponsor Canonical explains it (on its www.maas.io site), it's a tool for automating the provisioning of physical servers in much the same way as a cloud platform might provision fleets of virtual machines.

MaaS comes in two flavors:

- Region (`regiond`) controllers that are configured to provide high-availability networking and provisioning services by way of a tiered system of rack controllers.
- Rack (`rackd`) controllers, using resources provided from the upstream region controllers, respond to requests for managing the servers in their care.

MaaS lets you fully automate the management of Ubuntu, CentOS, RHEL, and Windows servers in your system. If you have no clue what that's all about, then you can safely assume you don't need it and go with the Ubuntu option in this dialog.

Subsequent pages in the server installation process will offer you the chance to configure a network interface—including how Ubuntu will acquire an IP address (meaning, either through a local DHCP server or a manually defined static address). Figure 9.10 shows the drop-down menu allowing you to toggle between DHCP and static IP addressing.

FIGURE 9.10

Choosing Manual IPv4 configurations lets you define a static IP address.

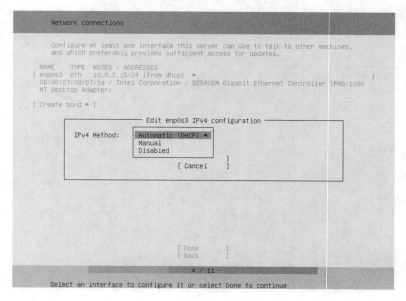

The archive mirror menu—shown in Figure 9.11—lets you tell Ubuntu where you'd prefer your software downloads to originate. Ubuntu will try to find a repository that's geographically close to you, but you might have, say, a repo that's managed by your organization that you need to use instead.

FIGURE 9.11

Selecting a mirror for downloading software archives.

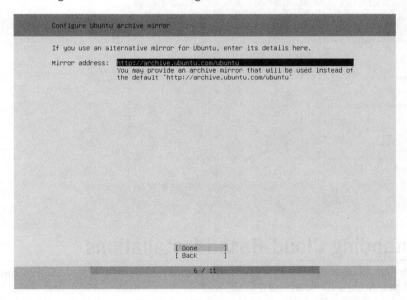

Configuration pages that follow will let you set up your drives and partitions just as you would using the desktop GUI. What is shown in Figure 9.12, however, is specific to servers. Ubuntu offers you an exhaustive list of packages that can be installed right from the start through the Snap software package management system. These choices include Canonical's version of the Kubernetes ("microk8s") container management system, a Nextcloud document collaboration server, Docker, and even public cloud command-line interfaces (like Amazon's AWS-CLI). These options can really shorten the setup process once your server is running. You use the up and down arrow keys to highlight an item and press the Space key to select or deselect it.

When that's done, you'll be all set to finish your installation.

9

FIGURE 9.12

Select software packages for popular server workloads.

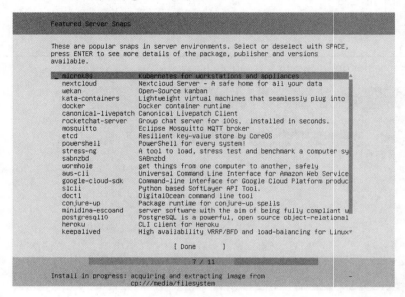

```
Featured Server Snaps

These are popular snaps in server environments. Select or deselect with SPACE,
press ENTER to see more details of the package, publisher and versions
available.

  microk8s             Kubernetes for workstations and appliances
  nextcloud            Nextcloud Server - A safe home for all your data
  wekan                Open-Source kanban
  kata-containers      Lightweight virtual machines that seamlessly plug into
  docker               Docker container runtime
  canonical-livepatch  Canonical Livepatch Client
  rocketchat-server    Group chat server for 100s, installed in seconds.
  mosquitto            Eclipse Mosquitto MQTT broker
  etcd                 Resilient key-value store by CoreOS
  powershell           PowerShell for every system!
  stress-ng            A tool to load, stress test and benchmark a computer sy
  sabnzbd              SABnzbd
  wormhole             get things from one computer to another, safely
  aws-cli              Universal Command Line Interface for Amazon Web Service
  google-cloud-sdk     Command-line interface for Google Cloud Platform produc
  slcli                Python based SoftLayer API Tool.
  doctl                DigitalOcean command line tool
  conjure-up           Package runtime for conjure-up spells
  minidlna-escoand     server software with the aim of being fully compliant w
  postgresql10         PostgreSQL is a powerful, open source object-relational
  heroku               CLI client for Heroku
  keepalived           High availability VRRP/BFD and load-balancing for Linux

                           [ Done      ]

                              7 / 11

Install in progress: acquiring and extracting image from
                     cp:///media/filesystem
```

Understanding Cloud-Based Installations

When you install a Linux system on a physical computer, the installer can see the computer's hard drive, network interfaces, CPUs, and other hardware components. When you install Linux in a cloud environment, those physical components are abstracted into a pool of resources. So, to install a Linux distribution in an Amazon EC2, Google Compute Engine, or OpenStack cloud platform, you need to go about things differently.

The common way of installing Linux in a cloud is to start with a file that is an image of an installed Linux system. Typically, that image includes all of the files needed by a basic, running Linux system. Metadata is added to that image from a configuration file or by filling out a form from a cloud controller that creates and launches the operating system as a virtual machine.

The kind of information added to the image might include a particular hostname, root password, and new user account. You might also want to choose to have a specific amount of disk space, a particular network configuration, and a certain number of CPU processors and RAM.

Methods for installing Linux in a cloud environment are discussed in Chapter 27, "Deploying Linux to the Public Cloud."

Installing Linux in the Enterprise

If you were managing dozens, hundreds, even thousands of Linux systems in a large enterprise, it would be terribly inefficient to have to go to each computer to type and click through each installation. Fortunately, you can automate installation in such a way that all you need to do is to turn on a computer and boot from the computer's network interface card to get your desired Linux installation.

There are many other ways to launch a Linux installation and many ways to complete an installation. The following descriptions briefly step through the installation process and describe ways of changing that process along the way:

Launch the installation medium.

You can launch an installation from any medium that you can boot from a computer: CD, DVD, USB drive, hard disk, or network interface card with PXE support. The computer goes through its boot order and looks at the master boot record on the physical medium or looks for a PXE server on the network.

Automate remote server provisioning.

Boot options (described later in this chapter) can be executed remotely using systems like Canonical's MaaS (described earlier). Automated control systems can closely manage the full lifecycle of physical server or desktop machines, allowing administrators to define, provision, allocate, and, when necessary, decommission machines.

Find software packages.

Software packages don't have to be on the installation medium. This allows you to launch an installation from a boot medium that contains only a kernel and initial RAM disk. From scripts or from an option you add manually to an installer/provisioner, you can identify the location of the repository holding the packages. That location can be a local CD (cdrom), website (https), FTP site (ftp), NFS share (nfs), NFS ISO (nfsiso), or local disk (hd).

Exploring Common Installation Topics

Some of the installation topics touched upon earlier in this chapter require further explanation for you to be able to implement them fully. Read through the following sections to get a greater understanding of specific installation topics.

Upgrading or installing from scratch

If you have an earlier version of Ubuntu already installed on your computer, Ubuntu can, in some cases, offer a direct upgrade option—in particular between long-term support (LTS) releases.

Upgrading lets you move a Linux system from one major release to the next.

TIP

Installing Linux from scratch goes faster than an upgrade. It also results in a cleaner Linux system. So, if you don't need the data on your system (or if you have a backup of your data), it often makes more sense to do a fresh installation. Then you can restore your data to a freshly installed system.

Dual booting

It is possible to have multiple operating systems installed on the same computer. One way to do this is by having multiple partitions on a hard disk and/or multiple hard disks and then installing different operating systems on different partitions. As long as the boot loader contains boot information for each of the installed operating systems, you can choose which one to run at boot time.

CAUTION

Although tools for resizing Windows partitions and setting up multi-boot systems have improved in recent years, there is still some risk of losing data on Windows/Linux dual-boot systems. Different operating systems often have different views of partition tables and master boot records that can cause your machine to become unbootable (at least temporarily) or lose data permanently. Always back up your data before you try to resize a Windows filesystem to make space for Linux.

If the computer you are using already has a Windows system on it, quite possibly the entire hard disk is devoted to Windows. Although you can always run a live Linux session without touching the hard disk, to do a more permanent installation, you'll want to find disk space outside of the Windows installation. There are a few ways to do this:

Add a hard disk.   Instead of messing with your Windows partition, you can simply add a hard disk and devote it to Linux.

Resize your Windows partition.   If you have available space on a Windows partition, you can shrink that partition so that free space is available on the disk to devote to Linux. Commercial tools such as Acronis Disk Director (www.acronis.com/en-us/personal/disk-manager) are available to resize your disk partitions and set up a workable boot manager. Some Linux distributions (particularly bootable Linux distributions used as rescue media) include a tool called GParted (which includes software from the Linux-NTFS project for resizing Windows NTFS partitions).

NOTE

Type `apt-get install gparted` to install GParted. Run `gparted` as root to start it.

Before you try to resize your Windows partition, you might need to defragment it. To defragment your disk on some Windows systems so that all your used space is put in order on the disk, open My Computer, right-click your hard disk icon (typically C:), select Properties, click Tools, and select Defragment Now.

Defragmenting your disk can be a fairly long process. The result of defragmentation is that all of the data on your disk are contiguous, creating lots of contiguous free space at the end of the partition. Sometimes, you have to complete the following special tasks to make this true:

- If the Windows swap file is not moved during defragmentation, you must remove it. Then, after you defragment your disk again and resize it, you need to restore the swap file. To remove the swap file, open the Control Panel, open the System icon, click the Performance tab, and select Virtual Memory. To disable the swap file, click Disable Virtual Memory.

- If your DOS partition has hidden files that are on the space you are trying to free up, you need to find them. In some cases, you can't delete them. In other cases, such as swap files created by a program, you can safely delete those files. This is a bit tricky because some files should not be deleted, such as DOS system files. You can use the `attrib -s -h` command from the root directory to deal with hidden files.

After your disk is defragmented, you can use commercial tools described earlier (Acronis Disk Director) to repartition your hard disk to make space for Linux. Or, you can use the Open source alternative GParted.

After you have cleared enough disk space to install Linux (see the disk space requirements described earlier in this chapter), you can install Ubuntu. As you set up your boot loader during installation, you can identify Windows, Linux, and any other bootable partitions so that you can select which one to boot when you start your computer.

Installing Linux to run virtually

Using virtualization technology such as KVM, VMware, VirtualBox, or Xen, you can configure your computer to run multiple operating systems simultaneously. Typically, you have a host operating system running (such as your Linux or Windows desktop), and then you configure guest operating systems to run within that environment.

If you have a Windows system, you can use commercial VMware products to run Linux on your Windows desktop. Get a trial of VMware Workstation (www.vmware.com/try-vmware) to see if you like it. Then run your installed virtual guests with the free VMware Player. With a full-blown version of VMware Workstation, you can run multiple distributions at the same time.

Open source virtualization products that are available with Linux systems include VirtualBox (www.virtualbox.org), Xen (www.xenproject.org), and KVM (www.linux-kvm.org). See Chapter 28, "Automating Apps and Infrastructure with Ansible," for information on installing Linux as a virtual machine on a Linux KVM host.

9

And don't forget that Windows 10 allows you to run Linux shell sessions on the Windows desktop through the Windows Subsystem for Linux without the need for external virtualization software. See docs.microsoft.com/en-us/windows/wsl/install-win10.

Using installation boot options

When the Linux kernel launches at boot time, boot options provided on the kernel command line modify the behavior of the installation process. By typing "**e**" within the GRUB boot menu with a particular Linux image selected, you can edit the default boot options to direct how the installation behaves. Figure 9.13 shows a GRUB menu with options to boot from one of two kernel versions and from a recovery mode version of each. You can force the GRUB menu to appear by pressing the Shift key early in the boot process.

The line identifying the kernel might look something like the following:

```
vmlinuz initrd=initrd.img ...
```

vmlinuz is the compressed kernel and initrd.img is the initial RAM disk (containing modules and other tools needed to start the installer). To add more options, just type them at the end of that line and press Enter.

FIGURE 9.13

A typical GRUB menu accessible at boot time

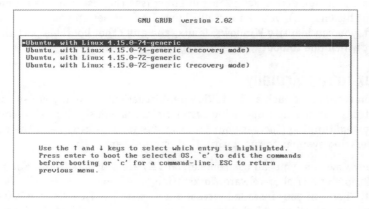

Boot options for disabling features

Sometimes, a Linux installation fails because the computer has some nonfunctioning or unsupported hardware. Often, you can get around those issues by passing options at boot time (through the GRUB menu, as in the previous section) that do such things as disable selected hardware when you need to select your own driver. Table 9.1 provides some examples.

TABLE 9.1 Boot Options for Disabling Features

INSTALLER OPTION	TELLS SYSTEM
nofirewire	Not to load support for Firewire devices
nodma	Not to load DMA support for hard disks
noide	Not to load support for IDE devices
nompath	Not to enable support for multipath devices
noparport	Not to load support for parallel ports
nopcmcia	Not to load support for PCMCIA controllers
noprobe	Not to probe hardware; instead prompt user for drivers
noscsi	Not to load support for SCSI devices
nousb	Not to load support for USB devices
noipv6	Not to enable IPV6 networking
nonet	Not to probe for network devices
numa-off	To disable the Non-Uniform Memory Access (NUMA) for AMD64 architecture
acpi=off	To disable the Advanced Configuration and Power Interface (ACPI)

Boot options for video problems

If you are having trouble with your video display, you can specify video settings as noted in Table 9.2.

TABLE 9.2 Boot Options for Video Problems

BOOT OPTION	TELLS SYSTEM
xdriver=vesa	Use standard vesa video driver
resolution=1024x768	Choose exact resolution to use
nofb	Don't use the VGA 16 framebuffer driver
skipddc	Don't probe DDC of the monitor (the probe can hang the installer)
graphical	Force a graphical installation

Boot options for special installation types

By default, installation runs in graphical mode with you sitting at the console answering questions. If you have a text-only console, or if the GUI isn't working properly, you can run an installation in plain-text mode: by typing **text**, you cause the installation to run in text mode.

If you want to start installation on one computer, but answer the installation questions from another computer, you can enable a VNC (virtual network computing) installation. After you start this type of installation, you can go to another system and open a `vnc viewer`, giving the viewer the address of the installation machine (such as `192.168.0.99:1`). Table 9.3 provides the necessary commands, along with what they tell the system to do.

TABLE 9.3   Boot Options for VNC Installations

Boot Option	Tells System	
vnc	Run installation as a VNC server	
vncconnect=*host name[:port]*	Connect to VNC client hostname and optional port	
vncpassword=*password*	Client uses password (at least 8 characters) to connect to installer	

Using specialized storage

In large enterprise computing environments, it is common to store the operating system and data outside of the local computer. Instead, some special storage device beyond the local hard disk is identified to the installer, and that storage device (or devices) can be used during installation.

Once identified, the storage devices that you indicate during installation can be used the same way that local disks are used. You can partition them and assign a structure (filesystem, swap space, and so on) or leave them alone and simply mount them where you want the data to be available.

The following types of specialized storage devices can be configured to work with Ubuntu installations:

Firmware RAID

A firmware RAID device is a type of device that has hooks in the BIOS, allowing it to be used to boot the operating system, if you choose.

Multipath devices

As the name implies, multipath devices provide multiple paths between the computer and its storage devices. These paths are aggregated, so these devices look like a single device to the system using them, while the underlying technology provides improved performance, redundancy, or both. Connections can be provided by iSCSI or Fibre Channel over Ethernet (FCoE) devices.

Other SAN devices

Any device representing a Storage Area Network (SAN).

While configuring these specialized storage devices is beyond the scope of this book, know that if you are working in an enterprise where iSCSI and FCoE devices are available, you can configure your Linux system to use them at installation time. You need the following types of information to do this:

iSCSI devices

Have your storage administrator provide you with the target IP address of the iSCSI device and the type of discovery authentication needed to use the device. The iSCSI device may require credentials.

Fibre Channel over Ethernet Devices (FCoE)   For FCoE, you need to know the network interface that is connected to your FCoE switch. You can search that interface for available FCoE devices.

Partitioning hard drives

The hard disk (or disks) on your computer provide the permanent storage area for your data files, applications programs, and the operating system itself. *Partitioning* is the act of dividing a disk into logical areas that can be worked with separately. With Linux there are several reasons you may want to have multiple partitions:

Multiple operating systems

If you install Linux on a PC that already has a Windows operating system, you may want to keep both operating systems on the computer. For all practical purposes, each operating system must exist on a completely separate partition. When your computer boots, you can choose which system to run.

Multiple partitions within an operating system

To protect their entire operating system from running out of disk space, people often assign separate partitions to different areas of the Linux filesystem. For example, if / home and /var were assigned to separate partitions, then a gluttonous user who fills up the /home partition wouldn't prevent logging daemons from continuing to write to log files in the /var/log directory.

Multiple partitions also make doing certain kinds of backups (such as an image backup) easier. For example, an image backup of /home would be much faster (and probably more useful) than an image backup of the root filesystem (/).

Different filesystem types

Different kinds of filesystems have different structures. Filesystems of different types must be on their own partitions. Also, you might need different filesystems to have different mount options for special features (such as read-only or user quotas). In most Linux systems, you need at least one filesystem type for the root of the filesystem (/) and one for your swap area. Filesystems on DVD use the iso9660 filesystem type.

> **TIP**
>
> When you create partitions for Linux, you usually assign the filesystem type as Linux native (using the ext2, ext3, ext4, or xfs type on most Linux systems). If the applications that you are running require particularly long filenames, large file sizes, or many inodes (each file consumes an inode), you may want to choose a different filesystem type.

Ubuntu lets you partition your hard disk during the installation process using graphical partitioning tools. Here are some quick insights into the dark art of Linux partitioning.

Understanding different partition types

Ubuntu gives you the option of selecting different partition types when you partition your hard disk during installation. Partition types include the following:

Linux partitions

Use this option to create a partition for an ext2, ext3, or ext4 filesystem type that is added directly to a partition on your hard disk (or other storage medium). The xfs filesystem type can also be used on a Linux partition.

LVM partitions

Create an LVM partition if you plan to create or add to an LVM volume group. LVMs give you more flexibility in growing, shrinking, and moving partitions later than regular partitions do.

RAID partitions

Create two or more RAID partitions to create a RAID array. These partitions should be on separate disks to create an effective RAID array. RAID arrays can help improve performance, reliability, or both as those features relate to reading, writing, and storing your data.

Swap partitions

Create a swap partition to extend the amount of virtual memory available on your system.

Refer to Chapter 12, "Managing Disks and Filesystems," for further information on configuring disk partitions.

Tips for creating partitions

Changing your disk partitions to handle multiple operating systems can be very tricky, in part because each operating system has its own ideas about how partitioning information should be handled as well as different tools for doing it. Here are some tips to help you get it right:

- If you are creating a dual-boot system, particularly for a Windows system, try to install the Windows operating system first after partitioning your disk. Otherwise, the Windows installation may make the Linux partitions inaccessible.

- The fdisk man page recommends that you use partitioning tools that come with an operating system to create partitions for that operating system. For example, the Windows fdisk knows how to create partitions that Windows will like, and the Linux fdisk will happily make your Linux partitions. After your hard disk is set up for dual boot, however, you should probably not go back to Windows-only partitioning tools. Use Linux fdisk or a product made for multi-boot systems (such as Acronis Disk Director).

- A master boot record (MBR) partition table can contain four primary partitions, one of which can be marked to contain 184 logical drives. On a GPT partition table, you can have a maximum of 128 primary partitions on most operating systems, including Linux. You typically won't need nearly that many partitions. If you need more partitions, use LVM and create as many logical volumes as you like.

If you are using Linux as a desktop system, you probably don't need lots of different partitions. However, some very good reasons exist for having multiple partitions for Linux systems that are shared by lots of users or are public web servers or file servers. These can include:

Protection from attacks

Denial-of-service attacks sometimes take actions that try to fill up your hard disk. If public areas, such as /var, are on separate partitions, a successful attack can fill up a partition without shutting down the whole computer. Because /var is the default location for web and FTP servers, and is expected to hold lots of data, entire hard disks often are assigned to the /var filesystem alone.

Protection from corrupted filesystems

If you have only one filesystem (/), its corruption can cause the whole Linux system to be damaged. Corruption of a smaller partition can be easier to fix and often allows the computer to stay in service while the correction is made.

Table 9.4 lists some directories that you may want to consider making into separate filesystem partitions.

TABLE 9.4   Assigning Partitions to Particular Directories

DIRECTORY	EXPLANATION
/boot	Sometimes, the BIOS in older PCs can access only the first 1024 cylinders of your hard disk. To make sure that the information in the /boot directory is accessible to the BIOS, many older systems created a separate disk partition for /boot. This is no longer a common design practice.
/usr	This directory structure contains most of the applications and utilities available to Linux users. The original theory was that if /usr were on a separate partition, you could mount that filesystem as read-only after the operating system had been installed. This would prevent attackers from replacing or removing important system applications with their own versions that may cause security problems. A separate /usr partition is also useful if you have diskless workstations on your local network. Using NFS, you can share /usr over the network with those workstations.
/var	Your FTP (/var/ftp) and web server (/var/www) directories are, by default in many Linux systems, stored under /var. Having a separate /var partition can prevent an attack on those facilities from corrupting or filling up your entire hard disk.
/home	Because your user account directories are located in this directory, having a separate /home account can prevent a reckless user from filling up the entire hard disk. It also conveniently separates user data from your operating system (for easy backups or new installs). Often, /home is created as an LVM logical volume, so it can grow in size as user demands increase. It may also be assigned user quotas to limit disk use.
/tmp	Protecting /tmp from the rest of the hard disk by placing it on a separate partition can ensure that applications that need to write to temporary files in /tmp can complete their processing, even if the rest of the disk fills up.

9

Although people who use Linux systems rarely see a need for lots of partitions, those who maintain and occasionally have to recover large systems are thankful when the system they need to fix has several partitions. Multiple partitions can limit the effects of deliberate damage (such as denial-of-service attacks), problems from errant users, and accidental filesystem corruption.

Using the GRUB 2 boot loader

We saw GRUB in action earlier in the chapter when discussing passing instructions as the Linux kernel loaded at boot time. Here we'll spend just a moment or two taking a deeper look at the way it works. First of all, GRUB stands for "GNU GRand Unified Bootloader." Next, GRUB's primary job is to find and start the operating system you want. If you're using GRUB 2, then it stands to reason that there must once have been a GRUB version 1. That, of course, is correct. But these days you'll have to look far and wide to find a modern system that starts up with the help of that legacy version of GRUB.

> **NOTE**
>
> SYSLINUX is another boot loader that you will encounter with Linux systems. The SYSLINUX boot loaders are not typically used for installed Linux systems. However, SYSLINUX is commonly used as the boot loader for bootable Linux CDs and DVDs. SYSLINUX is particularly good for booting ISO9660 CD images (isolinux) and USB sticks (syslinux) and for working on older hardware or for PXE booting (pxelinux) a system over the network.

GRUB's configuration file is named /boot/grub/grub.cfg or /etc/grub-efi.cfg (for systems booted with EFI).

Here are some things you should know about the grub.cfg file:

- Instead of editing grub.cfg by hand, grub.cfg is generated automatically from the contents of the /etc/default/grub file and the /etc/grub.d/ directory. You should modify or add to those files to configure GRUB yourself.
- The grub.cfg file can contain scripting syntax, including such things as functions, loops, and variables.
- Device names needed to identify the location of kernels and initial RAM disks can be more reliably identified using labels or universally unique identifiers (UUIDs). This prevents the possibility of a disk device such as /dev/sda being changed to /dev/sdb when you add a new disk (which would result in the kernel not being found).

There are many, many more features of GRUB that you can learn about if you want to dig deeper into your system's boot loader. The best documentation for GRUB is available by typing **info grub** at the shell. The info entry for GRUB provides lots of information for booting different operating systems, writing your own configuration files, working with GRUB image files, setting GRUB environment variables, and working with other GRUB features.

Summary

When you install Ubuntu, you need to deal with issues of disk partitioning, boot options, and configuring boot loaders.

In this chapter, you stepped through installation procedures for Ubuntu desktop and server deployments. You learned how deploying Linux in cloud environments can differ from traditional installation methods by combining metadata with prebuilt base operating system image files to run on large pools of compute resources.

The chapter also covered special installation topics, including using boot options and disk partitioning. With your Linux system now installed, Chapter 10, "Getting and Managing Software," describes how to begin managing the software on your Linux system.

Exercises

Use these exercises to test your knowledge of installing Linux. I recommend that you do these exercises on a computer that has no operating system or data on it that you would fear losing (in other words, one you don't mind erasing). If you have a computer that allows you to install virtual systems, that is a safe way to do these exercises as well. If you are stuck, solutions to the tasks are shown in Appendix A (although in Linux, there are often multiple ways to complete a task).

1. Start installing Ubuntu desktop from an Ubuntu ISO on VirtualBox using as many of the default options as possible.

2. After you have completely installed Ubuntu, update all of the packages on the system.

3. Start installing an Ubuntu server image. Complete the installation in any way you choose.

4. Start installing from an Ubuntu server image (using VirtualBox if you like) and set the disk partitioning as follows: a 1024MB /boot, / (6G), /var (2G), and /home (2G). Leave the rest as unused space. But before beginning, read the related caution that is described here.

> **CAUTION**
>
> Completing Exercise 4 on a physical device ultimately deletes all content on your existing hard disk. If you just want to use this exercise to practice partitioning, you can reboot your computer before clicking Accept Changes at the very end of this procedure without harming your hard disk. If you go forward and partition your disk, assume that all data that you have not explicitly changed has been deleted.

9

Getting and Managing Software

IN THIS CHAPTER

Installing software from the desktop

Installing and managing software using the APT system

Installing and managing software using the dpkg system

Installing software in the enterprise

I n Ubuntu, you don't need to know much about how software is packaged and managed to get the software you want. It has excellent software installation tools that automatically point to huge software repositories. Just a few clicks and you're using the software in little more time than it takes to download it.

The fact that Linux software management is so easy these days is a credit to the Linux community, which has worked diligently to create packaging formats, complex installation tools, and high-quality software packages. Not only is it easy to get the software, but after it's installed, it's easy to manage, query, update, and remove it.

This chapter begins by describing how to install software in Ubuntu using the new software graphical installation tool. If you are just installing a few desktop applications on your own desktop system, you may not need much more than that and occasional security updates.

To dig deeper into managing Linux software, next we'll describe what makes up Linux software packages, the underlying software management components, and commands (apt and dpkg) for managing software.

Managing Software on the Desktop

The Ubuntu Software window offers an intuitive way of choosing and installing desktop applications that does not align with typical Linux installation practices. With the Software window, the smallest software component you install is an application.

Figure 10.1 shows an example of the Software window.

FIGURE 10.1

Install and manage software packages from the Software window.

To get to the Software window in Ubuntu, select Activities, then type **ubuntu software**, and press Enter. Using the Software window is the best way to install desktop-oriented applications, such as word processors, games, graphics editors, and educational applications.

From the Software window, you can select the applications that you want to install from the Editor's Picks group (a handful of popular applications), choose from categories of applications (Audio & Video, Games, Graphics & Photography, and so on), or search by application name or description. Select the Install button to have the Software window download and install all of the software packages needed to make the application work.

Other features of this window let you see all installed applications (Installed tab) or view a list of applications that have updated packages available for you to install (Updates tab). If you want to remove an installed application, simply click the Remove button next to the package name.

If you are using Linux purely as a desktop system where you can write documents, play music, and do other common desktop tasks, the Software window might be all you need to get the basic software you want. By default, your system connects to the main Ubuntu software repository and gives you access to hundreds of software applications. You also have the option of accessing third-party applications that are still free for you to use but not redistribute.

Although the Software window lets you download and install some applications from the Ubuntu software repository, that repository actually contains tens of thousands of software packages. What packages can you *not* see from that repository? When might you want those other packages? And how can you gain access to those packages (as well as packages from other software repositories)?

Going Beyond the Software Window

If you are managing a single desktop system, you might be quite satisfied with the hundreds of packages that you can find through the Software window. Open-source versions of the most common types of desktop applications are available to you through the Software window after you have a connection to the Internet.

However, these are some of the reasons you might want to go beyond what you can do with the Software window:

More repositories   The repositories enabled by default contain only open source, freely distributable software. You may want to install some commercial software (such as Microsoft's Skype communication software) or software with restrictive licenses (like the latest build of the Chromium web browser).

Beyond desktop applications   Tens of thousands of software packages in the Ubuntu repository are not available through the Software window. Most of these packages are not associated with graphical applications at all. For example, some packages contain pure command-line tools, system services, programming tools, or documentation that doesn't show up in the Software window.

Flexibility   Although you may not know it, when you install an application through the Software window, you may actually be installing multiple Debian packages. This set of packages may just be a default package set that includes documentation, extra fonts, additional software plug-ins, or multiple language packs that you may or may not want. With the apt and dpkg commands, you have more flexibility on exactly which packages related to an application or other software feature are installed on your system.

More complex queries   Using commands such as apt and dpkg, you can get detailed information about packages, package groups, and repositories.

10

Software validation   Using `apt` and other tools, you can check whether a signed package has been modified before you installed it or whether any of the components of a package have been tampered with since the package was installed.

Managing software installation   Although the Software window works well if you are installing desktop software on a single system, it doesn't scale well for managing software on multiple systems. Other tools are built on top of the `apt` facility for doing that.

Before we discuss some of the command-line tools for installing and managing software in Linux, the next section describes how the underlying packaging and package management systems in Linux work. In particular, we focus on Deb packages, which are associated with Debian, Ubuntu, Linux Mint, and related distributions.

Understanding Linux Software Packaging

On the first Linux systems, if you wanted to add software, you would grab the source code from a project that produced it, compile it into executable binaries, and drop it onto your computer. If you were lucky, someone would have already compiled it into a form that would run on your computer.

The package format could be a Tarball containing executable files (commands), documentation, configuration files, and libraries. (A *Tarball* is a single file in which multiple files are gathered together for convenient storage or distribution.) When you install software from a Tarball, the files from that Tarball might be spread across your Linux system in appropriate directories (`/usr/share/man`, `/etc`, `/bin`, and `/lib`, to name just a few). Although it is easy to create a Tarball and just drop a set of software onto your Linux system, this method of installing software makes it difficult to do these things:

Satisfy software dependencies   You would need to know if the software you were installing depended on other software being installed for your software to work. Then you would have to track down that software and install it (which might have some of its own dependencies).

List the software   Even if you knew the name of the command, you might not know where its documentation or configuration files were located when you looked for it later.

Remove the software   Unless you kept the original Tarball, or a list of files, you wouldn't know where all the files were when it came time to remove them. Even if you knew, you would have to manually remove each one individually.

Update the software   Tarballs are not designed to hold metadata about the contents that they contain. After the contents of a Tarball are installed, you may not have a way to tell what version of the software you are using, making it difficult to track down bugs and get new versions of your software.

To deal with these problems, packages progressed from simple Tarballs to more complex packaging. With only a few notable exceptions (such as Gentoo, Slackware, and a few others), the majority of Linux distributions went to one of two packaging formats— DEB and RPM:

DEB (.deb) packaging   The Debian GNU/Linux project created .deb packaging, which is used by Debian and other distributions based on Debian (Ubuntu, Linux Mint, KNOPPIX, and so on). Using tools such as apt-get, apt, and dpkg, Linux distributions could install, manage, upgrade, and remove software.

RPM (.rpm) packaging   Originally named Red Hat Package Manager, but later recursively renamed RPM Package Manager, RPM is the preferred package format for SUSE, Red Hat distributions (RHEL and Fedora), and those based on Red Hat distributions (CentOS, Oracle Linux, and so on). The rpm command was the first tool to manage RPMs. Later, yum was added to enhance the RPM facility, and now dnf has become the default tool for many releases instead of yum.

This chapter will focus on DEB packaging and software management.

Working with Debian Packaging

Debian software packages hold multiple files and metadata related to some set of software in the format of an ar archive file. The files can be executables (commands), configuration files, documentation, and other software items. The metadata includes such things as dependencies, licensing, package sizes, descriptions, and other information. Multiple command-line and graphical tools are available for working with DEB files in Ubuntu, Debian, and other Linux distributions. Some of these include the following:

Ubuntu Software Center   Select the Ubuntu Software application from the GNOME Activities menu. The window that appears lets you search for applications and packages that you want by searching for keywords or navigating categories.

aptitude   The aptitude command is a package installation tool that provides a screen-oriented menu that runs in the shell. After you run the command, use arrow keys to highlight the selection you want, and press Enter to select it. You can upgrade packages, get new packages, or view installed packages.

apt*   There is a set of apt* commands (apt-get, apt, apt-config, apt-cache, and so on) that can be used to manage package installation.

APT basics

The Ubuntu Software Center is fairly intuitive for finding and installing packages. By comparison APT might seem less intuitive, but it actually is pretty handy as well. The following note lists a few examples of commands that can help you install and manage packages with apt* commands. In this case, you are looking for and installing the vsftpd package.

10

NOTE

Notice that the `apt*` commands are preceded by the `sudo` command in these examples. That's because package management is a system-wide process that requires admin privileges.

```
$ sudo apt update              Get the latest package versions
    $ sudo apt-get update          Get the latest package versions (alternate)
    $ sudo apt-cache search vsftpd  Find package by key word (such as vsftpd)
    $ sudo apt-cache show vsftpd    Display information about a package
    $ sudo apt install vsftpd       Install the vsftpd package
    $ sudo apt-get install vsftpd   Install the vsftpd package (alternate)
    $ sudo apt-get upgrade          Update installed packages if upgrade ready
    $ sudo apt-cache pkgnames       List all packages that are installed
```

Note how, in some cases, you can use either `apt` or `apt-get`. `apt` is a more modern toolset designed to fit the basic day-to-day needs of most users, most of the time, while leaving out some obscure and seldom-used functions. There are many other uses of `apt` commands that you can try out. I recommend that you run `man apt` to get an understanding of what the `apt` and related commands can do.

The most basic of all commands within the Debian universe is `apt update`. This command polls remote repositories for any recent changes to their software indexes and updates the local index. Without this update, your local system could never be sure it's installing the latest versions of the software you need. Run it yourself; it'll do you good:

```
$ sudo apt update
```

To apply the latest updates to all the packages currently installed on your system using a single command, run `apt upgrade`. If there are any updates, you'll be shown the files that could be changed and asked to confirm that's what you want. If you accept, APT will get to work applying the updates—including installing new versions of the Linux kernel itself.

```
$ sudo apt upgrade
Reading package lists... Done
Building dependency tree
Reading state information... Done
Calculating upgrade... Done
The following packages were automatically installed and are no
longer required:
  kde-cli-tools kde-cli-tools-data libfakekey0 libkf5su-bin
libkf5su-data
  libkf5su5 sshfs
Use 'sudo apt autoremove' to remove them.
The following packages will be upgraded:
```

```
    bsdutils fdisk gir1.2-ibus-1.0 ibus ibus-gtk ibus-gtk3 libasound2
    libasound2-data libblkid1 libfdisk1 libglib2.0-0 libglib2.0-bin
    libglib2.0-data libibus-1.0-5 libmount1 libsmartcols1 libuuid1
linux-base
    mount rfkill teamviewer util-linux uuid-runtime vim-common
vim-tiny xxd
26 upgraded, 0 newly installed, 0 to remove and 0 not upgraded.
Need to get 16.8 MB/23.4 MB of archives.
After this operation, 147 kB of additional disk space will be used.
Do you want to continue? [Y/n]
```

> **NOTE**
>
> Some updates—especially kernel updates—will require a system reboot before they're active. Since it can be difficult to reboot production servers, Canonical makes its Livepatch software available that can apply deep system changes even without the need for a reboot. If you're running server workloads, you can use Livepatch for free for up to three machines. You can learn more about Livepatch on its website: `ubuntu.com/livepatch`.

In the market for some new software but don't know what it's called? Suppose you're worried about heat building up inside your computer's case and want something to monitor temperature changes. You can search through the repositories using—you guessed it— `apt search`:

```
$ apt search sensor
```

That command will probably return way too many choices. You can always filter your results using `grep`. This example will return any result containing the words "sensor" and "temperature" along with the two lines preceding and following the reference. (Try running that without `-B 2 -A 2` to see the difference.)

```
$ apt search sensor | grep -B 2 -A 2 temperature
digitemp/bionic 3.7.1-2build1 amd64
    read temperature sensors in a 1-Wire net

dispcalgui/bionic 3.5.0.0-1 amd64
--
libsensors4/bionic 1:3.4.0-4 amd64
    library to read temperature/voltage/fan sensors
libsensors4-dev/bionic 1:3.4.0-4 amd64
--
lm-sensors/bionic 1:3.4.0-4 amd64
    utilities to read temperature/voltage/fan sensors
logdata-anomaly-miner/bionic 0.0.7-1 all
--
psensor/bionic 1.1.5-1ubuntu3 amd64
    display graphs for monitoring hardware temperature
psensor-common/bionic 1.1.5-1ubuntu3 all
--
```

10

Continues

Continued

```
wmtemp/bionic 0.0.6-3.3build1 amd64
  WM dock applet displaying lm_sensors temperature values
xfce4-goodies/bionic 4.12.4 amd64
```

psensor looks like the one we're after, but we'd like to learn a bit more. Now that we know the package name, that'll be easy:

```
$ apt show psensor
Package: psensor
Version: 1.1.5-1ubuntu3
Priority: optional
Section: universe/utils
Origin: Ubuntu
Maintainer: Ubuntu Developers <ubuntu-devel-discuss@lists.ubuntu.com>
Original-Maintainer: Jean-Philippe Orsini <jeanfi@gmail.com>
Bugs: https://bugs.launchpad.net/ubuntu/+filebug
Installed-Size: 367 kB
Depends: psensor-common (= 1.1.5-1ubuntu3), dconf-gsettings-backend
| gsettings-backend, libappindicator3-1 (>= 0.2.92), libatasmart4
(>= 0.13), libc6 (>= 2.14), libcairo2 (>= 1.2.4), libcurl3-gnutls
(>= 7.16.2), libglib2.0-0 (>= 2.30.0), libgtk-3-0 (>= 3.3.16),
libgtop-2.0-11 (>= 2.22.3), libjson-c3 (>= 0.10), libnotify4 (>=
0.7.0), libsensors4 (>= 1:3.0.0), libudisks2-0 (>= 2.0.0), libunity9
(>= 3.4.6), libx11-6, libxnvctrl0
Homepage: http://wpitchoune.net/psensor
Download-Size: 58.4 kB
APT-Sources: http://us-east-1.ec2.archive.ubuntu.com/ubuntu bionic/
universe amd64 Packages
Description: display graphs for monitoring hardware temperature
 Psensor is a GTK+ application for monitoring hardware sensors,
 including temperatures and fan speeds.
 .
 It displays a curve for each sensor, alerts user using Desktop
Notification
 and Application Indicator when a temperature is too high.
 .
 It can monitor:
  * the temperature of the motherboard and CPU sensors (using
lm-sensors).
  * the temperature of the NVidia GPUs (using XNVCtrl).
  * the temperature of the Hard Disk Drives (using hddtemp or
atasmart lib).
  * the rotation speed of the fans (using lm-sensors).
  * the sensors of a remote computer (using psensor-server).
```

The Description section is where you'll usually see helpful context information. Here's how you can display a list of the dependencies required by a package:

```
$ apt depends psensor
psensor
```

```
 Depends: psensor-common (= 1.1.5-1ubuntu3)
|Depends: dconf-gsettings-backend
 Depends: <gsettings-backend>
   dconf-gsettings-backend
 Depends: libappindicator3-1 (>= 0.2.92)
 Depends: libatasmart4 (>= 0.13)
 Depends: libc6 (>= 2.14)
 Depends: libcairo2 (>= 1.2.4)
 Depends: libcurl3-gnutls (>= 7.16.2)
 Depends: libglib2.0-0 (>= 2.30.0)
 Depends: libgtk-3-0 (>= 3.3.16)
 Depends: libgtop-2.0-11 (>= 2.22.3)
 Depends: libjson-c3 (>= 0.10)
 Depends: libnotify4 (>= 0.7.0)
 Depends: libsensors4 (>= 1:3.0.0)
 Depends: libudisks2-0 (>= 2.0.0)
 Depends: libunity9 (>= 3.4.6)
 Depends: libx11-6
 Depends: libxnvctrl0
```

When you're ready to pull the trigger and install a package, it'll be apt install you run:

```
$ sudo apt install psensor
```

Should you ever need to remove software, you'll want apt remove:

```
$ sudo apt remove psensor
```

apt remove will delete all the related program files that had been installed, but it'll leave behind any configuration files. If you don't want anything remaining from the program—which would let you reinstall from scratch later—then you'd run apt purge:

```
$ sudo apt purge psensor
```

Working with APT repositories

You can control which repositories various apt commands will use through configuration files in the /etc/apt directory. The primary resource used by APT to determine where to look for software is the sources.list file. While there will normally be commented-out lines describing the contents and, perhaps, some optional repositories, here's what it looks like with only active repositories listed. Feel free to take a look at the version on your own machine.

```
$ cat /etc/apt/sources.list
deb http://ca.archive.ubuntu.com/ubuntu/ bionic main restricted
deb http://ca.archive.ubuntu.com/ubuntu/ bionic-updates main
restricted
deb http://ca.archive.ubuntu.com/ubuntu/ bionic universe
deb http://ca.archive.ubuntu.com/ubuntu/ bionic-updates universe
deb http://ca.archive.ubuntu.com/ubuntu/ bionic multiverse
deb http://ca.archive.ubuntu.com/ubuntu/ bionic-updates multiverse
```

Continues

10

209

Continued

```
deb http://ca.archive.ubuntu.com/ubuntu/ bionic-backports main
restricted universe multiverse
deb http://security.ubuntu.com/ubuntu bionic-security main restricted
deb http://security.ubuntu.com/ubuntu bionic-security universe
deb http://security.ubuntu.com/ubuntu bionic-security multiverse
```

Third parties can, should you permit it, install their own repository information as files within the /etc/apt/sources.list.d directory. Here's how those contents might look:

```
$ ls /etc/apt/sources.list.d/
brave-browser-release.list   google-chrome.list   skype-stable.list
teamviewer.list
```

And here's the contents of the list file used by the Brave browser:

```
$ cat /etc/apt/sources.list.d/brave-browser-release.list
deb [arch=amd64] https://brave-browser-apt-release.s3.brave.com/
stable main
```

You may sometimes want to manually add a private repository to your APT configuration. This might be to manage your own software project, or because there's software you need that isn't part of the regular repositories. You can do this using Personal Package Archives (PPAs). Just make very sure that you trust the sources you add, as they're not scanned for malware or curated the way the mainstream repositories are.

You can add a PPA through the Software & Updates GUI dialog (from Activities, type **software** to open the dialog). Just select the Other Software tab, click the Add button, and enter the appropriate APT line. Running apt update will tell APT to add the new source to your repository list. From that point, you'll be able to install packages the normal way using APT.

Of course, it will be faster and more Linux-y to do this from the command line using the apt-add-repository command:

```
$ sudo apt-add-repository ppa:ansible/ansible
 Ansible is a radically simple IT automation platform that makes your
applications and systems easier to deploy. Avoid writing scripts or
custom code to deploy and update your applications— automate in a
language that approaches plain English, using SSH, with no agents to
install on remote systems.

http://ansible.com/
 More info: https://launchpad.net/~ansible/+archive/ubuntu/ansible
Press [ENTER] to continue or Ctrl-c to cancel adding it.

gpg: unknown option `import-export'
gpg: invalid import options
Failed to add key.
```

That example worked, but you'll notice the warning about the encryption keys. This is important, since we trust APT to ensure that packages that reach our computers are the same ones that left the repository. If the keys can't be confirmed, then there is no guarantee and you really shouldn't use the software.

In this case, you can blame it on the fact that that repository is old and outdated. We just used it for illustration. Nevertheless, it would be a good idea to remove the source from our configuration. One quick way to do that is by removing the source file from the /etc/apt/ sources.list.d/ directory and then running apt update again:

```
$ ls /etc/apt/sources.list.d/
alexlarsson-ubuntu-flatpak-bionic.list          ansible-ubuntu-ansible-
bionic.list
alexlarsson-ubuntu-flatpak-bionic.list.save
$
$ sudo rm /etc/apt/sources.list.d/ansible-ubuntu-ansible-bionic.list
$ sudo apt update
```

Working with dpkg

If APT is the Debian system's tool for dealing with software that lives in repositories, then dpkg is the way you deal directly with packages that happen to be lying around your local machine (although many dpkg tasks can also be run through the more user-friendly apt). Say, for instance, you were browsing the Internet and downloaded a .deb package containing some software that you'd like to try. Assuming that you trust the package's source, and are comfortable that it hasn't been altered in transit, you won't be able to use some apt install command to install it. Instead, installing, removing, building, and managing .deb packages is the job of dpkg. Here's how it works.

Let's assume your package is called brscan4-0.4.2-1.amd64.deb—which happens to be the name of a package of Linux printer drivers provided by the Brother company. Installing the package would be as simple as running dpkg -i followed by the package name. In this example, the package is in the current directory, so I don't need to provide a full path:

```
$ sudo dpkg -i brscan4-0.4.2-1.amd64.deb
(Reading database ... 58215 files and directories currently
installed.)
Preparing to unpack brscan4-0.4.2-1.amd64.deb ...
Unpacking brscan4 (0.4.2-1) over (0.4.2-1) ...
Setting up brscan4 (0.4.2-1) ...
This software is based in part on the work of the Independent
JPEG Group.
```

You can use dpkg to list all the packages that are currently installed on your system—even those packages that were installed by APT. Here's a truncated version of the output:

```
$ dpkg -l
Desired=Unknown/Install/Remove/Purge/Hold
| Status=Not/Inst/Conf-files/Unpacked/halF-conf/Half-inst/trig-
aWait/Trig-pend
|/ Err?=(none)/Reinst-required (Status,Err: uppercase=bad)
||/ Name             Version        Architecture Description
```

Continues

10

Continued

```
+++-=============-============-=============-
=================================
ii   accountsservic 0.6.45-1ubun amd64          query and manipulate
user account
ii   acl            2.2.52-3buil amd64          Access control
list utilities
ii   acpid          1:2.0.28-1ub amd64          Advanced Configuration
and Power
ii   adduser        3.116ubuntu1 all            add and remove users
and groups
ii   adwaita-icon-t 3.28.0-1ubun all            default icon theme of
GNOME (smal
ii   alsa-utils     1.1.3-1ubunt amd64          Utilities for
configuring and usi
ii   apache2        2.4.29-1ubun amd64          Apache HTTP Server
ii   apache2-bin    2.4.29-1ubun amd64          Apache HTTP Server
(modules and o
ii   apache2-data   2.4.29-1ubun all            Apache HTTP Server
(common files)
ii   apache2-utils  2.4.29-1ubun amd64          Apache HTTP Server
(utility progr
ii   apparmor       2.12-4ubuntu amd64          user-space parser
utility for App
ii   apport         2.20.9-0ubun all            automatically generate
crash repo
ii   apport-symptom 0.20         all            symptom scripts
for apport
[...]
```

There are a lot of packages on the system. Why not pipe that command to wc to see just how many?

```
$ dpkg -l | wc
   938    9444   122386
```

There are 938 packages (whose descriptions comprise 9,444 words and 122,386 characters), to be precise. How many are on your system?

You can narrow that output down if you know the name of the package you're looking for:

```
$ dpkg -l apache2
Desired=Unknown/Install/Remove/Purge/Hold
| Status=Not/Inst/Conf-files/Unpacked/halF-conf/Half-inst/trig-
aWait/Trig-pend
|/ Err?=(none)/Reinst-required (Status,Err: uppercase=bad)
||/ Name           Version      Architecture Description
+++-=============-============-=============-
=================================
ii   apache2        2.4.29-1ubun amd64          Apache HTTP Server
```

You can scan the inner workings of a package using -c, which will give us a list of all the included files and the filesystem locations where they'll be installed. This can be useful for administrating the software once it's installed. This output is only a small portion of what I got from this command:

```
$ dpkg -c brscan4-0.4.2-1.amd64.deb
drwxr-xr-x root/root 0 2013-09-25 05:35 ./
drwxr-xr-x root/root 0 2013-09-25 05:35 ./opt/
drwxr-xr-x root/root 0 2013-09-25 05:35 ./opt/brother/
drwxr-xr-x root/root 0 2013-09-25 05:35 ./opt/brother/scanner/
drwxr-xr-x root/root 0 2013-09-25 05:35 ./opt/brother/
scanner/brscan4/
drwxr-xr-x root/root 0 2013-09-25 05:35 ./opt/brother/scanner/
brscan4/models4/
-rw-r--r-- root/root 103 2013-09-25 05:35 ./opt/brother/scanner/
brscan4/models4/ext_5.ini
-rw-r--r-- root/root 141 2013-09-25 05:35 ./opt/brother/scanner/
brscan4/models4/ext_9.ini
-rw-r--r-- root/root 541 2013-09-25 05:35 ./opt/brother/scanner/
brscan4/models4/ext_4.ini
-rw-r--r-- root/root 426 2013-09-25 05:35 ./opt/brother/scanner/
brscan4/models4/ext_8.ini
-rw-r--r-- root/root 676 2013-09-25 05:35 ./opt/brother/scanner/
brscan4/models4/ext_3.ini
-rw-r--r-- root/root 213 2013-09-25 05:35 ./opt/brother/scanner/
brscan4/models4/ext_6.ini
-rw-r--r-- root/root 667 2013-09-25 05:35 ./opt/brother/scanner/
brscan4/models4/ext_7.ini
-rw-r--r-- root/root 79 2013-09-25 05:35 ./opt/brother/scanner/
brscan4/models4/ext_2.ini
-rw-r--r-- root/root 578 2013-09-25 05:35 ./opt/brother/scanner/
brscan4/models4/ext_1.ini
-rw-rw-rw- root/root 2 2013-09-25 05:35 ./opt/brother/scanner/
brscan4/brsanenetdevice4.cfg
[...]
```

Knowing everything you now know, removing a package is straightforward. But you'll first need the name Linux uses to describe it. Our brscan4-0.4.2-1.amd64.deb package has a dpkg name—and it's not brscan4-0.4.2-1.amd64.deb. One quick trick to get the information we're after is to run dkpg and filter the results for a minimal subset of that name:

```
$ dpkg -l | grep brscan
ii  brscan4  0.4.2-1  amd64  Brother Scanner Driver
```

Success. The package is known as brscan4. Now let's remove it:

```
$ sudo dpkg -r brscan4
(Reading database ... 58215 files and directories currently
installed.)
Removing brscan4 (0.4.2-1) ...
```

10

Finally, if any installed Debian package somehow becomes corrupted, you can reconfigure it using:

```
$ sudo dpkg --configure <package-name>
```

Summary

Software packaging in Ubuntu and related systems relies on DEB files. You can try easy-to-
use graphical tools such as Ubuntu Software for finding and installing packages. The primary command-line tools include `aptitude`, `apt`, and `dpkg`.

Using these software management tools, you can install, query, verify, update, and remove
packages. You can also do maintenance tasks.

With your system installed and the software packages that you need added, it's time to
configure your system further. If you expect to have multiple people using your system,
your next task could be to add and otherwise manage user accounts on your system. Chapter 11, "Managing User Accounts," describes user management in Ubuntu.

Exercises

These exercises test your knowledge of working with APT software packages. To do the
exercises, I recommend that you have an Ubuntu system in front of you that has an Internet connection.

You need to be able to reach the Debian repositories (which should be set up automatically).
If you are stuck, solutions to the tasks are shown in Appendix A (although in Linux, there
are often multiple ways to complete a task).

1. Search the APT repository for the package that provides the `pdftoppm` command.

2. Display information about the package that provides the `pdftoppm` command, and
   determine that package's home page (URL).

3. Install the package containing the `pdftoppm` command.

4. Delete the `pdftoppm` command from your system and verify its package against
   the APT database to see that the command is indeed missing.

5. Reinstall the package that provides the `pdftoppm` command, and make sure that
   the entire package is intact again.

Managing User Accounts

A dding and managing users are common tasks for Linux system administrators. *User accounts* keep boundaries between the people who use your systems and between the processes that run on your systems. *Groups* are a way of assigning rights to your system that can be assigned to multiple users at once.

This chapter describes not only how to create a new user, but also how to create predefined settings and files to configure the user's environment. Using tools such as the `adduser` and `usermod` commands, you can assign settings such as the location of a home directory, a default shell, a default group, and specific user ID and group ID values. With Cockpit, you can add and manage user accounts through a web UI.

Creating User Accounts

Every person who uses your Linux system should have a separate user account. Having a user account provides you with an area in which to store files securely as well as a means of tailoring your user interface (GUI, path, environment variables, and so on) to suit the way that you use the computer.

You can add user accounts to most Linux systems in several ways. *Cockpit* is a browser-based monitoring and administration tool that includes an Account selection for creating and managing user accounts. If Cockpit is not yet installed and enabled, do that as follows:

```
# apt install cockpit
# systemctl enable --now cockpit.socket
```

To create a user account through Cockpit, do the following:

1. Open the Cockpit interface from your web browser (`localhost:9090`). If you'd prefer to install and try Cockpit on a VM or remote machine and access it locally, you would use that machine's IP address instead of `localhost`. Note that, since you won't be using an encryption certificate from a certificate authority (CA), you will have to click past your browser's privacy warning to enter the site.

2. Log in as an existing user with `sudo` authority and select the "Reuse my password for privileged tasks" check box.

3. Select the Accounts link on the left side of the page and then Create New Account.

   Figure 11.1 shows an example of the Create New Account pop-up window.

FIGURE 11.1

Add and modify user accounts from Cockpit.

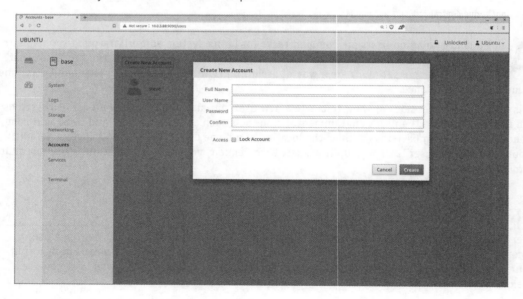

4. Begin adding a new user account to your Linux system. Here are the fields you need to fill in:

   Full Name   Use the user's real name, typically used with uppercase and lowercase letters, as the user would write it in real life. Technically, this information is stored in the comment field of the `passwd` file, but by convention, most Linux and UNIX systems expect this field to hold each user's full name.

User Name   This is the name used to log in as this user. When you choose a username, don't begin with a number (for example, 26jsmith). Also, it's best to use all lowercase letters, no control characters or spaces, and a maximum of eight characters, by convention. Having users named Jsmith and jsmith can cause confusion with programs (such as sendmail) that don't distinguish case.

Password, Confirm   Enter the password you want the user to have in the Password and Confirm fields. The password should be at least eight characters long and contain a mixture of uppercase and lowercase letters, numbers, and punctuation. It should not contain real words, repeated letters, or letters in a row on the keyboard. Through this interface, you must set a password that meets the preceding criteria. (If you want to add a password that doesn't meet these criteria, you can use the adduser command, described later in this chapter.) Bars underneath the password fields turn from red to green as you improve the strength of your password.

Access   To create an account that you are not quite ready to use, select the Lock Account check box. That prevents anyone from logging in to the account until you uncheck that box or change that information in the passwd file.

5. Select Create to add the user to the system. An entry for the new user account is added to the /etc/passwd file and the new group account to the /etc/group file. (I will describe those later in this chapter.)

The Cockpit Accounts screen lets you modify a small set of information about a regular user after it has been created. To modify user information later, do the following:

1. Select the user account that you want to change. A screen appears with available selections for that user account.

2. You can delete the user but not modify the username, but you can change the following information:

Full Name   Because the user's full name is just a comment, you can change that as you please.

Roles   By default, you have the opportunity to select check boxes that allow the user to be added to the role of Server Administrator (giving the user root privilege by being added to the sudo group). Other roles might be added to this list by other Cockpit components. If the user is logged in, that user must log out to obtain those privileges.

Access   You can choose Lock Account to lock the account. The "Never lock account" link lets you choose a specific date beyond which the account will be locked, or to never lock the account (setting no account expiration date).

Password   You can choose Set Password to set a new password for that user or Force Change to force the user to change their password the next time they log in. By default, passwords never expire. You can change that to have the password expire every set number of days.

Authorized Public SSH Keys If you have a public SSH key for the user, you can select the plus sign (+) for this field, paste that key into the text box, and select Add key. With that key in place, the user with the associated private key is allowed to log in to that user account via SSH without needing to enter a password.

3. Changes take effect immediately, so you can simply leave the window when you are done modifying the user account.

The Accounts area of the Cockpit web UI was designed to simplify the process of creating and modifying user accounts. More features associated with user accounts can be added or modified from the command line. The next section of this chapter describes how to add user accounts from the command line with `adduser` and change them with the `usermod` command.

Adding users with adduser

Sometimes, a Linux system doesn't have a desktop tool or web UI available for adding users. Other times, you might find it more convenient to add lots of users at once with a shell script or change user account features that are not available from Cockpit. For those cases, commands are available to enable you to add and modify user accounts from the command line.

The most straightforward method for creating a new user from the shell is the `adduser` command. After opening a Terminal window and gaining root authority, you simply invoke `adduser` at the command prompt, with details of the new account as parameters.

> **NOTE**
> Ubuntu recommends you use the `adduser` and `deluser` scripts rather than the `useradd` and `userdel` native binary commands that are more common for other distributions like Fedora. While they're similar from a feature perspective, `adduser` was built to be more user friendly and interactive. Both commands are available on Ubuntu.

The only required parameter is the login name of the user, but you'll sometimes want to include some additional information. Each item of account information is preceded by a single-letter option code with a dash in front of it. The following options are available with `adduser`:

--home *home_dir*: Manually set the home directory to use for the account. By default, a directory using the same as the login name will be created in /home. The –home argument can create that directory wherever you'd like.

--ingroup *group*: Place the new user in an existing group. In any case, a new group is created that is the same as the username and is used as that user's primary group.

--uid *ID*: Assign a specific UID for this user. By default, `adduser` will assign the user a new UID within the range defined in the /etc/adduser.conf file.

--shell *shell*: Specify a non-default command shell to use for this account. Replace *shell* with the command shell (for example, --shell /bin/csh).

Let's create an account for a new user. The user's full name is Sara Green, with a login name of sara. To begin, become root user and type the following command:

```
$ sudo adduser sara
Adding user `sara' ...
Adding new group `sara' (1001) ...
Adding new user `sara' (1001) with group `sara' ...
Creating home directory `/home/sara' ...
Copying files from `/etc/skel' ...
Enter new UNIX password:
Retype new UNIX password:
passwd: password updated successfully
Changing the user information for sara
Enter the new value, or press ENTER for the default
    Full Name []: Sara Green
    Room Number []:
    Work Phone []:
    Home Phone []:
    Other []:
Is the information correct? [Y/n]
```

The command creates the new user and assigns it group and user IDs for the new user and group that it creates. It will then create the user's new home directory (in /home/sara/) and copy files from the /etc/skel directory. (Any files you save to the skel directory will be automatically added to home directories of new users as their accounts are created.) You'll then be prompted to enter a new password for the user and may, optionally, add a full name and other contact information. When you're done, the account will be created.

> **NOTE**
>
> Keep in mind that creating new passwords as root user lets you add short or blank passwords that regular users cannot add themselves.

In creating the account for sara, the adduser command performs several actions:

- Reads the /etc/login.defs and /etc/adduser.conf files to get default values to use when creating accounts.
- Checks command-line parameters to find out which default values to override.
- Creates a new user entry in the /etc/passwd and /etc/shadow files based on the default values and command-line parameters.
- Creates any necessary entries for new groups in the /etc/group file.
- Creates a home directory based on the user's name in the /home directory.
- Copies any files located within the /etc/skel directory to the new home directory. This usually includes login and application startup scripts.

The preceding example uses only a few of the available adduser options. Most account settings are assigned using default values. You can set more values explicitly if you want to. Here's an example that uses a few more options to do so:

```
# adduser -g users -G wheel,apache -s /bin/tcsh -c "Sara Green" sara
```

This command line results in the following line being added to the /etc/passwd file:

```
sara:x:1001:1001:Sara Green,,,:/home/sara:/bin/bash
```

Each line in the /etc/passwd file represents a single user account record. Each field is separated from the next by a colon (:). The field's position in the sequence determines what it is. As you can see, the login name is first. The password field contains an x because, in this example, the shadow password file is used to store actual encrypted password data (in /etc/shadow).

The user ID selected by adduser is 1001. The primary group ID is also 1001, which corresponds to a new private sara group in the /etc/group file. The comment field was correctly set to Sara Green, the home directory was automatically assigned as /home/ sara, and the command shell was assigned as /bin/bash.

The /etc/group file holds information about the different groups on your Linux system and the users who belong to them. Groups are useful for enabling multiple users to share access to the same files while denying access to others. Here is the /etc/group entry created for sara:

```
sara:x:1001:
```

Each line in the group file contains the name of a group, a group password (usually filled with an x), the group ID number associated with it, and a list of users in that group. By default, each user is added to their own group, beginning with the next available GID, starting with 1000.

Setting user defaults

The adduser command determines the default values for new accounts by reading the / etc/login.defs and /etc/adduser.conf files. You can modify those defaults by editing the files manually with a standard text editor. Here is an example containing many of the settings that you might find in a typical login.defs file:

```
MAIL_DIR            /var/mail
FAILLOG_ENAB        yes
LOG_UNKFAIL_ENAB    no
LOG_OK_LOGINS       no
SYSLOG_SU_ENAB      yes
SYSLOG_SG_ENAB      yes
FTMP_FILE           /var/log/btmp
SU_NAME             su
HUSHLOGIN_FILE      .hushlogin
ENV_SUPATH  PATH=/usr/local/sbin:/usr/local/bin:/usr/sbin:/usr/
bin:/sbin:/bin
ENV_PATH    PATH=/usr/local/bin:/usr/bin:/bin:/usr/local/games:/usr/games
TTYGROUP    tty
TTYPERM             0600
ERASECHAR           0177
KILLCHAR            025
```

```
UMASK                022
PASS_MAX_DAYS        99999
PASS_MIN_DAYS        0
PASS_WARN_AGE        7
UID_MIN              1000
UID_MAX              60000
GID_MIN              1000
GID_MAX              60000
LOGIN_RETRIES        5
LOGIN_TIMEOUT        60
CHFN_RESTRICT        rwh
DEFAULT_HOME         yes
USERGROUPS_ENAB      yes
```

All uncommented lines contain keyword/value pairs. For example, the keyword PASS_MAX_DAYS is followed by some white space and the value 99999. This tells adduser that the user password needs to be updated after no more than 99,999 days. Or, in other words, there is currently no limit on how long users can keep their old passwords. Other lines let you customize the valid range of automatically assigned user ID numbers or group ID numbers. (This example starts at 1,000 and goes up to 60,000.)

A comment section that explains that keyword's purpose precedes each keyword (which I edited out here to save space). Altering a default value is as simple as editing the value associated with a keyword and saving the file before running the adduser command.

If you want to view other default settings, you can find them in the /etc/adduser.conf file.

Here's how that file can look:

```
DSHELL=/bin/bash
DHOME=/home
GROUPHOMES=no
LETTERHOMES=no
SKEL=/etc/skel
FIRST_SYSTEM_UID=100
LAST_SYSTEM_UID=999
FIRST_SYSTEM_GID=100
LAST_SYSTEM_GID=999
FIRST_UID=1000
LAST_UID=59999
FIRST_GID=1000
LAST_GID=59999
USERGROUPS=yes
USERS_GID=100
DIR_MODE=0755
SETGID_HOME=no
QUOTAUSER=""
SKEL_IGNORE_REGEX="dpkg-(old|new|dist|save)"
```

Other commands that are useful for working with user accounts include usermod (to modify settings for an existing account) and deluser (to delete an existing user account).

Modifying users with usermod

The usermod command provides a simple and straightforward method for changing account parameters. Many of the options available with it mirror those found in adduser. The options that can be used with this command include the following:

-c *username*: Change the description associated with the user account. Replace *username* with the name of the user account (-c jake). Use quotes to enter multiple words (for example, -c "Jake Jackson").

-d *home_dir*: Change the home directory to use for the account. The default is to name it the same as the login name and to place it in /home. Replace *home_dir* with the directory name to use (for example, -d /mnt/homes/jake).

-e *expire_date*: Assign a new expiration date for the account in *YYYY-MM-DD* format. Replace *expire_date* with a date you want to use. (For October 15, 2022, use -e 2022-10-15.)

-f *-1*: Change the number of days after a password expires until the account is permanently disabled. The default, -1, disables the option. Setting this to 0 disables the account immediately after the password has expired. Replace -1 with the number to use.

-g *group*: Change the primary group (as listed in the /etc/group file) the user will be in. Replace *group* with the group name (for example, -g sudo).

-G *grouplist*: Set the user's secondary groups to the supplied comma-separated list of groups. If the user is already in at least one group besides the user's private group, you must add the -a option as well (-Ga). If not, the user belongs to only the new set of groups and loses membership to any previous groups.

-l *login_name*: Change the login name of the account.

-L: Lock the account by putting an exclamation point at the beginning of the encrypted password in /etc/shadow. This locks the account while still allowing you to leave the password intact (the -U option unlocks it).

-m: Available only when –d is used. This causes the contents of the user's home directory to be copied to the new directory.

-o: Use only with -u uid to remove the restriction that UIDs must be unique.

-s *shell*: Specify a different command shell to use for this account. Replace *shell* with the command shell (for example, -s bash).

-u *user_id*: Change the user ID number for the account. Replace *user_id* with the ID number (for example, -u 1474).

-U: Unlock the user account (by removing the exclamation mark at the beginning of the encrypted password).

The following are examples of the usermod command:

```
# usermod -s /bin/csh chris
# usermod -Ga sales,marketing, chris
```

The first example changes the shell to the csh shell for the user named chris. In the second example, supplementary groups are added for the user chris. The -a option (-Ga) makes sure that the supplementary groups are added to any existing groups for the user chris. If the -a is not used, existing supplementary groups for chris are erased and the new list of groups includes the only supplementary groups assigned to that user.

Deleting users with deluser

Just as usermod is used to modify user settings and adduser is used to create users, deluser is used to remove users. The following command removes the user chris:

```
# deluser --remove-home chris
```

Here, the user chris is removed from the /etc/passwd file. The --remove-home option removes the user's home directory as well. If you choose not to use --remove-home, the home directory for chris is not removed:

```
# deluser chris
```

Keep in mind that simply removing the user account does not change anything about the files that user leaves around the system (except those that are deleted when you use --remove-home). However, ownership of files left behind appear as belonging to the previous owner's user ID number when you run ls -1 on the files.

Before you delete the user, you may want to run a find command to find all files that would be left behind by the user. After you delete the user, you could search on user ID to find files left behind. Here are two find commands to do those things:

```
# find / -user chris -ls
# find / -uid 504 -ls
```

Because files that are not assigned to any username are considered to be a security risk, it is a good idea to find those files and assign them to a real user account. Here's an example of a find command that finds all files in the filesystem that are not associated with any user (the files are listed by UID):

```
# find / -nouser -ls
```

Understanding Group Accounts

Group accounts are useful if you want to share a set of files with multiple users. You can create a group and configure the set of files to be associated with that group. The root user can assign users to that group so they can all have access to files based on that group's permission. Consider the following file and directory:

```
$ ls -ld /var/salesdocs /var/salesdocs/file.txt
drwxrwxr-x. 2 root sales 4096 Jan 14 09:32 /var/salesstuff/
-rw-rw-r--. 1 root sales    0 Jan 14 09:32 /var/salesstuff/file.txt
```

Looking at permissions on the directory /var/salesdocs (rwxrwxr-x), you see the second set of rwx shows that any member of the group (sales) has permission to read files in that directory (r is read), create and delete files from that directory (w is write), and change to that directory (x is execute). The file named file.txt can be read and changed by members of the sales group (based on the second rw-).

Using group accounts

Every user is assigned to a primary group. In Ubuntu, by default, that group is a new group with the same name as the user. So, if the user were named sara, the group assigned to her would also be sara. The primary group is indicated by the number in the third field of each entry in the /etc/passwd file; for example, the group ID 1001 here:

```
sara:x:1001:1001:Sara Green:/home/sara:/bin/tcsh
```

That entry points to an entry in the /etc/group file:

```
sara:x:1001:
```

Let's turn to the sara user and group accounts for examples. Here are a few facts about using groups:

- When sara creates a file or directory, by default, that file or directory is assigned to sara's primary group (also called sara).
- The user sara can belong to zero or more supplementary groups. If sara were a member of groups named sales and marketing, those entries could look like the following in the /etc/group file:

```
sales:x:1302:joe,bill,sally,sara

marketing:x:1303:mike,terry,sara
```

- The user sara can't add herself to a supplementary group. She can't even add another user to her sara group. Only someone with root privilege can assign users to groups.
- Any file assigned to the sales or marketing group is accessible to sara with group and other permissions (whichever provides the most access). If sara wants to create a file with the sales or marketing groups assigned to it, she could use the newgrp command. In this example, sara uses the newgrp command to have sales become her primary group temporarily and creates a file:

```
[sara]$ touch file1

[sara]$ newgrp sales

[sara]$ touch file2

[sara]$ ls -l file*

-rw-rw-r--. 1 sara sara  0 Jan 18 22:22 file1

-rw-rw-r--. 1 sara sales 0 Jan 18 22:23 file2

[sara]$ exit
```

It is also possible to allow users to become a member of a group temporarily with the new-grp command without actually being a member of that group. To do that, someone with root permission can use gpasswd to set a group password (such as gpasswd sales). After that, any user can type newgrp sales into a shell and temporarily use sales as their primary group by simply entering the group password when prompted.

Creating group accounts

As the root user, you can create new groups from the command line with the addgroup command. Also, groups are created automatically when a user account is created.

Group ID numbers from 0 through 999 are assigned to special administrative groups. For example, the root group is associated with GID 0. Regular groups begin at 1000 for Ubuntu. On the first UNIX systems, GIDs went from 0 to 99. Other Linux systems reserve GIDs between 0 and 500 for administrative groups.

Here are some examples of creating a group account with the addgroup command:

```
# addgroup kings
# addgroup --gid 1325 jokers
```

In the examples just shown, the group named kings is created with the next available group ID. After that, the group jokers is created using the 1325 group ID. Some adminis-trators like using an undefined group number above 200 and under 1000 so that the group they create doesn't intrude on the group designations above 1000 (so UID and GID numbers can go along in parallel).

To change a group later, use the groupmod command, as in the following example:

```
# groupmod -g 330 jokers
# groupmod -n jacks jokers
```

In the first example, the group ID for jokers is changed to 330. In the second, the name jokers is changed to jacks. If you then wanted to assign any of the groups as supple-mentary groups to a user, you can use the usermod command (as described earlier in this chapter).

Managing Users in the Enterprise

The basic Linux method of handling user and group accounts has not changed since the first UNIX systems were developed decades ago. However, as Linux systems have become used in more complex ways, features for managing users, groups, and the permissions associated with them have been added on to the basic user/group model so that it could be more flexible and more centralized:

More flexible In the basic model, only one user and one group can be assigned to each file. Also, regular users have no ability to assign specific permissions to different users or groups and very little flexibility setting up collaborative files/directories. Enhancements to this model allow regular users to set up special collaborative directories (using features such as sticky bit and set GID bit directories). Using Access Control Lists (ACLs), any user can also assign specific permissions to files and directories to any users and groups they like.

More centralized   When you have only one computer, storing user information for all users in the /etc/passwd file is probably not a big deal. However, if you need to authenticate the same set of users across thousands of Linux systems, centralizing that information can save lots of time and heartache. Linux includes features that enable you to authenticate users from LDAP servers or Microsoft Active Directory servers.

The following sections describe how to use features such as ACLs and shared directories (sticky bit and set GID bit directories) to provide powerful ways to share files and directories selectively.

Setting permissions with Access Control Lists

The *Access Control List (ACL)* feature was created so that regular users could share their files and directories selectively with other users and groups. With ACLs, a user can allow others to read, write, and execute files and directories without leaving those filesystem elements wide open or requiring the root user to change the user or group assigned to them.

Here are a few things to know about ACLs:

- For ACLs to be used, they must be enabled on a filesystem when that filesystem is mounted.
- If you create a filesystem after installation (such as when you add a hard disk), you need to make sure that the acl mount option is used when the filesystem is mounted (more on that later).
- To add ACLs to a file, you use the setfacl command; to view ACLs set on a file, you use the getfacl command.
- To set ACLs on any file or directory, you must be the actual owner (user) assigned to it. In other words, being assigned user or group permissions with setfacl does not give you permission to change ACLs on those files yourself.
- Because multiple users and groups can be assigned to a file/directory, the actual permission a user has is based on a union of all user/group designations to which they belong. For example, if a file has read-only permission (r--) for the sales group and read/write/execute (rwx) for the market group, and mary belonged to both, mary would have rwx permission.

NOTE

If ACLs are not enabled on the filesystem you are trying to use with setfacl, see the section "Enabling ACLs" later in this chapter for information on how to mount a filesystem with ACLs enabled.

Setting ACLs with setfacl

Using the `setfacl` command, you can modify permissions (-m) or remove ACL permissions (-x). The following is an example of the syntax of the `setfacl` command:

```
setfacl -m u:username:rwx filename
```

In the example just shown, the modify option (-m) is followed by the letter u, indicating that you are setting ACL permissions for a user. After a colon (:), you indicate the username, followed by another colon and the permissions that you want to assign. As with the `chmod` command, you can assign read (r), write (w), and/or execute (x) permissions to the user or group (in the example, full `rwx` permission is given). The last argument is replaced by the actual filename you are modifying.

The following are some examples of the user `mary` using the `setfacl` command to add permission for other users and groups on a file:

```
[mary]$ touch /tmp/memo.txt
[mary]$ ls -l /tmp/memo.txt
-rw-rw-r--. 1 mary mary 0 Jan 21 09:27 /tmp/memo.txt
[mary]$ setfacl -m u:bill:rw /tmp/memo.txt
[mary]$ setfacl -m g:sales:rw /tmp/memo.txt
```

In the preceding example, `mary` created a file named /tmp/memo.txt. Using the `setfacl` command, she modified (-m) permissions for the user named `bill` so that he now has read/write (`rw`) permissions to that file. Then she modified permissions for the group `sales` so that anyone belonging to that group would also have read/write permissions. Look at `ls -l` and `getfacl` output on that file now:

```
[mary]$ ls -l /tmp/memo.txt
-rw-rw-r--+ 1 mary mary 0 Jan 21 09:27 /tmp/memo.txt
[mary]$ getfacl /tmp/memo.txt
# file: tmp/memo.txt
# owner: mary
# group: mary
user::rw-
user:bill:rw-
group::rw-
group:sales:rw-
mask::rw-
other::r--
```

From the `ls -l` output, notice the plus sign (+) in the `rw-rw-r--+` output. The plus sign indicates that ACLs are set on the file, so you know to run the `getfacl` command to see how ACLs are set. The output shows `mary` as owner and group (same as what you see with `ls -l`), the regular user permissions (`rw-`), and permissions for ACL user `bill` (`rw-`). The same is true for group permissions and permissions for the group `sales`. Other permissions are `r--`.

The `mask` line (near the end of the previous `getfacl` example) requires some special discussion. As soon as you set ACLs on a file, the regular group permission on the file sets a mask of the maximum permission an ACL user or group can have on a file. So, even if you provide an individual with more ACL permissions than the group permissions allow, the individual's effective permissions do not exceed the group permissions as in the following example:

```
[mary]$ chmod 644 /tmp/memo.txt
[mary]$ getfacl /tmp/memo.txt
# file: tmp/memo.txt
# owner: mary
# group: mary
user::rw-
user:bill:rw-    #effective:r--
group::rw-       #effective:r--
group:sales:rw-  #effective:r--
mask::r--
other::r--
```

Notice in the preceding example that even though the user `bill` and group `sales` have `rw-` permissions, their effective permissions are `r--`. So, `bill` or anyone in `sales` would not be able to change the file unless `mary` were to open permissions again (for example, by typing `chmod 664 /tmp/memo.txt`).

Setting default ACLs

Setting default ACLs on a directory enables your ACLs to be inherited. This means that when new files and directories are created in that directory, they are assigned the same ACLs. To set a user or group ACL permission as the default, you add a `d:` to the user or group designation. Consider the following example:

```
[mary]$ mkdir /tmp/mary
[mary]$ setfacl -m d:g:market:rwx /tmp/mary/
[mary]$ getfacl /tmp/mary/
# file: tmp/mary/
# owner: mary
# group: mary
user::rwx
group::rwx
other::r-x
default:user::rwx
default:group::rwx
default:group:sales:rwx
default:group:market:rwx
default:mask::rwx
default:other::r-x
```

To make sure that the default ACL worked, create a subdirectory. Then run getfacl again. You will see that default lines are added for user, group, mask, and other, which are inherited from the directory's ACLs:

```
[mary]$ mkdir /tmp/mary/test
[mary]$ getfacl /tmp/mary/test
# file: tmp/mary/test
# owner: mary
# group: mary
user::rwx
group::rwx
group:sales:rwx
group:market:rwx
mask::rwx
other::r-x
default:user::rwx
default:group::rwx
default:group:sales:rwx
default:group:market:rwx
default:mask::rwx
default:other::r-x
```

Notice that when you create a file in that directory, the inherited permissions are different. Because a regular file is created without execute permission, the effective permission is reduced to rw-:

```
[mary@cnegus ~]$ touch /tmp/mary/file.txt
[mary@cnegus ~]$ getfacl /tmp/mary/file.txt
# file: tmp/mary/file.txt
# owner: mary
# group: mary
user::rw-
group::rwx          #effective:rw-
group:sales:rwx     #effective:rw-
group:market:rwx    #effective:rw-
mask::rw-
other::r--
```

Enabling ACLs

In recent Ubuntu systems, xfs and ext filesystem types (ext2, ext3, and ext4) are automatically created with ACL support. On other Linux systems, or on filesystems created on other Linux systems, you can add the acl mount option in several ways:

- Add the acl option to the fifth field in the line in the /etc/fstab file that automatically mounts the filesystem when the system boots up.
- Implant the acl line in the Default mount options field in the filesystem's super block, so that the acl option is used whether the filesystem is mounted automatically or manually.
- Add the acl option to the mount command line when you mount the filesystem manually with the mount command.

To check that the `acl` option has been added to an ext filesystem, determine the device name associated with the filesystem, and run the `tune2fs -l` command to view the implanted mount options, as in this example:

```
$ mount | grep sda
/dev/sda2 on / type ext4 (rw,relatime,errors=remount-ro)
# tune2fs -l /dev/sda2 | grep mount
Last mounted on:          /
Default mount options:    user_xattr acl
Last mount time:          Wed Mar 25 07:50:52 2020
```

First, I typed the `mount` command to see a list of all filesystems that are currently mounted, limiting the output by grepping for the string `sda` (because I wanted to confirm the existence of the filesystem mounted on `/dev/sda2`). I used that as an option to `tune2fs -l` to find the default mount options line. There, I filtered for the string `mount` and saw that both `user_xattr` (for controlling extended file system attributes) and `acl` were implanted in the filesystem super block so that they would be used when the filesystem was mounted.

If the `Default mount options` field is blank (such as when you have just created a new filesystem), you can add the `acl` mount option using the `tune2fs -o` command. For example, on a different Linux system, I created a filesystem on a removable USB drive that was assigned as the `/dev/sdc1` device. To implant the `acl` mount option and check that it is there, I ran the following commands:

```
# tune2fs -o acl /dev/sdc1
# tune2fs -l /dev/sdc1 | grep "mount options"
Default mount options:    acl
```

You can test that this worked by remounting the filesystem and trying to use the `setfacl` command on a file in that filesystem.

A second way to add `acl` support to a filesystem is to add the `acl` option to the line in the `/etc/fstab` file that automatically mounts the filesystem at boot time. The following is an example of what a line would look like that mounts the ext4 filesystem located on the `/dev/sdc1` device to the `/var/stuff` directory:

```
/dev/sdc1       /var/stuff     ext4     acl       1 2
```

Instead of the `defaults` entry in the fourth field, I added `acl`. If there were already options set in that field, add a comma after the last option and add `acl`. The next time the filesystem is mounted, ACLs are enabled. If the filesystem were already mounted, I could type the following `mount` command as root to remount the filesystem using `acl` or any other values added to the `/etc/fstab` file:

```
# mount -o remount /dev/sdc1
```

A third way that you can add ACL support to a filesystem is to mount the filesystem by hand and specifically request the `acl` mount option. So, if there were no entry for the filesystem in the /etc/fstab file, after creating the mount point (/var/stuff), type the following command to mount the filesystem and include ACL support:

```
# mount -o acl /dev/sdc1 /var/stuff
```

Keep in mind that the mount command only mounts the filesystem temporarily. When the system reboots, the filesystem is not mounted again, unless you add an entry to the /etc/fstab file.

Adding directories for users to collaborate

A special set of three permission bits are typically ignored when you use the chmod command to change permissions on the filesystem. These bits can set special permissions on commands and directories. The focus of this section is setting the bits that help you create directories to use for collaboration.

As with read, write, and execute bits for user, group, and other, these special file permission bits can be set with the chmod command. If, for example, you run chmod 775 /mnt/xyz, the implied permission is actually 0775. To change permissions, you can replace the number 0 with any combination of those three bits (4, 2, and 1), or you can use letter values instead. (Refer to Chapter 4, "Moving Around the Filesystem," if you need to be reminded about how permissions work.) The letters and numbers are shown in Table 11.1.

TABLE 11.1   Commands to Create and Use Files

NAME	NUMERIC VALUE	LETTER VALUE
Set user ID bit	4	u+s
Set group ID bit	2	g+s
Sticky bit	1	o+t

The bits in which you are interested for creating collaborative directories are the set group ID bit (2) and sticky bit (1). If you are interested in other uses of the set user ID and set group ID bits, refer to the sidebar "Using Set UID and Set GID Bit Commands."

Creating group collaboration directories (set GID bit)

When you create a set GID directory, any files created in that directory are assigned to the group assigned to the directory itself. The idea is to have a directory where all members of a group can share files but still protect them from other users. Here's a set of steps for creating a collaborative directory for all users in the group I created called sales:

1. Create a group to use for collaboration:

   ```
   # addgroup --gid 301 sales
   ```

2. Add to the group some users with which you want to be able to share files (I used mary):

   ```
   # usermod -aG sales mary
   ```

3. Create the collaborative directory:

```
# mkdir /mnt/salestools
```

Using Set UID and Set GID Bit Commands

The set UID and set GID bits are used on special executable files that allow commands to be run differently than most. Normally, when a user runs a command, that command runs with that user's permissions. In other words, if I run the vi command as chris, that instance of the vi command would have the permissions to read and write files that the user chris could read and write.

Commands with the set UID or set GID bits set are different. It is the owner and group assigned to the command, respectively, that determines the permissions the command has to access resources on the computer. So, a set UID command owned by root would run with root permissions; a set GID command owned by Apache would have Apache group permissions.

Examples of applications that have set UID bits turned on are the su and newgrp commands. In both of those cases, the commands must be able to act as the root user to do their jobs. However, to actually get root permissions, a user must provide a password. You can tell su is a set UID bit command because of the s where the first execute bit (x) usually goes:

```
$ ls -l /bin/su
-rwsr-xr-x. 1 root root  30092 Jan 30 07:11 su
```

4. Assign the group sales to the directory:

```
# chgrp sales /mnt/salestools
```

5. Change the directory permission to 2775. This turns on the set group ID bit (2), full rwx for the user (7), rwx for group (7), and r-x (5) for other:

```
# chmod 2775 /mnt/salestools
```

6. Become mary (run su - mary). As mary, create a file in the shared directory and look at the permissions. When you list permissions, you can see that the directory is a set GID directory because a lowercase s appears where the group execute permission should be (rwxrw**s**r-x):

```
# su - mary
[mary]$ touch /mnt/salestools/test.txt
[mary]$ ls -ld /mnt/salestools/ /mnt/salestools/test.txt
drwxrwsr-x. 2 root sales 4096 Jan 22 14:32 /mnt/salestools/
-rw-rw-r--. 1 mary sales    0 Jan 22 14:32 /mnt/salestools/test.txt
```

Typically, a file created by mary would have the group mary assigned to it. But because test.txt was created in a set group ID bit directory, the file is assigned to the sales group. Now, anyone who belongs to the sales group can read from or write to that file, based on group permissions.

Creating restricted deletion directories (sticky bit)

A *restricted deletion directory* is created by turning on a directory's sticky bit. What makes a restricted deletion directory different than other directories? Normally, if write permission is open to a user on a file or directory, that user can delete that file or directory. However, in a restricted deletion directory, unless you are the root user or the owner of the directory, you can never delete another user's files.

Typically, a restricted deletion directory is used as a place where lots of different users can create files. For example, the /tmp directory is a restricted deletion directory:

```
$ ls -ld /tmp
drwxrwxrwt. 116 root root 36864 Jan 22 14:18 /tmp
```

You can see that the permissions are wide open, but instead of an x for the execute bit for other, the t indicates that the sticky bit is set. The following is an example of creating a restricted deletion directory with a file that is wide open for writing by anyone:

```
[mary]$ mkdir /tmp/mystuff
[mary]$ chmod 1777 /tmp/mystuff
[mary]$ cp /etc/services /tmp/mystuff/
[mary]$ chmod 666 /tmp/mystuff/services
[mary]$ ls -ld /tmp/mystuff /tmp/mystuff/services
drwxrwxrwt. 2 mary mary   4096 Jan 22 15:28 /tmp/mystuff/
-rw-rw-rw-. 1 mary mary 640999 Jan 22 15:28 /tmp/mystuff/services
```

With permissions set to 1777 on the /tmp/mystuff directory, you can see that all permissions are wide open, but a t appears instead of the last execute bit. With the /tmp/mystuff/services file open for writing, any user could open it and change its contents. However, because the file is in a sticky bit directory, only root and mary can delete that file.

Centralizing User Accounts

Although the default way of authenticating users in Linux is to check user information against the /etc/passwd file and passwords from the /etc/shadow file, you can authenticate in other ways as well. In most large enterprises, user account information is stored in a centralized authentication server, so each time you install a new Linux system, instead of adding user accounts to that system, you have the Linux system query the authentication server when someone tries to log in.

As with local passwd/shadow authentication, configuring centralized authentication requires that you provide two types of information: account information (username, user/group IDs, home directory, default shell, and so on) and authentication method (different types of encrypted passwords, smart cards, retinal scans, and so on). Linux provides ways of configuring those types of information.

Authentication domains that are supported in Linux include LDAP, NIS, and Windows Active Directory.

Supported centralized database types include the following:

LDAP   The *Lightweight Directory Access Protocol (LDAP)* is a popular protocol for providing directory services (such as phone books, addresses, and user accounts). It is an open standard that is configured in many types of computing environments.

NIS   The *Network Information Service (NIS)* was originally created by Sun Microsystems to propagate information such as user accounts, host configuration, and other types of system information across many UNIX systems. Because NIS passes information in clear text, most enterprises now use the more secure LDAP or Winbind protocols for centralized authentication.

Winbind   Selecting *Winbind* from the Authentication Configuration window enables you to authenticate your users against a Microsoft Active Directory (AD) server. Many large companies extend their desktop authentication setup to do server configuration as well as using an AD server.

If you are looking into setting up your own centralized authentication services and you want to use an open-source project, check out the OpenLDAP implementation. The `ldap-utils` package can be installed through the regular APT repos.

Summary

Having separate user accounts is the primary method of setting secure boundaries between the people who use your Linux system. Regular users typically can control the files and directories within their own home directories but very little outside of those directories.

In this chapter, you learned how to add user and group accounts, how to modify them, and even how to extend user and group accounts beyond the boundaries of the local `/etc/passwd` file. You also learned that authentication can be done by accessing centralized LDAP servers.

The next chapter introduces another basic topic needed by Linux system administrators: how to manage disks. In that chapter, you learn how to partition disks, add filesystems, and mount them so the contents of the disk partitions are accessible to those using your system.

Exercises

Use these exercises to test your knowledge of adding and managing user and group accounts in Linux. These tasks assume that you are running an Ubuntu system (although some tasks work on other Linux systems as well). If you are stuck, solutions to the tasks are shown in Appendix A (although in Linux, you often have multiple ways to complete a task).

1. Add a local user account to your Linux system that has a username of `jbaxter` and a full name of John Baxter and that uses `/bin/sh` as its default shell. Let the UID be assigned by default. Set the password for `jbaxter` to: `My1N1teOut!`

2. Create a group account named `testing` that uses group ID 315.

3. Add `jbaxter` to the `testing` group and the `bin` group.

4. Open a shell as `jbaxter` (either a new login session or using a current shell) and temporarily have the `testing` group be your default group so that when you type `touch /home/jbaxter/file.txt`, the `testing` group is assigned as the file's group.

5. Note what user ID has been assigned to `jbaxter`, and delete the user account without deleting the home directory assigned to `jbaxter`.

6. Find any files in the `/home` directory (and any subdirectories) that are assigned to the user ID that recently belonged to the user named `jbaxter`.

7. Copy the `/etc/services` file to the default skeleton directory so that it shows up in the home directory of any new user. Then add a new user to the system named `mjones`, with a full name of Mary Jones and a home directory of `/home/maryjones`.

8. Find all files under the `/home` directory that belong to `mjones`. Are there any files owned by `mjones` that you didn't expect to see?

9. Log in as `mjones`, and create a file called `/tmp/maryfile.txt`. Using ACLs, assign the `bin` user read/write permission to that file. Then assign the `lp` group read/write permission to that file.

10. Still as `mjones`, create a directory named `/tmp/mydir`. Using ACLs, assign default permissions to that directory so that the `adm` user has read/write/execute permission to that directory and any files or directories created in it. Create the `/tmp/mydir/testing/` directory and `/tmp/mydir/newfile.txt` file, and make sure that the `adm` user was also assigned full read/write/execute permissions. (Note that despite `rwx` permission being assigned to the `adm` user, the effective permission on `newfile.txt` is only `rw`. What could you do to make sure that `adm` gets execute permission as well?)

Managing Disks and Filesystems

IN THIS CHAPTER

Creating disk partitions

Creating logical volumes with LVM

Adding filesystems

Mounting filesystems

Unmounting filesystems

Your operating system, applications, and data need to be kept on some kind of permanent storage so that when you turn your computer off and then on again, it is all still there. Traditionally, that storage has been provided by a hard disk in your computer. To organize the information on that disk, the disk is usually divided into partitions, with most partitions given a structure referred to as a *filesystem*.

This chapter describes how to work with hard drives. Hard drive tasks include partitioning, adding filesystems, and managing those filesystems in various ways. Storage devices that are attached to the systems such as removable devices, including hard disk drives (HDDs) and solid-state drives (SSDs), and network devices can be partitioned and managed in the same ways.

After covering basic partitions, I describe how Logical Volume Manager (LVM) can be used to make it easier to grow, shrink, and otherwise manage filesystems more efficiently.

Understanding Disk Storage

The basics of how data storage works are the same in most modern operating systems. When you install the operating system, the disk is divided into one or more partitions. Each partition is formatted with a filesystem. In the case of Linux, some of the partitions may be specially formatted for elements such as swap area or LVM physical volumes. Disks are used for permanent storage; *random access memory (RAM)* and swap partitions are used for temporary storage. For example, when you run a command, that command is copied from the hard disk into RAM so that your computer processor (CPU) can access it more quickly.

Your CPU can access data much faster from RAM than it can from a hard disk, although SSDs are becoming more like RAM than HDDs. However, a disk is usually much larger than RAM, RAM is much more expensive, and RAM is erased when the computer reboots. Think of your office as a metaphor for RAM and disk. A disk is like a file cabinet where you store folders of information you need. RAM is like the top of your desk, where you put the folder of papers while you are using it but put it back in the file cabinet when you are not. (Warning: this metaphor doesn't work for people with permanently messy desks!)

If RAM fills up by running too many processes or a process that doesn't return its unused memory (called a "memory leak"), new processes will fail—unless your system can find a way to extend system memory. That's where a swap area comes in. A *swap space* is a hard disk swap partition or a swap file where your computer can "swap out" data from RAM that isn't being used at the moment and then "swap in" the data back to RAM when it is needed again. Although it is better never to exceed your RAM (performance takes a hit when you swap), swapping out is better than having processes just fail.

Another special partition is a *Logical Volume Manager (LVM)* physical volume. LVM physical volumes enable you to create pools of storage space called *volume groups*. From those volume groups, you have much more flexibility for growing and shrinking logical volumes than you have resizing disk partitions directly.

For Linux, at least one disk partition is required, assigned to the root (/) of the entire Linux filesystem. However, it is more common to have separate partitions that are assigned to particular directories, such as /home, /var, and/or /tmp. Each of the partitions is connected to the larger Linux filesystem by mounting it to a point in the filesystem where you want that partition to be used. Any file added to the mount point directory of a partition, or a subdirectory, is stored on that partition.

> **NOTE**
>
> The word *mount* refers to the action of connecting a filesystem from a hard disk, USB drive, or network storage device to a particular point in the filesystem. This action is done using the mount command, along with options to tell the command where the storage device is located and to which directory in the filesystem to connect it.

The business of connecting disk partitions to the Linux filesystem is done automatically and is invisible to the end user. How does this happen? Each regular disk partition created when you install Linux is associated with a device name. An entry in the /etc/fstab file tells Linux each partition's device name and where to mount it (as well as other bits of information). The mounting is done when the system boots.

Most of this chapter focuses on understanding how your computer's disk is partitioned and connected to form your Linux filesystem as well as how to partition disks, format filesystems and swap space, and have those items used when the system boots. The chapter then covers how to do partitioning and filesystem creation manually.

Coming from Windows

Filesystems are organized differently in Linux than they are in Microsoft Windows operating systems. Instead of drive letters (for example, A:, B:, C:) for each local disk, network filesystem, CD-ROM, or other type of storage medium, everything fits neatly into the Linux directory structure.

Some drives are connected (mounted) automatically into the filesystem when you insert removable media. For example, a CD might be mounted on /media/cdrom. If the drive isn't mounted automatically, it is up to an administrator to create a mount point in the filesystem and then connect the disk to that point.

Linux can understand VFAT filesystems, which are often the default format when you buy a USB flash drive. A VFAT and exFAT USB flash drive provides a good way to share data between Linux and Windows systems. Linux kernel support is available for NTFS filesystems, which are usually used with Windows these days. However, NTFS, and sometimes exFAT, require that you install additional kernel drivers in Linux.

VFAT filesystems are often used when files need to be exchanged between different types of operating systems. Because VFAT was used in MS-DOS and early Windows operating systems, it offers a good lowest common denominator for sharing files with many types of systems (including Linux). NTFS is the filesystem type most commonly used with modern Microsoft Windows systems.

12

Partitioning Hard Disks

Linux provides several tools for managing your hard disk partitions. You need to know how to partition your disk if you want to add a disk to your system or change your existing disk configuration.

The following sections demonstrate disk partitioning using a removable USB flash drive and a fixed hard disk. To be safe, I use a USB flash drive that doesn't contain any data that I want to keep in order to practice partitioning.

Changing partitioning can make a system unbootable!

I don't recommend using your system's primary hard disk to practice editing partitions because a mistake can make your system unbootable. Even if you use a separate USB flash drive to practice, a bad entry in /etc/fstab can hang your system on reboot.

Understanding partition tables

PC architecture computers have traditionally used *master boot record (MBR) partition tables* to store information about the sizes and layouts of the hard disk partitions. There are many tools for managing MBR partitions that are stable and reliable. A few years ago, however, a new standard called *Globally Unique Identifier (GUID) partition tables* was introduced as part of the UEFI computer architecture to replace the older BIOS method of booting systems.

Many Linux partitioning tools have been updated to handle GUID partition tables (GPTs). Other tools for handling GUID partition tables have been added. Because the popular fdisk command has not always supported GPT partitions, the parted command is used to illustrate partitioning in this chapter.

Limitations imposed by the MBR specification brought about the need for GUID partitions. In particular, MBR partitions are limited to 2TB in size. GUID partitions can create partitions up to 9.4ZB (zettabytes).

Viewing disk partitions

To view disk partitions, use the parted command with the -l option. The following is an example of partitioning on a 160GB fixed hard drive:

```
# parted -l /dev/sda
Disk /dev/sda: 160.0 GB, 160000000000 bytes, 312500000 sectors
Units = sectors of 1 * 512 = 512 bytes
Sector size (logical/physical): 512 bytes / 512 bytes
I/O size (minimum/optimal): 512 bytes / 512 bytes
Disk label type: dos
Disk identifier: 0x0008870c
    Device Boot      Start        End       Blocks   Id  System
  /dev/sda1   *        2048    1026047      512000   83  Linux
  /dev/sda2         1026048  304281599   151627776   8e  Linux LVM
```

When a USB flash drive is inserted, it is assigned to the next available sd device. The following (truncated) example shows the two partitions on a 500GB SSD drive (/dev/sda) and a USB drive where /dev/sdb is assigned as the USB device name (the second disk on the system). This USB drive is a 4GB USB flash drive:

```
#  fdisk -l | less

Device        Start       End    Sectors   Size Type
/dev/sda1      2048   1050623    1048576   512M EFI System
/dev/sda2   1050624 976771071  975720448 465.3G Linux filesystem

Device     Boot Start       End Sectors  Size Id Type
/dev/sdb1   *    2048   7811071 7809024  3.7G  c W95 FAT32 (LBA)
```

Although this USB drive was assigned to /dev/sdb, your drive might be assigned to a different device name. Here are some things to look for:

- A SCSI or USB storage device, represented by an *sd?* device (such as sda, sdb, sdc, and so on) can have up to 16 minor devices (for example, the main /dev/sdc device and /dev/sdc1 through /dev/sdc15). So, there can be 15 partitions total. An NVMe SSD storage device, represented by a nvme device (such as nvme0, nvme1, nvme2, and so on) can be divided into one or more namespaces (most devices just use the first namespace) and partitions. For example, / dev/nvme0n1p1 represents the first partition in the first namespace on the first NVMe SSD.

- For x86 computers, disks can have up to four primary partitions. So, to have more than four total partitions, one must be an extended partition. Any partitions beyond the four primary partitions are logical partitions that use space from the extended partition.

- The type field indicates the type of partition. Notice that there is a Linux filesystem partition in the first example, and FAT32 in the second.

The first partition on the system described by the following lsblk command is roughly 512MB and is mounted on the /boot/efi directory. The second partition (465GB) is mounted on the / (root) partition.

```
$ lsblk
sda       8:0     0  465.8G  0 disk
└sda1     8:1     0    512M  0 part /boot/efi
└sda2     8:2     0  465.3G  0 part /
sdb       8:16    1    3.7G  0 disk
└sdb1     8:17    1    3.7G  0 part /media/local/LUBUNTU 19_
```

For the moment, I recommend that you leave the hard disk alone and find a USB flash drive that you do not mind erasing. You can try the commands I demonstrate on that drive.

Creating a single-partition disk

To add a new storage medium (hard disk, USB flash drive, or similar device) to your computer so that it can be used by Linux, you first need to connect the disk device to your computer and then partition the disk. Here's the general procedure:

1. Install the new hard drive or insert the new USB flash drive.

2. Partition the new disk.

3. Create the filesystems on the new disk.

4. Mount the filesystems.

The easiest way to add a disk or flash drive to Linux is to have the entire disk devoted to a single Linux partition. You can have multiple partitions, however, and assign them each to different types of filesystems and different mount points if you like.

The following process takes you through partitioning a USB flash drive to be used for Linux that has only one partition. If you have a USB flash drive (any size) that you don't mind erasing, you can work through this procedure as you read. The section following this describes how to partition a disk with multiple partitions.

WARNING

If you make a mistake partitioning your disk with `parted`, make sure that you correct that change. Unlike `fdisk`, where you could just type q to exit without saving your changes, `parted` makes your changes immediately, so you are not able just to quit to abandon changes.

1. For a USB flash drive, just plug it into an available USB port. Going forward, I use a 128GB USB flash drive, but you can get a USB flash drive of any size.

2. Determine the device name for the USB drive. Using `sudo`, type the following **journalctl** command, and then insert the USB flash drive. Messages appear, indicating the device name of the drive you just plugged in (press Ctrl+C to exit the `tail` command when you are finished):

```
# journalctl -f
kernel: usb 4-1: new SuperSpeed Gen 1 USB device number 3
using xhci_hcd
kernel: usb 4-1: New USB device found, idVendor=0781,
                 idProduct=5581, bcdDevice= 1.00
kernel: usb 4-1: New USB device strings: Mfr=1, Product=2, SerialNumber=3
kernel: usb 4-1: Product: Ultra
kernel: usb 4-1: Manufacturer: SanDisk
...
kernel: sd 6:0:0:0: Attached scsi generic sg2 type 0
kernel:  sdb: sdb1
kernel: sd 6:0:0:0: [sdb] Attached SCSI removable disk
udisksd[809]: Mounted /dev/sdb1 at /run/media/chris/7DEB-B010
              on behalf of uid 1000
```

3. From the output, you can see that the USB flash drive was found and assigned to /dev/sdb. (Your device name may be different.) It also contains a single formatted partition: sdb1. Be sure you identify the correct disk or you could lose all data from disks you may want to keep!

4. If the USB flash drive mounts automatically, unmount it. Here is how to find the USB partitions in this example and unmount them:

```
# mount | grep sdb
/dev/sdb1 on /media/local/...
# umount /dev/sdb1
```

5. Use the `parted` command to create partitions on the USB drive. For example, if you are formatting the second USB, SATA, or SCSI disk (sdb), you can type the following:

```
# parted /dev/sdb
GNU Parted 3.2
Using /dev/sdb
Welcome to GNU Parted! Type 'help' to view a list of commands.
(parted)
```

Now you are in `parted` command mode, where you can use the `parted` single-letter command set to work with your partitions.

6. If you start with a new USB flash drive, it may have one partition that is entirely devoted to a Windows-compatible filesystem (such as VFAT or fat32). Use `p` to view all partitions and `rm` to delete the partition. Here's what it looked like when I did that:

```
(parted) p
Model: SanDisk Ultra (scsi)
Disk /dev/sdb: 123GB
Sector size (logical/physical): 512B/512B
Partition Table: msdos
Disk Flags:

Number  Start    End    Size   Type     File system  Flags
 1      16.4kB   123GB  123GB  primary  fat32        lba
(parted) rm
Partition number? 1
```

7. Relabel the disk as having a GPT partition table:

```
(parted) mklabel gpt
Warning: The existing disk label on /dev/sdb will be destroyed
and all data
on this disk will be lost. Do you want to continue?
Yes/No? Yes
(parted)
```

8. To create a new partition, type **mkpart**. You are prompted for the filesystem type, then the start and end of the partition. This example names the partition `alldisk`, uses `xfs` as the file system type, starts the partition at 1M and ends at 123GB:

```
(parted) mkpart
Partition name?  []? alldisk
File system type?  [ext2]? xfs
Start? 1
End? 123GB
```

9. Double-check that the drive is partitioned the way you want by pressing **p**. (Your output will differ, depending on the size of your drive.)

```
(parted) p
Model: SanDisk Ultra (scsi)
Disk /dev/sdb: 123GB
Sector size (logical/physical): 512B/512B
Partition Table: gpt
Disk Flags:

Number  Start    End    Size   File system  Name     Flags
 1      1049kB   123GB  123GB  xfs          alldisk
```

12

10. Although the partitioning is done, the new partition is not yet ready to use. For that, you have to create a filesystem on the new partition. To create a filesystem on the new disk partition, use the mkfs command. By default, this command creates an ext2 filesystem, which is usable by Linux. However, in most cases you want to use a journaling filesystem (such as ext3, ext4, or xfs). To create an xfs filesystem on the first partition of the second hard disk, type the following:

```
# mkfs -t xfs /dev/sdb1
```

> **TIP**
>
> You can use different commands or options to this command to create other filesystem types. For example, use mkfs.exfat to create a VFAT filesystem, mkfs.msdos for DOS, or mkfs.ext4 for the ext4 filesystem type. You may want a VFAT or exFAT (available with Ubuntu) filesystem if you want to share files among Linux, Windows, and Mac systems.

11. To be able to use the new filesystem, you need to create a mount point and mount it to the partition. Here is an example of how to do that. You then check to make sure that the mount succeeded.

```
# mkdir /mnt/test
# mount /dev/sdb1 /mnt/test
# df -h /mnt/sdb1
Filesystem          Size  Used Avail Use% Mounted on
/dev/sdb1           115G   13M  115G   1% /mnt/test
```

The df command shows that /dev/sdb1 is mounted on /mnt/test and that it offers about 115GB of disk space. The mount command shows all mounted filesystems, but here I just list sdb1 to show that it is mounted.

Any files or directories that you create later in the /mnt/test directory, and any of its subdirectories, are stored on the /dev/sdb1 device.

12. When you are finished using the drive, you can unmount it with the umount command, after which you can safely remove the drive (see the description of the umount command later if this command fails):

```
# umount /dev/sdb1
```

13. You don't usually set up a USB flash drive to mount automatically every time the system boots because it mounts automatically when you plug it in. But if you decide that you want to do that, edit /etc/fstab and add a line describing what and where to mount. Here is an example of a line you might add:

```
/dev/sdb1      /mnt/test      xfs     defaults    0 1
```

In this example, the partition (/dev/sdb1) is mounted on the /mnt/test directory as an xfs filesystem. The defaults keyword causes the partition to be mounted at boot time. The number 0 tells the system not to back up files automatically from this filesystem with the dump command (dump is rarely used anymore, but the field is here). The 1 in the last column tells the system to check the partition for errors after a certain number of mounts.

At this point, you have a working, permanently mounted disk partition. The next section describes how to partition a disk that has multiple partitions.

Creating a multiple-partition disk

Now that you understand the basic process of partitioning a disk, adding a filesystem, and making that filesystem available (temporarily and permanently), it is time to try a more complex example. Taking that same 128GB USB flash drive, I ran the procedure described later in this section to create multiple partitions on one disk.

In this procedure, I configure a master boot record (MBR) partition to illustrate how extended partitions work and to use the older fdisk command. I create two partitions of 5GB (sdb1 and sdb2), two 3GB (sdb3 and sdb5), and one 4GB (sdb6). The sdb4 device is an extended partition, which consumes all remaining disk space. Space from the sdb5 and sdb6 partitions is taken from the extended partition. This leaves plenty of space to create new partitions.

As before, insert the USB flash drive and determine the device name (in my case, /dev/sdb). Also, be sure to unmount any partitions that mount automatically when you insert the USB flash drive.

TIP

When you indicate the size of each partition, type the plus sign and the number of megabytes or gigabytes you want to assign to the partition. For example, +1024M to create a 1024-megabyte partition or +10G for a 10-gigabyte partition. Be sure to remember the plus sign (+) and the M or G! If you forget the M or G, fdisk thinks you mean sectors and you get unexpected results.

1. I started this procedure by overwriting the USB drive with the dd command (dd if=/dev/zero of=/dev/sdb bs=1M count=100). This allowed me to start with a fresh master boot record. Please be careful to use the right drive number, or you could erase your operating system!

2. Create six new partitions as follows:

```
# fdisk /dev/sdb
Welcome to fdisk (util-linux 2.33.2).
Changes will remain in memory only, until you decide to write them.
Be careful before using the write command.

Device does not contain a recognized partition table.
Created a new DOS disklabel with disk identifier 0x8933f665.

Command (m for help): n
Partition type
```

Continues

Continued

```
     p   primary (0 primary, 0 extended, 4 free)
     e   extended (container for logical partitions)
Select (default p): p
Partition number (1-4, default 1): 1
First sector (2048-240254975, default 2048):
Last sector, +/-sectors or +/-size{K,M,G,T,P} (2048-240254975,
default 240254975): +5G

Created a new partition 1 of type 'Linux' and of size 5 GiB.

Command (m for help): n
Partition type
     p   primary (1 primary, 0 extended, 3 free)
     e   extended (container for logical partitions)
Select (default p): p
Partition number (2-4, default 2): 2
First sector (10487808-240254975, default 10487808):
Last sector, +/-sectors or +/-size{K,M,G,T,P} (10487808-240254975,
default 240254975): +5G

Created a new partition 2 of type 'Linux' and of size 5 GiB.

Command (m for help): n
Partition type
     p   primary (2 primary, 0 extended, 2 free)
     e   extended (container for logical partitions)
Select (default p): p
Partition number (3,4, default 3): 3
First sector (20973568-240254975, default 20973568):
Last sector, +/-sectors or +/-size{K,M,G,T,P} (20973568-240254975,
default 240254975): +3G

Created a new partition 3 of type 'Linux' and of size 3 GiB.

Command (m for help): n
Partition type
     p   primary (3 primary, 0 extended, 1 free)
     e   extended (container for logical partitions)
Select (default e): e

Selected partition 4
First sector (27265024-240254975, default 27265024):
Last sector, +/-sectors or +/-size{K,M,G,T,P} (27265024-240254975,
default 240254975): <ENTER>

Created a new partition 4 of type 'Extended' and of size 101.6 GiB.

Command (m for help): n
All primary partitions are in use.
```

```
Adding logical partition 5
First sector (27267072-240254975, default 27267072):
Last sector, +/-sectors or +/-size{K,M,G,T,P} (27267072-240254975, default
240254975): +3G

Created a new partition 5 of type 'Linux' and of size 3 GiB.

Command (m for help): n
All primary partitions are in use.
Adding logical partition 6
First sector (33560576-240254975, default 33560576):
Last sector, +/-sectors or +/-size{K,M,G,T,P} (33560576-240254975, default
240254975): +4G

Created a new partition 6 of type 'Linux' and of size 4 GiB.
```

3. Check the partitioning before saving by typing **p**. Notice that there are five usable partitions (sdc1, sdc2, sdc3, sdc5, and sdc6) and that the sectors between the Start and End for sdc4 are being consumed by sdc5 and sdc6.

```
Command (m for help): p
...
Device     Boot    Start       End    Sectors   Size Id Type
/dev/sdb1           2048  10487807   10485760    5G 83 Linux
/dev/sdb2       10487808  20973567   10485760    5G 82 Linux
/dev/sdb3       20973568  27265023    6291456    3G 83 Linux
/dev/sdb4       27265024 240254975  212989952 101.6G  5 Extended
/dev/sdb5       27267072  33558527    6291456    3G 83 Linux
/dev/sdb6       33560576  41949183    8388608    4G 83 Linux
```

4. The default partition type is Linux. But now I think I want to use some of the partitions for swap space (type 82), FAT32 (type x), and Linux LVM (type 8e). To do that, I type **t** and indicate which partition type to use. Type **L** to see a list of partition types.

```
Command (m for help): t
Partition number (1-6): 2
Hex code (type L to list codes): 82
Changed type of partition 'Linux' to 'Linux swap / Solaris'.

Command (m for help): t
Partition number (1-6): 5
Hex code (type L to list codes): c
Changed type of partition 'Linux' to 'W95 FAT32 (LBA)'.

Command (m for help): t
Partition number (1-6): 6
Hex code (type L to list codes): 8e
Changed type of partition 'Linux' to 'Linux LVM'.
```

5. I check that the partition table is the way I want it and then write the changes:

```
Command (m for help): p
...
Device     Boot    Start        End    Sectors   Size Id Type
/dev/sdb1           2048   10487807   10485760    5G 83 Linux
/dev/sdb2       10487808   20973567   10485760    5G 82 Linux
swap / Solaris
/dev/sdb3       20973568   27265023    6291456    3G 83 Linux
/dev/sdb4       27265024  240254975  212989952 101.6G  5 Extended
/dev/sdb5       27267072   33558527    6291456    3G  c W95 FAT32
(LBA)
/dev/sdb6       33560576   41949183    8388608    4G 8e Linux LVM

Command (m for help): w
The partition table has been altered!
The kernel still uses the old partitions. The new table will be
used at the next reboot.
Syncing disks
```

6. After the write is completed, check that the kernel knows about the changes to the partition table. To do that, search the /proc/partitions for sdb. If the new devices are not there, run the partprobe /dev/sdb command on the drive or reboot your computer.

```
# grep sdb /proc/partitions
    8      16  120127488 sdb
    8      17  120125440 sdb1
# partprobe /dev/sdb
# grep sdb /proc/partitions
    8      16  120127488 sdb
    8      17    5242880 sdb1
    8      18    5242880 sdb2
    8      19    3145728 sdb3
    8      20          1 sdb4
    8      21    3145728 sdb5
    8      22    4194304 sdb6
```

7. While the partitions are now set for different types of content, other commands are needed to structure the partitions into filesystems or swap areas. Here's how to do that for the partitions just created:

sdb1: To make this into a regular Linux ext4 filesystem, type the following:

```
# mkfs -t ext4 /dev/sdb1
```

sdb2: To format this as a swap area, type the following:

```
# mkswap /dev/sdb2
```

sdb3: To make this into an ext2 filesystem (the default), type the following:

```
# mkfs /dev/sdb3
```

sdb5: To make this into a VFAT filesystem (the default), type the following:

```
# mkfs -t vfat /dev/sdb5
```

sdb6: To make this into an LVM physical volume, type the following:

```
# pvcreate /dev/sdb6
```

These partitions are now ready to be mounted, used as swap area, or added to an LVM volume group. See the next section, "Using Logical Volume Manager Partitions," to see how LVM physical volumes are used to ultimately create LVM logical volumes from volume groups. See the section "Mounting Filesystems" for descriptions of how to mount filesystems and enable swap areas.

Using Logical Volume Manager Partitions

Basic disk partitioning in Linux has its shortcomings. What happens if you run out of disk space? In the old days, a common solution was to copy data to a bigger disk, restart the system with the new disk, and hope that you don't run out of space again anytime soon. This process meant downtime and inefficiency.

Logical Volume Manager (LVM) offers lots of flexibility and efficiency in dealing with constantly changing storage needs. With LVM, physical disk partitions are added to pools of space called volume groups. Logical volumes are assigned space from volume groups as needed. This gives you these abilities:

- Add more space to a logical volume from the volume group while the volume is still in use.
- Add more physical volumes to a volume group if the volume group begins to run out of space.
- Move data from one physical volume to another so you can remove smaller disks and replace them with larger ones while the filesystems are still in use—again, without downtime.

With LVM, it is also easier to shrink filesystems to reclaim disk space, although shrinking does require that you unmount the logical volume (but no reboot is needed). LVM also supports advanced features, such as mirroring and working in clusters.

Checking an existing LVM

Let's start by looking at an existing LVM example. The following command displays the partitions on my first hard disk:

```
# fdisk -l /dev/sda | grep /dev/sda
Disk /dev/sda: 160.0 GB, 160000000000 bytes
/dev/sda1    *         2048     1026047        512000    83   Linux
/dev/sda2    *      1026048   312498175     155736064    8e   Linux LVM
```

On this system, the 160GB hard drive is divided into one 500MB Linux partition (sda1) and a second (Linux LVM) partition that consumes the rest of the disk (sda2). Next, I use the pvdisplay command to see if that partition is being used in an LVM group:

```
# pvdisplay /dev/sda2
  --- Physical volume ---
  PV Name               /dev/sda2
  VG Name               vg_abc
  PV Size               148.52 GiB / not usable 2.00 MiB
  Allocatable           yes (but full)
  PE Size               4.00 MiB
  Total PE              38021
  Free PE               0
  Allocated PE          38021
  PV UUID               wlvuIv-UiI2-pNND-f39j-oH0X-9too-AOII7R
```

You can see that the LVM physical volume represented by /dev/sda2 has 148.52GiB of space, all of which has been totally allocated to a volume group named vg_abc. The smallest unit of storage that can be used from this physical volume is 4.0MiB, which is referred to as a *Physical Extent (PE)*.

> **NOTE**
>
> Notice that LVM tools show disk space in MiB and GiB. One MB is 1,000,000 bytes (10^6), while a MiB is 1,048,576 bytes (2^20). An MiB is a more accurate way to reflect how data are stored on a computer. But marketing people tend to use MB because it makes the hard disks, CDs, and DVDs they sell look like they have more capacity than they do. Keep in mind that most tools in Linux display storage data in MiB and GiB, although some can display MB and GB as well.

Next, you want to see information about the volume group:

```
# vgdisplay vg_abc
  --- Volume group ---
  VG Name               vg_abc
  System ID
  Format                lvm2
  Metadata Areas        1
  Metadata Sequence No  4
  VG Access             read/write
  VG Status             resizable
  MAX LV                0
  Cur LV                3
  Open LV               3
  Max PV                0
  Cur PV                1
  Act PV                1
  VG Size               148.52 GiB
  PE Size               4.00 MiB
```

```
Total PE           38021
Alloc PE / Size    38021 / 148.52 GiB
Free  PE / Size    0 / 0
VG UUID            c2SGHM-KU9H-wbXM-sgca-EtBr-UXAq-UnnSTh
```

You can see that all of the 38,021 PEs have been allocated. Using lvdisplay as follows, you can see where they have been allocated (I have snipped some of the output):

```
# lvdisplay vg_abc
  --- Logical volume ---
  LV Name                /dev/vg_abc/lv_root
  VG Name                vg_abc
  LV UUID                33VeDc-jd0l-hlCc-RMuB-tkcw-QvFi-cKCZqa
  LV Write Access        read/write
  LV Status              available
  # open                 1
  LV Size                50.00 GiB
  Current LE             12800
  Segments               1
  Allocation             inherit
  Read ahead sectors     auto
  - currently set to     256
  Block device           253:0
  --- Logical volume ---
  LV Name                /dev/vg_abc/lv_home
  VG Name                vg_abc
  ...
  LV Size                92.64 GiB
  --- Logical volume ---
  LV Name                /dev/vg_abc/lv_swap
  VG Name                vg_abc
  ...
  LV Size                5.88 GiB
```

There are three logical volumes drawing space from vg_abc. Each logical volume is associated with a device name that includes the volume group name and the logical volume name: /dev/vg_abc/lv_root (50GB), /dev/vg_abc/lv_home (92.64GB), and /dev/vg_abc/lv_swap (5.88GB). Other devices linked to these names are located in the /dev/mapper directory: vg_abc-lv_home, vg_abc-lv_root, and vg_abc-lv_swap. Either set of names can be used to refer to these logical volumes.

The root and home logical volumes are formatted as ext4 filesystems, whereas the swap logical volume is formatted as swap space. Let's look in the /etc/fstab file to see how these logical volumes are used:

```
# grep vg_ /etc/fstab
/dev/mapper/vg_abc-lv_root /      ext4   defaults    1 1
/dev/mapper/vg_abc-lv_home /home  ext4   defaults    1 2
/dev/mapper/vg_abc-lv_swap swap   swap   defaults    0 0
```

Figure 12.1 illustrates how the different partitions, volume groups, and logical volumes relate to the complete Linux filesystem. The sda1 device is formatted as a filesystem and mounted on the /boot directory. The sda2 device provides space for the vg_abc volume group. Then logical volumes lv_home and lv_root are mounted on the /home and / directories, respectively.

FIGURE 12.1

LVM logical volumes can be mounted like regular partitions on a Linux filesystem.

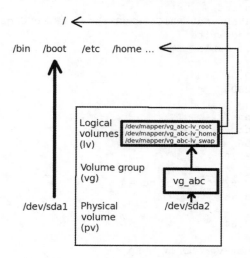

If you run out of space on any of the logical volumes, you can assign more space from the volume group. If the volume group is out of space, you can add another hard drive or network storage drive and add space from that drive to the volume group so more is available.

Now that you know how LVM works, the next section shows you how to create LVM logical volumes from scratch.

Creating LVM logical volumes

LVM logical volumes are used from the top down, but they are created from the bottom up. As illustrated in Figure 12.1 in the previous section, first you create one or more physical volumes (pv), use the physical volumes to create volume groups (vg), and then create logical volumes (lv) from the volume groups.

Commands for working with each LVM component begin with the letters pv, vg, and lv. For example, pvdisplay shows physical volumes, vgdisplay shows volume groups, and lvdisplay shows logical volumes.

The following procedure takes you through the steps of creating LVM volumes from scratch. To do this procedure, you could use the USB flash drive and partitions that I described earlier in this chapter.

1. Obtain a disk with some spare space on it and create a disk partition on it of the LVM type (8e). Then use the `pvcreate` command to identify this partition as an LVM physical volume. The process of doing this is described in the section "Creating a multiple-partition disk" using the /dev/sdb6 device in that example.

2. To add that physical volume to a new volume group, use the `vgcreate` command. The following command shows you how to create a volume group called `myvg0` using the /dev/sdb6 device:

   ```
   # vgcreate myvg0 /dev/sdc6
      Volume group "myvg0" successfully created
   ```

3. To see the new volume group, type the following:

   ```
   # vgdisplay myvg0
     --- Volume group ---
     VG Name                myvg0
     ...
     VG Size                <4.00 GiB
     PE Size                4.00 MiB
     Total PE               1023
     Alloc PE / Size        0 / 0
     Free  PE / Size        1023 / <4.00 MiB
   ```

4. All of the 1023 physical extents (PEs, 4.00 MiB each) are available. Here's how to create a logical volume from some of the space in that volume group and then check that the device for that logical volume exists:

   ```
   # lvcreate -n music -L 1G myvg0
     Logical volume "music" created
   # ls /dev/mapper/myvg0*
   /dev/mapper/myvg0-music
   ```

5. As you can see, the procedure created a device named /dev/mapper/myvg0-music. That device can now be used to put a filesystem on and mount it, just as you did with regular partitions in the first part of this chapter. For example:

   ```
   # mkfs -t ext4 /dev/mapper/myvg0-music
   # mkdir /mnt/mymusic
   # mount /dev/mapper/myvg0-music /mnt/mymusic
   # df -h /mnt/mymusic
   Filesystem               Size  Used Avail Use%  Mounted on
   /dev/mapper/myvg0-music  976M  2.6M  987M   1%  /mnt/mymusic
   ```

6. As with regular partitions, logical volumes can be mounted permanently by adding an entry to the /etc/fstab file, such as:

   ```
   /dev/mapper/myvg0-music /mnt/mymusic  ext4 defaults 1 2
   ```

12

The next time you reboot, the logical volume is automatically mounted on /mnt/mymusic. (Be sure to unmount the logical volume and remove this line if you want to remove the USB flash drive from your computer.)

Growing LVM logical volumes

If you run out of space on a logical volume, you can add more without even unmounting it. To do that, you must have unused space available in the volume group, grow the logical volume, and grow the filesystem to fill it. Building on the procedure in the previous section, here's how to do that:

1. Note how much space is currently on the logical volume, and then check that space is available in the logical volume's volume group:

```
# vgdisplay myvg0
...
  VG Size                <4.00 MiB
  PE Size                4.00 MiB
  Total PE               1023
  Alloc PE / Size        256 / 1.00 GiB
  Free  PE / Size        767 / <3.00 GiB
# df -h /mnt/mymusic/
Filesystem                 Size  Used Avail Use% Mounted on
/dev/mapper/myvg0-music    976M  2.6M  987M   1% /mnt/mymusic
```

2. Expand the logical volume using the lvextend command:

```
# lvextend -L +1G /dev/mapper/myvg0-music
  Size of logical volume myvg0/music changed
         from 1.00GiB to 2.00 GiB (512 extents).
  Logical volume myvg0/music successfully resized
```

3. Resize the filesystem to fit the new logical volume size:

```
# resize2fs -p /dev/mapper/myvg0-music
```

4. Check to see that the filesystem is now resized to include the additional disk space:

```
# df -h /mnt/mymusic/
Filesystem                 Size  Used Avail Use% Mounted on
/dev/mapper/myvg0-music    2.0G  3.0M  1.9G   1% /mnt/mymusic
```

You can see that the filesystem is now about 1G larger.

Mounting Filesystems

Now that you've had a chance to play with disk partitioning and filesystems, I'm going to step back and talk about how filesystems can be connected permanently to your Linux system.

Most of the hard disk partitions created when you install Linux are mounted automatically for you when the system boots. But you could also manually create partitions yourself and indicate the mount points for those partitions.

When you boot Linux, usually all of the Linux partitions on your hard disk are listed in your /etc/fstab file and are mounted. For that reason, the following sections describe what you might expect to find in that file. It also describes how you can mount other partitions so that they become part of your Linux filesystem.

The mount command is used not only to mount local storage devices, but also to mount other kinds of filesystems on your Linux system. For example, mount can be used to mount directories (folders) over the network from NFS or Samba servers. It can be used to mount filesystems from a new hard drive or USB flash drive that is not configured to automount. It can also mount filesystem image files using loop devices.

12

> **NOTE**
>
> With the addition of automatic mounting features and changes in how removable media are identified, since the release of the Linux 2.6 kernel (using features such as Udev and Hardware Abstraction Layer), you no longer need to mount removable media manually for many Linux desktop systems. Understanding how to mount and unmount filesystems manually on a Linux server, however, can be a very useful skill if you want to mount remote filesystems or temporarily mount partitions in particular locations.

Supported filesystems

To see filesystem types that are currently loaded in your kernel, type **cat /proc/filesystems**. The list that follows shows a sample of filesystem types that are currently supported in Linux, although they may not be in use at the moment or even available on the Linux distribution you are using:

befs: Filesystem used by the BeOS operating system.

btrfs: A copy-on-write filesystem that implements advanced filesystem features. It offers fault tolerance and easy administration. The btrfs filesystem has recently grown in popularity for enterprise applications.

cifs: Common Internet Filesystem (CIFS), the virtual filesystem used to access servers that comply with the SNIA CIFS specification. CIFS is an attempt to refine and standardize the SMB protocol used by Samba and Windows file sharing.

ext4: Successor to the popular ext3 filesystem. It includes many improvements over ext3, such as support for volumes up to 1 exbibyte and file sizes up to 16 tebibytes. (This has replaced ext3 as the default filesystem used in Ubuntu.)

ext3: Ext filesystems are the most common in most Linux systems. Compared ext2, the ext3 filesystem, also called the third extended filesystem, includes journaling features that, compared to ext2, improve a filesystem's capability to recover from crashes.

ext2: The default filesystem type for earlier Linux systems. Features are the same as ext3, except that ext2 doesn't include journaling features.

ext: This is the first version of ext3. It is not used very often anymore.

iso9660: Evolved from the High Sierra filesystem (the original standard for CD-ROMs). Extensions to the High Sierra standard (called Rock Ridge extensions) allow iso9660 filesystems to support long filenames and UNIX-style information (such as file permissions, ownership, and links). Data CD-ROMs typically use this filesystem type.

kafs: AFS client filesystem. Used in distributed computing environments to share files with Linux, Windows, and Macintosh clients.

minix: Minix filesystem type, used originally with the Minix version of UNIX. It supports filenames of up to only 30 characters.

msdos: An MS-DOS filesystem. You can use this type to mount media that comes from old Microsoft operating systems.

vfat: Microsoft extended FAT (VFAT) filesystem.

exfat: Extended FAT (exFAT) filesystem that has been optimized for SD cards, USB drives, and other flash memory.

umsdos: An MS-DOS filesystem with extensions to allow features that are similar to UNIX (including long filenames).

proc: Not a real filesystem, but rather a filesystem interface to the Linux kernel. You probably won't do anything special to set up a proc filesystem. However, the /proc mount point should be a proc filesystem. Many utilities rely on /proc to gain access to Linux kernel information.

reiserfs: ReiserFS journaled filesystem. ReiserFS was once a common default filesystem type for several Linux distributions. However, ext and xfs filesystems are by far more common filesystem types used with Linux today.

swap: Used for swap partitions. Swap areas are used to hold data temporarily when RAM is used up. Data is swapped to the swap area and then returned to RAM when it is needed again.

squashfs: Compressed, read-only filesystem type. Squashfs is popular on live CDs, where there is limited space and a read-only medium (such as a CD or DVD).

nfs: Network Filesystem (NFS) type of filesystem. NFS is used to mount filesystems on other Linux or UNIX computers.

hpfs: Filesystem is used to do read-only mounts of an OS/2 HPFS filesystem.

ncpfs: A filesystem used with Novell NetWare. NetWare filesystems can be mounted over a network.

ntfs: Windows NT filesystem. Depending upon the distribution you have, it may be supported as a read-only filesystem (so that you can mount and copy files from it).

ufs: Filesystem popular on Sun Microsystems's operating systems (that is, Solaris and SunOS).

jfs: A 64-bit journaling filesystem by IBM that is relatively lightweight for the many features it has.

xfs: A high-performance filesystem originally developed by Silicon Graphics that works extremely well with large files.

gfs2: A shared disk filesystem that allows multiple machines to all use the same shared disk without going through a network filesystem layer such as CIFS, NFS, and so on.

To see the list of filesystems that come with the kernel you are using, type **ls /lib/ modules/`uname -r`/kernel/fs/**. The actual modules are stored in subdirectories of that directory. Mounting a filesystem of a supported type causes the filesystem module to be loaded, if it is not already loaded.

Type **man fs** to see descriptions of Linux filesystems.

Enabling swap areas

A *swap area* is an area of the disk that is made available to Linux if the system runs out of memory (RAM). If your RAM is full and you try to start another application without a swap area, that application will fail.

With a swap area, Linux can temporarily swap out data from RAM to the swap area and then get it back when needed. You take a performance hit, but it is better than having processes fail.

To create a swap area from a partition or a file, use the mkswap command. To enable that swap area temporarily, you can use the swapon command. For example, here's how to check your available swap space, create a swap file, enable the swap file, and then check that the space is available on your system:

```
# free -m

          total      used      free    shared  buffers  cached
Mem:       1955       663      1291         0       42     283
-/+ buffers/cache:              337      1617
Swap:       819         0       819

# dd if=/dev/zero of=/var/tmp/myswap bs=1M count=1024
# mkswap /var/opt/myswap
# swapon /var/opt/myswap
# free -m

          total      used      free   shared  buffers    cached
Mem:       1955      1720       235        0       42      1310
-/+ buffers/cache:              367      1588
Swap:      1843         0      1843
```

The free command shows the amount of swap before and after creating, making, and enabling the swap area with the swapon command. That amount of swap is available immediately and temporarily to your system. To make that swap area permanent, you need to add it to your /etc/fstab file. Here is an example:

```
/var/opt/myswap   swap    swap     defaults   0 0
```

This entry indicates that the swap file named /var/opt/myswap should be enabled at boot time. Because there is no mount point for swap area, the second field is just set to swap, as is the partition type. To test that the swap file works before rebooting, you can enable it immediately (swapon -a) and check that the additional swap area appears:

```
# swapon -a
```

Disabling swap area

If at any point you want to disable a swap area, you can do so using the swapoff command. You might do this, in particular, if the swap area is no longer needed and you want to reclaim the space being consumed by a swap file or remove a USB drive that is providing a swap partition.

First, make sure that there aren't any applications using space on the swap device (using the free command), and then use swapoff to turn off the swap area so that you can reuse the space. Here is an example:

```
# free -m
            total       used       free     shared    buffers     cached
Mem:         1955       1720        235          0         42       1310
-/+ buffers/cache: 367             1588
Swap:        1843          0       1843
# swapoff /var/opt/myswap
# free -m
            total       used       free     shared    buffers     cached
Mem:         1955       1720        235          0         42       1310
-/+ buffers/cache: 367             1588
Swap:         819          0        819
```

Notice that the amount of available swap was reduced after running the swapoff command.

Using the fstab file to define mountable filesystems

The hard disk partitions on your local computer and the remote filesystems that you use every day are probably set up to mount automatically when you boot Linux. The /etc/fstab file contains definitions for each partition, along with options describing how the partition is mounted. Here's an example of an /etc/fstab file:

```
$ cat /etc/fstab
# /etc/fstab: static file system information.
# Use 'blkid' to print the universally unique identifier for a
# device; this may be used with UUID= as a more robust way to name devices
# that works even if disks are added and removed. See fstab(5).
#
```

```
# <file system> <mount point>   <type>  <options> <dump>  <pass>
# / was on /dev/sda2 during installation
UUID=c0e513f0-f840-4174-912d-241d30fd2e26 / ext4  errors=remount-ro
0   1
# /boot/efi was on /dev/sda1 during installation
UUID=15C2-F100   /boot/efi   vfat   umask=0077  0   1
/swapfile   none   swap   sw   0      0
/dev/sdb1                     /win    vfat   ro            1 2
192.168.0.27:/nfsstuff        /remote nfs    users,_netdev 0 0
//192.168.0.28/myshare        /share  cifs   guest,_netdev 0 0
```

The /etc/fstab file just shown is from a default Ubuntu install.

In general, the first column of /etc/fstab shows the device or share (what is mounted), while the second column shows the mount point (where it is mounted). That is followed by the type of filesystem, any mount options (or defaults), and two numbers (used to tell commands such as dump and fsck what to do with the filesystem).

The first two entries represent the disk partitions assigned to the root of the filesystem (/) and the /boot/efi directory. The first is an ext4 filesystem, while the boot partition uses vfat. The third line is a swap device (used to store data when RAM overflows).

The /boot partition is on its own physical partition, /dev/sda1. Instead of using /dev/sda1, however, a unique identifier (UUID) identifies the device. Why use a UUID instead of /dev/sda1 to identify the device? Suppose you plugged another disk into your computer and booted up. Depending on how your computer iterates through connected devices on boot, it is possible that the new disk might be identified as /dev/sda, causing the system to look for the contents of /boot on the first partition of that disk.

To see all of the UUIDs assigned to storage devices on your system, type the blkid command, as follows:

```
# blkid
/dev/sda1: UUID="15C2-F100" TYPE="vfat" PARTLABEL="EFI System
Partition" PARTUUID="5277724a-b124-4030-85cb-d80d430f8edb"
/dev/sda2: UUID="c0e513f0-f840-4174-912d-241d30fd2e26" TYPE="ext4"
PARTUUID="addb5440-c9ce-4d29-b50c-8cdba8cd60e0"
/dev/sdb1: LABEL="LUBUNTU 19_" UUID="4C35-A5E6" TYPE="vfat" PARTUUID="00262d60-01"
```

Any of the device names can be replaced by the UUID designation in the left column of an /etc/fstab entry.

I added the next three entries in /etc/fstab to illustrate some different kinds of entries. I connected a hard drive from an old Microsoft Windows system and had it mounted on the /win directory. I added the ro option so it would mount read-only.

```
/dev/sdb1                     /win    vfat   ro            1 2
192.168.0.27:/nfsstuff        /remote nfs    users,_netdev 0 0
//192.168.0.28/myshare        /share  cifs   guest,_netdev 0 0
```

The next two entries represent remote filesystems. On the /remote directory, the /nfs-stuff directory is mounted read/write (rw) from the host at address 192.168.0.27 as an

NFS share. On the `/share` directory, the Windows share named `myshare` is mounted from the host at `192.168.0.28`. In both cases, I added the `_netdev` option, which tells Linux to wait for the network to come up before trying to mount the shares. For more information on mounting CIFS and NFS shares, refer to Chapters 19, "Configuring a Windows File Sharing (Samba) Server," and 20, "Configuring an NFS File Server," respectively.

To help you understand the contents of the `/etc/fstab` file, here is what is in each field of that file:

Field 1: Name of the device representing the filesystem. This field can include the `LABEL` or `UUID` option with which you can indicate a volume label or universally unique identifier (`UUID`) instead of a device name. The advantage to this approach is that because the partition is identified by volume name, you can move a volume to a different device name and not have to change the `fstab` file. (See the description of the `mkfs` command in the section "Using the `mkfs` Command to Create a Filesystem" for information on creating and using labels.)

Field 2: Mount point in the filesystem. The filesystem contains all data from the mount point down the directory tree structure unless another filesystem is mounted at some point beneath it.

Field 3: Filesystem type. Valid filesystem types are described in the section "Supported filesystems" earlier in this chapter (although you can only use filesystem types for which drivers are included for your kernel).

Field 4: Use `defaults` or a comma-separated list of options (no spaces) that you want to use when the entry is mounted. See the `mount` command manual page (under the `-o` option) for information on other supported options.

> **TIP**
>
> Typically, only the root user is allowed to mount a filesystem using the `mount` command. However, to allow any user to mount a filesystem (such as a filesystem on a CD), you could add the `user` option to Field 4 of `/etc/fstab`.

Field 5: The number in this field indicates whether the filesystem needs to be dumped (that is, have its data backed up). A `1` means that the filesystem needs to be dumped, and a `0` means that it doesn't. (This field is no longer particularly useful because most Linux administrators use more sophisticated backup options than the `dump` command. Most often, a `0` is used.)

Field 6: The number in this field indicates whether the indicated filesystem should be checked with `fsck` when the time comes for it to be checked: `1` means it needs to be checked first, `2` means to check after all those indicated by `1` have already been checked, and `0` means don't check it.

If you want to find out more about mount options as well as other features of the `/etc/fstab` file, there are several man pages to which you can refer, including `man 5 nfs` and `man 8 mount`.

Using the mount command to mount filesystems

Linux systems automatically run mount -a (mount all filesystems from the /etc/ fstab file) each time you boot. For that reason, you generally use the mount command only for special situations. In particular, the average user or administrator uses mount in two ways:

- To display the disks, partitions, and remote filesystems currently mounted
- To mount a filesystem temporarily

Any user can type mount (with no options) to see what filesystems are currently mounted on the local Linux system. The following is an example of the mount command. It shows a single hard disk partition (/dev/sda1) containing the root (/) filesystem and proc and devpts filesystem types mounted on /proc and /dev, respectively.

```
$ mount
/dev/sda3 on / type ext4 (rw)
/dev/sda2 on /boot type ext4 (rw)
/dev/sda1 on /mnt/win type vfat (rw)
/dev/proc on /proc type proc (rw)
/dev/sys on /sys type sysfs (rw)
/dev/devpts on /dev/pts type devpts (rw,gid=5,mode=620)
/dev/shm on /dev/shm type tmpfs (rw)
none on /proc/sys/fs/binfmt_misc type binfmt_misc (rw)
/dev/cdrom on /media/MyOwnDVD type iso9660 (ro,nosuid,nodev)
```

Traditionally, the most common devices to mount by hand are removable media, such as DVDs or CDs. However, depending on the type of desktop you are using, CDs and DVDs may be mounted for you automatically when you insert them. (In some cases, applications are launched as well when media is inserted. For example, a music player or photo editor may be launched when your inserted USB medium has music or digital images on it.)

Occasionally, however, you may find it useful to mount a filesystem manually. For example, you want to look at the contents of an old hard disk, so you install it as a second disk on your computer. If the partitions on the disk did not automount, you could mount partitions from that disk manually. For example, to mount as read-only a disk partition sdb1 that has an older ext3 filesystem, you could type this:

```
# mkdir /mnt/temp
# mount -t ext3 -o ro /dev/sdb1 /mnt/temp
```

Another reason to use the mount command is to remount a partition to change its mount options. Suppose that you want to remount /dev/sdb1 as read/write, but you do not want to unmount it (maybe someone is using it). You could use the remount option as follows:

```
# mount -t ext3 -o remount,rw /dev/sdb1
```

Mounting a disk image in loopback

Another valuable way to use the mount command has to do with disk images. If you download an SD card or DVD ISO image file from the Internet and you want to see what it contains, you can do so without burning it to DVD or other medium. With the image on your hard disk, create a mount point and use the -o loop option to mount it locally. Here's an example:

```
# mkdir /mnt/mydvdimage
# mount -o loop whatever-i686-disc1.iso /mnt/mydvdimage
```

In this example, the /mnt/mydvdimage directory is created, and then the disk image file (whatever-i686-disc1.iso) residing in the current directory is mounted on it. You can now cd to that directory, view the contents of it, and copy or use any of its contents. This is useful for downloaded DVD images from which you want to install software without having to burn the image to DVD. You could also share that mount point over NFS, so you could install the software from another computer. When you are finished, just type umount /mnt/mydvdimage to unmount it.

Other options to mount are available only for specific filesystem types. See the mount manual page for those and other useful options.

Using the umount command

When you are finished using a temporary filesystem, or you want to unmount a permanent filesystem temporarily, use the umount command. This command detaches the filesystem from its mount point in your Linux filesystem. To use umount, you can give it either a directory name or a device name, as shown in this example:

```
# umount /mnt/test
```

This unmounts the device from the mount point /mnt/test. You can also unmount using this form:

```
# umount /dev/sdb1
```

In general, it's better to use the directory name (/mnt/test) because the umount command will fail if the device is mounted in more than one location. (Device names all begin with /dev.)

If you get the message device is busy, the umount request has failed because either an application has a file open on the device or you have a shell open with a directory on the device as a current directory. Stop the processes or change to a directory outside the device you are trying to unmount for the umount request to succeed.

An alternative for unmounting a busy device is the -l option. With umount -l (a lazy unmount), the unmount happens as soon as the device is no longer busy. To unmount a remote NFS filesystem that's no longer available (for example, the server went down), you can use the umount -f option to forcibly unmount the NFS filesystem.

> **TIP**
>
> A really useful tool for discovering what's holding open a device you want to unmount is the `lsof` command. Type `lsof` with the name of the partition that you want to unmount (such as `lsof /mnt/test`). The output shows you what commands are holding files open on that partition. The `fuser -v /mnt/test` command can be used in the same way.

Using the mkfs Command to Create a Filesystem

You can create a filesystem for any supported filesystem type on a disk or partition that you choose. You do so with the `mkfs` command. Although this is most useful for creating filesystems on hard disk partitions, you can create filesystems on USB flash drives or rewritable DVDs as well.

Before you create a new filesystem, make sure of the following:

- You have partitioned the disk as you want (using the `fdisk` command).
- You get the device name correct, or you may end up overwriting your hard disk by mistake. For example, the first partition on the second SCSI or USB flash drive on your system is /dev/sdb1 and the third disk is /dev/sdc1.
- To unmount the partition if it's mounted before creating the filesystem.

The following are two examples of using `mkfs` to create a filesystem on two partitions on a USB flash drive located as the first and second partitions on the third SCSI disk (/dev/sdc1 and /dev/sdc2). The first creates an xfs partition, while the second creates an ext4 partition:

```
# mkfs -t xfs /dev/sdc1
meta-data=/dev/sda3              isize=256      agcount=4, agsize=256825 blks
         =                       sectsz=512     attr=2, projid32bit=1
         =                       crc=0
data     =                       bsize=4096     blocks=1027300, imaxpct=25
         =                       sunit=0        swidth=0 blks
naming   =version 2              bsize=4096     ascii-ci=0 ftype=0
log      =internal log           bsize=4096     blocks=2560, version=2
         =                       sectsz=512     sunit=0 blks, lazy-count=1
realtime =none                   extsz=4096     blocks=0, rtextents=0

# mkfs -t ext4 /dev/sdc2
mke2fs 1.44.6 (5-Mar-2019)
Creating filesystem with 524288 4k blocks and 131072 inodes
Filesystem UUID: 6379d82e-fa25-4160-8ffa-32bc78d410eee
Superblock backups stored on blocks:
        32768, 98304, 163840, 229376, 294912
Allocating group tables: done
Writing inode tables: done
Creating journal (16384 blocks): done
Writing superblocks and filesystem accounting information: done
```

You can now mount either of these filesystems (for example, `mkdir /mnt/myusb` ; `mount /dev/sdc1 /mnt/myusb`), change to /mnt/myusb as your current directory (`cd /mnt/myusb`), and create files on it as you please.

Managing Storage with Cockpit

Most of the features described in this chapter for working with disk partitions and filesystems using command-line tools can be accomplished using the Cockpit web user interface. With Cockpit running on your system, open the Web UI (`hostname:9090`) and select the Storage tab. Figure 12.2 shows an example of the Cockpit Storage tab on an Ubuntu system:

FIGURE 12.2

View storage devices, filesystems, and activities from the Cockpit Storage page.

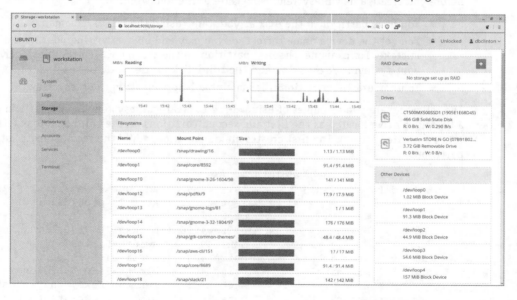

The Storage tab provides a solid overview of your system's storage. It charts read and write activity of your storage devices every minute. It displays the local filesystems and storage (including RAID devices and LVM volume groups) as well as remotely mounted NFS shares and iSCSI targets. Each hard disk, DVD, and other physical storage device is also displayed on the Storage tab.

Select a mounted filesystem, and you can see and change partitioning for that filesystem. For example, by selecting the entry for an attached USB drive, you can see all of the partitions for the device it is on (/dev/sdb1 in this case). Figure 12.3 shows that partition's page and the options available for deleting it or creating a new partition table.

FIGURE 12.3

View and change disk partitions for a select storage device.

With the storage device information displayed, you could reformat the entire storage device (Create partition table) or, assuming that space is available on the device, add a new partition (Create partition).

If you decide that you want to format the disk or USB drive, change the Erase setting to allow all of the data on the drive to be overwritten and then choose the type of partitioning. Select Format to unmount any mounted partitions from the drive and create a new partition table. After that, you can add partitions to the storage device, choosing the size, filesystem type, and whether or not to encrypt data. You can even choose where in the operating system's filesystem to mount the new partition. With just a few selections, you can quickly create the disk layouts that you want in ways that are more intuitive than methods for doing comparable steps from the command line.

Summary

Managing filesystems is a critical part of administering a Linux system. Using commands such as `fdisk`, you can view and change disk partitions. Filesystems can be added to partitions using the `mkfs` command. Once created, filesystems can be mounted and unmounted using the `mount` and `umount` commands, respectively.

Logical Volume Manager (LVM) offers a more powerful and flexible way of managing disk partitions. With LVM, you create pools of storage, called volume groups, which can allow you to grow and shrink logical volumes as well as extend the size of your volume groups by adding more physical volumes.

For a more intuitive way of working with storage devices, Cockpit offers an intuitive, Web-based interface for viewing and configuring storage on your Linux system. Using the Web UI, you can see both local and networked storage as well as reformat disks and modify disk partitions.

With most of the basics needed to become a system administrator covered at this point in the book, Chapter 13, "Understanding Server Administration," introduces concepts for extending those skills to manage network servers. Topics in that chapter include information on how to install, manage, and secure servers.

Exercises

Use these exercises to test your knowledge of creating disk partitions, Logical Volume Manager, and working with filesystems. You need a USB flash drive that is at least 1GB, which you can erase for these exercises.

These tasks assume that you are running Ubuntu (although some tasks work on other Linux systems as well). If you are stuck, solutions to the tasks are shown in Appendix A (although in Linux, there are often multiple ways to complete a task).

1. Run a command as root to watch the system journal in a Terminal as fresh data comes in, and insert your USB flash drive. Determine the device name of the USB flash drive.
2. Run a command to list the partition table for the USB flash drive.
3. Delete all the partitions on your USB flash drive, save the changes, and make sure the changes were made both on the disk's partition table and in the Linux kernel.
4. Add three partitions to the USB flash drive: 100MB Linux partition, 200MB swap partition, and 500MB LVM partition. Save the changes.
5. Put an ext4 filesystem on the Linux partition.
6. Create a mount point called /mnt/mypart and mount the Linux partition on it.
7. Enable the swap partition and turn it on so that additional swap space is immediately available.
8. Create a volume group called abc from the LVM partition, create a 200MB logical volume from that group called data, add a VFAT partition, and then temporarily mount the logical volume on a new directory named /mnt/test. Check that it was successfully mounted.
9. Grow the logical volume from 200MB to 300MB.
10. Do what you need to do to remove the USB flash drive safely from the computer: unmount the Linux partition, turn off the swap partition, unmount the logical volume, and delete the volume group from the USB flash drive.

Part IV

Becoming a Linux Server Administrator

IN THIS PART

Understanding Server Administration

A lthough some system administration tasks are needed even on a desktop system (installing software, setting up printers, and so on), many new tasks appear when you set up a Linux system to act as a server. That's especially true if the server that you configure is made public to anyone on the Internet, where you can be overloaded with requests from good guys while needing to be constantly on guard against attacks from bad guys.

Dozens of different kinds of servers are available for Linux systems, and it's often possible for a single machine to play multiple server roles. Most servers serve up data to remote clients, but others serve the local system (such as those that gather logging messages or kick off maintenance tasks at set times using the `cron` facility). Many servers are represented by processes that run continuously in the background and respond to requests. These processes are referred to as *daemon* processes.

As the name implies, servers exist to serve. The data that they serve can include web pages, files, database information, email, and lots of other types of content. As a server administrator, some of the additional challenges to your system administration skills include the following:

Remote access   To use a desktop system, you typically sit at its console. Server systems, by contrast, tend to be housed in racks in climate-controlled environments under lock and key. More often than not, after the physical computers are in place, most administration of those machines is done using remote access tools. Often, no graphical interface is available, so you must rely on command-line tools or browser-based interfaces to do things such as remote login, remote copying, and remote execution. The most common of these tools are built on the Secure Shell (SSH) facility.

Diligent security   To be useful, a server must be able to accept requests for content from remote users and systems. Unlike desktop systems, which can simply close down all network ports that allow incoming requests for access, a server must make itself vulnerable by allowing some access to its ports. That's why as a server administrator, it is important to open ports to services that are needed and lock down ports that are not needed. You can secure services using `iptables` and other firewall tools and kernel security controls like AppArmor (to limit the resources a service can access from the local system).

Continuous monitoring   Although you typically turn off your laptop or desktop system when you are not using it, servers usually stay on 24/7, 365 days a year. Because you don't want to sit next to each server without taking your eyes off it, you can configure tools to automate monitoring, gather log messages, and even forward suspicious messages to an email account of your choice. You can enable system activity reporters to gather data around the clock on CPU usage, memory usage, network activity, and disk access.

In this chapter, I lay out some of the basic tools and techniques that you need to know to administer remote Linux servers. You'll learn to use SSH tools to access your server securely, transfer data back and forth, and even launch remote desktops or graphical applications and have them appear on your local system. You'll also learn to use remote logging and system activity reports to monitor system activities continuously.

Getting Started with Server Administration

Whether you are installing a file server, web server, or any of the other server facilities available with Linux systems, many of the steps required for getting the server up and running are the same. Where server setup diverges is in the areas of configuration and tuning.

In later chapters, I describe specific servers and how they differ. In each of the server-related chapters that follow, you'll go through these same basic steps for getting that server started and available to be used by your clients.

Step 1: Install the server

Although most server software is not preinstalled on the typical Linux system, any general-purpose Linux system offers access to the software packages needed to supply every major type of server available. Here are some widely used server configurations that can be easily installed on an Ubuntu machine:

System logging server   The `rsyslog` service allows a local system to gather and organize log messages delivered from a variety of active system processes. It can also act as a remote logging server, gathering logging messages sent from other servers. (The `rsyslog` service is described later in this chapter.) On `systemd` machines, log messages are gathered in a binary journal, which can be viewed and managed locally through the `journalctl` command, or picked up and redirected by the `rsyslog` service. `rsyslog` is installed by default on Debian-based systems.

Print server The Common UNIX Printing System (`cups` package) is used most often to provide print server features on Linux systems. Packages that provide graphical administration of CUPS (`system-config-printer`) and printer drivers (`foomatic` and others) are also available when you install CUPS. (See Chapter 16, "Configuring a Print Server.")

Web server The Apache web server (available through the `apache2` package) is the software used most often to serve web pages (HTTP content). Related packages include modules to help serve particular types of content (Perl, Python, PHP, and SSL connections). Likewise, there are packages for monitoring web data (`webalizer`) and tools for providing web proxy services (`squid`). (See Chapter 17, "Configuring a Web Server.")

FTP server The Very Secure FTP daemon (`vsftpd` package) provides FTP services that include encryption—as the original FTP protocol is highly insecure. (See Chapter 18, "Configuring an FTP Server.")

Windows file server Samba (`samba` package) allows a Linux system to act as a Windows file and print server. (See Chapter 19, "Configuring a Windows File Sharing [Samba] Server.")

NFS file server Network File System (NFS) is the standard Linux and UNIX protocol for providing shared directories to other systems over a network. The `nfs-kernel-server` package provides NFS services and related commands. (See Chapter 20, "Configuring an NFS File Server.")

Mail server Mail server packages let you configure Mail Transport Agent (MTA) servers. You have several choices of email servers, including `sendmail` and `postfix`. Related packages, such as `dovecot`, allow the mail server to deliver email to clients.

Directory server Packages in this category provide remote and local authentication services. These include Kerberos (`krb5-server`), LDAP (`openldap-servers`), and NIS (`ypserv`).

DNS server The Berkeley Internet Name Domain service (`bind 9`) provides the software needed to configure a server to resolve hostnames into IP addresses.

Network Time Protocol server The `ntpd` or `chronyd` package provides a service that you can enable to sync your system clock with clocks from public or private NTP servers.

SQL server The PostgreSQL (`postgresql` and `postgresql-server` packages) service is an object-relational database management system. Related packages provide PostgreSQL documentation and related tools. The MySQL (`mysql` and `mysql-server` packages) service is another popular open source SQL database server. A community-developed branch of MySQL called MariaDB has recently gained popularity over MySQL for many workloads.

13

Step 2: Configure the server

Most server software packages are installed with a default configuration that leans more toward security than immediate full use. Here are some things to think about when you set out to configure a server.

Using configuration files

Traditionally, Linux server software was configured by editing plain-text files in the /etc directory (or subdirectories). Often, there is a primary configuration file, although there could also be a related configuration directory in which files ending in .conf can be incorporated into the main configuration.

The apache2 package (Apache web server) is an example of a server package that has a primary configuration file and a directory where other configuration files can be dropped in and be included with the service. The main configuration file in Ubuntu is /etc/apache2/ apache2.conf, while configuration directories exist within the /etc/apache2/ directory.

```
$ ls /etc/apache2
apache2.conf    conf-enabled  magic              mods-enabled  sites-available
conf-available  envvars       mods-available     ports.conf    sites-enabled
```

The one downside to plain-text configuration files is that you don't get the kind of immediate error checking you get when you use graphical administration tools. You either have to run a test command (if the service includes one) or actually try to start the service to see if there is any problem with your configuration file.

Checking the default configuration

Most server software packages are installed with a minimal and locked-down configuration. Some packages prompt you to create authentication credentials during the installation process, but others just do their work and leave it up to you to figure out the details— including where associated files have been saved and how to get the program running.

Two examples of servers that are installed with limited functionality are mail servers (sendmail or postfix packages) and DNS servers (bind 9 package). Both of these servers come with default configurations and will start up on reboot. However, both also only listen for requests on your localhost. So, until you configure them, people who are not logged in to your local server cannot send you mail or use your computer as a public DNS server.

Step 3: Start the server

Most services that you install in Linux are configured to start up when the system boots and then run continuously, listening for requests, until the system is shut down. These days, nearly all Linux systems manage services through systemd.

It's your job to do things such as set whether you want the service to automatically launch when the system boots and to manually start, stop, and reload it as needed (possibly to load new configuration files or temporarily stop access to the service). Commands for doing these tasks are described in Chapter 15, "Starting and Stopping Services."

Most, but not all, services are implemented as daemon processes. Here are a few things that you should know about those processes:

User and group permissions   Daemon processes often run as users and groups other than `root`. For example, an Apache server often runs as www-data and an NTP server runs as the ntp user. The reason for this is that if someone cracks these daemons, they would not have permissions to access files beyond what the services can access.

Daemon configuration files   Often, a service has a configuration file for the daemon stored in the `/lib/systemd/system` directory. This is different than the service configuration file in that its job is often just to pass arguments to the server process itself rather than configure the service. For example, options you set in the `/lib/systemd/system/apache2.service` file are passed to the `apache` daemon when it starts up. You can tell the daemon, for example, what to do in the event of an unexpected abort.

Port numbers   Packets of data go to and from your system over network interfaces through ports for each supported protocol (usually UDP or TCP). Most standard services have specific port numbers to which daemons listen and to which clients connect. Unless you are trying to hide the location of a service, you typically don't change the ports on which a daemon process listens. When you go to secure a service, you must make sure that the port to the service is open on the firewall (see Chapter 25, "Securing Linux on a Network," for information on `iptables` and UFW firewalls).

> **NOTE**
>
> One reason for changing port numbers on a service is "security by obscurity." For example, the `sshd` service is a well-known target for people trying to break into a system by guessing logins and passwords on TCP port 22.
>
> Some admins change their Internet-facing `sshd` service to listen on some other port number (perhaps some unused, very high port number). Then they tell their contacts to log in to their machine from SSH by pointing to this other port. The idea is that port scanners looking to break into a system might be less likely to scan the normally unused port.
>
> The problem is that, using port scanners, experienced hackers could detect the port you're actually using in seconds.

Not all services run continuously as daemon processes. Some older UNIX services ran on demand using the `xinetd` super server. Other services just run once on startup and exit. Still others run only a set number of times, being launched when the `crond` daemon sees that the service was configured to run at the particular time.

In recent years, older `xinetd` services such as `telnet` and `tftp`, have been converted to `systemd` sockets. Many newer services, including `cockpit`, use `systemd` sockets to achieve the same results.

13

Step 4: Secure the server

Opening your system to allow remote users to access it over the network is not a decision to be taken lightly. Crackers all over the world run programs to scan for vulnerable servers that they can take over for their data or their processing power. Luckily, there are measures that you can put in place on Linux systems to protect your servers and services from attacks and abuse.

Some common security techniques are described in the following sections. These and other topics are covered in more depth in Part V, "Learning Linux Security Techniques."

Password protection

Good passwords and password policies are the first line of defense in protecting a Linux system. If someone can log in to your server via SSH as the root user with a password of pa$$word, expect to be cracked. A good technique is to disallow direct login by root and require every user to log in as a regular user and then use su or sudo to become root.

You can also use the Pluggable Authentication Module (PAM) facility to adjust the number of times that someone can have failed login attempts before blocking access to that person. PAM also includes other features for locking down authentication to your Linux server. For a description of PAM, see Chapter 23, "Understanding Advanced Linux Security."

Of course, you can bypass passwords altogether by requiring public key authentication. To use that type of authentication, you must make sure that any user you want to have access to your server has their public key copied to the server (such as through ssh-copy-id). Then they can use ssh, scp, or related commands to access that server without typing their password. See the section "Using key-based (passwordless) authentication" later in this chapter for further information.

Firewalls

The iptables firewall service can track and respond to every packet coming from and going to network interfaces on your computer. Using iptables, you can drop or reject every packet making requests for services on your system except for those few that you have enabled. Further, you can tell iptables to allow service requests only from certain IP addresses (good guys) or not allow requests from other addresses (bad guys).

In recent Ubuntu versions, the Uncomplicated Firewall (UFW) feature adds a layer of functionality to Linux firewall rules. With UFW, you can insert firewall rules into the kernel through a much more user-friendly CLI interface.

In each of the server chapters coming up, I describe what ports need to be open to allow access to services. Descriptions of how iptables and UFW work are included in Chapter 25.

TCP Wrappers

TCP Wrappers, which use /etc/hosts.allow and /etc/hosts.deny files to allow and deny access in a variety of ways to selected services, was used primarily to secure older

UNIX services, and it is no longer considered to be very secure. While the use of the TCP Wrapper program (/usr/sbin/tcpd) is only common on systems that use xinetd, the /etc/hosts.allow and /etc/hosts.deny files that the TCP Wrapper program checked before granting access to network services are often checked by daemons that are configured to do so. The configuration option within the configuration files for these daemons is often labeled as TCP Wrapper support.

AppArmor

Ubuntu comes with the mandatory access control (MAC) AppArmor kernel security module. Although the default targeted mode doesn't have much impact on most applications that you run in Linux, it has a major impact on most major services.

A major function of AppArmor is to protect the contents of your Linux system from the processes running on the system. In other words, AppArmor makes sure a web server, FTP server, Samba server, or DNS server can access the appropriate system files and allows only appropriate system behavior.

Details about how to use AppArmor are contained in Chapter 24, "Enhancing Linux Security with AppArmor."

Security settings in configuration files

Within the configuration files of most services are values that you can set to secure the service further. For example, for file servers and web servers, you can restrict access to certain files or data based on username, hostname, IP address of the client, or other attributes.

Step 5: Monitor the server

Because you can't be there to monitor every service, every minute, you need to put monitoring tools in place to watch your servers for you and make it easy for you to find out when something needs attention. Some of the tools that you can use to monitor your servers are described in the sections that follow.

Configure logging

Using the rsyslog service, you can gather critical information and error conditions into log files about many different services. By default, log messages from applications are directed into log files in the /var/log directory. For added security and convenience, log messages can also be directed to a centralized server, providing a single location to view and manage logging for a group of systems. For example, journalctl manages logs in parallel with rsyslog on most systems these days.

Several different software packages are available to work with rsyslog and manage log messages. The logwatch feature scans your log files each night and sends critical information gathered from those files to an email account of your choice. The logrotate feature backs up log files into compressed archives when the logs reach a certain size or pass a set amount of time since the previous backup.

The features for configuring and managing system logging are described in the section "Configuring System Logging" later in this chapter.

Run system activity reports

The `sar` facility (which is enabled by the `sysstat` package) can be configured to watch activities on your system such as memory usage, CPU usage, disk latency, network activities, and other resource drains. By default, the `sar` facility launches the `sadc` program every few minutes, day and night, to gather data. Viewing that data later can help you go back and figure out where and when demand is spiking on your system. The `sar` facility is described in the section "Checking System Resources with `sar`" later in this chapter.

Watch activity live with Cockpit

With Cockpit running on your system, you can watch system activity in real time. To see what's happening on your own, local system, open your web browser to display the Cockpit console (`localhost:9090`). In real time, you can watch percentage of CPU use, memory and swap consumption, how much data is written to and from disk (disk I/O), and network traffic as it is gathered and displayed across the screen. Figure 13.1 shows an example of the System area of the Cockpit console, displaying activity data.

FIGURE 13.1

The System page of Cockpit

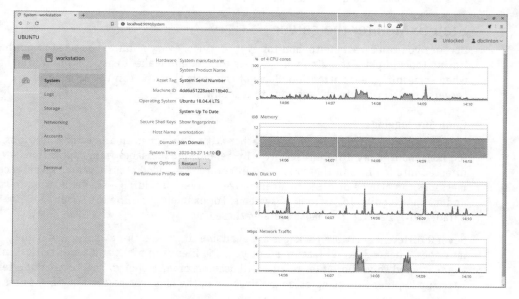

Keep system software up to date

As security holes are discovered and patched, you must make sure that the updated software packages containing those patches are installed on your servers. With mission-critical servers—as for all Ubuntu computers—the safest and most efficient solution is to apply APT updates immediately to all of your servers. And the best way to do that is to automate those updates using a tool like unattended-upgrades (apt install unattended-upgrades). Of course, if you're worried that unattended updates might break an important application, then you'll have no choice but to watch carefully during patches.

To ensure that your personal server and desktop systems remain up to date, there are various graphical tools to add software and to check for updates. Running apt update && apt upgrade will keep things honest.

Check the filesystem for signs of crackers

To check your filesystem for possible intrusion, you can run commands such like debsums -c (after installing with apt install debsums) to check for any commands, document files, or configuration files that have been tampered with.

Now that you have an overview of how Linux server configuration is done, the next sections of this chapter focus on the tools that you need to access, secure, and maintain your Linux server systems.

Checking and Setting Servers

If you're tasked with managing a Linux server, the following sections include a bunch of items that you can check. Keep in mind that nowadays many servers in large data centers are deployed and managed by larger platforms. So, know how the server is managed before you make any changes to it. Your changes might be overwritten automatically if you changed the defined state of that system.

Managing Remote Access with the Secure Shell Service

The *Secure Shell tools* are a set of client and server applications that allow you to do basic communications between client computers and your Linux server. The tools include ssh, scp, sftp, and many others. Because communication is encrypted between the server and the clients, these tools are more secure than similar, older tools. For example, instead of using older remote login commands such as telnet or rlogin, you could use ssh. The ssh command can also replace older remote execution commands, such as rsh. Remote copy commands, such as rcp, can be replaced with secure commands such as scp and rsync.

With Secure Shell tools, both the authentication process and all communications that follow are encrypted. Communications from `telnet` and the older `r` commands expose passwords and all data to someone sniffing the network. Today, `telnet` and similar commands should be used only for testing access to remote ports, providing public services such as PXE booting, or doing other tasks that don't expose your private data.

> **NOTE**
> For a deeper discussion of encryption techniques, refer to Chapter 23.

Most Linux systems include secure shell clients, and many include the secure shell server as well. The client and server software packages that contain the `ssh` tools are found in the `openssh-client` and `openssh-server` packages.

By default, Ubuntu usually comes with only the `openssh-client` package installed. If you need the server installed so clients can log in to your system using SSH, use the `sudo apt install openssh-server` command.

Starting the openssh-server service

Linux systems that come with the `openssh-server` package already installed are sometimes not configured for it to start automatically. Running `systemctl start ssh` will cure you of that problem.

Although Ubuntu usually installs without any running firewalls, if any network restrictions do exist, you'll need to allow the `openssh-client` to access port 22 (firewalls are covered in Chapter 25). After the service is up and running and the firewall is properly configured, you should be able to use `ssh` client commands to access your system via the `ssh` server.

Any further server-side configurations for what the `sshd` daemon is allowed to do are handled in the `/etc/ssh/sshd_config` file. At a minimum, set the `PermitRootLogin` setting to no. This stops anyone from remotely logging in as `root`.

```
# grep PermitRootLogin /etc/ssh/sshd_config
PermitRootLogin no
```

After you have changed the `sshd_config` file, restart the `ssh` service. After that point, if you use `ssh` to log in to that system from a remote client, you must do so as a regular user and then use `su` or `sudo` to become the `root` user.

Using SSH client tools

Many tools for accessing remote Linux systems have been created to make use of the SSH service. The most frequently used of those tools is the `ssh` command, which can be used for remote login, remote execution, and other tasks. Commands such as `scp` and `rsync` can copy one or more files at a time between SSH client and server systems. The `sftp` command provides an FTP-like interface for traversing a remote filesystem and getting and putting files between the systems interactively.

By default, all of the SSH-related tools authenticate using standard Linux usernames and passwords, all done over encrypted connections. However, SSH also supports key-based authentication, which can be used to configure key-based and possibly passwordless authentication between clients and SSH servers, as described in the section "Using key-based (passwordless) authentication" later in this chapter.

Using ssh for remote login

Use the ssh command from another Linux computer to test that you can log in to the Linux system running your ssh service. The ssh command is one that you will use often to access a shell on the servers you are configuring.

Try logging in to your Linux server from another Linux system using the ssh command. (If you don't have another Linux system, you can simulate this by typing localhost instead of the IP address and logging in as a local user.) The following is an example of remotely logging in to johndoe's account on 10.140.67.23:

```
$ ssh johndoe@10.140.67.23
The authenticity of host '10.140.67.23 (10.140.67.23)'
     can't be established.
RSA key fingerprint is
     a4:28:03:85:89:6d:08:fa:99:15:ed:fb:b0:67:55:89.
Are you sure you want to continue connecting (yes/no)? yes
Warning: Permanently added '10.140.67.23' (RSA) to the
     list of known hosts.
johndoe@10.140.67.23's password: *********
```

If this is the very first time that you have logged in to that remote system using the ssh command, the system asks you to confirm that you want to connect. Type **yes** (the full word: not just "y"), and press Enter. When prompted, enter the user's password.

When you type yes to continue, you accept the remote host's public key. At that point, the remote host's public key is downloaded to the client in the client's ~/.ssh/known_hosts file. Now data exchanged between these two systems can be encrypted and decrypted using RSA asymmetric encryption (see Chapter 23). After you are logged in to the remote system, you can begin typing shell commands. The connection functions like a normal login. The only difference is that the data is encrypted as it travels over the network.

When you are finished, type **exit** to end the remote connection. The connection is closed, and you are returned to the command prompt on your local system. (If the local shell doesn't return after you exit the remote shell, typing ~. usually closes the connection.)

```
$ exit
logout
Connection to 10.140.67.23 closed
```

After you have remotely connected to a system, a file in your local system subdirectory, ~.ssh/known_hosts, will exist. This file contains the public key of the remote host along with its IP address. Your server's public and private keys are stored in the /etc/ssh directory.

13

```
$ ls .ssh
known_hosts
$ cat .ssh/known_hosts
10.140.67.23 ssh-rsa
AAAAB3NzaC1yc2EAAAABIwAAAQEAoyfJK1YwZhNmpHE4yLPZAZ9ZNEdRE7I159f3I
yGiH21Ijfqs
NYFR10ZlBLlYyTQi06r/9O19GwCaJ753InQ8FWHW+OOYOG5pQmghhn
/x0LD2uUb6egOu6zim1NEC
JwZf5DWkKdy4euCUEMSqADh/WYeuOSoZ0pp2IAVCdh6
w/PIHMF1HVR069cvdv+OTL4vD0X8llSpw
OozqRptz2UQgQBBbBjK1RakD7fY1TrWv
NQhYG/ugt gPaY4JDYeY6OBzcadpxZmf7EYUw0ucXGVQ1a
NP/erIDOQ9rA0YNzCRv
y2LYCm2/9adpAxc+UYi5UsxTw4ewSBjmsXYq//Ahaw4mjw==
```

> **TIP**
>
> Any later attempts by this user to contact the server at `10.140.67.23` are authenticated using this stored key. If the server should change its key (which happens if the operating system is reinstalled or if keys are rotated), attempts to `ssh` to that system result in a refused connection and dire warnings that you may be under attack. If you know that the key has indeed changed, in order to be able to `ssh` to that address again, just remove the host's key (the whole line) from your `known_hosts` file and you can copy over the new key. The warning message will probably include a command suitable for cutting and pasting that will get this done for you.

Using SSH for remote execution

Besides logging in to a remote shell, the `ssh` command can be used to execute a command on the remote system and have the output returned to the local system. Here is an example:

```
$ ssh johndoe@10.140.67.23 hostname
johndoe@10.140.67.23's password: **********
host01.example.com
```

In the example just shown, the `hostname` command runs as the user `johndoe` on the Linux system located at IP address `10.140.67.23`. The output of the command is the name of the remote host (in this case, `host01.example.com`), which appears on the local screen.

If you run a remote execution command with `ssh` that includes options or arguments, be sure to surround the whole remote command line in quotes. Keep in mind that if you refer to files or directories in your remote commands, relative paths are interpreted in relation to the user's home directory, as shown here:

```
$ ssh johndoe@10.140.67.23 "cat myfile"
johndoe@10.140.67.23's password: **********
Contents of the myfile file located in johndoe's home directory.
```

The `ssh` command just shown goes to the remote host located at `10.140.67.23` and runs the `cat myfile` command as the user `johndoe`. This causes the contents of the `myfile` file from that system to be displayed on the local screen.

Another type of remote execution that you can do with `ssh` is X11 forwarding. If X11 forwarding is enabled on the server (`X11Forwarding yes` is set in the host's `/etc/sshd/sshd_config` file), you can run graphical applications from the server securely over the SSH connection using `ssh -X`. For a new server administrator, this means that if there are graphical administration tools installed on a server, you can run those tools without having to sit at the console, as in this example:

```
$ ssh -X johndoe@10.140.67.23 system-config-printer
johndoe@10.140.67.23's password: **********
```

After running this command, you are prompted for the remote user's `sudo` password. After that, the Printers window appears, ready for you to configure a printer. Just close the window when you are finished, and the local prompt returns. You can do this for any graphical administration tool or just regular X applications (such as the `gedit` graphical editor, so that you don't have to use `vi`).

If you want to run several X commands and don't want to have to reconnect each time, you can use X11 forwarding directly from a remote shell as well. Put them in the background and you can have several remote X applications running on your local desktop at once. Here's an example:

```
$ ssh -X johndoe@10.140.67.23
johndoe@10.140.67.23's password: **********
$ system-config-printer &
$ gedit &
$ exit
```

After you have finished using the graphical applications, close them as you would normally. Then type **exit**, as shown in the preceding code, to leave the remote shell and return to your local shell.

Copying files between systems with scp and rsync

The `scp` command is similar to the old UNIX `rcp` command for copying files to and from Linux systems, except that all communications are encrypted. Files can be copied from the remote system to the local system or local to remote. You can also copy files recursively through a whole directory structure if you choose.

The following is an example of using the `scp` command to copy a file called memo from the home directory of the user `chris` to the `/tmp` directory on a remote computer as the user `johndoe`:

```
$ scp /home/chris/memo johndoe@10.140.67.23:/tmp
johndoe@10.140.67.23's password: ***************
memo           100%|***************|   153    0:00
```

You must enter the password for `johndoe`. After the password is accepted, the file is copied to the remote system successfully.

You can do recursive copies with `scp` using the `-r` option. Instead of a file, pass a directory name to the `scp` command and all files and directories below that point in the filesystem are copied to the other system.

13

```
$ scp -r johndoe@10.140.67.23:/usr/share/man/man1/ /tmp/
johndoe@10.140.67.23's password: ***************
volname.1.gz                                   100%  543    0.5KB/s   00:00
mtools.1.gz                                    100% 6788    6.6KB/s   00:00
roqet.1.gz                                     100% 2496    2.4KB/s   00:00
...
```

As long as the user johndoe has access to the files and directories on the remote system and the local user can write to the target directory (both are true in this case), the directory structure from /usr/share/man/man1 down is copied to the local /tmp directory.

The scp command can be used to back up files and directories over a network. However, if you compare scp to the rsync command, you see that rsync (which also works over SSH connections) is a better backup tool. Try running the scp command shown previously to copy the man1 directory (you can simulate the command using localhost instead of the IP address if you only have one accessible Linux system). Now enter the following on the system to which you copied the files:

```
$ ls -l /usr/share/man/man1/batch* /tmp/man1/batch*
-rw-r--r--.1 johndoe johndoe 2628 Apr 15 15:32 /tmp/man1/batch.1.gz
lrwxrwxrwx.1 root root 7 Feb 14 17:49 /usr/share/man/man1/batch.1.gz
       -> at.1.gz
```

Next, run the scp command again and list the files once more:

```
$ scp johndoe@10.140.67.23:/usr/share/man/man1/ /tmp/
johndoe@10.140.67.23's password: ***************
$ ls -l /usr/share/man/man1/batch* /tmp/man1/batch*
-rw-r--r--.1 johndoe johndoe 2628 Apr 15 15:40 /tmp/man1/batch.1.gz
lrwxrwxrwx.1 root root 7 Feb 14 17:49 /usr/share/man/man1/batch.1.gz
       -> at.1.gz
```

The output of those commands tells you a few things about how scp works:

Attributes lost   Permissions or date/time stamp attributes were not retained when the files were copied. If you were using scp as a backup tool, you would probably want to keep permissions and time stamps on the files if you needed to restore the files later.

Symbolic links lost   The batch.1.gz file is actually a symbolic link to the at.1.gz file. Instead of copying the link, scp follows the link and actually copies the file. Again, if you were to restore this directory, batch.1.gz would be replaced by the actual at.1.gz file instead of a link to it.

Copy repeated unnecessarily   If you watched the second scp output, you would notice that all files were copied again, even though the exact files being copied were already on the target. The updated modification date confirms this. By contrast, the rsync command can determine that a file has already been copied and not copy the file again.

The `rsync` command is a better network backup tool because it can overcome some of the shortcomings of `scp` just listed. Try running an `rsync` command to do the same action that `scp` just did, but with a few added options:

```
$ rm -rf /tmp/man1/
$ rsync -avl johndoe@10.140.67.23:/usr/share/man/man1/ /tmp/
johndoe@10.140.67.23's password: ***************
sending incremental file list
man1/
man1/HEAD.1.gz
man1/Mail.1.gz -> mailx.1.gz
...
$ rsync -avl johndoe@10.140.67.23:/usr/share/man/man1/ /tmp/
johndoe@10.140.67.23's password: ***************
sending incremental file list
sent 42362 bytes  received 13 bytes  9416.67 bytes/sec
total size is 7322223  speedup is 172.80
$ ls -l /usr/share/man/man1/batch* /tmp/man1/batch*
lrwxrwxrwx.1 johndoe johndoe 7 Feb 14 17:49 /tmp/man1/batch.1.gz
       -> at.1.gz
lrwxrwxrwx.1 root root 7 Feb 14 17:49 /usr/share/man/man1/batch.1.gz
       -> at.1.gz
```

After removing the `/tmp/man1` directory, you run an `rsync` command to copy all of the files to the `/tmp/man1` directory, using -a (recursive archive), -v (verbose), and -l (copy symbolic links). Then run the command immediately again and notice that nothing is copied. The `rsync` command knows that all of the files are there already, so it doesn't copy them again. This can be a tremendous savings of network bandwidth for directories with gigabytes of files where only a few megabytes change.

Also notice from the output of `ls -l` that the symbolic links have been preserved on the `batch.1.gz` file and so has the date/time stamp on the file. If you need to restore those files later, you can put them back exactly as they were.

This use of `rsync` is good for backups. But what if you wanted to mirror two directories, making the contents of two directory structures exactly the same on two machines? The following commands illustrate how to create an exact mirror of the directory structure on both machines using the directories shown with the previous `rsync` commands.

First, on the remote system, copy a new file into the directory being copied:

```
# cp /etc/services /usr/share/man/man1
```

Next, on the local system, run `rsync` to copy across any new files (in this case, just the directory and the new file, `services`):

```
$ rsync -avl johndoe@10.140.67.23:/usr/share/man/man1 /tmp
johndoe@10.140.67.23's password:
***************
```

Continues

Continued

```
sending incremental file list
man1/
man1/services
```

After that, go back to the remote system and remove the new file:

```
$ sudo rm /usr/share/man/man1/services
```

Now, on the local system, run `rsync` again and notice that nothing happens. At this point, the remote and local directories are different because the local system has the services file and the remote doesn't. That is correct behavior for a backup directory. (You want to have files on the backup in case something was removed by mistake.) However, if you want the remote and local directories to be mirrored, you would have to add the `--delete` option. The result is that the services file is deleted on the local system, making the remote and local directory structures in sync.

```
$ rsync -avl /usr/share/man/man1 localhost:/tmp
johndoe@10.140.67.23's password: ***************
sending incremental file list
man1/
$ rsync -avl --delete johndoe@10.140.67.23:/usr/share/man/man1 /tmp
johndoe@10.140.67.23's password: ***************
sending incremental file list
deleting man1/services
```

Interactive copying with sftp

If you don't know exactly what you want to copy to or from a remote system, you can use the `sftp` command to create an interactive FTP-style session over the SSH service. Using `sftp`, you can connect to a remote system over SSH, change directories, list directory contents, and then (given proper permission) get files from and put files on the server. Keep in mind that, despite its name, `sftp` has nothing to do with the FTP protocol and doesn't use FTP servers. It simply uses an FTP style of interaction between a client and a `sshd` server.

The following example shows the user johndoe connecting to jd.example.com:

```
$ sftp johndoe@jd.example.com
Connecting to jd.example.com
johndoe@jd.example.com's password: ***************
sftp>
```

At this point, you can begin an interactive FTP session. You can use `get` and `put` commands on files as you would with any FTP client, but with the comfort of knowing that you are working on an encrypted and secure connection. Because the FTP protocol passes usernames, passwords, and data in clear text, using `sftp` over SSH, if possible, is a much better alternative for allowing your users to copy files interactively from the system.

Using key-based (passwordless) authentication

If you are using SSH tools to connect to the same systems throughout the day, you might find it inconvenient to be entering your password over and over again. Instead of using password-based authentication, SSH allows you to set up key-based authentication to use instead. Here's how it works:

- You create a public key and a private key.
- You guard the private key but copy the public key across to the user account on the remote host to which you want to do key-based authentication.
- With your key copied to the proper location, you use any SSH tools to connect to the user account on the remote host, but instead of asking you for a password, the remote SSH service compares the public key and the private key and allows you access if the two keys match.

When you create the keys, you are given the option to add a passphrase to your private key. If you decide to add a passphrase, even though you don't need to enter a password to authenticate to the remote system, you still need to enter your passphrase to unlock your private key. If you don't add a passphrase, you can communicate using your public/private key pairs in a way that is completely passwordless. However, if someone should get ahold of your private key, they could act as you in any communication that required that key.

The following procedure demonstrates how a local user named chris can set up key-based authentication to a remote user named johndoe at IP address 10.140.67.23. If you don't have two Linux systems, you can simulate this by using two user accounts on your local system. I start by logging in as the local user named chris and typing the following to generate my local public/private key pair:

```
$ ssh-keygen
Generating public/private rsa key pair.
Enter file in which to save the key (/home/chris/.ssh/id_rsa): ENTER
Enter passphrase (empty for no passphrase): ENTER
Enter same passphrase again: ENTER
Your identification has been saved in /home/chris/.ssh/id_rsa.
Your public key has been saved in /home/chris/.ssh/id_rsa.pub.
The key fingerprint is:
bf:06:f8:12:7f:f4:c3:0a:3a:01:7f:df:25:71:ec:1d chris@abc.example.com
The key's randomart image is:
   . . .
```

I accepted the default RSA key (DSA keys are also allowed) and pressed Enter twice to have a blank passphrase associated with the key. As a result, my private key (id_rsa) and public key (id_rsa.pub) are copied to the .ssh directory in my local home directory. The next step is to copy that key over to a remote user so that I can use key-based authentication each time I connect to that user account with ssh tools:

```
$ ssh-copy-id -i ~/.ssh/id_rsa.pub johndoe@10.140.67.23
johndoe@10.140.67.23's password:
***************
```

When prompted, I entered `johndoe`'s password. With that accepted, the public key belonging to `chris` is copied to the `authorized_keys` file in `johndoe`'s `.ssh` directory on the remote system. Now, the next time `chris` tries to connect to `johndoe`'s account, the SSH connection is authenticated using those keys. Because no passphrase is put on the private key, no passphrase is required to unlock that key when it is used.

Log in to the machine with `ssh johndoe@10.140.67.23`, and check in `$HOME/.ssh/authorized_keys` to make sure that you haven't added extra keys that you weren't expecting:

```
[chris]$ ssh johndoe@10.140.67.23
Last login: Sun Apr 17 10:12:22 2016 from  10.140.67.22
[johndoe]$ cat .ssh/authorized_keys
```

With the keys in place, `chris` could now use `ssh`, `scp`, `rsync`, or any other SSH-enabled command to do key-based authentication. Using these keys, for example, an `rsync` command could go into a `cron` script and automatically back up `johndoe`'s home directory every night.

Want to secure your remote system further? After you have the keys in place on your remote system for everyone you want to allow to log in to that system, you can set the `sshd` service on the remote system to not allow password authentication by changing the `PasswordAuthentication` setting in the `/etc/ssh/sshd_config` file to no, so that it appears as follows:

```
PasswordAuthentication no
```

Then restart the `ssh` service (`systemctl restart ssh`). After that, anyone with a valid key is still accepted. Anyone who tries to log in without a key gets the following failure message and doesn't even get a chance to enter a username and password:

```
Permission denied (publickey,gssapi-keyex,gssapi-with-mic).
```

Configuring System Logging

With the knowledge of how to access your remote server using SSH tools, you can log in to the server and set up some of the services needed to make sure that it's running smoothly. System logging is one of the basic services configured for Linux to keep track of what is happening on the system.

The `rsyslog` service provides the features to gather log messages from software running on the Linux system and direct those messages to local log files, devices, or remote logging hosts. Configuration of `rsyslog` is similar to the configuration of its predecessor, `syslog`. However, `rsyslog` allows you to add modules to manage and direct log messages more specifically.

In recent Ubuntu releases, the `rsyslog` facility leverages messages that are gathered and stored in the `systemd` journal. To display journal log messages directly from the `systemd` journal, instead of viewing them from files in the `/var/log` directory, use the `journalctl` command.

Enabling system logging with rsyslog

Most of the files in the `/var/log` directory are populated with log messages directed to them from the `rsyslog` service. The `rsyslogd` daemon is the system logging daemon. It accepts log messages from a variety of other programs and writes them to the appropriate log files. This is better than having every program write directly to its own log file because it enables you to manage centrally how log files are handled.

Configuring `rsyslogd` to record varying levels of detail in the log files is possible. It can be told to ignore all but the most critical messages, or it can record every detail.

The `rsyslogd` daemon can even accept messages from other computers on your network. This remote logging feature is particularly handy because it enables you to centralize the management and review of the log files from many systems on your network. There is also a major security benefit to this practice.

With remote logging, if a system on your network is broken into, the cracker cannot delete or modify the log files because those files are stored on a separate computer. It is important to remember, however, that those log messages are not, by default, encrypted (though encryption can be enabled). Anyone tapping into your local network can eavesdrop on those messages as they pass from one machine to another. Also, although crackers may not be able to change old log entries, they can affect the system such that any new log messages should not be trusted.

Running a dedicated loghost, a computer that serves no purpose other than to record log messages from other computers on the network, is not uncommon. Because this system runs no other services, it is unlikely that it will be broken into. This makes it nearly impossible for crackers to erase their tracks completely.

Understanding the rsyslog.conf file

The `/etc/rsyslog.conf` file is the primary configuration file for the `rsyslog` service. In the `/etc/rsyslog.conf` file, a modules section lets you include or not include specific features in your `rsyslog` service. The following is an example of the modules section of `/etc/rsyslog.conf`:

```
module(load="imuxsock") # provides support for local system logging
#module(load="immark")  # provides --MARK-- message capability

# provides UDP syslog reception
#module(load="imudp")
#input(type="imudp" port="514")

# provides TCP syslog reception
#module(load="imtcp")
#input(type="imtcp" port="514")

# provides kernel logging support and enable non-kernel klog messages
module(load="imklog" permitnonkernelfacility="on")
```

13

Entries beginning with `module(load=` load the modules that follow. Modules that are currently disabled are preceded by a pound sign (#). The `imuxsock` module is needed to accept messages from the local system. (It should not be commented out—preceded by a pound sign—unless you have a specific reason to do so.) The `imklog` module logs kernel messages.

Modules not enabled by default include the `immark` module, which allows --MARK-- messages to be logged (used to indicate that a service is alive). The `imudp` and `imtcp` modules and related port number entries are used to allow the `rsyslog` service to accept remote logging messages and are discussed in more detail in the section "Setting up and using a loghost with `rsyslogd`."

Most of the work done by `rsyslog` is based on rules found in files in the `/etc/rsyslog.d` directory:

```
$ ls /etc/rsyslog.d/
20-ufw.conf  50-default.conf  postfix.conf
```

Rules entries come in two columns. In the left column are designations of what messages are matched; the right column shows where matched messages go. Messages are matched based on facility (`mail`, `cron`, `kern`, and so on) and priority (starting at `debug`, `info`, `notice`, and up to `crit`, `alert`, and `emerg`), separated by a dot (.). So `mail.info` matches all messages from the mail service that are info level and above. An asterisk (*) means that all priority levels are to be logged. Here's a sample from a typical `/etc/rsyslog.d/50-default.conf` file:

```
# First some standard log files.  Log by facility.
#
auth,authpriv.*                 /var/log/auth.log
*.*;auth,authpriv.none          -/var/log/syslog
#cron.*                         /var/log/cron.log
#daemon.*                       -/var/log/daemon.log
kern.*                          -/var/log/kern.log
#lpr.*                          -/var/log/lpr.log
mail.*                          -/var/log/mail.log
#user.*                         -/var/log/user.log

#mail.info                      -/var/log/mail.info
#mail.warn                      -/var/log/mail.warn
mail.err                        /var/log/mail.err
```

As for where the messages go, most messages are directed to files in the `/var/log` directory. You can, however, direct messages to a device (such as `/dev/console`) or a remote loghost (such as `@loghost.example.com`). The at sign (@) indicates that the name that follows is the name of the loghost.

The `mail`, `authpriv` (authentication messages), and `cron` (cron facility messages) services each has its own log files, as listed in the columns to their right. To understand the format of those and other log files, the format of the `/var/log/messages` file is described next.

Understanding log messages

Because of the many programs and services that record information to log files, understanding their format is important. You can get a good early warning of problems developing on your system by examining some examples. Each line is a single message recorded by some program or service. Here is a snippet of an actual messages log file:

```
Feb 25 11:04:32 toys network: Bringing up loopback:  succeeded
Feb 25 11:04:35 toys network: Bringing up interface eth0:  succeeded
Feb 25 13:01:14 toys vsftpd(pam_unix)[10565]: authentication failure;
     logname= uid=0 euid=0 tty= ruser= rhost=10.0.0.5  user=chris
Feb 25 14:44:24 toys su(pam_unix)[11439]: session opened for
     user root by chris(uid=500)
```

The default message format is divided into five main parts.

When you view messages in files from the /var/log directory, from left to right, message parts are as follows:

- The date and time that the message was logged
- The name of the computer from which the message came
- The program or service name to which the message pertains
- The process number (enclosed in square brackets) of the program sending the message
- The actual text message

Take another look at the preceding file snippet. In the first two lines, you can see that the network was restarted. The next line shows that the user named chris tried and failed to get to the FTP server on this system from a computer at address 10.0.0.5. (He typed the wrong password and authentication failed.) The last line shows chris using the su command to become root user.

By occasionally reviewing the /var/log/auth.log file, you could catch a cracking attempt before it is successful. If you see an excessive number of connection attempts for a particular service, especially if they are coming from systems on the Internet, you may be under attack.

Setting up and using a loghost with rsyslogd

To redirect your computer's log files to another computer's rsyslogd, you must make changes to both the local and remote rsyslog configuration file, /etc/rsyslog.conf. Become root using the su - command, and then open the /etc/rsyslog.conf file in a text editor (such as vi).

On the client side

To send the messages to another computer (the loghost) instead of a file, start by replacing the log file name with the @ character followed by the name of the loghost. For example, to direct the output of messages that are being sent to the syslog and mail.log log files to a loghost as well, add the lines in bold to the messages file:

```
authpriv.*                          @10.0.3.24:514
mail.*                              @10.0.3.24:514
```

The messages are now sent to the `rsyslogd` running on the computer named loghost. The name `loghost` was not an arbitrary choice. Creating such a hostname and making it an alias to the actual system acting as the loghost is customary. That way, if you ever need to switch the loghost duties to a different machine, you need to change only the loghost alias; you do not need to re-edit the `syslog.conf` file on every computer.

On the loghost side

The loghost that is set to accept the messages must listen for those messages on standard ports (514 UDP, although it can be configured to accept messages on 514 TCP as well). Here is how you would configure the Linux loghost that is also running the `rsyslog` service:

- Edit the `/etc/rsyslog.conf` file on the loghost system and uncomment the lines that enable the `rsyslogd` daemon to listen for remote log messages. Uncomment the first two lines to enable incoming UDP log messages on port 514 (default); uncomment the two lines after that to allow messages that use TCP protocol (also port 514):

```
module(load="imudp") # needs to be done just once

input(type="imudp" port="514")

module(load="imtcp") # needs to be done just once

input(type="imtcp" port="514")
```

- If there's a firewall running, you'll need to open port 514 to allow new messages to be directed to your loghost. (See Chapter 25 for a description of how to open specific ports to allow access to your system.)
- Restart the `rsyslog` service (**systemctl restart rsyslog**).
- If the service is running, you should be able to see that the service is listening on the ports that you enabled (UDP and/or TCP ports 514). Run the `netstat` command as follows to see that the `rsyslogd` daemon is listening on IPv4 and IPv6 ports 514 for both UDP and TCP services:

```
# netstat -tupln | grep 514
tcp    0    0 0.0.0.0:514    0.0.0.0:*    LISTEN    25341/rsyslogd
tcp    0    0 :::514         :::*         LISTEN    25341/rsyslogd
udp    0    0 0.0.0.0:514    0.0.0.0:*              25341/rsyslogd
udp    0    0 :::514         :::*                   25341/rsyslogd
```

Watching logs with logwatch

The `logwatch` service runs in most Linux systems that do system logging with `rsyslog`. Because logs on busy systems can become very large over time, it doesn't take long for there to be too many messages for a system administrator to watch every message in every log. To install the `logwatch` facility, enter the following:

```
# apt install logwatch
```

What logwatch does is gather messages once each night that look like they might represent a problem, put them in an email message, and send it to any email address the administrator chooses. To enable logwatch, all you have to do is install the logwatch package.

The logwatch service runs from a cron job (0logwatch) placed in /etc/cron.daily. The /etc/logwatch/conf/logwatch.conf file holds local settings. The default options used to gather log messages are available in the /usr/share/logwatch/default. conf/logwatch.conf file (which you can easily copy to your /etc/logwatch/conf/ directory).

Some of the default settings define the location of log files (/var/log), location of the temporary directory (/var/cache/logwatch), and the recipient of the daily logwatch email (the local root user). Unless you expect to log in to the server to read logwatch messages, you probably want to change the MailTo setting in the /etc/logwatch/conf/ logwatch.conf file:

```
MailTo = chris@example.com
```

When the service is enabled (which is done by simply installing the logwatch package), you will see a message each night in the root user's mailbox (you may need to install the mailutils package to make this work: apt install mailutils. When you are logged in as root, you can use the old mail command to view the root user's mailbox:

```
# mail
Heirloom Mail version 12.5 7/5/10.  Type ? for help.
"/var/spool/mail/root": 2 messages 2 new
>N  1 logwatch@abc.ex  Sun Feb 15 04:02 45/664    "Logwatch for abc"
    2 logwatch@abc.ex  Mon Feb 16 04:02 45/664    "Logwatch for abc"
& 1
& x
```

In mail, you should see email messages from logwatch run each day (here at 4:02 a.m.). Type the number of the message that you want to view and page through it with the spacebar or line by line by pressing Enter. Type **x** to exit when you are finished.

The kind of information that you see includes kernel errors, installed packages, authentication failures, and malfunctioning services. Disk space usage is reported, so you can see if your storage is filling up. Just by glancing through this logwatch message, you should get an idea whether sustained attacks are underway or if some repeated failures are taking place.

Checking System Resources with sar

The System Activity Reporter (sar) is one of the oldest system monitoring facilities created for early UNIX systems—predating Linux by years. The sar command itself can display system activity continuously, at set intervals (every second or two), and display it on the screen. It can also display system activity data that was gathered earlier.

The `sar` command is part of the `sysstat` package. When you install `sysstat` you might need to edit the `/etc/default/sysstat` file, changing `ENABLED="false"` to `ENABLED="true"` and then enabling the `sysstat` service. Your system should immediately begin gathering system activity data that can be reviewed later using certain options to the `sar` command.

```
# systemclt enable sysstat
# systemctl start sysstat
```

To read the data in the `/var/log/sa/sa??` files, you can use some of the following `sar` commands (it may take time before the data is populated):

```
# sar -u
Linux 5.3.8-200.fc30.x86_64 (ubuntu) 11/28/2019  _x86_64_  (1 CPU)

23:27:46      LINUX RESTART (1 CPU)

11:30:05 PM  CPU    %user  %nice %system  %iowait   %steal    %idle
11:40:06 PM  all     0.90   0.00    1.81     1.44     0.28    95.57
Average:     all     0.90   0.00    1.81     1.44     0.28    95.57
```

The `-u` option shows CPU usage. By default, the output starts at midnight on the current day and then shows how much processing time is being consumed by different parts of the system. The output continues to show the activity every 10 minutes until the current time is reached.

To see disk activity output, run the `sar  -d` command. Again, output comes in 10-minute intervals starting at midnight.

```
# sar -d
Linux 5.3.8-200.fc30.x86_64 (ubuntu)  11/28/2019 _x86_64_  (1 CPU)

23:27:46      LINUX RESTART  (1 CPU)

11:30:05 PM      DEV   tps   rkB/s   wkB/s   areq-sz   aqu-sz   await...
11:40:06 PM    dev8-0 49.31 5663.94   50.38   115.89     0.03    1.00
11:40:06 PM  dev253-0 48.99 5664.09    7.38   115.78     0.05    0.98
11:40:06 PM  dev253-1 10.84    0.01   43.34     4.00     0.04    3.29
Average:       dev8-0 49.31 5663.94   50.38   115.89     0.03    1.00
Average:     dev253-0 48.99 5664.09    7.38   115.78     0.05    0.98
Average:     dev253-1 10.84    0.01   43.34     4.00     0.04    3.29
```

If you want to run `sar` activity reports live, you can do that by adding counts and time intervals to the command line, as shown here:

```
# sar -n DEV 5 2
Linux 5.3.8-200.fc30.x86_64 (ubuntu)  11/28/2019  _x86_64_  (1 CPU)
11:19:36 PM IFACE rxpck/s txpck/s  rxkB/s  txkB/s rxcmp/s txcmp/s...
11:19:41 PM    lo    5.42    5.42    1.06    1.06    0.00    0.00...
11:19:41 PM  ens3    0.00    0.00    0.00    0.00    0.00    0.00...
...
```

```
Average:  IFACE rxpck/s txpck/s rxkB/s txkB/ rxcmp/s txcmp/s rxmcst/s
Average:     lo    7.21    7.21   1.42  1.42    0.00    0.00    0.00
Average:   ens3    0.00    0.00   0.00  0.00    0.00    0.00    0.00
Average:  wlan0    4.70    4.00   4.81  0.63    0.00    0.00    0.00

Average:   pan0    0.00    0.00   0.00  0.00    0.00    0.00    0.00
Average:   tun0    3.70    2.90   4.42  0.19    0.00    0.00    0.00
```

With the -n Dev example just shown, you can see how much activity came across the different network interfaces on your system. You can see how many packets were transmitted and received and how many KB of data were transmitted and received. In that example, samplings of data were taken every five seconds and repeated twice.

Refer to the sar, sadc, sa1, and sa2 man pages for more information on how sar data can be gathered and displayed.

Checking System Space

Although logwatch can give you a daily snapshot of space consumption on your system disks, the df and du commands can help you immediately see how much disk space is available. The following sections show examples of those commands.

Displaying system space with df

You can display the space available in your filesystems using the df command. To see the amount of space available on all of the mounted filesystems on your Linux computer, type **df** with no options:

```
$ df
Filesystem   1k-blocks     Used  Available  Use%  Mounted on
/dev/sda3    30645460  2958356   26130408   11%  /
/dev/sda2       46668     8340      35919   19%  /boot
...
```

This example output shows the space available on the hard disk partition mounted on the / (root) directory (/dev/sda1) and /boot partition (/dev/sda2). Disk space is shown in 1KB blocks. To produce output in a more human-readable form, use the -h option:

```
$ df -h
Filesystem      Size  Used  Avail  Use%  Mounted on
/dev/sda3       29G   2.9G    24G   11%  /
/dev/sda2       46M   8.2M    25M   19%  /boot
...
```

With the df -h option, output appears in a friendlier megabyte or gigabyte listing. Other options with df enable you to do the following:

- Print only filesystems of a particular type (-t type).
- Exclude filesystems of a particular type (-x type). For example, type df -x tmpfs -x devtmpfs to exclude temporary filesystem types (limiting output to filesystems that represent real storage areas).

- Include filesystems that have no space, such as /proc and /dev/pts (-a).
- List only available and used inodes (-i).
- Display disk space in certain block sizes (--block-size=#).

Checking disk usage with du

To find out how much space is being consumed by a particular directory (and its subdirectories), use the du command. With no options, du lists all directories below the current directory, along with the space consumed by each directory. At the end, du produces total disk space used within that directory structure.

The du command is a good way to check how much space is being used by a particular user (du /home/jake) or in a particular filesystem partition (du /var). By default, disk space is displayed in 1KB block sizes. To make the output friendlier (in kilobytes, megabytes, and gigabytes), use the -h option as follows:

```
$ du -h /home/jake
114k    /home/jake/httpd/stuff
234k    /home/jake/httpd
137k    /home/jake/uucp/data
701k    /home/jake/uucp
1.0M    /home/jake
```

The output shows the disk space used in each directory under the home directory of the user named jake (/home/jake). Disk space consumed is shown in kilobytes (k) and megabytes (M). The total space consumed by /home/jake is shown on the last line. Add the —s option to see total disk space used for a directory and its subdirectories.

Finding disk consumption with find

The find command is a great way to find file consumption of your hard disk using a variety of criteria. You can get a good idea of where disk space can be recovered by finding files that are over a certain size or were created by a particular person.

> **NOTE**
>
> You must be the root user to run this command effectively, unless you are just checking your personal files. If you are not the root user, there are many places in the filesystem for which you do not have permission to check. Regular users can usually check their own home directories but not those of others.

In the following example, the find command searches the root filesystem (/) for any files owned by the user named jake (-user jake) and prints the filenames. The output of the find command is organized in a long listing in size order (ls -ldS). Finally, that output is sent to the file /tmp/jake. When you view the file /tmp/jake (for example, less /tmp/jake), you will find all of the files that are owned by the user jake listed in size order. Here is the command line:

```
# find / -xdev -user jake -print | xargs ls -ldS > /tmp/jake
```

Here's another example, except that instead of looking for a user's files, we're looking for files larger than 100 kilobytes (-size +100M):

```
# find / -xdev -size +100M | xargs ls -ldS > /tmp/size
```

You can save yourself lots of disk space just by removing some of the largest files that are no longer needed. In this example, you can see that large files are sorted by size in the /tmp/size file.

Managing Servers in the Enterprise

Most of the server configurations covered in this book describe how to install systems manually and work directly on host computers. Having to set up each host individually would be far too inefficient for modern data centers consisting of dozens, hundreds, or even thousands of computers. To make the process of setting up Linux servers in a large data center more efficient, some of the following are employed:

Automated deployments   One way to install systems without having to step through a manual install process is with PXE booting. By setting up a PXE server and booting a computer on that network from a PXE-enabled network interface card, you can start a full install of that system simply by booting the system. Once the install is done, the system can reboot to run from the installed system.

Generic host systems   By making your host systems as generic as possible, individual installation, configuration, and upgrades can be greatly simplified. This can be automated in layers, where the base system is installed by PXE booting, configuration is done through features such as cloud-int, and applications can bring along their own dependencies when they run. On the application level, this can be done by running an application from inside a virtual machine or container. When the application is done running, it can be discarded without leaving its dependent software on the host.

Separation of management and worker systems   Instead of individually managing host systems, a separate platform can offer a way to manage large sets of systems. To do this, a platform such as OpenStack or OpenShift can have management nodes (in some cases called *control plane* or *master nodes*) to manage the machines where the workload actually runs (sometimes called *workers*, *slaves*, or just *nodes*). This separation of tasks by host type makes it possible to have applications deployed on any available worker that meets the needs of the application (such as available memory or CPU).

13

Keep in mind that understanding how individual applications are configured and services are run is still the foundation for these more advanced ways of managing data center resources. Although in-depth coverage of enterprise deployment and monitoring tools is outside the scope of this book, refer to Part VI, "Engaging with Cloud Computing," for an introduction to how different Linux-based cloud platforms manage these issues.

Summary

Although many different types of servers are available with Linux systems, the basic procedure for installing and configuring a server is essentially the same. The normal course of events is to install, configure, start, secure, and monitor your servers. Basic tasks that apply to all servers include using networking tools (particularly SSH tools) to log in, copy files, or execute remote commands.

Because an administrator can't be logged in watching servers all the time, tools for gathering data and reviewing the log data later are very important when administering Linux servers. The `rsyslog` facility can be used for local and remote logging. The `sar` facility gathers live data or plays back data gathered earlier at 10-minute intervals. Cockpit lets you watch CPU, memory, disk, and networking activity live from a web user interface. To watch disk space, you can run `df` and `du` commands.

The skills described in this chapter are designed to help you build a foundation to do enterprise-quality system administration in the future. Although these skills are useful, to manage many Linux systems at the same time, you need to extend your skills by using automating deployment and monitoring tools, as described in the cloud computing section of this book.

Although it is easy to set up networking to reach your servers in simple, default cases, more complex network configuration requires a knowledge of networking configuration files and related tools. The next chapter describes how to set up and administer networking in Linux.

Exercises

The exercises in this section cover some of the basic tools for connecting to and watching over your Linux servers. As usual, you can accomplish the tasks here in several ways. So, don't worry if you don't go about the exercises in the same way as shown in the answers, as long as you get the same results. If you are stuck, solutions to the tasks are shown in Appendix A.

Some of the exercises assume that you have a second Linux system available that you can log in to and try different commands. On that second system, you need to make sure that the `sshd` service is running, that the firewall is open, and that `ssh` is allowed for the user account that you are trying to log in to (`root` is often blocked by `sshd`).

If you have only one Linux system, you can create an additional user account and simply simulate communications with another system by connecting to the name localhost instead, as shown in this example:

```
# adduser joe
# passwd joe
# ssh joe@localhost
```

1. Using the ssh command, log in to another computer (or the local computer) using any account to which you have access. Enter the password when prompted.

2. Using remote execution with the ssh command, display the output from a remote command on the local system.

3. Use the ssh command to use X11 forwarding to display a gedit window on your local system; then save a file in the remote user's home directory.

4. Recursively copy all of the files from the /etc/apt/ directory on a remote system to the /tmp directory on your local system in such a way that all of the modification times on the files are updated to the time on the local system when they are copied.

5. Recursively copy all of the files from the /usr/share/logwatch directory on a remote system to the /tmp directory on your local system in such a way that all of the modification times on the files from the remote system are maintained on the local system.

6. Create a public/private key pair to use for SSH communications (no passphrase on the key), copy the public key file to a remote user's account with ssh-copy-id, and use key-based authentication to log in to that user account without having to enter a password.

7. Create an entry in /etc/rsyslog.d/50-default.conf that stores all authentication messages (authpriv) info level and higher into a file named /var/log/myauth. From one terminal, watch the file as data comes into it, and in another terminal, try to ssh into your local machine as any valid user with a bad password.

8. Use the du command to determine the largest directory structures under /usr/share, sort them from largest to smallest, and list the top 10 of those directories in terms of size.

9. Use the df command to show the space that is used and available from all of the filesystems currently attached to the local system but exclude any tmpfs or devtmpfs filesystems.

10. Find any files in the /usr directory that are more that 10MB in size.

Administering Networking

C onnecting a single desktop system or laptop to a network, particularly one that connects to the Internet, is easy. If you are trying to connect your Ubuntu desktop system to the Internet, here's what you can try given an available wired or wireless network interface:

Wired network   If your home or office has a wired Ethernet port that provides a path to the Internet and your computer has an Ethernet port, use an Ethernet cable to connect the two ports. After you turn on your computer, boot up Linux and log in. Clicking the NetworkManager icon on the desktop should show you that you are connected to the Internet or allow you to connect with a single click.

Wireless network   For a wireless computer running Linux, log in and click the NetworkManager icon on the desktop. From the list of wireless networks that appear, select the one you want and, when prompted, enter the required password. Each time you log in from that computer from the same location, it automatically connects to that wireless network.

If either of those types of network connections works for you, and you are not otherwise curious about how networking works in Linux, that may be all you need to know. However, what if your Linux system doesn't automatically connect to the Internet? What if you want to configure your desktop to talk to a private network at work (VPN)? What if you want to lock down network settings on your server or configure your Linux system to work as a router?

NOTE

The software running networking on your Ubuntu machine will depend on your particular release. The Linux community has been adopting and rejecting networking tools at an alarming rate over the past few years. This chapter will assume you're using NetworkManager, but older environments might have instead (or additionally) used `ifupdown` or the `/etc/network/interfaces` file. And newer releases are likely to use an entirely different tool: Netplan—perhaps on top of `systemd-networkd`. Be prepared for change. We'll see an example of Netplan in action a bit later in this chapter.

In this chapter, topics related to networking are divided into networks for desktops, servers, and enterprise computing. The general approach to configuring networking in these three types of Linux systems is as follows:

Desktop/laptop networking   On desktop or laptop systems, NetworkManager runs by default in order to manage network interfaces. With NetworkManager, you can automatically accept the address and server information that you need to connect to the Internet. However, you can also set address information manually. You can configure things such as proxy servers or virtual private network connections to allow your desktop to work from behind an organization's firewall or to connect through a firewall, respectively.

Server networking   Although NetworkManager originally worked best on desktop and laptop network configurations, it now works extremely well on servers. Today, features that are useful for configuring servers, such as Ethernet channel bonding and configuring aliases, can be found in NetworkManager.

Enterprise networking   Explaining how to configure networking in a large enterprise can fill several volumes itself. However, to give you a head start using Linux in an enterprise environment, I discuss basic networking technologies, such as DHCP and DNS servers, which make it possible for desktop systems to connect to the Internet automatically and find systems based on names and not just IP addresses.

Configuring Networking for Desktops

Whether you connect to the Internet from Linux, Windows, a smartphone, or any other kind of network-enabled device, certain things must be in place for that connection to work. The computer must have a network interface (wired or wireless), a unique IP address, an assigned DNS server, and a route to the Internet (identified by a gateway device).

Before I discuss how to change your networking configuration in Linux, let's look at what happens when Linux tries to connect to the Internet automatically with NetworkManager:

Activate network interfaces   NetworkManager looks to see what network interfaces (wired or wireless) are available. By default, external interfaces are usually set to start automatically using DHCP, although static names and addresses can be defined at install time instead.

Request DHCP service   The Linux system acts as a DHCP client to send out a request for DHCP service on each enabled interface. It uses the MAC address of the network interface to identify itself in the request.

Get response from DHCP server   A DHCP server, possibly running on a wireless router, cable modem, or other device providing a route to the Internet from your location, responds to the DHCP request with necessary information. That information probably contains at least the following:

IP address   The DHCP server typically has a range of Internet Protocol (IP) addresses that it can hand out to any system on the network that requests an address. In more secure environments, or one in which you want to be sure that machines get specific addresses, the DHCP server provides a static IP address to requests from specific MAC addresses. (MAC addresses are made to be unique among all network interface cards and are assigned by the manufacturer of each card.)

Subnet mask   When the DHCP client is assigned an IP address, the accompanying subnet mask tells that client which part of the IP address identifies the subnet and which identifies the host. For example, an IP address of 192.168.0.100 and subnet mask of 255.255.255.0 tell the client that the network is 192.168.0 and the host part is 100.

Lease time   When an IP address is dynamically allocated to the DHCP client, that client is assigned a lease time. The client doesn't own that address but must lease it again when the time expires and request it once again when the network interface restarts. Usually, the DHCP server remembers the client and assigns the same address when the system starts up again or asks to renew the lease—but that isn't guaranteed. The default lease time is typically 86,400 seconds (24 hours) for IPV4 addresses. The more plentiful IPV6 addresses are assigned for 2,592,000 seconds (30 days) by default.

Domain name server   Because computers like to think in numbers (such as IP addresses like 192.168.0.100) and people tend to think in names (such as the hostname www.example.com), computers need a way to translate hostnames into IP addresses and sometimes the reverse as well. The Domain Name System (DNS) was designed to handle that problem by providing a hierarchy of servers to perform name-to-address mapping on the Internet. The location of one or more DNS servers is usually assigned to the DHCP client from the DHCP host.

Default gateway   Although the Internet has one unique namespace, it is actually organized as a series of interconnected subnetworks. In order for a network request to leave your local network, it must know what node on your network provides a route to addresses outside of your local network. The DHCP server usually provides the default gateway IP address. By having network interfaces on both your subnet and the next network on the way to the ultimate destination of your communication, a gateway can route your packets to their destination.

Other information   A DHCP server can be configured to provide all kinds of information to help the DHCP client. For example, it can provide the location of an NTP server (to sync time between clients), font server (to get fonts for your X display), IRC server (for online chats), or print server (to designate available printers).

14

Update local network settings   After the settings are received from the DHCP server, they are implemented as appropriate on the local Linux system. For example, the IP address is set on the network interface, the DNS server entries are added to the local `/etc/resolv.conf` file (by NetworkManager), and the lease time is stored by the local system so it knows when to request that the lease be renewed.

All of the steps just described typically happen without your having to do anything but turn on your Linux system and log in. Now suppose that you want to be able to verify your network interfaces or change some of those settings. You can do that using the tools described in the next sections.

Checking your network interfaces

There are both graphical and command-line tools for viewing information about your network interfaces in Linux. From the desktop, NetworkManager tools and the Cockpit web user interface are good places to start.

Checking your network from NetworkManager

The easiest way to check the basic setting for a network interface is to open the pull-down menu at the upper-right corner of your desktop and select your active network interface. Figure 14.1 shows the WiFi settings for an active network on a GNOME 3 desktop.

FIGURE 14.1

Checking network interfaces with NetworkManager

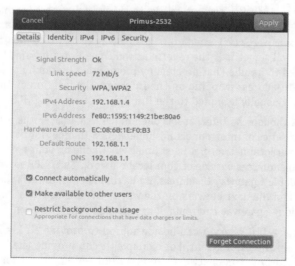

As you can see in Figure 14.1, both IPv4 and IPv6 addresses are assigned to the interface. The IP address 192.168.1.1 offers both a DNS service and a route to external networks.

To see more about how your Linux system is configured, click one of the tabs at the top of the window. For example, Figure 14.2 shows the Security tab, where you can select the type of security connection to the network and set the password needed to connect to that network.

FIGURE 14.2

Viewing security for a wireless network using NetworkManager

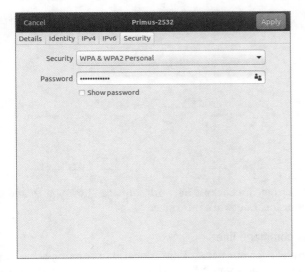

Checking your network from Cockpit

Provided you have enabled Cockpit, you can see and change information about your network interfaces through your web browser. On your local system, you open `https://localhost:9090/network` to go directly to the Cockpit Networking page for your local system. Figure 14.3 shows an example of this.

From the Cockpit Networking page, you can see information about all of your network interfaces at once. In this case, there are three network managed interfaces: `enp8s0` (an inactive wired interface), `wlxec086b1ef0b3` (an active wireless interface), and `lxdbr0` (an active bridge to local LXD containers).

At the top of the Cockpit Networking page, you can see data being sent from and received on the local system. Select a network interface to see a page displaying activities for that particular interface.

14

FIGURE 14.3

Viewing and changing network settings from Cockpit

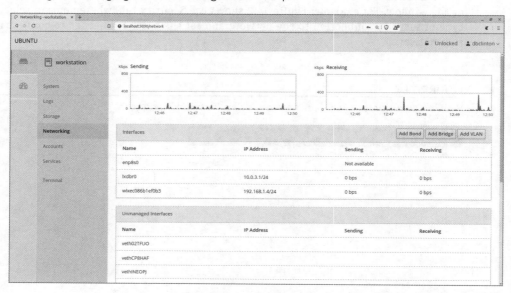

More advanced features available from the Cockpit Networking page allow you to add bonds, teams, bridges, and VLANs to your local network interfaces.

Checking your network from the command line

To get more detailed information about your network interfaces, try running some commands. There are commands that can show you information about your network interfaces, routes, hosts, and traffic on the network.

Viewing network interfaces

To see information about each network interface on your local Linux system, enter the following:

```
# ip addr show
1: lo: <LOOPBACK,UP,LOWER_UP> mtu 65536 qdisc noqueue state UNKNOWN
group default qlen 1000
    link/loopback 00:00:00:00:00:00 brd 00:00:00:00:00:00
    inet 127.0.0.1/8 scope host lo
       valid_lft forever preferred_lft forever
    inet6 ::1/128 scope host
       valid_lft forever preferred_lft forever
2: enp0s3: <BROADCAST,MULTICAST,UP,LOWER_UP> mtu 1500 qdisc fq_codel
state UP group default qlen 1000
```

```
        link/ether 08:00:27:45:24:e1 brd ff:ff:ff:ff:ff:ff
        inet 192.168.1.13/24 brd 192.168.1.255 scope global
dynamic enp0s3
          valid_lft 86342sec preferred_lft 86342sec
        inet6 fe80::a00:27ff:fe45:24e1/64 scope link
          valid_lft forever preferred_lft forever
3: enp0s8: <BROADCAST,MULTICAST> mtu 1500 qdisc noop state DOWN group
default qlen 1000
        link/ether 08:00:27:f1:5e:a9 brd ff:ff:ff:ff:ff:ff
4: enp0s9: <BROADCAST,MULTICAST> mtu 1500 qdisc noop state DOWN group
default qlen 1000
        link/ether 08:00:27:2d:a8:ba brd ff:ff:ff:ff:ff:ff
```

The `ip addr show` output displays information about your network interfaces. The `lo` entry in the first line of the output shows the loopback interface, which is used to allow network commands to run on the local system to connect to the local system. The IP address for localhost is 127.0.0.1/8 (the /8 is CIDR notation, indicating that 127. is the network number and 0.0.1 is the host number). Add a -s option (`ip -s addr show`) to see statistics of packet transmissions and errors associated with each interface.

In this case, the wired Ethernet interfaces (`enp0s8 and enp0s9`) are down (no cable), but `enp0s3` is up. The MAC address on that interface is 08:00:27:45:24:e1 and the Internet (IPv4) address is 192.168.1.13. An IPv6 address is also enabled.

Older versions of Linux used to assign more generic network interface names, such as `eth0` and `wlan0`. Now interfaces are given predictable names based on their locations on the computer's bus.

An older (and now deprecated) command for seeing network interface information was `ifconfig`. By default, `ifconfig` shows similar information to that of `ip addr`, but `ifconfig` also shows the number of packets received (RX) and transmitted (TX) by default, as well as the amount of data and any errors or dropped packets.

```
# ifconfig wlp2s0
wlp2s0: flags=4163<UP,BROADCAST,RUNNING,MULTICAST>  mtu 1500
        inet 192.168.1.83  netmask 255.255.255.0
           broadcast 192.168.1.255
        inet6 2600:1700:722:a10:b55a:fca6:790d:6aa6
           prefixlen 64   scopeid 0x0<global>
        inet6 fe80::25ff:8129:751b:23e3
           prefixlen 64   scopeid 0x20<link>
        inet6 2600:1700:722:a10::489
           prefixlen 128   scopeid 0x0<global>
        ether e0:06:e6:83:ac:c7  txqueuelen 1000  (Ethernet)
        RX packets 208402  bytes 250962570 (239.3 MiB)
        RX errors 0  dropped 4  overruns 0  frame 0
        TX packets 113589  bytes 13240384 (12.6 MiB)
        TX errors 0  dropped 0 overruns 0  carrier 0  collisions 0
Checking connectivity to remote systems
```

To make sure that you can reach systems that are available on the network, you can use the ping command. As long as the computer responds to ping requests (not all do), you can use ping to send packets to that system in a way that asks them to respond. Here is an example:

```
$ ping host1
PING host1 (192.168.1.15 ) 56(84) bytes of data.
64 bytes from host1 (192.168.1.15 ): icmp_seq=1 ttl=64 time=0.062 ms
64 bytes from host1 (192.168.1.15 ): icmp_seq=2 ttl=64 time=0.044 ms
^C
--- host1 ping statistics ---
2 packets transmitted, 2 received, 0% packet loss, time 1822ms
rtt min/avg/max/mdev = 0.044/0.053/0.062/0.009 ms
```

The ping command shown here continuously pings the host named host1. After a few pings, press Ctrl+C to end the pings, and the last few lines show you how many of the ping requests succeeded.

You could have used the IP address (192.168.1.15, in this case) to see that you could reach the system. However, using the hostname gives you the additional advantage of knowing that your name-to-IP-address translation (being done by your DNS server or local hosts file) is working properly as well. In this case, however, host1 appeared in the local /etc/hosts file.

Checking routing information

Routing is the next thing that you can check with respect to your network interfaces. The following snippets show you how to use the ip and route commands to do that:

```
# ip route show
default via 192.168.1.1 dev enp0s3 proto dhcp src 192.168.1.13
metric 100
192.168.1.0/24 dev enp0s3 proto kernel scope link src 192.168.1.13
192.168.1.1 dev enp0s3 proto dhcp scope link src 192.168.1.13 metric 100
```

The ip route show command example illustrates that the 192.168.1.13 address provides the route to the host from a local network interface (enp0s3). Communication to any address in the 192.168.1.0/24 range from that machine (192.168.1.13) goes over that interface. The route command can provide similar information:

```
# route
Kernel IP routing table
Destination     Gateway      Genmask          Flags Metric Ref    Use Iface
default         _gateway     0.0.0.0          UG    100    0        0 enp0s3
192.168.1.0     0.0.0.0      255.255.255.0    U     0      0        0 enp0s3
_gateway        0.0.0.0      255.255.255.255  UH    100    0        0 enp0s3
```

Here's a more complex routing table:

```
# route
Kernel IP routing table
Destination    Gateway        Genmask          Flags Metric Ref Use Iface
default        gateway        0.0.0.0          UG    600    0     0 wlp3s0
10.0.0.0       vpn.example.   255.0.0.0        U     50     0     0 tun0
10.10.135.0    0.0.0.0        255.255.217.0    U     50     0     0 tun0
vpn.example.   gateway        255.255.255.255  UGH   600    0     0 wlp3s0
172.17.0.0     0.0.0.0        255.255.0.0      U     0      0     0 docker0
192.168.1.0    *              255.255.255.0    U     600    0     0 wlp3s0
```

In the route example just shown, there is a wireless interface (wlp3s0) as well as an interface representing a virtual private network (VPN) tunnel. A VPN provides a way to have encrypted, private communications between a client and a remote network over an insecure network (such as the Internet). Here the tunnel goes from the local system over the wlan0 interface to a host named vpn.example.com (some of the name is truncated).

All communication to the 192.168.1.0/24 network still goes directly over the wireless LAN. However, packets destined for the 10.10.135.0/24 and 10.0.0.0/8 networks are routed directly to vpn.example.com for communication with hosts on the other side of the VPN connection over the tunneled interface (tun0).

A special route is set up for communications to containers (docker0) running on the local system on network 172.17.0.0. All other packets go to the default route via the address 192.168.1.0. As for the flags shown in the output, a U says the route is up, a G identifies the interface as a gateway, and an H says the target is a host (as is the case with the VPN connection).

So far, I have shown you the routes to leave the local system. If you want to follow the entire route to a host from beginning to end, you can use the traceroute command (apt install traceroute). For example, to trace the route a packet takes from your local system to the www.google.com site, type the following traceroute command:

```
# traceroute google.com
traceroute to google.com (74.125.235.136), 30 hops max, 60 byte pkts
...
 7  rrcs-70-62-95-197.midsouth.biz.rr.com (70.62.95.197)  ...
 8  ge-2-1-0.rlghncpop-rtr1.southeast.rr.com (24.93.73.62)  ...
 9  ae-3-0.cr0.dca10.tbone.rr.com (66.109.6.80) ...
10  107.14.19.133 (107.14.19.133)  13.662 ms  ...
11  74.125.49.181 (74.125.49.181)  13.912 ms ...
12  209.85.252.80 (209.85.252.80)  61.265 ms ...
13  66.249.95.149 (66.249.95.149)  18.308 ms ...
14  66.249.94.22 (66.249.94.22)  18.344 ms ...
15  72.14.239.83 (72.14.239.83)  85.342 ms ...
16  64.233.174.177 (64.233.174.177)  167.827 ms ...
17  209.85.255.35 (209.85.255.35)  169.995 ms  ...
18  209.85.241.129 (209.85.241.129)  170.322 ms  ...
19  nrt19s11-in-f8.1e100.net (74.125.235.136)  169.360 ms  ...
```

14

I truncated part of the output to drop off some of the initial routes and the amount of time (in milliseconds) that the packets were taking to traverse each route. Using `traceroute`, you can see where the bottlenecks are along the way if your network communication is stalling.

Viewing the host and domain names

To see the hostname assigned to the local system, type `hostname`. To just see the domain portion of that name (assuming a DNS name has been assigned), use the `dnsdomainname` command:

```
# hostname
spike.example.com
# dnsdomainname
example.com
```

Configuring network interfaces

If you don't want to have your network interfaces assigned automatically from a DHCP server (or if there is no DHCP server), you can configure network interfaces manually. This can include assigning IP addresses, the locations of DNS servers and gateway machines, and routes. This basic information can be set up using NetworkManager.

Setting IP addresses manually

To change the network configuration for your wired network interface through Network-Manager, do the following:

1. Select the Settings icon from the drop-down menu in the upper-right corner of the desktop and select Network.

2. Assuming that you have a wired NIC that is not yet in use, select the settings button (small gear icon) next to the interface that you want to change.

3. Choose IPv4 and change the IPv4 Method setting from Automatic (DHCP) to Manual.

4. Fill in the following information (only Address and Netmask are required):

   a. **Address:** The IP address that you want to assign to your local network interface. For example, 192.168.100.100.

   b. **Netmask:** The subnetwork mask that defines which part of the IP address represents the network and which part identifies the host. For example, a netmask of 255.255.255.0 would identify the network portion of the previous address as 192.168.100 and the host portion as 100.

   c. **Gateway:** The IP address of the computer or device on the network that acts as the default route. The default route will route packets from the local network to any address that is not available on the local network or via some other custom route.

   d. **DNS servers:** Fill in the IP addresses for the system providing DNS service to your computer. If there is more than one DNS server, add the others in a comma-separated list of servers.

5. Click the Apply button. The new information is saved, and the network is restarted using the new information. Figure 14.4 shows an example of those network settings.

FIGURE 14.4

Changing network settings with NetworkManager

Setting IP address aliases

You can attach multiple IP addresses to a single network interface. In the same NetworkManager screen, this is done by simply filling in a subsequent Addresses box and adding the new IP address information. Here are a few things you should know about adding address aliases:

- A netmask is required for each address, but a gateway is not required.
- The Apply button stays grayed out until you include valid information in the fields.
- The new address does not have to be on the same subnetwork as the original address, although it is listening for traffic on the same physical network.

After adding the address 192.168.100.103 to my wired interface, running `ip addr show enp4s0` displays the following indication of the two IP addresses on the interface:

```
2: enp4s0: <BROADCAST,MULTICAST,UP,LOWER_UP> mtu 1500 qdisc fq_codel
state UP group default qlen 1000
    link/ether 30:85:a9:04:9b:f9 brd ff:ff:ff:ff:ff:ff
    inet 192.168.100.100/24 brd 192.168.100.255 scope
        global noprefixroute enp4s0
    valid_lft forever preferred_lft forever
    inet 192.168.100.103/24 brd 192.168.100.255 scope
        global secondary noprefixroute enp4s0
    valid_lft forever preferred_lft forever
```

14

For information on setting up aliases directly in configuration files, refer to the section "Setting alias network interfaces" later in this chapter.

Setting routes

When you request a connection to an IP address, your system looks through your routing table to determine the path on which to connect to that address. Information is sent in the form of packets. A packet is routed in the following different ways, depending on its destination:

- The local system is sent to the lo interface.
- A system on your local network is directed through your NIC directly to the intended recipient system's NIC.
- Any other system is sent to the gateway (router) that directs the packet on to its intended address on the Internet.

Of course, what I have just described here is one of the simplest cases. You may, in fact, have multiple NICs with multiple interfaces connected to different networks. You may also have multiple routers on your local network that provide access to other private networks. For example, suppose you have a router (or other system acting as a router) on your local network; you can add a custom route to that router via NetworkManager. Using the NetworkManager example shown previously, scroll down the page to view the Routes section. Then add the following information:

Address   The network address of the subnet you route to. For example, if the router (gateway) will provide you access to all systems on the 192.168.200 network, add the address 192.168.200.0.

Netmask   Add the netmask needed to identify the subnet. For example, if the router provides access to the address 192.168.200, you could use the netmask 255.255.255.0.

Gateway   Add the IP address for the router (gateway) that provides access to the new route. For example, if the router has an IP address on your 192.168.1 network of 192.168.1.199, add that address in this field.

Click Apply to apply the new routing information. You may have to restart the interface for this to take effect (for example, ifup enp4s0). Enter **route -n** to make sure the new routing information has been applied.

```
# route -n
Kernel IP routing table
Destination     Gateway         Genmask         Flags Metric Ref Use Iface
0.0.0.0         192.168.100.1   0.0.0.0         UG    1024   0     0 p4p1
192.168.100.0   0.0.0.0         255.255.255.0   U     0      0     0 p4p1

192.168.200.0   192.168.1.199   255.255.255.0 UG    1      0     0 p4p1
```

In the example just shown, you can see that the default gateway is 192.168.100.1. However, any packets destined for the 192.168.200 network are routed through the gateway host at IP address 192.168.1.199. Presumably that host has a network interface that faces the 192.168.200 network, and it is set up to allow other hosts to route through it to that network.

See the section "Setting custom routes" later in this chapter for information on how to set routes directly in configuration files.

Configuring a network proxy connection

If your desktop system is running behind a corporate firewall, you might not have direct access to the Internet. Instead, you might have to reach the Internet via a proxy server. Instead of allowing you full access to the Internet, a proxy server lets you make requests only for certain services outside of the local network. The proxy server then passes those requests on to the Internet or another network.

Proxy servers typically provide access to web servers (http:// and https://) and FTP servers (ftp://). However, a proxy server that supports SOCKS can provide a proxy service for different protocols outside of the local network. (*SOCKS* is a network protocol that allows client computers to access the Internet through a firewall.) You can identify a proxy server in NetworkManager and have communications for selected protocols go through that server (from the Settings window, select Network and then select Network Proxy).

Instead of identifying a proxy server to your network interfaces (via NetworkManager), you can configure your browser to use a proxy server directly by changing your Firefox preferences to use a proxy server. Here's how to define a proxy server from the Firefox window:

1. From Firefox, select Preferences. The Firefox Preferences window appears.

2. From the Firefox Preferences window, scroll down to Network Settings and select Settings.

3. From the Connection Settings window that appears, you can try to autodetect the proxy settings or, if you set the proxy in NetworkManager, you can choose to use system proxy settings. You can also select Manual Proxy Configuration, fill in the following information, and click OK.

   a. **HTTP Proxy**: The IP address of the computer providing the proxy service. This causes all requests for web pages (http:// protocol) to be forwarded to the proxy server.

   b. **Port**: The port associated with the proxy service. By default, the port number is 3128, but it can differ.

14

c. **Use this proxy server for all protocols:** Select this box to use the same proxy server and port associated with the HTTP proxy for all other service requests. This causes other proxy settings to be grayed out. (Instead of selecting this box, you can set those proxy services separately.)

d. **No Proxy for:** Add the hostname or IP address for any system that you want to be able to contact with Firefox directly without going through the proxy server. You don't need to add localhost and the local IP address (127.0.0.1) in this box, since those addresses are already set not to redirect.

After you click OK, all requests from the Firefox browser to locations outside of the local system are directed to the proxy server, which forwards those requests on to the appropriate server.

Configuring Networking from the Command Line

While NetworkManager does a great job of autodetecting wired networks or presenting you with lists of wireless networks, sometimes you need to abandon the NetworkManager GUI and use the terminal or Cockpit to configure the features that you need. These are some of the networking features described in the coming sections:

Basic configuration: See how to use nmtui to configure basic networking with a menu-based interface from a shell. This tool provides an intuitive interface for configuring networking on servers that have no graphical interface for running GUI-based tools.

Configuration files: Understand configuration files associated with Linux networking and how to configure them directly.

Ethernet channel bonding: Set up Ethernet channel bonding (multiple network cards listening on the same IP address).

Configure networking with nmtui

Many servers don't have graphical interfaces available. So, if you want to configure networking, you must be able to do so from the shell. One way to do that is to edit networking configuration files directly. Another method is to use menu-based commands that let you press arrow and Tab keys to navigate and forms you fill in to configure your network interface.

The nmtui command provides a menu-based interface that runs in the shell. As root, enter **nmtui** to see a screen similar to the one presented in Figure 14.5.

Use arrow keys and the Tab key to move around the interface. With the item you want to select highlighted, press Enter to select it. The interface is limited to modifying the following kinds of information: Edit or Activate a connection (network interface cards) and Set system hostname (hostname and DNS configuration).

FIGURE 14.5

Configuring networking with NetworkManager TUI

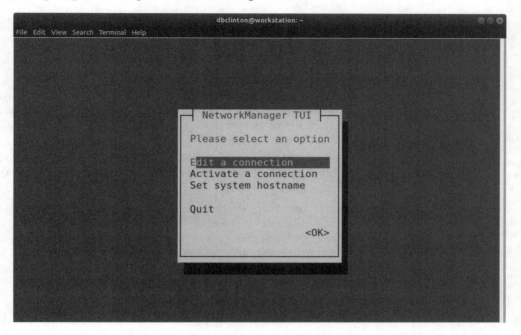

Editing a NetworkManager TUI connection

From the NetworkManager TUI screen displayed, here is how to edit an existing connection:

1. **Edit a connection:** With "Edit a connection" highlighted, press Enter. A list of network devices (usually wired or wireless Ethernet cards) is displayed, along with any wireless networks to which you have connected in the past.

2. **Network devices:** Highlight one of the network devices (in my case, I chose a wired Ethernet interface) and press Enter.

3. **IPv4 Configuration:** Move to the IPv4 Configuration Show button and press Enter. The Edit Connection window that appears lets you change information relating to the selected network device.

4. **Change to Manual:** You can leave the Profile Name and Device fields as they are. By default, Automatic is enabled. Automatic is what allows the network interface to come up automatically on the network if a DHCP service is available. To enter address and other information yourself, use the Tab key to highlight the Automatic field and press the spacebar; then use the arrow keys to highlight Manual and press Enter.

14

5. **Addresses:** Now fill in the address information (IP address and netmask). For example, 192.168.0.150/24 (where 24 is the CIDR equivalent for the 255.255.255.0 netmask).

6. **Gateway:** Type in the IP address for the computer or router that is supplying the route to the Internet.

7. **DNS servers:** Type in the IP addresses of either one or two DNS servers to tell the system where to go to translate hostnames you request into IP addresses.

8. **Search domains:** The Search domains entries are used when you request a host from an application without using a fully qualified domain name. For example, if you type `ping host1` with an `example.com` search path, the command would try to send ping packets to `host1.example.com`.

9. **Routing:** You can set custom routes by highlighting Edit in the Routing field and pressing Enter. Fill in the Destination/Prefix and Next Hop fields and select OK to save the new custom route.

10. **Other selections:** Of the other selections on the screen, consider setting "Never use this network for default route" if the network doesn't connect to wider networks and "Ignore automatically obtained routes" if you don't want those features to be set automatically from the network. Tab to the OK button and press the spacebar. Then click Quit to exit.

Understanding networking configuration files

Whether you change your network setup using NetworkManager or `nmtui`, most of the same configuration files are updated. In Ubuntu, network interfaces and custom routes are set in files in the `/etc/NetworkManager/system-connections` directory. However, you'll need to be sure that interfaces (besides `lo`) aren't already being defined in the `/etc/network/interfaces` file.

Here's how a typical WiFi interface connection is described by a file within `/etc/NetworkManager/system-connections`:

```
[connection]
id=BackRoom
uuid=39cea31a-9582-40b7-9fc6-f74c23e2fd9d
type=wifi
permissions=

[wifi]
mac-address=EC:00:6F:1E:F0:B3
mac-address-blacklist=
mode=infrastructure
ssid=BackRoom

[wifi-security]
auth-alg=open
key-mgmt=wpa-psk
psk=L87theQQ3ww
```

```
[ipv4]
dns-search=
method=auto

[ipv6]
addr-gen-mode=stable-privacy
dns-search=
method=auto
```

Bear in mind that those files might include plain-text copies of your passwords. For this reason, they're only readable using `sudo`. And, no, the password in that example is not real.

Other networking files

In addition to the network interface files, there are other network configuration files that you can edit directly to configure Linux networking. Here are some of those files.

/etc/hostname file

Your system's hostname is stored in the `/etc/hostname` file. For example, if the file included the hostname `host1.example.com`, that hostname would be set each time the system booted up. You can check how the current hostname is set at any time by typing the `hostname` command.

/etc/hosts file

Before DNS was created, translating hostnames to IP addresses was done by passing around a single hosts file. While there were only a few dozen and then a few hundred hosts on the Internet, this approach worked pretty well. But as the Internet grew, the single hosts file became unscalable and DNS was invented.

The `/etc/hosts` file still exists on Linux systems. It can still be used to map IP addresses to hostnames. The `/etc/hosts` file is a way to set up names and addresses for a small local network or just create aliases in order to make it easier to access the systems that you use all the time.

Here's an example of an `/etc/hosts` file:

```
127.0.0.1   localhost localhost.localdomain
::1         localhost localhost.localdomain
192.168.0.201  node1.example.com node1 joe
192.168.0.202  node2.example.com node2 sally
```

The first two lines (`127.0.0.1` and `::1`) set addresses for the local system. The IPv4 address for the local host is `127.0.0.1`; the IPv6 address for the local host is `::1`. There are also entries for two IP addresses. You could reach the first IP address (192.168.0.201) by the names `node1.example.com`, `node1`, or `joe`. For example, typing `ping joe` results in packets being sent to 192.168.0.201.

14

/etc/resolv.conf file

DNS servers and search domains are set in the /etc/resolv.conf file. If NetworkManager is enabled and running, you should not edit this file directly. Using the DNS servers specified in the nameservers section in /etc/netplan/*.yaml files, NetworkManager overwrites the /etc/resolv.conf file so that you would lose any entries you add to that file. Here's an example of the /etc/resolv.conf file that was modified by NetworkManager:

```
# Generated by NetworkManager
nameserver 192.168.0.2
nameserver 192.168.0.3
```

Each nameserver entry identifies the IP address of a DNS server. The order defines the order in which the DNS servers are checked. It's normal to have two or three nameserver entries, in case the first is not available. More than that and it can take too long for an unresolvable hostname to get checked for each server.

Another type of entry that you can add to this file is a search entry. A *search entry* lets you indicate domains to be searched when a hostname is requested by its base name instead of its entire fully qualified domain name. You can have multiple search entries by identifying one or more domain names after the search keyword, as in this example:

```
search example.com example.org example.net
```

The search options are separated by spaces or tabs.

/etc/nsswitch.conf and systemd

Unlike in earlier releases, name service switch functionality (which controls available DNS sources) is managed by systemd rather than the /etc/nsswitch.conf file on its own. Here's an example of an /etc/nsswitch.conf file that's properly configured for systemd:

```
passwd:         compat systemd
group:          compat systemd
shadow:         compat
gshadow:        files

hosts:          files mdns4_minimal [NOTFOUND=return] dns myhostname
networks:       files

protocols:      db files
services:       db files
ethers:         db files
rpc:            db files

netgroup:       nis
```

If you want to check that your DNS servers are being queried properly, you can use the host or dig commands, as in, for example:

```
$ host ubuntu.com

ubuntu.com has address 91.189.88.180
ubuntu.com has address 91.189.88.181
ubuntu.com has address 91.189.91.44
ubuntu.com has address 91.189.91.45
ubuntu.com has IPv6 address 2001:67c:1360:8001::2b
ubuntu.com has IPv6 address 2001:67c:1360:8001::2c
ubuntu.com has IPv6 address 2001:67c:1562::1f
ubuntu.com has IPv6 address 2001:67c:1562::20
ubuntu.com mail is handled by 10 mx.canonical.com.
$ dig ubuntu.com

; <<>> DiG 9.11.3-1ubuntu1.11-Ubuntu <<>> ubuntu.com
;; global options: +cmd
;; Got answer:
;; ->>HEADER<<- opcode: QUERY, status: NOERROR, id: 55254
;; flags: qr rd ra; QUERY: 1, ANSWER: 4, AUTHORITY: 0, ADDITIONAL: 1

;; OPT PSEUDOSECTION:
; EDNS: version: 0, flags:; udp: 65494
;; QUESTION SECTION:
;ubuntu.com.                 IN      A

;; ANSWER SECTION:
ubuntu.com.             55      IN      A       91.189.91.45
ubuntu.com.             55      IN      A       91.189.91.44
ubuntu.com.             55      IN      A       91.189.88.181
ubuntu.com.             55      IN      A       91.189.88.180

;; Query time: 0 msec
;; SERVER: 127.0.0.53#53(127.0.0.53)
;; WHEN: Sun Mar 29 14:55:42 EDT 2020
;; MSG SIZE  rcvd: 103
```

By default, the host command produces simpler output for DNS queries. It shows the IP address for ubuntu.com and the names of the mail servers (MX records) that serve ubuntu .com. The dig command shows information similar to what appears in the files that hold DNS records. The QUESTION SECTION part of the output shows that the address section asked for the address of ubuntu.com and the ANSWER SECTION part shows the answer (91.189.91.45). You can also see the address of the DNS server that was queried.

The host and dig commands are only used to query DNS servers. To identify other places to query, such as the local hosts file you would have to use the getent command:

```
# getent hosts node1
192.168.0.201   node1
```

This getent example finds a host named node1 that was entered into my local /etc/ hosts file. The getent command can be used to query any information settings. For example, typing getent passwd root shows the entry for the root user account in the local file, but it can also query a remote LDAP database for user information if you have configured that feature.

Setting alias network interfaces

Sometimes you might want your network interface card listening on multiple IP addresses. For example, if you were setting up a web server that was serving secure content (https) for multiple domains (example.com, example.org, and so on), each domain would require a separate IP address (associated with a separate certificate). In that case, instead of adding multiple network interface cards to the computer, you could simply create multiple aliases on a single NIC.

To create an alias network interface using the ip tool, you could specify the new IP address and subnet and then apply it to the appropriate interface. Here's how that might look:

```
sudo ip addr add 192.168.1.77/24 dev enp0s3
ip a
1: lo: <LOOPBACK,UP,LOWER_UP> mtu 65536 qdisc noqueue state UNKNOWN
group default qlen 1000
    link/loopback 00:00:00:00:00:00 brd 00:00:00:00:00:00
    inet 127.0.0.1/8 scope host lo
       valid_lft forever preferred_lft forever
    inet6 ::1/128 scope host
       valid_lft forever preferred_lft forever
2: enp0s3: <BROADCAST,MULTICAST,UP,LOWER_UP> mtu 1500 qdisc fq_codel
state UP group default qlen 1000
    link/ether 08:00:27:45:24:e1 brd ff:ff:ff:ff:ff:ff
    inet 192.168.1.13/24 brd 192.168.1.255 scope global dynamic enp0s3
       valid_lft 79131sec preferred_lft 79131sec
    inet 192.168.1.77/24 scope global secondary enp0s3
       valid_lft forever preferred_lft forever
    inet6 fe80::a00:27ff:fe45:24e1/64 scope link
       valid_lft forever preferred_lft forever
```

Note how the enp0s3 interface now has two IP addresses (192.168.1.13 and 192.168.1.77) associated with it. Removing the alias is as simple as running ip addr del 192.168.1.77/24 dev enp0s3.

The problem with the ip tool is that changes won't survive a system reboot. To create permanent interface configurations, you can use the Netplan tool. Netplan is installed by default on Ubuntu 18.04 but the renderer: NetworkManager line in the 01-network-manager-all.yaml file that might be in the /etc/netplan/ directory hands control over the NetworkManager. If you want to use Netplan to manage your networks, simply remove that line.

To add multiple static IP addresses to an interface, edit your .yaml file in /etc/netplan/ to look something like this:

```
network:
    ethernets:
        enp0s3:
            addresses:
                - 192.168.1.75/24
                - 10.1.0.5/16
            gateway4: 192.168.1.1
            dhcp4: false
    version: 2
```

Make sure the interface (enp0s3 in this example) is the one you want to edit. When you're done, run sudo netplan apply.

Setting up Ethernet channel bonding

Ethernet channel bonding allows you to have more than one network interface card on a computer associated with a single IP address. There are several reasons you might want to do this:

High availability   Multiple NICs on the same IP address can ensure that if one subnet goes down or one NIC breaks, the address can still be reached on a NIC connected to another subnet.

Performance   If there is too much network traffic to be handled by one NIC, you can spread that traffic across multiple NICs.

You'll first need to make sure the bonding kernel module is active. These commands will add the module (if necessary) and confirm it's active:

```
$ sudo modprobe bonding
$ lsmod | grep bond
bonding                163840  0
```

Once again, the ip command will do all the heavy lifting for us.

This series of commands will start by creating a new bond called bond0. I'll then set each of two existing interfaces to join bond0 and confirm it all happened by running ip addr:

```
$ sudo ip link add bond0 type bond mode 802.3ad
$ sudo ip link set enp0s8 master bond0
$ sudo ip link set enp0s9 master bond0
$ ip addr
1: lo: <LOOPBACK,UP,LOWER_UP> mtu 65536 qdisc noqueue state UNKNOWN
group default qlen 1000
    link/loopback 00:00:00:00:00:00 brd 00:00:00:00:00:00
    inet 127.0.0.1/8 scope host lo
       valid_lft forever preferred_lft forever
    inet6 ::1/128 scope host
       valid_lft forever preferred_lft forever
```

Continues

14

Continued

```
2: enp0s3: <BROADCAST,MULTICAST,UP,LOWER_UP> mtu 1500 qdisc fq_codel
state UP group default qlen 1000
    link/ether 08:00:27:45:24:e1 brd ff:ff:ff:ff:ff:ff
    inet 192.168.1.13/24 brd 192.168.1.255 scope global
dynamic enp0s3
       valid_lft 78563sec preferred_lft 78563sec
    inet6 fe80::a00:27ff:fe45:24e1/64 scope link
       valid_lft forever preferred_lft forever
3: enp0s8: <BROADCAST,MULTICAST,SLAVE,UP,LOWER_UP> mtu 1500 qdisc
fq_codel master bond0 state UP group default qlen 1000
    link/ether 08:00:27:f1:5e:a9 brd ff:ff:ff:ff:ff:ff
4: enp0s9: <BROADCAST,MULTICAST,SLAVE,UP,LOWER_UP> mtu 1500 qdisc
fq_codel master bond0 state UP group default qlen 1000
    link/ether 08:00:27:f1:5e:a9 brd ff:ff:ff:ff:ff:ff
5: bond0: <BROADCAST,MULTICAST,MASTER> mtu 1500 qdisc noop state DOWN
group default qlen 1000
    link/ether 08:00:27:f1:5e:a9 brd ff:ff:ff:ff:ff:ff
```

If you prefer to leave NetworkManager active on your machine, and you want this to persist across multiple boots, you can use the nmcli tool:

```
$ sudo nmcli con add type bond ifname bond0
Connection 'bond-bond0' (29765620-fe97-4c34-9866-c7650bb2161c)
successfully added.
$ sudo nmcli con add type ethernet ifname enp0s8 master bond0
Connection 'bond-slave-enp0s8' (4a6d107e-df4b-4431-aeb3-af37cb5a4697)
successfully added.
$ sudo nmcli con add type ethernet ifname enp0s9 master bond0
Connection 'bond-slave-enp0s9' (815e0e80-b24f-461c-b3fb-b8d646921a83)
successfully added.
```

Feel free to reboot your system to confirm that the changes have persisted.

Setting custom routes

On a simple network configuration, communications that are destined for the local network are directed to the appropriate interface on your LAN, while communications for hosts outside of your LAN go to a default gateway to be sent on to remote hosts. As an alternative, you can set custom routes to provide alternative paths to specific networks.

You can view the routes that are currently configured on your system using ip route:

```
$ ip route
default via 192.168.1.1 dev wlp3s0 proto dhcp metric 600
169.254.0.0/16 dev wlp3s0 scope link metric 1000
192.168.1.0/24 dev wlp3s0 proto kernel scope link src 192.168.1.6
metric 600
```

If you'd like to connect your network connection to work through a different server whose gateway address is, say, 192.168.4.1/24, then you'll first have to bring down the current route (192.168.1.0/24 in our example) and the default route setting, too:

```
# ip route delete 192.168.1.0/24 dev enp0s3
#
# ip route delete default dev enp0s3
#
$ ip route
10.1.46.0/24 dev cni0 proto kernel scope link src 10.1.46.1
192.168.1.1 dev enp0s3 proto dhcp scope link src 192.168.1.14
metric 100
```

Finally, you can add a new route pointing to your new gateway address, and then set it as default:

```
# sudo ip route add 192.168.4.0/24 dev enp0s3
# sudo ip route add default dev enp0s3
$ ip route
default dev enp0s3 scope link
10.1.46.0/24 dev cni0 proto kernel scope link src 10.1.46.1
192.168.4.1 dev enp0s3 proto dhcp scope link src 192.168.4.5
metric 100
```

The standard warnings about ensuring you've got physical access to your machine before playing around with network configurations apply.

Configuring Networking in the Enterprise

So far, the network configuration described in this chapter has centered on setting up single systems to connect to a network. Features available in Linux can go well beyond that by providing software that supports the actual network infrastructure needed by host computers to communicate.

The following sections introduce you to a few of the network infrastructure types of services available in Linux. Full implementation of these features is beyond the scope of this book, but know that if you find yourself needing to manage network infrastructure features, the following sections will give you a sense of how those features are implemented in Linux.

Configuring Linux as a router

If you have more than one network interface on a computer (typically two or more NICs), you can configure Linux as a router. To make this happen, all that is needed is a change to one kernel parameter that allows packet forwarding. To turn on the ip _ forward parameter immediately and temporarily, enter the following as root:

```
# cat /proc/sys/net/ipv4/ip_forward
0
# echo 1 > /proc/sys/net/ipv4/ip_forward
# cat /proc/sys/net/ipv4/ip_forward
1
```

Packet forwarding (routing) is disabled by default, with the value of ip_forward set to 0. By setting it to 1, packet forwarding is immediately enabled. To make this change permanent, you must add that value to the /etc/sysctl.conf file, so that it appears as follows:

```
net.ipv4.ip_forward = 1
```

With that file modified as shown, each time the system reboots, the value for ip_forward is reset to 1. (Notice that net.ipv4.ip _ forward reflects the actual location of the ip_forward file, minus /proc/sys, and with dots replacing slashes. You can change any kernel parameters set in the /proc/sys directory structure in this way.)

When a Linux system is used as a router, it is often also used as a firewall between a private network and a public network, such as the Internet. If that is the case, you might also want to use that same system for network address translation (NAT) and DHCP service, so the systems on the private network can route through the Linux system using private IP addresses. (See Chapter 25, "Securing Linux on a Network," for information on working with Linux firewall rules using the iptables utility.)

Configuring Linux as a DHCP server

Not only can a Linux system use a DHCP server to get its IP address and other information, it can also be configured to act as a DHCP server itself. In its most basic form, a DHCP server can hand out IP addresses from a pool of addresses to any system that requests an IP address. Usually, however, the DHCP server also distributes the locations of DNS servers and the default gateway.

Configuring a DHCP server is not something that should be done without some thought. Don't add a DHCP server on a network that is not under your control and that already has a working DHCP server. Many clients are set up to get address information from any DHCP server that will hand it out.

DHCP service is provided by the isc-dhcp-server package in Ubuntu. The service is named dhcpd. The primary configuration file is /etc/dhcp/dhcpd.conf for IPv4 networks (there is a dhcpd6.conf file in the same directory to provide DHCP service for IPv6 networks). By default, the dhcpd daemon listens on UDP port 67, so remember to keep that port open on your firewall.

When you install some virtualization and cloud services on a Linux system, a DHCP server is set up by default for you within that system. When you launch virtual machines, they are given IP addresses in that range. When you install and start the Docker service on those Linux distributions, it likewise sets up a private network and hands out IP addresses to Docker containers launched on that system.

Configuring Linux as a DNS server

In Linux, most professional Domain Name System (DNS) servers are implemented using the Berkeley Internet Name Domain (BIND) service. This is implemented in Ubuntu by installing the bind9 and bind9utils packages.

By default, `bind9` is configured by editing the `/etc/named.conf` file. Hostname-to-IP-address mapping is done in zone files located in the `/var/named` directory.

If you are interested in trying out `bind9`, I recommend that you first try it out by configuring DNS for a small home network behind a firewall as a way to make it easier for the people in your household to communicate with each other. You can lock down the IP addresses of the machines in your home by attaching MAC addresses of each computer's network interface card to specific IP addresses on a DHCP server and then mapping those names to addresses in a DNS server.

OTHER

Before you create a public DNS server, keep in mind that it is very important to secure it properly. A cracked public DNS server can be used to redirect traffic to any server the bad guys choose. So, if you are using that server, you are in danger of being presented with sites that are not the sites you think they are.

Configuring Linux as a proxy server

A proxy server provides a means of restricting network traffic from a private network to a public one, such as the Internet. Such servers provide an excellent way to lock down a computer lab at a school or restrict websites that employees can visit from work.

By physically setting up Linux as a router but configuring it as a proxy server, all of the systems on your home or business network can be configured to access the Internet using only certain protocols and only after you filter the traffic.

Using the Squid Proxy Server, which comes with most Linux systems (`squid` package in Ubuntu), you can enable the system to accept requests to web servers (HTTP and HTTPS), file servers (FTP), and other protocols. You can restrict which systems can use your proxy server (by hostname or IP address) and even limit which sites they can visit (by specific address, range of addresses, hostname, or domain names).

Configuring a squid proxy server can be as simple as installing the `squid` package, editing the `/etc/squid/squid.conf` file, and starting the `squid` service. The file comes with a recommended minimal configuration. However, you might want to define the hosts (based on IP address or name) that you want to allow to use the service. There are blacklists available with `squid` that allow you to deny access to whole sets of sites that might be inappropriate for children to visit.

Summary

Most network connections from a Linux desktop or laptop system can be made with little or no user intervention. If you use NetworkManager over a wired or wireless Ethernet connection, address and server information needed to start up can be automatically obtained from a DHCP server.

14

With NetworkManager's graphical interface, you can do some network configuration, if you like. You can set static IP addresses and select the name server and gateway computers to use. To do more manual and complex network configuration, consider working more directly with network configuration files.

Network configuration files in Linux can be used to set up more advanced features such as Ethernet channel bonding.

Beyond the basics of network connectivity in Linux, features are available that enable you to provide network infrastructure types of services. This chapter introduced services and features such as routing, DHCP, and DNS that you need to know when working with more advanced networking features in Linux.

With your networking configured, you can now begin configuring services to run over your networks. Chapter 15, "Starting and Stopping Services," describes the tools that you need to enable, disable, start, stop, and check the status of the services that are configured for your Linux system.

Exercises

The exercises in this section help you to examine and change the network interfaces on your Linux system as well as understand how to configure more advanced networking features. Start these exercises on a Linux system that has an active network connection but that is *not* in the middle of some critical network activity.

I recommend that you do these exercises directly from your computer console (in other words, don't SSH into the computer to do them). Some of the commands that you run may interrupt your network connectivity, and some of the configuration you do, if you make a mistake, can result in your computer being temporarily unavailable from the network.

There are often multiple ways to complete the tasks described in these exercises. If you are stuck, refer to the task solutions that are provided in Appendix A.

1. Use the desktop to check that NetworkManager has successfully started your network interface (wired or wireless) to the network. If it has not, then try to start your network interface.

2. Run a command to check the active network interfaces available on your computer.

3. Try to contact google.com from the command line in a way that ensures that DNS is working properly.

4. Run a command to check the routes being used to communicate outside of your local network.

5. Trace the route being taken to connect to google.com.

6. View the network activity of your Linux system from the Cockpit web user interface.

7. Create a host entry that allows you to communicate with your local host system using the name `myownhost`.

8. Determine the addresses of the DNS name servers that are being used to resolve hostnames to IP addresses on your system, then check which is queried from your system to find the IP address for `google.com`.

9. Check to see if your system has been configured to allow IPv4 packets to be routed between network interfaces on your system.

14

Starting and Stopping Services

IN THIS CHAPTER

The primary job of a Linux server system is to offer services to local or remote users. A server can provide access to web pages, files, database information, streaming music, or other types of content. Name servers can provide access to lists of host computer or usernames. Hundreds of these and other types of services can be configured on your Linux systems.

Ongoing services offered by a Linux system, such as access to a printer service or login service, are typically implemented by what is referred to as a *daemon* process. Most Linux systems have a method of managing each daemon process as a *service* using one of several popular initialization systems (also referred to as init systems). Advantages of using init systems include the ability to do the following:

- **Identify runlevels:** Put together sets of services in what are referred to as *runlevels* or *targets*.
- **Establish dependencies:** Set service dependencies so, for example, a service that requires network interfaces won't start until all network startup services have started successfully.
- **Set the default runlevel:** Select which runlevel or target starts up when the system boots (a *default runlevel*).
- **Manage services:** Run commands that tell individual services to start, stop, pause, restart, or even reload configuration files.

Several different init systems are in use with Linux systems today. The one you use depends on the Linux distribution and release that you are using. In this chapter, I cover the following init systems that have been used in Ubuntu and many other Linux distributions:

- **SysVinit:** This traditional init system was created for UNIX System V systems in the early 1980s. It offers an easy-to-understand method of starting and stopping services based on runlevel. Most UNIX and Linux systems up until a few years ago used SysVinit.
- **Systemd:** The latest versions of Ubuntu use the systemd init system. It is the most complex of the init systems, but it also offers much more flexibility. systemd offers not only features for starting and working with services, but also lets you manage sockets, devices, mount points, swap areas, and other unit types.

> **Note**
> If you are using an older version of Ubuntu, you probably used Upstart (a modification of SysVinit) as your initialization system. Beginning with Ubuntu 15.04 (released April 28, 2015), Upstart was replaced by the systemd initialization daemon. Thus, Upstart will not be described in this book.

This chapter describes the sysVinit and systemd init systems. In the process of using the init system that matches your Linux distribution, you learn how the boot process works to start services, how you can start and stop services individually, and how you enable and disable services.

Understanding the Initialization Daemon (init or systemd)

In order to understand service management, you need to understand the initialization daemon. The initialization daemon can be thought of as the "mother of all processes." This daemon is the first process to be started by the kernel on the Linux server. For Linux distributions that use SysVinit, the init daemon is literally named init. For systemd, the init daemon is named systemd.

The Linux kernel has a process ID (PID) of 0. Thus, the initialization process (init or systemd) daemon has a parent process ID (PPID) of 0, and a PID of 1. Once started, init is responsible for spawning (launching) processes configured to be started at the server's boot time, such as the login shell (agetty or mingetty process). It is also responsible for managing services.

The Linux init daemon was based on the UNIX System V init daemon. Thus, it is called the SysVinit daemon. However, it was not the only classic init daemon. The init daemon is not part of the Linux kernel. Therefore, it can come in different flavors, and Linux distributions can choose which flavor to use. Another classic init daemon was based on Berkeley UNIX, also called BSD. Therefore, the two original Linux init daemons were BSD init and SysVinit.

The classic `init` daemons worked without problems for many years. However, these daemons were created to work within a static environment. As new hardware, such as USB devices, came along, the classic `init` daemons had trouble dealing with these and other hot-plug devices. Computer hardware had changed from static to event based. New `init` daemons were needed to deal with these fluid environments.

In addition, as new services came along, the classic `init` daemons had to deal with starting more and more services. Thus, the entire system initialization process was less efficient and ultimately slower.

The modern initialization daemons have tried to solve the problems of inefficient system boots and non-static environments. The most popular of the new initialization daemons is `systemd`. Like other modern Linux systems, Ubuntu has made the move to the `systemd` daemon while maintaining backward compatibility to the classic SysVinit, Upstart, or BSD `init` daemons.

The `systemd` daemon was written primarily by Lennart Poettering, a Red Hat developer. However, it is also currently used by Ubuntu and other distributions. The official documentation is available from `docs.fedoraproject.org/en-US/quick-docs/understanding-and-administering-systemd`.

In order to manage your services properly, you need to know which initialization daemon your server has. Figuring that out can be a little tricky. The initialization process running on a SysVinit or Upstart is named `init`. For the first `systemd` systems, it was also called `init` but is now named `systemd`. Running `ps -e` can immediately tell you if yours is a `systemd` system:

```
# ps -e | head
   PID TTY          TIME CMD
   PID TTY          TIME CMD
     1 ?        00:00:18 systemd
     2 ?        00:00:00 kthreadd
     3 ?        00:00:00 rcu_gp
     4 ?        00:00:00 rcu_par_gp
     6 ?        00:00:00 kworker/0:0H-kb
     9 ?        00:00:00 mm_percpu_wq
    10 ?        00:00:00 ksoftirqd/0
    11 ?        00:00:13 rcu_sched
    12 ?        00:00:00 migration/0
```

If PID 1 is the `init` daemon for your system, try looking on the init Wikipedia page (`wikipedia.org/wiki/Init`) under "Other implementations." This will help you understand if your `init` daemon is SysVinit, Upstart, or some other initialization system.

Understanding the classic init daemons

The classic `init` daemons, SysVinit and BSD init, are worth understanding, even if your Linux server has a different `init` daemon. Not only is backward compatibility to the classics often used in the newer `init` daemons, but many are based upon them.

15

The classic SysVinit and BSD init daemons operate in a very similar fashion. Although in the beginning they may have been rather different, over time very few significant differences remained. For example, the older BSD init daemon would obtain configuration information from the /etc/ttytab file. Now, like the SysVinit daemon, the BSD init daemon's configuration information is taken at boot time from the /etc/inittab file. The following is a classic SysVinit /etc/inittab file:

```
# cat /etc/inittab
# inittab  This file describes how the INIT process should set up
# Default runlevel. The runlevels used by RHS are:
#   0 - halt (Do NOT set initdefault to this)
#   1 - Single user mode
#   2 - Multiuser, no NFS (Same as 3, if you do not have networking)
#   3 - Full multiuser mode
#   4 - unused
#   5 - X11
#   6 - reboot (Do NOT set initdefault to this)
#
id:5:initdefault:

# System initialization.
si::sysinit:/etc/rc.d/rc.sysinit

l0:0:wait:/etc/rc.d/rc 0
l1:1:wait:/etc/rc.d/rc 1
l2:2:wait:/etc/rc.d/rc 2
l3:3:wait:/etc/rc.d/rc 3
l4:4:wait:/etc/rc.d/rc 4
l5:5:wait:/etc/rc.d/rc 5
l6:6:wait:/etc/rc.d/rc 6

# Trap CTRL-ALT-DELETE
ca::ctrlaltdel:/sbin/shutdown -t3 -r now
pf::powerfail:/sbin/shutdown -f -h +2
"Power Failure; System Shutting Down"


# If power was restored before the shutdown kicked in, cancel it.
pr:12345:powerokwait:/sbin/shutdown -c
"Power Restored; Shutdown Cancelled"


# Run gettys in standard runlevels
1:2345:respawn:/sbin/mingetty tty1
2:2345:respawn:/sbin/mingetty tty2
3:2345:respawn:/sbin/mingetty tty3
4:2345:respawn:/sbin/mingetty tty4
5:2345:respawn:/sbin/mingetty tty5
6:2345:respawn:/sbin/mingetty tty6
```

```
# Run xdm in runlevel 5
x:5:respawn:/etc/X11/prefdm -nodaemon
```

The /etc/inittab file tells the init daemon which runlevel is the default runlevel. A *runlevel* is a categorization number that determines what services are started and what services are stopped. In the preceding example, a default runlevel of 5 is set with the line id:5:initdefault:. Table 15.1 shows the standard seven Linux runlevels.

TABLE 15.1 **Standard Linux Runlevels**

RUNLEVEL #	NAME	DESCRIPTION
0	Halt	All services are shut down, and the server is stopped.
1 or S	Single User Mode	The root account is automatically logged in to the server. Other users cannot log in to the server. Only the command-line interface is available. Network services are not started.
2	Multi-user Mode	Users can log in to the server, but only the command-line interface is available. On some systems, network interfaces and services are started; on others they are not. Originally, this runlevel was used to start dumb terminal devices so that users could log in (but no network services were started).
3	Extended Multi-user Mode	Users can log in to the server, but only the command-line interface is available. Network interfaces and services are started. This is a common runlevel for servers.
4	User Defined	Users can customize this runlevel.
5	Graphical Mode	Users can log in to the server. Command-line and graphical interfaces are available. Network services are started. This is a common runlevel for desktop systems.
6	Reboot	The server is rebooted.

Linux distributions can differ slightly on the definition of each runlevel as well as which runlevels are offered.

Other

The only runlevels that should be used in the /etc/inittab file are 2 through 5. The other runlevels could cause problems. For example, if you put runlevel 6 in the /etc/inittab file as the default, when the server reboots, it would go into a loop and continue to reboot over and over again.

15

The runlevels are not only used as a default runlevel in the /etc/inittab file. They can also be called directly using the init daemon itself. Thus, if you want to halt your server immediately, you type **init 0** at the command line:

```
# init 0
...
System going down for system halt NOW!
```

The init command accepts any of the runlevel numbers in Table 15.1, allowing you to switch your server quickly from one runlevel category to another. For example, if you need to perform troubleshooting that requires the graphical interface to be down, you can type **init 3** at the command line:

```
# init 3
INIT: Sending processes the TERM signal
starting irqbalance:                      [ OK ]
Starting setroubleshootd:
Starting fuse:  Fuse filesystem already available.
...
Starting console mouse services:          [ OK ]
```

To see your Linux server's current runlevel, simply type in the command **runlevel**. The first item displayed is the server's previous runlevel, which in the following example is 5. The second item displayed shows the server's current runlevel, which in this example is 3.

```
$ runlevel
5 3
```

In addition to the init command, you can use the telinit command, which is functionally the same. In the example that follows, the telinit command is used to reboot the server by taking it to runlevel 6:

```
# telinit 6
INIT: Sending processes the TERM signal
Shutting down smartd:                      [ OK ]
Shutting down Avahi daemon:                [ OK ]
Stopping dhcdbd:                           [ OK ]
Stopping HAL daemon:                       [ OK ]
...
Starting killall:
Sending all processes the TERM signal...   [ OK ]
Sending all processes the KILL signal...   [ OK ]
...
Unmounting filesystems                     [ OK ]
Please stand by while rebooting the system
...
```

On a freshly booted Linux server, the current runlevel number should be the same as the default runlevel number in the /etc/inittab file. However, notice that the previous runlevel in the example that follows is N. The N stands for "Nonexistent" and indicates that the server was freshly booted to the current runlevel.

```
$ runlevel
N 5
```

How does the server know which services to stop and which ones to start when a particular runlevel is chosen? When a runlevel is chosen, the scripts located in the /etc/rc.d/rc#.d directory (where # is the chosen runlevel) are run. These scripts are run whether the runlevel is chosen via a server boot using the /etc/inittab initdefault setting or the init or telinit command is used. For example, if runlevel 5 is chosen, then all of the scripts in the /etc/rc.d/rc5.d directory are run; your list will be different, depending on what services you have installed and enabled.

```
# ls /etc/rc.d/rc5.d
K01smolt                          K88wpa_supplicant    S22messagebus
K02avahi-dnsconfd                 K89dund              S25bluetooth
K02NetworkManager                 K89netplugd          S25fuse
K02NetworkManagerDispatcher       K89pand              S25netfs
K05saslauthd                      K89rdisc             S25pcscd
K10dc_server                      K91capi              S26hidd
K10psacct                         S00microcode_ctl     S26udev-post
K12dc_client                      S04readahead_early   S28autofs
K15gpm                            S05kudzu             S50hplip
K15httpd                          S06cpuspeed          S55cups
K20nfs                            S08ip6tables         S55sshd
K24irda                           S08iptables          S80sendmail
K25squid                          S09isdn              S90ConsoleKit
K30spamassassin                   S10network           S90crond
K35vncserver                      S11auditd            S90xfs
K50netconsole                     S12restorecond       S95anacron
K50tux                            S12syslog            S95atd
K69rpcsvcgssd                     S13irqbalance        S96readahead_later
K73winbind                        S13mcstrans          S97dhcdbd
K73ypbind                         S13rpcbind           S97yum-updatesd
K74nscd                           S13setroubleshoot    S98avahi-daemon
K74ntpd                           S14nfslock           S98haldaemon
K84btseed                         S15mdmonitor         S99firstboot
K84bttrack                        S18rpcidmapd         S99local
K87multipathd                     S19rpcgssd           S99smartd
```

Notice that some of the scripts within the /etc/rc.d/rc5.d directory start with a K and some start with an S. The K refers to a script that will kill (stop) a process. The S refers to a script that will start a process. Also, each K and S script has a number before the name of the service or daemon that they control. This allows the services to be stopped or started in a particular controlled order. You would not want your Linux server's network services to be started before the network itself was started.

An /etc/rc.d/rc#.d directory exists for all the standard Linux runlevels. Each one contains scripts to start and stop services for its particular runlevel.

```
# ls -d /etc/rc.d/rc?.d
/etc/rc.d/rc0.d  /etc/rc.d/rc2.d  /etc/rc.d/rc4.d  /etc/rc.d/rc6.d
/etc/rc.d/rc1.d  /etc/rc.d/rc3.d  /etc/rc.d/rc5.d
```

15

Actually, the files in the /etc/rc.d/rc#.d directories are not scripts but instead symbolic links to scripts in the /etc/rc.d/init.d directory. Thus, there is no need to have multiple copies of particular scripts.

```
# ls -l /etc/rc.d/rc5.d/K15httpd
lrwxrwxrwx 1 root root 15 Oct 10 08:15
 /etc/rc.d/rc5.d/K15httpd -> ../init.d/httpd
# ls /etc/rc.d/init.d
anacron              functions    multipathd                rpcidmapd
atd                  fuse         netconsole                rpcsvcgssd
auditd               gpm          netfs                     saslauthd
autofs               haldaemon    netplugd                  sendmail
avahi-daemon         halt         network                   setroubleshoot
avahi-dnsconfd       hidd         NetworkManager            single
bluetooth            hplip        NetworkManagerDispatcher  smartd
btseed               hsqldb       nfs                       smolt
bttrack              httpd        nfslock                   spamassassin
capi                 ip6tables    nscd                      squid
ConsoleKit           iptables     ntpd                      sshd
cpuspeed             irda         pand                      syslog
crond                irqbalance   pcscd                     tux
cups                 isdn         psacct                    udev-post
cups-config-daemon   killall      rdisc                     vncserver
dc_client            kudzu        readahead_early           winbind
dc_server            mcstrans     readahead_later           wpa_supplicant
dhcdbd               mdmonitor    restorecond               xfs
dund                 messagebus   rpcbind                   ypbind
firstboot            microcode    rpcgssd                   yum-updatesd
```

Notice that each service has a single script in /etc/rc.d/init.d. There aren't separate scripts for stopping and starting a service. These scripts will stop or start a service depending upon what parameter is passed to them by the init daemon.

Each script in /etc/rc.d/init.d takes care of all that is needed for starting or stopping a particular service on the server. The following is a partial example of the httpd script on a Linux system that uses the SysVinit daemon. It contains a case statement for handling the parameter ($1) that was passed to it, such as start, stop, status, and so on.

```
# cat /etc/rc.d/init.d/httpd
#!/bin/bash
#
# httpd        Startup script for the Apache HTTP Server
#
# chkconfig: - 85 15
# description: Apache is a World Wide Web server.
#              It is used to serve \
#              HTML files and CGI.
# processname: httpd
# config: /etc/httpd/conf/httpd.conf
```

```
# config: /etc/sysconfig/httpd
# pidfile: /var/run/httpd.pid

# Source function library.
. /etc/rc.d/init.d/functions
...
# See how we were called.
case "$1" in
  start)
        start
        ;;
  stop)
        stop
        ;;
  status)
        status $httpd
        RETVAL=$?
        ;;
...
esac

exit $RETVAL
```

After the runlevel scripts linked from the appropriate /etc/rc.d/rc#.d directory are executed, the SysVinit daemon's process spawning is complete. The final step the init process takes at this point is to do anything else indicated in the /etc/inittab file (such as spawn mingetty processes for virtual consoles and start the desktop interface, if you are in runlevel 5).

Understanding systemd initialization

The systemd initialization daemon is the newer replacement for the SysVinit and the Upstart init daemons. It is backward compatible with both SysVinit and Upstart. System initialization time is reduced by systemd because it can start services in a parallel manner.

Learning systemd basics

With the SysVinit daemon, services are stopped and started based upon runlevels. The systemd service is concerned with runlevels, but it implements them in a different way with what are called *target units*. Although the main job of systemd is to start and stop services, it can manage other types of things referred to as units. A *unit* is a group consisting of a name, type, and configuration file, and it is focused on a particular service or action. There are 12 systemd unit types:

- automount
- device
- mount

15

- path
- service
- snapshot
- socket
- target
- timer
- swap
- slice
- scope

The two primary `systemd` units with which you need to be concerned for dealing with services are service units and target units. A *service unit* is for managing daemons on your Linux server. A *target unit* is simply a group of other units.

The example that follows shows several `systemd` service units and target units. The service units have familiar daemon names, such as `cups` and `ssh`. Note that each service unit name ends with `.service`. The target units shown have names like `sysinit.` (`sysinit` is used for starting up services at system initialization.) The target unit names end with `.target`.

```
# systemctl list-units | grep .service
...
accounts-daemon.service       loaded active    running
Accounts Service
acpid.service                 loaded active    running   ACPI
event daemon
alsa-restore.service          loaded active    exited    Save/Restore
Sound Card State
apparmor.service              loaded active    exited    AppArmor
initialization
apport.service                loaded active    exited    LSB:
automatic crash report generation
atd.service                   loaded active    running   Deferred
execution scheduler
avahi-daemon.service          loaded active    running   Avahi mDNS/
DNS-SD Stack
binfmt-support.service        loaded active    exited    Enable
support for additional executable binary formats
bolt.service                  loaded active    running   Thunderbolt
system service
colord.service                loaded active    running   Manage,
Install and Generate Color Profiles
console-setup.service         loaded active    exited    Set console
font and keymap
cron.service                  loaded active    running   Regular
background program processing daemon
```

```
cups-browsed.service            loaded active    running   Make remote
CUPS printers available locally
cups.service                    loaded active    running   CUPS Scheduler
dbus.service                    loaded active    running   D-Bus System
Message Bus
ddclient.service                loaded active    running   LSB: Update
dynamic domain name service entries
...
# systemctl list-units | grep .target
basic.target            loaded active     active    Basic System
cryptsetup.target       loaded active     active    Local
Encrypted Volumes
getty.target            loaded active     active    Login Prompts
graphical.target        loaded active     active    Graphical Interface
local-fs-pre.target     loaded active     active    Local File
Systems (Pre)
local-fs.target         loaded active     active    Local File Systems
multi-user.target       loaded active     active    Multi-User System
network-online.target loaded active       active    Network is Online
network-pre.target      loaded active     active    Network (Pre)
network.target          loaded active     active    Network
nss-lookup.target       loaded active     active    Host and Network
Name Lookups
nss-user-lookup.targetloaded active       active    User and Group
Name Lookups
paths.target            loaded active     active    Paths
printer.target          loaded active     active    Printer
remote-fs.target        loaded active     active    Remote File Systems
slices.target           loaded active     active    Slices
sockets.target          loaded active     active    Sockets
sound.target            loaded active     active    Sound Card
swap.target             loaded active     active    Swap
sysinit.target          loaded active     active    System
Initialization
time-sync.target        loaded active     active    System Time
Synchronized
timers.target           loaded active     active    Timers
```

The Linux system unit configuration files are located in the /lib/systemd/system and /etc/systemd/system directories. You could use the ls command to look through those directories, but the preferred method is to use an option on the systemctl command as follows:

```
# systemctl list-unit-files --type=service
UNIT FILE                               STATE
...
cups.service                            enabled
...
```

Continues

Continued

```
    dbus.service                                        static
    ...
    NetworkManager.service                              enabled
    ...
    poweroff.service                                    static
    ...
    sshd.service                                        enabled
    sssd.service                                        disabled
    ...
    276 unit files listed.
```

The unit configuration files shown in the preceding code are all associated with a service unit. Configuration files for target units can be displayed via the following method:

```
    # systemctl list-unit-files --type=target
    UNIT FILE                       STATE     VENDOR PRESET
    basic.target                    static    enabled
    blockdev@.target                static    enabled
    bluetooth.target                static    enabled
    boot-complete.target            static    enabled
    cloud-config.target             static    enabled
    cloud-init.target               static    enabled
    cryptsetup-pre.target           static    disabled
    cryptsetup.target               static    enabled
    ctrl-alt-del.target             disabled  enabled
    default.target                  static    enabled
    emergency.target                static    enabled
    exit.target                     disabled  disabled
    final.target                    static    enabled
    friendly-recovery.target        static    enabled
    getty-pre.target                static    disabled
    getty.target                    static    enabled
    graphical.target                static    enabled
    [...]
    time-sync.target                static    disabled
    timers.target                   static    enabled
    umount.target                   static    enabled

    68 unit files listed.
```

Notice that both of the configuration units' file examples display units with a status of static, enabled, or disabled. The enabled status means that the unit is currently enabled (meaning that it will load automatically on system boot). The disabled status means that the unit is currently disabled. The next status, static, is slightly confusing. It stands for "statically enabled," and it means that the unit is enabled by default and cannot be disabled, even by root.

The service unit configuration files contain lots of information, such as what other services must be started, when this service can be started, which environmental file to use, and so on. The following example shows the ssh daemon's unit configuration file:

```
$ cat /lib/systemd/system/ssh.service
[Unit]
Description=OpenBSD Secure Shell server
After=network.target auditd.service
ConditionPathExists=!/etc/ssh/sshd_not_to_be_run

[Service]
EnvironmentFile=-/etc/default/ssh
ExecStartPre=/usr/sbin/sshd -t
ExecStart=/usr/sbin/sshd -D $SSHD_OPTS
ExecReload=/usr/sbin/sshd -t
ExecReload=/bin/kill -HUP $MAINPID
KillMode=process
Restart=on-failure
RestartPreventExitStatus=255
Type=notify
RuntimeDirectory=sshd
RuntimeDirectoryMode=0755

[Install]
WantedBy=multi-user.target
Alias=sshd.service
```

This basic service unit configuration file includes the following options:

Description: A free-form description (comment line) of the service.

After: Configures ordering. In other words, it lists which units should be activated before this service is started.

Environment File: The service's configuration files.

ExecStart: The command used to start this service.

ExecReload: The command used to reload this service.

WantedBy: The target unit to which this service belongs.

Notice that the target unit, multi-user.target, is used in the sshd service unit configuration file. The sshd service unit is wanted by the multi-user.target. In other words, when the multi-user.target unit is activated, the sshd service unit is started.

You can view the various units that a target unit will activate by using the following command:

15

```
# systemctl show --property "Wants" multi-user.target
Wants=binfmt-support.service plymouth-quit.service getty.target
snapd.seeded.service NetworkManager.service dns-clean.service snap-
gnome\x2dsy
```

Unfortunately, the systemctl command does not format the output for this well. It runs off the right edge of the screen so you cannot see the full results. Also, you must enter **q** to return to the command prompt. To fix this problem, pipe the output through some formatting commands to produce a nice, alphabetically sorted display, as shown in the example that follows:

```
# systemctl show --property "Wants" multi-user.target \
    | fmt -10 | sed 's/Wants=//g' | sort
anacron.service
apport.service
atd.service
avahi-daemon.service
binfmt-support.service
console-setup.service
cron.service
...
```

This display shows all of the services and other units that will be activated (started), including sshd, when the multi-user.target unit is activated. Remember that a target unit is simply a grouping of other units, as shown in the preceding example. Also notice that the units in this group are not all service units. There are path units and other target units as well.

A target unit has both *Wants* and requirements, called *Requires*. A *Wants* means that all of the units listed are triggered to activate (start). If they fail or cannot be started, no problem—the target unit continues on its merry way. The preceding example is a display of Wants only.

A Requires is much more stringent than a Wants and potentially catastrophic. A *Requires* means that all of the units listed are triggered to activate (start). If they fail or cannot be started, the entire unit (group of units) is deactivated.

You can view the various units a target unit Requires (must activate or the unit will fail), using the command in the example that follows. Notice that the Requires output is much shorter than the Wants for the multi-user.target. Thus, no special formatting of the output is needed.

```
# systemctl show --property "Requires" multi-user.target
Requires=basic.target
```

The target units also have configuration files, as do the service units. The following example shows the contents of the multi-user.target configuration file:

```
# cat /lib/systemd/system/multi-user.target
#  This file is part of systemd.
#
...
```

```
[Unit]
Description=Multi-User
Documentation=man:systemd.special(7)
Requires=basic.target
Conflicts=rescue.service rescue.target
After=basic.target rescue.service rescue.target
AllowIsolate=yes
```

This basic target unit configuration file has the following options:

Description: This is just a free-form description of the target.

Documentation: Lists the appropriate systemd man page.

Requires: If this multi-user.target gets activated, the listed target unit is also activated. If the listed target unit is deactivated or fails, then multi-user.target is deactivated. If there are no After and Before options, then both multi-user .target and the listed target unit activate simultaneously.

Conflicts: This setting avoids conflicts in services. Starting multi-user.target stops the listed targets and services, and vice versa.

After: This setting configures ordering. In other words, it determines which units should be activated before starting this service.

AllowIsolate: This option is a Boolean setting of yes or no. If this option set to yes, then this target unit, multi-user.target, is activated along with its dependencies and all others are deactivated.

To get more information on these configuration files and their options, enter **man systemd .service**, **man systemd.target**, and **man systemd.unit** at the command line.

For the Linux server using systemd, the boot process is easier to follow now that you understand systemd target units. At boot, systemd activates the default.target unit. This unit is aliased either to multi-user.target or graphical.target. Thus, depending upon the alias set, the services targeted by the target unit are started.

If you need more help understanding the systemd daemon, you can enter **man -k systemd** at the command line to get a listing of the various systemd utilities' documentation in the man pages.

Learning systemd's backward compatibility to SysVinit

The systemd daemon has maintained backward compatibility to the SysVinit daemon. This allows Linux distributions time to migrate slowly to systemd.

While runlevels are not truly part of systemd, the systemd infrastructure has been created to provide compatibility with the concept of runlevels. There are seven target unit configuration files specifically created for backward compatibility to SysVinit:

- runlevel0.target

15

- `runlevel1.target`
- `runlevel2.target`
- `runlevel3.target`
- `runlevel4.target`
- `runlevel5.target`
- `runlevel6.target`

As you probably have already figured out, there is a target unit configuration file for each of the seven classic SysVinit runlevels. These target unit configuration files are symbolically linked to target unit configuration files that most closely match the idea of the original runlevel. In the example that follows, the symbolic links are shown for runlevel target units. Notice that the runlevel target units for runlevel 2, 3, and 4 are all symbolically linked to `multi-user.target`. The `multi-user.target` unit is similar to the legacy extended multi-user mode.

```
# ls -l /lib/systemd/system/runlevel*.target
lrwxrwxrwx. 1 root root 15 Apr  9 04:25 /lib/systemd/system/
runlevel0.target
     -> poweroff.target
lrwxrwxrwx. 1 root root 13 Apr  9 04:25 /lib/systemd/system/
runlevel1.target
     -> rescue.target
lrwxrwxrwx. 1 root root 17 Apr  9 04:25 /lib/systemd/system/
runlevel2.target
     -> multi-user.target
lrwxrwxrwx. 1 root root 17 Apr  9 04:25 /lib/systemd/system/
runlevel3.target
     -> multi-user.target
lrwxrwxrwx. 1 root root 17 Apr  9 04:25 /lib/systemd/system/
runlevel4.target
     -> multi-user.target
lrwxrwxrwx. 1 root root 16 Apr  9 04:25 /lib/systemd/system/
runlevel5.target
     -> graphical.target
lrwxrwxrwx. 1 root root 13 Apr  9 04:25 /lib/systemd/system/
runlevel6.target
     -> reboot.target
```

The old `/etc/inittab` file hasn't existed on Ubuntu systems for many years. But wherever you do still find copies (on RHEL, for instance), here's what it'll look like:

```
# cat /etc/inittab
# inittab is no longer used.
#
# ADDING CONFIGURATION HERE WILL HAVE NO EFFECT ON YOUR SYSTEM.
#
# Ctrl-Alt-Delete is handled by
# /etc/systemd/system/ctrl-alt-del.target
```

```
#
# systemd uses 'targets' instead of runlevels.
# By default, there are two main targets:
#
# multi-user.target: analogous to runlevel 3
# graphical.target: analogous to runlevel 5
#
# To view current default target, run:
# systemctl get-default
#
# To set a default target, run:
# systemctl set-default TARGET.target
```

The capability to switch runlevels using the init or telinit command is still available. When issued, either of the commands is translated into a systemd target unit activation request. Therefore, typing **init 3** at the command line really issues the command systemctl isolate multi-user.target. Also, you can still use the runlevel command to determine the current legacy runlevel, but it is strongly discouraged.

The classic SysVinit /etc/inittab handled spawning the getty or mingetty processes. The systemd init handles this via the getty.target unit. The getty.target is activated by the multi-user.target unit. You can see how these two target units are linked by executing the following command:

```
# systemctl show --property "WantedBy" getty.target
WantedBy=multi-user.target
```

Now that you have a basic understanding of classic and modern init daemons, it's time to do some practical server administrator actions that involve the initialization daemon.

Checking the Status of Services

As a Linux administrator, you need to check the status of the services being offered on your server. For security reasons, you should disable and remove any unused system services discovered through the process. Most important for troubleshooting purposes, you need to be able to know quickly what should and should not be running on your Linux server.

Of course, knowing which initialization service is being used by your Linux server is the first piece of information to obtain. How to determine this was covered in the section "Understanding the Initialization Daemon" earlier in this chapter. The following sections are organized into subsections on the various initialization daemons.

Checking services for SysVinit systems

To see all of the services that are being offered by a Linux server using the classic SysVinit daemon, use the chkconfig command. The example that follows shows the services available on a classic SysVinit Linux server. Note that each runlevel (0–6) is shown for each

15

service with a status of on or off. The status denotes whether a particular service is started (on) or not (off) for that runlevel.

```
# chkconfig --list
ConsoleKit        0:off   1:off   2:off   3:on    4:on    5:on    6:off
NetworkManager    0:off   1:off   2:off   3:off   4:off   5:off   6:off
...
crond             0:off   1:off   2:on    3:on    4:on    5:on    6:off
cups              0:off   1:off   2:on    3:on    4:on    5:on    6:off
...
sshd              0:off   1:off   2:on    3:on    4:on    5:on    6:off
syslog            0:off   1:off   2:on    3:on    4:on    5:on    6:off
tux               0:off   1:off   2:off   3:off   4:off   5:off   6:off
udev-post         0:off   1:off   2:off   3:on    4:on    5:on    6:off
vncserver         0:off   1:off   2:off   3:off   4:off   5:off   6:off
winbind           0:off   1:off   2:off   3:off   4:off   5:off   6:off
wpa_supplicant    0:off   1:off   2:off   3:off   4:off   5:off   6:off
xfs               0:off   1:off   2:on    3:on    4:on    5:on    6:off
ypbind            0:off   1:off   2:off   3:off   4:off   5:off   6:off
```

Some services in the example are never started, such as vncserver. Other services, such as the cups daemon, are started on runlevels 2 through 5.

Using the chkconfig command, you cannot tell if a service is currently running. To do that, you need to use the service command. To help isolate only those services that are currently running, the service command is piped into the grep command and then sorted, as follows:

```
# service --status-all | grep running... | sort
anacron (pid 2162) is running...
atd (pid 2172) is running...
auditd (pid 1653) is running...
automount (pid 1952) is running...
console-kit-daemon (pid 2046) is running...
crond (pid 2118) is running...
cupsd (pid 1988) is running...
...
sshd (pid 2002) is running...
syslogd (pid 1681) is running...
xfs (pid 2151) is running...
```

You can also use both the chkconfig and the service commands to view an individual service's settings. Using both commands in the example that follows, you can view the cups daemon's settings:

```
# chkconfig --list cups
cups                0:off   1:off   2:on    3:on    4:on    5:on    6:off
#
# service cups status
cupsd (pid 1988) is running...
```

You can see that the `cupsd` daemon is set to start on every runlevel but 0, 1, and 6, and from the `service` command, you can see that it is currently running. Also, the process ID (PID) number is given for the daemon.

To see all of the services that are being offered by a Linux server using `systemd`, use the following command:

```
# systemctl list-unit-files --type=service | grep -v disabled
UNIT FILE                              STATE        VENDOR PRESET
accounts-daemon.service                enabled      enabled
alsa-restore.service                   static       enabled
alsa-state.service                     static       enabled
alsa-utils.service                     masked       enabled
anacron.service                        enabled      enabled
apparmor.service                       enabled      enabled
apport-autoreport.service              static       enabled
apport-forward@.service                static       enabled
apport.service                         generated    enabled
apt-daily-upgrade.service              static       enabled
apt-daily.service                      static       enabled
autovt@.service                        enabled      enabled
avahi-daemon.service                   enabled      enabled
[...]
wpa_supplicant.service                 enabled      enabled
x11-common.service                     masked       enabled

219 unit files listed.
```

Remember that the three status possibilities for a `systemd` service are enabled, disabled, or static. There's no need to include disabled to see which services are set to be active, which is effectively accomplished by using the `-v` option on the `grep` command, as shown in the preceding example. The state of static is essentially enabled and thus should be included.

To see if a particular service is running, use the following command:

```
# systemctl status cups.service
● cups.service - CUPS Scheduler
   Loaded: loaded (/lib/systemd/system/cups.service; enabled; vendor
preset: ena
   Active: active (running) since Mon 2020-03-30 07:49:16 EDT; 9h ago
     Docs: man:cupsd(8)
 Main PID: 986 (cupsd)
    Tasks: 4 (limit: 4915)
   CGroup: /system.slice/cups.service
           986 /usr/sbin/cupsd -l
           /usr/lib/cups/notifier/dbus dbus://
           /usr/lib/cups/notifier/dbus dbus://

Mar 30 07:49:16 workstation systemd[1]: Started CUPS Scheduler.
```

15

The `systemctl` command can be used to show the status of one or more services. In the preceding example, the printing service was chosen. Notice that the name of the service is `cups.service`. A great deal of helpful information about the service is given here, such as the fact that it is enabled and active, its start time, and its process ID (PID).

Now that you can check the status of services and determine some information about them, you need to know how to accomplish starting, stopping, and reloading the services on your Linux server.

Stopping and Starting Services

The tasks of starting, stopping, and restarting services typically refer to immediate needs—in other words, managing services without a server reboot. For example, if you want to stop a service temporarily, then you are in the right place. However, if you want to stop a service and not allow it to be restarted at server reboot, then you actually need to disable the service, which is covered in the section "Enabling Persistent Services" later in this chapter.

Stopping and starting SysVinit services

The primary command for stopping and starting SysVinit services is the `service` command. With the `service` command, the name of the service that you want to control comes second in the command line. The last option is what you want to do to the service: `stop`, `start`, `restart`, and so on. The following example shows how to stop the `cups` service. Notice that an `OK` is given, which lets you know that `cupsd` has been successfully stopped:

```
# service cups status
cupsd (pid 5857) is running...
# service cups stop
Stopping cups:          [  OK  ]
# service cups status
cupsd is stopped
```

To start a service, you simply use a `start` option instead of a `stop` option on the end of the `service` command, as follows:

```
# service cups start
Starting cups:          [  OK  ]
# service cups status
cupsd (pid 6860) is running...
```

To restart a SysVinit service, the `restart` option is used. This option stops the service and then immediately starts it again:

```
# service cups restart
Stopping cups:          [  OK  ]
Starting cups:          [  OK  ]
```

```
# service cups status
cupsd (pid 7955) is running...
```

When a service is already stopped, a restart generates a FAILED status on the attempt to stop it. However, as shown in the example that follows, the service is successfully started when a restart is attempted:

```
# service cups stop
Stopping cups:             [  OK  ]
# service cups restart
Stopping cups:             [FAILED]
Starting cups:             [  OK  ]
# service cups status
cupsd (pid 8236) is running...
```

Reloading a service is different from restarting a service. When you reload a service, the service itself is not stopped. Only the service's configuration files are loaded again. The following example shows how to reload the cups daemon:

```
# service cups status
cupsd (pid 8236) is running...
# service cups reload
Reloading cups:            [  OK  ]
# service cups status
cupsd (pid 8236) is running...
```

If a SysVinit service is stopped when you attempt to reload it, you get a FAILED status. This is shown in the following example:

```
# service cups status
cupsd is stopped
# service cups reload
Reloading cups: [FAILED]
Stopping and starting systemd services
```

For the systemd daemon, the systemctl command works for stopping, starting, reloading, and restarting services. The options to the systemctl command should look familiar.

Stopping a service with systemd

In the example that follows, the status of the cups daemon is checked and then stopped using the systemctl stop cups.service command:

```
# systemctl status cups.service
cups.service - CUPS Printing Service
    Loaded: loaded (/lib/systemd/system/cups.service; enabled)
    Active: active (running) since Mon, 20 Apr 2020 12:36:3...
  Main PID: 1315 (cupsd)
    CGroup: name=systemd:/system/cups.service
            1315 /usr/sbin/cupsd -f
# systemctl stop cups.service
# systemctl status cups.service
```

Continues

15

Continued

```
cups.service - CUPS Printing Service
    Loaded: loaded (/lib/systemd/system/cups.service; enabled)
    Active: inactive (dead) since Tue, 21 Apr 2020 04:43:4...
    Process: 1315 ExecStart=/usr/sbin/cupsd -f
 (code=exited, status=0/SUCCESS)
    CGroup: name=systemd:/system/cups.service
```

Notice that when the status is taken, after stopping the cups daemon, the service is inactive (dead) but still considered enabled. This means that the cups daemon is still started upon server boot.

Starting a service with systemd

Starting the cups daemon is just as easy as stopping it. The example that follows demonstrates this ease:

```
# systemctl start cups.service
# systemctl status cups.service
cups.service - CUPS Printing Service
    Loaded: loaded (/lib/systemd/system/cups.service; enabled)
    Active: active (running) since Tue, 21 Apr 2020 04:43:5...
  Main PID: 17003 (cupsd)
    CGroup: name=systemd:/system/cups.service
            &boxur;  17003 /usr/sbin/cupsd -f
```

After the cups daemon is started, using systemctl with the status option shows the service is active (running). Also, its process ID (PID) number, 17003, is shown.

Restarting a service with systemd

Restarting a service means that a service is stopped and then started again. If the service was not currently running, restarting it simply starts the service.

```
# systemctl restart cups.service
# systemctl status cups.service
cups.service - CUPS Printing Service
    Loaded: loaded (/lib/systemd/system/cups.service; enabled)
    Active: active (running) since Tue, 21 Apr 2020 04:45:2...
  Main PID: 17015 (cupsd)
    CGroup: name=systemd:/system/cups.service
            &boxur;  17015 /usr/sbin/cupsd -f
```

You can also perform a conditional restart of a service using systemctl. A conditional restart only restarts a service if it is currently running. Any service in an inactive state is not started.

```
# systemctl status cups.service
cups.service - CUPS Printing Service
    Loaded: loaded (/lib/systemd/system/cups.service; enabled)
    Active: inactive (dead) since Tue, 21 Apr 2020 06:03:32...
    Process: 17108 ExecStart=/usr/sbin/cupsd -f
```

```
    (code=exited, status=0/SUCCESS)
      CGroup: name=systemd:/system/cups.service
  # systemctl condrestart cups.service
  # systemctl status cups.service
  cups.service - CUPS Printing Service
    Loaded: loaded (/lib/systemd/system/cups.service; enabled)
    Active: inactive (dead) since Tue, 21 Apr 2020 06:03:32...
   Process: 17108 ExecStart=/usr/sbin/cupsd -f
   (code=exited, status=0/SUCCESS)
      CGroup: name=systemd:/system/cups.service
```

Notice in the example that the cups daemon was in an inactive state. When the conditional restart was issued, no error messages were generated! The cups daemon was not started because conditional restarts affect active services. Thus, it is always a good practice to check the status of a service after stopping, starting, conditionally restarting, and so on.

Reloading a service with systemd

Reloading a service is different from restarting a service. When you reload a service, the service itself is not stopped. Only the service's configuration files are loaded again. Note that not all services are implemented to use the reload feature.

```
  # systemctl status sshd.service
  sshd.service - OpenSSH server daemon
    Loaded: loaded (/usr/lib/systemd/system/sshd.service; enabled)
    Active: active (running) since Wed 2019-09-18 17:32:27 EDT; 3
  days ago
   Main PID: 1675 (sshd)
    CGroup: /system.slice/sshd.service
            1675 /usr/sbin/sshd -D
  # systemctl reload sshd.service
  # systemctl status sshd.service
  sshd.service - OpenSSH server daemon
    Loaded: loaded (/lib/systemd/system/sshd.service; enabled)
    Active: active (running) since Wed 2019-09-18 17:32:27 EDT; 3
  days ago
   Process: 21770 ExecReload=/bin/kill -HUP $MAINPID (code=exited,
  status=0/SUCCESS)
         (code=exited, status=0/SUCCESSd)
   Main PID: 1675 (sshd)
    CGroup: /system.slice/sshd.service
            1675 /usr/sbin/sshd -D ...
```

Doing a reload of a service, instead of a restart, prevents any pending service operations from being aborted. A reload is a better method for a busy Linux server.

Now that you know how to stop and start services for troubleshooting and emergency purposes, you can learn how to enable and disable services.

15

Enabling Persistent Services

You use `stop` and `start` for immediate needs, not for services that need to be persistent. A *persistent service* is one that is started at server boot time or at a particular runlevel. Services that need to be set as persistent are typically new services that the Linux server is offering.

Configuring persistent services for SysVinit

One of the nice features of the classic SysVinit daemon is that making a particular service persistent or removing its persistence is very easy to do. Consider the following example:

```
# chkconfig --list cups
cups              0:off  1:off  2:off  3:off  4:off  5:off  6:off
```

On this Linux server, the `cups` service is not started at any runlevel, as shown with the `chkconfig` command. You can also check and see if any start (S) symbol links are set up in each of the seven runlevel directories, `/etc/rc.d/rc?.d`. Remember that SysVinit keeps symbolic links here for starting and stopping various services at certain runlevels. Each directory represents a particular runlevel; for example, `rc5.d` is for runlevel 5. Notice that only files starting with a `K` are listed, so there are links for killing off the `cups` daemon. None are listed with `S`, which is consistent with `chkconfig` because the `cups` daemon does not start at any runlevel on this server.

```
# ls /etc/rc.d/rc?.d/*cups
/etc/rc.d/rc0.d/K10cups    /etc/rc.d/rc3.d/K10cups
/etc/rc.d/rc1.d/K10cups    /etc/rc.d/rc4.d/K10cups
/etc/rc.d/rc2.d/K10cups    /etc/rc.d/rc5.d/K10cups
/etc/rc.d/rc6.d/K10cups
```

To make a service persistent at a particular runlevel, the `chkconfig` command is used again. Instead of the `--list` option, the `--level` option is used, as shown in the following code:

```
# chkconfig --level 3 cups on
# chkconfig --list cups
cups              0:off  1:off  2:off  3:on   4:off  5:off  6:off
# ls /etc/rc.d/rc3.d/S*cups
/etc/rc.d/rc3.d/S56cups
```

The service's persistence at runlevel 3 is verified by using both the `chkconfig --list` command and looking at the `rc3.d` directory for any files starting with the letter *S*.

To make a service persistent on more than one runlevel, you can do the following:

```
# chkconfig --level 2345 cups on
# chkconfig --list cups
cups              0:off  1:off  2:on   3:on   4:on   5:on   6:off
# ls /etc/rc.d/rc?.d/S*cups
```

```
/etc/rc.d/rc2.d/S56cups  /etc/rc.d/rc4.d/S56cups
/etc/rc.d/rc3.d/S56cups  /etc/rc.d/rc5.d/S56cups
```

Disabling a service is just as easy as enabling one with SysVinit. You just need to change the on in the `chkconfig` command to `off`. The following example demonstrates using the `chkconfig` command to disable the `cups` service at runlevel 5:

```
# chkconfig --level 5 cups off
# chkconfig --list cups
cups            0:off  1:off  2:on   3:on   4:on   5:off   6:off
# ls /etc/rc.d/rc5.d/S*cups
ls: cannot access /etc/rc.d/rc5.d/S*cups: No such file or directory
```

As expected, there is now no symbolic link, starting with the letter *S*, for the `cups` service in the /etc/rc.d/rc5.d directory.

For the `systemd` daemon, again the `systemctl` command is used. With it, you can disable and enable services on the Linux server.

Enabling a service with systemd

Using the `enable` option on the `systemctl` command sets a service to always start at boot (be persistent). The following shows exactly how to accomplish this:

```
# systemctl status cups.service
cups.service - CUPS Printing Service
   Loaded: loaded (/lib/systemd/system/cups.service; disabled)
   Active: inactive (dead) since Tue, 21 Apr 2020 06:42:38 ...
 Main PID: 17172 (code=exited, status=0/SUCCESS)
   CGroup: name=systemd:/system/cups.service
# systemctl enable cups.service
Created symlink /etc/systemd/system/printer.target.wants/cups.service
       /usr/lib/systemd/system/cups.service.
Created symlink /etc/systemd/system/sockets.target.wants/cups.socket
       /usr/lib/systemd/system/cups.socket.
Created symlink /etc/systemd/system/multi-user.target.wants/cups.path
       /usr/lib/systemd/system/cups.path.
# systemctl status cups.service
cups.service - CUPS Printing Service
   Loaded: loaded (/lib/systemd/system/cups.service; enabled)
   Active: inactive (dead) since Tue, 21 Apr 2020 06:42:38...
 Main PID: 17172 (code=exited, status=0/SUCCESS)
   CGroup: name=systemd:/system/cups.service
```

Notice that the status of `cups.service` changes from disabled to enabled after using the `enable` option on `systemctl`. Also, notice that the `enable` option simply creates a few symbolic links. You may be tempted to create these links yourself. However, the preferred method is to use the `systemctl` command to accomplish this.

15

Disabling a service with systemd

You can use the `disable` option on the `systemctl` command to keep a service from starting at boot. However, it does not immediately stop the service. You need to use the `stop` option discussed in the section "Stopping a service with `systemd`." The following example shows how to `disable` a currently `enabled` service:

```
# systemctl disable cups.service
rm '/etc/systemd/system/printer.target.wants/cups.service'
rm '/etc/systemd/system/sockets.target.wants/cups.socket'
rm '/etc/systemd/system/multi-user.target.wants/cups.path'
# systemctl status cups.service
cups.service - CUPS Printing Service
   Loaded: loaded (/lib/systemd/system/cups.service; disabled)
   Active: active (running) since Tue, 21 Apr 2020 06:06:41...
 Main PID: 17172 (cupsd)
   CGroup: name=systemd:/system/cups.service
              17172 /usr/sbin/cupsd -f
```

The `disable` option simply removes a few files via the preferred method of the `systemctl` command. Notice also in the preceding example that although the `cups` service is now disabled, the `cups` daemon is still active (running) and needs to be stopped manually. With `systemd`, some services cannot be disabled. These services are static services. Consider the following service, `dbus.service`:

```
# systemctl status dbus.service
dbus.service - D-Bus System Message Bus
  Loaded: loaded (/lib/systemd/system/dbus.service; static)
  Active: active (running) since Mon, 20 Apr 2020 12:35:...
 Main PID: 707 (dbus-daemon)
 ...
# systemctl disable dbus.service
# systemctl status dbus.service
dbus.service - D-Bus System Message Bus
  Loaded: loaded (/lib/systemd/system/dbus.service; static)
  Active: active (running) since Mon, 20 Apr 2020 12:35:...
 Main PID: 707 (dbus-daemon)
 ...
```

When the `systemctl disable` command is issued on `dbus.service`, it is simply ignored. Remember that static means that the service is enabled by default and cannot be disabled, even by root. Sometimes, disabling a service is not enough to make sure that it does not run. For example, you might want `network.service` to replace `networkManager.service` for starting network interfaces on your system. Disabling NetworkManager would keep the service from starting on its own. However, if some other service listed NetworkManager as a dependency, that service would try to start NetworkManager when it started.

To disable a service in a way that prevents it from ever running on your system, you can use the `mask` option. For example, to set the NetworkManager service so that it never runs, type the following:

```
# systemctl mask NetworkManager.service
ln -s '/dev/null' '/etc/systemd/system/NetworkManager.service'
```

As the output shows, the `networkManager.service` file in /etc is linked to /dev/null. So even if someone tried to run that service, nothing would happen. To be able to use the service again, you could type `systemctl unmask networkManager.service`.

Now that you understand how to enable individual services to be persistent (and how to disable or mask individual services), you need to look at service groups as a whole. Next, I cover how to start groups of services at boot time.

Configuring a Default Runlevel or Target Unit

Whereas a persistent service is one that is started at server boot time, a persistent (default) runlevel or target unit is a group of services that are started at boot time. Both classic Sys-Vinit and Upstart define these groups of services as runlevels, while `systemd` calls them target units.

Configuring the SysVinit default runlevel

You set the persistent runlevel for a Linux server using SysVinit in the /etc/inittab file. A portion of this file is shown here:

```
# cat /etc/inittab
#
# inittab      This file describes how the INIT process should
#              set up the system in a certain run-level.
...
id:5:initdefault:
...
```

The `initdefault` line in the example shows that the current default runlevel is runlevel 5. To change this, simply edit the /etc/inittab file using your favorite editor and change the 5 to one of the following runlevels: 2, 3, or 4. Do not use the runlevels 0 or 6 in this file! This would cause your server either to halt or reboot when it is started up.

For `systemd`, the term *target units* refers to groups of services to be started. The following shows the various target units that you can configure to be persistent and their equivalent backward-compatible, runlevel-specific target units:

15

- multi-user.target =
  - runlevel2.target
  - runlevel3.target
  - runlevel4.target

- graphical.target = runlevel5.target

The persistent target unit is set via a symbolic link to the `default.target` unit file. Consider the following:

```
# ls -l /etc/systemd/system/default.target
lrwxrwxrwx. 1 root root 36 Mar 13 17:27
 /etc/systemd/system/default.target ->
 /lib/systemd/system/runlevel5.target
# ls -l /lib/systemd/system/runlevel5.target
lrwxrwxrwx. 1 root root 16 Mar 27 15:39
 /lib/systemd/system/runlevel5.target ->
 graphical.target
```

The example shows that the current persistent target unit on this server is `runlevel5.target` because `default.target` is a symbolic link to the `runlevel5.target` unit file. However, notice that `runlevel5.target` is also a symbolic link and it points to `graphical.target`. Thus, this server's current persistent target unit is `graphical.target`.

To set a different target unit to be persistent, you simply need to change the symbolic link for `default.target`. To be consistent, stick with the runlevel target units if they are used on your server.

The following `systemctl` example changes the server's persistent target unit from `graphical.target` to `multi-user.target`:

```
# systemctl get-default
graphical.target
#
 systemctl set-default runlevel3.target
Removed /etc/systemd/system/default.target.
Created symlink /etc/systemd/system/default.target → /usr/lib/
systemd/system/multi-user.target.
# systemctl get-default
multi-user.target
```

When the server is rebooted, the `multi-user.target` is the persistent target unit. Any services in the `multi-user.target` unit are started (activated) at that time.

Adding New or Customized Services

Occasionally, you need to add a new service to your Linux server. Also, you may have to customize a particular service. When these needs arise, you must follow specific steps for your Linux server's initialization daemon to either take over the management of the service or recognize the customization of it.

Adding new services to SysVinit

When adding a new or customized service to a Linux SysVinit server, you must complete four steps in order to have the service managed by SysVinit:.

1. Create a new or customized service script file.
2. Move the new or customized service script to the proper location for SysVinit management.
3. Set appropriate permission on the script.
4. Add the service to a specific runlevel.

Step 1: Create a new or customized service script file

If you are customizing a service script, simply make a copy of the original unit file from /etc/rc.d/init.d and add any desired customizations.

If you are creating a new script, you need to make sure you handle all of the various options that you want the `service` command to accept for your service, such as `start`, `stop`, `restart`, and so on.

For a new script, especially if you have never created a service script before, it would be wise to make a copy of a current service script from /etc/rc.d/init.d and modify it to meet your new service's needs. Consider the following partial example of the `cupsd` service's script:

```
# cat /etc/rc.d/init.d/cups
#!/bin/sh
#
...
#    chkconfig: 2345 25 10

...
start () {
        echo -n $"Starting $prog: "
        # start daemon
        daemon $DAEMON
        RETVAL=$?
        echo
        [ $RETVAL = 0 ] && touch /var/lock/subsys/cups
        return $RETVAL
}

stop () {
        # stop daemon
        echo -n $"Stopping $prog: "
        killproc $DAEMON
        RETVAL=$?
        echo         [ $RETVAL = 0 ] && rm -f /var/lock/subsys/cups
}
```

15

Continues

Continued

```
restart() {
        stop
        start
}

case $1 in
...
```

The `cups` service script starts out by creating functions for each of the `start`, `stop`, and `restart` options. If you feel uncomfortable with shell script writing, review Chapter 7, "Writing Simple Shell Scripts," to improve your skills.

One line you should be sure to check and possibly modify in your new script is the `chkconfig` line that is commented out; for example:

```
#   chkconfig: 2345 25 10
```

When you add the service script in a later step, the `chkconfig` command reads that line to set runlevels at which the service starts (2, 3, 4, and 5), its run order when the script is set to start (25), and its kill order when it is set to stop (10).

Check the boot order in the default runlevel before adding your own script, as shown in this example:

```
# ls /etc/rc5.d
...
/etc/rc5.d/S22messagebus
/etc/rc5.d/S23NetworkManager
/etc/rc5.d/S24nfslock
/etc/rc5.d/S24openct
/etc/rc5.d/S24rpcgssd
/etc/rc5.d/S25blk-availability
/etc/rc5.d/S25cups
/etc/rc5.d/S25netfs
/etc/rc5.d/S26acpid
/etc/rc5.d/S26haldaemon
/etc/rc5.d/S26hypervkvpd
/etc/rc5.d/S26udev-post

...
```

In this case, the `chkconfig` line in the `S25my_new_service` script will cause the script to be added after `S25cups` and before `S25netfs` in the boot order. You can change the `chkconfig` line in the service script if you want the service to start earlier (use a smaller number) or later (use a larger number) in the list of service scripts.

Step 2: Add the service script to /etc/rc.d/init.d

After you have modified or created and tested your service's script file, you can move it to the proper location, /etc/rc.d/init.d:

```
# cp My_New_Service /etc/rc.d/init.d
# ls /etc/rc.d/init.d/My_New_Service
/etc/rc.d/init.d/My_New_Service
```

Step 3: Set appropriate permission on the script

The script should be executable:

```
# chmod 755 /etc/rc.d/init.d/My_New_Service
```

Step 4: Add the service to runlevel directories

This final step sets up the service script to start and stop at different runlevels and checks that the service script works.

1. To add the script based on the chkconfig line in the service script, type the following:

   ```
   # chkconfig --add My_New_Service
   # ls /etc/rc?.d/*My_New_Service
   /etc/rc0.d/K10My_New_Service   /etc/rc4.d/S25My_New_Service
   /etc/rc1.d/K10My_New_Service   /etc/rc5.d/S25My_New_Service
   /etc/rc2.d/S25My_New_Service   /etc/rc6.d/K10My_New_Service
   /etc/rc3.d/S25My_New_Service
   ```

   Based on the previous example (chkconfig: 2345 25 10), symbolic links to the script set the service to start in the position 25 (s25) for runlevels 2, 3, 4, and 5. Also, links are set to stop (or not start) at runlevels 0, 1, and 6.

2. After you have made the symbolic link(s), test that your new or modified service works as expected before performing a server reboot:

   ```
   # service My_New_Service start
   Starting My_New_Service:        [  OK  ]
   # service My_New_Service stop
   ```

After everything is in place, your new or modified service starts at every runlevel that you have selected on your system. Also, you can start or stop it manually using the service command.

Adding new services to systemd

When adding a new or customized service to a Linux systemd server, you have to complete three steps in order to have the service managed by systemd:

1. Create a new or customized service configuration unit file for the new or customized service.

2. Move the new or customized service configuration unit file to the proper location for systemd management.

3. Add the service to a specific target unit's Wants to have the new or customized service start automatically with other services.

15

Step 1: Create a new or customized service configuration unit file

If you are customizing a service configuration unit file, simply make a copy of the original unit file from /lib/systemd/system and add any desired customizations.

For new files, obviously, you are creating a service unit configuration file from scratch. Consider the following basic service unit file template. At bare minimum, you need description and execStart options for a service unit configuration file:

```
# cat My_New_Service.service
[Unit]
Description=My New Service
[Service]
ExecStart=/usr/bin/My_New_Service
```

For additional help on customizing or creating a new configuration unit file and the various needed options, you can use the man pages. At the command line, type **man systemd.service** to find out more about the various service unit file options.

Step 2: Move the service configuration unit file

Before you move the new or customized service configuration unit file, you need to be aware that there are two potential locations to store service configuration unit files. The one you choose determines whether the customizations take effect and if they remain persistent through software upgrades.

You can place your system service configuration unit file in one of the following two locations:

- /etc/systemd/system
    - This location is used to store customized local service configuration unit files.
    - Files in this location are not overwritten by software installations or upgrades. Files here are used by the system *even* if there is a file of the same name in the /lib/systemd/system directory.
- /lib/systemd/system
    - This location is used to store system service configuration unit files.
    - Files in this location are overwritten by software installations and upgrades.

    Files here are used by the system only if there is no file of the same name in the /etc/systemd/system directory.

Thus, the best place to store your new or customized service configuration unit file is in /etc/systemd/system.

> **Tip**
> When you create a new or customized service, in order for the change to take effect without a server reboot, you need to issue a special command. At the command line, type systemctl daemon-reload.

Step 3: Add the service to the Wants directory

This final step is optional. It needs to be done only if you want your new service to start with a particular `systemd` target unit. For a service to be activated (started) by a particular target unit, it must be in that target unit's `wants` directory.

First, add the line `wantedBy=desired.target` to the bottom of your service configuration unit file. The following example shows that the desired target unit for this new service is `multi-user.target`:

```
# cat /etc/systemd/system/My_New_Service.service
[Unit]
Description=My New Fake Service
[Service]
ExecStart=/usr/bin/My_New_Service
[Install]
WantedBy=multi-user.target
```

To add a new service unit to a target unit, you need to create a symbolic link. The following example shows the files located in the `multi-user.target` unit's `wants` directory. Previously, in the section "Understanding `systemd` initialization," the `systemctl` command was used to list Wants, and it is still the preferred method. Notice that in this directory, the files are symbolic links pointing to service unit configuration files in the `/lib/systemd/system` directory.

```
# ls /etc/systemd/system/multi-user.target.wants
abrt-ccpp.service      cups.path            remote-fs.target
abrtd.service          fcoe.service         rsyslog.service
abrt-oops.service      irqbalance.service   sendmail.service
abrt-vmcore.service    lldpad.service       sm-client.service
atd.service            mcelog.service       sshd-keygen.service
auditd.service         mdmonitor.service    sshd.service
...
# ls -l /etc/systemd/system/multi-user.target.wants
total 0
lrwxrwxrwx. 1 root root 37 Nov  2 22:29 abrt-ccpp.service ->
    /lib/systemd/system/abrt-ccpp.service
lrwxrwxrwx. 1 root root 33 Nov  2 22:29 abrtd.service ->
    /lib/systemd/system/abrtd.service
...
lrwxrwxrwx. 1 root root 32 Apr 26 20:05 sshd.service ->
    /lib/systemd/system/sshd.service
```

The following illustrates the process of adding a symbolic link file for my_new_service:

```
# ln -s /etc/systemd/system/My_New_Service.service
 /etc/systemd/system/multi-user.target.wants/My_New_Service.service
```

15

A symbolic link is created in the `multi-user.target.wants` directory. Now the new service, `my_new_service`, is activated (started) when the `multi-user.target` unit is activated.

> **Tip**
>
> If you want to change the `systemd` target unit for a service, you need to change the symbolic link to point to a new target `Wants` directory location. Use the `ln -sf` command to force any current symbolic link to be broken and the new designated symbolic link to be enforced.

Together, the three steps get your new or customized service added to a Linux `systemd` server. Remember that at this point, a new service is not running until a server reboot. To start the new service before a reboot, review the commands in the section "Stopping and Starting Services."

Summary

How you start and stop services is dependent upon what initialization daemon is used by your Linux server: SysVinit, Upstart, or Systemd. Before you do any service management, be sure to use the examples in this chapter to help you determine your Linux server's initialization daemon.

The concepts of starting and stopping services go along with other service management concepts, such as making a service persistent, starting certain services at server boot time, reloading a service, and restarting a service. Understanding these concepts is very helpful as you learn about configuring and managing a Linux print server in the next chapter.

Exercises

Refer to the material in this chapter to complete the tasks that follow. If you are stuck, solutions to the tasks are shown in Appendix A (although in Linux, there are often multiple ways to complete a task). Try each of the exercises before referring to the answers. These tasks assume that you are running an Ubuntu Linux system (although some tasks work on other Linux systems as well).

1. Determine which initialization daemon your server is currently using.
2. What command can you use to check the status of the `sshd` daemon, depending on the initialization daemon in use on your Linux server?
3. Determine your server's previous and current runlevel.
4. How can you change the default runlevel or target unit on your Linux server?
5. For each initialization daemon, what commands list services running (or active) on your server?

6. List the running (or active) services on your Linux server.

7. For each initialization daemon, what commands show a particular service's current status?

8. Show the status of the cups daemon on your Linux server.

9. Attempt to restart the cups daemon on your Linux server.

10. Attempt to reload the cups daemon on your Linux server.

15

Configuring a Print Server

You can configure your Linux system to use printers that are connected directly to it (via a USB port) or that are available for printing over the network. Likewise, any printer that you configure on your local system can be shared with users on other Linux, Windows, or Mac systems by opening up your printer as a print server.

You configure a printer as a native Linux printer in Linux systems with the *Common UNIX Printing System (CUPS)*. To configure a printer to work as a Microsoft Windows style of print server, you can use the Samba service in Linux.

This chapter focuses on CUPS. In particular, it shows you the graphical front end to CUPS, called the *Print Settings window*, which comes with Ubuntu right out of the box. Using Print Settings, you can also configure your printers as print servers so that people can access your printer from their own computers.

If you don't have a desktop or you want to print from within a shell script, this chapter shows you how to use printing commands. From the command line, print commands such as `lpr` are available. Commands also exist for querying print queues (`lpstat`), manipulating print queues (`cupsenable`, `cupsdisable`, and `cupsreject`), and removing print jobs (`cancel`). Note that an older set of print commands are also available for backward compatibility that includes `lpr`, `lpq`, and `lprm`.

Common UNIX Printing System

Common UNIX Printing System (CUPS) has become the standard for printing from Linux and other UNIX-like operating systems. It was designed to meet today's needs for standardized printer definitions and sharing on Internet Protocol–based networks (as most computer networks are today). Like nearly every Linux distribution today, Ubuntu comes with CUPS as its printing service. Here are some of the service's features:

IPP   CUPS is based on the Internet Printing Protocol (www.pwg.org/ipp), a standard that was created to simplify how printers are shared over IP networks. In the IPP model, printer servers and clients who want to print can exchange information about the model and features of a printer using the HTTP (that is, web content) protocol. A server can also broadcast the availability of a printer so that a printing client can easily find a list of locally available printers without configuration.

Drivers   CUPS also standardized how printer drivers are created. The idea was to have a common format that could be used by printer manufacturers so that a driver could work across all types of UNIX systems. That way, a manufacturer had to create the driver only once to work for Linux, macOS, and a variety of UNIX derivatives.

Printer classes   You can use printer classes to create multiple print server entries that point to the same printer or one print server entry that points to multiple printers. In the first case, multiple entries can each allow options (such as pointing to a particular paper tray or printing with certain character sizes or margins). In the second case, you can have a pool of printers so that printing is distributed. In this instance, a malfunctioning printer, or a printer that is dealing with very large documents, won't bring all printing to a halt. CUPS also supports *implicit classes*, which are print classes that form by merging identical network printers automatically.

Printer browsing   With printer browsing, client computers can see any CUPS printers on your local network with browsing enabled. As a result, clients can simply select the printers that they want to use from the printer names broadcast on the network, without needing to know in advance what the printers are named and where they are connected. You can turn off the feature to prevent others on the local network from seeing a printer.

UNIX print commands   To integrate into Linux and other UNIX environments, CUPS offers versions of standard commands for printing and managing printers that have been traditionally offered with UNIX systems.

Instead of using the Print Settings window, you can configure CUPS printing in other ways as well:

Configuring CUPS from a browser   The CUPS project itself offers a web-based interface for adding and managing printers. With the cupsd service running, type **localhost:631** from a web browser on the computer running the CUPS service to manage printing. (See the section "Using web-based CUPS administration" later in this chapter.)

Configuring CUPS manually   You can also edit the CUPS configuration files and start the cupsd daemon from the command line. Configuration files for CUPS are contained in the /etc/cups directory. In particular, you might be interested in the cupsd.conf file, which identifies permissions, authentication, and other information for the printer daemon; and printers.conf, which identifies addresses and options for configured printers. Use the classes.conf file to define local printer classes.

Printing Directly from Windows to CUPS

You can print to CUPS from non-UNIX systems as well. For example, you can use a PostScript printer driver to print directly from a Windows system to your CUPS server. You can use CUPS without modification by configuring the Windows computer with a PostScript driver that uses http://*printserver-name*:631/printers/*targetPrinter* as its printing port.

You may also be able to use the native Windows printer drivers for the printer instead of the PostScript driver. If the native Windows driver does not work right out of the box on your CUPS print queue, you can create a Raw Print Queue under CUPS and use that instead. The Raw Print Queue directly passes through the data from the Windows native print driver to the printer.

To use CUPS, you must have the cups package installed. If for some reason it's not installed, install it by typing the following:

```
# apt install cups cups-client
```

Setting Up Printers

Although using the printer administration tools specifically built for Linux is usually best, many Linux systems—including Ubuntu—simply rely on the tools that come with the CUPS software package.

The following sections explore how to use CUPS web-based administration tools that come with Ubuntu. Then it examines the Print Settings tool system-config-printer, which you can use to set up your printers. In most cases, no installation or configuration will be necessary, because connected printers are automatically detected and configured. If necessary, you can install the tool using:

```
# apt install system-config-printer
```

Adding a printer automatically

CUPS printers can be configured to broadcast their availability on the network automatically so that a client system can detect and use them without configuration. Connect a USB printer to your computer, and the printer can be automatically detected and made available. If the print driver is not yet installed, you'll be prompted to install the necessary software packages.

The first time you go to print a document or view your Print Settings tool, the printers are ready to use. Further configuration can be done using the web-based CUPS administration tool or the Print Settings window.

Using web-based CUPS administration

CUPS offers its own web-based administrative tool for adding, deleting, and modifying printer configurations on your computer. The CUPS print service (using the cupsd daemon) listens on port 631 to provide access to the CUPS web-based administrative interface and share printers.

If CUPS is already running on your computer, you can immediately use CUPS web-based administration from your web browser. To see whether CUPS is running and to start setting up your printers, open a web browser on the local computer and type this into its location box: **localhost:631**.

A prompt for a valid login name and password may appear when you request functions that require it. If so, type the login name and password of an account with sudo access and click OK. A screen similar to the one shown in Figure 16.1 appears.

FIGURE 16.1

CUPS provides a web-based administration tool.

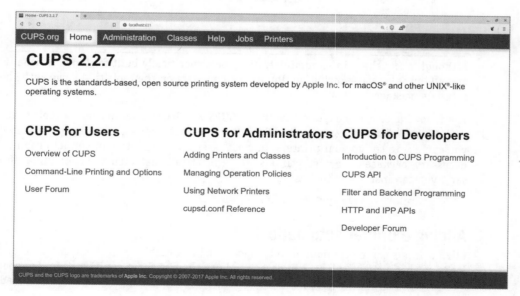

Allow remote printing administration

By default, web-based CUPS administration is available only from the local host. To access web-based CUPS administration from another computer, from the main CUPS page:

1. Select the Administration tab.
2. Select the check box next to "Allow remote administration."
3. Select the Change Settings button.

If you're behind a firewall you'll need to allow connections to TCP port 631. After that, from any browser that has access to your local network, you can access the CUPS Administration page by going to port 631 on the CUPS server (for example, `host.example.com:631`).

You may need to restart CUPS for the change to take effect: **`systemctl restart cups.service`**.

Add a printer not automatically detected

To configure a printer that is not automatically detected, you can add a printer from the Administration screen. With the Administration screen displayed, you can add a printer as follows:

1. Click the Add Printer button. The Add New Printer screen appears.
2. Your printer may be displayed on the list. If it is, select it and click Continue. Otherwise, select the device to which the printer is connected. The printer can be connected locally to a parallel, SCSI, serial, or USB port directly on the computer. Alternatively, you can select a network connection type for Apple printers (AppSocket or HP JetDirect), Internet Printing Protocol (`http`, `https`, `ipps`, or `ipp`), or a Windows printer (using Samba or SMB).
3. If prompted for more information, you may need to describe the connection to the printer further. For example, you might be asked for the network address for an IPP or Samba printer.
4. Type a name, location, and description for the printer; select if you want to share this printer and click Continue.
5. Select the make of the print driver. If you don't see the manufacturer of your printer listed, choose PostScript for a PostScript printer or HP for a PCL printer. For the manufacturer you choose, you can select a specific model.
6. Set options. If you are asked to set options for your printer, you may do so. Then select Set Printer Options to continue.
7. Your printer should be available. If the printer is added successfully, click the name of your printer to have the new printer page appear; from the printer page, you can select Maintenance or Administration to print a test page or modify the printer configuration.

With the basic printer configuration done, you can now do further work with your printers. Here are a few examples of what you can do:

List print jobs   Click Show All Jobs to see completed or pending print jobs on any of the printers configured for this server. Click Show Completed Jobs to see information about only jobs that are already printed.

Create a printer class   Click the Administration tab, choose Add Class, and identify a name, description, and location for a printer class. From the list of Printers (Members) configured on your server, select the ones to go into this class.

Cancel or move a print job   If you print a 100-page job by mistake, or if the printer is spewing out junk, the Cancel feature can be very handy. Likewise, if you sent a print job to the wrong printer, the Manage Jobs selection can be useful. From the Administration tab, click Manage Jobs; then click Show Active Jobs to see what print jobs are currently in the queue for the printer. Select the Cancel Job button next to the print job that you want to cancel or select Move Job to move the print job to a different printer.

View printers   You can click the Printers tab from the top of any of the CUPS web-based administration pages to view the printers that you have configured. For each printer that appears, you can select Maintenance or Administrative tasks. Under Maintenance, click Pause Printer (to stop the printer from printing but still accept print jobs for the queue), Reject Jobs (to not accept any further print jobs for the moment), Move All Jobs (to move them to another printer), Cancel All Jobs (to delete all print jobs), or Print Test Page (to print a page). Figure 16.2 shows the information on the Printers tab for a specific printer.

Using the Print Settings window

You can also use the Print Settings window to set up your printers. In fact, I recommend that you use it instead of CUPS web administration because the resulting printer configuration files are tailored to work with the way the CUPS service is started on those systems. After the package is installed (`apt install system-config-printer` if necessary), to install a printer from your GNOME desktop, start the Printers window by clicking Additional Printer Settings in the **Printers** section of GNOME Settings, or as root user by typing `system-config-printer`. This tool enables you to add and delete printers and edit printer properties.

The key here is that you are configuring printers that are managed by your print daemon (`cupsd` for the CUPS service). After a printer is configured, users on your local system can use it. You can refer to the section "Configuring Print Servers" to learn how to make the server available to users from other computers on your network.

The printers that you set up can be connected directly to your computer (as on a USB port) or to another computer on the network (for example, from another UNIX system or Windows system).

FIGURE 16.2

You can do administration tasks from the Printers tab.

Configuring local printers with the Print Settings window

Add a local printer (in other words, a printer connected directly to your computer) with the Printers window using the procedure that follows.

> **TIP**
> Even if Ubuntu doesn't successfully install your printer on its own, some printer manufacturers make Ubuntu-friendly scripts and drivers available on their websites that can prove easier to work with than the process that follows. It's worth looking for those before going further.

Adding a local printer

To add a local printer from a GNOME desktop, follow these steps:

1. Type the following to open the Print Settings window:

   ```
   # system-config-printer &
   ```

   The Printing window appears.

2. Click Add. (If asked, click the Adjust Firewall button to allow access to the printer port 631.) A New Printer window appears.

3. If the printer that you want to configure is detected, simply select it and click Forward. If it is not detected, choose the device to which the printer is connected (LPT #1 and Serial Port #1 are the first parallel and serial ports, respectively) and click Forward. (Type **/usr/sbin/lpinfo -v | less** in a shell to see printer connection types.) You are asked to identify the printer's driver.

4. To use an installed driver for your printer, choose Select Printer From Database, and then choose the manufacturer of your printer. As an alternative, you could select Provide PPD File and supply your own PPD file (for example, if you have a printer that is not supported in Linux and you have a driver that was supplied with the printer). (PPD stands for PostScript Printer Description.) Select Forward to see a list of printer models from which you can choose.

> **TIP**
>
> If your printer doesn't appear on the list but supports PCL (HP's Printer Control Language), try selecting one of the HP printers (such as HP LaserJet). If your printer supports PostScript, select the PostScript printer from the list. Selecting Raw Print Queue enables you to send documents that are already formatted for a particular printer type to a specific printer.

5. With your printer model selected, click the driver that you want to use with it and then click Forward to continue.

6. Add the following information, and click Forward:

   a. **Printer Name:** Add the name that you want to give to identify the printer. The name must begin with a letter, but after the initial letter, it can contain a combination of letters, numbers, dashes (-), and underscores (_). For example, an HP printer on a computer named *maple* could be named *hp-maple*.

   b. **Description:** Add a few words describing the printer, such as its features (for example, an HP LaserJet 2100M with PCL and PS support).

   c. **Location:** Add some words that describe the printer's location (for example, "In Room 205 under the coffee maker").

7. When the printer is added, click No or Yes if you're prompted to print a test page. The new printer entry appears in the Print Settings window. Double-click the printer to see the Properties window for that printer.

8. If you want the printer to be your default printer, right-click the printer and select Set As Default. As you add other printers, you can change the default printer by selecting the one you want and selecting Set As Default again.

9. Make sure that the printer is working. Open a Terminal window and use the lp command to print a file (such as lp /etc/hosts). (If you want to share this printer with other computers on your network, refer to the section "Configuring Print Servers" later in this chapter.)

Editing a local printer

After double-clicking the printer that you want to configure, choose from the following menu options to change its configuration:

Settings: The Description, Location, Device URI, and Make and Model information you created earlier are displayed in this dialog box.

Policies: Click Policies to set the following items:

State: Select check boxes to indicate whether the printer will print jobs that are in the queue (Enabled), accept new jobs for printing (Accepting Jobs), and be available to be shared with other computers that can communicate with your computer (Shared). You also must select Server Settings and click the "Share Published printers connected to this system" check box before the printer will accept print jobs from other computers.

Policies: In case of error, the stop-printer selection causes all printing to that printer to stop. You can also select to have the job discarded (abort-job) or retried (retry-job) in the event of an error condition.

Banner: There are no starting or ending banner pages by default for the printer. Choose starting or ending banner pages that include text such as *Classified*, *Confidential*, *Secret*, and so on.

Access Control: If your printer is a shared printer, you can select this window to create a list that either allows users access to the printer (with all others denied) or denies users access to the printer (with all others allowed).

Printer Options: Click Printer Options to set defaults for options related to the printer driver. The available options are different for different printers. Many of these options can be overridden when someone prints a document. Here are examples of a few of the options that you might (or might not) have available:

Watermark: Several Watermark settings are available to enable you to add and change watermarks on your printed pages. By default, Watermark and Overlay are off (None). By selecting Watermark (behind the text) or Overlay (over the text), you can set the other Watermark settings to determine how watermarks and overlays are done. Watermarks can go on every page (All) or only the first page (First Only). Select Watermark Text to choose what words are used for the watermark or overlay (Draft, Copy, Confidential, Final, and so on). You can then select the font type, size, style, and intensity of the watermark or overlay.

Resolution Enhancement: You can use the printer's current settings or choose to turn resolution enhancement on or off.

Page Size: The default is US letter size, but you can also ask the printer to print legal size, envelopes, ISO A4 standard, or several other page sizes.

Media Source: Choose which tray to print from. Select Tray 1 to insert pages manually.

Levels of Gray: Choose to use the printer's current levels of gray or have enhanced or standard gray levels turned on.

Resolution: Select the default printing resolution (such as 300, 600, or 1,200 dots per inch). Higher resolutions result in better quality but take longer to print.

EconoMode: Either use the printer's current setting or choose a mode where you save toner or one where you have the highest possible quality.

Job Options: Click Job Options to set common default options that will be used for this printer if the application printing the job doesn't already set them. These include Common Options (number of copies, orientation, scale to fit, and pages per side), Image Options (scaling, saturation, hue, and gamma), and Text Options (characters/inch, lines/inch, and margin settings).

Ink/Toner Levels: Click Ink/Toner Levels to see information on how much ink or toner your printer has left. (Not all printers report these values.)

Click Apply when you are satisfied with the changes you made to the local printer.

Configuring remote printers

To use a printer that's available on your network, you must identify that printer to your Linux system. Supported remote printer connections include Networked CUPS (IPP) printers, Networked UNIX (LPD) printers, Networked Windows (Samba) printers, and JetDirect printers. (Of course, both CUPS and UNIX print servers can be run from Linux systems as well as other UNIX systems.)

In each case, you need a network connection from your Linux system to the servers to which those printers are connected. To use a remote printer requires that someone set up that printer on the remote server computer. See the section "Configuring Print Servers" later in this chapter for information on how to do that on your Linux server.

Use the Print Settings window (`system-config-printer`) to configure each of the remote printer types. This is how it is done:

1. From GNOME Settings, select Devices, Printers, and then Additional Printer Settings.

2. Click Add. The New Printer window appears.

3. Depending on the type of ports that you have on your computer, select one of the following:

   a. **LPT #1:** Use this for a printer connected to your parallel port.

   b. **Serial Port #1:** Use this for a printer connected to your serial port.

   c. **Network Printer:** Under this heading, you can search for network printers (by hostname or IP address) or type in the URI for several different printer types:

      i. **Find Network Printer:** Instead of entering a printer URI, you can provide a hostname or IP address for the system that has the printer to which you want to print. Any printers found on that host appear on the window, ready for you to add.

ii. **AppleSocket/HP JetDirect**: Use this for a JetDirect printer.

iii. **Internet Printing Protocol (IPP)**: Use this for a CUPS or other IPP printer. Most Linux and macOS printers fall into this category.

iv. **Internet Printing Protocol (HTTPS)**: Use this for a CUPS or other IPP printer being shared over a secure connection (valid certificates required).

v. **LPD/LPR Host or Printer**: Use this for a UNIX printer.

vi. **Windows Printer via SAMBA**: Use this for a Windows system printer.

Continue with the steps in whichever of the following sections is appropriate.

Adding a remote CUPS printer

If you chose to add a CUPS (IPP) printer that is accessible over your local network from the Print Settings window, you must add the following information to the window that appears:

Host This is the hostname of the computer to which the printer is attached (or otherwise accessible). This can be an IP address or TCP/IP hostname for the computer. The TCP/IP name is accessible from your /etc/hosts file or through a DNS name server.

Queue This is the printer name on the remote CUPS print server. CUPS supports printer instances, which allows each printer to have several sets of options. If the remote CUPS printer is configured this way, you can choose a particular path to a printer, such as hp/300dpi or hp/1200dpi. A slash character separates the print queue name from the printer instance.

Complete the rest of the procedure as you would for a local printer (see the section "Adding a local printer" earlier in this chapter).

Adding a remote UNIX (LDP/LPR) printer

If you chose to add a UNIX printer (LPD/LPR) from the Print Settings window, you must add the following information to the window that appears:

Host This is the hostname of the computer to which the printer is attached (or otherwise accessible). This is the IP address or hostname for the computer (the hostname is accessible from your /etc/hosts file or through a DNS name server). Select the Probe button to search for the host.

Queue This is the printer name on the remote UNIX computer.

Complete the rest of the procedure as you would for a local printer (see the section "Adding a local printer" earlier in this chapter).

> **TIP**
> If the print job you send to test the printer is rejected, the print server computer may not have allowed you access to the printer. Ask the remote computer's administrator to add your hostname to the /etc/lpd.perms file. (Enter `lpstat -d printer` to see the status of your print job.)

Adding a Windows (SMB) printer

Enabling your computer to access an SMB printer (the Windows printing service) involves adding an entry for the printer in the Select Connection window.

When you choose to add a Windows printer to the Print Settings window (Windows Printer via Samba), select Browse to see a list of computers on your network that have been detected as offering SMB services (file and/or printing service). You can configure the printer from this window as follows:

1. Type the URI of the printer, excluding the leading `smb:/`. For example, you might type `/host1/myprinter` or `/mygroup/host1/myprinter`.
2. Select either "Prompt user if authentication is required" or "Set authentication details now."
3. If you chose "Set authentication details now," fill in the username and password needed to access the SMB printer; then click Verify to check that you can authenticate to the server.
4. Click Forward to continue.

Alternatively, you can identify a server that does not appear on the list of servers. Type the information needed to create an SMB URI that contains the following information:

Workgroup   This is the workgroup name assigned to the SMB server. Using the workgroup name isn't necessary in all cases.

Server   This is the NetBIOS name or IP address for the computer, which may or may not be the same as its TCP/IP name. To translate this name into the address needed to reach the SMB host, Samba checks several places where the name may be assigned to an IP address. Samba checks the following (in the order shown) until it finds a match: the local `/etc/hosts` file, the local `/etc/samba/lmhosts` file, a WINS server on the network, and responses to broadcasts on each local network interface to resolve the name.

Share   This is the name under which the printer is shared with the remote computer. It may be different from the name by which local users of the SMB printer know the printer.

User   A username is required by the SMB server system to give you access to the SMB printer. A username is not necessary if you are authenticating the printer based on share-level rather than user-level access control. With share-level access, you can add a password for each shared printer or file system.

Password   Use the password associated with the SMB username or the shared resource, depending on the kind of access control being used.

> **CAUTION**
>
> When you enter a username and password for SMB, the information is stored unencrypted in the `/etc/cups/printers.conf` file. Be sure that the file remains readable only by root.

The following is an example of the SMB URI that you could add to the SMB:// box:

```
jjones:my9passswd@FSTREET/NS1/hp
```

The URI shown here identifies the username (jjones), the user's password (my9passswd), the workgroup (FSTREET), the server (NS1), and the printer queue name (hp).

Complete the rest of the procedure as you would for a local printer (see the section "Adding a local printer" earlier in this chapter).

If everything is set up properly, you can use the standard lp command to print the file to the printer. Using this example, employ the following form for printing:

```
$ cat file1.ps | lp -P NS1-PS
```

TIP

If you are receiving failure messages, make sure that the computer to which you are printing is accessible. For the Printer NS1 hp example, you can type smbclient -L NS1 -U jjones. Then type the password (my9passswd, in this case). The −L asks for information about the server; the −U jjones says to log in the user jjones. If you get a positive name query response after you enter a password, you should see a list of shared printers and files from that server. Check the names and try printing again.

Working with CUPS Printing

Tools such as CUPS web-based administration and the Printers window effectively hide the underlying CUPS facility. Sometimes, however, you want to work directly with the tools and configuration files that come with CUPS. The following sections describe how to use some special CUPS features.

Configuring the CUPS server (cupsd.conf)

The cupsd daemon process listens for requests to your CUPS print server and responds to those requests based on settings in the /etc/cups/cupsd.conf file. The configuration variables in the cupsd.conf file are in the same form as those in the Apache configuration file (apache2.conf). Type **man cupsd.conf** to see details on any of the settings.

The Printers window adds access information to the cupsd.conf file. For other Linux systems, or if you don't have a desktop on your server, you may need to configure the cupsd.conf file manually. You can step through the cupsd.conf file to tune your CUPS server further. Most of the settings are optional or can just be left as the default. Let's look at some of the settings that you can use in the cupsd.conf file.

The term *browsing* refers to the act of broadcasting information about your printer on your local network and listening for other print servers' information. The BrowseLocalProtocols setting is used to control browsing of shared, remote printers. Browsing is on by default for all local networks (@LOCAL). Browsing information is broadcast, by default, on address 255.255.255.255. Here are some browsing settings:

```
Browsing On
BrowseLocalProtocols dnssd

<Location />
  # Allow shared printing...
  Order allow,deny
  Allow @LOCAL
</Location>

Port 631
```

To enable web-based CUPS administration and to share printers with others on the network, the cupsd daemon can be set to listen on port 631 for all network interfaces to your computer. By default, it listens on the local interface only on many Linux systems.

This is a good way to enable users on several connected LANs to discover and use printers on other nearby LANs.

As you can see from the following lines from the file, administration tasks will require sudo password authentication:

```
<Location /admin/conf>
  AuthType Default
  Require user @SYSTEM
  Order allow,deny
</Location>
```

Starting the CUPS server

For Linux systems that use System V–style startup scripts, starting and shutting down the CUPS print service is done via the chkconfig command. Run the cups startup script to have the CUPS service start immediately.

```
# chkconfig cups on
# service cups start
```

If the CUPS service was already running, you should use restart instead of start. Using the restart option is also a good way to reread any configuration options that you may have changed in the cupsd.conf file (although, if CUPS is already running, service cups reload rereads configuration files without restarting).

In systemd, you use the systemctl command instead of service to start and stop services:

```
# systemctl status cups.service

* cups.service - CUPS Printing Service
   Loaded: loaded (/usr/lib/systemd/system/cups.service; enabled)
```

```
        Active: active (running) since Sat 2016-07-23 22:41:05 EDT; 18h ago
      Main PID: 20483 (cupsd)
        Status: "Scheduler is running..."
        CGroup: /system.slice/cups.service
                └─20483 /usr/sbin/cupsd -f
```

You can tell the CUPS service is running because the status shows the `cupsd` daemon active with `PID 20483`. If that service were not running, you could start the CUPS service as follows:

```
# systemctl start cups.service
```

See Chapter 15, "Starting and Stopping Services," for more information on the `systemctl` and `service` commands for working with services.

Configuring CUPS printer options manually

If your Ubuntu machine doesn't have a graphical means of configuring CUPS, you can edit configuration files directly. For example, when a new printer is created from the Print Settings window, it is defined in the /etc/cups/printers.conf file. This is what a printer entry looks like:

```
# Printer configuration file for CUPS v2.2.7
# Written by cupsd
# DO NOT EDIT THIS FILE WHEN CUPSD IS RUNNING
<Printer DCP-7060D>
UUID urn:uuid:33579cfe-b80b-356d-5a92-f2aa6513fb32
Info Brother DCP-7060D
MakeModel Brother DCP-7065DN, using brlaser v4
DeviceURI usb://Brother/DCP-7060D?serial=U62711H3N846958
State Idle
StateTime 1558972243
ConfigTime 1553624304
Type 4180
Accepting Yes
Shared Yes
JobSheets none none
QuotaPeriod 0
PageLimit 0
KLimit 0
OpPolicy default
ErrorPolicy retry-job
</Printer>
```

This is an example of a local printer that serves as the default printer for the local system. The `Shared Yes` value is set because the printer is currently available across the network. The most interesting information relates to `DeviceURI`, which shows that the printer is connected to a USB port usb://. The state is `Idle` (ready to accept printer jobs), and the `Accepting` value is `Yes` (the printer is accepting print jobs by default).

The `DeviceURI` has several ways to identify the device name of a printer, reflecting where the printer is connected. Here are some examples listed in the `printers.conf` file:

```
DeviceURI parallel:/dev/plp
DeviceURI serial:/dev/ttyd1?baud=38400+size=8+parity=none+flow=soft
DeviceURI scsi:/dev/scsi/sc1d610
DeviceURI usb://hostname:port
DeviceURI socket://hostname:port
DeviceURI tftp://hostname/path
DeviceURI ftp://hostname/path
DeviceURI http://hostname[:port]/path
DeviceURI ipp://hostname/path
DeviceURI smb://hostname/printer
```

The first four examples show the form for local printers (`parallel`, `serial`, `scsi`, and `usb`). The other examples are for remote hosts. In each case, *hostname* can be the host's name or IP address. Port numbers or paths identify the locations of each printer on the host. For example, *hostname* could be `myhost.example.com:631` and *path* could be replaced by any name you like, such as `printers/myprinter`.

Using Printing Commands

To remain backward compatible with older UNIX and Linux printing facilities, CUPS supports many of the old commands for working with printing. Most command-line printing with CUPS can be performed with the `lp` command. Word processing applications such as LibreOffice, OpenOffice, and AbiWord are set up to use this facility for printing.

You can use the Print Settings window to define the filters needed for each printer so that the text can be formatted properly. Options to the `lp` command can add filters to process the text properly. Other commands for managing printed documents include `lpstat` (for viewing the contents of print queues), `cancel` (for removing print jobs from the queue), and `lpstat -t` (for controlling printers).

Printing with lp

You can use the `lp` command to print documents to both local and remote printers (provided the printers are configured locally). Document files can be either added to the end of the `lp` command line or directed to the `lp` command using a pipe (|). Here's an example of a simple `lp` command:

```
$ lp doc1.ps
```

When you specify just a document file with `lp`, output is directed to the default printer. As an individual user, you can change the default printer by setting the value of the `PRINTER` variable. Typically, you add the `PRINTER` variable to one of your startup files, such as

$HOME/.bashrc. Adding the following line to your .bashrc file, for example, sets your default printer to lp3:

```
export PRINTER=lp3
```

To override the default printer, specify a particular printer on the lp command line. The following example uses the -d option to select a different printer:

```
$ lp -d canyonps doc1.ps
```

The lp command has a variety of options that enable lp to interpret and format several different types of documents. These include *-n num*, where *num* is replaced by the number of copies to print (from 1 to 100) and -o (which causes a document to be sent in raw mode, presuming that the document has already been formatted). To learn more options to lp, type **man lp**.

Listing status with lpstat -t

Use the lpstat -t command to list the status of your printers. Here is an example:

```
$ lpstat -t

scheduler is running
no system default destination
device for DCP-7060D: usb://Brother/DCP-7060D?serial=U62711H3N846958
DCP-7060D accepting requests since Mon 27 May 2019 11:50:43 AM EDT
printer DCP-7060D is idle.  enabled since Mon 27 May 2019
11:50:43 AM EDT
```

This output shows one active printer: the Brother DCP-7060D.

Removing print jobs with cancel

Users can remove their own print jobs from the queue with the cancel command. Used alone on the command line, cancel removes all of the user's print jobs from the default printer. To remove jobs from a specific printer, use the -P option, as follows:

```
$ cancel -P lp0
```

To remove all print jobs for the current user, type the following:

```
$ cancel -a
```

The root user can remove all of the print jobs for a specific user by indicating that user on the cancel command line. For example, to remove all print jobs for the user named mike, the root user types the following:

```
# cancel -u mike
```

To remove an individual print job from the queue, indicate its job number on the cancel command line. To find the job number, type the lpstat command.

Configuring Print Servers

You've configured a printer so that you and the other users on your computer can print to it. Now you want to share that printer with other people in your home, school, or office. Basically, that means configuring the printer as a print server.

The printers configured on your Linux system can be shared in different ways with other computers on your network. Not only can your computer act as a Linux print server (by configuring CUPS), but it can also appear as an SMB (Windows) print server to client computers. After a local printer is attached to your Linux system and your computer is connected to your local network, you can use the procedures in the following sections to share the printer with client computers using a Linux (UNIX) or SMB interface.

Configuring a shared CUPS printer

Making the local printer added to your Linux computer available to other computers on your network is fairly easy. If a TCP/IP network connection exists between the computers sharing the printer, you simply grant permission to all hosts, individual hosts, or users from remote hosts to access your computer's printing service.

To configure a printer entry manually in the /etc/cups/printers.conf file to accept print jobs from all other computers, make sure that the Shared Yes line is set. The following example from a printers.conf entry earlier in this chapter demonstrates what the new entry would look like:

```
<DefaultPrinter printer>
Info HP LaserJet 2100M
Location HP LaserJet 2100M in hall closet
DeviceURI parallel:/dev/lp0
State Idle
Accepting Yes
Shared Yes
JobSheets none none
QuotaPeriod 0
PageLimit 0
KLimit 0
</Printer>
```

On Linux systems that use the Print Settings window described earlier in this chapter, it's best to set up your printer as a shared printer using that window. Here's how to do that using Ubuntu:

1. From the Printers window (accessible through GNOME Settings) click the Additional Printer Settings button.

2. Select Server ⇨ Settings. The Basic Server Settings pop-up appears.

3. Select the check box next to "Publish shared printers connected to this system" and click OK. You may be asked to modify your firewall to open the necessary ports for remote systems to access your printers.

4. To allow or restrict printing for a particular printer further, double-click the name of the printer that you want to share. (If the printer is not yet configured, refer to the section "Setting Up Printers" earlier in this chapter.)

5. Choose the Policies heading and select Shared so that a check mark appears in the box.

6. If you want to restrict access to the printer to selected users, select the Access Control heading and choose one of the following options:

   a. **Allow Printing for Everyone Except These Users**. With this selected, all users are allowed access to the printer. By typing usernames into the Users box and clicking Add, you exclude selected users.

   b. **Deny Printing for Everyone Except These Users**. With this selected, all users are excluded from using the printer. Type usernames into the Users box, and click Add to allow access to the printer for only those names that you enter.

   Now you can configure other computers to use your printer, as described in the section "Setting Up Printers" earlier in this chapter. If you try to print from another computer and it doesn't work, try these troubleshooting tips:

   a. **Open your firewall**. If you have a restrictive firewall, it may not permit printing. You must enable access to TCP port 631 to allow access to printing on your computer.

   b. **Check names and addresses**. Make sure that you entered your computer's name and print queue properly when you configured it on the other computer. Try using the IP address instead of the hostname. (If that works, it indicates a DNS name resolution problem.) Running a tool such as tcpdump enables you to see where the transaction failed.

   c. **Check which addresses cupsd is listening on**. The cupsd daemon must be listening outside of the localhost for remote systems to print to it. Use the netstat command (as the root user) as follows to check this. The first example shows cupsd only listening on local host (127.0.0.1:631); the second shows cupsd listening on all network interfaces (0 0.0.0.0:631):

```
# netstat -tupln | grep 631
tcp   0   0 127.0.0.1:631   0.0.0.0:*     LISTEN    6492/cupsd
# netstat -tupln | grep 631
tcp   0   0 0.0.0.0:631     0.0.0.0:*     LISTEN    6492/cupsd
```

Access changes to your shared printer are made in the cupsd.conf and printers.conf files in your /etc/cups directory.

Configuring a shared Samba printer

Your Linux printers can be configured as shared SMB printers so that they appear to be available from Windows systems. To share your printer as if it were a Samba (SMB) printer, simply configure basic Samba server settings as described in Chapter 19, "Configuring a

Windows File Sharing (Samba) Server." All your printers should be shared on your local network by default. The next section shows what the resulting settings look like and how you might want to change them.

Understanding smb.conf for printing

When you configure Samba, the /etc/samba/smb.conf file is constructed to enable all of your configured printers to be shared. Here are a few lines from the smb.conf file that relate to printer sharing:

```
[global]
   workgroup = WORKGROUP
        server string = %h server (Samba, Ubuntu)
;    wins server = w.x.y.z
   dns proxy = no
;    interfaces = 127.0.0.0/8 eth0
;    bind interfaces only = yes
   log file = /var/log/samba/log.%m
   max log size = 1000
   syslog = 0
```

You can read the comment lines to learn more about the file's contents. Lines beginning with a semicolon (;) indicate the default setting for the option on a comment line. Remove the semicolon to change the setting.

The last few lines are the actual printers' definition. By changing the browseable option from no to yes, you give users the ability to print to all printers (printable = yes). You can also store Windows native print drivers on your Samba server. When a Windows client uses your printer, the driver automatically becomes available. You do not need to download a driver from the vendor's website. To enable the printer driver share, add a Samba share called print$ that looks like the following:

```
[print$]
   comment = Printer Drivers
   path = /var/lib/samba/printers
   browseable = yes
   read only = yes
   guest ok = no
   write list = root, @lpadmin
```

After you have the share available, you can start copying Windows print drivers to the /var/lib/samba/drivers directory.

Setting up SMB clients

Chances are good that if you are configuring a Samba printer on your Linux computer, you want to share it with Windows clients. If Samba is set up properly on your computer and the client computers can reach you over the network, users should have no trouble finding and using your printer.

For many Windows 10 systems, click Start ⇨ Printers and Scanners and select the printer from the list to configure it.

After your shared printer appears in the window, configure a pointer to that printer by opening (double-clicking) the printer icon. A message tells you that you must set up the printer before you can use it. Click Yes to proceed to configure the printer for local use. The Add Printer Wizard appears. Answer the questions that ask you how you intend to use the printer and add the appropriate drivers. When you are finished, the printer appears in your printer window.

Summary

Providing networked printing services is essential on today's business networks. With the use of a few network-attached devices, you can focus your printer spending on a few high-quality devices that multiple users can share instead of numerous lower-cost devices. In addition, a centrally located printer can make it easier to maintain the printer while still enabling everyone to get their printing jobs done.

The default printing service in Ubuntu is the Common UNIX Printing System (CUPS), and Ubuntu offers the CUPS web-based administrative interface for configuring CUPS printing. It also offers configuration files in the /etc/cups directory for configuring printers and the CUPS service (cupsd daemon).

You can configure your printer with the printing configuration windows available in both KDE and GNOME desktops. A variety of drivers makes it possible to print to different kinds of printers as well as to printers that are connected to computers on the network.

You can set up your computer as a Linux print server, and you can also have your computer emulate an SMB (Windows) print server. After your network is configured properly and a local printer is installed, sharing that printer over the network as a UNIX or SMB print server is not very complicated.

Exercises

Use these exercises to test your knowledge of configuring printers in Linux. These tasks assume that you are running an Ubuntu system (although some tasks work on other Linux systems as well). If you are stuck, solutions to the tasks are shown in Appendix A (although in Linux, you can often complete a task in multiple ways).

1. Use the Printers window (system-config-printer package) to add a new printer called myprinter to your system. (The printer does not have to be connected to set up a print queue for the new printer.) Make it a generic PostScript printer connected to a local serial, LPT, or other port.

2. Use the lpstat -t command to see the status of all of your printers.

3. Use the `lp` command to print the `/etc/hosts` file to that printer.

4. Check the print queue for that printer to see that the print job is there.

5. Remove the print job from the queue (cancel it).

6. Using the Printers window, set the basic server setting that publishes your printers so that other systems on your local network can print to your printers.

7. Allow remote administration of your system from a web browser.

8. Demonstrate that you can do remote administration of your system by opening a web browser to port 631 from another system to the Linux system running your print server.

9. Use the `netstat` command to see on which addresses the `cupsd` daemon is listening (the printing port is 631).

10. Delete the `myprinter` printer entry from your system.

Configuring a Web Server

W eb servers are responsible for serving up the content you view on the Internet every day. The most popular web server is the Apache HTTP web server, which is sponsored by the Apache Software Foundation (www.apache.org). Apache is an open source project that is available with Ubuntu.

You can configure a basic web server to run in Linux in just a few minutes. However, there's no end of customization you can apply to it. You can configure an Apache web server to serve content for multiple domains (virtual hosting), provide encrypted communications (HTTPS), and secure some or all of a website using different kinds of authentication.

This chapter takes you through the steps to install and configure an Apache web server. These steps include procedures for securing your server as well as using a variety of modules so that you can incorporate different authentication methods and scripting languages into your web server. Then I describe how to generate certificates to create an HTTPS Transport Layer Security (TLS) website.

Understanding the Apache Web Server

Apache HTTPD Server provides the service with which the client web browsers communicate. The daemon process (apache2) runs in the background on your server and waits for requests from web clients. Web browsers provide those connections to the HTTP daemon and send requests, which the daemon interprets, sending back the appropriate data (such as a web page or other content).

Apache HTTP Server includes an interface that allows modules to tie into the process to handle specific portions of a request. Among other things, modules are available to handle the processing of scripting languages, such as Perl or PHP, within web documents and to add encryption to connections between clients and the server.

Apache began as a collection of patches and improvements from the National Center for Supercomputing Applications (NCSA), University of Illinois, Urbana-Champaign, to the HTTP daemon. The NCSA HTTP daemon was the most popular HTTP server at the time, but it had started to show its age after its author, Rob McCool, left NCSA in mid-1994.

> **NOTE**
> Another project that came from NCSA is Mosaic. Most modern web browsers can trace their origins to Mosaic.

In early 1995, a group of developers formed the Apache Group and began making extensive modifications to the NCSA HTTPD code base. Apache soon replaced NCSA HTTPD as the most popular web server, a title it still holds today.

The Apache Group later formed the Apache Software Foundation (ASF) to promote the development of Apache and other free software. With the start of new projects at ASF, the Apache server became known as The Apache HTTP Server Project although the two terms are still used interchangeably. Currently, ASF has more than 350 open source initiatives, including Tomcat (which includes open source Java Servlet and JavaServer Pages technologies), Hadoop (a project providing highly available, distributed computing), and SpamAssassin (an email filtering program).

Getting and Installing Your Apache Web Server

All you need to start a simple Apache web server is the package containing the Apache daemon itself (/usr/sbin/apache2) and its related files. The Apache web server comes in the apache2 package.

Installing Apache is simple:

```
# apt install apache2
Reading package lists... Done
Building dependency tree
Reading state information... Done
The following package was automatically installed and is no longer required:
  libfreetype6
Use 'apt autoremove' to remove it.
The following additional packages will be installed:
  apache2-bin apache2-data apache2-utils libapr1 libaprutil1 libaprutil1-dbd-
sqlite3 libaprutil1-ldap liblua5.2-0 ssl-cert
```

```
Suggested packages:
  www-browser apache2-doc apache2-suexec-pristine | apache2-suexec-
custom openssl-blacklist
The following NEW packages will be installed:
  apache2 apache2-bin apache2-data apache2-utils libapr1 libaprutil1
libaprutil1-dbd-sqlite3 libaprutil1-ldap liblua5.2-0 ssl-cert
0 upgraded, 10 newly installed, 0 to remove and 26 not upgraded.
Need to get 1409 kB/1729 kB of archives.
After this operation, 6986 kB of additional disk space will be used.
Do you want to continue? [Y/n]
```

On Ubuntu, that'll be all it takes to get the server up and running. You can confirm everything is working by loading the new site's home page using `curl`:

```
curl localhost
```

You'll see the contents of the `index.html` file that Apache saved to the web document root directory, /var/www/html/. If you want to see how that file is meant to be viewed, open a browser and point it to the address used by the host. If your browser is on the same machine, that could be `localhost`. Otherwise, use the host's IP address. Figure 17.1 shows you part of what you'll see.

FIGURE 17.1

The Ubuntu version of the Apache2 introduction page

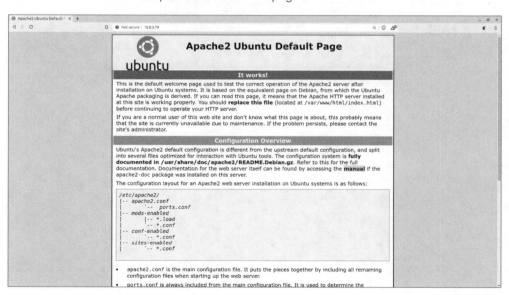

Take a look in that /var/www/html/ directory. Right now there's only a single file: the index.html file you just viewed in your browser. But you can edit that file or add new files and directories to create a website that fits your needs.

```
$ ls /var/www/html
index.html
```

By default, browsers will look for and load any file in your document root that's named either default.html or default.php. You can also load specific files by simply including them in the uniform resource locator (URL) you type into your browser. Let's create a new file called myfile.html and save it to the web root:

```
# nano /var/www/html/myfile.html
```

You could enter some text like this into the file:

```
<h1>Hello!</h1>
<h3>Welcome to my web site.</h3>
```

Now, when you add /myfile.html to the address in your browser, you'll see what's shown in Figure 17.2.

FIGURE 17.2

A custom HTML page within a simple Apache website

Naturally, you'll want to replace the default index.html page to fit your needs, but it does contain some useful information. That includes the helpful document tree showing you where, within the /etc/apache2/ directory hierarchy, the key configuration files are kept. The main configuration is done at the top level, particularly in the apache2. conf file. Module add-on configurations are in the mods-enabled/ directory, and virtual domain hosting information is kept in the sites-enabled/ directory.

Controlling Apache

You stop, start, and enable Apache using the regular systemctl tools:

```
# systemctl status apache2
• apache2.service - The Apache HTTP Server
    Loaded: loaded (/lib/systemd/system/apache2.service; enabled;
vendor preset:
   Drop-In: /lib/systemd/system/apache2.service.d
            └─apache2-systemd.conf
    Active: active (running) since Wed 2020-04-01 13:52:04 UTC; 59min ago
  Main PID: 1113 (apache2)
     Tasks: 54 (limit: 4915)
    CGroup: /system.slice/apache2.service
            └─1113 /usr/sbin/apache2 -k start
            └─1115 /usr/sbin/apache2 -k start
            └─1116 /usr/sbin/apache2 -k start

Apr 01 13:52:04 apache systemd[1]: Starting The Apache HTTP Server...
Apr 01 13:52:04 apache systemd[1]: Started The Apache HTTP Server.
```

Securing Apache

To secure Apache, you need to be aware of standard Linux security features (permissions, ownership, firewalls, and AppArmor) as well as security features that are specific to Apache. The following sections describe security features that relate to Apache.

Apache file permissions and ownership

The apache2 daemon process runs as the user www-data and group www-data. By default, HTML content is stored in the /var/www/html directory (as determined by the value of DocumentRoot in the sites-available/000-default.conf file).

For the apache2 daemon to be able to access that content, standard Linux permissions apply: if read permission is not on for other users, it must be on for the apache user or group for the files to be read and served to clients. Likewise, any directory the apache2 daemon must traverse to get to the content must have execute permission on for the www-data user, www-data group, or other user.

Although you cannot log in as the `www-data` user (`/usr/sbin/nologin` is the default shell), you can create content as root and change its ownership (`chown` command) or permission (`chmod` command). Often, however, separate user or group accounts are added to create content that is readable by everyone (other) but only writable by that special user or group.

Apache and firewalls

If you've locked down access to your computer using a firewall, you'll need to open network ports for clients to be able to talk to Apache through the firewall. Standard web service (HTTP) is accessible over TCP port 80; secure web service (HTTPS) is accessible via TCP port 443. (Port 443 only appears if you have configured encryption, as described later.)

To verify which ports are being used by the `httpd` server, use the `netstat` command:

```
$ netstat -tupln | grep apache2
tcp6   0   0 :::80        :::*        LISTEN       1113/apache2
```

The output shows that the `apache2` daemon (process ID 1113) is listening on all addresses for port 80 (`:::80`). The port is associated with the TCP protocol (`tcp6`). You'll need to open that port with a new rule if you've got a firewall running.

Out of the box, Ubuntu servers will generally not activate a firewall, so this won't be a problem.

Naturally, if your computer is part of a private network sitting behind a router, clients won't be able to access your website unless you configure port forwarding on the router. Similarly, if the computer is a virtual machine running on a public cloud platform like Amazon Web Services, you'll need to create a security group rule permitting incoming traffic on port 80 and, for encrypted traffic, port 443.

We'll talk about firewalls in Chapter 25, "Securing Linux on a Network."

Apache and AppArmor

AppArmor is a mandatory access control (MAC) kernel security module that permits carefully defined controls over who and what can access individual Linux programs. AppArmor is the Ubuntu equivalent of RHEL's *Security Enhanced Linux (SELinux)*. When configured to manage access to Apache resources, AppArmor provides an additional layer of security. We'll discuss AppArmor in greater detail in Chapter 24, "Enhancing Linux Security with AppArmor."

Here, we'll just dig deeply enough into AppArmor to make sure it's protecting Apache. The `policy` command will confirm that AppArmor is installed and active:

```
# apt policy apparmor
apparmor:
  Installed: 2.12-4ubuntu5.1
  Candidate: 2.12-4ubuntu5.1
  Version table:
```

```
*** 2.12-4ubuntu5.1 500
        500 http://archive.ubuntu.com/ubuntu bionic-updates/main amd64 Packages
        500 http://security.ubuntu.com/ubuntu bionic-security/main amd64 Packages
        100 /var/lib/dpkg/status
    2.12-4ubuntu5 500
        500 http://archive.ubuntu.com/ubuntu bionic/main amd64 Packages
```

There's an `apparmor_status` command just bursting with helpful information about the tool's current settings:

```
# apparmor_status
apparmor module is loaded.
15 profiles are loaded.
15 profiles are in enforce mode.
   /sbin/dhclient
   /usr/bin/lxc-start
   /usr/bin/man
   /usr/lib/NetworkManager/nm-dhcp-client.action
   /usr/lib/NetworkManager/nm-dhcp-helper
   /usr/lib/connman/scripts/dhclient-script
   /usr/lib/snapd/snap-confine
   /usr/lib/snapd/snap-confine//mount-namespace-capture-helper
   /usr/sbin/tcpdump
   lxc-container-default
   lxc-container-default-cgns
   lxc-container-default-with-mounting
   lxc-container-default-with-nesting
   man_filter
   man_groff
0 profiles are in complain mode.
0 processes have profiles defined.
0 processes are in enforce mode.
0 processes are in complain mode.
0 processes are unconfined but have a profile defined.
```

Note that there's no reference to Apache and, there are currently no processes set to "complain" (meaning: issue alerts for non-compliant activities) or "enforce" policies.

To get Apache on board with all this, we will need to install a couple of packages:

```
apt install apparmor-utils libapache2-mod-apparmor
```

That will add a file to the /etc/apparmor.d/ directory called usr.sbin.apache2. That'll include some helpful instructions for getting everything set up along with configuration settings. Next, I'll shut down the Apache service and make some changes. In this case, I'll have to disable the mpm_event module so I can successfully enable mpm _ prefork. Next, I'll enable the `apparmor` module and run `aa-enforce` to enable protection for Apache and restart Apache.

```
# systemctl stop apache2
# a2dismod mpm_event
Module mpm_event disabled.
To activate the new configuration, you need to run:
  systemctl restart apache2
# a2enmod mpm_prefork
Considering conflict mpm_event for mpm_prefork:
Considering conflict mpm_worker for mpm_prefork:
Enabling module mpm_prefork.
To activate the new configuration, you need to run:
  systemctl restart apache2
# a2enmod apparmor
Enabling module apparmor.
To activate the new configuration, you need to run:
  systemctl restart apache2
# systemctl restart apache2
# aa-enforce /etc/apparmor.d/usr.sbin.apache2
Setting /etc/apparmor.d/usr.sbin.apache2 to enforce mode.
# systemctl start apache2
```

Now, if we run `apparmor_status` once again, we can see that Apache is a big part of the mix:

```
# apparmor_status
apparmor module is loaded.
18 profiles are loaded.
18 profiles are in enforce mode.
  /sbin/dhclient
  /usr/bin/lxc-start
  /usr/bin/man
  /usr/lib/NetworkManager/nm-dhcp-client.action
  /usr/lib/NetworkManager/nm-dhcp-helper
  /usr/lib/connman/scripts/dhclient-script
  /usr/lib/snapd/snap-confine
  /usr/lib/snapd/snap-confine//mount-namespace-capture-helper
  /usr/sbin/apache2
  /usr/sbin/apache2//DEFAULT_URI
  /usr/sbin/apache2//HANDLING_UNTRUSTED_INPUT
  /usr/sbin/tcpdump
  lxc-container-default
  lxc-container-default-cgns
  lxc-container-default-with-mounting
  lxc-container-default-with-nesting
  man_filter
  man_groff
```

```
0 profiles are in complain mode.
6 processes have profiles defined.
6 processes are in enforce mode.
   /usr/sbin/apache2 (2096)
   /usr/sbin/apache2//HANDLING_UNTRUSTED_INPUT (2097)
   /usr/sbin/apache2//HANDLING_UNTRUSTED_INPUT (2098)
   /usr/sbin/apache2//HANDLING_UNTRUSTED_INPUT (2099)
   /usr/sbin/apache2//HANDLING_UNTRUSTED_INPUT (2100)
   /usr/sbin/apache2//HANDLING_UNTRUSTED_INPUT (2101)
0 processes are in complain mode.
0 processes are unconfined but have a profile defined.
```

Understanding the Apache configuration files

The configuration files for Apache are incredibly flexible, meaning that you can configure the server to behave in almost any manner you want. This flexibility comes at the cost of increased complexity in the form of a large number of configuration options (called *directives*). In practice, however, you need to be familiar with only a few directives in most cases.

> **NOTE**
>
> See httpd.apache.org/docs/current/mod/directives.html for a complete list of directives supported by Apache.

In Ubuntu, the Apache configuration is stored in text files read by the Apache server, beginning with /etc/apache2/apache2.conf. Configuration is read from start to finish, with most directives being processed in the order in which they are read.

Using directives

The scope of many configuration directives can be altered based on context. In other words, some parameters may be set on a global level and then changed for a specific file, directory, or virtual host. Other directives are always global in nature, such as those specifying on which IP addresses the server listens. Still others are valid only when applied to a specific location.

Locations are configured in the form of a start tag containing the location type and a resource location, followed by the configuration options for that location, and finishing with an end tag. This form is often called a *configuration block*, and it looks very similar to HTML code. A special type of configuration block, known as a *location block*, is used to limit the scope of directives to specific files or directories. These blocks take the following form:

```
<locationtag specifier>
(options specific to objects matching the specifier go within this
block)
</locationtag>
```

Different types of location tags exist and are selected based on the type of resource location that is being specified. The specifier included in the start tag is handled based on the type of location tag. The location tags that you generally use and encounter are `Directory`, `Files`, and `Location`, which limit the scope of the directives to specific directories, files, or locations, respectively.

- `Directory` tags are used to specify a path based on the location on the filesystem. For instance, `<Directory />` refers to the root directory on the computer. Directories inherit settings from directories above them, with the most specific `Directory` block overriding less specific ones, regardless of the order in which they appear in the configuration files.

- `Files` tags are used to specify files by name. `Files` tags can be contained within a `Directory` block to limit them to files under that directory. Settings within a `Files` block override the ones in `Directory` blocks.

- `Location` tags are used to specify the URI used to access a file or directory. This is different from `Directory` in that it relates to the address contained within the request and not to the real location of the file on the drive. `Location` tags are processed last and override the settings in `Directory` and `Files` blocks.

Match versions of these tags—`DirectoryMatch`, `FilesMatch`, and `LocationMatch`—have the same function but can contain regular expressions in the resource specification. `FilesMatch` and `LocationMatch` blocks are processed at the same time as `Files` and `Location`, respectively. `DirectoryMatch` blocks are processed after `Directory` blocks.

Apache can also be configured to process configuration options contained within files with the name specified in the `AccessFileName` directive (which is generally set to `.htaccess`). Directives in access configuration files are applied to all objects under the directory they contain, including subdirectories and their contents. Access configuration files are processed at the same time as `Directory` blocks, using a similar "most specific match" order.

> **NOTE**
>
> Access control files are useful for allowing users to change specific settings without having access to the server configuration files. The configuration directives permitted within an access configuration file are determined by the `AllowOverride` setting on the directory in which they are contained. Some directives do not make sense at that level and generally result in a "server internal error" message when trying to access the URI. The `AllowOverride` option is covered in detail at httpd.apache.org/docs/mod/core.html#allowoverride.

Three directives commonly found in location blocks and access control files are `DirectoryIndex`, `Options`, and `ErrorDocument`:

- `DirectoryIndex` tells Apache which file to load when the URI contains a directory but not a filename. This directive doesn't work in `Files` blocks.

- `Options` is used to adjust how Apache handles files within a directory. The `Exec-CGI` option tells Apache that files in that directory can be run as CGI scripts, and the `Includes` option tells Apache that server-side includes (SSIs) are permitted. Another common option is the `Indexes` option, which tells Apache to generate a list of files if one of the filenames found in the `DirectoryIndex` setting is missing. An absolute list of options can be specified, or the list of options can be modified by adding + or - in front of an option name. See httpd.apache.org/docs/mod/core.html#options for more information.

- `ErrorDocument` directives can be used to specify a file containing messages to send to web clients when a particular error occurs. The location of the file is relative to the `/var/www` directory. The directive must specify an error code and the full URI for the error document. Possible error codes include `403` (access denied), `404` (file not found), and `500` (server internal error). You can find more information about the `ErrorDocument` directive at httpd.apache.org/docs/mod/core.html#errordocument. As an example, when a client requests a URL from the server that is not found, the following `ErrorDocument` line causes the 404 error code to send the client an error message that is listed in the `/var/www/error/HTTP_NOT_FOUND.html.var` file:

```
ErrorDocument 404 /error/HTTP_NOT_FOUND.html.var
```

Another common use for location blocks and access control files is to limit or expand access to a resource. The `Allow` directive can be used to permit access to matching hosts, and the `Deny` directive can be used to forbid it. Both of these options can occur more than once within a block and are handled based on the `Order` setting. Setting `Order` to `Deny,Allow` permits access to any host that is not listed in a `Deny` directive. A setting of `Allow,Deny` denies access to any host not allowed in an `Allow` directive.

As with most other options, the most specific `Allow` or `Deny` option for a host is used, meaning that you can `Deny` access to a range and `Allow` access to subsets of that range. By adding the `Satisfy` option and some additional parameters, you can add password authentication. For more information on `Allow` or `Deny`, `Satisfy`, or other directives, refer to the Apache Directive Index: httpd.apache.org/docs/current/mod/directives.html.

Understanding default settings

The reason you can start using your Apache web server as soon as you install it is that the `apache2.conf` file includes default settings that tell the server where to find web content, scripts, log files, and other items that the server needs to operate. It also includes settings that tell the server how many server processes to run at a time and how directory contents are displayed.

If you want to host a single website (such as for the www.example.com domain), you can simply add content to the `/var/www/html` directory and add the address of your website to a DNS server so that others can browse to it. You can then change directives, such as those described in the previous section, as needed.

To help you understand the settings that come in the default `apache2.conf` file, I've displayed some of those settings with descriptions in the following examples. I have removed comments and rearranged some of the settings for clarity.

The following settings show locations where the `apache` server is getting and putting content by default:

```
ServerRoot "/etc/apache2"
IncludeOptional conf-enabled/*.conf
IncludeOptional sites-enabled/*.conf
ErrorLog ${APACHE_LOG_DIR}/error.log
```

The `ServerRoot` directive identifies `/etc/apache2` as the location where configuration files are stored.

At the point in the file where the `Include` line appears, any files ending in `.conf` from the `/conf-enabled` and `/sites-enabled` subdirectories are included in the `apache2.conf` file. Configuration files are often associated with Apache modules (and are often included in the software package with a module) or with virtual host blocks (which you might add yourself to virtual host configurations in separate files). See the section "Adding a virtual host to Apache" later in this chapter.

As errors are encountered and content is served, messages about those activities are placed in files indicated by the `ErrorLog` and `CustomLog` entries. From the entries shown here (based on the contents of the `envars` file), those logs are stored in the `/var/log/apache2` directory. Here are some settings found in other configuration files, specifically, `sites-available/000-default.conf` and `conf-available/serve-cgi-bin.conf`:

```
DocumentRoot /var/www/html
ScriptAlias /cgi-bin/ /usr/lib/cgi-bin/
```

The `DocumentRoot` and `ScriptAlias` directives determine where content that is served by your `Apache` server is stored. Traditionally, you would place an `index.html` file in the `DocumentRoot` directory (`/var/www/html`, by default) as the home page and add other content as needed. The `ScriptAlias` directive tells the `httpd` daemon that any scripts requested from the `cgi-bin` directory should be found in the `/usr/lib/cgi-bin` directory. For example, a client could access a script located in `/usr/lib/cgi-bin/script.cgi` by entering a URL such as `http://www.example.com/cgi-bin/script.cgi`.

In addition to file locations, you can find other information in the `apache2.conf` file. Here are some examples:

```
User ${APACHE_RUN_USER}
Group ${APACHE_RUN_GROUP}
AccessFileName .htaccess
```

The `User` and `Group` directives tell Apache to run as `www-data` for both the user and group (again: based on the `APACHE_RUN_USER=www-data` and `APACHE_RUN_GROUP=www-data` values in the `envars` file).

An `AccessFileName` directive can be added to tell Apache to use the contents of the
`.htaccess` file if it exists in a directory to read in settings that apply to access to that
directory. For example, the file could be used to require password protection for the directory or to indicate that the contents of the directory should be displayed in certain ways.
For this file to work, however, a `Directory` container (described next) would have to have
`AllowOverride` opened. (By default, the `AllowOverride None` setting prevents the
`.htaccess` file from being used for any directives.)

The following `Directory` containers define behavior when the root directory (/), /var/
www, and /var/www/html directories are accessed:

```
<Directory />
    AllowOverride none
    Require all denied
</Directory>
<Directory "/var/www">
    AllowOverride None
    # Allow open access:
    Require all granted
</Directory>
<Directory "/var/www/html">
    Options Indexes FollowSymLinks
    AllowOverride None
    Require all granted
</Directory>
```

The first `Directory` container (/) indicates that if Apache tries to access any files in the
Linux filesystem, access is denied. The `AllowOverride none` directive prevents .htac-
cess files from overriding settings for that directory. Those settings apply to any subdirectories that are not defined in other `Directory` containers.

Content access is relaxed within the /var/www directory. Access is granted to content
added under that directory, but overriding settings is not allowed.

The /var/www/html `Directory` container follows symbolic links and does not allow
overrides. With `Require all granted` set, `httpd` doesn't prevent any access to
the server.

If all of the settings just described work for you, you can begin adding the content that you
want to the /var/www/html and /var/www/cgi-bin `html` directories. One reason you
might not be satisfied with the default setting is that you might want to serve content for
multiple domains (such as www.example.com, www.example.org, and www.example.net). To
do that, you need to configure virtual hosts. Virtual hosts, which are described in greater
detail in the next section, are a convenient (and almost essential) tool for serving different
content to clients based on the server address or name to which a request is directed. Most
global configuration options are applied to virtual hosts, but they can be overridden by
directives within the `VirtualHost` block.

Adding a virtual host to Apache

Apache supports the creation of separate websites within a single server to keep content separate. Individual sites are configured on the same server in what are referred to as *virtual hosts*.

Virtual hosts are really just a way to have the content for multiple domain names available from the same Apache server. Instead of needing to have one physical system to serve content for each domain, you can serve content for multiple domains from the same operating system.

An Apache server that is doing virtual hosting may have multiple domain names that resolve to the IP address of the server. The content that is served to a web client is based on the name used to access the server.

For example, if a client got to the server by requesting the name www.example.com, the client would be directed to a virtual host container that had its ServerName (found in the sites-available/000-default.conf file) set to respond to www.example.com. The container would provide the location of the content and possibly different error logs or Directory directives from the global settings. This way, each virtual host could be managed as if it were on a separate machine.

To use name-based virtual hosting, add as many VirtualHost containers as you like. Here's how to configure a virtual host:

> **NOTE**
> After you enable your first VirtualHost, your default DocumentRoot (/var/www/html) is no longer used if someone accesses the server by IP address or some name that is not set in a VirtualHost container. Instead, the first VirtualHost container is used as the default location for the server.

While you could create a new *.conf file for each domain, the "Ubuntu" way of doing things involves adding new definition blocks to the /etc/apache2/sites-available/000-default.conf file. Here's what two domain definitions on a single server might look like:

```
<VirtualHost *:80>
    ServerName example1.com
    DocumentRoot /var/www/html/example1/
    ServerAlias www.example1.com
</VirtualHost>

<VirtualHost *:80>
    ServerName example2.com
    DocumentRoot /var/www/html/example2/
    ServerAlias www.example2.com
</VirtualHost>
```

This example includes the following settings:

- The `*:80` specification in each `VirtualHost` block indicates to what address and port this virtual host applies. With multiple IP addresses associated with your Linux system, the `*` can be replaced by a specific IP address. The port is optional for `VirtualHost` specifications but should always be used to prevent interference with SSL virtual hosts (which use port 443 by default).

- The `ServerName` and `ServerAlias` lines tell Apache which names this virtual host should be recognized as, so replace them with names appropriate to your site. You can leave out the `ServerAlias` line if you do not have any alternate names for the server, and you can specify more than one name per `ServerAlias` line or have multiple `ServerAlias` lines if you have several alternate names. Believe it or not, www is an alias and is not considered the same as the domain name itself.

- The `DocumentRoot` specifies where the web documents (content served for this site) are stored. Although our examples show a subdirectory that was created under the default `DocumentRoot` (`/var/www/html`), you could point the configuration to any other location in your filesystem. Often, sites are attached to the home directories of specific users (such as `/home/chris/public_html`) so that each site can be managed by a different user.

With the host enabled, use `apachectl` to check the configuration, and then do a `graceful` restart:

```
# apachectl configtest
Syntax OK
# apachectl graceful
```

Provided that you have registered the system with a DNS server, a web browser should be able to access this website using either www.example1.com or www.example2.com. If that works, you can start adding other virtual hosts to the system as well.

Another way to extend the use of your website is to allow multiple users to share their own content on your server. You can enable users to add content that they want to share via your web server in a subdirectory of their home directories, as described in the next section.

> **NOTE**
>
> Keeping individual virtual hosts in separate files is a convenient way to manage them. However, you should be careful to keep your primary virtual host in a file that will be read before the others because the first virtual host receives requests for site names that don't match any in your configuration. In a commercial web-hosting environment, it is common to create a special default virtual host that contains an error message indicating that no site by that name has been configured.

17

Allowing users to publish their own web content

In situations where you do not have the ability to set up a virtual host for every user for whom you want to provide web space, you can easily make use of the mod_userdir module in Apache. With this module enabled (which it is not by default), the public_html directory under every user's home directory is available to the web at http:// servername/~username/.

For example, a user named wtucker on www.example.org stores web content in /home/ wtucker/public_html. That content would be available from http://www.example .org/~wtucker.

Make these changes to the /etc/apache2/mods-available/userdir.conf file to allow users to publish web content from their own home directories. Not all versions of Apache have these blocks in their httpd.conf file, so you might have to create them from scratch:

1. Edit the IfModule block and edit the Options and Require lines in the Directory block so that they look like this:

```
<IfModule mod_userdir.c>
        UserDir public_html
        UserDir disabled root
        <Directory /home/*/public_html>
                AllowOverride All
                Options MultiViews Indexes SymLinksIfOwnerMatch
                <Limit GET POST OPTIONS>
                        Require all granted
                </Limit>
                <LimitExcept GET POST OPTIONS>
                        Require all denied
                </LimitExcept>
        </Directory>
</IfModule>
```

2. Have your users create their own public_html directories in their own home directories:

```
$ mkdir $HOME/public_html
```

3. Set the execute permission (as root user) to allow the Apache daemon to access the home directory:

```
# chmod +x /home /home/*
```

4. Enable the usermod module:

```
# a2enmod userdir
Enabling module userdir.
To activate the new configuration, you need to run:
  systemctl restart apache2
```

5. Restart or reload Apache.

   At this point, you should be able to access content placed in a user's `public_html` directory by pointing a web browser to `http://hostname/~chris`.

Securing your web traffic with TLS

Any data that you share from your website using standard HTTP protocol is sent in clear text. This means that anyone who can watch the traffic on a network between your server and your client can view your unprotected data. To secure that information, you can add certificates to your site (so a client can validate who you are) and encrypt your data (so nobody can sniff your network and see your data).

Electronic commerce applications, such as online shopping and banking, must always be encrypted using the Transport Layer Security (TLS) specification. TLS is based on version 3.0 of the Secure Sockets Layer (SSL) specifications, so they are very similar in nature. Because of this similarity—and because SSL is older—the SSL acronym is often used to refer to either variety. For web connections, the SSL connection is established first, and then normal HTTP communication is tunneled through it.

> **NOTE**
> Because SSL negotiation takes place before any HTTP communication, name-based virtual hosting (which occurs at the HTTP layer) does not work easily with SSL. As a consequence, every SSL virtual host you configure should have a unique IP address. (See the Apache site for more information: `httpd.apache.org/docs/vhosts/name-based.html`.)

While you are establishing a connection between an SSL client and an SSL server, asymmetric (public key) cryptography is used to verify identities and establish the session parameters and the session key. A symmetric encryption algorithm is then used with the negotiated key to encrypt the data that are transmitted during the session. The use of asymmetric encryption during the handshaking phase allows safe communication without the use of a preshared key, and the symmetric encryption is faster and more practical for use on the session data.

For the client to verify the identity of the server, the server must have a previously generated private key as well as a certificate containing the public key and information about the server. This certificate must be verifiable using a public key that is known to the client.

Certificates are generally digitally signed by a third-party *certificate authority (CA)* that has verified the identity of the requester and the validity of the request to have the certificate signed. In most cases, the CA is a company that has made arrangements with the web browser vendor to have its own certificate installed and trusted by default client installations. The CA then charges the server operator for its services.

Commercial certificate authorities vary in price, features, and browser support, but remember that price is not always an indication of quality. Some popular CAs are InstantSSL (`www.instantssl.com`), Let's Encrypt (`www.letsencrypt.org`), and DigiCert (`www.digicert.com`).

You also have the option of creating self-signed certificates, although these should be used only for testing or when a very small number of people will be accessing your server, and you do not plan to have certificates on multiple machines. Directions for generating a self-signed certificate are included in the section "Generating an SSL key and self-signed certificate" later in this chapter.

The last option is to run your own certificate authority. This is probably practical only if you have a small number of expected users and the means to distribute your CA certificate to them (including assisting them with installing it in their browsers). The process for creating a CA is too elaborate to cover in this book, but it is a worthwhile alternative to generating self-signed certificates.

The following section describes how HTTPS communications are configured when you install the mod_ssl package. After that, I describe how to configure SSL communications better by generating your own SSL keys and certificates to use with the web server configured in this chapter.

Understanding how SSL is configured

It's important to understand how all this works, but for most people, as you'll soon see, you won't need to actually do this yourself any more.

If you have installed the mod_ssl package, a self-signed certificate and private key are created when the package is installed. This allows you to use HTTPS protocol immediately to communicate with the web server.

Although the default configuration of mod_ssl allows you to have encrypted communications between your web server and clients, because the certificate is self-signed, a client accessing your site is warned that the certificate is untrusted. To begin exploring the SSL configuration for your Apache web server, make sure that the mod_ssl package is installed on the server running your Apache (httpd) service:

```
# a2enmod ssl
Considering dependency setenvif for ssl:
Module setenvif already enabled
Considering dependency mime for ssl:
Module mime already enabled
Considering dependency socache_shmcb for ssl:
Enabling module socache_shmcb.
Enabling module ssl.
See /usr/share/doc/apache2/README.Debian.gz on how to configure SSL
and create self-signed certificates.
To activate the new configuration, you need to run:
  systemctl restart apache2
```

After installing the `mod_ssl` package and reloading the configuration file, you can test that the default certificate is working by following these steps:

1. Open a connection to the website from a web browser, using the HTTPS protocol. For example, if you are running Firefox on the system where the web server is running, type **https://localhost** into the location box and press Enter. This page warns you that there is no way of verifying the authenticity of this site. That is because there is no way to know who created the certificate that you are accepting.

2. Because you are accessing the site via a browser on the local host, click Advanced and then View to see the certificate that was generated. It includes your hostname, information on when the certificate was issued and when it expires, and other organization information.

3. Select Accept the Risk and Continue to allow connections to this site.

4. Close that window, and then select Confirm Security Exception to accept the connection. You should now see your default web page using HTTPS protocol. From now on, your browser will accept HTTPS connections to the web server using that certificate and encrypt all communications between the server and browser.

Because you don't want your website to scare off users, the best thing to do is to get a valid certificate to use with your site. The next best thing to do is to create a self-signed certificate that at least includes better information about your site and organization. The following section describes how to do that.

Generating an SSL key and self-signed certificate

To begin setting up SSL, use the `openssl` command, which is part of the `openssl` package, to generate your public and private key. After that, you can generate your own self-signed certificate to test the site or to use internally.

1. If the `openssl` package is not already installed, install it as follows:

```
# apt install openssl
```

2. Generate a 2048-bit RSA private key and save it to a file. You'll be asked to provide a passphrase. When that's done, you'll set the key filenames.

```
$ openssl genrsa -des3 -out server.key 2048
Generating RSA private key, 2048 bit long modulus (2 primes)
.......................................................+++++
........+++++
e is 65537 (0x010001)
Enter pass phrase for server.key:
140238233633216:error:28078065:UI routines:UI_set_result_ex:result
too small:../crypto/ui/ui_lib.c:903:You must type in 4 to 1023
characters
Enter pass phrase for server.key:
```

Continues

Continued

```
Verifying - Enter pass phrase for server.key:
$ openssl rsa -in server.key -out server.key.insecure
Enter pass phrase for server.key:
writing RSA key
$ mv server.key server.key.secure
$ mv server.key.insecure server.key
```

> **NOTE**
>
> You can use a filename other than `server.key` and should do so if you plan to have more than one SSL host on your machine (which requires more than one IP address). Just make sure that you specify the correct filename in the Apache configuration later.

3. If you want to request a certificate from a traditional certificate authority (CA), you can generate the request file using the `openssl req` command. You'll answer the questions so OpenSSL can populate the request file with the appropriate values that reflect your organization.

```
$ openssl req -new -key server.key -out server.csr
139789130899904:error:2406F079:random number generator:RAND_load_file:
Cannot open file:../crypto/rand/randfile.c:88:Filename=/root/.rnd
You are about to be asked to enter information that will be
incorporated
into your certificate request.
What you are about to enter is what is called a Distinguished
Name or a DN.
There are quite a few fields but you can leave some blank.
For some fields there will be a default value,
If you enter '.', the field will be left blank.
-----
Country Name (2 letter code) [AU]:CA
State or Province Name (full name) [Some-State]:Ontario
Locality Name (eg, city) []:Toronto
Organization Name (eg, company) [Internet Widgits Pty
Ltd]:Bootstrap IT
Organizational Unit Name (eg, section) []:
Common Name (e.g. server FQDN or YOUR name) []:
Email Address []:info@bootstrap-it.com

Please enter the following 'extra' attributes
to be sent with your certificate request
A challenge password []:
An optional company name []:
```

4. As our goal here is to create a self-signed certificate, you'll run this command, which will generate a .csr file:

```
$ openssl x509 -req -days 365 -in server.csr -signkey server.key
-out server.crt
Signature ok
subject=C = CA, ST = Ontario, L = Toronto, O = Bootstrap IT,
emailAddress = info@bootstrap-it.com
Getting Private key
```

5. The final step is to install that certificate on your local server (as the root user):

```
# cp server.crt /etc/ssl/certs
# cp server.key /etc/ssl/private
```

You'll need to tell Apache about the new certificate. You do that by editing the /etc/apache2/sites-available/default-ssl.conf file so that the SSLCertificate-File and SSLCertificateKeyFile lines look like this:

```
SSLCertificateFile      /etc/ssl/certs/server.crt
SSLCertificateKeyFile /etc/ssl/private/server.key
```

Don't forget to restart Apache. For internal use or testing, a self-signed certificate might work for you. However, for public websites, you should use a certificate that is validated by a certificate authority (CA). The procedure for doing that is covered next.

Generating a certificate signing request

Once upon a time, CAs would issue you valid certificates when you manually sent them a request—and some money. However some years ago, the tech industry–supported Let's Encrypt project (www.letsencrypt.org) was created to convince as many website owners as possible to add valid encryption to their site configurations. Since then, things have become much simpler. And adding encryption won't cost you anything.

To make it all happen, the Electronic Frontier Foundation created a tool called Certbot that will manage all the configuration heavy lifting for you. You get started by going to the Certbot instructions page (certbot.eff.org/instructions). You'll be asked what software and OS you're using; you'll choose Apache and the appropriate release of Ubuntu. As you can see in Figure 17.3, the appropriate instructions will appear below on the page.

Those instructions will show you how to add the Certbot PPA to your repositories and then install the certbot and python-cerbot-apache packages:

```
# apt-get update
# apt-get install software-properties-common
# add-apt-repository universe
# add-apt-repository ppa:certbot/certbot
# apt-get update
# apt-get install certbot python-certbot-apache
```

All that will remain for you is to run the certbot tool specifying Apache as your web server and answering the questions you're asked. The tool will create and configure any

Apache files that need updating. When you're done—and assuming you've configured your domain to correctly point to your server—you'll have an enterprise-strength HTTPS server.

```
# certbot --apache
```

FIGURE 17.3

The Certbot instructions page

Troubleshooting Your Web Server

In any complex environment, you occasionally run into problems. The following sections include tips for isolating and resolving the most common errors that you may encounter.

Checking for configuration errors

You may occasionally run into configuration errors or script problems that prevent Apache from starting or that prevent specific files from being accessible. Most of these problems can be isolated and resolved using two Apache-provided tools: the apachectl program and the system error log.

When encountering a problem, first use the `apachectl` program with the `configtest` parameter to test the configuration. In fact, it's a good idea to develop the habit of running this every time you make a configuration change:

```
# apachectl configtest
Syntax OK
# apachectl graceful
/usr/sbin/apachectl graceful: httpd gracefully restarted
```

In the event of a syntax error, `apachectl` indicates where the error occurs and also does its best to give a hint about the nature of the problem. You can then use the `graceful` restart option (`apachectl graceful`) to instruct Apache to reload its configuration without disconnecting any active clients.

> **NOTE**
>
> The `graceful` restart option in `apachectl` automatically tests the configuration before sending the reload signal to `apache`, but getting in the habit of running the manual configuration test after making any configuration changes is still a good idea.

Some configuration problems pass the syntax tests performed by `apachectl` but cause the HTTP daemon to exit immediately after reloading its configuration. If this happens, use the `tail` command to check Apache's error log for useful information. The error log is in /var/log/apache2/error.log.

You might encounter an error message that looks something like this:

```
[crit] (98)Address already in use: make_sock: could not bind to port 80
```

This error often indicates that something else is bound to port 80, that another Apache process is already running (`apachectl` usually catches this), or that you have told Apache to bind the same IP address and port combination in more than one place.

You can use the `netstat` command to view the list of programs (including Apache) with TCP ports in the `LISTEN` state:

```
# netstat -nltp
Active Internet connections (only servers)
Proto  Local Address  Foreign Address  State   PID/Program name
tcp6   :::80          :::*             LISTEN  2105/httpd
```

The output from `netstat` (which was shortened to fit here) indicates that an instance of the `httpd` process with a process ID of 2105 is listening (as indicated by the `LISTEN` state) for connections to any local IP address (indicated by `:::80`) on port 80 (the standard HTTP port). If a different program is listening to port 80, it is shown there. You can use the `kill` command to terminate the process, but if it is something other than `httpd`, you should also find out why it is running.

If you don't see any other processes listening on port 80, it could be that you have accidentally told Apache to listen on the same IP address and port combination in more than one place. Three configuration directives can be used for this: BindAddress, Port, and Listen.

- BindAddress enables you to specify a single IP address on which to listen, or you can specify all IP addresses using the * wildcard. You should never have more than one BindAddress statement in your configuration file.
- Port specifies on which TCP port to listen, but it does not enable you to specify the IP address. Port is generally not used more than once in the configuration.
- Listen enables you to specify both an IP address and a port to bind to. The IP address can be in the form of a wildcard, and you can have multiple Listen statements in your configuration file.

To avoid confusion, it is generally a good idea to use only one of these directive types. Of the three, Listen is the most flexible, so it is probably the one you want to use the most. A common error when using Listen is to specify a port on all IP addresses (*:80) as well as that same port on a specific IP address (1.2.3.4:80), which results in the error from make_sock.

Configuration errors relating to SSL commonly result in Apache starting improperly. Make sure that all key and certificate files exist and that they are in the proper format (use openssl to examine them).

For other error messages, try doing a web search to see whether somebody else has encountered the problem. In most cases, you can find a solution within the first few matches.

If you aren't getting enough information in the ErrorLog, you can configure it to log more information using the LogLevel directive. The options available for this directive, in increasing order of verbosity, are emerg, alert, crit, error, warn, notice, info, and debug. Select only one of these.

Any message that is at least as important as the LogLevel that you select is stored in the ErrorLog. On a typical server, LogLevel is set to warn. You should not set it to any value lower than crit, and you should avoid leaving it set to debug because that can slow down the server and result in a very large ErrorLog.

As a last resort, you can also try running apache2 -X manually to check for crashes or other error messages. The -X runs Apache so that it displays debug and higher messages on the screen.

Access forbidden and server internal errors

The two common types of errors that you may encounter when attempting to view specific pages on your server are permission errors and server internal errors. Both types of errors can usually be isolated using the information in the error log. After making any of the changes described in the following list to attempt to solve one of these problems, try the request again and check the error log to see whether the message has changed (for example, to show that the operation completed successfully).

File permissions   A "File permissions prevent access" error indicates that the `apache2` process is running as a user that is unable to open the requested file. By default, `apache2` is run by the `www-data` user and group. Make sure that the account has execute permissions on the directory and every directory above it as well as read permissions on the files themselves. Read permissions on a directory are also necessary if you want Apache to generate an index of files. See the manual page for `chmod` for more information about how to view and change permissions.

Access denied   A "Client denied by server configuration" error indicates that Apache was configured to deny access to the object. Check the configuration files for `Location` and `Directory` sections that might affect the file that you are trying to access. Remember that settings applied to a path are also applied to any paths below it. You can override these by changing the permissions only for the more specific path to which you want to allow access.

Index not found   The "Directory index forbidden by rule" error indicates that Apache could not find an index file with a name specified in the `DirectoryIndex` directive and was configured not to create an index containing a list of files in a directory. Make sure that your index page, if you have one, has one of the names specified in the relevant `DirectoryIndex` directive, or add an `Options Indexes` line to the appropriate `Directory` or `Location` section for that object.

Script crashed   "Premature end of script headers" errors can indicate that a script is crashing before it finishes. On occasion, the errors that caused this also show up in the error log. When using `suexec` or `suPHP`, this error may also be caused by a file ownership or permissions error. These errors appear in log files in the `/var/log/apache2` directory

Summary

The open source Apache project is the world's most popular web server. Although Apache offers tremendous flexibility, security, and complexity, a basic Apache web server can be configured in just a few minutes.

The chapter described the steps for installing, configuring, securing, and troubleshooting a basic Apache web server. You learned how to configure virtual hosting and secure SSL hosts. You also learned how to configure Apache to allow any user account on the system to publish content from their own `public_html` directory.

Continuing on the topic of server configuration, in Chapter 18, "Configuring an FTP Server," you will learn how to set up an FTP server in Linux. The examples illustrate how to configure an FTP server using the `vsftpd` package.

Exercises

The exercises in this section cover topics related to installing and configuring an Apache web server. As usual, I recommend that you use a spare system to do the exercises. Don't do these exercises on a production machine because these exercises modify the Apache configuration files and service, and they could damage services that you have currently configured. Try to use a virtual machine or find a computer where it will do no harm to interrupt services on the system.

These exercises assume that you are starting with an Ubuntu installation on which the Apache server (`apache2` package) is not yet installed.

If you are stuck, solutions to the tasks are shown in Appendix A. These show you one approach to each task, although Linux may offer multiple ways to complete a task.

1. From an Ubuntu machine, install Apache.
2. Create a file called `index.html` in the directory assigned to `DocumentRoot` in the main Apache configuration file. The file should have the words "My Own Web Server" inside.
3. Start the Apache web server and set it to start up automatically at boot time. Check that it is available from a web browser on your local host.
4. Use the `netstat` command to see on which ports the `httpd` server is listening.
5. Try to connect to your Apache web server from a web browser that is outside of the local system. If it fails, correct any problems that you encounter by investigating the firewall and other security features.
6. Using the `openssl` or similar command, create your own private RSA key and self-signed SSL certificate.

7. Configure your Apache web server to use your key and self-signed certificate to serve secure (HTTPS) content.

8. Use a web browser to create an HTTPS connection to your web server and view the contents of the certificate that you created.

9. Add the text joe.example.org to the end of the localhost entry in your /etc/ hosts file on the machine that is running the web server. Then type **http://joe .example.org** into the location box of your web browser. You should see "Welcome to the House of Joe" when the page is displayed.

17

Configuring an FTP Server

IN THIS CHAPTER

Learning how FTP works

Getting a `vsftpd` server installed

Choosing security settings for `vsftpd`

Setting up `vsftpd` configuration files

Running FTP clients

The *File Transfer Protocol (FTP)* is one of the oldest protocols in existence for sharing files over networks. Although there are more secure protocols for network file sharing, FTP is still sometimes used for making files available on the Internet.

Several FTP server projects are available with Linux today. However, the one often used with Ubuntu and other Linux distributions is the Very Secure FTP Daemon (`vsftpd` package). This chapter describes how to install, configure, use, and secure an FTP server using the `vsftpd` package.

Understanding FTP

FTP operates in a client/server model. An FTP server daemon listens for incoming requests on TCP port 21 from FTP clients. The client presents a login and password. If the server accepts the login information, the client can interactively traverse the filesystem, list files and directories, and then download (and sometimes upload) files.

What makes FTP insecure is that everything sent between the FTP client and server is done in clear text. The FTP protocol was created at a time when most computer communication was done on private lines or over dial-up, where encryption was not thought to be critical. If you use FTP over a public network, someone sniffing the line anywhere between the client and server would be able to see not only the data being transferred but also the authentication process (login and password information).

So, FTP is not good for sharing files privately (use SSH commands such as sftp, scp, or rsync if you need private, encrypted file transfers). However, if you are sharing public documents, open source software repositories, or other openly available data, FTP is a good choice. Regardless of the operating system people use, they surely have an FTP file transfer application available to get files that you offer from your FTP server.

When users authenticate to an FTP server in Linux, their usernames and passwords are authenticated against the standard Linux user accounts and passwords. There is also a special, non-authenticated account used by the FTP server called anonymous. The anonymous account can be accessed by anyone because it does not require a valid password. In fact, the term *anonymous FTP server* is often used to describe a public FTP server that does not require (or even allow) authentication of a legitimate user account.

After the authentication phase (on the control port, TCP port 21), a second connection is made between the client and server. FTP supports both active and passive connection types. With an *active FTP connection*, the server sends data from its TCP port 20 to some random port the server chooses above port 1023 on the client. With a *passive FTP connection*, the client requests the passive connection and requests a random port from the server.

Many browsers support passive FTP mode so that if the client has a firewall, it doesn't block the data port that the FTP server might use in active mode. Supporting passive mode requires some extra work on the server's firewall to allow random connections to ports above 1023 on the server.

After the connection is established between the client and server, the client's current directory is established. For the anonymous user, the /srv/ftp directory is the home directory. The anonymous user cannot go outside of the /srv/ftp directory structure. If a regular user, let's say joe, logs in to the FTP server, /home/joe is joe's current directory, but joe can change to any part of the filesystem for which he has permission.

Command-oriented FTP clients (such as lftp and ftp commands) go into an interactive mode after connecting to the server. From the prompt, you can run many commands that are similar to those that you would use from the shell. You could use pwd to see your current directory, ls to list directory contents, and cd to change directories. When you see a file that you want, you use the get and put commands to download files from or upload them to the server, respectively.

With graphical tools for accessing FTP servers (such as a web browser), you type the URL of the site that you want to visit (such as ftp://docs.example.com) into the location box of the browser. If you don't add a username or password, an anonymous connection is made, and the contents of the home directory of the site are displayed. Click links to directories to change to those directories. Click links to files to display or download those files to your local system.

Armed with some understanding of how FTP works, you are now ready to install an FTP server (vsftpd package) on your Linux system.

Installing the vsftpd FTP Server

Setting up the Very Secure FTP server requires only one package in Ubuntu: vsftpd. Assuming you have a connection to your software repository, just type the following as root:

```
# apt install vsftpd
```

If you want to get more information about vsftpd, follow the URL listed to the related website (security.appspot.com/vsftpd.html). You can get additional documentation and information about the latest revisions of vsftpd.

To see the documentation files in the vsftpd package, visit the /usr/share/doc/vsftpd directory:

```
$ ls /usr/share/doc/vsftpd
AUDIT          NEWS.Debian.gz    README.ssl    SPEED                copyright
BENCHMARKS     README            REWARD        TODO                 examples
BUGS           README.Debian     SECURITY      TUNING
FAQ.gz         README.security   SIZE          changelog.Debian.gz
```

In the /usr/share/doc/vsftpd/examples directory structure, there are sample configuration files included to help you configure vsftpd in ways that are appropriate for an Internet site, multiple IP address site, and virtual hosts. The main /usr/share/doc/vsftpd directory contains an FAQ (frequently asked questions), installation tips, and version information.

The man pages might have the most useful information when you set out to configure the vsftpd server. Type **man vsftpd.conf** to read about the configuration file and **man vsftpd** to read about the daemon process and how to manage it as a systemd service.

To list the configuration files, type the following:

```
$ cat /var/lib/dpkg/info/vsftpd.conffiles
/etc/ftpusers
/etc/init.d/vsftpd
/etc/logrotate.d/vsftpd
/etc/pam.d/vsftpd
/etc/vsftpd.conf
```

The main configuration file is /etc/vsftpd.conf. The ftpusers file in the same directory stores information about user accounts that are restricted from accessing the server. The /etc/pam.d/vsftpd file sets how authentication is done to the FTP server. The /etc/logrotate.d/vsftpd file configures how log files are rotated over time.

Now you have vsftpd installed and have taken a quick look at its contents. The next step is to start up and test the vsftpd service.

18

Controlling the vsftpd Service

No configuration or manual launch is required to start the `vsftpd` service if you just want to use the default settings. This is what the default values will give you:

- The `vsftpd` service starts the `vsftpd` daemon, which runs in the background.
- The standard port on which the `vsftpd` daemon listens is TCP port 21. By default, data is transferred to the user, after the connection is made, on TCP port 20. TCP port 21 must be open in the firewall to allow new connections to access the service. Both IPv4 and IPv6 connections are available by default. This procedure changes to the TCP IPv4 service.
- The `vsftpd` daemon reads `vsftpd.conf` to determine what features the service allows.
- Linux user accounts (excluding administrative users) can access the FTP server. The anonymous user account (no password required) can be enabled.
- The anonymous user has access only to the `/srv/ftp` directory and its subdirectories. A regular user starts with their home directory as the current directory but can access any directory to which the user would be able to gain access via a regular login or SSH session. Lists of users in the `/etc/ftpusers` file define some administrative and special users who do not have access to the FTP server (root, bin, daemon, and others).
- By default, the anonymous user can neither download files from the server nor upload them. A regular user can upload or download files, based on regular Linux permissions.
- Log messages detailing file uploads or downloads are written in the `/var/log/vsftpd.log` file. Those log messages are stored in a standard xferlog format.

Once you're happy with your configurations, you control the `vsftp` life cycle the usual systemd way, using `systemctl start`, `stop`, `enable`, and `status`:

```
$ systemctl status vsftpd
• vsftpd.service - vsftpd FTP server
   Loaded: loaded (/lib/systemd/system/vsftpd.service; enabled;
vendor preset: e
   Active: active (running) since Thu 2020-04-02 20:17:34 UTC; 25min ago
 Main PID: 3294 (vsftpd)
    Tasks: 1 (limit: 4915)
   CGroup: /system.slice/vsftpd.service
           └─3294 /usr/sbin/vsftpd /etc/vsftpd.conf

Apr 02 20:17:34 apache systemd[1]: Starting vsftpd FTP server...
Apr 02 20:17:34 apache systemd[1]: Started vsftpd FTP server.
```

You could check that the service is running using the `netstat` command:

```
# netstat -tupln | grep vsftpd
tcp6    0    0 :::21    :::*    LISTEN        3294/vsftpd
```

From the `netstat` output, you can see that the `vsftpd` process (process ID of 3294) is listening (`LISTEN`) on all IP addresses for incoming connections on port 21 (0.0.0.0:21) for the TCP (`tcp6`) protocol.

You'll need to enable anonymous access. To do that, edit the `anonymous_enable` line in the /etc/vsftpd.conf file to read:

```
anonymous_enable=YES
```

You'll then need to restart the service using `systemctl`. A quick way to check that vsftpd is working is to put a file in the /srv/ftp directory and try to open it from your web browser on the local host:

```
# echo "Hello From Your New FTP Server" > /srv/ftp/hello.txt
```

From a web browser on the local system, type the following into the location box of Brave or another browser:

```
ftp://localhost/hello.txt
```

If the text `Hello From Your New FTP Server` appears in the web browser (or you get a prompt to download it), the `vsftpd` server is working and accessible from your local system. Next, try this again from a web browser on another system on your network, replacing `localhost` with your host's IP address or fully qualified hostname. If that works, the `vsftpd` server is publicly accessible. If it doesn't, which it quite possibly may not, you need to open firewalls and modify other security features to allow access and otherwise secure your FTP server.

Securing your FTP server

Even though it is easy to get a `vsftpd` FTP server started, that doesn't mean that it is immediately fully accessible. If you have a firewall in place on your Linux system, it is probably blocking access to all services on your system except for those that you have explicitly allowed.

If you decide that the default `vsftpd` configuration works for you as described in the previous section, you can set to work allowing the appropriate access and providing security for your `vsftpd` service. To help you secure your `vsftpd` server, the next section describes how to configure your system to prevent unauthorized resource access.

Consult Chapter 24, "Enhancing Linux Security with AppArmor," and Chapter 25, "Securing Linux on a Network," for more details about safely controlling access to your services.

Integrating Linux file permissions with vsftpd

The vsftpd server relies on standard Linux file permissions to allow or deny access to files and directories. As you would expect, for an anonymous user to view or download a file, at least read permission must be open for other (------r--). To access a directory, at least execute permission must be on for other (--------x).

For regular user accounts, the general rule is that if a user can access a file from the shell, that user can access the same file from an FTP server. So, typically, regular users should at least be able to get (download) and put (upload) files to and from their own home directories, respectively. After permissions and other security provisions are in place for your FTP server, you may want to consider other configuration settings for your FTP server.

Configuring Your FTP Server

Most of the configuration for the vsftpd service is done in the /etc/vsftpd.conf file. Examples of vsftpd.conf for different types of sites are included in the /usr/share/doc/vsftpd directory. Depending on how you want to use your FTP site, the following sections discuss a few ways to configure your FTP server.

Remember to restart the vsftpd service after making any configuration changes.

Setting up user access

The vsftpd server comes with all local Linux users (those listed in the /etc/passwd file) configured to access the server and the anonymous user prevented. This is based on the following vsftpd.conf settings:

```
anonymous_enable=NO
local_enable=YES
```

Some web server hosts let users use FTP to upload the content for their own web servers. In some cases, the users have FTP-only accounts, meaning that they cannot log in to a shell, but they can log in via FTP to manage their content. Creating a user account that has no default shell (actually, /usr/sbin/nologin) is how you can keep a user from logging in to a shell but still allow FTP access. For example, the /etc/passwd entry for the FTP-only user account bill might look something like the following:

```
bill:x:1000:1000:Bill Jones:/home/bill:/usr/sbin/nologin
```

With the user account set with /usr/sbin/nologin as the default shell, any attempts to log in from a console or via ssh as the user bill are denied. However, as long as bill has a password and local account access to the FTP server is enabled, bill should be able to log in to the FTP server via an FTP client.

Not every user with an account on the Linux system has access to the FTP server. You can add the setting userlist_enable=YES to the end of vsftpd.conf to deny access to the FTP server to all accounts listed in the /etc/ftpusers file. That list includes administrative users root, bin, daemon, adm, lp, and others. You can add to that list other users to whom you would like to deny access.

If you change userlist_enable to NO, the user_list file becomes a list of only those users who do have access to the server. In other words, setting userlist_enable=NO, removing all usernames from the user_list file, and adding the usernames chris, joe, and mary to that file cause the server to allow only those three users to log in to the server.

No matter how the value of userlist_enable is set, the /etc/ftpusers file always includes users who are denied access to the server. Like the userlist_enable file, the ftpusers file includes a list of administrative users. You can add more users to that file if you want them to be denied FTP access.

One way to limit access to users with regular user accounts on your system is to use chroot settings. Here are examples of some chroot settings:

```
chroot_local_user=YES
chroot_list_enable=YES
chroot_list_file=/etc/chroot_list
```

With the settings just shown uncommented, you could create a list of local users and add them to a /etc/vsftpd.chroot_list file. After one of those users logged in, that user would be prevented from going to places in the system that were outside of that user's home directory structure.

If uploads to your FTP server are allowed, the directories a user tries to upload to must be writeable by that user. However, uploads can be stored under a username other than that of the user who uploaded the file. This is one of the features discussed next, in the section "Allowing uploading."

Allowing uploading

To allow any form of writing to the vsftpd server, you must have write_enable=YES set in the vsftpd.conf file (which it is, by default). Because of that, if local accounts are enabled, users can log in and immediately begin uploading files to their own home directories. However, anonymous users are denied the ability to upload files by default.

To allow anonymous uploads with vsftpd, you must have the first option in the following code example, and you may want the second line of code as well (both can be enabled by uncommenting them from the vsftpd.conf file). The first allows anonymous users to upload files; the second allows them to create directories:

```
anon_upload_enable=YES
anon_mkdir_write_enable=YES
```

The next step is to create a directory where anonymous users can write. Any directory under the /srv/ftp directory that has write permissions for the user ftp, the ftp group, or other can be written to by an anonymous user. A common thing is to create an uploads

18

directory with permission open for writing. The following are examples of commands to run on the server:

```
# mkdir /srv/ftp/uploads
# chown ftp:ftp /srv/ftp/uploads
# chmod 775 /srv/ftp/uploads
```

As long as the firewall is open, an anonymous user can cd to the uploads directory and put a file from the user's local system into the uploads directory. On the server, the file would be owned by the ftp user and ftp group. The permissions set on the directory (775) would allow you to see the files that were uploaded but not change or overwrite them.

One reason for allowing anonymous FTP, and then enabling it for anonymous uploads, is to allow people you don't know to drop files into your uploads folder. Because anyone who can find the server can write to this directory, some form of security needs to be in place. You want to prevent an anonymous user from seeing files uploaded by other users, taking files, or deleting files uploaded by other anonymous FTP users. One form of security is the chown feature of FTP.

By setting the following two values, you can allow anonymous uploads. The result of these settings is that when an anonymous user uploads a file, that file is immediately assigned ownership of a different user. The following is an example of some chown settings that you could put in your vsftpd.conf file to use with your anonymous upload directory:

```
chown_uploads=YES
chown_username=joe
```

If an anonymous user were to upload a file after vsftpd was restarted with these settings, the uploaded file would be owned by the user joe and the ftp group. Permissions would be read/write for the owner and nothing for anyone else (rw-------).

So far, you have seen configuration options for individual features on your vsftpd server. Some sets of vsftp.conf variables can work together in ways that are appropriate for certain kinds of FTP sites. The next section contains one of these examples, represented by a sample vsftpd.conf configuration file that comes with the vsftpd package. That file can be copied from a directory of sample files to the /etc/vsftpd.conf file to use for an FTP server that is available on the Internet.

Setting up vsftpd for the Internet

To share files from your FTP server safely to the Internet, you can lock down your server by limiting it only to allow downloads and only from anonymous users. To start with a configuration that is designed to share vsftpd files safely over the Internet, back up your current /etc/vsftpd.conf file and copy this file to overwrite your vsftpd.conf:

```
/usr/share/doc/vsftpd/examples/INTERNET_SITE/vsftpd.conf
```

The following paragraphs describe the contents of that `vsftpd.conf`. Settings in the first section set the access rights for the server:

```
# Access rights
anonymous_enable=YES
local_enable=NO
write_enable=NO
anon_upload_enable=NO
anon_mkdir_write_enable=NO
anon_other_write_enable=NO
```

Turning on `anonymous_enable` (YES) and turning off `local_enable` (NO) ensures that no one can log in to the FTP server using a regular Linux user account. Everyone must come in through the anonymous account. No one can upload files (`write_enable=NO`). Then, the anonymous user cannot upload files (`anon_upload_enable=NO`), create directories (`anon_mkdir_write_enable=NO`), or otherwise write to the server (`anon_other_write_enable=NO`). Here are the security settings:

```
# Security
anon_world_readable_only=YES
connect_from_port_20=YES
hide_ids=YES
pasv_min_port=50000
pasv_max_port=60000
```

Because the `vsftpd` daemon can read files assigned to the `ftp` user and group, setting `anon_world_readable_only=YES` ensures that anonymous users can see files where the read permission bit is turned on for `other` (`------r--`) but not write files. The `connect_from_port_20=YES` setting gives the `vsftpd` daemon slightly more permission to send data the way a client might request by allowing PORT-style data communications.

Using `hide_ids=YES` hides the real permissions set on files, so to the user accessing the FTP site, everything appears to be owned by the `ftp` user. The two `pasv` settings restrict the range of ports that can be used with passive FTP (where the server picks a higher number port on which to send data) to between 50000 and 60000.

The next section contains features of the `vsftpd` server:

```
# Features
xferlog_enable=YES
ls_recurse_enable=NO
ascii_download_enable=NO
async_abor_enable=YES
```

With `xferlog_enable=YES`, all file transfers to and from the server are logged to the `/var/log/vsftpd.log` file. Setting `ls_recurse_enable=NO` prevents users from recursively listing the contents of an FTP directory (in other words, it prevents the type of

18

listing that you could get with the `ls -R` command) because on a large site, that could drain resources. Disabling ASCII downloads forces all downloads to be in binary mode (preventing files from being translated in ASCII, which is inappropriate for binary files). The `async_abor_enable=YES` setting ensures that some FTP clients, which might hang when aborting a transfer, will not hang.

The following settings have an impact on performance:

```
# Performance
one_process_model=YES
idle_session_timeout=120
data_connection_timeout=300
accept_timeout=60
connect_timeout=60
anon_max_rate=50000
```

With `one_process_model=YES` set, performance can improve because `vsftpd` launches one process per connection. Reducing the `idle_session_timeout` from the default 300 seconds to 120 seconds causes FTP clients that are idle more than 2 minutes to be disconnected. Thus, less time is spent managing FTP sessions that are no longer in use. If a data transfer stalls for more than `data_connection_timeout` seconds (300 seconds here), the connection to the client is dropped.

The `accept_timeout` setting of 60 seconds allows 1 minute for a PASV connection to be accepted by the remote client. The `connect_timeout` sets how long a remote client has to respond to a request to establish a PORT-style data connection. Limiting the transfer rate to 50000 (bytes per second) with `anon_max_rate` can improve overall performance of the server by limiting how much bandwidth each client can consume.

Using FTP Clients to Connect to Your Server

Many client programs come with Linux, which you can use to connect to your FTP server. If you simply want to do an anonymous download of some files from an FTP server, any modern web browser will provide an easy interface to do that. For more complex interactions between your FTP client and server, you can use command-line FTP clients. The following sections describe some of these tools.

Accessing an FTP server from a browser

A web browser provides a quick and easy way to test access to your FTP server or to access any public FTP server. On your own system, type **ftp://localhost** into the location box. You are prompted to log in, which you can do as a regular user or the anonymous user if your server is accessible via anonymous FTP. As the anonymous user, you should see something similar to the example shown in Figure 18.1.

FIGURE 18.1

Accessing a remote FTP server from the Brave browser

To log in to an FTP server as a particular user from your browser, you can precede the host-name with a username:password@ notation, as shown in the following example of logging in to a local server:

```
ftp://chris:MypassWd5@localhost
```

If you provide the correct username and password, you should immediately see the contents of your home directory. Click a folder to open it. Click a file to download or view the file.

Accessing an FTP server with the lftp command

To test your FTP server from the command line, you can use the lftp command. To install the lftp command in Ubuntu, enter the following from the command line:

```
# apt install lftp
```

If you use the lftp command with just the name of the FTP server you're trying to access, the command tries to connect to the FTP server as the anonymous user. This example logs in to a local server as anonymous:

```
$ lftp localhost
lftp localhost:~> ls
```

Continues

Continued

```
-rwxrwxrwx    1 0          0              31 Apr 02 20:48 Hello.txt
lftp localhost:/>
```

By adding the -u *username*, you can enter the user's password when prompted and gain access to the FTP server as the user you logged in as.

After you have added your user and password information, you get an lftp prompt, ready for you to start typing commands:

```
$ lftp localhost -u ubuntu
Password:
lftp ubuntu@localhost:~> ls
drwxrwxr-x    4 1000       1000           4096 Apr 02 13:40 my-ca
drwxr-xr-x    2 1000       1000           4096 Apr 01 23:49 public_html
lftp ubuntu@localhost:~>
```

The connection is made to the server when you type your first command. You can use the commands to move around the FTP server and then use the get and put commands to download and upload files.

The following example shows how to use commands as just described. It assumes that the FTP server (and associated security measures) has been configured to allow local users to connect and to read and write files:

```
$ lftp -u ubuntu localhost
Password:
lftp ubuntu@localhost:~> pwd
ftp://ubuntu@localhost
lftp ubuntu@localhost:~> !pwd
/home/ubuntu
lftp ubuntu@localhost:~> ls
drwxr-xr-x    3 1000       1000              4096 Apr 27 23:36 aws
-rw-rw-r--    1 1000       1000          32738339 May 05 13:46 awscliv2.zip
drwxrwxr-x    3 1000       1000              4096 May 01 21:18 cloud
-rw-rw-r--    1 1000       1000               101 May 05 15:09 my_script.txt
-r--------    1 1000       1000              1671 May 05 14:23
newcluster.pem
-rw-rw-r--    1 1000       1000               368 May 05 14:45 script.yaml
lftp ubuntu@localhost:~> !ls
aws  awscliv2.zip  cloud  my_script.txt  newcluster.pem  script.yaml
```

After providing the username (-u ubuntu), lftp prompts for the ubuntu user's password. Typing **!pwd** shows that ubuntu is logged in to the local host and that /home/ubuntu is the current directory. Just as you would from a regular Linux command-line shell, you can use cd to change to another directory and ls to list that directory's contents. The ! character runs your command on the client system. As this example is run locally, the remote and client directories are the same.

This is good to know because if you get a file from the server without specifying its destination, it goes to the client's current directory (in this case, /root). Other commands you might run so that they are interpreted by the client system include !cd (to change directories) and !ls (to list files).

Assuming that you have read permission for a file on the server and write permission from the current directory on the initiating system, you can use the get command to download a file from the server (get survey-20141023.txt). If you have write and upload permission on the current directory on the server, you can use put to copy a file to the server (put /etc/hosts).

Running an ls command shows that the /etc/hosts file was uploaded to the server. Running the !ls command lets you see that the survey-20141023.txt file was downloaded from the server to the initiating system.

Using the gFTP client

Many other FTP clients are available with Linux as well. Another FTP client that you could try is gFTP. The gFTP client provides an interface that lets you see both the local and remote sides of your FTP session. To install gFTP in Ubuntu, run the following command to install the gftp package:

```
# apt install gftp
```

To start gFTP, launch it from the applications menu or run gftp & from the shell. To use it, type the URL of the FTP server to which you wish to connect, enter the username you want to use (such as anonymous), and press Enter. Figure 18.2 shows an example of gFTP being used to connect to an FTP site on my network.

18

FIGURE 18.2

The gFTP FTP client lets you see both sides of an FTP session.

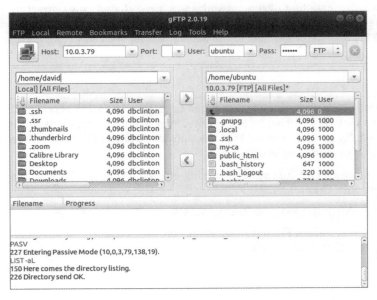

To traverse the FTP site from gFTP, just double-click folders (as you would from a file manager window). The full paths to the local directory (on the left) and remote directory (on the right) are shown above the listings of files and folders below.

To transfer a file from the remote side to the local side, select the file that you want from the right and click the arrow in the middle of the screen pointing to the left. Watch the progress of the file transfer from messages on the bottom of the screen. When the transfer completes, the file appears in the left pane.

You can bookmark the address information that you need to connect to an FTP site. That address is added to a set of bookmarks already stored under the Bookmarks menu. You can select sites from the list to try out the gFTP. Most of the sites are for Linux distributions and other open source software sites.

Summary

Setting up an FTP server is an easy way to share files over a TCP network. The Very Secure FTP Daemon (vsftpd package) is available for Ubuntu and other Linux systems.

A default vsftpd server allows anonymous users to download files from the server and regular Linux users to upload or download files (provided the correct security settings are applied). Moving around on an FTP server is similar to moving around a Linux filesystem. You move up and down the directory structure to find the content that you want.

There are both graphical and text-based FTP clients. A popular text-based client for Linux is lftp. As for graphical FTP clients, you can use a regular web browser, such as Brave, or dedicated FTP clients, such as gFTP.

FTP servers are not the only way to share files over a network from Linux. The Samba service provides a way to share files over a network so that the shared Linux directory looks like a shared directory from a Windows system. Chapter 19, "Configuring a Windows File Sharing (Samba) Server," describes how to use Samba to offer Windows-style file sharing.

Exercises

The exercises in this section describe tasks related to setting up an FTP server in Ubuntu and connecting to that server using an FTP client. If you are stuck, solutions to the tasks are shown in Appendix A. Keep in mind that the solutions shown in Appendix A are usually just one of multiple ways to complete a task.

Don't do these exercises on a Linux system running a public FTP server because they almost certainly interfere with that server.

1. Determine which package provides the Very Secure FTP Daemon service.

2. Install the Very Secure FTP Daemon package on your system, and search for the configuration files in that package.

3. Enable anonymous FTP and disable local user login for the Very Secure FTP Daemon service.

4. Start the Very Secure FTP Daemon service and set it to start when the system boots.

5. On the system running your FTP server, create a file named `test` in the anonymous FTP directory that contains the words "Welcome to your vsftpd server."

6. From a web browser on the system running your FTP server, open the `test` file from the anonymous FTP home directory. Be sure that you can see that file's contents.

7. From a web browser outside of the system that is running the FTP server, try to access the `test` file in the anonymous FTP home directory.

8. Configure your `vsftpd` server to allow file uploads by anonymous users to a directory named `in`.

9. Install the `lftp` FTP client (if you don't have a second Linux system, install `lftp` on the same host running the FTP server). If you cannot upload files to the `in` directory, check that your firewall and TCP wrappers are configured to allow access to that file.

10. Using any FTP client you choose, visit the `/pub/debian-meetings` directory on the `ftp.gnome.org` site and list the contents of that directory.

18

Configuring a Windows File Sharing (Samba) Server

IN THIS CHAPTER

Getting and installing Samba

Using Samba security features

Editing the `smb.conf` configuration file

Accessing Samba from Linux and Windows clients

Using Samba in the enterprise

S amba is the project that implements open source versions of protocols used to share files and printers among Windows systems as well as authenticate users and restrict hosts. Samba offers a number of ways to share files among Windows, Linux, and macOS systems that are well known and readily available to users of those systems.

This chapter steps you through the process of installing and configuring a Samba server. It describes the security features that you need to know to share your file and printer resources and describes how to access those resources from Linux and Windows systems.

Understanding Samba

Samba (www.samba.org) is a suite of programs that allows Linux, UNIX, and other systems to interoperate with Microsoft Windows file and printer sharing protocols. Windows, macOS, and other client systems can access Samba servers to share files and printers in the same ways that they would from Windows file and print servers.

With Samba, you can use standard TCP/IP networking to communicate with clients. For name service, Samba supports regular TCP/IP hostnames as well as NetBIOS names. For that reason, Samba doesn't require the NetBEUI (Microsoft Raw NetBIOS frame) protocol. File sharing is done using Server Message Block (SMB) protocol, which is sometimes referred to as the *Common Internet File System (CIFS)*.

The Samba project has gone to great lengths to make its software secure and robust. In fact, many people prefer using Samba servers over Windows file servers because of the added security that is inherent in running Windows-style file sharing services on Linux or other UNIX-like operating systems.

Beyond all of the technical mumbo-jumbo, however, the end result is that Samba makes it easy to share files and printers between Linux servers and Windows desktop systems. For the server, only a few configuration files and tools are needed to manage Samba. For the clients, shared resources just show up under the Network selection in the File Explorer (formerly Windows Explorer) application or in the Network Neighborhood on older Windows systems.

To configure the Samba service, you directly edit Samba configuration files (particularly `smb.conf`) and run a few commands. Graphical and web-based interfaces, such as `system-config-samba` and Samba SWAT, are no longer included with the latest Linux systems.

To begin using Samba on Ubuntu, you need to install a few software packages, as described in the next section.

Installing Samba

To configure a Samba file and print server, installing the `samba` package gets you everything you need to start. Among other components, the `samba` package includes the Samba service daemon (`/usr/sbin/smbd`) and NetBIOS name server daemon (`/usr/sbin/nmbd`). There's also an optional `samba-common` package that contains server configuration files (`smb.conf`, `lmhosts`, and others) and commands for adding passwords and testing configuration files, along with other Samba features.

Features from other packages are referenced in this chapter, so I describe those as well. Those include the following:

> **smbclient:** Contains command-line tools such as `smbclient` (for connecting to Samba or Windows shares), `nmblookup` (for looking up host addresses), and `findsmb` (to find SMB hosts on the network).
>
> **winbind:** Includes components that allow your Samba server in Linux to become a complete member of a Windows domain, including using Windows user and group accounts in Linux.

Go ahead and install those packages:

```
# apt install samba smbclient winbind
```

After that's done, look at the configuration files. Go ahead and install those packages.

The `/etc/logrotate.d/samba` file is usually not modified. It sets how files in `/var/log/samba` log files are rotated (copied to other files and removed) over time.

Most configuration files that you would modify for Samba are in the `/etc/samba` directory. The `smb.conf` file is the primary configuration file where you put global settings for the Samba server as well as individual file and printer share information (more on that later).

Although it doesn't exist by default, you can create a file named /etc/samba/smbusers to map Linux usernames into Windows usernames. As you configure your Samba server, you can refer to the smb.conf man page (man smb.conf). There are also man pages for Samba commands, such as smbpasswd (to change passwords), smbclient (to connect to a Samba server), and nmblookup (to look up NetBIOS information).

After you have installed Samba packages and completed a quick survey of what they contain, try starting up the Samba service and see what you get in a default configuration.

Controlling Samba

With samba and samba-common installed, you can start the server and investigate how it runs in the default configuration. Two main services are associated with a Samba server, each of which has its own service daemon:

smb: This service controls the smbd daemon process, which provides the file and print sharing services that can be accessed by Windows clients.

nmb: This service controls the nmbd daemon. By providing NetBIOS name service name-to-address mapping, nmbd can map requests from Windows clients for NetBIOS names so that they can be resolved into IP addresses.

To share files and printers with other Linux systems with Samba, only the smb service is required. The next section describes how to start and enable the smb service.

Viewing Samba processes

Samba is controlled by the smbd daemon, which makes files and printers available from your local system to other computers on the network.

The usual systemctl commands will manage smdb:

```
$ systemctl status smbd
• smbd.service - Samba SMB Daemon
   Loaded: loaded (/lib/systemd/system/smbd.service; enabled; vendor preset: ena
   Active: active (running) since Fri 2020-04-03 13:20:42 UTC; 43min ago
     Docs: man:smbd(8)
           man:samba(7)
           man:smb.conf(5)
 Main PID: 1230 (smbd)
   Status: "smbd: ready to serve connections..."
    Tasks: 4 (limit: 4915)
   CGroup: /system.slice/smbd.service
           └─230 /usr/sbin/smbd --foreground --no-process-group
           └─1232 /usr/sbin/smbd --foreground --no-process-group
           └─1233 /usr/sbin/smbd --foreground --no-process-group
           └─1235 /usr/sbin/smbd --foreground --no-process-group
```

19

The first nmb daemon is controlled through nmbd:

```
$ systemctl status nmbd
• nmbd.service - Samba NMB Daemon
   Loaded: loaded (/lib/systemd/system/nmbd.service; enabled; vendor
preset: ena
   Active: active (running) since Fri 2020-04-03 13:20:42 UTC; 44min ago
     Docs: man:nmbd(8)
           man:samba(7)
           man:smb.conf(5)
 Main PID: 1297 (nmbd)
   Status: "nmbd: ready to serve connections..."
    Tasks: 1 (limit: 4915)
   CGroup: /system.slice/nmbd.service
           └─1297 /usr/sbin/nmbd --foreground --no-process-group
```

When you look at the smdb.service file (as shown in the following code snippet), you'll see that the Samba daemon process (smbd) must start up only after the network, nmbd, and winbind processes. The WantedBy line indicates that smb.service should start when the system boots up into multi-user mode (multi-user.target), which it does by default.

```
$ cat /lib/systemd/system/smbd.service
[Unit]
Description=Samba SMB Daemon
Documentation=man:smbd(8) man:samba(7) man:smb.conf(5)
After=network.target nmbd.service winbind.service

[Service]
Type=notify
NotifyAccess=all
PIDFile=/var/run/samba/smbd.pid
LimitNOFILE=16384
EnvironmentFile=-/etc/default/samba
ExecStart=/usr/sbin/smbd --foreground --no-process-group $SMBDOPTIONS
ExecReload=/bin/kill -HUP $MAINPID
LimitCORE=infinity

[Install]
WantedBy=multi-user.target
```

Similarly, the NetBIOS (nmbd) name service file (/lib/systemd/system/nmbd.ser-vice) requires that the network-online.target be true before it can load and is controlled by the environment file /etc/default/samba:

```
$ cat /lib/systemd/system/nmbd.service
[Unit]
Description=Samba NMB Daemon
Documentation=man:nmbd(8) man:samba(7) man:smb.conf(5)
After=network-online.target
Wants=network-online.target
```

```
[Service]
Type=notify
NotifyAccess=all
PIDFile=/var/run/samba/nmbd.pid
EnvironmentFile=-/etc/default/samba
ExecStart=/usr/sbin/nmbd --foreground --no-process-group $NMBDOPTIONS
ExecReload=/bin/kill -HUP $MAINPID
LimitCORE=infinity

[Install]
WantedBy=multi-user.target
```

You can check access to the Samba server using the smbclient command. You can get basic information about the local resources available to a Samba server using -L:

```
# smbclient -L localhost
Enter SAMBA\root's password: <ENTER>
Anonymous login successful

    Sharename   Type      Comment
    ---------   ----      -------
    print$      Disk      Printer Drivers
    IPC$        IPC       IPC Service
 (Samba Server Version 4.10.10)
    deskjet     Printer   deskjet
Reconnecting with SMB1 for workgroup listing.
Anonymous login successful
    Server          Comment
    ---------       -------

    Workgroup       Master
    ---------       -------
```

The smbclient output allows you see what services are available from the server. By default, anonymous login is allowed when querying the server (so I just pressed Enter when prompted for a password).

You can discern a number of things about the default Samba server setup from this output:

- All printers that are shared via the CUPS server on your Linux system are, by default, also made available from the Samba server running on that same system.
- No directories are shared yet from the server.
- There is no NetBIOS name service running yet from the Samba server.

Next, you can decide whether you want to run the NetBIOS name service on your Samba server.

If no Windows domain server is running on the network, as is the case here, you use systemctl to start the nmb service on the Samba host to provide that service. This nmplookup command displays the IP addresses and status of all available Samba servers–there's only the one on our local machine available on this network.

```
$ nmblookup -S '*'
10.0.3.79 *<00>
Looking up status of 10.0.3.79
      APACHE         <00> -          B <ACTIVE>
      APACHE         <03> -          B <ACTIVE>
      APACHE         <20> -          B <ACTIVE>
      WORKGROUP      <00> - <GROUP>  B <ACTIVE>
      WORKGROUP      <1e> - <GROUP>  B <ACTIVE>
      MAC Address = 00-00-00-00-00-00
```

Normally there would be one or more Windows printer or file server available on the network–after all, that is why you're installing Samba, right? But for now we'll have to make do with just this Linux server.

Another way to canvass Samba servers and their resources is through the smbtree command:

```
$ smbtree
WORKGROUP
    \\WORKSTATION                        workstation server (Samba, Ubuntu)
        \\WORKSTATION\vpn-videos
        \\WORKSTATION\DCP-7060D          Brother DCP-7060D
        \\WORKSTATION\IPC$               IPC Service (workstation server
(Samba, Ubuntu))
        \\WORKSTATION\print$             Printer Drivers
    \\APACHE                             apache server (Samba, Ubuntu)
        \\APACHE\IPC$                    IPC Service (apache server
(Samba, Ubuntu))
        \\APACHE\print$                  Printer Drivers
Securing Samba
```

If you have an active firewall protecting your network or computer, you'll need to make sure these ports are open:

TCP port 445: This is the primary port on which the Samba smbd daemon listens. Your firewall must support incoming packet requests on this port for Samba to work.

TCP port 139: The smbd daemon also listens on TCP port 139 in order to handle sessions associated with NetBIOS hostnames. It is possible to use Samba over TCP without opening this port, but it is not recommended.

UDP ports 137 and 138: The nmbd daemon uses these two ports for incoming NetBIOS requests. If you are using the nmbd daemon, these two ports must be open for new packet requests for NetBIOS name resolution.

You'll learn more about firewalls in Chapter 25, "Securing Linux on a Network."

Within the smb.conf file itself, you can allow or restrict access to the entire Samba server or to specific shares based on the hosts or users trying to gain access.

You can do this by adding a valid users entry to a section of your `smb.conf` file. This example will permit the user `steve` and all members of the admins group access:

```
[printers]
   comment = All Printers
   browseable = no
   path = /var/spool/samba
   printable = yes
   valid users = steve @admins
   guest ok = no
   read only = yes
   create mask = 0700
```

The next section describes how to configure Samba, including how to identify which hosts, users, or network interfaces can access your Samba server.

Configuring Samba

Inside the `/etc/samba/smb.conf` file are settings for configuring your Samba server, defining shared printers, configuring how authentication is done, and creating shared directories. The file consists of the following predefined sections:

[global]: Settings that apply to the Samba server as a whole are placed in this section. This is where you set the server's description, its workgroup (domain), the location of log files, the default type of security, and other settings.

[homes]: This section determines whether users with accounts on the Samba server can see their home directories (browseable) or write to them.

[printers]: In this section, settings tell Samba whether to make printers available through Samba that are configured for Linux printing (CUPS).

[print$]: This section configures a directory as a shared printer drivers folder.

Inside the `smb.conf` file, lines beginning with pound signs (#) or semicolons (;) are comments. Removing the semicolons enables you to set up different kinds of shared information quickly. The # sign can also be used to comment out a line.

When you begin editing your `smb.conf` file, make a backup that you can revert to if something goes wrong. You can start by copying the `smb.conf.example` file to `smb.conf`, if you want to start with some examples.

Configuring the [global] section

Here is an example of a [global] section of the `smb.conf` file:

```
[global]
   workgroup = WORKGROUP
   server string = %h server (Samba, Ubuntu)
;    wins server = w.x.y.z
```

Continues

19

Continued

```
      dns proxy = no
;     interfaces = 127.0.0.0/8 eth0
;     bind interfaces only = yes
      log file = /var/log/samba/log.%m
      max log size = 1000
      syslog = 0
      panic action = /usr/share/samba/panic-action %d
      server role = standalone server
      passdb backend = tdbsam
      obey pam restrictions = yes
      unix password sync = yes
      passwd program = /usr/bin/passwd %u
      passwd chat = *Enter\snew\s*\spassword:* %n\n *Retype\snew\s*\
spassword:* %n\n *password\supdated\ssuccessfully* .
      pam password change = yes
      map to guest = bad user
;     logon path = \\%N\profiles\%U
;     logon drive = H:
;     logon script = logon.cmd
; add user script = /usr/sbin/adduser --quiet --disabled-password
--gecos "" %u
; add machine script = /usr/sbin/useradd -g machines -c "%u machine
account" -d /var/lib/samba -s /bin/false %u
; add group script = /usr/sbin/addgroup --force-badname %g
;     include = /home/samba/etc/smb.conf.%m
;     idmap uid = 10000-20000
;     idmap gid = 10000-20000
;     template shell = /bin/bash
;     usershare max shares = 100
      usershare allow guests = yes
```

The workgroup (also used as the domain name) is set to WORKGROUP in this example. When a client communicates with the Samba server, this name tells the client which workgroup the Samba server is in.

The passdb backend = tdbsam specifies to use a Samba backend database to hold passwords. You can use the smbpasswd command to set each user's password (as described later).

If you want to restrict access to the Samba server so that it only responds on certain interfaces, you can uncomment the interfaces line and add either the IP address or name (lo, eth0, eth1, and so on) of the network interfaces you want.

By default, your server's DNS hostname (enter **hostname** to see what it is) is used as your Samba server's NetBIOS name as well. You can override that and set a separate NetBIOS name by uncommenting the include = /home/samba/etc/smb.conf.%m line and adding the server name you want. For example, netbios name = myownhost.localhost is used as your NetBIOS name if it has not otherwise been set.

Configuring the [homes] section

The [homes] section is configured, by default, to allow any Samba user account to be able to access its own home directory via the Samba server. Here is what the default homes entry looks like:

```
; [homes]
;     comment = Home Directories
;     browseable = no
;     read only = yes
;     create mask = 0700
;     directory mask = 0700
;     valid users = %S
```

Setting valid users to %S substitutes the current service name, which allows any valid users of the service to access their home directories. The valid users are also identified by domain or workgroup (%D), winbind separator (%w), and name of current service (%S).

The browseable = No setting prevents the Samba server from displaying the avail-ability of the shared home directories. Users who can provide their own Samba usernames and passwords can read and write in their own home directories (read only = no). With inherit acls set to Yes, access control lists can be inherited to add another layer of security on the shared files.

Configuring the [printers] section

Any printer that you configure for CUPS printing on your Linux system is automatically shared to others over Samba, based on the [printers] section that is added by default.

Here's what the default printers section looks like in the smb.conf file:

```
[printers]
   comment = All Printers
   browseable = no
   path = /var/spool/samba
   printable = yes
   guest ok = no
   read only = yes
   create mask = 0700
```

The path tells Samba to store temporary print files in /var/spool/samba. The print-able = Yes line causes all of your CUPS printers on the local system to be shared by Samba. Printers are writeable and allow guest printing by default. The create mask = 0700 setting used here has the effect of removing write and execute bits for groups and others, within the ACL, when files are created in the path directory.

To see that local printers are available, you could run the smbclient -L command from a Linux system, as shown earlier. On a Windows system, you can select Network from the File Explorer window and select the icon representing your Samba server. All shared printers and folders appear in that window. (See the section "Accessing Samba Shares" later in this chapter for details on viewing and using shared printers.)

19

Creating a Samba shared folder

Before you can create a shared folder, that folder (directory) must exist and have the proper permissions set. In this example, the /var/salesdata directory is shared. You want the data to be writeable by the user named chris but visible to anyone on your network. To create that directory:

```
# mkdir /var/salesdata
# chmod 775 /var/salesdata
# chown chris:chris /var/salesdata
# touch /var/salesdata/test
```

Here's how we'll add the shared folder to Samba. With the /var/salesdata directory created and properly configured to be shared by Samba, here is what the shared folder (called salesdata) might look like in the smb.conf file:

```
[salesdata]
        comment = Sales data for current year
        path = /var/salesdata
        read only = no
        browseable = yes
        valid users = chris
```

Before this share was created, the /var/salesdata directory was created, with chris assigned as the user and group, and the directory was set to be readable and writeable by chris. The Samba username chris must be presented along with the associated password to access the share. After chris is connected to the share, chris has read and write access to it (read only = no).

Now that you have seen the default settings for Samba and an example of a simple shared directory (folder), read the next few sections to see how to configure shares even further. In particular, the examples demonstrate how to make shares available to particular users, hosts, and network interfaces.

Checking the Samba share

Before our user Chris will be able to log in to a Samba share, he'll need a password. You can create this password by running the smbpasswd -a chris command.

For the changes to your Samba configuration to take effect, you need to restart the smb service. After that's done, check that the Samba share you created is available and that any user you assigned to the share can access it. To do those things, enter the following as root user from a shell on the Samba server:

```
# systemctl restart smbd
# smbclient -L localhost -U chris

Enter WORKGROUP\chris's password:
```

```
Sharename       Type      Comment
---------       ----      -------
homes           Disk      Home Directories
print$          Disk      Printer Drivers
salesdata       Disk      Sales data for current year
IPC$            IPC       IPC Service (apache server
(Samba, Ubuntu))
Reconnecting with SMB1 for workgroup listing.

Server                    Comment
---------                 -------

Workgroup                 Master
---------                 -------
WORKGROUP
```

Here you can see the share name (salesdata), the domain, and the description entered earlier (Sales data for current year). Next, a quick way to test access to the share is to use the smbclient command. You can use the hostname or IP address with smbclient to access the share. Because I am on the local system in this example, I just use the name localhost and the user I added (chris):

```
$ smbclient -U chris //localhost/salesdata
WARNING: The "syslog" option is deprecated
Enter WORKGROUP\chris's password:
Try "help" to get a list of possible commands.
smb: \> ls
  .                                D        0  Fri Apr  3
18:48:20 2020
  ..                               D        0  Fri Apr  3
18:47:37 2020
  test                             N        0  Fri Apr  3
18:48:20 2020

    479152840 blocks of size 1024. 278637884 blocks available
smb: \> quit
$
```

A Samba share is in the form //host/share or \\host\share. However, when you identify a Samba share from a Linux shell in the latter case, the backslashes need to be escaped. So, as an argument, the first example of the share would have to appear as \\\\ localhost\\salesdata. Thus, the first form is easier to use.

> **NOTE**
>
> Escaping a character that you type from the shell is done by putting a backslash (\) in front of that character. It tells the shell to use the character following the backslash literally, instead of giving the character a special meaning to the shell. (The * and ? characters are examples of characters with special meaning.) Because the backslash itself has special meaning to the shell, if you want to use a backslash literally, you need to precede it with a backslash. That is why when you want to type a Samba address that includes two backslashes, you actually have to enter four backslashes.

When prompted, enter the Samba password for that user (it may be different from the Linux user's password). The Samba user's password was set earlier with smbpasswd in this example. You see the smb: \> prompt after that.

At this point, you have a session open to the Samba host that is similar to an ftp session for traversing an FTP server. The lcd /etc command makes /etc the current directory on the local system. The put hosts command uploads the hosts file from the local system to the shared directory. Typing ls shows that the file exists on the server. The quit command ends the session.

Restricting Samba access by network interface

To restrict access to all of your shares, you can set the global interfaces setting in the smb. conf file. Samba is designed more for local file sharing than for sharing over wide area networks. If your computer has a network interface connected to a local network and one connected to the Internet, consider allowing access only to the local network.

To set which interfaces Samba listens on, uncomment the interfaces line shown in an earlier example in the [global] section of the smb.conf file. Then add the interface names or IP address ranges of those computers that you want to allow access to your computer. Here is an example:

```
interfaces = lo 192.168.22.15/24
```

This interface entry allows access to the Samba service to all users on the local system (lo). It also allows access to any systems on the 192.168.22 network. See the smb.conf man page's description of different ways of identifying hosts and network interfaces.

Restricting Samba access by host

Host access to the Samba server can be set for the entire service or for single shares.

Here are some examples of hosts allow and hosts deny entries that can be added to the networking section of smb.conf:

```
hosts allow = 192.168.22. EXCEPT 192.168.22.99
hosts allow = 192.168.5.0/255.255.255.0
hosts allow = .example.com market.example.net
hosts deny = evil.example.org 192.168.99.
```

The first example allows access to any host in the 192.168.22. network except for 192.168.22.99, which is denied. Note that a dot is required at the end of the network number. The 192.168.5.0/255.255.255.0 example uses netmask notation to identify 192.168.5 as the set of addresses that are allowed.

In the third line of the sample code, any host from the .example.com network is allowed, as is the individual host market.example.net. The hosts deny example shows that you can use the same form to identify names and IP addresses in order to prevent access from certain hosts.

Restricting Samba access by user

Particular Samba users and groups can be allowed access to specific Samba shares by identifying those users and groups within a share in the smb.conf file. Aside from guest users, which you may or may not allow, the default user authentication for Samba requires you to add a Samba (Windows) user account that maps into a local Linux user account.

As we've seen, to allow a user to access the Samba server, you need to create a password for the user. Here is an example of how to add a Samba password for the user jim:

```
# smbpasswd -a jim
New SMB password: *******
Retype new SMB password: *******
```

After running that smbpasswd command, jim can use that username and password to access the Samba server. The /var/lib/samba/private/passdb.tdb file holds the password just entered for jim. After that, the user jim can change the password by simply typing smbpasswd when he is logged in. The root user can change the password by rerunning the command shown in the example but dropping the -a option.

If you wanted to give jim access to a share, you could add a valid users line to that shared block in the smb.conf file. For example, to provide both chris and jim access to a share, you could add the following line:

```
valid users = jim, chris
```

If the read only option is set to no for the share, both users could potentially write files to the share (depending on file permissions). If read only is set to yes, you could still allow access to jim and chris to write files by adding a write list line as follows:

```
write list = jim, chris
```

The write list can contain groups (that is, Linux groups contained in the /etc/group file) to allow write permission to any Linux user that belongs to a particular Linux group. You can add write permission for a group by putting a plus (+) character in front of a name. For example, the following adds write access for the market group to the share with which this line is associated:

```
write list = jim, chris, +market
```

There are many ways to change and extend the features of your shared Samba resources. For further information on configuring Samba, be sure to examine the smb.conf file itself (which includes many useful comments) and the smb.conf man page.

Accessing Samba Shares

After you have created some shared directories in Samba, many client tools are available in both Linux and Windows for accessing those shares. Command-line tools in Linux include the smbclient command, demonstrated earlier in this chapter. For a graphical means of accessing shares, you can use the file managers available in both Windows (File Explorer) and Linux (Nautilus, with the GNOME desktop).

Accessing Samba shares in Linux

Once a Samba share is available, it can be accessed from remote Linux and Windows systems using file managers or remote mount commands.

Accessing Samba shares from a Linux file manager

Opening a file manager in Linux can provide you with access to the shared directories from Linux (Samba) and Windows (SMB). How you access the file manager is different on different Linux desktops. In GNOME 3, you can click the Files icon. In other desktops, open the Home folder.

With the Nautilus window manager displayed, select Other Locations in the left navigation bar. Available networks (such as Windows Network) should appear. Look to the box at the bottom of the window identified as Connect to Server, and then enter the location of an available Samba share. Given the previous examples, you would be able to use either of these shares:

```
smb://10.0.3.79/chris
smb://10.0.3.79/salesdata
```

Click to connect. From the window that appears, you can select to connect as a registered user. If you do that, you can enter your username, Samba domain name, and the password for your user. You can also select whether or not to save that password.

Click Connect. If the user and password are accepted, you should see the contents of the remote directory. If you have write access to the share, you can open another Nautilus window and drag and drop files between the two systems.

You can also access your remote share from the command line. This command will drop you into a Samba shell session from a remote Samba client (with the `cifs-utils` package installed):

```
smbclient -U chris //10.0.3.79/salesdata
Enter WORKGROUP\chris's password:
Try "help" to get a list of possible commands.
smb: \> ls
  .                              D        0  Fri Apr  3 18:48:20 2020
  ..                             D        0  Fri Apr  3 18:47:37 2020
  test                           N        0  Fri Apr  3 18:48:20 2020

    479152840 blocks of size 1024. 278680468 blocks available
smb: \>
```

Mounting a Samba share from a Linux command line

Because a Samba shared directory can be viewed as a remote filesystem, you can use common Linux tools to connect a Samba share (temporarily or permanently) to your Linux system. Using the standard `mount` command, you can mount a remote Samba share as a

CIFS filesystem in Linux. This example mounts the salesdata share on the host at IP address 10.0.3.79 on the local directory /mnt/sales:

```
# apt install cifs-utils
# mkdir /mnt/sales
# mount -t cifs -o user=chris \
     //10.0.3.79/salesdata /mnt/sales
Password for chris@//192.168.122.119/salesdata: *******
# ls /mnt/sales
hosts   memos  test  whitepapers
```

When prompted, enter the Samba password for chris. Given that the user chris in this example has read-write permission to the shared directory, users on your system should be able to read and write to the mounted directory. Regardless of who saves files on the shared directory, on the server those files are owned by the user chris. This mount lasts until the system is rebooted or you run the umount command on the directory. If you want the share to be mounted permanently (that is, every time the system boots up) in the same location, you can do some additional configuration. First, open the /etc/fstab file and add an entry similar to the following:

```
//192.168.0.119/salesdata /mnt/sales cifs credentials=/root/cif.txt 0 0
```

Next, create a credentials file (in this example, /root/cif.txt). In that file, put the name of the user and the user's password that you want to present when the system tries to mount the filesystem. Here is an example of the contents of that file:

```
user=chris
pass=mypass
```

Before you reboot to check that the entry is correct, try mounting it from the command line. A mount -a command tries to mount any filesystem listed in the /etc/fstab file that is not already mounted. The df command shows information about disk space for the mounted directory, as in the following example:

```
# mount -a
# df -h /mnt/sales
Filesystem                    Size  Used  Avail  Ues%  Mounted on
//192.168.0.119/salesdata     20G   5.7G  14G    30%   /mnt/sales
```

You should now be able to use the shared Samba directory as you do any directory on the local system.

NOTE

For security reasons, by default, mounting remote Samba shares is not allowed in containers (which we'll discuss in Chapter 26, "Shifting to Clouds and Containers"). If you want a Linux container to access the contents of a remote Samba share, you will need to run the container as a privileged container, as well as ensure that AppArmor is configured to allow the execution of privileged containers.

19

Accessing Samba shares in Windows

As with Linux, you can access Samba shares from the file manager window, in this case Windows File Explorer. To do this, open any folder in Windows and select Network from the left panel. An icon representing the Samba server should appear on the screen. Click that icon and enter a password if prompted for one. You should see all shared printers and folders from that server.

There should be two shared folders (directories): `chris` and `salesdata`. There are also several shared printers. To use the folders, double-click them and enter the required authentication information. Because printers are set up to use raw drivers by default, you need to obtain Windows drivers to use any of the Samba printers.

> **NOTE**
>
> To access Samba shares from macOS, in the Finder app, select Connect to Server from the Go menu. In the Connect to Server window, you can type `smb://host/share` and click Connect.

Using Samba in the Enterprise

Although it's beyond the scope of this book, Windows file and printer sharing via Samba servers is a very popular application in large enterprises. Despite the fact that Linux has begun to dominate the enterprise-quality server market, Microsoft Windows systems are still the predominant systems used on the desktop.

The major features needed to integrate Samba servers into a large enterprise with many Microsoft Windows desktops are related to authentication. Most large enterprises use Microsoft Active Directory Services (ADS) servers for authentication. On the Linux side, that means configuring Kerberos on the Linux system and using ADS (instead of user) for the type of security in the `smb.conf` file.

The advantage of central authentication is that users only have to remember one set of credentials throughout the enterprise, and system administrators need to manage fewer user accounts and passwords.

Summary

Because of the popularity of Windows desktops, Samba servers have become popular for sharing files and printers among Windows and Linux systems. Samba provides a way to interoperate with Windows systems by implementing the Server Message Block (SMB) or Common Internet File System (CIFS) protocol for sharing resources over a network.

This chapter stepped through the process of installing, starting, securing, configuring, and accessing Samba servers on a Linux system. Using command-line tools, I demonstrated how to set up a Samba server. I showed you both command-line and desktop tools for getting to Samba shares from Linux and Windows systems.

The next chapter describes the Network File System (NFS) facility. NFS is the native Linux facility for sharing and mounting filesystems over networks with other Linux and UNIX systems.

Exercises

The exercises in this section describe tasks related to setting up a Samba server in Linux and accessing that server using a Samba client. As usual, there are often several ways to accomplish some of the tasks here. So don't worry if you don't go about the exercises in exactly the same way as shown in the answers, as long as you get the same results. See Appendix A for suggested solutions.

Don't do these exercises on a Linux system running a Samba server because they will almost certainly interfere with that server. These exercises were tested on an Ubuntu system. Some of the steps might be slightly different on another Linux system.

1. Install the `samba` and `samba-client` packages.

2. Start and enable the `smb` and `nmb` services.

3. Set the Samba server's workgroup to `TESTGROUP` and the server string to `Samba Test System`.

4. Add a Linux user named `phil` to your system, and add a Linux password and Samba password for `phil`.

5. Set the `[homes]` section so that home directories are browseable (`yes`) and write-able (`yes`) and `phil` is the only valid user.

6. From the local system, use the `smbclient` command to list that the `homes` share is available.

7. From a Nautilus (file manager) window on the local system, connect to the `homes` share for the user `phil` on the local Samba server in a way that allows you to drag and drop files to that folder.

19

Configuring an NFS File Server

Instead of representing storage devices as drive letters (A:, B:, C:, and so on), as they are in Microsoft operating systems, Linux systems invisibly connect filesystems from multiple hard disks, USB drives, CD-ROMs, and other local devices to form a single Linux filesystem. The Network File System (NFS) facility enables you to extend your Linux filesystem to connect filesystems on other computers to your local directory structure.

An NFS file server provides an easy way to share large amounts of data among the users and computers in an organization. An administrator of a Linux system that is configured to share its filesystems using NFS has to perform the following tasks to set up NFS:

1. **Set up the network**. NFS is typically used on private networks as opposed to public networks, such as the Internet.

2. **Start the NFS service**. Several service daemons need to start up and run to have a fully operational NFS service. On Ubuntu, you can start up the `nfs-server` service.

3. **Choose what to share from the server**. Decide which directories (folders) on your Linux NFS server to make available to other computers. You can choose any point in the filesystem and make all files and directories below that point accessible to other computers.

4. **Set up security on the server**. You can use several different security features to apply the level of security with which you are comfortable. *Mount-level security* enables you to restrict the computers that can mount a resource and, for those allowed to mount it, enables you to specify whether it can be mounted read/write or read-only. In NFS, user-level security is implemented by mapping users from the client systems to users on the NFS server (based on UID and not username) so that they can rely on standard Linux read/write/execute permissions, file ownership, and group permissions to access and protect files.

447

5. **Mount the filesystem on the client.** Each client computer that is allowed access to the server's NFS shared filesystem can mount it anywhere the client chooses. For example, you may mount a filesystem from a computer called oak on the /mnt/ oak directory in your local filesystem. After it is mounted, you can view the contents of that directory by typing **ls /mnt/oak**.

Although it is often used as a file server (or other type of server), Linux is a general-purpose operating system, so any Linux system can share, or export, filesystems as a server or use another computer's filesystems (mount) as a client.

> **NOTE**
>
> A *filesystem* is usually a structure of files and directories that exists on a single device (such as a hard disk partition or CD-ROM). The term *Linux filesystem* refers to the entire directory structure (which may include filesystems from several disk partitions, NFS, or a variety of network resources), beginning from root (/) on a single computer. A shared directory in NFS may represent all or part of a computer's filesystem, which can be attached (from the shared directory down the directory tree) to another computer's filesystem.

If you already have the NFS and Cockpit services running on your system, you can mount NFS shares and view mounted shares from the Cockpit Web UI. Here's how to do that:

1. Log in to your Cockpit interface (port 9090) through your web browser and select Storage. The URL to get to storage in the Cockpit service on your local system should be something like https://host1.example.com:9090/storage.

2. If there are mounted NFS shares on your system, they should appear under the NFS Mounts section.

3. To mount a remote NFS share, select the plus (+) sign on the NFS Mounts line. Fill in the address or hostname of the NFS server, the shared directory on the NFS share, and the point on the local filesystem where you will mount that share. Then select Add, as shown in Figure 20.1.

At this point, you should be able to access the content from the remote NFS share from the mount point on your local filesystem. By default, the NFS mount information is added to the /etc/fstab file, so the NFS share will be made available each time the system reboots. Now that you have seen the easy way to use NFS, the rest of the chapter describes how to use NFS from the ground up.

Installing an NFS Server

To run an NFS server, you need a set of kernel modules (which are delivered with the kernel itself) plus some user-level tools to configure the service, run daemon processes, and query the service in various ways. Everything you'll need will be included with the nfs-kernel-server package:

```
# apt install nfs-kernel-server
```

FIGURE 20.1

Add a new NFS mount using Cockpit Web UI.

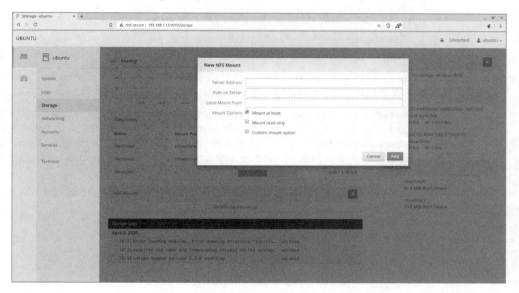

Besides a few documents in the /usr/share/doc/nfs-common and /usr/share/doc/nfs-kernel-server directories, most documentation for the package comes with the man pages for its various components.

There are tools and man pages for both the NFS server side (for sharing a directory with others) and the client side (for mounting a remote NFS directory locally). To configure a server, you can refer to the exports man page (to set up the /etc/exports file to share your directories). The man page for the exportfs command describes how to share and view the list of directories that you share from the /etc/exports file.

Man pages on the client side include the mount.nfs man page (to see what mount options you can use when mounting remote NFS directories on your local system). There is also an nfsmount.conf man page, which describes how to use the /etc/nfsmount.conf file to configure how your system behaves when you mount remote resources locally. The showmount man page describes how to use the showmount command to see what shared directories are available from NFS servers.

Starting the NFS Service

As with other systemd services, you control your NFS server using systemctl running against nfs-server:

```
$ systemctl status nfs-server
• nfs-server.service - NFS server and services
   Loaded: loaded (/lib/systemd/system/nfs-server.service; enabled;
vendor prese
   Active: active (exited) since Sun 2020-04-05 14:25:12 UTC; 35min ago
 Main PID: 15282 (code=exited, status=0/SUCCESS)
    Tasks: 0 (limit: 1108)
   CGroup: /system.slice/nfs-server.service

Apr 05 14:25:12 ubuntu systemd[1]: Starting NFS server and services...
Apr 05 14:25:12 ubuntu systemd[1]: Started NFS server and services.
```

You can see from the status that the nfs-server service is enabled and active. Peeking inside the /etc/systemd/system/multi-user.target.wants/nfs-server.service file shows us that the NFS service also requires that the RPC service be running (rpcbind). The nfs-server service automatically starts the rpcbind service, if it is not already running.

```
$  cat /etc/systemd/system/multi-user.target.wants/nfs-server.service
[Unit]
Description=NFS server and services
DefaultDependencies=no
Requires=network.target proc-fs-nfsd.mount
Requires=nfs-mountd.service
Wants=rpcbind.socket
Wants=nfs-idmapd.service
[...]
```

Sharing NFS Filesystems

To share an NFS filesystem from your Linux system, you need to export it from the server system. Exporting is done in Linux by adding entries into the /etc/exports file. Each entry identifies a directory in your local filesystem that you want to share with other computers. The entry also identifies the other computers that can access the resource (or opens it to all computers) and includes other options that reflect permissions associated with the directory.

Remember that when you share a directory, you are sharing all files and subdirectories below that directory as well (by default). You need to be sure that you want to share everything in that directory structure. You can still restrict access within that directory structure in many ways; those are discussed later in this chapter.

Configuring the /etc/exports file

To make a directory from your Linux system available to other systems, you need to export that directory. Exporting is done on a permanent basis by adding information about an exported directory to the /etc/exports file.

Here's the format of the /etc/exports file:

```
Directory    Host(Options...)   Host(Options...)   # Comments
```

In this example, *Directory* is the name of the directory that you want to share, and *Host* indicates the client computer to which the sharing of this directory is restricted. *Options* can include a variety of options to define the security measures attached to the shared directory for the host. (You can repeat Host and Option pairs.) *Comments* are any optional comments that you want to add (following the # sign).

The exports man page (man exports) contains details about the syntax of the /etc/exports file. In particular, you can see the options that you can use to limit access and secure each shared directory.

As root user, you can use any text editor to configure /etc/exports to modify shared directory entries or add new ones. Here's an example of an /etc/exports file:

```
/cal    *.linuxtoys.net(rw)              # Company events
/pub    *(ro,insecure,all_squash)        # Public dir
/home   maple(rw,root_squash) spruce(rw,root_squash)
```

The /cal entry represents a directory that contains information about events related to the company. Any computer in the company's domain (*.linuxtoys.net) can mount that NFS share. Users can write files to the directory as well as read them (indicated by the rw option). The comment (# Company events) simply serves to remind you of what the directory contains.

The /pub entry represents a public directory. It allows any computer and user to read files from the directory (indicated by the ro option) but not to write files. The insecure option enables any computer, even one that doesn't use a secure NFS port, to access the directory. The all_squash option causes all users (UIDs) and groups (GIDs) to be mapped to the nobody user (UID 65534), giving them minimal permission to files and directories.

The /home entry enables a set of users to have the same /home directory on different computers. Suppose, for example, that you are sharing /home from a computer named oak. The computers named maple and spruce could each mount that directory on their own /home directories. If you gave all users the same username/UID on all machines, you could have the same /home/*user* directory available for each user, regardless of which computer they are logged in to. The root_squash is used to exclude the root user from another computer from having root privilege to the shared directory.

These are just examples; you can share any directories that you choose, including the entire filesystem (/). Of course, there are security implications of sharing the whole filesystem or sensitive parts of it (such as /etc). Security options that you can add to your /etc/exports file are described throughout the sections that follow.

Hostnames in /etc/exports

You can use the /etc/exports file to define which host computers can have access to your shared directory. If you want to associate multiple hostnames or IP addresses with a particular shared directory, be sure to leave a space before each hostname. However, add no spaces between a hostname and its options. Here's an example:

```
/usr/local maple(rw) spruce(ro,root_squash)
```

Notice that there is a space after (rw) but none after maple. You can identify hosts in several ways:

Individual host   Enter one or more TCP/IP hostnames or IP addresses. If the host is in your local domain, you can simply indicate the hostname. Otherwise, use the full host.domain format. These are valid ways to indicate individual host computers:

```
maple
maple.handsonhistory.com
10.0.0.11
```

IP network   Allow access to all hosts from a particular network address by indicating a network number and its netmask, separated by a slash (/). Here are valid ways to designate network numbers:

```
10.0.0.0/255.0.0.0 172.16.0.0/255.255.0.0
192.168.18.0/255.255.255.0
192.168.18.0/24
```

TCP/IP domain   Using wildcards, you can include all or some host computers from a particular domain level. Here are some valid uses of the asterisk and question mark wildcards:

```
*.handsonhistory.com
*craft.handsonhistory.com
???.handsonhistory.com
```

The first example matches all hosts in the handsonhistory.com domain. The second example matches woodcraft, basketcraft, or any other hostnames ending in craft in the handsonhistory.com domain. The final example matches any three-letter hostnames in the domain.

NIS groups   You can allow access to hosts contained in an NIS group. To indicate an NIS group, prefix the group name with an at (@) sign (for example, @group).

Access options in /etc/exports

You don't have to just give away your files and directories when you export a directory with NFS. In the options part of each entry in /etc/exports, you can add options that allow or limit access by setting read/write permission. These options, which are passed to NFS, are as follows:

ro: Client can mount this exported filesystem read-only. The default is to mount the filesystem read/write.

rw: Explicitly asks that a shared directory be shared with read/write permissions. (If the client chooses, it can still mount the directory as read-only.)

User mapping options in /etc/exports

In addition to options that define how permissions are handled generally, you can use options to set the permissions that specific users have to NFS shared filesystems.

One method that simplifies this process is to have each user with multiple user accounts have the same username and UID on each machine. This makes it easier to map users so they have the same permissions on a mounted filesystem as they do on files stored on their local hard disks. If that method is not convenient, user IDs can be mapped in many other ways. Here are some methods of setting user permissions and the /etc/exports option that you use for each method:

root user The client's root user is mapped by default into the nobody username (UID 65534). This prevents a client computer's root user from being able to change all files and directories in the shared filesystem. If you want the client's root user to have root permission on the server, use the no_root_squash option.

> **TIP**
>
> Keep in mind that even though root is squashed, the root user from the client can still become any other user account and access files for those user accounts on the server. So, be sure that you trust root with all of your user data before you share it read/write with a client.

nfsnobody or nobody user/group By using the 65534 user ID and group ID, you essentially create a user/group with permissions that do not allow access to files that belong to any real users on the server, unless those users open permission to everyone. However, files created by the 65534 user or group are available to anyone assigned as the 65534 user or group. To set all remote users to the 65534 user/group, use the all_squash option.

The 65534 UIDs and GIDs are used to prevent the ID from running into a valid user or group ID. Using anonuid or anongid options, you can change the 65534 user or group, respectively. For example, anonuid=175 sets all anonymous users to UID 175, and anongid=300 sets the GID to 300. (Only the number is displayed when you list file permissions unless you add entries with names to /etc/passwd and /etc/group for the new UIDs and GIDs.)

User mapping If a user has login accounts for a set of computers (and has the same ID), NFS, by default, maps that ID. This means that if the user named mike (UID 110) on maple has an account on pine (mike, UID 110), he can use his own remotely mounted files on either computer from either computer.

If a client user who is not set up on the server creates a file on the mounted NFS directory, the file is assigned to the remote client's UID and GID. (Running ls -l on the server shows the UID of the owner.)

20

Exporting the shared filesystems

After you have added entries to your `/etc/exports` file, run the `exportfs` command to have those directories exported (made available to other computers on the network). Updates will also be applied whenever you reboot your computer or restart the NFS service—the `exportfs` command will run automatically to export your directories.

> **TIP**
>
> Running the `exportfs` command after you change the exports file is a good idea. If any errors are in the file, `exportfs` identifies them for you.

Here's an example of the `exportfs` command:

```
# /usr/sbin/exportfs -a -r -v
exporting maple:/pub
exporting spruce:/pub
exporting maple:/home
exporting spruce:/home
exporting *:/mnt/win
```

The `-a` option indicates that all directories listed in `/etc/exports` should be exported. The `-r` resyncs all exports with the current `/etc/exports` file (disabling those exports no longer listed in the file). The `-v` option says to print verbose output. In this example, the `/pub` and `/home` directories from the local server are immediately available for mounting by those client computers that are named (`maple` and `spruce`). The `/mnt/win` directory is available to all client computers.

Securing Your NFS Server

The NFS facility was created at a time when encryption and other security measures were not routinely built into network services (such as remote login, file sharing, and remote execution). Therefore, NFS (even up through version 3) suffers from some rather glaring security issues.

NFS security issues made it an inappropriate facility to use over public networks and even made it difficult to use securely within an organization. These are some of the issues:

Remote `root` users Even with the default `root_squash` (which prevents `root` users from having `root` access to remote shares), the `root` user on any machine to which you share NFS directories can gain access to any other user account. Therefore, if you are doing something like sharing home directories with read/write permission, the `root` user on any box to which you are sharing has complete access to the contents of those home directories.

Unencrypted communications Because NFS traffic is unencrypted, anyone sniffing your network can see the data that is being transferred.

User mapping   Default permissions to NFS shares are mapped by user ID. So, for example, a user with UID 1000 on an NFS client has access to files owned by UID 1000 on the NFS server. This is regardless of the usernames used.

Filesystem structure exposed   Up to NFSv3, if you shared a directory over NFS, you exposed the location of that directory on the server's filesystem. (In other words, if you shared the /var/stuff directory, clients would know that /var/stuff was its exact location on your server.)

That's the bad news. The good news is that most of these issues are addressed in NFSv4 but require some extra configuration. By integrating Kerberos support, NFSv4 lets you configure user access based on each user obtaining a Kerberos ticket. For you, the extra work is configuring a Kerberos server. As for exposing NFS share locations, with NFSv4 you can bind shared directories to an /exports directory, so when they are shared, the exact location of those directories is not exposed.

Visit help.ubuntu.com/community/NFSv4Howto for details on NFSv4 features in Ubuntu.

As for standard Linux security features associated with NFS, iptables firewalls, and TCP wrappers can all play a role in securing and providing access to your NFS server from remote clients. In particular, getting firewall features working with NFS can be particularly challenging. We'll be discussing firewalls in Chapter 25, "Securing Linux on a Network." But we'll talk about TCP wrappers right here.

For network services such as vsftpd, sshd, and NFS, TCP wrappers in Linux enable you to add information to /etc/hosts.allow and /etc/hosts.deny files to indicate which hosts can or cannot access the service. Although the nfsd server daemon itself is not enabled for TCP wrappers, the rpcbind service is.

For NFSv3 and earlier versions, simply adding a line such as the following to the /etc/hosts.deny file would deny access to the rpcbind service, but it would also deny access to your NFS service:

```
rpcbind: ALL
```

For servers running NFSv4 by default, however, the rpcbind: ALL line just shown prevents outside hosts from getting information about RPC services (such as NFS) using commands like showmount. However, it does not prevent you from mounting an NFS shared directory.

Using NFS Filesystems

After a server exports a directory over the network using NFS, a client computer connects that directory to its own filesystem using the mount command. That's the same command used to mount filesystems from local hard disks, DVDs, and USB drives, but with slightly different options.

The mount command enables a client to mount NFS directories added to the /etc/fstab file automatically, just as it does with local disks. NFS directories can also be added to the

/etc/fstab file in such a way that they are not automatically mounted (so you can mount them manually when you choose). With a noauto option, an NFS directory listed in /etc/fstab is inactive until the mount command is used, after the system is up and running, to mount the filesystem.

In addition to the /etc/fstab file, you can set mount options using the /etc/nfs-mount.conf file. Within that file, you can set mount options that apply to any NFS directory you mount or only those associated with specific mount points or NFS servers.

Before you set about mounting NFS shared directories, however, you probably want to check out what shared directories are available via NFS using the showmount command.

Viewing NFS shares

From a client Linux system, you can use the showmount command to see what shared directories are available from a selected computer, such as in this example:

```
$ showmount -e server.example.com
/export/myshare client.example.com
/mnt/public     *
```

The showmount output shows that the shared directory named /export/myshare is available only to the host client.example.com. The /mnt/public shared directory, however, is available to anyone.

Manually mounting an NFS filesystem

After you know that the directory from a computer on your network has been exported (that is, made available for mounting), you can mount that directory manually using the mount command. This is a good way to make sure that it is available and working before you set it up to mount permanently. The following is an example of mounting the /stuff directory from a computer named maple on your local computer:

```
# mkdir /mnt/maple
# mount maple:/stuff /mnt/maple
```

The first command (mkdir) creates the mount point directory. (/mnt is a common place to put temporarily mounted disks and NFS filesystems.) The mount command identifies the remote computer and shared filesystem, separated by a colon (maple:/stuff), and the local mount point directory (/mnt/maple) follows.

> **NOTE**
>
> If the mount fails, make sure that the NFS service is running on the server and that the server's firewall rules don't deny access to the service. From the server, type `ps ax | grep nfsd` to see a list of nfsd server processes. If you don't see the list, try to start your NFS daemons as described earlier in this chapter. Check your firewall settings if you're worried that might be the problem. By default, the nfsd daemon listens for NFS requests on port number 2049. Your firewall must accept udp requests on ports 2049 (nfs) and 111 (rpc).

To ensure that the NFS mount occurred, type **mount -t nfs4**. This command lists all mounted NFS filesystems. Here is an example of the mount command and its output (with filesystems not pertinent to this discussion edited out):

```
# mount -t nfs4
192.168.1.15:/nfsshare on /home/nfs type nfs4 (rw,relatime,vers=4.2,
rsize=131072,wsize=131072,namlen=255,hard,proto=tcp,timeo=600,retrans
=2,sec=sys,clientaddr=192.168.1.11,local_lock=none,addr=192.168.1.15)
```

The output from the mount -t nfs4 command shows only those filesystems mounted from NFS file servers. The NFS filesystem is the /nfsshare directory from 192.168.1.15. It's mounted on /home/nfs, and its mount type is nfs4. The filesystem was mounted read/write (rw). Many other settings related to the mount are shown as well, such as the read and write sizes of packets and the NFS version number.

The mount operation just shown temporarily mounts an NFS filesystem on the local system. The next section describes how to make the mount more permanent (using the /etc/fstab file) and how to select various options for NFS mounts.

Mounting an NFS filesystem at boot time

To set up an NFS filesystem to mount automatically on a specified mount point each time you start your Linux system, you need to add an entry for that NFS filesystem to the /etc/fstab file. That file contains information about all different kinds of mounted (and available to be mounted) filesystems for your system.

Here's the format for adding an NFS filesystem to your local system:

```
host:directory      mountpoint    nfs     options      0    0
```

The first item (*host:directory*) identifies the NFS server computer and shared directory. *mountpoint* is the local mount point on which the NFS directory is mounted. It is followed by the filesystem type (nfs). Any options related to the mount appear next in a comma-separated list. (The last two zeros configure the system not to dump the contents of the filesystem and not to run fsck on the filesystem.)

The following are examples of NFS entries in /etc/fstab:

```
maple:/stuff    /mnt/maple nfs    bg,rsize=8192,wsize=8192  0 0
oak:/apps       /oak/apps  nfs    noauto,ro                 0 0
```

In the first example, the remote directory /stuff from the computer named maple (maple:/stuff) is mounted on the local directory /mnt/maple (the local directory must already exist). If the mount fails because the share is unavailable, the bg causes the mount attempt to go into the background and retry again later.

The filesystem type is nfs, and read (rsize) and write (wsize) buffer sizes (discussed in the section "Using mount options," later in this chapter) are set at 8192 to speed data transfer associated with this connection. In the second example, the remote directory is /apps on the computer named oak. It is set up as an NFS filesystem (nfs) that can be

20

mounted on the /oak/apps directory locally. This filesystem is not mounted automatically (noauto), however, and it can be mounted only as read-only (ro) using the mount command after the system is already running.

> **TIP**
>
> The default is to mount an NFS filesystem as read/write. However, the default for exporting a filesystem is read-only. If you are unable to write to an NFS filesystem, check that it was exported as read/write from the server.

Mounting noauto filesystems

Your /etc/fstab file may also contain devices for other filesystems that are not mounted automatically. For example, you might have multiple disk partitions on your hard disk or an NFS shared filesystem that you want to mount only occasionally. A noauto filesystem can be mounted manually. The advantage is that when you type the mount command, you can type less information and have the rest filled in by the contents of the /etc/fstab file. So, for example, you could type

```
# mount /oak/apps
```

With this command, mount knows to check the /etc/fstab file to get the filesystem to mount (oak:/apps), the filesystem type (nfs), and the options to use with the mount (in this case ro, for read-only). Instead of typing the local mount point (/oak/apps), you could have typed the remote filesystem name (oak:/apps) and had other information filled in.

> **TIP**
>
> When naming mount points, incorporating the name of the remote NFS server into that name can help you remember where the files are actually being stored. For example, you might mount a filesystem from a machine called duck on the directory /mnt/duck.

Using mount options

You can add several mount options to the /etc/fstab file (or to a mount command line itself) to influence how the filesystem is mounted. When you add options to /etc/fstab, they must be separated by commas. For example, here the noauto, ro, and hard options are used when oak:/apps is mounted:

```
oak:/apps    /oak/apps  nfs    noauto,ro,hard    0 0
```

The following are some options that are valuable for mounting NFS filesystems. You can read about these and other NFS mount options you can put in the /etc/fstab file from the nfs man page (man 5 nfs):

hard   If this option is used, and the NFS server disconnects or goes down while a process is waiting to access it, the process hangs until the server comes back up. This is helpful if it is critical that the data with which you are working stay in sync with the programs that are accessing it. (This is the default behavior.)

soft If the NFS server disconnects or goes down, a process trying to access data from the server times out after a set period when this option is on. An input/output error is delivered to the process trying to access the NFS server.

rsize This is the size of the blocks of data (in bytes) that the NFS client will request be used when it is reading data from an NFS server. The default is 1024. Using a larger number (such as 8192) gets you better performance on a network that is fast (such as a LAN) and is relatively error-free (that is, one that doesn't have lots of noise or collisions).

wsize This is the size of the blocks of data (in bytes) that the NFS client will request to be used when it is writing data to an NFS server. The default is 1024. Performance issues are the same as with the `rsize` option.

timeo=# This sets the time after an RPC time-out occurs that a second transmission is made, where # represents a number in tenths of a second. The default value is seven-tenths of a second. Each successive time-out causes the time-out value to be doubled (up to 60 seconds maximum). Increase this value if you believe that time-outs are occurring because of slow response from the server or a slow network.

retrans=# This sets the number of minor time-outs and retransmissions that need to happen before a major time-out occurs.

retry=# This sets how many minutes to continue to retry failed mount requests, where # is replaced by the number of minutes to retry. The default is 10,000 minutes (which is about one week).

bg If the first mount attempt times out, try all subsequent mounts in the background. This option is very valuable if you are mounting a slow or sporadically available NFS filesystem. When you place mount requests in the background, your system can continue to mount other filesystems instead of waiting for the current one to complete.

> **NOTE**
>
> If a nested mount point is missing, a time-out to allow for the needed mount point to be added occurs. For example, if you mount `/usr/trip` and `/usr/trip/extra` as NFS filesystems and `/usr/trip` is not yet mounted when `/usr/trip/extra` tries to mount, `/usr/trip/extra` times out. If you're lucky, `/usr/trip` comes up and `/usr/trip/extra` mounts on the next retry.

fg If the first mount attempt times out, try subsequent mounts in the foreground. This is the default behavior. Use this option if it is imperative that the mount be successful before continuing (for example, if you were mounting `/usr`).

Not all NFS mount options need to go into the `/etc/fstab` file. On the client side, the `/etc/nfsmount.conf` file can be created or edited to configure the `MountPoint`, `Server`, and `NFSMount_Global_Options` sections. In the Mount section, you can indicate which mount options are used when an NFS filesystem is mounted to a particular

20

mount point. The Server section lets you add options to any NFS filesystem mounted from a particular NFS server. Global options apply to all NFS mounts from this client.

The following entry in the /etc/nfsmount.conf file sets a 32KB read and write block size for any NFS directories mounted from the system named thunder.example.com:

```
[ Server "thunder.example.com" ]
  rsize=32k
  wsize=32k
```

Here are the contents of a typical /etc/nfsmount.conf file:

```
[ NFSMount_Global_Options ]
   Proto=Tcp

[ Server "nfsserver.foo.com" ]
   rsize=32k
   wsize=32k
proto=udp6

 [ MountPoint "/export/home" ]
   Background=True
```

Using autofs to mount NFS filesystems on demand

Improvements to autodetecting and mounting removable devices have meant that you can simply insert or plug in those devices to have them detected, mounted, and displayed. However, to make the process of detecting and mounting remote NFS filesystems more automatic, you still need to use a facility such as autofs (short for *automatically mounted filesystems*).

The autofs facility mounts network filesystems on demand when someone tries to use the filesystems. With the autofs facility configured and turned on, you can cause any available NFS shared directories to mount on demand. To use the autofs facility, you need to have the autofs package installed. (**apt install autofs** will get that package installed.)

Automounting to the /net directory

Even once autofs is enabled, you'll need to set up a default mount directory in the /etc/auto.master file. You can uncomment this line to define /net as the default host:

```
#/net    -hosts
```

Now, simply change (cd) to the autofs mount directory (/net in this case). This causes the shared resource to be automatically mounted and made accessible to you.

You should then restart the service using systemctl restart autofs.

Believe it or not, that's all you have to do. If you have a network connection to the NFS servers from which you want to share directories, try to access a shared NFS directory.

For example, if you know that the /usr/local/share directory is being shared from the computer on your network named shuttle, you can do the following:

```
$ cd /net/shuttle/
```

If that computer has any shared directories that are available to you, you can successfully change to that directory.

You also can type the following:

```
$ ls
usr
```

You should be able to see that the usr directory is part of the path to a shared directory. If there were shared directories from other top-level directories (such as /var or /tmp), you would see those as well. Of course, seeing any of those directories depends on how security is set up on the server.

Try going straight to the shared directory as well, as shown in this example:

```
$ cd /net/shuttle/usr/local/share
$ ls
info man music television
```

At this point, the ls should reveal the contents of the /usr/local/share directory on the computer named shuttle. What you can do with that content depends on how it was configured for sharing by the server.

This can be a bit disconcerting because you don't see any files or directories until you actually try to use them, such as changing to a network-mounted directory. The ls command, for example, doesn't show anything under a network-mounted directory until the directory is mounted, which may lead to a sometimes-it's-there-and-sometimes-it's-not impression. Just change to a network-mounted directory, or access a file on such a directory, and autofs takes care of the rest.

In the example shown, the hostname shuttle is used. However, you can use any name or IP address that identifies the location of the NFS server computer. For example, instead of shuttle, you might have used shuttle.example.com or an IP address such as 192.168.1.115.

Automounting home directories

Instead of just mounting an NFS filesystem under the /net directory, you might want to configure autofs to mount a specific NFS directory in a specific location. For example, you could configure a user's home directory from a centralized server that could be automounted from a different machine when a user logs in. Likewise, you could use a central authentication mechanism, such as LDAP (as described in Chapter 11, "Managing User Accounts"), to offer centralized user accounts as well.

The following procedure illustrates how to set up a user account on an NFS server and share the home directory of a user named joe from that server so that it can be automounted

20

when `joe` logs in to a different computer. In this example, instead of using a central authentication server, matching accounts are created on each system.

1. On the NFS server (`mynfs.example.com`) that provides a centralized user home directory for the user named `joe`, create a user account for `joe` with a home directory of `/home/shared/joe` as its name (using the `useradd` program instead of `adduser` will make this go faster). Also find `joe`'s user ID number from the `/etc/passwd` file (third field) so that you can match it when you set up a user account for `joe` on another system.

```
# mkdir /home/shared
# useradd -c "Joe Smith" -d /home/shared/ joe
# grep joe /etc/passwd
joe:x:1000:1000:Joe Smith:/home/shared/joe:/bin/bash
```

2. On the NFS server, export the `/home/shared/` directory to any system on your local network (I use 192.168.0.* here), so that you can share the home directory for `joe` and any other users you create by adding this line to the `/etc/exports` file:

```
# /etc/exports file to share directories under /home/shared
# only to other systems on the 192.168.0.0/24 network:
/home/shared 192.168.0.*(rw,insecure)
```

> **NOTE**
> In the exports file example in step 2, the `insecure` option allows clients to use ports above port 1024 to make mount requests. Some NFS clients require this because they do not have access to NFS-reserved ports.

3. On the NFS server, restart the `nfs-server` service, or if it is already running, you can simply export the shared directory as follows:

```
# exportfs -a -r -v
```

4. On the NFS server, make sure that the appropriate ports are open on the firewall.

5. On the NFS client system, add an entry to the `/etc/auto.master` file that identifies the mount point where you want the remote NFS directory to be mounted and a file (of your choosing) where you will identify the location of the remote NFS directory. I added this entry to the `auto.master` file:

```
/home/remote /etc/auto.joe
```

6. On the NFS client system, add an entry to the file you just noted (`/etc/auto.joe` is what we used) that contains an entry like the following:

```
joe        -rw      mynfs.example.com:/home/shared/joe
```

7. On the NFS client system, restart the `autofs` service:

```
# systemctl restart autofs.service
```

8. On the NFS client system, create a user named `joe` using the `useradd` command. For that command line, you need to get the UID for `joe` on the server (507 in this

example) so that `joe` on the client system owns the files from `joe`'s NFS home directory. When you run the following command, the `joe` user account is created, but you will see an error message stating that the home directory already exists (which is correct):

```
# useradd -u 507 -c "Joe Smith" -d /home/remote/joe joe
# passwd joe
Changing password for user joe.
New password: ********
Retype new password: ********
```

9. On the NFS client system, log in as `joe`. If everything is working properly, when `joe` logs in and tries to access his home directory (`/home/remote/joe`), the directory `/home/share/joe` should be mounted from the `mynfs.example.com` server. The NFS directory was both shared and mounted as read/write with owner-ship to UID 507 (`joe` on both systems), so the user `joe` on the local system should be able to add, delete, change, and view files in that directory.

After `joe` logs off (actually, when he stops accessing the directory) for a time-out period (10 minutes, by default), the directory is unmounted.

Unmounting NFS Filesystems

After an NFS filesystem is mounted, unmounting it is simple. You use the `umount` command with either the local mount point or the remote filesystem name. For example, here are two ways that you could unmount `maple:/stuff` from the local directory `/mnt/maple`:

```
# umount maple:/stuff
# umount /mnt/maple
```

Either form works. If `maple:/stuff` is mounted automatically (from a listing in `/etc/fstab`), the directory is remounted the next time you boot Linux. If it was a temporary mount (or listed as `noauto` in `/etc/fstab`), it isn't remounted at boot time.

> **TIP**
> The command is `umount`, not unmount. This is easy to get wrong.

If you get the message `device is busy` when you try to unmount a filesystem, it means that the unmount failed because the filesystem is being accessed. Most likely, one of the directories in the NFS filesystem is the current directory for your shell (or the shell of someone else on your system). The other possibility is that a command is holding a file open in the NFS filesystem (such as a text editor). Check your Terminal windows and other shells, and then `cd` out of the directory if you are in it, or just close the Terminal windows.

20

If an NFS filesystem doesn't unmount, you can force it (umount -f /mnt/maple) or unmount and clean up later (umount -l /mnt/maple). The -l option is usually the better choice because a forced unmount can disrupt a file modification that is in progress. Another alternative is to run fuser -u *mountpoint* to see what users are holding your mounted NFS share open and then fuser -k *mountpoint* to kill all of those processes.

Summary

Network File System (NFS) is one of the oldest computer file sharing products in existence today. It is still the most popular for sharing directories of files between UNIX and Linux systems. NFS allows servers to designate specific directories to make available to designated hosts and then allows client systems to connect to those directories by mounting them locally.

NFS can be secured using firewall (iptables) rules, and TCP wrappers (to allow and deny host access). Although NFS was inherently insecure when it was created (data is shared unencrypted and user access is fairly open), features in NFS version 4 have helped improve the overall security of NFS.

This NFS chapter is the last of the book's server chapters. Chapter 21, "Troubleshooting Linux," covers a wide range of desktop and server topics as it helps you understand techniques for troubleshooting your Linux system.

Exercises

Exercises in this section take you through tasks related to configuring and using an NFS server in Linux. If possible, have two Linux systems available that are connected on a local network. One of those Linux systems will act as an NFS server while the other will be an NFS client.

To get the most from these exercises, I recommend that you don't use a Linux server that has NFS already up and running. You can't do all of the exercises here without disrupting an NFS service that is already running and sharing resources.

See Appendix A for suggested solutions.

1. On the Linux system you want to use as an NFS server, install the packages needed to configure an NFS service.

2. What file will contain all the requirements for the NFS server process?

3. On the NFS server, determine the name of the NFS service and start it.

4. On the NFS server, check the status of the NFS service you just started.

5. On the NFS server, create the /var/mystuff directory and share it from your NFS server with the following attributes: available to everyone, read-only, and the root user on the client has root access to the share.

6. On a second Linux system (NFS client), view the shares available from the NFS server. (If you don't have a second system, you can do this from the same system.) If you do not see the shared NFS directory, go back to the previous question and try again.

7. On the NFS client, create a directory called /var/remote and temporarily mount the /var/mystuff directory from the NFS server on that mount point.

8. On the NFS client, unmount /var/remote, add an entry so that the same mount is done automatically when you reboot (with a bg mount option), and test that the entry you created is working properly.

9. From the NFS server, copy some files to the /var/mystuff directory. From the NFS client, make sure that you can see the files just added to that directory and make sure that you can't write files to that directory from the client.

20

Troubleshooting Linux

IN THIS CHAPTER

Troubleshooting boot loaders

Troubleshooting system initialization

Fixing software packaging problems

Checking network interface issues

Dealing with memory problems

I n any complex operating system, lots of things can go wrong. You can fail to save a file because you are out of disk space. An application can crash because the system is out of memory. The system can fail to boot up properly for, well, lots of different reasons.

In Linux, the dedication to openness, and the focus on making the software run with maximum efficiency, has led to an amazing number of tools that you can use to troubleshoot every imaginable problem. In fact, if the operating system isn't working as you would like, you even rewrite the code yourself (although I don't cover how to do that here).

This chapter takes on some of the most common problems that you can run into on a Linux system, and it describes the tools and procedures that you can use to overcome those problems. Topics are broken down by category, including the boot process, software packages, networking, and memory issues.

Boot-Up Troubleshooting

Before you can begin troubleshooting a running Linux system itself, that system needs to boot up. For a Linux system to boot up, a series of things has to happen. A Linux system installed directly on a PC architecture computer goes through the following steps:

- Turning on the power
- Starting the hardware (from Basic Input/Output System [BIOS] or Unified Extensible Firmware Interface [UEFI] firmware)
- Finding the location of the boot loader and starting it
- Choosing an operating system from the boot loader

- Starting the kernel and initial RAM disk for the selected operating system
- Starting the initialization process (`systemd`)
- Starting all of the services associated with the selected level of activity (default target)

The exact activities that occur at each of these points have undergone a transformation in recent years. Boot loaders are changing to accommodate new kinds of hardware. The initialization process is changing so that services can start more efficiently, based on dependencies and in reaction to the state of the system (such as what hardware is plugged in or what files exist) rather than a static boot order.

Troubleshooting the Linux boot process begins when you turn on your computer, and it ends when all of the services are up and running. At that point, typically a graphical or text-based login prompt is available from the console, ready for you to log in.

After reading the short descriptions of startup methods, go to the section "Starting from the firmware (BIOS or UEFI)" in order to understand what happens at each stage of the boot process and where you might need to troubleshoot.

Understanding startup

It's up to the individual Linux distribution how the services associated with the running Linux system are started. After the boot loader starts the kernel, how the rest of the activities (mounting filesystems, setting kernel options, running services, and so on) are done is all managed by the initialization process.

So it makes sense to begin with `systemd`'s initialization functionality.

The `systemd` facility is quickly becoming the present and future of the initialization process for many Linux systems. Back in 2015, it replaced Upstart in Debian and Ubuntu (version 15.04). Although `systemd` is more complex than the older System V `init`, it also offers many more features, including:

Targets Instead of runlevels, `systemd` focuses on targets. A *target* can start a set of services as well as create or start other types of units (such as directory mounts, sockets, swap areas, and timers).

System V compatibility There are targets that align with System V runlevels, if you are used to dealing with runlevels. For example, `graphical.target` aligns with runlevel 5 while `multi-user.target` is essentially runlevel 3. However, there are many more targets than runlevels, giving you the opportunity to manage sets of units more finely. Likewise, `systemd` supports System V `init` scripts and commands, such as `chkconfig` and `service` for manipulating those services if System V `init` services happen to be installed.

Dependency-based startup When the system starts up, any service in the default target (`graphical.target` for desktops and `multi-user.target` for most servers) that has had its dependencies met can start. This feature can speed up the boot process by ensuring that a single stalled service doesn't stall other services from starting if they don't need the stalled service.

Resource usage   With `systemd`, you can use `cgroups` to limit how much of your system's resources are consumed by a service. For example, you can limit the amount of memory, CPU, or other resources an entire service can consume, so a runaway process or a service that spins off an unreasonable number of child processes cannot consume more than the entire service is allowed.

When a `systemd`-enabled Linux system starts up, the first running process (Process ID [PID] 1) is the `systemd` daemon (instead of the `init` daemon). Later, the primary command for managing `systemd` services is the `systemctl` command. Managing `systemd` journal (log) messages is done with the `journalctl` command. You also have the ability to use old-style System V `init` commands such as `init`, `poweroff`, `reboot`, `runlevel`, and `shutdown` to manage services.

Starting from the firmware (BIOS or UEFI)

When you physically turn on a computer, firmware is loaded to initialize the hardware and find an operating system to boot. On PC architectures, that firmware has traditionally been referred to as *BIOS (Basic Input Output System)*. In recent years, a new type of firmware called *UEFI (Unified Extensible Firmware Interface)* has become available to replace BIOS on some computers. The two are mutually exclusive.

UEFI was designed to allow a secure boot feature, which can be used to ensure that only operating systems whose components have been signed can be used during the boot process. UEFI can still be used with non-signed operating systems by disabling the secure boot feature.

For Ubuntu, secure boot was first supported in 12.04.2. The main job of BIOS and UEFI firmware is to initialize the hardware and then hand off control of the boot process to a boot loader. The *boot loader* then finds and starts the operating system. After an operating system is installed, you should typically just let the firmware do its work and not interrupt it.

There are, however, occasions when you want to interrupt the firmware. For this discussion, we focus on how BIOS generally works. Right after you turn on the power, you should see a BIOS screen that usually includes a few words noting how to go into Setup mode and change the boot order. If you press the function key noted (often F1, F2, or F12) to choose one of those two items, here's what you can do:

Setup utility   The setup utility lets you change settings in the BIOS. These settings can be used to enable or disable certain hardware components or turn on or off selected hardware features.

Boot order   Computers are capable of starting an operating system—or more specifically, a boot loader that can start an operating system—from any one of several different devices attached to the computer. Those devices can include a CD drive, DVD drive, hard disk, USB drive, or network interface card. The boot order defines the order in which those devices are checked. By modifying the boot order, you can tell the computer to ignore the default boot order temporarily and try to boot from the device that you select.

It's common to need to press the F2, F9, or Del key to go to into Setup, or F12 to change the boot order temporarily. The next sections explore what you can troubleshoot from the Setup and Boot Order screens.

Troubleshooting BIOS setup

As we already noted, you can usually let the BIOS start without interruption and have the system boot up to the default boot device (probably the hard drive). However, here are some instances when you may want to go into Setup mode and change something in the BIOS:

To see an overview of your hardware   If your problem is hardware related, the BIOS setup is a great place to start examining your system. The Setup screen tells you the type of system, its BIOS version, its processors, its memory slots and types, whether it is 32-bit or 64-bit, which devices are in each slot, and many details about the types of devices attached to the system.

If you can't get an operating system booted at all, the BIOS Setup screen may be the only way to determine the system model, processor type, and other information you'll need to search for help or call for support.

To disable/enable a device   Most devices connected to your computer are enabled and made available for use by the operating system. To troubleshoot a problem, you may need to disable a device.

For example, let's say that your computer has two network interface cards (NICs). You want to use the second NIC to install Linux over a network, but the installer keeps trying to use the first NIC to connect to the network. You can disable the first NIC so that the installer doesn't even see it when it tries to connect to the network. Or, you can keep the NIC visible to the computer but simply disable the NIC's ability to Preboot Execution Environment (PXE) boot.

Maybe you have a plug-in audio card and you want to disable the integrated audio on the motherboard. That can be done in the BIOS as well.

Conversely, sometimes you want to enable a device that has been disabled. Perhaps you were given a computer that had a device disabled in the BIOS. From the operating system, for example, it may look like you don't have front USB ports or a CD drive. Looking at the BIOS tells you whether those devices are not available simply because they have been disabled in the BIOS.

To change a device setting   Sometimes, the default settings that come in your BIOS don't work for your situation. You might want to change the following settings in the BIOS:

NIC PXE boot settings   Most modern NICs are capable of booting from servers found on the network. If you need to do that, and you find that the NIC doesn't come up as a bootable device on your Boot Order screen, you may have to enable that feature in the BIOS.

Virtualization settings   If you want to run a Linux system as a virtual host, the computer's CPU must include Intel Virtual Technology or AMD Secure Virtual Machine (SVM) support. It is possible, however, that even if your CPU comes with this support, it may not be enabled in the BIOS. To enable it, go to the BIOS Setup screen and look for a Virtualization selection (possibly under the Performance category). Make sure that it is set to On.

Troubleshooting boot order

Depending on the hardware attached to your computer, a typical boot order might boot a CD/DVD drive first, then the hard drive, then a USB device, and finally the network interface card. The BIOS would go to each device, looking for a boot loader in the device's master boot record. If the BIOS finds a boot loader, it starts it. If no boot loader is located, the BIOS moves on to the next device until all are tried. If no boot loader is found, the computer fails to boot.

One problem that could occur with the boot order is that the device you want to boot may not appear in the boot order at all. In that case, going to the Setup screen, as described in the previous section, either to enable the device or change a setting to make it bootable, may be the thing to do.

If the device from which you want to boot does appear in the boot order, typically you just have to move the arrow key to highlight the device you want and press Enter. The following are reasons for selecting your own device to boot:

Recovery mode   If Linux does not boot from the hard disk, selecting the CD drive or a USB drive allows you to boot to a recovery mode that can help you repair the hard disk on an unbootable system.

Fresh install   Sometimes, the boot order has the hard disk listed first. If you decide that you need to do a fresh install of the operating system, you need to select the boot device that is holding your installation medium (CD, DVD, USB, or NIC).

Assuming that you get past any problems you have with the BIOS, the next step is for the BIOS to start the boot loader.

GRUB 2 boot loader

Follow these instructions for interrupting the GNU GRand Unified Bootloader (GRUB) boot prompt for the most recent Ubuntu systems:

1. After you turn on your computer and just after you see the BIOS screen, press the Shift key. You should see several menu items representing different kernels to boot.

2. From the available entries, the default is to boot the latest available kernel, which should be highlighted and ready to boot. However, you can choose a different entry if any of the following applies:

   ■ The current kernel is broken, and you want to choose an older kernel that you know is working.

- You want to run an entry that represents a totally different operating system that is installed on your disk.
- You want to run a rescue kernel.

3. Assuming you want to run a Linux kernel, highlight the kernel you want (using up and down arrows) and type **e**. You will see commands that are run to start the system, as shown in Figure 21.1.

FIGURE 21.1

Interrupt the GRUB boot loader to modify the boot process.

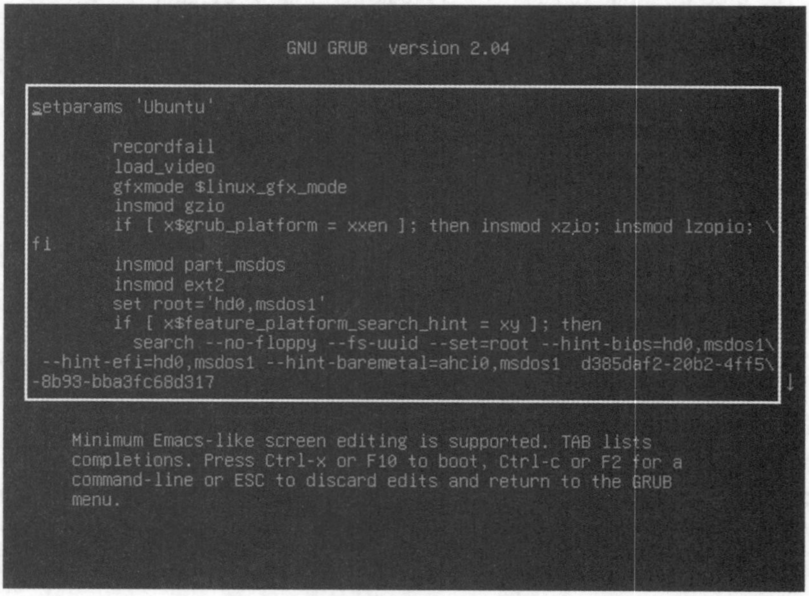

```
                    GNU GRUB   version 2.04

setparams 'Ubuntu'

        recordfail
        load_video
        gfxmode $linux_gfx_mode
        insmod gzio
        if [ x$grub_platform = xxen ]; then insmod xzio; insmod lzopio; \
fi
        insmod part_msdos
        insmod ext2
        set root='hd0,msdos1'
        if [ x$feature_platform_search_hint = xy ]; then
          search --no-floppy --fs-uuid --set=root --hint-bios=hd0,msdos1\
 --hint-efi=hd0,msdos1 --hint-baremetal=ahci0,msdos1  d385daf2-20b2-4ff5\
-8b93-bba3fc68d317

    Minimum Emacs-like screen editing is supported. TAB lists
    completions. Press Ctrl-x or F10 to boot, Ctrl-c or F2 for a
    command-line or ESC to discard edits and return to the GRUB
    menu.
```

4. To add arguments to the kernel, move your cursor to the end of the line beginning with "linux" and type the arguments you want. See `kernel.org/doc/Documentation/admin-guide/kernel-parameters.txt` for a list of kernel parameters.

5. Once you are done adding arguments, press Ctrl+X to boot the system with the kernel arguments you added.

Starting the kernel

After the kernel starts, there isn't much to do except to watch out for potential problems. If you want to watch messages detailing the boot process scroll by rather than the colorful splash screen, press the Esc key.

At this point, the kernel tries to load the drivers and modules needed to use the hardware on the computer. The main things to look for at this point (although they may scroll by quickly) are hardware failures that may prevent some feature from working properly. Although much rarer than it used to be, there may be no driver available for a piece of hardware, or the wrong driver may get loaded and cause errors. The messages appear as components are detected, such as your CPU, memory, network cards, hard drives, and so on.

In addition to scrolling past on the screen, messages produced when the kernel boots are copied to the *kernel ring buffer*. As its name implies, the kernel ring buffer stores kernel messages in a buffer, throwing out older messages after that buffer is full. After the computer boots up completely, you can log in to the system and enter the following command to capture these kernel messages in a file (then view them with the `less` command):

```
$ dmesg > /tmp/kernel_msg.txt
$ less /tmp/kernel_msg.txt
```

I like to direct the kernel messages into a file (choose any name you like) so that the messages can be examined later or sent to someone who can help debug any problems.

In Linux systems that support `systemd`, kernel messages are stored in the `systemd` journal. So, besides the `dmesg` command, you can also run `journalctl` to see kernel messages from boot time to the present. For example, here are kernel messages output from an Ubuntu 20.04 system:

```
$ journalctl -k
-- Logs begin at Tue 2019-05-07 09:16:36 EDT, end at Sun 2020-04-05 21:11:32 EDT
Apr 05 07:47:44 workstation kernel: Linux version 5.3.0-45-generic (buildd@lcy01
Apr 05 07:47:44 workstation kernel: Command line: BOOT_IMAGE=/boot/vmlinuz-5.3.0
Apr 05 07:47:44 workstation kernel: KERNEL supported cpus:
Apr 05 07:47:44 workstation kernel:    Intel GenuineIntel
Apr 05 07:47:44 workstation kernel:    AMD AuthenticAMD
Apr 05 07:47:44 workstation kernel:    Hygon HygonGenuine
Apr 05 07:47:44 workstation kernel:    Centaur CentaurHauls
Apr 05 07:47:44 workstation kernel:    zhaoxin   Shanghai
Apr 05 07:47:44 workstation kernel: x86/fpu: Supporting XSAVE feature 0x001: 'x8
Apr 05 07:47:44 workstation kernel: x86/fpu: Supporting XSAVE feature 0x002: 'SS
Apr 05 07:47:44 workstation kernel: x86/fpu: Supporting XSAVE feature 0x004: 'AV
Apr 05 07:47:44 workstation kernel: x86/fpu: xstate_offset[2]:  576, xstate_size
Apr 05 07:47:44 workstation kernel: x86/fpu: Enabled xstate features 0x7, contex
Apr 05 07:47:44 workstation kernel: BIOS-provided physical RAM map:
Apr 05 07:47:44 workstation kernel: BIOS-e820: [mem 0x0000000000000000-0x0000000
Apr 05 07:47:44 workstation kernel: BIOS-e820: [mem 0x00000000000a0000-0x0000000
```

What you want to look for are drivers that fail to load or messages that show certain features of the hardware failing to be enabled. For example, I once had a TV tuner card (for watching television on my computer screen) that set the wrong tuner type for the card that was detected. Using information about the TV card's model number and the type of failure, I found that passing an option to the card's driver allowed me to try different settings until I found the one that matched my tuner card.

In describing how to view kernel startup messages, I have gotten ahead of myself a bit. Before you can log in and see the kernel messages, the kernel needs to finish bringing up the system. As soon as the kernel is done initially detecting hardware and loading drivers, it passes off control of everything else that needs to be done to boot the system to the initialization system.

Troubleshooting the initialization system

The first process to run on a system where the kernel has just started is systemd. Although systemd is more complex than System V init, systemd also offers more ways to analyze what is happening during initialization.

Understanding the systemd boot process

When the systemd daemon (/lib/systemd/systemd) is started after the kernel starts up, it sets in motion all of the other services that are set to start up. In particular, it keys off of the contents of the target file being booted. For a typical server session, that could be /lib/systemd/system/multi-user.target, which may look like this:

```
$ cat /lib/systemd/system/multi-user.target
[Unit]
Description=Multi-User System
Documentation=man:systemd.special(7)
Requires=basic.target
Conflicts=rescue.service rescue.target
After=basic.target rescue.service rescue.target
AllowIsolate=yes
```

A desktop launch would load the directives found in the graphical.target file:

```
$ cat /lib/systemd/system/graphical.target
[Unit]
Description=Graphical Interface
Documentation=man:systemd.special(7)
Requires=multi-user.target
Wants=display-manager.service
Conflicts=rescue.service rescue.target
After=multi-user.target rescue.service rescue.target display-manager
.service
AllowIsolate=yes
```

The main difference between the two is the display-manager. service that's required for the graphical target. In addition, note how, ultimately, both launch types rely on the basic target, which looks like this:

```
$ cat /lib/systemd/system/basic.target
[Unit]
Description=Basic System
Documentation=man:systemd.special(7)
Requires=sysinit.target
Wants=sockets.target timers.target paths.target slices.target
```

```
After=sysinit.target sockets.target paths.target slices.target
tmp.mount

RequiresMountsFor=/var /var/tmp
Wants=tmp.mount
```

To see services the `multi-user.target` starts, list contents of the `/etc/systemd/system/multi-user.target.wants` directory, as in this example:

```
$ ls /etc/systemd/system/multi-user.target.wants/
anacron.service                 snap-drawing-16.mount
atd.service                     snapd.seeded.service
avahi-daemon.service            snapd.service
binfmt-support.service          'snap-gnome\x2d3\x2d26\x2d1604-97.mount'
console-setup.service           'snap-gnome\x2d3\x2d26\x2d1604-98.mount'
cron.service                    'snap-gnome\x2d3\x2d28\x2d1804-110.mount'
cups-browsed.service            'snap-gnome\x2d3\x2d28\x2d1804-116.mount'
cups.path                       'snap-gnome\x2d3\x2d32\x2d1804-96.mount'
dns-clean.service               'snap-gnome\x2d3\x2d32\x2d1804-97.mount'
ebtables.service                'snap-gnome\x2dcalculator-544.mount'
irqbalance.service              'snap-gnome\x2dcalculator-704.mount'
kerneloops.service              'snap-gnome\x2dcharacters-399.mount'
lxcfs.service                   'snap-gnome\x2dcharacters-495.mount'
lxd-containers.service          'snap-gnome\x2dlogs-81.mount'
ModemManager.service            'snap-gnome\x2dlogs-93.mount'
networkd-dispatcher.service     'snap-gnome\x2dsystem\x2dmonitor-127.mount'
networking.service              'snap-gnome\x2dsystem\x2dmonitor-135.mount'
NetworkManager.service          'snap-gtk\x2dcommon\x2dthemes-1440.mount'
nmbd.service                    'snap-gtk\x2dcommon\x2dthemes-1474.mount'
ondemand.service                'snap-onlyoffice\x2ddesktopeditors-38.mount'
postfix.service                 snap-pdftk-9.mount
pppd-dns.service                snap-slack-21.mount
remote-fs.target                snap-slack-22.mount
rsync.service                   snap-spotify-36.mount
rsyslog.service                 snap-spotify-41.mount
smartd.service                  ssh.service
smbd.service                    sysstat.service
'snap-aws\x2dcli-130.mount'     systemd-resolved.service
'snap-aws\x2dcli-151.mount'     teamviewerd.service
snap-core18-1668.mount          thermald.service
snap-core18-1705.mount          ufw.service
snap-core-8689.mount            unattended-upgrades.service
snap-core-8935.mount            whoopsie.service
snapd.autoimport.service        wpa_supplicant.service
snapd.core-fixup.service
```

These files are symbolic links to files that define what starts for each of those services. On your system, these may include remote shell (`ssh`), printing (`cups`), networking (`NetworkManager`), and others. Those links were added to that directory either when the package for a service was installed or when the service was enabled from a `systemctl enable` command.

Keep in mind that, unlike System V init, `systemd` can start, stop, and otherwise manage unit files that represent more than just services. It can manage devices, automounts, paths, sockets, and other things. After `systemd` has started everything, you can log in to the system to investigate and troubleshoot any potential problems.

After you log in, running the `systemctl` command lets you see every unit file that `systemd` tried to start up.

From the `systemctl` output, you can see whether any unit file failed. To investigate a failure, you can run `journalctl -u` specifying that service to see any error messages that were reported.

Analyzing the systemd boot process

To see exactly what happened during the boot process for a system using the `systemd` service, `systemd` provides the `systemd-analyze` tool. If you want to see if there are services that are stalling, or you want to look for a place to put in your own `systemcd` service, you can use this command to analyze the entire startup process. Here are some examples:

```
$ systemd-analyze time
Startup finished in 18.624s (firmware) + 4.604s (loader) + 2.930s
(kernel) + 25.443s (userspace) = 51.603s
graphical.target reached after 11.858s in userspace
```

The `time` option lets you see how long each phase of the startup process took, from the start of the kernel to the end of the default target. You can use `plot` to create an SVG graphic of each component of the startup process (I show `eog` here to display the output):

```
$ systemd-analyze plot > /tmp/systemd-plot.svg
$ eog /tmp/systemd-plot.svg
```

Figure 21.2 shows a small snippet of output from the much larger graphic.

From this snippet, you can see services that start after the `NetworkManager.service` starts up. Parts in dark red show the time it took the service or target to start. If the service continues to run, that is shown in light red. If the bar to the right is white, that indicates that the service is not running. At this point, you could use the `journalctl` command, as described earlier, to debug the problem.

The next section describes how to troubleshoot issues that can arise with your software packages.

Troubleshooting Software Packages

Software packaging facilities are designed to make it easier for you to manage your system software. (See Chapter 10, "Getting and Managing Software," for the basics on how to

FIGURE 21.2

Snippet from *systemd-analyze* startup plot

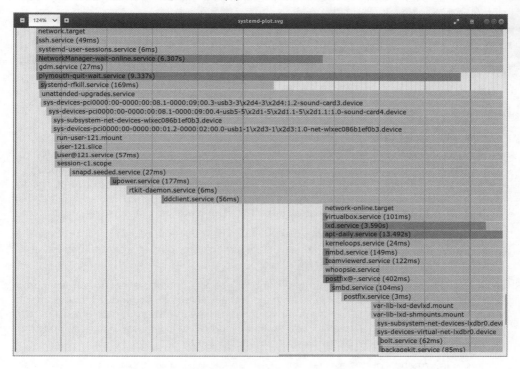

manage software packages.) Despite efforts to make it all work, however, sometimes software packaging can break.

As always, however, prevention beats troubleshooting every time. If you keep your software packages properly patched and updated and—wherever possible—restrict yourself to official, supported software repositories, then you're much less likely to run into trouble.

You can sync your local APT package database with the currently available online sources using apt update. The apt upgrade command will download and install available patches for all the software you've currently got installed on your system. Run those regularly—once a day is great. Automating the process is even better. See the "Using cron for Software Updates" sidebar for a guide to setting that up.

When things do go wrong, there are plenty of tools that can help. And these are really well-designed tools that, in our experience, are far more likely to work than not work.

Using cron for Software Updates

The cron facility provides a means of running commands at predetermined times and intervals. You can set the exact minute, hour, day, or month that a command runs. You can configure a command to run every five minutes, every third hour, or at a particular time on Friday afternoon.

If you want to use cron to set up nightly software updates, you can do that as the admin user by running the crontab -e command. That opens a file using your default editor that you can configure as a crontab file. Here's an example of what the crontab file you create might look like:

```
# min  hour  day/month  month  day/week  command
  59   23    *          *      *         apt update && apt -y
upgrade | mail
root@localhost
```

A crontab file consists of five fields, designating day and time, and a sixth field, containing the command line to run. I added the comment line to indicate the fields. Here, the apt update && apt -y upgrade commands are run, with the output mailed to the user root@localhost. The command is run at 59 minutes after hour 23 (11:59 p.m.). The asterisks (*) are required as placeholders, instructing cron to run the command on every day of the month, during every month, and on every day of the week.

When you create a cron entry, make sure that you either direct the output to a file or pipe the output to a command that can deal with the output. If you don't, any output is sent to the user that ran the crontab -e command (in this case, root).

In a crontab file, you can have a range of numbers or a list of numbers, or you can skip numbers. For example, 1, 5, or 17 in the first field causes the command to be run 1, 5, and 17 minutes after the hour. An */3 in the second field causes the command to run every three hours (midnight, 3 a.m., 6 a.m., and so on). A 1-3 in the fourth field tells cron to run the command in January, February, and March. Days of the week and months can be entered as numbers or words.

For more information on the format of a crontab file, type **man 5 crontab**. To read about the crontab command, type **man 1 crontab**.

Sometimes an installation process can be interrupted by a sudden and unintended system shutdown. This can leave one or more packages in an unusable state. The Debian package management system can attempt to repair itself:

```
# apt-get update --fix-broken
```

If a particular package is misbehaving and you think it might be due to a configuration mistake, rather than uninstalling it and starting from scratch, you can start over again with a clean state using dpkg:

```
# dpkg --reconfigure <package-name>
```

If you find yourself running short of disk space, you might be able to make some more room by removing software dependencies that are no longer being used. Finding those and then actually removing them could be a process that easily stretches on for hours. But the simple autoremove feature can do it all in one go:

```
# apt autoremove
Reading package lists... Done
Building dependency tree
Reading state information... Done
The following packages will be REMOVED:
  kde-cli-tools kde-cli-tools-data libfakekey0 libkf5su-bin libkf5su-data
  libkf5su5 sshfs
0 upgraded, 0 newly installed, 7 to remove and 9 not upgraded.
After this operation, 5,385 kB disk space will be freed.
Do you want to continue? [Y/n]
```

Sometimes a package just won't download—even though you asked APT ever so nicely. You might see an error message like "E: Unable to locate package package-name." Here are some common causes for that error:

1. You haven't updated the local repo database for a while (or ever, in the case of new Ubuntu installations). Run apt update and then try the install one more time.

2. You spelled the package name incorrectly. It happens to the best of us.

3. The package exists but isn't available for your Ubuntu release. Try searching for the package using apt search package-name.

4. Make sure the package is part of a repository that's already enabled in one of the sources files in your /etc/apt directory.

The next section covers information about network troubleshooting.

Troubleshooting Networking

With more and more of the information, images, video, and other content that we use every day now available outside of our local computers, a working network connection is required on almost every computer system. So, if you drop your network connection or can't reach the systems with which you wish to communicate, it's good to know that there are many tools in Linux for looking at the problem.

For client computers (laptops, desktops, and handheld devices), you want to connect to the network to reach other computer systems. On a server, you want your clients to be able to reach you. The following sections describe different tools for troubleshooting network connectivity for Linux client and server systems.

Troubleshooting outgoing connections

Let's say that you open your web browser but are unable to get to any website. You suspect that you are not connected to the network. Maybe the problem is with name resolution, but it may be with the connection outside of your local network.

To check whether your outgoing network connections are working, you can use many of the commands described in Chapter 14, "Administering Networking." You can test connectivity using a simple ping command. To see if name-to-address resolution is working, use host and dig.

The following sections cover problems that you can encounter with network connectivity for outgoing connections and what tools to use to uncover the problems.

View network interfaces

To see the status of your network interfaces, use the ip command. The following output shows that the loopback interface (lo) is up (so you can run network commands on your local system), but eth0 (your first wired network card) is down (state DOWN). If the interface had been up, an inet line would show the IP address of the interface. Here, only the loopback interface has an inet address (127.0.0.1):

```
# ip addr show
1: lo: <LOOPBACK,UP,LOWER_UP> mtu 16436 qdisc noqueue state UNKNOWN
    link/loopback 00:00:00:00:00:00 brd 00:00:00:00:00:00
    inet 127.0.0.1/8 scope host lo
    inet6 ::1/128 scope host
        valid_lft forever preferred_lft forever
2: eth0: <NO-CARRIER,BROADCAST,MULTICAST,UP> mtu 1500 state DOWN qlen 1000
    link/ether f0:de:f1:28:46:d9 brd ff:ff:ff:ff:ff:ff
```

By default, network interfaces are now named based on how they are connected to the physical hardware. For example, you might see a network interface of enp11s0. That would indicate that the NIC is a wired Ethernet card (en) on PCI board 11 (p11) and slot 0 (s0). A wireless card would start with wl instead of en. The intention is to make the NIC names more predictable, because when the system is rebooted, it is not guaranteed which interfaces would be named eth0, eth1, and so on by the operating system.

Check physical connections

For a wired connection, make sure that your computer is plugged into the port on your network switch. If you have multiple NICs, make sure that the cable is plugged into the correct one. If you know the name of a network interface (eth0, p4p1, or other), to find which NIC is associated with the interface, enter **ethtool -p eth0** at the command line and look behind your computer to see which NIC is blinking (Ctrl+C stops the blinking). Plug the cable into the correct port. You may need to install the ethtool package to make this work. (If you see a "Cannot identify NIC: Operation not supported" error message, it might mean that your network adapter doesn't support this kind of action.)

If instead of seeing an interface that is down, the ip command shows no interface at all, check that the hardware isn't disabled. For a wired NIC, the card may not be fully seated in its slot or the NIC may have been disabled in the BIOS.

On a wireless connection, you may click the NetworkManager icon and not see an available wireless interface. Again, it could be disabled in the BIOS. However, on a laptop, check to see if there is a tiny switch that disables the NIC. I've seen several people shred their networking configurations only to find out that this tiny switch on the front or side of their laptops had been switched to the off position.

Check routes

If your network interface is up but you still can't reach the host you want, try checking the route to that host. Start by checking your default route. Then try to reach the local network's gateway device to the next network. Finally, try to ping a system somewhere on the Internet:

```
$ ip route show
default via 192.168.122.1 dev ens3 proto dhcp metric 100
192.168.122.0/24 dev ens3 proto kernel scope link src 192.168.122.194
metric 100
```

The default line shows that the default gateway is at address 192.168.122.1 and that the address can be reached over the ens3 card. Because there is only the ens3 interface here and only a route to the 192.168.122.0 network is shown, all communication not addressed to a host on the 192.168.122.0/24 network is sent through the default gateway (192.168.122.1). The default gateway is more properly referred to as a router.

To make sure that you can reach your router, try to ping it, as in this example:

```
# ping -c 2 192.168.122.1
PING 192.168.122.1 (192.168.122.1) 56(84) bytes of data.
64 bytes from 192.168.122.1: icmp_seq=1 ttl=64 time=0.757 ms
64 bytes from 192.168.122.1: icmp_seq=2 ttl=64 time=0.538 ms

--- 192.168.122.1 ping statistics ---
2 packets transmitted, 2 received, 0% packet loss, time 65ms
rtt min/avg/max/mdev = 0.538/0.647/0.757/0.112 ms
```

A "Destination Host Unreachable" message tells you that the router is either turned off or not physically connected to you (maybe the router isn't connected to the switch you share). If the ping succeeds and you can reach the router, the next step is to try an address beyond your router.

Try to ping a widely accessible IP address. For example, the IP address for the Google public DNS server is 8.8.8.8. Try to ping that (ping -c 2 8.8.8.8). If that ping succeeds, your network is probably fine, and it is most likely your hostname-to-address resolution that is not working properly.

If you can reach a remote system but the connection is very slow, you can use the traceroute command to follow the route to the remote host. For example, this command shows each hop taken en route to www.google.com:

```
$ traceroute google.com
traceroute to google.com (172.217.1.14), 30 hops max, 60 byte packets
 1  ControlPanel.Home (192.168.1.1)  411.607 ms  412.686 ms  413.813 ms
```

Continues

Continued

```
   2   dsl-173-206-32-1.tor.primus.ca (173.206.32.1)   429.830 ms
432.166 ms   438.998 ms
   3   10.201.117.2 (10.201.117.2)   450.030 ms   450.417 ms   450.796 ms
   4   74.125.48.46 (74.125.48.46)   451.044 ms   470.842 ms   472.093 ms
   5   108.170.250.241 (108.170.250.241)   472.412 ms 108.170.250.225
(108.170.250.225)   472.407 ms   481.666 ms
   6   216.239.35.233 (216.239.35.233)   484.464 ms   407.747 ms   407.604 ms
   7   iad23s25-in-f14.1e100.net (172.217.1.14)   406.466 ms   586.899 ms
354.843 ms
```

The output shows the time taken to make each hop along the way to the Google site.

Check hostname resolution

If you cannot reach remote hosts by name, but you can reach them by pinging IP addresses, your system is having a problem with hostname resolution. Systems connected to the Internet do name-to-address resolution by communicating to a domain name system (DNS) server that can provide them with the IP addresses of the requested hosts.

The DNS server your system uses can be entered manually or picked up automatically from a Dynamic Host Configuration Protocol (DHCP) server when you start your network interfaces. In either case, the names and IP addresses of one or more DNS servers end up in your /etc/resolv.conf file. Here is an example of that file:

```
search example.com
nameserver 192.168.0.254
nameserver 192.168.0.253
```

When you ask to connect to a hostname the /etc/hosts file is searched; then the name server entries in resolv.conf are queried in the order that they appear. Here are some ways of debugging name-to-address resolution:

Check if the DNS server can be reached.   Knowing the name server addresses, you can try to ping each name server's IP address to see if it is accessible. For example: ping -c 2 192.168.0.254. If the IP address can be reached, it could be that you were either assigned the wrong address for the DNS server or it is currently down.

Check if the DNS server is working.   You specifically try to use each DNS server with the host or dig command. For example, either of these two commands can be used to see if the DNS server at 192.168.0.254 can resolve the hostname www.google .com into an IP address. Repeat this for each name server's IP address until you find which ones work:

```
# host google.com 192.168.0.254
Using domain server:
Name: 192.168.0.254
Address: 192.168.0.254#53
Aliases:
www.google.com has address 172.217.13.228
www.google.com has IPv6 address 2607:f8b0:4004:809::2004
# dig @192.168.0.254 www.google.com
...
```

```
;; QUESTION SECTION:
;www.google.com.                  IN  A

;; ANSWER SECTION:
www.google.com.          67  IN  A    172.217.13.228
...
```

Correct your DNS servers.   If you determine that you have the wrong IP addresses set for your DNS servers, changing them can be a bit tricky. Search /var/log/sys-log or the output of journalctl for your DNS servers' IP addresses. If Network-Manager is used to start your networking and connect to a DHCP server, you should see name server lines with the IP addresses being assigned. If the addresses are wrong, you can override them.

If you're using Netplan to manage your network devices, you can edit the file named /etc/netplan/01-network-manager-all.yaml (or something similar). Assuming your DNS server addresses are 8.8.8.8 and 8.8.4.4, the new entry should look like this:

```
nameservers:
   addresses: [8.8.8.8,8.8.4.4]
```

Don't forget to run sudo netplan apply when you're done.

The procedures just described for checking your outgoing network connectivity apply to any type of system, whether it is a laptop, desktop, or server. For the most part, incoming connections are not an issue with laptops or desktops because most requests are simply denied. However, for servers, the next section describes ways of making your server accessible if clients are having trouble reaching the services you provide from that server.

Troubleshooting incoming connections

If you are troubleshooting network interfaces on a server, there are different considerations than on a desktop system. Because most Linux systems are configured as servers, you should know how to troubleshoot problems encountered by those who are trying to reach your Linux servers.

I'll start with the idea of an Apache web server running on your Linux system which, for some strange reason, no web clients can reach. The following sections describe things that you can try to locate the problem.

Check if the client can reach your system at all

To be a public server, your system's hostname should be resolvable so that any client on the Internet can reach it. That means locking down your system to a particular, public IP address and registering that address with a public DNS server. You can use a domain registrar (such as www.networksolutions.com or Amazon's Route 53) to do that.

When clients cannot reach your website by name from their web browsers, if the client is a Linux system, you can go through ping, host, traceroute, and other commands described in the previous section to track down the connectivity problem. Windows systems have their own version of ping that you can use from those systems.

If the name-to-address resolution is working to reach your system and you can ping your server from the outside, the next thing to try is the availability of the service.

Check if the service is available to the client

From a Linux client, you can check if the service you are looking for (Apache in this case) is available from the server. One way to do that is using the nmap command.

The nmap command is a favorite tool for system administrators checking for various kinds of information on networks. However, it is a favorite cracker tool as well because it can scan servers, looking for potential vulnerabilities. So, it is fine to use nmap to scan your own systems to check for problems, but know that using nmap on another system is like checking the doors and windows on someone's house to see if you can get in. You look like an intruder.

Checking your own system to see what ports to your server are open to the outside world (essentially, checking what services are running) is perfectly legitimate and easy to do. After nmap is installed (apt install nmap), use your system hostname or IP address to use nmap to scan your system to see what is running on common ports:

```
# nmap 192.168.0.119
Starting Nmap 6.40 ( http://nmap.org ) at 2019-12-08 13:28 EST
Nmap scan report for spike (192.168.0.119)
Host is up (0.0037s latency).
Not shown: 995 filtered ports
PORT     STATE   SERVICE
21/tcp   open    ftp
22/tcp   open    ssh
80/tcp   open    http
443/tcp  open    https
631/tcp  open    ipp
MAC Address: 00:1B:21:0A:E8:5E (Intel Corporate)
Nmap done: 1 IP address (1 host up) scanned in 4.77 seconds
```

The preceding output shows that TCP ports are open to the regular (http) and secure (https) web services. When you see that the state is open, it indicates that a service is listening on the port as well. If you get to this point, it means that your network connection is fine and you should direct your troubleshooting efforts to how the service itself is configured (for example, you might look in /etc/apache2/sites-available to see if specific hosts are allowed or denied access).

If TCP ports 80 and/or 443 are not shown, it means that they are being filtered. You need to check whether your firewall is blocking (not accepting packets to) those ports. If the port is not filtered but the state is closed, it means that the Apache service either isn't running or isn't listening on those ports. The next step is to log in to the server and check those issues. While you're there, you can check any active firewalls to see if they're blocking your requests. We'll discuss firewalls in Chapter 25, "Securing Linux on a Network."

Check the service on the server

If there seems to be nothing blocking client access to your server through the actual ports providing the service that you want to share, it is time to check the service itself. Assuming that the service is running (`systemctl status apache2` to check), the next thing to check is that it is listening on the proper ports and network interfaces.

The `netstat` command is a great general-purpose tool for checking network services. The following command lists the names and process IDs (`p`) for all processes that are listening (`l`) for TCP (`t`) and UDP (`u`) services, along with the port number (`n`) on which they are listening. The command line filters out all lines except those associated with the `apache2` process:

```
# netstat -tupln | grep apache2
tcp    0   0 :::80          :::*          LISTEN      2567/apache2
tcp    0   0 :::443         :::*          LISTEN      2567/apache2
```

The preceding example shows that the `apache2` process is listening on port 80 and 443 for all interfaces. It is possible that Apache might be listening on selected interfaces. For example, if the `apache2` process were only listening on the local interface (127.0.0.1) for HTTP requests (port 80), the entry would appear as follows:

```
tcp    0   0 127.0.0.1:80 :::*          LISTEN      2567/apache2
```

For Apache, as well as for other network services that listen for requests on network interfaces, you can edit the service's main configuration file (in this case, `/etc/apache2/apache2.conf`) to tell it to listen on port 80 for all addresses (`Listen 80`) or a specific address (`Listen 192.168.0.100:80`).

Troubleshooting Memory

Troubleshooting performance problems on your computer is one of the most important, although often elusive, tasks you'll face. Maybe you have a system that was working fine, but it begins to slow down to a point where it is practically unusable. Maybe applications just begin to crash for no apparent reason. Finding and fixing the problem may take some detective work.

Linux comes with many tools for watching activities on your system and figuring out what's happening. Using a variety of Linux utilities, you can do things such as finding out which processes are consuming large amounts of memory or placing high demands on your processors, disks, or network bandwidth. Solutions can include the following:

Adding capacity Your computer may be trying to do what you ask of it, but failures might occur because you don't have enough memory, processing power, disk space, or network capacity to get reasonable performance. Even nearing the boundaries of resource exhaustion can cause performance problems. Improving your computer hardware capacity is often the easiest way of solving performance problems.

Tuning the system Linux comes with default settings that define how it internally saves data, moves data around, and protects data. System tunable parameters can be changed if the default settings don't work well for the types of applications you have on your system.

Uncovering problem applications or users   Sometimes, a system performs poorly because a user or an application is doing something wrong. Misconfigured or broken applications can hang or gobble up all of the resources they can find. An inexperienced user might mistakenly start multiple instances of a program that drain system resources. As a system administrator, you want to know how to find and fix these problems.

To troubleshoot performance problems in Linux, you use some of the basic tools for watching and manipulating processes running on your system. Refer to Chapter 6, "Managing Running Processes," if you need details on commands such as ps, top, kill, and killall. In the following sections, I add commands such as memstat to dig a little deeper into what processes are doing and where things are going wrong.

The most complex area of troubleshooting in Linux relates to managing virtual memory. The next sections describe how to view and manage virtual memory.

Uncovering memory issues

Computers have ways of storing data permanently (hard disks) and temporarily (*random access memory*, or *RAM*, and *swap space*). Think of yourself as a CPU, working at a desk trying to get your work finished. You would put data that you want to keep permanently in a filing cabinet across the room (that's like hard disk storage). You would put information that you are currently using on your desk (that's like RAM memory on a computer).

Swap space is a way of extending RAM. It is really just a place to put temporary data that doesn't fit in RAM but is expected to be needed by the CPU at some point. Although swap space is on the hard disk, it is not a regular Linux filesystem in which data is stored permanently.

Compared to disk storage, random access memory has the following attributes:

Nearer the processor   Like the desk being near to you as you work, memory is physically near the CPU on the computer's motherboard. So, any data the CPU needs, it can just grab immediately if the data is in RAM.

Faster   Its proximity to the CPU and the way that it is accessed (solid state versus mechanical hard disks) makes it much faster for the CPU to get information from RAM than it can from a hard disk. It's quicker to look at a piece of paper on your desk (a small, close space) than to walk to a row of file cabinets and to start searching for what you want.

Less capacity   A new computer might have a 10 TB or larger hard drive but only 8 GB or 16 GB of RAM. Although it would make the computer run faster to put every file and every piece of data that the processor may need into RAM, in most cases there just wouldn't be enough room. Also, both the physical memory slots on the computer and the computer system itself (64-bit computers can address more RAM than 32-bit computers) can limit how much RAM a computer is capable of having.

More expensive   Although RAM is much more affordable than it was a decade or two ago, it is still more expensive (per GB) than hard disks.

Temporary   RAM holds data and metadata that the CPU is using now for the work it is doing (plus some content the Linux kernel is keeping around because it suspects a process will need it before long). When you turn off the computer, however, everything in RAM is lost. When the CPU is done with data, that data is discarded if it is no longer needed, left in RAM for possible later use, or marked to be written to disk for permanent storage if it needs to be saved.

It is important to understand the difference between temporary (RAM) and permanent (hard disk) storage, but that doesn't tell the whole story. If the demand for memory exceeds the supply of RAM, the kernel can temporarily move data out of RAM to an area called *swap space*.

If we revisit the desk analogy, this would be like saying, "There is no room left on my desk, yet I have to add more papers to it for the projects I'm currently working on. Instead of storing papers I'll need soon in a permanent file cabinet, I'll have one special file cabinet (like a desk drawer) to hold those papers that I'm still working with but that I'm not ready to store permanently or throw away."

Refer to Chapter 12, "Managing Disks and Filesystems," for more information on swap files and partitions and how to create them. For the moment, however, there are a few things that you should know about these kinds of swap areas and when they are used:

- When data is swapped from RAM to a swap area (swapped out), you get a performance hit. Remember, writing to disk is much slower than writing to RAM.
- When data is returned from swap to RAM because it is needed again (swapped in), you get another performance hit.
- When Linux runs out of space in RAM, swapping is like losing a high gear on a car. The car might have to run in a lower gear, but it would not stop altogether. In other words, all your processes stay active and they don't lose any data or fail completely, but the system performance can significantly slow down.
- If both RAM and swap are full and no data can be discarded or written to disk, your system can reach an out-of-memory (OOM) condition. When that happens, the kernel OOM killer kicks in and begins killing off processes, one by one, to regain as much memory as the kernel needs to begin functioning properly again.

The general rule has always been that swapping is bad and should be avoided. However, some would argue that, in certain cases, more aggressive swapping can actually improve performance.

Think of the case where you open a document in a text editor and then minimize it on your desktop for several days as you work on different tasks. If data from that document were swapped out to disk, more RAM would be available for more active applications that could put that space to better use. The performance hit would come the next time you needed to access the data from the edited document and the data was swapped in from disk to RAM. The settings that relate to how aggressively a system swaps are referred to as *swappiness*.

As much as possible, Linux wants to make everything that an open application needs immediately available. So, using the desk analogy, if I am working on nine active projects and there is space on the desk to hold the information I need for all nine projects, why not leave them all within reach on the desk? Following that same way of thinking, the kernel sometimes keeps libraries and other content in RAM that it thinks you might eventually need—even if a process is not looking for it immediately.

The fact that the kernel is inclined to store information in RAM that it expects may be needed soon (even if it is not needed now) can cause an inexperienced system administrator to think that the system is almost out of RAM and that processes are about to start failing. That is why it is important to know the different kinds of information being held in memory—so that you can tell when real out-of-memory situations can occur. The problem is not just running out of RAM; it is running out of RAM when only non-swappable data is left.

Keep this general overview of *virtual memory* (RAM and swap) in mind, as the next section describes ways to go about troubleshooting issues related to virtual memory.

Checking for memory problems

Let's say that you are logged in to a Linux desktop, with lots of applications running, and everything begins to slow down. To find out if the performance problems have occurred because you have run out of memory, you can try commands such as top and ps to begin looking for memory consumption on your system.

To run the top command to watch for memory consumption, type **top** and then type a capital **M**. Here is an example:

```
# top
top - 22:48:24 up  3:59,  2 users,  load average: 1.51, 1.37, 1.15
Tasks: 281 total,   2 running, 279 sleeping,   0 stopped,   0 zombie
Cpu(s): 16.6%us,  3.0%sy,  0.0%ni, 80.3%id,  0.0%wa,  0.0%hi,  0.2%si,  0.0%st
Mem:   3716196k total,  2684924k used,  1031272k free,   146172k buffers
Swap:  4194296k total,        0k used,  4194296k free,   784176k cached
  PID USER      PR  NI  VIRT  RES  SHR S %CPU %MEM    TIME+  COMMAND
 6679 cnegus    20   0 1665m 937m  32m S  7.0 25.8  1:07.95 firefox
 6794 cnegus    20   0  743m 181m  30m R 64.8  5.0  1:22.82 npviewer.bin
 3327 cnegus    20   0 1145m 116m  66m S  0.0  3.2  0:39.25 soffice.bin
 6939 cnegus    20   0  145m  71m  23m S  0.0  2.0  0:00.97 acroread
 2440 root      20   0  183m  37m  26m S  1.3  1.0  1:04.81 Xorg
 2795 cnegus    20   0 1056m  22m  14m S  0.0  0.6  0:01.55 nautilus
```

There are two lines (Mem and Swap) and four columns of information (VIRT, RES, SHR, and %MEM) relating to memory in the top output. In this example, you can see that RAM is not exhausted from the Mem line (only 268492k of 3716196k is used) and that nothing is being swapped to disk from the Swap line (0 k used).

However, adding up just these first six lines of output in the VIRT column, you would see that 4937MB of memory has been allocated for those applications, which exceeds the 3629MB of total RAM (3716196k) that is available. That's because the VIRT column shows only the amount of memory that has been promised to the application. The RES line shows the amount of non-swappable memory that is actually being used, which totals only 1364MB.

Notice that, when you ask to sort by memory usage by typing a capital **M**, top knows to sort on that RES column. The SHR column shows memory that could potentially be shared by other applications (such as libraries), and %MEM shows the percentage of total memory consumed by each application.

If you think that the system is reaching an out-of-memory state, here are a few things to look for:

- The free space shown on the Mem line would be at or near zero.
- The used space shown on the Swap line would be non-zero and would continue to grow. That should be accompanied with a slowdown of system performance.
- As the top screen redraws every few seconds, if there is a process with a memory leak (continuously asking for and using more memory, but not giving any memory back), the amount of VIRT memory grows, but more important, the RES memory continues to grow for that process.
- If the Swap space actually runs out, the kernel starts to kill off processes to deal with this out-of-memory condition.

If you have Cockpit installed and enabled, you can watch memory usage live from your web browser. Open Cockpit and then select System ⇨ Memory & Swap.

Dealing with memory problems

In the short term, you can do several things to deal with this out-of-memory condition:

Kill a process   If the memory problem is due to one errant process, you can simply kill that process. Assuming that you are logged in as root or as the user who owns the runaway process, type **k** from the top window, then enter the PID of the process that you want to kill and choose 15 or 9 as the signal to send.

Drop page caches   If you just want to clear up some memory right now as you otherwise deal with the problem, you can tell the system to drop inactive page caches. When you do this, some memory pages are written to disk; others are just discarded (because they are stored permanently and can be gotten again from disk when they are needed).

This action is the equivalent of cleaning your desk and putting all but the most critical information into the trash or into a file cabinet. You may need to retrieve information again shortly from a file cabinet, but you almost surely don't need it all immediately. Keep top running in one Terminal window to see the Mem line change as you type the following (as root) into another Terminal window:

```
# echo 3 > /proc/sys/vm/drop_caches
```

Kill an out-of-memory process   Sometimes, memory exhaustion has made the system so unusable that you may not be able to get a response from a shell or GUI.

In those cases, you might be able to use Alt+SysRq keystrokes to kill an out-of-memory process. The reason you can use Alt+SysRq keystrokes on an otherwise unresponsive system is that the kernel processes Alt+SysRq requests ahead of other requests.

To enable Alt+SysRq keystrokes, the system must have already set /proc/sys/kernel/sysrq to 1. An easy way to do this is to add kernel.sysrq = 1 to the /etc/sysctl.conf file. Also, you must run the Alt+SysRq keystrokes from a text-based interface (such as the virtual console you see when you press Ctrl+Alt+F2).

With kernel.sysrq set to 1, you can kill the process on your system with the highest OOM score by pressing Alt+SysRq+f from a text-based interface. A listing of all processes running on your system appears on the screen with the name of the process that was killed listed at the end. You can repeat those keystrokes until you have killed enough processes to be able to access the system normally from the shell again.

> **NOTE**
>
> There are many other Alt+SysRq keystrokes that you can use to deal with an unresponsive system. For example, Alt+SysRq+e terminates all processes except for the init process. Alt+SysRq+t dumps a list of all current tasks and information about those tasks to the console. To reboot the system, press Alt+SysRq+b. See the sysrq .txt file in the /usr/share/doc/kernel-doc*/Documentation directory for more information about Alt+SysRq keystrokes.

Summary

Troubleshooting problems in Linux can start from the moment you turn on your computer. Problems can occur with your computer BIOS, boot loader, or other parts of the boot process that you can correct by intercepting them at different stages of the boot process.

After the system has started, you can troubleshoot problems with software packages, network interfaces, or memory exhaustion. Linux comes with many tools for finding and correcting any part of the Linux system that might break down and need fixing.

The next chapter covers the topic of Linux security. Using the tools described in that chapter, you can provide access to those services that you and your users need while blocking access to system resources that you want to protect from harm.

Exercises

The exercises in this section enable you to try out useful troubleshooting techniques in Linux. Because some of the techniques described here can potentially damage your system, I recommend that you do not use a production system that you cannot risk damaging. See Appendix A for suggested solutions.

These exercises relate to troubleshooting topics in Linux. They assume that you are booting a PC with standard BIOS. To do these exercises, you need to be able to reboot your computer and interrupt any work it may be doing.

1. Boot your computer, and as soon as you see the BIOS screen, go into Setup mode as instructed on the BIOS screen.

2. From the BIOS Setup screen, determine if your computer is 32-bit or 64-bit, if it includes virtualization support, and if your network interface card is capable of PXE booting.

3. Reboot, and just after the BIOS screen disappears, when you see the countdown to booting the Linux system, press a key to get to the GRUB boot loader.

4. From the GRUB boot loader, add an option to boot up to runlevel 1 so that you can do some system maintenance.

5. After the system boots up, look at the messages that were produced in the kernel ring buffer that show the activity of the kernel as it booted up.

6. Use APT to download and install any available package versions and patches.

7. Check to see what processes are listening for incoming connections on your system.

8. Check to see what ports are open on your external network interface.

9. Run the `top` command in a Terminal window. Open a second Terminal window, clear your page cache, and note on the `top` screen if more RES memory is now available.

10. With Cockpit enabled on your system, access Cockpit to view details on the system's on-going memory and swap usage.

Part V

Learning Linux Security Techniques

IN THIS PART

Understanding Basic Linux Security

IN THIS CHAPTER

A t its most basic level, securing an Ubuntu system starts with physical security, data security, user accounts protection, and software security. Over time, you need to monitor that system to make sure it remains safe.

Some of the questions that you need to ask yourself include the following:

- Who can get to the system physically?
- Are backup copies of data being made in case of disaster?
- How well are user accounts secured?
- Does the software come from a secure Ubuntu distribution, and are security patches up to date?
- Have you been monitoring the system to make sure that it hasn't been cracked or corrupted?

This chapter starts by covering basic Ubuntu security topics. Subsequent chapters go deeper into advanced security mechanisms.

Implementing Physical Security

A lock on the computer server room door is the first line of defense. Although a very simple concept, it's often ignored. Access to the physical server means access to all of the data that it contains. No security software can fully protect your systems if someone with malicious intent has physical access to the Linux server.

Basic server room physical security includes items such as these:

- A lock or security alarm on the server room door
- Access controls that allow only authorized access and that identify who accessed the room and when the access occurred, such as a card key entry system

- A sign stating "no unauthorized access allowed" on the door
- Policies on who can access the room and when that access may occur for groups such as the cleaning crew, server administrators, and others

Physical security includes environmental controls. Appropriate fire suppression systems and proper ventilation for your server room must be implemented.

Implementing disaster recovery

Disaster recovery plans should include these things:

- What data is to be included in backups
- Where backups are to be stored
- How long backups are maintained
- How backup media is rotated through storage

Backup data, media, and software should be included in your Access Control Matrix checklist.

It is important to determine how many backup copies of each object should be maintained. While you may need only three backup copies of one particular object, another object may be important enough to require maintaining more copies.

Backup utilities on a Linux system include the following:

- amanda (Advanced Maryland Automatic Network Disk Archiver)
- cpio
- dump/restore
- tar
- rsync

The cpio and tar utilities are typically pre-installed on an Ubuntu distribution. A simple, yet effective tool for backing up data over networks is the rsync utility. With rsync, you can set up a cron job to keep copies of all data in selected directories or mirror exact copies of directories on remote machines.

Of the tools just mentioned, only amanda is not typically installed by default. However, amanda is popular because it comes with a great deal of flexibility and can even back up a Windows system. If you need more information on the amanda backup utility, see www.amanda .org. Ultimately, the utility you select must meet your organization's particular security needs for backup.

Securing user accounts

User accounts are part of the authentication process allowing users into the Linux system. Proper user account management enhances a system's security. Setting up user accounts was covered in Chapter 11, "Managing User Accounts." However, a few additional rules are necessary to increase security through user account management:

- Allow one user per user account.
- Limit access to the root user account.
- Set expiration dates on temporary accounts.
- Remove unused user accounts.

One user per user account

Accounts should enforce accountability. Thus, multiple people should not be logging in to one account. When multiple people share an account, there is no way to prove a particular individual completed a particular action.

Limiting access to the root user account

If multiple people can log in to the root account, you have another repudiation situation. You cannot track individual use of the root account. To allow tracking of root account use by individuals, a policy for using sudo (see Chapter 8, "Learning System Administration") instead of logging in to root should be instituted. By default, Ubuntu systems don't provide the root user with login credentials, thereby discouraging its use.

Instead of using the root user, you should grant root access on a per-command basis with the sudo command. Using sudo provides the following security benefits:

- The root password does not have to be given out.
- You can fine-tune command access.
- All sudo use (who, what, when) is recorded in /var/log/auth.log, including any failed sudo access attempts. Recent Linux systems also store all sudo access in the systemd journal (type **journalctl -f** to watch live sudo access attempts, along with other system messages).
- After you grant someone sudo permission, you can try to restrict root access to certain commands in the /etc/sudoers file (with the visudo command). However, after you grant root permission to a user, even in a limited way, it is difficult to be sure that a determined user can't find ways to gain full root access to your system and do what they want to it.

One way to keep a misbehaving administrator in check is to have security messages intended for the /var/log/auth.log file sent to a remote log server to which none of the local administrators have access. In that way, any misuse of root privilege is attached to a particular user and is logged in a way that the user can't cover their tracks.

Setting expiration dates on temporary accounts

If you have consultants, interns, or temporary employees who need access to your Linux systems, it's important to set up their user accounts with expiration dates. The expiration date is a safeguard, in case you forget to remove their accounts when they no longer need access to your organization's systems.

22

To set a user account with an expiration date, use the `usermod` command. The format is `usermod -e yyyy-mm-dd user_name`. In the following code, the account `tim` has been set to expire on January 1, 2021:

```
# usermod -e 2021-01-01 tim
```

To verify that the account has been properly set to expire, double-check yourself by using the `chage` command. The `chage` command is primarily used to view and change a user account's password aging information. However, it also can access account expiration information. The `-l` option allows you to list various information to which `chage` has access. To keep it simple, pipe the output from the `chage` command into `grep` and search for the word *Account*. This produces only the user account's expiration date.

```
# chage -l tim | grep Account
Account expires                          :  Jan  01,  2021
```

As you can see, the account expiration date was successfully changed for `tim` to January 1, 2021.

> **TIP**
>
> If you do not use the `/etc/shadow` file for storing your account passwords, the `chage` utility doesn't work. In most cases, this is not a problem because the `/etc/shadow` file is configured to store password information by default on most Linux systems.

Set account expiration dates for all transitory employees. In addition, consider reviewing all user account expiration dates as part of your security monitoring activities. These activities help to eliminate any potential backdoors to your Linux system.

Removing unused user accounts

Keeping old expired accounts around is asking for trouble. After a user has left an organization, it is best to perform a series of steps to remove their account along with data:

1. Find files on the system owned by the account, using the *find / -user username* command.

2. Expire or disable the account.

3. Back up the files.

4. Remove the files or reassign them to a new owner.

5. Delete the account from the system.

Problems occur when step 5 is forgotten and expired or disabled accounts are still on the system. A malicious user gaining access to your system could renew the account and then masquerade as a legitimate user.

To find these accounts, search through the /etc/shadow file. The account's expiration date is in the eighth field of each record. It would be convenient if a date format were used. Instead, this field shows the account's expiration date as the number of days since January 1, 1970.

You can use a two-step process to find expired accounts in the /etc/shadow file automatically. First, set up a shell variable (see Chapter 7, "Writing Simple Shell Scripts") with today's date in "days since January 1, 1970" format. Then, using the gawk command (apt install gawk), you can obtain and format the information needed from the /etc/shadow file.

Setting up a shell variable with the current date converted to the number of days since January 1, 1970 is not particularly difficult. The date command can produce the number of seconds since January 1, 1970. To get what you need, divide the result from the date command by the number of seconds in a day: 86,400. The following demonstrates how to set up the shell variable TODAY:

```
$ TODAY=$(echo $(($(date --utc --date "$1" +%s)/86400)))
$ echo $TODAY
16373
```

Next, the accounts and their expiration dates are pulled from the /etc/shadow file using gawk. The gawk command is the GNU's Not Unix (GNU) version of the awk program used in UNIX. The command's output is shown in the code that follows. As you would expect, many of the accounts do not have an expiration date. However, two accounts, Consultant and Intern, show an expiration date in the "days since January 1, 1970" format. Note that you can skip this step. It is just for demonstration purposes.

```
# gawk -F: '{print $1,$8}' /etc/shadow
...
chrony
tcpdump
johndoe
Consultant 13819
Intern 13911
```

The $1 and $8 in the gawk command represent the username and expiration date fields in the /etc/shadow file records. To check those accounts' expiration dates and see if they are expired, a more refined version of the gawk command is needed:

```
# gawk -F: '{if (($8 > 0) && ($TODAY > $8)) print $1}' /etc/shadow
Consultant
Intern
```

Only accounts with an expiration date are collected by the ($8 > 0) portion of the gawk command. To make sure that these expiration dates are past the current date, the TODAY variable is compared with the expiration date field, $8. If TODAY is greater than the account's expiration date, the account is listed. As you can see in the preceding example, two expired accounts still exist on the system and need to be removed.

That is all you need to do. Set up your TODAY variable and execute the gawk command. All of the expired accounts in the /etc/shadow file are listed for you. To remove these accounts, use the deluser command.

User accounts are only a portion of the authentication process allowing users into the Linux system. User account passwords also play an important role in the process.

Securing passwords

Passwords are the most basic security tool of any modern operating system and, consequently, the most commonly attacked security feature. It is natural for users to want to choose a password that is easy to remember, but often this means that they choose a password that is also easy to guess.

Brute force methods are commonly employed to gain access to a computer system. Trying the popular passwords often yields results. Some of the most common passwords are as follows:

- 123456
- Password
- princess
- rockyou
- abc123

Just use your favorite Internet search engine and look for "common passwords." If you can find these lists, then malicious attackers can too. Obviously, choosing good passwords is critical to having a secure system.

Choosing good passwords

In general, a password must not be easy to guess, be common or popular, or be linked to you in any way. Here are some rules to follow when choosing a password:

- Do not use any variation of your login name or your full name.
- Do not use a dictionary word.
- Do not use proper names of any kind.
- Do not use your phone number, address, family, or pet names.
- Do not use website names.
- Do not use any contiguous line of letters or numbers on the keyboard (such as "qwerty" or "asdfg").
- Do not use any of the above with added numbers or punctuation at the front or end or typed backward.
- Do not reuse passwords across multiple accounts.

So now that you know what not to do, look at the two primary items that make a strong password:

1. A password should be at least 15 to 25 characters in length.
2. A password should contain all of the following:

   ■ Lowercase letters
   ■ Uppercase letters
   ■ Numbers
   ■ Special characters, such as : ! $ % * ( ) - + = , < > : : " '

Twenty-five characters is a long password. However, the longer the password, the more secure it is. What your organization chooses as the minimum password length depends on its security needs.

22

> **TIP**
>
> Gibson Research Center has some excellent material on strong passwords, including an article called "How big is your haystack. . .and how well hidden is your needle?" at `grc.com/haystack.htm`.

Choosing a good password can be difficult. It has to be hard enough not to be guessed and easy enough for you to remember. A good way to choose a strong password is to take the first letter from each word of an easily remembered sentence. Be sure to add numbers, special characters, and varied case. The sentence you choose should have meaning only to you and should not be publicly available.

In the real world, when we're working with real human beings, building passwords that are both strong and likely to be remembered is practically impossible. A better alternative is to use four random five-letter words, something like: HorseTabletMarchBound. According to the Gibson Research Center referenced above, this easy-to-remember password would require 3.52 quadrillion centuries to crack. That should keep you safe for now—at least until quantum computers become widely available.

Setting and changing passwords

You set your own password using the `passwd` command. Type the **passwd** command and it allows you to change your password. First, it prompts you to enter your old password. To protect against someone shoulder surfing and learning your password, neither your old nor new password is displayed as you type.

Assuming that you type your old password correctly, the `passwd` command prompts you for the new password. When you type your new password, it is checked using a utility called `cracklib` to determine whether it is a good or bad password. Non-root users are required to try a different password if the one they have chosen is not a good password.

The root user is the only user who is permitted to assign bad passwords. After the password has been accepted by `cracklib`, the `passwd` command asks you to enter the new password a second time to make sure that there are no typos (which are hard to detect when you can't see what you are typing).

When running as root, changing a user's password is possible by supplying that user's login name as a parameter of the `passwd` command, as in this example:

```
# passwd joe
Changing password for user joe.
New UNIX password: ********
Retype new UNIX password: ********
passwd: all authentication tokens updated successfully.
```

Here, the `passwd` command prompts you twice to enter a new password for `joe`. It does not prompt for his old password in this case.

Enforcing best password practices

Now you know what a good password looks like and how to change a password, but how do you enforce it on your Linux system? One place to start is with the Pluggable Authentication Modules (PAM) facility. With PAM, you can define exact requirements that passwords must meet. For example, to ensure that passwords must be 12 characters long, with at least 2 numbers, 3 uppercase letters, and 2 lowercase letters, and are different than the previous 4 passwords, you can add the following line to either the /etc/pam.d/common-password or /etc/pam.d/common-auth file:

```
password requisite pam_cracklib.so minlen=12, dcredit=2, ucredit=3,
lcredit=2, difok=4
```

The next question is, how can you make people change passwords? It can become tiresome to come up with new, strong passwords every 30 days! That's why some enforcing techniques are often necessary.

> **TIP**
>
> Current best practice security policies no longer recommend forcing users to regularly change their passwords. For one thing, human nature being human nature, users will most likely "cheat" the system, choosing easy-to-remember sequences of passwords like "NewWord-january, NewWord-february..." and so on. But more significantly, why do you think a hacker will hold off using stolen passwords until after they've been renewed at the end of each update cycle? In the real world, by the time your users update their passwords, the hackers will have done their dirty work and be long gone. Nevertheless, we'll include instructions for forcing regular password renewal here just for old time's sake.

Default values in the /etc/login.defs file for new accounts were covered in Chapter 11. Within the login.defs file are some settings affecting password aging and length (PASS_MIN_LEN):

```
PASS_MAX_DAYS      30
PASS_MIN_DAYS      5
PASS_MIN_LEN       16
PASS_WARN_AGE      7
```

In this example, the maximum number of days, PASS_MAX_DAYS, until the password must be changed is 30. The number that you set here is dependent upon your particular account setup. For organizations that practice one person to one account, this number can be much larger than 30. If you do have shared accounts or multiple people know the root password, it is imperative that you change the password often. This practice effectively refreshes the list of those who know the password.

To keep users from changing their password to a new password and then immediately changing it right back, you need to set the PASS_MIN_DAYS to a number larger than 0. In the preceding example, the soonest a user could change their password again is 5 days.

The PASS_WARN_AGE setting is the number of days a user is warned before being forced to change their password. People tend to need lots of warnings and prodding, so the preceding example sets the warning time to 7 days.

For accounts that have already been created, you need to control password aging via the chage command. The options needed to control password aging with chage are listed in Table 22.1. Notice that there is not a password length setting in the chage utility.

TABLE 22.1 chage Options

Option	Description
-M	Sets the maximum number of days before a password needs to be changed. Equivalent to PASS_MAX_DAYS in /etc/login.defs.
-m	Sets the minimum number of days before a password can be changed again. Equivalent to PASS_MIN_DAYS in /etc/login.defs.
-W	Sets the number of days a user is warned before being forced to change the account password. Equivalent to PASS_WARN_AGE in /etc/login.defs.

The example that follows uses the chage command to set password aging parameters for the tim account. All three options are used at once.

```
# chage -l tim | grep days
Minimum number of days between password change          : 0
Maximum number of days between password change          : 99999
Number of days of warning before password expires       : 7
# chage -M 30 -m 5 -W 7 tim
# chage -l tim | grep days
Minimum number of days between password change          : 5
Maximum number of days between password change          : 30
Number of days of warning before password expires       : 7
```

You can also use the chage command as another method of account expiration, which is based upon the account's password expiring. Earlier, the usermod utility was used for account expiration. Use the chage command with the -M and the -I options to lock the account. In the code that follows, the `tim` account is viewed using `chage -l`. Only the information for `tim`'s password settings are extracted.

```
# chage -l tim | grep Password
Password expires                : never
Password inactive               : never
```

You can see that there are no settings for password expiration (`Password expires`) or password inactivity (`Password inactive`). In the following code, the account is set to be locked 5 days after `tim`'s password expires by using only the `-I` option:

```
# chage -I 5 tim
# chage -l tim | grep Password
Password expires                : never
Password inactive               : never
```

Notice that no settings changed! Without a password expiration set, the `-I` option has no effect. Thus, using the `-M` option, the maximum number of days is set before the password expires and the setting for the password inactivity time should take hold.

```
# chage -M 30 -I 5 tim
# chage -l tim | grep Password
Password expires                : Mar 03, 2017
Password inactive               : Mar 08, 2017
```

Now, `tim`'s account will be locked 5 days after his password expires. This is helpful in situations where an employee has left the company but their user account has not yet been removed. Depending upon your organization's security needs, consider setting all accounts to lock a certain number of days after passwords have expired.

Understanding the password files and password hashes

Early Linux systems stored their passwords in the `/etc/passwd` file. The passwords were hashed. A *hashed password* is created using a one-way mathematical process. After you create the hash, you cannot re-create the original characters from the hash. Here's how it works:

When a user enters the account password, the Linux system rehashes the password and then compares the hash result to the original hash in `/etc/passwd`. If they match, the user is authenticated and allowed into the system.

The problem with storing these password hashes in the `/etc/passwd` file has to do with the filesystem security settings (see Chapter 4, "Moving Around the Filesystem"). The filesystem security settings for the `/etc/passwd` file are listed here:

```
# ls -l /etc/passwd
-rw-r--r--. 1 root root 1644 Feb  2 02:30 /etc/passwd
```

As you can see, everyone can read the password file. You might think that this is not a problem because the passwords are all hashed. However, individuals with malicious intent have created files called *rainbow tables*. A rainbow table is simply a dictionary of potential passwords that have been hashed. For instance, the rainbow table would contain the hash for the popular password "Password," which is as follows:

```
$6$dhN5ZMUj$CNghjYIteau5xl8yX.f6PTOpendJwTOcXjlTDQUQZhhy
V8hKzQ6Hxx6Egj8P3VsHJ8Qrkv.VSR5dxcK3QhyMc.
```

Because of the ease of access to the password hashes in the /etc/passwd file, it is only a matter of time before a hashed password is matched in a rainbow table and the plain-text password is uncovered.

NOTE

Security experts will tell you that the passwords are not just hashed but also salted. *Salting a hash* means that a randomly generated value is added to the original password before it is hashed. This makes it even more difficult for the hashed password to be matched to its original password. However, in Linux, the hash salt is also stored with the hashed passwords (how else would the system be able to confirm passwords when they're entered?). So read access to the /etc/passwd file means that you have the hash value and its salt.

22

Thus, the hashed passwords were moved to a new configuration file, /etc/shadow, many years ago. This file has the following security settings:

```
# ls -l /etc/shadow
-rw-r----- 1 root shadow 1320 Apr  3 19:50 /etc/shadow
```

Root (and members of the shadow group), but no other user, can view this file. Thus, the hashed passwords are protected. Here is the tail end of a /etc/shadow file. You can see that there are long, nonsensical character strings in each user's record. Those are the hashed passwords.

```
# tail -2 /etc/shadow
johndoe:$6$jJjdRN9/qELmb8xWM1LgOYGhEIxc/:15364:0:99999:7:::
Tim:$6$z760AJ42$QXdhFyndpbVPVM5oVtNHs4B/:15372:5:30:7:16436::
```

You may inherit a Linux system that still uses the old method of keeping the hashed passwords in the /etc/passwd file. It is easy to fix. Just use the pwconv command, and the /etc/shadow file is created and hashed passwords moved to it.

The following are also stored in the /etc/shadow file, in addition to the account name and hashed password:

- Number of days (since January 1, 1970) since the password was changed
- Number of days before the password can be changed
- Number of days before a password must be changed
- Number of days to warn a user before a password must be changed
- Number of days after a password expires that an account is disabled
- Number of days (since January 1, 1970) that an account has been disabled

This should sound familiar, as they are the settings for password aging covered earlier in the chapter. Remember that the chage command does not work if you do not have an /etc/shadow file set up or if the /etc/login.defs file is not available.

Obviously, filesystem security settings are very important for keeping your Linux system secure. This is especially true with all Linux systems' configuration files and others.

Securing the filesystem

Another important part of securing your Linux system is setting proper filesystem security. The basics for security settings were covered in Chapter 4 and Access Control Lists (ACLs) in Chapter 11. However, there are a few additional points about which you should be aware.

Managing dangerous filesystem permissions

If you gave full rwxrwxrwx (777) access to every file on the Linux system, you can imagine the chaos that would follow. In many ways, similar chaos can occur by not closely managing the set UID (SUID) and the set GID (SGID) permissions (see Chapter 4 and Chapter 11).

Files with the SUID permission in the Owner category and execute permission in the Other category allow anyone to become the file's owner temporarily while the file is being executed in memory. The riskiest case is if the file's owner is root.

Similarly, files with the SGID permission in the Group category and execute permission in the Other category allow anyone temporarily to become a group member of the file's group while the file is being executed in memory. SGID can also be set on directories. This sets the group ID of any files created in the directory to the group ID of the directory.

Executable files with SUID or SGID are favorites of malicious users. Thus, it is best to use them sparingly. However, some files do need to keep these settings. Two examples are the passwd and the sudo commands that follow. Each of these files should maintain their SUID permissions.

```
$ ls -l /usr/bin/passwd
-rwsr-xr-x. 1 root root 28804 Aug 17 20:50 /usr/bin/passwd
$ ls -l /usr/bin/sudo
---s--x--x. 2 root root 77364 Nov 3 08:10 /usr/bin/sudo
```

Commands such as passwd and sudo are designed to be used as SUID programs. Even though those commands run as root user, as a regular user you can only change your own password with passwd and can only escalate to root permission with sudo if you were given permission in the /etc/sudoers file. A more dangerous situation would be if a hacker created a SUID bash command; anyone running that command could effectively change everything on the system that had root access.

Using the find command, you can search your system to see if there are any hidden or otherwise inappropriate SUID and SGID commands on your system. Here is an example:

```
# find / -perm /6000 -ls
4597316 52 -rwxr-sr-x 1 root games 51952 Dec 21 2013 /usr/bin/atc
```

```
4589119 20 -rwxr-sr-x 1 root tty    19552 Nov 18 2013 /usr/bin/write
4587931 60 -rwsr-xr-x 1 root root   57888 Aug  2 2013 /usr/bin/at
4588045 60 -rwsr-xr-x 1 root root   57536 Sep 25 2013 /usr/bin/crontab
4588961 32 -rwsr-xr-x 1 root root   32024 Nov 18 2013 /usr/bin/su
...
5767487 85 -rwsrwsr-x 1 root  root 68928 Sep 13 11:52 /var/.bin/myvi
...
```

Notice that `find` uncovers `SUID` and `SGID` commands that regular users can run to escalate their permission for particular reasons. In this example, there is also a file that a user tried to hide (`myvi`). This is a copy of the `vi` command that, because of permission and ownership, can change files owned by root. This is obviously a user doing something that they should not be doing.

Securing the password files

The `/etc/passwd` file is the file the Linux system uses to check user account information and was covered earlier in the chapter. The `/etc/passwd` file should have the following permissions settings:

- Owner: `root`
- Group: `root`
- Permissions: (644) Owner: `rw-` Group: `r--` Other: `r--`

The example that follows shows that the `/etc/passwd` file has the appropriate settings:

```
# ls -l /etc/passwd
-rw-r--r--. 1 root root 1644 Feb  2 02:30 /etc/passwd
```

These settings are needed so that users can log in to the system and see usernames associated with user ID and group ID numbers. However, users should not be able to modify the `/etc/passwd` directly. For example, a malicious user could add a new account to the file if write access were granted to `Other`.

The next file is the `/etc/shadow` file. Of course, it is closely related to the `/etc/passwd` file because it is also used during the login authentication process. This `/etc/shadow` file should have the following permissions settings:

- Owner: `root`
- Group: `root`
- Permissions: (640) Owner: `-rw-` Group: `r--` Other: `---`

The code that follows shows that the `/etc/shadow` file has the appropriate settings:

```
# ls -l /etc/shadow
-rw-r----- 1 root shadow 1320 Apr  3 19:50 /etc/shadow
```

The `/etc/passwd` file has read access for the owner, group, and other. Notice how much more the `/etc/shadow` file is restricted than the `/etc/passwd` file. For the `/etc/shadow` file, there is sharply limited access permission, although the root user can still access the file. So, if only root can view this file, how can users change their passwords, which are stored in /etc/shadow? The passwd utility, /usr/bin/passwd, uses the special permission SUID. This permission setting is shown here:

```
# ls -l /usr/bin/passwd
-rwsr-xr-x. 1 root root 28804 Aug 17 20:50 /usr/bin/passwd
```

Thus, the user running the passwd command temporarily becomes root while the command is executing in memory and can then write to the /etc/shadow file, but only to change the user's own password-related information.

The /etc/group file (see Chapter 11) contains all of the groups on the Linux system. Its file permissions should be set exactly as the /etc/passwd file:

- Owner: root
- Group: root
- Permissions: (644) Owner: rw- Group: r-- Other: r--

Locking down the filesystem

The filesystem table (see Chapter 12, "Managing Disks and Filesystems"), /etc/fstab, needs some special attention, too. The /etc/fstab file is used at boot time to mount storage devices on filesystems. It is also used by the mount command, the dump command, and the fsck command. The /etc/fstab file should have the following permission settings:

- Owner: root
- Group: root
- Permissions: (644) Owner: rw- Group: r-- Other: r--

Within the filesystem table, there are some important security settings that need to be reviewed. Besides your root, boot, and swap partitions, filesystem options are fairly secure by default. However, you may want to also consider the following:

- Typically, you put the /home subdirectory, where user directories are located, on its own partition. When you add mount options to mount that directory in /etc/fstab, you can set the nosuid option to prevent SUID and SGID permission-enabled executable programs from running from there. Programs that need SUID and SGID permissions should not be stored in /home and are most likely malicious. You can set the nodev option so that no device file located there will be recognized. Device files should be stored in /dev and not in /home. You can set the noexec option so that no executable programs, which are stored in /home, can be run.
- You can put the /tmp subdirectory, where temporary files are located, on its own partition and use the same options settings as for /home:
  - nosuid
  - nodev
  - noexec

- You can put the /usr subdirectory, where user programs and data are located, on its own partition and set the nodev option so that no device file located there is recognized. After software is installed, the /usr directory often has little or no change (sometimes, it is even mounted read-only for security reasons).

- If the system is configured as a server, you probably want to put the /var directory on its own partition. The /var directory is meant to grow, as log messages and content for web, FTP, and other servers are added. You can use the same mount options with the /var partition as you do for /home:

  - nosuid
  - nodev
  - noexec

Putting the preceding mount options into your /etc/fstab would look similar to the following:

```
/dev/sdb1      /home    ext4    defaults,nodev,noexec,nosuid    1 2
/dev/sdc1      /tmp     ext4    defaults,nodev,noexec,nosuid    1 1
/dev/sdb2      /usr     ext4    defaults,nodev                  1 2
/dev/sdb3      /var     ext4    defaults,nodev,noexec,nosuid    1 2
```

These mount options will help to lock down your filesystem further and add another layer of protection from those with malicious intent. Again, managing the various file permissions and fstab options should be part of your security policy. The items you choose to implement must be determined by your organization's security needs.

Managing software and services

Often, the administrator's focus is on making sure that the needed software and services are on a Linux system. From a security standpoint, you need to take the opposite viewpoint and make sure that the unneeded software and services are not on a Linux system.

Updating software packages

In addition to removing unnecessary services and software, keeping current software up to date is critical for security. The latest bug fixes and security patches are obtained via software updates. Software package updates were covered in Chapter 9, "Installing Linux," and Chapter 10, "Getting and Managing Software."

Software updates need to be done on a regular basis. How often and when you do it, of course, depends upon your organization's security needs.

You can easily automate software updates, but like removing services and software, it would be wise to test the updates in a test environment first. When updated software shows no problems, you can then update the software on your production Linux systems.

Keeping up with security advisories

As security flaws are found in Linux software, the Common Vulnerabilities and Exposures (CVE) project tracks them and helps to quickly get fixes for those flaws worked on by the Linux community.

22

Companies such as Canonical provide updated packages to fix the security flaws and deliver them.

For more information on how security updates are handled in Ubuntu, refer to the Security Notices page on the Ubuntu website (usn.ubuntu.com/). You can also search for CVEs and related packages on the people.canonical.com/~ubuntu-security/cve page.

Advanced implementation

You should be aware of several other important security topics as you are planning your deployments. They include cryptography, Pluggable Authentication Modules (PAM), and AppArmor. These advanced and detailed topics have been put into separate chapters, Chapter 23, "Understanding Advanced Linux Security," and Chapter 24, "Enhancing Linux Security with AppArmor".

Monitoring Your Systems

If you do a good job of planning and implementing your system's security, most malicious attacks will be stopped. However, if an attack should occur, you need to be able to recognize it. Monitoring is an activity that needs to be going on continuously.

Monitoring your system includes watching over log files, user accounts, and the filesystem itself. In addition, you need some tools to help you detect intrusions and other types of malware.

Monitoring log files

Understanding how message logging is done is critical to maintaining and troubleshooting a Linux system. Before the systemd facility was used to gather messages in what is referred to as the systemd journal, messages generated by the kernel and system services were directed to files in the /var/log directory. While that is still true to a great extent with systemd, you can now also view log messages directly from the systemd journal using the journalctl command.

The log files for your Linux system are primarily located in the /var/log directory. Most of the files in the /var/log directory are directed there from the systemd journal through the rsyslogd service (see Chapter 13, "Understanding Server Administration").

Most of the log files are displayed using the commands cat, head, tail, more, or less. However, a few of them have special commands for viewing (see Table 22.2).

TABLE 22.2 Viewing Log Files That Need Special Commands

Filename	View Command
btmp	dump-utmp btmp
dmesg	dmesg
lastlog	lastlog
wtmp	dump-utmp wtmp

With the change to `systemd` (which manages the boot process and services), as noted ear-lier, the mechanism for gathering and displaying log messages associated with the kernel and system services has changed as well. Those messages are directed to the `systemd` journal and can be displayed with the `journalctl` command.

To page through kernel messages, type the following command:

```
$ journalctl -k
-- Logs begin at Tue 2019-05-07 09:16:36 EDT, end at Tue 2020-04-07
12:25:01 EDT
Apr 07 07:49:08 workstation kernel: Linux version 5.3.0-46-generic
(buildd@lcy01
Apr 07 07:49:08 workstation kernel: Command line: BOOT_IMAGE=/boot/
vmlinuz-5.3.0
Apr 07 07:49:08 workstation kernel: KERNEL supported cpus:
Apr 07 07:49:08 workstation kernel:    Intel GenuineIntel
Apr 07 07:49:08 workstation kernel:    AMD AuthenticAMD
Apr 07 07:49:08 workstation kernel:    Hygon HygonGenuine
Apr 07 07:49:08 workstation kernel:    Centaur CentaurHauls
Apr 07 07:49:08 workstation kernel:    zhaoxin    Shanghai
Apr 07 07:49:08 workstation kernel: x86/fpu: Supporting XSAVE feature
0x001: 'x8
Apr 07 07:49:08 workstation kernel: x86/fpu: Supporting XSAVE feature
0x002: 'SS
Apr 07 07:49:08 workstation kernel: x86/fpu: Supporting XSAVE feature
0x004: 'AV
Apr 07 07:49:08 workstation kernel: x86/fpu: xstate_offset[2]:   576,
xstate_size
Apr 07 07:49:08 workstation kernel: x86/fpu: Enabled xstate features
0x7, contex
Apr 07 07:49:08 workstation kernel: BIOS-provided physical RAM map:
Apr 07 07:49:08 workstation kernel: BIOS-e820: [mem
0x0000000000000000-0x0000000
...
```

To view messages associated with a particular service, use the `-u` option followed by the service name to see log messages for any service, as in this example:

```
$ journalctl -u NetworkManager.service
$ journalctl -u apache2.service
$ journalctl -u avahi-daemon.service
```

If you think that a security breach is in progress, you can watch all or selected messages as they come in by following messages. For example, to follow kernel messages or Apache mes-sages as they come in, add the `-f` option (press Ctrl+C when you are finished):

```
$ journalctl -k -f
$ journalctl -f -u apache2.service
```

To check just boot messages, you can list the boot IDs for all system boots and then boot the particular boot instance that interests you. The following examples display boot IDs and then show boot messages for a selected boot ID:

```
$ journalctl -list-boots
[...]
 -11 24f2850c6b4a42d1ae44945d6c088393 Fri 2020-03-27 07:48:51 EDT-Fri
2020-03-27 17:46:47 EDT
 -10 e26956a6a4ac4bacbd1c35fdf373facf Sat 2020-03-28 20:53:35 EDT-Sun
2020-03-29 00:09:42 EDT
  -9 05c00d086c1b49ccab24ba118c7f1e38 Sun 2020-03-29 07:46:35 EDT-Mon
2020-03-30 00:12:54 EDT
  -8 7eb56eef2bb242c4b0d347bb30fe9d53 Mon 2020-03-30 07:49:14 EDT-Tue
2020-03-31 00:21:25 EDT
  -7 7ea9b4f75ad849e8929bb5ec6a58d760 Tue 2020-03-31 07:47:07 EDT-Wed
2020-04-01 00:16:47 EDT
  -6 82b2d7e9067e45198e53076fda8fa9a4 Wed 2020-04-01 07:49:09 EDT-Thu
2020-04-02 00:19:14 EDT
  -5 0e3cc11227364c5c9cf9322aa87064c4 Thu 2020-04-02 07:49:08 EDT-Fri
2020-04-03 00:13:10 EDT
  -4 7f432f43ee6d427d91a79b200543bd69 Fri 2020-04-03 07:48:35 EDT-Fri
2020-04-03 18:07:30 EDT
  -3 246bbe00e58740138636b5386f12a4fb Sat 2020-04-04 21:02:22 EDT-Sat
2020-04-04 23:25:21 EDT
  -2 3ffc709d76884c8bbcc26e239c570744 Sun 2020-04-05 07:47:44 EDT-Mon
2020-04-06 00:04:48 EDT
  -1 0b2c500ca05549d09e2083c343abea66 Mon 2020-04-06 07:49:37 EDT-Tue
2020-04-07 00:11:23 EDT
   0 02d1fc2469794ebc83026d47e02b97fa Tue 2020-04-07 07:49:08 EDT-Tue
2020-04-07 12:39:58 EDT
```

Monitoring user accounts

User accounts are often used in malicious attacks on a system by gaining unauthorized access to a current account, by creating new bogus accounts, or by leaving an account behind to access later. To avoid such security issues, watching over user accounts is an important activity.

Detecting counterfeit accounts and privileges

Accounts created without going through the appropriate authorization should be considered counterfeit. Also, modifying an account in any way that gives it a different unauthorized user identification (UID) number or adds unauthorized group memberships is a form of rights escalation. Keeping an eye on the /etc/passwd and /etc/group files will monitor these potential breaches.

To help you monitor the /etc/passwd and /etc/group files, you can use the audit daemon. The audit daemon is an extremely powerful auditing tool that allows you to select system events to track and record them, and it provides reporting capabilities.

To begin auditing the `/etc/passwd` and `/etc/group` files, you need to use the `auditctl` command (`apt install auditd`). Two options at a minimum are required to start this process:

-w *filename*: Place a watch on *filename*. The audit daemon tracks the file by its inode number. An *inode number* is a data structure that contains information concerning a file, including its location.

-p *trigger(s—)*: If one of these access types occurs (r=read, w=write, x=execute, a=attribute change) to *filename*, then trigger an audit record.

In the following example, a watch has been placed on the `/etc/passwd` file using the `auditctl` command. The audit daemon will monitor access, which consists of any reads, writes, or file attribute changes:

```
# auditctl -w /etc/passwd -p rwa
```

After you have started a file audit, you may want to turn it off at some point. To turn off an audit, use the command

```
auditctl -W filename -p trigger(s)
```

To see a list of current audited files and their watch settings, type **auditctl -l** at the command line.

To review the audit logs, use the audit daemon's `ausearch` command. The only option needed here is the `-f` option, which specifies which records you want to view from the audit log. The following is an example of the `/etc/passwd` audit information:

```
# ausearch -f /etc/passwd
time->Fri Feb  7 04:27:01 2020
type=PATH msg=audit(1328261221.365:572):
item=0 name="/etc/passwd" inode=170549
dev=fd:01 mode=0100644 ouid=0 ogid=0
rdev=00:00 obj=system_u:object_r:etc_t:s0
type=CWD msg=audit(1328261221.365:572):  cwd="/"
...
time->Fri Feb  7 04:27:14 2020
type=PATH msg=audit(1328261234.558:574):
item=0 name="/etc/passwd" inode=170549
dev=fd:01 mode=0100644 ouid=0 ogid=0
rdev=00:00 obj=system_u:object_r:etc_t:s0
type=CWD msg=audit(1328261234.558:574):
cwd="/home/johndoe"
type=SYSCALL msg=audit(1328261234.558:574):
arch=40000003 syscall=5 success=yes exit=3
a0=3b22d9 a1=80000 a2=1b6 a3=0 items=1 ppid=3891
pid=21696 auid=1000 uid=1000 gid=1000 euid=1000
suid=1000 fsuid=1000 egid=1000 sgid=1000 fsgid=1000
tty=pts1 ses=2 comm="vi" exe="/bin/vi"
 subj=unconfined_u:unconfined_r:unconfined_t:s0-s0:c0.c1023"
----
```

22

This is a lot of information to review. A few items will help you see what audit event happened to trigger the bottom record:

time: The time stamp of the activity

name: The filename, /etc/passwd, being watched

inode: The /etc/passwd's inode number on this filesystem

uid: The user ID, 1000, of the user running the program

exe: The program, /bin/vi, used on the /etc/passwd file

To determine what user account is assigned the UID of 1000, look at the /etc/passwd file. In this case, the UID of 1000 belongs to the user johndoe. Thus, from the audit event record just displayed, you can determine that account johndoe has attempted to use the vi editor on the /etc/passwd file. It is doubtful that this was an innocent action, and it requires more investigation.

> **NOTE**
> The ausearch command returns nothing if no watch events on a file have been triggered.

The audit daemon and its associated tools are extremely rich. To learn more about it, look at the man pages for the following audit daemon utilities and configuration files:

auditd: The audit daemon

/etc/audit/auditd.conf: The audit daemon configuration file

autditctl: Controls the auditing system

/etc/audit/audit.rules: Configuration rules loaded at boot

ausearch: Searches the audit logs for specified items

aureport: Report creator for the audit logs

audispd: Sends audit information to other programs

The audit daemon is one way to keep an eye on important files. You should also review your account and group files on a regular basis with a human eye to see if anything looks irregular.

Important files, such as /etc/passwd, do need to be monitored for unauthorized account creation. However, just as bad as a new unauthorized user account is an authorized user account with a bad password.

Detecting bad account passwords

Even with all your good efforts, bad passwords will slip in. Therefore, you do need to monitor user account passwords to ensure they that are strong enough to withstand an attack.

One password strength monitoring tool that you can use is the same one malicious users use to crack accounts, John the Ripper. John the Ripper is a free, open source tool that you can use at the Linux command line. It's not installed by default. You can install it using `apt install john`.

In order to use John the Ripper to test user passwords, you must first extract account names and passwords using the `unshadow` command. This information needs to be redirected into a file for use by `john`, as shown here:

```
# unshadow /etc/passwd /etc/shadow > password.file
```

Now edit the `password.file` using your favorite text editor to remove any accounts without passwords. Because it is wise to limit John the Ripper to testing a few accounts at a time, remove any account names that you do not wish to test presently.

> The `john` utility is extremely CPU-intensive. It does set its `nice` value to 19 in order to lower its priority. However, it would be wise to run it on a non-production system or during off-peak hours and for only a few accounts at a time.

Now use the `john` command to attempt password cracks. To run `john` against the created password file, issue the command `john filename`. In the following code snippet, you can see the output from running `john` against the sample `password.file`. For demonstration purposes, only one account was left in the sample file. Further, the account `Samantha` was given the bad password of `password`. You can see how little time it took for John the Ripper to crack the password.

```
# john password.file
Loaded 1 password hash (generic crypt(3) [?/32])
password        (Samantha)
guesses: 1  time: 0:00:00:44 100% (2)  c/s: 20.87
 trying: 12345 - missy
Use the "--show" option to display all of the
  cracked passwords reliably
```

To demonstrate how strong passwords are vital, consider what happens when the `Samantha` account's password is changed from `password` to `Password1234`. Even though `Password1234` is still a weak password, it takes longer than 7 days of CPU time to crack it. In the code that follows, `john` was finally aborted to end the cracking attempt:

```
# passwd Samantha
Changing password for user Samantha.
...
# john password.file
Loaded 1 password hash (generic crypt(3) [?/32])
...
time: 0:07:21:55 (3)  c/s: 119  trying: tth675 - tth787
Session aborted
```

As soon as the password cracking attempts have completed, the `password.file` should be removed from the system. To learn more about John the Ripper, visit openwall.com/john.

Monitoring the filesystem

Malicious programs often modify files. They also can try to cover their tracks by posing as ordinary files and programs. However, there are ways to uncover them through the various monitoring tactics covered in the following sections.

Verifying software packages

Typically, if you install a software package from a standard repository or download a reputable site's package, you won't have any problems. But it is always good to double-check your installed software packages to see if they have been compromised. The **dpkg -V** *package_name* command will check for a valid md5sum hash. You can also run **dpkg --audit** *package_name* to check for configuration issues or problems with control data or files. In this example, dpkg correctly discovered a configuration issue with the auditd package:

```
# dpkg --audit auditd
The following packages are only half configured, probably due
to problems
configuring them the first time.  The configuration should be
retried using
dpkg --configure <package> or the configure menu option in dselect:
 auditd                 User space tools for security auditing
```

When you verify the software, information from the installed package files is compared against the package metadata (see Chapter 10) in the APT database. If no problems are found, the command returns nothing. However, if there are discrepancies, you get a coded listing.

> **NOTE**
>
> You could also use the debsums utility. To check all installed packages, use the debsums -a command. To check one package, type debsums packagename.

Scanning the filesystem

Unless you've recently updated your system, binary files should not have been modified for any reason. Commands such as find can help you determine if a binary file has been tampered with.

To check for binary file modification, find can use the file's modify time, or mtime. The file mtime is the time when the contents of a file were last modified. Also, find can monitor the file's create/change time, or ctime.

If you suspect malicious activity, you can quickly scan your filesystem to see if any binaries were modified or changed today (or yesterday, depending upon when you think the intrusion took place). To do this scan, use the find command.

In the example that follows, a scan is made of the /sbin directory. To see if any binary files were modified less than 24 hours ago, the command find /sbin -mtime -1 is used. In the example, several files are displayed, showing that they were modified recently. This indicates that malicious activity is taking place on the system. To investigate further, review each individual file's times, using the **stat** *filename* command, as shown here:

```
# find /sbin -mtime -1
/sbin
/sbin/init
/sbin/reboot
/sbin/halt
#
# stat /sbin/init
  File: '/sbin/init' -> '../bin/systemd'
  Size: 14      Blocks: 0        IO Block: 4096    symbolic link
Device: fd01h/64769d    Inode: 9551           Links: 1
Access: (0777/lrwxrwxrwx)
Uid: (    0/    root)   Gid: (    0/    root)
Context: system_u:object_r:bin_t:s0
Access: 2016-02-03 03:34:57.276589176 -0500
Modify: 2016-02-02 23:40:39.139872288 -0500
Change: 2016-02-02 23:40:39.140872415 -0500
 Birth: -
```

You could create a database of all of the binary's original mtimes and ctimes and then run a script to find current mtimes and ctimes, compare them against the database, and note any discrepancies. However, this type of program has already been created and works well. It's called an Intrusion Detection System, and it is covered later in this chapter.

You need to perform several other filesystem scans on a regular basis. Favorite files or file settings of malicious attackers are listed in Table 22.3. The table also lists the commands to perform the scans and why the file or file setting is potentially problematic.

TABLE 22.3 Additional Filesystem Scans

File or Setting	Scan Command	Problem with File or Setting
SUID permission	find / -perm -4000	Allows anyone to become the file's owner temporarily while the file is being executed in memory.
SGID permission	find / -perm -2000	Allows anyone to become a group member of the file's group temporarily while the file is being executed in memory.
rhost files	find /home -name .rhosts	Allows a system to trust another system completely. It should not be in /home directories.
Ownerless files	find / -nouser	Indicates files that are not associated with any username.
Groupless files	find / -nogroup	Indicates files that are not associated with any group name.

These filesystem scans help monitor what is going on in your system and help detect malicious attacks. However, other types of attacks can threaten your files, including viruses and rootkits.

Detecting viruses and rootkits

Two popular malicious attack tools are viruses and rootkits because they stay hidden while performing their malicious activities. Linux systems need to be monitored for both such intrusions.

Monitoring for viruses

A *computer virus* is malicious software that can attach itself to already installed system software, and it has the ability to spread through media or networks. It is a misconception that there are no Linux viruses. The malicious creators of viruses do often focus on the more popular desktop operating systems, such as Windows. However, that does not mean that viruses are not created for the Linux systems.

Even more important, Linux systems are often used to handle services, such as mail servers, for Windows desktop systems. Therefore, Linux systems used for such purposes need to be scanned for Windows viruses as well.

Antivirus software scans files using virus signatures. A *virus signature* is a hash created from a virus's binary code. The hash will positively identify that virus. Antivirus programs have a virus signature database that is used to compare against files to see if there is a signature match. Depending upon the number of new threats, a virus signature database can be updated often to provide protection from these new threats.

A good antivirus software choice for your Linux system, which is open source and free, is ClamAV. To install ClamAV and the virus database, install these two packages:

```
# apt install clamav clamav-freshclam
```

You can find out more about ClamAV at clamav.net, where there is documentation on how to set up and run the antivirus software.

Monitoring for rootkits

A rootkit is a little more insidious than a virus. A *rootkit* is a malicious program that does the following:

- Hides itself, often by replacing system commands or programs
- Maintains high-level access to a system
- Is able to circumvent software created to locate it

The purpose of a rootkit is to get and maintain root-level access to a system. The term was created by putting together *root*, which means that it has to have administrator access, and *kit*, which means it is usually several programs that operate in concert.

A rootkit detector that can be used on a Linux system is chkrootkit. To install chkrootkit issue the command **apt install chkrootkit**.

Finding a rootkit with `chkrootkit` is simple. After installing the package or booting up the Live CD, type in **chkrootkit** at the command line. It searches the entire file structure denoting any infected files.

The code that follows shows a run of `chkrootkit` on an infected system. The `grep` command was used to search for the keyword `INFECTED`. Notice that many of the files listed as infected are Bash shell command files. This is typical of a rootkit.

```
# chkrootkit | grep INFECTED
Checking 'du'... INFECTED
Checking 'find'... INFECTED
Checking 'ls'... INFECTED
Checking 'lsof'... INFECTED
Checking 'pstree'... INFECTED
Searching for Suckit rootkit... Warning: /sbin/init INFECTED
```

In the last line of the preceding `chkrootkit` code is an indication that the system has been infected with the Suckit rootkit. It actually is not infected with this rootkit. When running utilities, such as antivirus and rootkit-detecting software, you often get a number of false positives. A *false positive* is an indication of a virus, rootkit, or other malicious activity that does not really exist. In this particular case, this false positive is caused by a known bug.

The `chkrootkit` utility should have regularly scheduled runs and, of course, should be run whenever a rootkit infection is suspected. To find more information on `chkrootkit`, go to www.chkrootkit.org.

> **TIP**
>
> Another rootkit detector that might interest you is called Rootkit Hunter (`rkhunter` package). Run the `rkhunter` script to check your system for malware and known rootkits. Configure `rkhunter` in the `/etc/rkhunter.conf` file. For a simple example, run `rkhunter -c` to check the filesystem for a variety of rootkits and vulnerabilities.

Detecting an intrusion

Intrusion Detection System (IDS) software—a software package that monitors a system's activities (or its network) for potential malicious activities and reports these activities—can help you monitor your system for potential intrusions. Closely related to Intrusion Detection System software is a software package that prevents an intrusion, called *Intrusion Prevention System* software. Some of these packages are bundled together to provide Intrusion Detection and Prevention.

Several Intrusion Detection System software packages are available for a Linux system. A few of the more popular utilities are listed in Table 22.4. You should know that `tripwire` is no longer open source. However, the original `tripwire` code is still available. See the `tripwire` website listed in Table 22.4 for more details.

TABLE 22.4 **Popular Linux Intrusion Detection Systems**

IDS Name	Installation	Website
aide	apt install aide	aide.sourceforge.net
Snort	apt install snort	www.snort.org
tripwire	apt install tripwire	www.tripwire.org

The Advanced Intrusion Detection Environment (aide) IDS uses a method of comparison to detect intrusions. When you were a child, you may have played the game of comparing two pictures and finding what was different between them. The aide utility uses a similar method. A "first picture" database is created. At some time later, another database "second picture" is created, and aide compares the two databases and reports what is different.

To begin, you need to take that "first picture." The best time to create this picture is when the system has been freshly installed. The command to create the initial database is aide. wrapper -i and it takes a long time to run. Some of its output follows:

```
# aide.wrapper -i
Start timestamp: 2020-04-07 19:19:33 +0000 (AIDE 0.16)
AIDE initialized database at /var/lib/aide/aide.db.new
Verbose level: 6

Number of entries:    183088


------------------------------------------------------
The attributes of the (uncompressed) database(s):
------------------------------------------------------

/var/lib/aide/aide.db.new
  RMD160   : CPYeo30jdCLFv5K982ikAF9tpoo=
  TIGER    : 3faY0oxurQbvrlj17IWWXGHX2fx+EHPN
  SHA256   : 6diJ2c8p6elfCkiRSxUJ5LV7icCUOmC5
             NO+z4iZ9suM=
  SHA512   : hDtBFYWmDGAFQUxL4PlgSKiSRRJRiQBV
             rUXrRUuLSgAiQCnQ9EWnLtBjNQxmDt9h
             tiN4IoON+LWWk0xXUK5AHw==
  CRC32    : KVke8Q==
  HAVAL    : SMq9Po82Dg1SOod3vHtgG6D/Xqd0X91/
             wkKX9aTbx4w=
  GOST     : L0JMMPR9WoMJpa1Bgj9C4Z4p2Aila5UC
             9ruHH/RC47I=

End timestamp: 2020-04-07 19:23:41 +0000 (run time: 4m 8s)
```

The next step is to move the initial "first picture" database to a new location. This protects the original database from being overwritten. Plus, the comparison does not work unless the database is renamed. The command to rename the new database is as follows:

```
# cp /var/lib/aide/aide.db.new /var/lib/aide/aide.db
```

When you are ready to check whether your files have been tampered with, you need to create a new database, "second picture," and compare it to the original database, "first picture." The check option on the `aide` command, `-c`, creates a new database and runs a comparison against the old database:

```
# aide.wrapper -C
```

Where `aide` databases are created, what comparisons are made, and several other configuration settings are handled in the /etc/aide/aide.conf file, along with files in the /etc/aide/aide.conf.d and /etc/aide/aide.settings.d directories.

An Intrusion Detection System can be a big help in monitoring the system. When potential intrusions are detected, comparing the output to information from other commands and log files can help you better understand and correct any attacks on your system.

Auditing and Reviewing Linux

You must understand two important terms when you are auditing the health of your Linux system. A *compliance review* is an audit of the overall computer system environment to ensure that the policies and procedures you have set for the system are being carried out correctly. A *security review* is an audit of current policies and procedures to ensure that they follow accepted best security practices.

Conducting compliance reviews

Similar to audits in other fields, such as accounting, audits can be conducted internally or by external personnel. These reviews can be as simple as someone sitting down and comparing implemented security to your company's stated policies. However, it's more popular to conduct audits using penetration testing.

Penetration testing is an evaluation method used to test a computer system's security by simulating malicious attacks. It is also called pen testing and ethical hacking. No longer do you have to gather tools and the local neighborhood hacker to help you conduct these tests.

Kali Linux (www.kali.org/) is a distribution created specifically for penetration testing. It can be used from a live DVD or a flash drive.

While penetration testing is lots of fun, for a thorough compliance review, a little more is needed. You should also use checklists from industry security sites.

Conducting security reviews

Conducting a security review requires that you know current best security practices. There are several ways to stay informed about best security practices. The following is a brief list of organizations that can help you:

- United States Cybersecurity and Infrastructure Security Agency (CISA)
  - URL: www.us-cert.gov
  - Offers the National Cyber Alert System
  - Offers RSS feeds on the latest security threats
- The SANS Institute
  - URL: sans.org/security-resources
  - Offers Computer Security Research newsletters
  - Offers RSS feeds on the latest security threats
- Gibson Research Corporation
  - URL: grc.com
  - Offers the *Security Now!* security netcast

Information from these sites will assist you in creating stronger policies and procedures. Given how fast the best security practices change, it would be wise to conduct security reviews often, depending upon your organization's security needs.

Now you understand a lot more about basic Linux security. The hard part is actually putting all of these concepts into practice.

Summary

Basic Linux security practices, such as managing user accounts, securing passwords, and managing software and services, form the foundation for all other security on your Linux system. With that foundation in place, ongoing monitoring of your system includes watching over system log files, checking for malicious intrusions, and monitoring the filesystem.

Regular reviews of your security policies are also important. Audits assist in ensuring that your Linux system is secured and the proper security policies and practices are in place.

You have completed your first step of gathering basic security procedures and principles knowledge. It is not enough just to know the basics. You need to add advanced Linux security tools to your security toolbox. In the next chapter, advanced security topics of cryptography and authentication modules are covered.

Exercises

Refer to the material in this chapter to complete the tasks that follow. If you are stuck, solutions to the tasks are shown in Appendix A (although in Linux, there are often multiple ways to complete a task). Try each of the exercises before referring to the answers. These tasks assume that you are running an Ubuntu system (although some tasks will work on other Linux systems as well).

1. Check log messages from the `systemd` journal for the following services: `NetworkManager.service`, `sshd.service`, and `auditd.service`.

2. List the permissions of the file containing your system's user passwords and determine if they are appropriate.

3. Determine your account's password aging and if it will expire using a single command.

4. Start auditing writes to the `/etc/shadow` file with the `auditd` daemon and then check your audit settings.

5. Create a report from the `auditd` daemon on the `/etc/shadow` file, and then turn off auditing on that file.

6. Install the lemon package, damage the `/usr/bin/lemon` file (perhaps copy `/etc/services` there), verify that the file has been tampered with, and remove the lemon package.

7. You suspect that you have had a malicious attack on your system today and important binary files have been modified. What command should you use to find these modified files?

8. Install and run `chkrootkit` to see if the malicious attack from the exercise 7 installed a rootkit.

9. Find files with the `SUID` or `SGID` permission set.

10. Install the `aide` package, run the `aide` command to initialize the aide database, copy the database to the correct location, and run the `aide` command to check if any important files on your system have been modified.

22

Understanding Advanced Linux Security

Due to ever-changing and growing threats, implementing basic computer security is no longer enough. As malicious users gain access to and knowledge of advanced tools, so must a Linux system administrator. Understanding advanced computer security topics and tools must be part of your preparation.

In this chapter, you will learn about cryptography basics, such as ciphers and encryption. You will also learn how the authentication module utility can simplify your administrative duties, even though it is an advanced security topic.

Implementing Linux Security with Cryptography

Using cryptography enhances the security of your Linux system and its network communications. *Cryptography* is the science of concealing information. It has a long and rich history that goes back far before computers were around. Because of its heavy use of mathematical algorithms, cryptography has easily transitioned to computers. Linux comes with many cryptographic tools ready for you to use.

To understand cryptographic concepts and the various Linux tools, you should know a few cryptography terms:

Plain text: Text that a human or machine can read and comprehend

Ciphertext: Text that a human or machine cannot read and comprehend

Encryption: The process of converting plain text into ciphertext using an algorithm

Decryption: The process of converting ciphertext into plain text using an algorithm

Cipher: The algorithm used to encrypt plain text into ciphertext and decrypt cipher-text into plain text

Block cipher: A cipher that breaks data into blocks before encrypting

Stream cipher: A cipher that encrypts the data without breaking it up

Key: A piece of data required by the cipher to encrypt or decrypt data successfully

Parents of young children often use a form of cryptography. They spell words instead of speaking them. A parent may take the plain-text word "candy" and turn it into ciphertext by saying to the other parent "C-A-N-D-Y." The other parent decrypts the word by using the same spelling cipher and recognizes that the word is *candy*. Unfortunately, it does not take children long to learn how to decrypt via the spelling cipher.

You may have noticed that hashing was not included in the preceding cryptography definition list. Hashing needs some special attention because it is often confused with encryption.

Understanding hashing

Hashing is not encryption, but it is a form of cryptography. Remember from Chapter 22, "Understanding Basic Linux Security," that *hashing* is a one-way mathematical process used to create ciphertext. However, unlike encryption, after you create a hash, you cannot de-hash it back to its original plain text.

In order for a hashing algorithm to be used in computer security, it needs to be *collision-free*, which means that the hashing algorithm does not output the same hash for two totally different inputs. Each input must have a unique hashed output. Thus, *cryptographic hashing* is a one-way mathematical process that is collision-free.

By default, cryptography is already in use on a Linux system. For example, the /etc/ shadow file contains hashed passwords. Hashing is used on Linux systems for the following:

- Passwords (Chapter 22)
- Verifying files
- Digital signatures
- Virus signatures (Chapter 22)

A hash is also called a *message digest, checksum, fingerprint,* or *signature.* One Linux utility that produces message digests is sha256sum. In Chapter 10, "Getting and Managing Software," you learned about getting software for your Linux system. When you download a software file, you can make sure that the file was not corrupted on download.

Even—perhaps especially—the integrity of the Ubuntu operating system images you download should be confirmed using checksum hashes. You can find links to md5, sha1, and sha256 hashes for all Ubuntu images on from this page: help.ubuntu.com/community/ UbuntuHashes.

To generate the hash, run the `sha256sum` command on, say, an ISO image after you've download it. The `sha256sum` hash results for the downloaded software file are shown in the code that follows:

```
$ sha256sum ubuntu-20-04-focal-live-server-amd64.iso
7d3e2e0c6ba036c7567084d25595a4556288e290a39aeae6bc547fee82ce3460
ubuntu-20-04-focal-live-server-amd64.iso
```

If the resulting hash *does* match the one available from the website, it means that the downloaded ISO file has not been corrupted and is ready for use.

You can implement even more cryptography besides hashing on your Linux system. The Linux utilities to do so are very easy to use. However, first you need to understand a few more underlying cryptography concepts.

Understanding encryption/decryption

The primary use of cryptography on a Linux system is to encode data to hide it (encryption) from unauthorized eyes and then decode the data (decryption) for authorized eyes. On a Linux system, you can encrypt the following:

- Individual files
- Partitions and volumes
- Web page connections
- Network connections
- Backups
- Zip files

These encryption/decryption processes use special math algorithms to accomplish their task. The algorithms are called *cryptographic ciphers*.

Understanding cryptographic ciphers

One of the original ciphers, called the *Caesar Cipher*, was created and used by Julius Caesar. It was terribly easy to crack, however. Today, many more secure ciphers are available. Understanding how each cipher works is important because the strength of the cipher you choose should directly relate to the security needs of your data. Table 23.1 lists a few modern ciphers.

Understanding cryptographic cipher keys

Cryptographic ciphers require a piece of data, called a *key*, to complete their mathematical process of encryption/decryption. The key can be either a single key or a pair of keys.

Notice the different cipher key sizes listed in Table 23.1. The key size is directly related to how easily the cipher is cracked. The bigger the key size, the less the chance of cracking the cipher. For example, DES is no longer considered secure because of its small 56-bit key size. However, a cipher with a key size of 256 bits or 512 bits is considered secure because (at least until quantum computing becomes widely available) it would take many years to brute-force crack such a keyed cipher.

TABLE 23.1 **Cryptography Ciphers**

Method	Description
AES (Advanced Encryption Standard), also called Rijndael	*Symmetric cryptography.* Block cipher, encrypting data in 128-, 192-, 256-, 512-bit blocks using a 128-, 192-, 256, or 512-bit key for encrypting/decrypting.
Blowfish	*Symmetric cryptography.* Block cipher, encrypting data in 64-bit blocks using the same 32-bit to 448-bit keys for encrypting/decrypting.
CAST5	*Symmetric cryptography.* Block cipher, encrypting data in 64-bit blocks using the same up to 128-bit key for encrypting/decrypting.
DES (Data Encryption Standard)	No longer considered secure. *Symmetric cryptography.* Block cipher, encrypting data in 64-bit blocks using the same 56-bit key for encrypting/decrypting.
3DES	Improved DES cipher. *Symmetric cryptography.* Data is encrypted up to 48 times with three different 56-bit keys before the encryption process is completed.
El Gamal	*Asymmetric cryptography.* Uses two keys derived from a logarithm algorithm.
Elliptic Curve Cryptosystems	*Asymmetric cryptography.* Uses two keys derived from an algorithm containing two randomly chosen points on an elliptic curve.
IDEA	*Symmetric cryptography.* Block cipher, encrypting data in 64-bit blocks using the same 128-bit key for encrypting/decrypting.
RC4 also called Arc-Four or ARC4	Stream cipher, encrypting data in 64-bit blocks using a variable key size for encrypting/decrypting.
RC5	*Symmetric cryptography.* Block cipher, encrypting data in 32-, 64-, or 128-bit blocks using the same up to 2,048-bit keys for encrypting/decrypting.
RC6	*Symmetric cryptography.* Same as RC5, but slightly faster.
Rijndael also called AES	*Symmetric cryptography.* Block cipher, encrypting data in 128-, 192-, 256-, 512-bit blocks using a 128-, 192-, 256-, or 512-bit key for encrypting/decrypting.
RSA	Most popular *asymmetric cryptography.* Uses two keys derived from an algorithm containing a multiple of two randomly generated prime numbers.

Symmetric key cryptography

Symmetric cryptography, also called *secret key* or *private key* cryptography, encrypts plain text using a single keyed cipher. The same key is needed in order to decrypt the data. The advantage of symmetric key cryptography is speed. The disadvantage is the need to share the single key if the encrypted data is to be decrypted by another person.

An example of symmetric key cryptography on a Linux system is accomplished using the OpenPGP utility, GNU Privacy Guard, gpg. Although it's often installed by default, some Ubuntu releases require manual installation of the gnupg package.

Encrypting and decrypting a tar archive file

The simple example that follows—that won't require that you first generate keys—shows the tar command used to create a compressed tar archive (backup.tar.gz) and the gpg utility used to encrypt the file, applying a one-time passphrase. The original file is kept and a new encrypted file, backup.tar.gz.gpg, is created.

```
# sudo tar czvf backup.tar.gz /etc
$ gpg --batch --output backup.tar.gz.gpg \
    --passphrase mypassword --symmetric backup.tar.gz
$ ls | grep backup
backup.tar.gz
backup.tar.gz.gpg
```

The single key used to encrypt the file is protected by a passphrase. This passphrase is simply a password or phrase chosen by the user at the time of encryption. It's now safe to transmit the encrypted file to your recipient via email or remote connection. Well, if I had used a better password than "mypassword" it would be safe, at any rate.

To decrypt the file, use the gpg utility installed on the recipient's machine. The recipient would run gpg with the --decrypt option, specify the name of the encrypted file and the output filename, and include the passphrase for the secret key.

```
$ gpg --batch --output backup.tar.gz \
    --passphrase mypassword --decrypt backup.tar.gz.gpg
gpg: AES256 encrypted data
gpg: encrypted with 1 passphrase
```

Symmetric key cryptography is rather simple and easy to understand. Asymmetric cryptography is much more complicated and often is a point of confusion in cryptography.

Asymmetric key cryptography

Asymmetric cryptography, also called private/public key cryptography, uses two keys, called a *key pair*. A key pair consists of a public key and a private key. The public key is just that—public. There is no need to keep it secret. The private key needs to be kept secret.

The general idea of asymmetric key cryptography is shown in Figure 23.1. A plain-text file is encrypted using a public key of a key pair. The encrypted file then can be securely transmitted to another person. To decrypt the file, the private key is used. This private key must

23

be from the public/private key pair. Thus, data that has been encrypted with the public key can only be decrypted with its private key. The advantage of asymmetric cryptography is heightened security. The disadvantage is speed and key management.

FIGURE 23.1

Basic asymmetric key cryptography

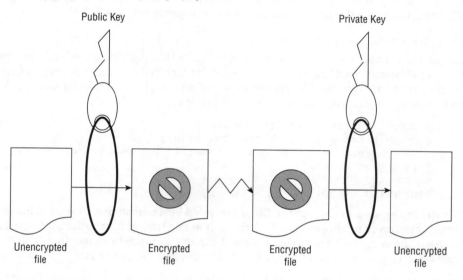

| Public Key | | Private Key |

| Unencrypted file | Encrypted file | Encrypted file | Unencrypted file |

Generating a key pair

You can perform asymmetric encryption on your Linux system using gpg. It is a very versatile cryptographic utility. Before you can encrypt a file, you must first create your key pair and a "key ring." In the example that follows, the gpg --gen-key command was used. This command creates a public/private key pair for the user johndoe, according to his desired specifications. It also generates a key ring to store his keys.

```
$ gpg --gen-key
gpg (GnuPG) 2.2.4; Copyright (C) 2017 Free Software Foundation, Inc.
This is free software: you are free to change and redistribute it.
There is NO WARRANTY, to the extent permitted by law.
Note: Use "gpg --full-generate-key" for a full featured key
generation dialog.
GnuPG needs to construct a user ID to identify your key.

Real name: steve
Email address: steve@mydomain.com
You selected this USER-ID:
    "steve <steve@mydomain.com>"
```

```
Change (N)ame, (E)mail, or (O)kay/(Q)uit? O
We need to generate a lot of random bytes. It is a good idea
to perform
some other action (type on the keyboard, move the mouse, utilize the
disks) during the prime generation; this gives the random number
generator a better chance to gain enough entropy.
gpg: /home/steve/.gnupg/trustdb.gpg: trustdb created
gpg: key B8536FC71908786C marked as ultimately trusted
gpg: directory '/home/steve/.gnupg/openpgp-revocs.d' created
gpg: revocation certificate stored as '/home/myname/.gnupg/openpgp-
revocs.d/08C228855F6E21848CE4A044B8536FC71908786C.rev'
public and secret key created and signed.

pub   rsa3072 2020-04-26 [SC] [expires: 2022-04-26]
      08C228855F6E21848CE4A044B8536FC71908786C
uid                      steve <steve@mydomain.com>
sub   rsa3072 2020-04-26 [E] [expires: 2022-04-26]
```

In the preceding example, the gpg utility asks for several specifications to generate the desired public/private keys:

User ID: This identifies the public key portion of the public/private key pair.

Email Address: This is the email address associated with the key.

Passphrase: This is used to identify and protect the private key portion of the public/private key pair.

The user steve can check his key ring by using the gpg --list-keys command, as shown in the code that follows. Notice the User ID (UID) of the public key is displayed just as it was created, containing steve's real name, comment, and email address.

```
$ gpg --list-keys
gpg: checking the trustdb
gpg: marginals needed: 3  completes needed: 1  trust model: pgp
gpg: depth: 0  valid:   1  signed:   0  trust: 0-, 0q, 0n, 0m, 0f, 1u
gpg: next trustdb check due at 2022-04-26
/home/steve/.gnupg/pubring.kbx
-------------------------------
pub   rsa3072 2020-04-26 [SC] [expires: 2022-04-26]
      08C228855F6E21848CE4A044B8536FC71908786C
uid           [ultimate] steve <steve@mydomain.com>
sub   rsa3072 2020-04-26 [E] [expires: 2022-04-26]
```

After the key pair and key ring are generated, files can be encrypted and decrypted. First, the public key must be extracted from the key ring so that it can be shared. In the example that follows, the gpg utility is used to extract the public key from myname's key ring. The extracted key is put into a file to be shared. The filename can be any name you wish it to be. In this case, the user steve chose the filename steve.pub.

```
$ gpg --export steve > steve.pub
$ ls *.pub
steve.pub
$ file steve.pub
steve.pub: GPG key public ring, created Sun Apr 26 02:31:22 2020
```

Sharing a public key

The file containing the public key can be shared in any number of ways. It can be sent as an attachment via email or even posted on a web page. The public key is considered public, so there is no need to hide it. In the example that follows, steve has given the file containing his public key to the user jill. She adds steve's public key to her key ring using the gpg --import command. The user jill verifies that steve's public key is added using the gpg --list-keys command to view her key ring.

```
$ ls *.pub
steve.pub
$ gpg --import steve.pub
gpg: key B8536FC71908786C: public key "steve <steve@mydomain
.com>" imported
gpg: Total number processed: 1
gpg:                 imported: 1
$ gpg --list-keys
/home/jill/.gnupg/pubring.kbx
---------------------------------
pub   rsa3072 2020-04-26 [SC] [expires: 2022-04-26]
      08C228855F6E21848CE4A044B8536FC71908786C
uid            [ unknown] steve <steve@mydomain.com>
sub   rsa3072 2020-04-26 [E] [expires: 2022-04-26]
```

Encrypting an email message

After the key is added to the key ring, that public key can be used to encrypt data for the public key's original owner. In the example code that follows, note that jill has created a text file, MessageForSteve.txt, for user johndoe.

- She encrypts the file using *his* public key.
- The encrypted file, MessageForSteve, is created by the --out option.
- The option --recipient identifies steve's public key using only the real name portion of his public key's UID in quotation marks, "Steve".

```
$ gpg --out MessageForSteve --recipient "Steve" \
    --encrypt MessageForSteve.txt
...
$ ls
steve.pub  MessageForSteve  MessageForSteve.txt
```

The encrypted message file, MessageForSteve, created from the plain-text file, MessageForSteve.txt, can be securely sent to the user steve. In order to decrypt this message, steve uses *his* private key, identified and protected by the secret passphrase used to create the key originally. After `steve` provides the proper passphrase, `gpg` decrypts the message file and puts it into the file `JillsMessage`, designated by the `--out` option. Once it's decrypted, he can read the plain-text message.

```
$ ls MessageForSteve
MessageForSteve
$ gpg --out JillsMessage --decrypt MessageForSteve
<A pop-up window prompts you for a passphrase>
gpg: encrypted with 2048-bit RSA key, ID D9EBC5F7317D3830, created
2019-10-27
      "Steve <steve@mydomain.com>"
$ cat JillsMessage
I know you are not the real Steve.
```

To review, the steps needed for encryption/decryption of files using asymmetric keys include the following:

1. Generate the key pair and the key ring.
2. Export a copy of your public key to a file.
3. Share the public key file.
4. Individuals who want to send you encrypted files add your public key to their key ring.
5. A file is encrypted using *your* public key.
6. The encrypted file is sent to you.
7. You decrypt the file using *your* private key.

You can see why asymmetric keys can cause confusion! Remember that in asymmetric cryptography, each public and private key is a paired set that works together.

Understanding digital signatures

A *digital signature* is an electronic originator used for authentication and data verification. A digital signature is not a scan of your physical signature. Instead, it is a cryptographic token sent with a file, so the file's receiver can be assured that the file came from you and has not been modified in any way.

When you create a digital signature, the following steps occur:

1. You create a file or message.
2. Using the `gpg` utility, you create a hash or message-digest of the file.
3. The `gpg` utility then encrypts the hash and the file, using an asymmetric key cipher. For the encryption, the private key of the public/private key pair is used. This is now a digitally signed encrypted file.
4. You send the encrypted hash (aka digital signature) and file to the receiver.
5. The receiver re-creates the hash or message digest of the received encrypted file.

23

6. Using the `gpg` utility, the receiver decrypts the received digital signature using the public key, to obtain the original hash or message digest.

7. The `gpg` utility compares the original hash to the re-created hash to see if they match. If they match, the receiver is told the digital signature is good.

8. The receiver can now read the decrypted file.

Notice in step 3 that the private key is used first. In the description of asymmetric key cryptography, the public key was used first. Asymmetric key cryptography is flexible enough to allow you to use your private key to encrypt and the receiver to use your public key to decrypt.

> **NOTE**
>
> Digital signatures have their own special ciphers. While several ciphers can handle both encryption and creating signatures, there are a few whose only job is to create digital signatures. Previously, the most popular cryptographic ciphers to use in creating signatures were RSA and Digital Signature Algorithm (DSA). The RSA algorithm can be used for both encryption and creating signatures, while DSA can be used only for creating digital signatures. Today, Ed25519 is considered to be more secure and faster than RSA, and ECDSA provides better protection than DSA.

As you can see, a digital signature contains both cryptographic hashing and asymmetric key cryptography. This complicated process is often handled by an application that has been configured to do so, instead of being directly handled by Linux system users. However, you can manually add your own digital signatures to documents.

Signing a file with a digital signature

Let's say that user `johndoe` is going to send a message to the user `jill`, along with his digital signature. He has created a file containing the plain-text message to send. He uses the `gpg` utility to create the signature file and encrypt the message file. The `--sign` option tells the `gpg` utility that `MessageForJill.txt` is the file to encrypt and use to create the digital signature. In response, the `gpg` utility does the following:

- Creates a message digest (aka hash) of the message file
- Encrypts the message digest, which creates the digital signature
- Encrypts the message file
- Places the encrypted contents into the file specified by the `--output` option, `JohnDoe.DS`

The file `JohnDoe.DS` now contains an encrypted and digitally signed message. The following code demonstrates this process:

```
$ gpg --output JohnDoe.DS --sign MessageForJill.txt
```

After the user `jill` receives the signed and encrypted file, she can use the `gpg` utility to check the digital signature and decrypt the file in one step. In the code that follows, the `--decrypt` option is used along with the name of the digitally signed file, `JohnDoe.DS`.

The file's message is decrypted and shown. The digital signature of the file is checked and found to be valid.

```
$ gpg --decrypt JohnDoe.DS
I am the real John Doe!
gpg: Signature made Sun 27 Oct 2019 07:03:21 PM EDT
gpg:                using RSA key
7469BCD3D05A43130F1786E0383D645D9798C173
gpg: Good signature from "John Doe <jdoe@example.com>" [unknown]
...
```

Without `johndoe`'s public key on her key ring, `jill` would not be able to decrypt this message and check the digital signature.

> **TIP**
>
> The previous example of digitally signing a document allows anyone with the public key the ability to decrypt the document. In order to keep it truly private, use the public key of the recipient to encrypt with the `gpg` options: `--sign` and `--encrypt`. The recipient can decrypt with their private key.

Understanding a few cryptography basics will help you get started on securing your Linux system with encryption. Keep in mind that we've covered just the basics in this chapter. There are many more cryptography topics, such as digital certificates and public key infrastructure, that would be worth your time to learn.

Implementing Linux cryptography

Many cryptography tools are available on your Linux system. Which ones you choose to use depend upon your organization's security requirements. The following is a brief review of some of the Linux cryptography tools available.

Ensuring file integrity

Earlier in this chapter, an ISO's file integrity was checked using the message digest utility `sha256sum`.

Related message digest utilities include the following:

- `sha224sum`
- `sha256sum`
- `sha384sum`
- `sha512sum`

These tools work just like the `sha1sum` command, except of course they use the SHA-2 cryptographic hash standard. The only difference between the various SHA-2 tools is the key length they use. The `sha224sum` command uses a key length of 224 bits, the `sha-256sum` command uses a key length of 256 bits, and so on. Remember that the longer the key length, the less the chance of cracking the cipher.

The SHA-2 cryptographic hash standard was created by the National Security Agency (NSA). SHA-3 is another cryptographic hash standard, which was released by NIST in August, 2015.

Encrypting a Linux filesystem at installation

You may need to encrypt an entire filesystem on your Linux server. This can be done in a number of different ways, including using a Free and Open Source Software (FOSS) third-party tool such as Linux Unified Key Setup (LUKS) (gitlab.com/cryptsetup/cryptsetup).

One of your options in Linux is to encrypt your root partition upon installation (see Chapter 9, "Installing Linux"). You can include an encryption option during the installation process.

After you select this option during installation, you are asked for a password. This is symmetric key cryptography with a password protecting the single key.

If you select this encryption option, whenever you boot the system, you are asked for the symmetric key password.

If you inherit a system with an encrypted disk, using root privileges, you can use the `lvs` and `cryptsetup` commands and the `/etc/crypttab` file to help. In the following, the `lvs` command shows all of the logical volumes currently on the system and their underlying device names. See Chapter 12, "Managing Disks and Filesystems," for a review of different Logical Volume Manager (LVM) commands.

```
# lvs -o devices
  Devices
  /dev/mapper/luks-b099fbbe-0e56-425f-91a6-44f129db9f4b(56)
  /dev/mapper/luks-b099fbbe-0e56-425f-91a6-44f129db9f4b(0)
```

On this system, notice that the underlying device names start with `luks`. This indicates that the Linux Unified Key Setup (LUKS) standard for hard disk encryption has been used.

> **NOTE**
> You might need to install the `lvs` command through the `lvm2` package.

The encrypted logical volumes are mounted at boot time using the information from the `/etc/fstab` file. However, contents of the `/etc/crypttab` file, which are used to trigger the capture of the password at boot time, will decrypt the `/etc/fstab` entries as they are mounted. This is shown in the following code. Notice that the `luks` names are the same as those listed by the `lvs` command in the previous example.

```
# cat /etc/crypttab
luks-b099fbbe-0e56-425f-91a6-44f129db9f4b
     UUID=b099fbbe-0e56-425f-91a6-44f129db9f4b none
```

You can also use the `cryptsetup` command to help you uncover more information about your Linux system's encrypted volumes. In the example that follows, the `status` option is used along with the `luks` device name to determine further information.

```
# cryptsetup status luks-b099fbbe-0e56-425f-91a6-44f129db9f4b
/dev/mapper/luks-b099fbbe-0e56-425f-91a6-44f129db9f4b
 is active and is in use.
  type:    LUKS1
  cipher:  aes-xts-plain64
  keysize: 512 bits
  device:  /dev/sda3
  offset:  4096 sectors
  size:    493819904 sectors
  mode:    read/write
```

Encrypting a Linux directory

You can also use the `ecryptfs` utility to encrypt on a Linux system. The `ecryptfs` utility (which is installed through the `ecryptfs-utils` package) is not a filesystem type, as the name would imply. Instead, it is a Portable Operating System Interface (POSIX)-compliant utility that allows you to create an encryption layer on top of any filesystem.

> **TIP**
>
> Because the `ecryptfs` utility is used for encryption, it is a common mistake to put the letter `n` after the letter `e` in the syntax `ecryptfs`. If you get an error while using the `ecryptfs` utilities, make sure that you did not use the syntax `encryptfs` by mistake.

In the example that follows, the user `johndoe` will have a subdirectory encrypted using the `ecryptfs` utility. First, there should be no files currently residing in the directory before it is encrypted. If there are files located there, move them to a safe place until after the encryption has been completed. If you do not move them, you cannot access them while the directory is encrypted.

Now, to encrypt the directory /home/johndoe/Secret, use the `mount` command. You must have root privileges to mount and unmount the encrypted directory in this method. Look at the `mount` command used in the example that follows. It is somewhat similar to the regular `mount` command, except that the partition type used is `ecryptfs`. The item to mount and its mount point are the same directory! You are literally encrypting the directory and mounting it upon itself. The other unusual item about this `mount` command is that it kicks off the `ecryptfs` utility, which asks a few interactive questions.

```
# mount -t ecryptfs /home/johndoe/Secret /home/johndoe/Secret
Select key type to use for newly created files:
 1) tspi
 2) passphrase
 3) pkcs11-helper
 4) openssl
Selection: 2
Passphrase: *********
Select cipher:
 1) aes: blocksize = 16;
```

Continues

Continued

```
    min keysize = 16; max keysize = 32 (loaded)
 2) blowfish: blocksize = 16;
    min keysize = 16; max keysize = 56 (not loaded)
 3) des3_ede: blocksize = 8;
    min keysize = 24; max keysize = 24 (not loaded)
 4) twofish: blocksize = 16;
    min keysize = 16; max keysize = 32 (not loaded)
 5) cast6: blocksize = 16;
    min keysize = 16; max keysize = 32 (not loaded)
 6) cast5: blocksize = 8;
    min keysize = 5; max keysize = 16 (not loaded)
Selection [aes]: 1
Select key bytes:
 1) 16
 2) 32
 3) 24
Selection [16]: 16
Enable plaintext passthrough (y/n) [n]: n
Enable filename encryption (y/n) [n]: n
Attempting to mount with the following options:
  ecryptfs_unlink_sigs
  ecryptfs_key_bytes=16
  ecryptfs_cipher=aes
  ecryptfs_sig=70993b8d49610e67
WARNING: Based on the contents of [/root/.ecryptfs/sig-cache.txt]
it looks like you have never mounted with this key
before. This could mean that you have typed your
passphrase wrong.

Would you like to proceed with the mount (yes/no)? : yes
Would you like to append sig [70993b8d49610e67] to
[/root/.ecryptfs/sig-cache.txt]
in order to avoid this warning in the future (yes/no)? : yes
Successfully appended new sig to user sig cache file
Mounted eCryptfs
```

The `ecryptfs` utility allows you to choose the following:

- Key type
- Passphrase
- Cipher
- Key size (in bytes)
- To enable or disable plain text to pass through
- To enable or disable filename encryption

It also warns you when you are first mounting this encrypted directory because the key has not been used before. The utility allows you to apply a digital signature to the mounted directory so that if you mount it again, it just mounts the directory and does not require a passphrase.

To verify that the encrypted directory is now mounted, you can use the mount command again. In the example that follows, the mount command is used and then piped into grep to search for the /home/johndoe/Secret directory. As you can see, the directory is mounted with an ecryptfs type.

```
# mount | grep /home/johndoe/Secret

/home/johndoe/Secret on /home/johndoe/Secret type ecryptfs
(rw,relatime,ecryptfs_sig=70993b8d49610e67,ecryptfs_cipher=aes,
ecryptfs_key_bytes=16,ecryptfs_unlink_sigs)
```

So far, you have not seen the effects of this mounted and encrypted directory. In the text that follows, the file my_secret_file is copied to the encrypted directory. User johndoe can still use the cat command to display the file in plain text. The file is automatically decrypted by the ecryptfs layer.

```
$ cp my_secret_file Secret
$ cat /home/johndoe/Secret/my_secret_file
Shh... It's a secret.
```

The root user also can use the cat command to display the file in plain text.

```
# cat /home/johndoe/Secret/my_secret_file
Shh... It's a secret.
```

However, after the encrypted directory is unmounted using the umount command, the files are no longer automatically decrypted. The file my _ secret _ file is now gibberish and cannot be read, even by the root user.

```
# umount /home/johndoe/Secret
```

Thus, the ecryptfs utility allows you to create a location on the filesystem to encrypt and decrypt files quickly. However, after that directory is no longer mounted as an ecryptfs type, the files are secure and cannot be decrypted.

23

Encrypting a Linux file

The most popular tool for file encryption on a Linux system is the OpenPGP utility GNU Privacy Guard, gpg. Its flexibility and variety of options, along with the fact that it is installed by default on Ubuntu, add to its appeal.

> **CAUTION**
>
> If your organization uses a third-party cloud storage company, you need to know that some of these companies, such as Dropbox, do not encrypt the files until they are received. This means that the company has the keys required to decrypt your files and can leave your organization's data vulnerable. Encrypting files on your Linux system before they are sent to the cloud adds the extra layer of protection needed.

However, you can use several other cryptography tools on a Linux system to encrypt files. Just like gpg, many of these tools allow you to do much more than merely file encryption. The following are some of the popular Linux cryptography tools that you can use to encrypt files:

- **aescrypt**: It uses the symmetric key cipher Rijndael, also called AES. This third-party FOSS tool is available for download from www.aescrypt.com.

- **bcrypt**: This tool uses the symmetric key cipher *blowfish*. It is not installed by default. After bcrypt is installed (sudo apt-+get install bcrypt), man pages are available.

- **ccrypt**: This tool uses the symmetric key cipher Rijndael, also called AES. It was created to replace the standard Unix crypt utility and is not installed by default. After ccrypt is installed (using sudo apt-get install ccrypt), man pages are available.

- **gpg**: This utility can use either asymmetric key pairs or a symmetric key. It is installed by default, and it is the cryptography tool of choice for Linux servers. The default cipher to use is set in the gpg.conf file. There are man pages available as well as info gpg.

Keep in mind that this list covers only the more popular tools. Also, remember that many of these tools can be used for more than just file cryptography.

Encrypting Linux with miscellaneous tools

You can apply *cryptography*, defined as the act of writing or generating codes meant to keep secrets, to just about everything in Linux. Besides filesystems, directories, and files, you can also encrypt backups, Zip files, network connections, and more.

Table 23.2 lists some of the miscellaneous Linux cryptography tools and what they do. If you want to see a full list of your currently installed cryptography tools, type **man -k crypt** at the command line.

TABLE 23.2   Linux Miscellaneous Cryptography Tools

Tool	Description
Duplicity	Encrypts backups. To install on Ubuntu, type **sudo apt-get install duplicity**.
gpg-zip	Uses GNU Privacy Guard to encrypt or sign files into an archive. Installed by default.
OpenSSL	A toolkit that implements Secure Sockets Layer (SSL) and Transport Layer Security (TLS) protocols. These protocols require encryption. Installed by default.
Seahorse	A GNU Privacy Guard encryption key manager. Installed by default on Ubuntu.
SSH	Encrypts remote access across a network. Installed by default.
Zipcloak	Encrypts entries in a Zip file. Installed by default.

Like many other items on a Linux system, the available cryptography tools are rich and plentiful. This gives you the flexibility and variety that you need in order to implement the cryptography standards your particular organization requires.

Using Encryption from the Desktop

The Passwords and Keys window provides a means of viewing and managing keys and passwords from the GNU Network Object Model Environment (GNOME) desktop. This window can be launched by selecting the Passwords and Keys icon from the Activities screen or by running the seahorse command. With the window that appears, you can work with the following:

Passwords: When you access a website, from a Chromium or Chrome web browser, and enter a username and password (and you select to save that password), it is stored on your system for the next time that you visit that site. Select the Login entry under the Passwords heading to see each of these saved usernames and passwords.

Certificates: You can view certificates associated with the GNOME Key Storage, User Key Storage, System Trust, and Default Trust.

PGP keys: You can view the GPG keys that you create by selecting the GnuPG keys entry.

Secure Shell: You can create public and private OpenSSH keys that let you log in to remote systems using those keys instead of passwords for authentication with ssh, scp, rsync, sftp, and related commands. Select OpenSSH keys to view any keys that you have created for this purpose. (See the section "Using key-based [password-less] authentication" in Chapter 13, "Understanding Server Administration," for information on creating these types of keys.)

Another extremely powerful security tool available on Linux is Pluggable Authentication Modules (PAM). The next sections in this chapter cover basic PAM concepts and how you can use this tool to enhance even further your Linux system's security.

Implementing Linux Security with PAM

Pluggable Authentication Modules (PAM) was invented by Sun Microsystems and originally implemented in the Solaris operating system. The Linux-PAM project began in 1997. Ubuntu, like most Linux distributions today, uses PAM.

23

PAM simplifies the authentication management process. Remember that authentication (see Chapter 22) is the process of determining that a subject (aka user or process) is who they say they are. This process is sometimes called "identification and authentication." PAM is a centralized method of providing authentication for the Linux system and applications.

Applications can be written to use PAM; such applications are called "PAM-aware." A PAM-aware application does not have to be rewritten and recompiled to have its authentication settings changed. Any required changes are made within a PAM configuration file for the PAM-aware applications. Thus, authentication management for these applications is centralized and simplified.

To see whether a particular Linux application or utility is PAM-aware check whether it's compiled with the PAM library, libpam.so. In the example that follows, the crontab application is being checked for PAM awareness. The ldd command checks a file's shared library dependencies. To keep it simple, grep is used to search for the PAM library. As you can see, crontab on this particular Linux system is PAM-aware.

```
# ldd /usr/bin/crontab | grep pam
libpam.so.0 => /lib64/libpam.so.0 (0x00007fbee19ce000)
```

The benefits of using PAM on your Linux system include the following:

- Simplified and centralized authentication management from the administrator viewpoint
- Simplified application development, because developers can write applications using the documented PAM library instead of writing their own authentication routines
- Flexibility in authentication:
  - Allow or deny access to resources based on traditional criteria, such as identification
  - Allow or deny access based on additional criteria, such as time-of-day restrictions
  - Set subject limitations, such as resource usage

Although the benefits of PAM simplify authentication management, the way that PAM actually works is not so simple.

Understanding the PAM authentication process

When a subject (user or process) requests access to a PAM-aware application or utility, two primary components are used to complete the subject authentication process:

- The PAM-aware application's configuration file
- The PAM modules the configuration file uses

Each PAM-aware application configuration file is at the center of the process. The PAM configuration files call upon particular PAM modules to perform the needed authentication.

PAM modules authenticate subjects from system authorization data, such as a centralized user account using Lightweight Directory Access Protocol (LDAP) (see Chapter 11, "Managing User Accounts").

Linux comes with many applications that are PAM-aware, with their needed configuration files and PAM modules already installed. If you have any special authentication needs, you can most likely find a PAM module that has already been written for that need. However, before you start tweaking PAM, you need to understand more about how PAM operates.

A series of steps is taken by PAM using the modules and configuration files in order to ensure that proper application authentication occurs:

1. A subject (user or process) requests access to an application.

2. The application's PAM configuration file, which contains an access policy, is open and read. The access policy is set via a list of all the PAM modules to be used in the authentication process. This PAM module(s) list is called a *stack*.

3. The PAM modules in the stack are invoked in the order in which they are listed.

4. Each PAM module returns either a success or failure status.

5. The stack continues to be read in order, and it is not necessarily stopped by a single returned failure status.

6. The status results of all of the PAM modules are combined into a single overall result of authentication success or failure.

Typically, if a single PAM module returns a failure status, access to the application is denied. However, this is dependent upon the configuration file settings. Most PAM configuration files are located in /etc/pam.d. The general format of a PAM configuration file is

```
context    control flag    PAM module [module options]
```

Understanding PAM contexts

PAM modules have standard functions that provide different authentication services. These standard functions within a PAM module can be divided into function types called *contexts*. Contexts can also be called *module interfaces* or *types*. In Table 23.3, the different PAM contexts are listed along with what type of authentication service they provide.

TABLE 23.3 PAM Contexts

Context	Service Description
auth	Provides authentication management services, such as verifying account passwords
account	Provides account validation services, such as time-of-day access restrictions
password	Manages account passwords, such as password length restrictions

Understanding PAM control flags

In a PAM configuration file, control flags are used to determine the overall status, which are returned to the application. A control flag is either of the following:

Simple keyword: The only concern here is if the corresponding PAM module returns a response of either "failed" or "success." See Table 23.4 for how these statuses are handled.

Series of actions: The returned module status is handled through the series of actions listed in the file.

Table 23.4 shows the various keyword control flags and their responses to the returned module status. Notice that a few of the control flags need to be carefully placed within the configuration file's stack. Some control flags cause the authentication process to stop immediately and the rest of the PAM modules are not called. The control flags simply control how the PAM module status results are combined into a single overall result. Table 23.4 demonstrates how the status results are combined.

TABLE 23.4 **PAM Configuration Control Flags and Response Handling**

required	If failed, returns a failure status to the application, after the rest of the contexts have been run in the stack. For example, a requisite control might cause a login to fail if someone types in an invalid user. But the user might not be told of the failure until after entering a password, hiding the fact that it was the bad username that caused the failure.
requisite	If failed, returns a failure status to the application immediately without running the rest of the stack. (Be careful where you place this control in the stack.) For example, a requisite control might require key-based authentication and fail immediately when a valid key is not provided. In that case, it could fail before even prompting for a username/password.
sufficient	If failed, the module status is ignored. If successful, then a success status is immediately returned to the application without running the rest of the stack. (Be careful where you place this control in the stack.)
optional	This control flag is important only for the final overall return status of success or failure. Think of it as a tiebreaker. When the other modules in the configuration file stack return statuses that are neither clear-cut failure nor success statuses, this optional module's status is used to determine the final status or break the tie. In cases where the other modules in the stack are returning a clear-cut path of failure or success, this status is ignored.
include	Get all the return statuses from this particular PAM configuration file's stack to include in this stack's overall return status. It's as if the entire stack from the named configuration file is now in this configuration file.
substack	Similar to the include control flag, except for how certain errors and evaluations affect the main stack. This forces the included configuration file stack to act as a substack to the main stack. Thus, certain errors and evaluations affect only the substack and not the main stack.

You should know that that the PAM modules return many more status result codes than just "success" or "failure." For example, a module may return the status code of PAM_ACCT_ EXPIRED, which means that the user account has expired. This would be deemed a "failure."

Understanding PAM modules

A PAM module is actually a suite of shared library modules (DLL files) stored in /usr/ lib64/security (64-bit). You can see a list of the various installed PAM modules on your system by entering **sudo find / -name pam*.so** at the command line.

Your Linux system comes with many of the PAM modules needed already installed. If you do need a module not already installed, most likely someone else has already written it. Check out sources such as these:

- openwall.com/pam/
- puszcza.gnu.org.ua/software/pam-modules/download.html

Understanding PAM system event configuration files

So far, the focus has been on PAM-aware applications and their configuration files. However, other system events, such as logging in to the Linux system, also use PAM. Thus, these events also have configuration files.

The following is a partial directory listing of the PAM configuration file directory. Notice that there are PAM-aware application configuration files, like the one for Cockpit.

```
# ls -l /etc/pam.d
total 136
-rw-r--r-- 1 root root  250 Feb 20  2018 atd
-rw-r--r-- 1 root root  384 Jan 25  2018 chfn
-rw-r--r-- 1 root root   92 Jan 25  2018 chpasswd
-rw-r--r-- 1 root root  581 Jan 25  2018 chsh
-rw-r--r-- 1 root root 1018 Mar 21  2018 cockpit
...
```

CAUTION

Modifying or deleting PAM system event configuration files incorrectly can lock you out of your own system. Make sure that you test any changes in a virtual or test environment before modifying your production Linux servers.

These PAM system event configuration files operate in exactly the same way as the PAM-aware application configuration files. They have the same format, use the same syntax, and call upon PAM modules. However, many of these files are symbolically linked (see Chapter 4, "Moving Around the Filesystem"). Therefore, these configuration files require a few extra steps when changes are made to them. The "how-tos" are covered later in this chapter.

TIP

Many of the PAM configuration files have a man page associated with them. For example, to find out more information on the pam_unix module, type **man pam_unix** at the command line.

Even though Linux comes with many PAM-aware applications, various configuration files, and PAM modules already installed, you cannot just hope that PAM will take care of itself. Certain administrative steps are needed to manage PAM.

Administering PAM on your Linux system

The task of administering PAM on your Linux system is rather minimal. You need to verify that PAM is properly implemented and make adjustments to meet your particular organization's security needs.

Also, PAM does a little more than just the application authentication steps described previously. PAM can also limit resources, restrict access times, enforce good password selection, and so on.

Managing PAM-aware application configuration files

You should review PAM configuration files for your PAM-aware applications and utilities in order to ensure that their authentication process matches your organization's desired authentication process. Your Access Control Matrix (see Chapter 22) and the information on understanding PAM provided in this chapter should help you conduct an audit of the PAM configuration files.

Each PAM-aware application should have its very own PAM configuration file. Each configuration file defines what particular PAM modules are used for that application. If no configuration file exists, a security hole may be created for that application. This hole could be used for malicious intent. As a safety precaution, PAM comes with the "other" configuration file. If a PAM-aware application does not have a PAM configuration file, it defaults to using the "other" PAM configuration file.

You can verify whether your Linux system has the /etc/pam.d/other configuration file by using the ls command. The example that follows shows that the /etc/pam.d/other PAM configuration file does exist on this system:

```
$ ls /etc/pam.d/other
/etc/pam.d/other
```

The PAM /etc/pam.d/other configuration file should deny all access, which in terms of security is referred to as Implicit Deny. In computer security access control, *Implicit Deny* means that if certain criteria are not clearly met, access must be denied. In this case, if no configuration file exists for a PAM-aware application, all access to it is denied. The following shows a /etc/pam.d/other file's contents:

```
$ cat /etc/pam.d/other
# /etc/pam.d/other - specify the PAM fallback behavior
#
# Note that this file is used for any unspecified service;
for example
#if /etc/pam.d/cron  specifies no session modules but cron calls
#pam_open_session, the session module out of /etc/pam.d/other is
```

```
#used.  If you really want nothing to happen then use pam_permit.so or
#pam_deny.so as appropriate.
# We fall back to the system default in /etc/pam.d/common-*
@include common-auth
@include common-account
@include common-password
@include common-session
```

Even with the "other" configuration file in place, if a PAM configuration file for a PAM-aware application is not there, it must be created. Add this item to your PAM audit checklist. You should also review your PAM "other" configuration file on your Linux system to ensure that it enforces Implicit Deny.

Implementing resources limits with PAM

Managing resources is not just a system administration task. It is also a security administration task. Setting resource limitations helps you avoid many adverse problems on your Linux system. Problems such as fork bombs can be averted by limiting the number of processes a single user can create. A *fork bomb* occurs when a process spawns one process after another in a recursive manner until system resources are consumed. Fork bombs can be malicious or just accidental; that is, created simply by poor program code development.

The PAM module `pam-limits` uses a special configuration file to set these resources limits: `/etc/security/limits.conf`. By default, this file has no resource limits set within it. Therefore, you need to review the file and set resources limits to match your organization's security needs.

23

> **NOTE**
>
> PAM configuration files are in the `/etc/pam.d` directory and the `/etc/security` directory.

The following snippet shows a version of the `/etc/security/limits.conf` file. The complete version on your system should contain plenty of illustrative examples.

```
$ cat /etc/security/limits.conf
# /etc/security/limits.conf
#
#This file sets the resource limits for the users logged in via PAM.
#It does not affect resource limits of the system services.
#
#Also note that configuration files in /etc/security/limits.d directory,
#which are read in alphabetical order, override the settings in this
#file in case the domain is the same or more specific.
...
#Each line describes a limit for a user in the form:
#
#<domain>        <type>  <item>  <value>
...
```

Continues

Continued

```
#*              soft    core        0
#*              hard    rss         10000
#@student       hard    nproc       20
#@faculty       soft    nproc       20
#@faculty       hard    nproc       50
#ftp            hard    nproc       0
#@student       -       maxlogins   4
# End of file
```

The format items *domain* and *type* need some further explanation than what is documented in the configuration file:

domain: The limit applies to the listed user or group. If the domain is *, it applies to *all* users.

type: A hard limit cannot be exceeded. A soft limit can be exceeded, but only temporarily.

Look at the limits.conf file setting example that follows. The group faculty is listed, but what you should notice is nproc. The nproc limit sets the maximum number of processes a user can start. This setting is what prevents a fork bomb. Notice that the type selected is hard; thus, the limit of 50 processes cannot be exceeded. Of course, this limit is not enforced because the line is commented out with a # symbol.

```
#@faculty       hard    nproc       50
```

Limit settings are set per login and only last for the duration of the login session. A malicious user could log in several times to create a fork bomb. Thus, setting the maximum number of logins for these user accounts is a good idea too.

Limiting the maximum number of logins may have to be done on a per-user basis. For example, johndoe needs to log in to the Linux system only once. To prevent others from using johndoe's account, set his account's maxlogins to 1:

```
johndoe         hard    maxlogins   1
```

To override any settings in the limits.conf file, add files named *.conf to the /etc/security/limits.d directory. This is a convenient way that to add and remove limits without needing to edit the limits.conf file directly.

The final step in limiting this resource is to ensure that the PAM module using limits.conf is included in one of the PAM system event configuration files. The PAM module using limits.conf is pam_limits. In the partial listing that follows, grep is used to verify that the PAM module is used within the system event configuration files:

```
$ grep -nr "pam_limits" /etc/pam.d/
/etc/pam.d/systemd-user:10:session      required pam_limits.so
/etc/pam.d/sshd:40:session              required pam_limits.so
/etc/pam.d/runuser:4:session            required pam_limits.so
/etc/pam.d/atd:9:session                required pam_limits.so
/etc/pam.d/cron:20:session              required pam_limits.so
```

```
/etc/pam.d/su:52:session              required pam_limits.so
/etc/pam.d/login:87:session           required pam_limits.so
```

Time limits for access to services and accounts are not handled by the PAM /etc/security/limits.conf configuration file. Instead, it is handled by the time.conf file.

Implementing time restrictions with PAM

PAM can make your entire Linux system operate on "PAM time." Time restrictions such as access to particular applications during certain times of the day, or allowing logins only during specified days of the week, are all handled by PAM.

The PAM configuration file that handles these restrictions is located in the /etc/security directory. The following code shows the well-documented /etc/security/time.conf PAM configuration file:

```
$ cat /etc/security/time.conf
# this is an example configuration file for the pam_time module.
Its syntax
# was initially based heavily on that of the shadow package
(shadow-960129).

#
# the syntax of the lines is as follows:
#
#        services;ttys;users;times
...
```

I recommend that you read through the contents of the time.conf file. Note that the format for each valid entry follows this syntax: services;ttys;users;times. Fields are separated by semicolons. The valid field values are documented in the time.conf configuration file.

While time.conf is well-documented, an example is always helpful. For instance, you might decide that regular users should be allowed to log in on terminals on weekdays only (Monday through Friday). They can log in from 7 a.m. to 7 p.m. on these weekdays. The following list describes what elements need to be set:

services: Login

ttys—*: Indicates that all terminals are to be included

users: Everyone but root (!root)

times: Allowed on weekdays (Wd) from 7 a.m. (0700) to 7 p.m. (1900)

The entry in time.conf would look like the following:

```
login; * ; !root ; Wd0700-1900
```

The final step in implementing this example time restriction is to ensure that the PAM module using time.conf is included in one of the PAM system event configuration files.

The PAM module using `time.conf` is `pam_time`. In the partial listing that follows, `grep` shows how the PAM module `pam_time` is used within system event configuration files:

```
$ grep -nr "pam_time" /etc/pam.d/
/etc/pam.d/su:29:# account    requisite  pam_time.so
/etc/pam.d/login:78:# account    requisite  pam_time.so
```

If pam _ time were not listed, you would need to modify the `/etc/pam.d/common-auth` file in order for PAM to enforce the time restrictions.

Add the following near the top of the "account" section of the configuration file. Now the pam _ time module checks the login restrictions you set within the `/etc/security/time.conf` file.

```
account    required    pam_time.so
```

Enforcing good passwords with PAM

When a password is modified, the PAM module pam _ cracklib is involved in the process. The module prompts the user for a password and checks its strength against a system dictionary and a set of rules for identifying poor choices.

Using `pam_cracklib`, you can check a newly chosen password for the following:

- Is it a dictionary word?
- Is it a palindrome?
- Is it the old password with the case changed?
- Is it too much like the old password?
- Is it too short?
- Is it a rotated version of the old password?
- Does it use the same consecutive characters?
- Does it contain the username in some form?

You can change the rules `pam_cracklib` uses for checking new passwords by making modifications to the `/etc/pam.d/common-password` file.

```
$ cat /etc/pam.d/passwd
#
# The PAM configuration file for the Shadow 'passwd' service
#
@include common-password
```

The current settings of the `common-password` file are shown here. Currently, one entry calls the pam _ cracklib PAM module.

```
$ cat /etc/pam.d/common-password
# /etc/pam.d/common-password - password-related modules common to
all services
#
# This file is included from other service-specific PAM config files,
# and should contain a list of modules that define the services to be
```

```
# used to change user passwords.  The default is pam_unix.
# here are the per-package modules (the "Primary" block)
password        [success=1 default=ignore]      pam_unix.so
obscure sha512
# here's the fallback if no module succeeds
password        requisite                        pam_deny.so
password        required                         pam_permit.so
# and here are more per-package modules (the "Additional" block)
password        optional
```

Encouraging sudo use with PAM

To allow tracking of root-account use by individuals and avoid a repudiation situation (see Chapter 22), you should restrict the use of the su command and force the use of sudo. If your organization has such a policy, you can accomplish this with PAM by simply uncommenting the appropriate line (# auth required pam_wheel.so deny group=nosu) in the su file that's partially listed here:

```
$ cat /etc/pam.d/su
#
# The PAM configuration file for the Shadow 'su' service
#
auth            sufficient pam_rootok.so
# Uncomment this if you want members of a specific group to not
# be allowed to use su at all.
# auth          required   pam_wheel.so deny group=nosu
session         required   pam_env.so readenv=1
session         required   pam_env.so readenv=1 envfile=/etc/
default/locale
session         optional   pam_mail.so nopen
session         required   pam_limits.so
@include common-auth
@include common-account
@include common-session
```

Obtaining more information on PAM

PAM is another rich and versatile security tool available to you on your Linux system. In your own Linux system's man pages, you can read about managing the PAM configuration files.

- To get more information on PAM configuration files, use the command **man pam.conf.**
- You can see all of the PAM modules available on your system by entering **ls /lib/ x86_64-linux-gnu/security/** at the command line. To get more information on each PAM module, enter **man pam_module_name**. Be sure to leave off the file extension of so for the **pam_module_name**. For example, enter **man pam_lastlog** to learn more about the pam_lastlog.so module. Several websites can provide additional information on PAM:

- **The Official Linux-PAM website:** www.linux-pam.org
- **The Linux-PAM System Administrator's Guide:** www.linux-pam.org/Linux-PAM-html/Linux-PAM _ SAG.html
- **PAM Module reference:** www.linux-pam.org/Linux-PAM-html/sag-module-reference.html

Summary

Cryptography tools offer ways of protecting and verifying the validity of the data you use on your Linux system. The PAM facility provides a means of creating policies to secure the tools that are used to authenticate users on your system.

Both the cryptography tools and PAM should be handled with care as you learn about Linux. Be sure to test any modifications that you make on a test Linux system or a virtualized Linux system before you implement them on a production machine.

The next chapter covers AppArmor. While cryptography and PAM are tools that you can use on your Linux system, AppArmor is an entire security enhancement layer.

Exercises

Use these exercises to test your knowledge of using cryptography tools and PAM. These tasks assume that you are running an Ubuntu Linux system (although some tasks work on other Linux systems as well). If you are stuck, solutions to the tasks are shown in Appendix A (although in Linux, there are often multiple ways to complete a task).

1. Encrypt a file using the gpg utility and a passphrase.
2. Generate a public key ring using the gpg utility.
3. List out the key ring you generated.
4. Encrypt a file and add your digital signature using the gpg utility.
5. Go to the Ubuntu download page: ubuntu.com. Select one of the versions to download. When the download is complete, verify your image.
6. Using the command which su, determine the su command's full filename. Next, determine whether the su command on your Linux system is PAM-aware.
7. Does the su command have a PAM configuration file? If so, display the configuration file on the screen and list what PAM contexts it uses.
8. List out the various PAM modules on your system to your screen.
9. Find the PAM "other" configuration file on your system. Does it exist? Does it enforce Implicit Deny?
10. Find the PAM limits configuration file. Does it have a setting to keep a fork bomb from occurring on your system?

Enhancing Linux Security with AppArmor

IN THIS CHAPTER

Learning about AppArmor benefits

Learning how AppArmor works

AppArmor configuration

Finding AppArmor resources

AppArmor is a name-based mandatory access control (MAC) security model that's currently supported by Canonical (the company behind Ubuntu). AppArmor has been included in the Linux kernel since version 2.6.36 (released back in 2010). AppArmor fills much of the same security needs as Red Hat's SELinux, but with significantly less complexity.

Understanding AppArmor

AppArmor is a security enhancement module deployed on top of Linux. It provides additional security measures and is installed and active by default. The thing about AppArmor—unlike its Red Hat equivalent SELinux—is that you can often use Ubuntu for years and never realize it's there. Now consider just how AppArmor works and why you need it.

You've already seen a number of traditional Linux features, including discretionary access controls (DAC) like object permissions. Such permissions are called *discretionary* because an entity (like a user) with legitimate access to a resource has the power to extend that access to other entities. Where you're concerned that this power might be abused—where, for instance, there's risk of a hacker executing a privilege escalation attack—you might want to impose mandatory access control. MACs are applied on processes rather than on resources themselves to ensure that, no matter which entity is active, it'll never be possible to extend permissions beyond their intended scope.

Any Linux program that's given an AppArmor profile at or after installation can be used in one of three ways:

- **The profile can be inactive:** No matter how it's configured, no actions will be restricted.
- **The profile could be set to *complain*:** Even though no actions will be restricted, violations of the current settings will be reported to the logging system. This can be a great way to test your configuration before sending it into production.
- **The profile could be set to *enforce*:** Any actions in violation of the profile settings will be blocked.

Configuration files exist in the /etc/apparmor/ directory:

```
$ ls /etc/apparmor
easyprof.conf  logprof.conf  parser.conf  subdomain.conf
init           notify.conf   severity.db
```

However, most AppArmor administration work happens within AppArmor profiles, and those live in the /etc/apparmor.d/ directory and are named after the location of their program binary file. Thus, the main LibreOffice profile would be found in a file called /etc/apparmor.d/usr.lib.libreoffice.program.soffice.bin. You administrate AppArmor using programs installed with the apparmor-utils package. If you're installing apparmor-utils, you might as well pick up a few more helpful tools at the same time:

```
# apt install apparmor-utils apparmor-easyprof apparmor-notify
```

When you want to change a profile's status, you would run either aa-enforce or aa-complain against the profile file. These examples would set the Apache web server service to either enforce or complain:

```
# aa-enforce /etc/apparmor.d/usr.sbin.apache2
# aa-complain /etc/apparmor.d/usr.sbin.apache2
```

You could also reset the mode of all profiles at once using either:

```
# aa-complain /etc/apparmor.d/*
```

or:

```
# aa-enforce /etc/apparmor.d/*
```

You can quickly view the status of all the profiles currently loaded using the apparmor_status command:

```
# apparmor_status
apparmor module is loaded.
28 profiles are loaded.
28 profiles are in enforce mode.
   /snap/snapd/7264/usr/lib/snapd/snap-confine
   /snap/snapd/7264/usr/lib/snapd/snap-confine//mount-namespace-
capture-helper
   /usr/bin/man
   /usr/lib/NetworkManager/nm-dhcp-client.action
```

```
/usr/lib/NetworkManager/nm-dhcp-helper
/usr/lib/connman/scripts/dhclient-script
/usr/lib/snapd/snap-confine
/usr/lib/snapd/snap-confine//mount-namespace-capture-helper
/usr/sbin/tcpdump
/{,usr/}sbin/dhclient
lsb_release
man_filter
man_groff
nvidia_modprobe
nvidia_modprobe//kmod
snap-update-ns.lxd
snap.lxd.activate
snap.lxd.benchmark
snap.lxd.buginfo
snap.lxd.check-kernel
snap.lxd.daemon
snap.lxd.hook.configure
snap.lxd.hook.install
snap.lxd.hook.remove
snap.lxd.lxc
snap.lxd.lxc-to-lxd
snap.lxd.lxd
snap.lxd.migrate
0 profiles are in complain mode.
0 processes have profiles defined.
0 processes are in enforce mode.
0 processes are in complain mode.
0 processes are unconfined but have a profile defined.
```

AppArmor events are logged to regular Linux logging systems. The best way to see what exciting stuff has been happening in your system's AppArmor world is to query the kernel ring buffer using dmesg:

```
$ dmesg | grep apparmor
```

Here's what a typical *denied* message will look like in dmesg:

```
[  234.104868] audit: type=1400 audit(1588030849.305:236):
apparmor="DENIED" operation="open" profile="/usr/bin/evince" name="/
etc/xdg/mimeapps.list" pid=10160 comm="evince" requested_mask="r"
denied_mask="r" fsuid=1000 ouid=0
```

In that example, the profile at the center of the event was evince (Ubuntu's default GUI document viewer), which tried to open the /etc/xdg/mimeapps.list file using the process ID, 10160. The /etc/xdg/ directory is for definitions controlling the way your desktop graphics will behave. The mimeapps.list file in particular defines the applications that will, by default, load a given file type. Upon seeing such a log message, you would probably want to dig a bit deeper to ensure that the evince utility hasn't been hijacked by an unauthorized user for some malicious purpose. Although, as it turns out, there's nothing like that happening in this particular case.

Working with AppArmor

To get an idea of how AppArmor works in the real world, consider the example of a simple profile. You'll use the profile managed by the /etc/apparmor.d/bin.ping file, which controls the way the ping command behaves. Here's the file itself:

```
#include <tunables/global>
profile ping /{usr/,}bin/{,iputils-}ping flags=(complain) {
  #include <abstractions/base>
  #include <abstractions/consoles>
  #include <abstractions/nameservice>

  capability net_raw,
  capability setuid,
  network inet raw,
  network inet6 raw,

  /{,usr/}bin/{,iputils-}ping mixr,
  /etc/modules.conf r,

  # Site-specific additions and overrides. See local/README for details.
  #include <local/bin.ping>
}
```

The #include line lets you incorporate common policy statements that are maintained in external documents. tunables/global refers to files referenced in the globals file found in the /etc/apparmor.d/tunables/ directory. Here's what that file might look like:

```
# All the tunables definitions that should be available to every profile
# should be included here

#include <tunables/home>
#include <tunables/multiarch>
#include <tunables/proc>
#include <tunables/alias>
#include <tunables/kernelvars>
#include <tunables/xdg-user-dirs>
#include <tunables/share>
```

The profile line of the ping file (/etc/apparmor.d/bin.ping) defines the path to the program binary itself (/bin/ping) and sets the mode (complain, in this case). A number of files in the /etc/apparmor.d/abstractions/ directory are also included. Those files contain some of the basic constraints that will govern the way ping will work. For instance, consider this line in the /etc/apparmor/abstractions/base file:

```
@{PROC}/meminfo                r,
```

The r tells the system that ping should be able to read the contents of the /proc/
meminfo file. But that meminfo file doesn't necessarily have to be in /proc/—the
actual location is determined by the contents of the /etc/apparmor.d/tunables/proc
file. The defaults will normally work just fine, but you can see how deeply customizable
all this is.

As you dive more deeply into AppArmor files, you'll see capabilities defined by strings of
letters including r, w, k, and m. The first two should be obvious: read and write. But you
may pause on seeing k and m. So know that k stands for *lock*—giving the process the
power to gain exclusive write access to a file to ensure no one else can edit it at the same
time. And m means the program can be mapped into memory. See man apparmor.d for
more details.

The capability and network lines in the /etc/apparmor.d/bin.ping file further
define ping behavior. inet and inet6, for instance, allow the program to operate using
both IPv4 and IPv6, and raw refers to the raw network transport protocol.

Now you'll install some new software and see how it can be integrated with AppArmor. This
example loosely follows a helpful tutorial found on the Ubuntu documentation site at
www.ubuntu.com/tutorials/beginning-apparmor-profile-development.

You'll install the certspotter package (which is used to monitor Internet domains for hos-
tile activity). To provide a place for certspotter to write data, you'll make a directory called
certspotter in the home directory and a file called watchlist within that directory.
Finally, you'll add at least one domain to that file that certspotter will monitor and run
the program.

```
# apt install certspotter
$ mkdir ~/.certspotter
$ touch ~/.certspotter/watchlist
$ echo "wiley.com" >> ~/.certspotter/watchlist
$ certspotter
certspotter: ctlog-gen2.api.venafi.com: 2020/04/28 18:32:16 Error
retrieving STH from log: Get https://ctlog-gen2.api.venafi.com/ct/
v1/get-sth: dial tcp: lookup ctlog-gen2.api.venafi.com: No address
associated with hostname
```

Now you can use aa-easyprof to generate a simple profile document and print it to
the screen:

```
$ aa-easyprof /usr/bin/certspotter
# vim:syntax=apparmor
# AppArmor policy for certspotter
# ###AUTHOR###
# ###COPYRIGHT###
# ###COMMENT###

#include <tunables/global>
```

Continues

continued

```
# No template variables specified

"/usr/bin/certspotter" {
  #include <abstractions/base>

  # No abstractions specified

  # No policy groups specified

  # No read paths specified

  # No write paths specified
}
```

Nothing much happening there, but it's a good place to start. You'll give it an appropriate name (using the binary location on the filesystem for inspiration) and move it to the /etc/apparmor.d/ directory. Then you'll add the profile to the kernel using apparmor_parser.

```
$ aa-easyprof /usr/bin/certspotter > ~/usr.bin.certspotter
# mv ~/usr.bin.certspotter /etc/apparmor.d/
# apparmor_parser -r /etc/apparmor.d/usr.bin.certspotter
```

The next time you run certspotter, it will fail outright. The error message you get might look something like this:

```
certspotter: /home/ubuntu/.certspotter/watchlist: open /home/ubuntu/
.certspotter/watchlist: permission denied
```

You can prove that it's AppArmor causing this failure by resetting the profile to complain and running certspotter again. This time it should work.

```
# aa-complain /etc/apparmor.d/usr.bin.certspotter
Setting /etc/apparmor.d/usr.bin.certspotter to complain mode.
$ certspotter
```

The aa-logprof program will scan the profiles and offer advice about possible changes and then, if you agree, apply them. Now see what it says about the certspotter profile:

```
# aa-logprof
Reading log entries from /var/log/syslog.
Updating AppArmor profiles in /etc/apparmor.d.
Complain-mode changes:

Profile:   /usr/bin/certspotter
Path:      /proc/sys/net/core/somaxconn
New Mode:  r
Severity:  6
```

```
   [1 - #include <abstractions/lxc/container-base>]
    2 - #include <abstractions/lxc/start-container>
    3 - /proc/sys/net/core/somaxconn r,
(A)llow / [(D)eny] / (I)gnore / (G)lob / Glob with (E)xtension / (N)
ew / Audi(t) / Abo(r)t / (F)inish
```

Press A and then S to accept and save the changes. Now take a look at the new parts of the updated document:

```
/usr/bin/certspotter flags=(complain) {
   #include <abstractions/base>
   #include <abstractions/lxc/container-base>
}
```

You can also manually add settings to the profile document. Perhaps you'd like to go the extra mile in preventing someone with malicious control over the certspotter program from accessing (and removing) private content. You should add the new entries within the `flags` section so that it looks like this:

```
# nano /etc/apparmor.d/usr.bin.certspotter
```

```
/usr/bin/certspotter flags=(complain) {
   #include <abstractions/base>
   #include <abstractions/lxc/container-base>

   deny @{HOME}/Documents/ rw,
   deny @{HOME}/Pictures/ rw,
   deny @{HOME}/Videos/ rw,
   deny @{HOME}/.config/ rw,
   deny @{HOME}/.ssh/ rw,
}
```

When that's done, you can reload your policy this way:

```
# apparmor_parser -r /etc/apparmor.d/usr.bin.certspotter
```

The way the parser behaves can be controlled through the `parser.conf` file in the /etc/ apparmor/ directory.

24

Summary

AppArmor provides a security enhancement to Linux, and it is installed by default on Ubuntu. In this chapter, you learned the benefits of AppArmor, how it works, how to set it up, and how to get more information about this important security enhancement.

You learned about the various steps available to configure AppArmor. Even though it comes preconfigured, you may need to make some modifications to meet your unique security needs. Each profile has its own configuration steps and settings to choose.

In the next chapter, you'll learn how to protect your Linux system on a network. You'll learn about controlling access, managing firewalls, and securing remote access.

Exercises

Use these exercises to test your knowledge of using AppArmor. These tasks assume that you are running an Ubuntu Linux system (although some tasks work on other Linux systems as well). If you are stuck, solutions to the tasks are shown in Appendix A (although in Linux, there are often multiple ways to complete a task).

1. Making no changes to configuration files, run a command that will change all of your AppArmor profiles to issue log messages for violations rather than prevent them.

2. Making no changes to configuration files, run a command that will change all of your AppArmor profiles to prevent violations rather than just issue log messages.

3. What command will view the current settings of all installed profiles?

4. Run a single command that will display the most recent kernel events involving AppArmor.

5. Identify the configuration file that contains virtual home directory values that can be used by all AppArmor profiles.

6. Run a program that will scan your profiles and suggest edits to your documents.

Securing Linux on a Network

S etting up your Linux system on a network, especially a public network, creates a whole new set of challenges when it comes to security. Of course, the best way to secure a computer is to keep it off all networks. However, that's rarely a workable option.

Entire books have been filled with information on how to secure a computer system on a network. Many organizations hire full-time network security administrators to watch over their network-attached Linux systems. Therefore, think of this chapter as just a brief introduction to the subject.

Auditing Network Services

Most Linux systems used for large enterprises are configured as servers that, as the name implies, offer services to remote clients over a network. A *network service* is any task that the computer performs requiring it to send and receive information over the network using some predefined set of rules. Routing email is a network service, as is serving web pages.

A Linux server has the potential to provide thousands of services. Many of them are listed in the /etc/services file. Consider the following sections from the /etc/services file:

```
$ cat /etc/services
# /etc/services:
# $Id: services,v 1.55 2013/04/14 ovasik Exp $
#
# Network services, Internet style
# IANA services version: last updated 2013-04-10
#
# Note that it is presently the policy of IANA to assign ...
# Each line describes one service, and is of the form:
#
```

Continues

Continued

```
# service-name    port/protocol   [aliases ...]      [# comment]
...
echo             7/tcp
echo             7/udp
discard          9/tcp           sink null
discard          9/udp           sink null
systat           11/tcp          users
systat           11/udp          users
daytime          13/tcp
daytime          13/udp
qotd             17/tcp          quote
qotd             17/udp          quote
...
chargen          19/tcp          ttytst source
chargen          19/udp          ttytst source
ftp-data         20/tcp
ftp-data         20/udp
# 21 is registered to ftp, but also used by fsp
ftp              21/tcp
...
http             80/tcp          www www-http    # WorldWideWeb HTTP
http             80/udp          www www-http    # HyperText
Transfer Protocol
http             80/sctp                         # HyperText
Transfer Protocol
kerberos         88/tcp          kerberos5 krb5  # Kerberos v5
kerberos         88/udp          kerberos5 krb5  # Kerberos v5
...
blp5             48129/udp                       # Bloomberg locator
com-bardac-dw    48556/tcp                       # com-bardac-dw
com-bardac-dw    48556/udp                       # com-bardac-dw
iqobject         48619/tcp                        # iqobject
iqobject         48619/udp                        # iqobject
```

After the comment lines, notice three columns of information. The left column contains the name of each service. The middle column defines the port number and protocol type used for that service. The right column contains an optional alias or list of aliases for the service.

Many servers can have unneeded network services running. An unnecessary service exposes your Linux system to malicious attacks. For example, if your machine is a dedicated printer server, then it should only be offering printing services. It should not also offer Apache Web Services. This would unnecessarily expose your printer server to any malicious attacks that take advantage of web service vulnerabilities.

Originally, restricting services on Linux systems meant setting up individual physical servers with only a few services running on each. Later, running multiple virtual machines on a physical host lets you lock down small sets of services on virtual machines. More recently, containerized applications can allow many more separate and secured services to run on each physical host.

Evaluating access to network services with nmap

A wonderful tool to help you review your network services from a network standpoint is the nmap security scanner. The nmap utility is available in most Linux distribution reposi- tories and has a web page full of information at www.nmap.org.

You install nmap the usual way:

```
# apt install nmap
```

The nmap utility's full name is Network Mapper. It has a variety of uses for security audits and network exploration. Using nmap to do various port scans allows you to see what ser- vices are running on all of the servers on your local network and whether they are advertis- ing their availability.

> **NOTE**
>
> What is a port? Ports, or more correctly *network ports*, are numeric values used by the TCP and UDP network pro- tocols as access points to services on a system. Standard port numbers are assigned to services so that a service knows to listen on a particular port number and a client knows to request the service on that port number.
>
> For example, port 80 is the standard network port for unencrypted (HTTP) traffic to a web service like Apache. So, if you ask for http://www.example.com from your web browser, the browser assumes that you mean to use TCP port 80 on the server that offers that web content. Think of a network port as a door to your Linux server. Each door is numbered. And behind every door is a particular service waiting to help whoever knocks on that door.

To audit your server's ports, the nmap utility offers several useful scan types. The nmap site has an entire manual on all of the port scanning techniques that you can use at nmap. org/book/man-port-scanning-techniques.html. Here are two basic port scans to get you started on your service auditing:

TCP Connect port scan   For this scan, nmap attempts to connect to ports using the Transmission Control Protocol (TCP) on the server. If a port is listening, the connec- tion attempt succeeds.

TCP is a network protocol used in the TCP/IP network protocol suite. TCP is a connec- tion-oriented protocol. Its primary purpose is to negotiate and initiate a connection using what is called a *three-way handshake*. TCP sends a synchronize packet (SYN) to a remote server specifying a specific port number in the packet. The remote server receives the SYN and replies with an acknowledgment packet (SYN-ACK) to the origi- nating computer. The original server then acknowledges (ACK) the response, and a TCP connection is officially established. This three-way handshake is often called a SYN- SYN-ACK or SYN, SYN-ACK, ACK.

25

If you select a TCP Connect port scan, the nmap utility uses this three-way handshake to do a little investigation on a remote server. Any services that use the TCP protocol will respond to the scan.

UDP port scan For this scan, nmap sends a UDP packet to every port on the system being scanned. *UDP* is another popular protocol in the TCP/IP network protocol suite. Unlike TCP, however, UDP is a *connectionless protocol*. If the port is listening and has a service that uses the UDP protocol, it responds to the scan.

> **TIP**
>
> Keep in mind that Free and Open Source Software (FOSS) utilities are also available to the bad guys. While you are doing these nmap scans, realize that the remote scan results that you see for your Linux server are the same scan results that others will see. This will help you evaluate your system's security settings in terms of how much information is being given out to port scans. Keep in mind that you should use tools like nmap only on your own systems, because scanning ports on other people's computers can give the impression that you are trying to break in.

When you run the nmap utility, it displays a report with information on the system you're scanning and the ports it sees. The ports are given a *state* status. nmap reports six possible port states:

open: This is the most dangerous state an nmap scan can report for a port. An open port indicates that a server has a service handling requests on this port. Think of it as a sign on the door, "Come on in! We are here to help you." Of course, if you are offering a public service, you want the port to be open.

closed: A closed port is accessible, but there is no service waiting on the other side of this door. However, the scan status still indicates that there is a live server at this particular IP address.

filtered: This is the best state to secure a port that you don't want anyone to access. It cannot be determined if a server is actually at the scanned IP address. It is possible that a service could be listening on a particular port, but the firewall is blocking access to that port, effectively preventing any access to the service through the particular network interface.

unfiltered: The nmap scan sees the port but cannot determine if the port is open or closed.

open|filtered: The nmap scan sees the port but cannot determine if the port is open or filtered.

closed|filtered: The nmap scan sees the port but cannot determine if the port is closed or filtered.

To help you better understand how to use the nmap utility, review the following example. For the purposes of building a network services list, the example nmap scans are conducted from inside an Ubuntu system. The first scan is a TCP Connect scan from the command line using the loopback address 127.0.0.1.

```
$ nmap -sT 127.0.0.1

Starting Nmap 7.60 ( https://nmap.org ) at 2020-04-29 12:29 EDT
Nmap scan report for localhost (127.0.0.1)
Host is up (0.000076s latency).
Not shown: 993 closed ports
PORT     STATE SERVICE
22/tcp   open  ssh
25/tcp   open  smtp
631/tcp  open  ipp

Nmap done: 1 IP address (1 host up) scanned in 0.05 seconds
```

The TCP Connect nmap scan reports that three TCP ports are open and have services listening on the localhost (127.0.0.1) for requests to these ports:

- Open SSH is listening at TCP port 22.
- Simple Mail Transfer Protocol (SMTP) is listening at TCP port 25.
- Internet Printing Protocol (IPP) is listening at TCP port 631.

The next nmap scan is a UDP scan on the Ubuntu system's loopback address.

```
# nmap -sU 127.0.0.1
[sudo] password for dbclinton:

Starting Nmap 7.60 ( https://nmap.org ) at 2020-04-29 12:31 EDT
Nmap scan report for localhost (127.0.0.1)
Host is up (0.000010s latency).
Not shown: 995 closed ports
PORT      STATE          SERVICE
68/udp    open|filtered  dhcpc
631/udp   open|filtered  ipp

Nmap done: 1 IP address (1 host up) scanned in 2.75 seconds
```

The UDP nmap scan reports that two UDP ports are open and have services listening on those ports:

- Dynamic Host Control Protocol client (dhcpc) is listening at port 68.
- Internet Printing Protocol (ipp) is listening at port 631.

Notice that port 631's IPP is listed under both nmap's TCP Connect scan and the UDP scan because the IPP service can communicate over both the TCP and the UDP protocol and thus is listed in both scans.

25

Using these two simple nmap scans, TCP Connect and UDP on your loopback address, you can build a list of the network services offered by your Linux server. Keep in mind that port numbers are associated with a particular protocol (TCP or UDP) and a particular network interface. For example, if you have one network interface card (NIC) on a computer that faces the Internet and another that faces a private network, you may want to offer a private service (like the Common UNIX Printing System (CUPS) service for printing) to the NIC on your private network. But you may want to filter that port (631) on the NIC that faces the Internet.

Using nmap to audit your network services' advertisements

You probably want lots of people to visit your website (httpd service). You probably don't want everyone on the Internet to be capable of accessing your server message block (SMB) file shares (smb service). To make sure that you are properly separating access to those two types of services, you want to be able to check what a malicious scanner can see of the services available on your public-facing network interfaces.

The idea here is to compare what your Linux server looks like from the inside versus what it looks like from the outside. If you determine that some network services are accessible that you intended to keep private, you can take steps to block access to them from external interfaces.

> **TIP**
>
> You may be tempted to skip the scans from inside your organization's internal network. Don't. Malicious activity often occurs by a company's own employees or by someone who has already penetrated external defenses. Again, the nmap utility is a great help here. To get a proper view of how your server's ports are seen, you need to conduct scans from several locations. For example, a simple audit would set up scans in these places:
>
> - On the server itself
> - From another server on the organization's same network
> - From outside the organization's network

In the following examples, part of a simple audit is conducted. The nmap utility is run on a system, designated as Host-A. Host-A is the Linux server whose network services are to be protected. Host-B is a Linux server using the Linux Mint distribution and is on the same network as Host-A.

> **TIP**
>
> Security settings on various network components, such as the server's firewall and the company's routers, should all be considered when conducting audit scans.

For this audit example, a scan is run from Host-A, using not the loopback address but the actual IP address. First, the IP address for Host-A is determined using the ip addr show command. The IP address is 10.140.67.23.

```
# ip addr show
1: lo: <LOOPBACK,UP,LOWER_UP> mtu 65536 qdisc noqueue state UNKNOWN
    group default qlen 1000
    link/loopback 00:00:00:00:00:00 brd 00:00:00:00:00:00
    inet 127.0.0.1/8 scope host lo
       valid_lft forever preferred_lft forever
    inet6 ::1/128 scope host
       valid_lft forever preferred_lft forever
2: ens3: <BROADCAST,MULTICAST,UP,LOWER_UP> mtu 1500 qdisc fq_codel
    state UP group default qlen 1000
    link/ether 52:54:00:c4:27:4e brd ff:ff:ff:ff:ff:ff
    inet 10.140.67.23/24 brd 10.140.67.255 scope global dynamic
       noprefixroute ens3
       valid_lft 3277sec preferred_lft 3277sec
    inet6 fe80::5036:9ec3:2ae8:7623/64 scope link noprefixroute
       valid_lft forever preferred_lft forever
```

Now, using the Host-A IP address, an nmap TCP Connect scan is issued from Host-A. The nmap scan goes out to the network to conduct the scan. All ports are reported as having a status of closed.

```
# nmap -sT 10.140.67.23
Starting Nmap 7.80 ( https://nmap.org ) at 2020-1-31 11:53 EDT

Nmap scan report for office (10.140.67.23)

Host is up (0.010s latency).
All 1000 scanned ports on 10.140.67.23 are closed

Nmap done: 1 IP address (1 host up) scanned in 1.48 seconds
```

The nmap scan is moved from originating at Host-A to originating on Host-B. Now the TCP Connect scan is attempted on Host-A's ports from Host-B's command line.

```
$ nmap -sT 10.140.67.23
Starting Nmap 7.80 ( https://nmap.org ) at 2020-1-31 11:57 EDT

Note: Host seems down. If it is really up,
 but blocking our ping probes, try -PN

Nmap done: 1 IP address (0 hosts up) scanned in 0.11 seconds
```

Here, nmap gives a helpful hint. Host-A appears to be down, or it could just be blocking the probes. So, another nmap scan is attempted from Host-B, using nmap's advice of disabling the scan's ping probes via the -PN option.

```
$ nmap -sT -PN 10.140.67.23
Starting Nmap 7.80 ( https://nmap.org ) at 2020-1-31 11:58 EDT
Nmap scan report for office (10.140.67.23)
```

25

Continues

Continued

```
Host is up (0.0015s latency).
All 1000 scanned ports on 10.140.67.23 are filtered

Nmap done: 1 IP address (1 host up) scanned in 5.54 seconds
```

You can see that Host-A (10.140.67.23) is up and running and all of its ports have a status of `filtered`. This means that there is a firewall in place on Host-A. These scans from Host-B give you a better idea of what a malicious scanner may see when scanning your Linux server. In this example, the malicious scanner would not see much.

> **NOTE**
>
> If you are familiar with `nmap`, you know that the TCP SYN scan is the default scan `nmap` uses. The TCP SYN scan does an excellent job of probing a remote system in a stealth manner. Because you are probing your own system for security auditing purposes, it makes sense to use the more heavy-duty `nmap` utility scans. If you still want to use the TCP SYN scan, the command is `nmap -sS ip_address`.

The services currently running on Host-A are not that "juicy." In the example that follows, another service, `sshd`, is started on Host-A using the `systemctl` command (see Chapter 15, "Starting and Stopping Services"). This should give the `nmap` utility a more interesting target to search for.

```
$ systemctl status ssh
● sshd.service - OpenSSH server daemon
● ssh.service - OpenBSD Secure Shell server
   Loaded: loaded (/lib/systemd/system/ssh.service; enabled; vendor
preset: enab
   Active: active (running) since Wed 2020-04-29 07:49:09 EDT; 5h 5min ago
 Main PID: 1144 (sshd)
    Tasks: 1 (limit: 4915)
   CGroup: /system.slice/ssh.service
           └1144 /usr/sbin/sshd -D

Apr 29 07:49:12 workstation systemd[1]: Reloading OpenBSD Secure
Shell server.
Apr 29 07:49:12 workstation sshd[1144]: Received SIGHUP; restarting.
Apr 29 07:49:12 workstation systemd[1]: Reloaded OpenBSD Secure
Shell server.
Apr 29 07:49:12 workstation sshd[1144]: Server listening on
0.0.0.0 port 22.
Apr 29 07:49:12 workstation sshd[1144]: Server listening on
:: port 22.
Apr 29 07:49:16 workstation systemd[1]: Reloading OpenBSD Secure
Shell server.
Apr 29 07:49:16 workstation sshd[1144]: Received SIGHUP; restarting.
Apr 29 07:49:16 workstation systemd[1]: Reloaded OpenBSD Secure
Shell server.
```

```
Apr 29 07:49:16 workstation sshd[1144]: Server listening on
0.0.0.0 port 22.
Apr 29 07:49:16 workstation sshd[1144]: Server listening on
:: port 22.
```

Also, because Host-A's firewall is blocking the nmap scans from Host-B, it would be interesting to see what an nmap scan can report when the firewall is down. The example that follows shows the Uncomplicated Firewall (UFW) firewall being disabled on Host-A:

```
# ufw disable
```

With a new service running and Host-A's firewall lowered, the nmap scans should find something. In the following, nmap scans are run again from Host-B. This time the nmap utility shows the ssh service running on open port 22. Notice that with the firewall down on Host-A, both nmap scans pick up much more information. This really demonstrates the importance of your Linux server's firewall.

```
# nmap -sT 10.140.67.23
Starting Nmap 7.80 ( http://nmap.org ) at 2020-1-31 11:58 EDT
Nmap scan report for 10.140.67.23
Host is up (0.016s latency).
Not shown: 999 closed ports

PORT    STATE SERVICE
22/tcp open  ssh

Nmap done: 1 IP address (1 host up) scanned in 0.40 seconds

# nmap -sU 10.140.67.23
[sudo] password for johndoe: ***************
Starting Nmap 5.21 ( http://nmap.org ) at 2020-1-31 11:59 EDT
Nmap scan report for 10.140.67.23
Host is up (0.00072s latency).
Not shown: 997 closed ports

PORT        STATE          SERVICE
68/udp      open|filtered  dhcpc
631/udp     open|filtered  ipp
...
Nmap done: 1 IP address (1 host up) scanned in 1081.83 seconds
```

In order to conduct a thorough audit, be sure to include the UDP scan. Also, there are additional nmap scans that may be beneficial to your organization. Look at the nmap utility's website for additional suggestions.

CAUTION

If you have been following along and lowered your server's firewall just for these nmap scans, be sure to raise it again. Enter sudo ufw enable.

25

You still need to implement controls for those services that your Linux server should offer. One way to accomplish this is via firewall rules.

Early versions of Linux use TCP Wrappers to allow or deny access to Linux services. It did this by offering /etc/hosts.allow and /etc/hosts.deny files where you could specifically indicate which services are available and which are blocked to particular outside system names and/or IP addresses. More recently, TCP Wrappers have been deprecated. However, some features, such as vsftpd, still honor those configuration files through other means.

Working with Firewalls

A firewall in a building is a fireproof wall that prevents the spread of fire throughout the building. A computer *firewall* blocks the transmission of malicious or unwanted data into and out of a computer system or network. For example, a firewall can block malicious scans from your Linux server ports. A firewall can also change network packets flowing through your system and redirect packets in various ways.

In Linux, *iptables* is the kernel-level firewall feature. It is most commonly used to allow or block access from outside systems to the services running on your local system. iptables works by allowing you to create rules that can be applied to every packet that tries to enter (INPUT), leave (OUTPUT), or cross through your system (FORWARD).

Although allowing or blocking packets trying to enter your system is the primary feature of iptables, you can also create rules for iptables that let you do the following:

- Block packets leaving your system to effectively prevent a process on your system from reaching a remote host, range of addresses, or selected services.
- Forward packets from one network interface on your system to another, effectively allowing your computer to act as a router between two networks.
- Port forward a packet intended for a selected port to be rerouted to another port on your local system, or to a remote system, so that other locations can handle the request from the packet.
- Change information in a packet header (called *mangling*) to redirect the packet or somehow mark it for more processing.
- Allow multiple computers on a private network (such as the computers, televisions, or other devices on your home network) to communicate with the Internet over a single public IP address. (This is referred to as *IP masquerading*.)

In the following sections, I describe many of these features but focus mostly on the rules to block or allow access to the services running on your Linux system.

Understanding firewalls

Although you may tend to think of a firewall as a complete barrier, a Linux firewall is really just a filter that checks each network packet or application request coming into or out of a computer system or network.

> **NOTE**
>
> What is a network packet? A *network packet* is data that has been broken up into transmittable chunks. The chunks, or packets, have additional data added to them as they traverse down the `OSI` model. It's like putting a letter inside an envelope at each stage as it moves down the protocol stack. One of the purposes of this additional data is to ensure the packet's safe and intact arrival at its destination. The additional data is stripped off of the packet as it traverses back up the OSI model at its destination (like taking off the outer envelope and handing the letter to the layer above).

Firewalls can be placed into different categories, depending upon their function. Each category has an important place in securing your server and network.

A firewall is either network or host-based.   A network-based firewall is one that is protecting the entire network or subnet. For example, a network firewall would be used in your workplace, where the network should be protected by a screening router's firewall.

A host-based firewall is one that is running on and protecting an individual host or server. You most likely have a firewall on your PC at home. This is a host-based firewall.

A firewall is either hardware- or software-based.   Firewalls can be located on network devices, such as routers. Their filters are configured in the router's firmware. In your home, your Internet service provider (ISP) may provide a router to let you gain access to the Internet. The router contains firewall firmware, and it is considered a hardware firewall.

Firewalls can be located on a computer system as an application. The application allows filtering rules to be set that filter the incoming traffic. This is an example of a software firewall. A software firewall is also called a rule-based firewall.

A firewall is either a network-layer or an application-layer filter.   A firewall that examines individual network packets is also called a *packet filter*. A *network-layer firewall* allows only certain packets into and out of the system. It operates on the lower layers of the OSI reference model.

An *application-layer firewall* filters at the higher layers of the OSI reference model. This firewall allows only certain applications access to and from the system.

You can see how these firewall categories overlap. The best firewall setup is a combination of all of the categories. As with many security practices, the more layers you have, the harder it is for malicious activity to penetrate.

25

Implementing firewalls

On a Linux system, the firewall is a host-based, network-layer, software firewall managed by the `iptables` utility and related kernel-level components. With `iptables`, you can create a series of rules for every network packet coming through your Linux server. You can fine-tune the rules to allow network traffic from one location but not from another. These rules essentially make up a network access control list for your Linux server.

While Fedora, RHEL, and related distributions use the `firewalld` service to provide a more user-friendly way to manage firewall rules, Ubuntu goes with their Uncomplicated Firewall (UFW). UFW acts as a front end for `nftables`.

> **TIP**
>
> The `iptables` utility manages the Linux firewall, called `netfilter`. Thus, you will often see the Linux firewall referred to as `netfilter/iptables`. The `iptables` syntax is still supported, but for recent Linux releases, `nftables` is actually doing all the hard work behind the scenes.

Starting with UFW

UFW may already be installed on your Linux system. To check this, type the following:

```
$ systemctl status ufw
• ufw.service - Uncomplicated firewall
   Loaded: loaded (/lib/systemd/system/ufw.service; enabled; vendor
preset: enabled)
   Active: active (exited) since Wed 2020-04-29 16:57:19
UTC; 20min ago
     Docs: man:ufw(8)
  Process: 410 ExecStart=/lib/ufw/ufw-init start quiet (code=exited,
status=0/SUCCESS)
 Main PID: 410 (code=exited, status=0/SUCCESS)

Warning: Journal has been rotated since unit was started. Log output
is incomplete or unavailable.
```

If it's not, you can install it using `apt install ufw`.

We'll take a quick look at some basic UFW operations so you won't be a complete stranger should you ever encounter it in the wild. To see the current state of UFW, check its status:

```
# ufw status
Status: inactive
```

If you'd like to activate UFW, you can do all the configuration work before actually applying your new rules. This can help you avoid unintentionally breaking important access (like locking yourself out of an Secure Shell (SSH) session).

Let's say you want to set your computer up as a web server for everyone, but that also permits SSH access only for administrators in your local network. You would first open the HTTP port 80:

```
# ufw allow 80
Rules updated
Rules updated (v6)
```

Two new rules were added to the UFW configuration permitting web access from anywhere using both IPv4 and IPv6 networking. However, you don't want to be quite so wide open with SSH, so you'll limit access to only clients coming from within your private subnet (that's 192.168.1.0/24 in my case):

```
# ufw allow from 192.168.1.0/24 to any port 22 proto tcp
Rules updated
```

Once you're satisfied that you've got the configuration exactly right, you can pull the trigger using enable:

```
# ufw enable
Command may disrupt existing ssh connections. Proceed with
operation (y|n)? y
Firewall is active and enabled on system startup
```

Go ahead and test the firewall. Make sure you can open a new SSH session on your server and, if you've got a web server like Apache installed, try accessing the home page from a browser. You could also try opening the Cockpit administration tool (which, you'll remember, uses port 9090) on a browser from a different computer. Hint: that one shouldn't work.

Check the UFW status once again:

```
# ufw status
Status: active

To                         Action      From
--                         ------      ----
22/tcp                     ALLOW       192.168.1.0/24
80                         ALLOW       Anywhere
80 (v6)                    ALLOW       Anywhere (v6)
```

Speaking of Cockpit, if you have it installed on your server, you can use it to administrate UFW from the Services menu. Scroll down to the Uncomplicated Firewall entry and click it. Although at this point, Cockpit-based tasks are pretty much limited to enabling and disabling.

If you don't need your firewall anymore, disable it this way:

```
# ufw disable
Firewall stopped and disabled on system startup
```

25

Understanding the iptables utility

Before you start changing the firewall rules via the `iptables` utility, you need to understand `netfilter/iptables` basics, which include the following:

- Tables
- Chains
- Policies
- Rules

Understanding these basics will help you set up and manage your Linux server firewall properly.

netfilter/iptables tables

The `iptables` firewall has the ability to do more than just low-level packet filtering. It defines what type of firewall functionality is taking place. There are four tables in the `iptables` utility. The tables offer the following functionalities:

filter: The `filter` table is the packet-filtering feature of the firewall. In this table, access control decisions are made for packets traveling to, from, and through your Linux system.

nat: The `nat` table is used for Network Address Translation (NAT). NAT table rules let you redirect where a packet goes.

mangle: As you would suspect, packets are mangled (modified) according to the rules in the `mangle` table. Using the `mangle` table directly is less common and typically done to change how a packet is managed.

raw: The `raw` table is used to exempt certain network packets from something called *connection tracking*. This feature is important when you are using Network Address Translation and virtualization on your Linux server.

Of all the tables listed, three focus on Network Address Translation. Therefore, the `filter` table is the primary table that this chapter focuses on for basic firewall packet filtering.

netfilter/iptables chains

The `netfilter/iptables` firewall categorizes network packets into categories, called *chains*. There are five chains (categories) to which a network packet can be designated:

INPUT: Network packets coming *into* the Linux server

FORWARD: Network packets coming into the Linux server that are to be *routed* out through another network interface on the server

OUTPUT: Network packets coming *out* of the Linux server

PREROUTING: Used by NAT for modifying network packets when they come into the Linux server

POSTROUTING: Used by NAT for modifying network packets before they come out of the Linux server

Which `netfilter/iptables` table you choose to work with determines what chains are available for categorizing network packets. Table 25.1 shows what chains are available for each table.

TABLE 25.1 Chains Available for Each netfilter/iptables Table

Table	Chains Available
filter	INPUT, FORWARD, OUTPUT
nat	PREROUTING, OUTPUT, POSTROUTING
mangle	INPUT, FORWARD, PREROUTING, OUTPUT, POSTROUTING
raw	PREROUTING, OUTPUT

After a network packet is categorized into a specific chain, `iptables` can determine what policies or rules apply to that particular packet.

netfilter/iptables rules, policies, and targets

For each network packet, a rule can be set up defining what to do with that individual packet. Network packets can be identified many ways by the `netfilter/iptables` firewall. These are a few of the ways:

- Source IP address
- Destination IP address
- Network protocol
- Inbound port
- Outbound port
- Network state

If no rule exists for a particular packet, then the overall policy is used. Each packet category or chain has a default policy. After a network packet matches a particular rule or falls to the default policy, then action on the packet can occur. The action taken depends upon what `iptables` target is set. Here are a couple of actions (targets) that can be taken:

ACCEPT: Network packet is accepted into the server.

REJECT: Network packet is dropped and not allowed into the server. A rejection message is sent.

DROP: Network packet is dropped and not allowed into the server. No rejection message is sent.

While REJECT gives a rejection message, DROP is quiet. You may consider using REJECT for internal employees who should be told that you are rejecting their outbound network traffic and why. Consider using DROP for inbound traffic so that any malicious personnel are unaware that their traffic is being blocked.

25

The `iptables` utility implements a software firewall using the `filter` table via policies and rules. Now that you have a general understanding of the software firewall implementation, you can begin to dig deeper into the specific commands for implementing the firewall via the `iptables` utility.

Using the iptables utility

Your Linux server should come with the firewall up and running. However, it's a good idea to check and see if it really is enabled.

If UFW is running, disable it using `sudo ufw disable`.

To see what policies and rules are currently in place for the `filter` (default) table, enter **iptables -vnL** at the command line:

```
# iptables -vnL
Chain INPUT (policy ACCEPT 0 packets, 0 bytes)...
```

Note that on systems where UFW has been enabled, there are many more iptables chains and rules listed by default than you might be used to on a system using iptables directly. This is done to offer more flexibility in building your firewalls by allowing your rules to be split into zones for different levels of security.

Only the first line of the iptables output is shown in the preceding example. That line shows that the INPUT chain's default policy is applied to all the network packets that don't match another rule. Currently, all of the default INPUT, FORWARD, and OUTPUT policies are set to ACCEPT. All network packets are allowed in, through, and out. A firewall in this state is essentially disabled until specific REJECT or DROP rules are added.

Modifying iptables policies and rules

Make sure you have direct (non-remote) access to the computer you're planning to use for `iptables` experiments. In case you accidentally mess up your network configuration, you'll always be able to log in physically to recover.

To get started, it is helpful to understand a few command options.

A few options for modifying the firewall follow:

-t *table*

> The iptables command listed along with this switch is applied to the *table*. By default, the filter table is used. Example:
>
> ```
> # iptables -t filter -P OUTPUT DROP
> ```

-P *chain target*

> Sets the overall policy for a particular *chain*. The rules in the *chain* are checked for matches. If no match occurs, then the *chain*'s listed target is used. Example:
>
> ```
> # iptables -P INPUT ACCEPT
> ```

-A *chain*

> Sets a rule called an *appended rule*, which is an exception to the overall policy for the *chain* designated. Example:
>
> ```
> # iptables -A OUTPUT -d 10.140.67.25 -j REJECT
> ```

-I *rule# chain*

> Inserts an appended rule into a specific location, designated by the *rule#*, in the appended rule list for the *chain* designated. Example:
>
> ```
> # iptables -I 5 INPUT -s 10.140.67.23 -j DROP
> ```

-D *chain rule#*

> Deletes a particular rule, designated by the *rule#*, from the *chain* designated. Example:
>
> ```
> # iptables -D INPUT 5
> ```

-j *target*

> If the criteria in the rule are met, the firewall should jump to this designated *target* for processing. Example:
>
> ```
> # iptables -A INPUT -s 10.140.67.25 -j DROP
> ```

-d *IP address*

> Assigns the rule listed to apply to the designated destination *IP address*. Example:
>
> ```
> # iptables -A OUTPUT -d 10.140.67.25 -j REJECT
> ```

-s *IP address*

> Assigns the rule listed to apply to the designated source *IP address*. Example:
>
> ```
> # iptables -A INPUT -s 10.140.67.24 -j ACCEPT
> ```

25

`-p protocol`

> Assigns the rule listed to apply to the *protocol* designated. For example, here incoming ping (`icmp`) requests are dropped:
>
> ```
> # iptables -A INPUT -p icmp -j DROP
> ```

`--dport port#`

> Assigns the rule listed to apply to certain protocol packets coming into the designated *port#*. Example:
>
> ```
> # iptables -A INPUT -p tcp --dport 22 -j DROP
> ```

`--sport port#`

> Assigns the rule listed to apply to certain protocol packets going out of the designated *port#*. Example:
>
> ```
> # iptables -A OUTPUT -p tcp --sport 22 -j ACCEPT
> ```

`-m state --state network_state`

> Assigns the rule listed to apply to the designated *network state*(s). Example:
>
> ```
> # iptables -A INPUT -m state --state RELATED,ESTABLISHED
> -j ACCEPT
> ```

To see how the `iptables` options work, consider the following example. You have a Linux server (Host-A) at IP address 10.140.67.23. There are two other Linux servers on your network. One is Host-B at IP address 10.140.67.22 and the other is Host-C at IP address 10.140.67.25. Your goal is to accomplish the following:

- Allow Host-C full access to Host-A.
- Block remote login connections using `ssh` from Host-B to Host-A.

Setting a policy of Drop

The following code shows the default policies of Host-A's firewall. In this example, the firewall is wide open with no restrictions implemented. No rules are set, and the policies are all set to ACCEPT.

```
# iptables -vnL

Chain INPUT (policy ACCEPT)
target     prot opt source              destination

Chain FORWARD (policy ACCEPT)
target     prot opt source              destination

Chain OUTPUT (policy ACCEPT)
target     prot opt source              destination
```

First, what would happen if the INPUT policy was changed from ACCEPT to DROP? Would that reach the goal? Look at what happens when this is tried. Remember that if no rules are listed for an incoming packet, then the chain's policy is followed. This change is made to Host-A's firewall in the example that follows.

```
# iptables -P INPUT DROP
# iptables -vnL

Chain INPUT (policy DROP)
target      prot opt source                   destination

Chain FORWARD (policy ACCEPT)
target      prot opt source                   destination

Chain OUTPUT (policy ACCEPT)
target      prot opt source                   destination
```

TIP

For policies, you cannot set the target to REJECT. It fails, and you receive the message "iptables: Bad policy name." Use DROP as your policy instead.

Host-B attempts to ping Host-A and then attempts an ssh connection, as shown in the example that follows. As you can see, both attempts fail. Because ping commands are blocked, this does not meet the objective to block only remote login connections using ssh from Host-B.

```
$ ping -c 2 10.140.67.23
PING 10.140.67.23 (10.140.67.23) 56(84) bytes of data.

--- 10.140.67.23 ping statistics ---
2 packets transmitted, 0 received, 100% packet loss, time 1007ms
$ ssh root@10.140.67.23

ssh: connect to host 10.140.67.23 port 22: Connection timed out
```

When Host-C attempts to ping Host-A and make an ssh connection, both attempts fail. Thus, it is confirmed that the firewall setting, INPUT policy equals DROP, is not what is needed to reach the goal.

```
$ ping -c 2 10.140.67.23
PING 10.140.67.23 (10.140.67.23) 56(84) bytes of data.

--- 10.140.67.23 ping statistics ---
2 packets transmitted, 0 received, 100% packet loss, time 1008ms
$ ssh root@10.140.67.23

ssh: connect to host 10.140.67.23 port 22: Connection timed out
```

25

Blocking a source IP address

What if instead only Host-B's IP address were blocked? That would allow Host-C to reach Host-A. Would this setting reach the desired goal?

In the example that follows, the policy of DROP must first be changed to ALLOW in Host-A's iptables. After that, a specific rule must be appended to block network packets from Host-B's IP address, 10.140.67.22, alone.

```
# iptables -P INPUT ACCEPT
# iptables -A INPUT -s 10.140.67.22 -j DROP
# iptables -vnL

Chain INPUT (policy ACCEPT)
target      prot opt source              destination
DROP        all  --  10.140.67.22             anywhere

Chain FORWARD (policy ACCEPT)
target      prot opt source              destination

Chain OUTPUT (policy ACCEPT)
target      prot opt source              destination
```

Host-C can now successfully `ping` and `ssh` into Host-A, meeting one of the set goals.

```
$ ping -c 2 10.140.67.23
PING 10.140.67.23 (10.140.67.23) 56(84) bytes of data.
64 bytes from 10.140.67.23: icmp_req=1 ttl=64 time=11.7 ms
64 bytes from 10.140.67.23: icmp_req=2 ttl=64 time=0.000 ms

--- 10.140.67.23 ping statistics ---
2 packets transmitted, 2 received, 0% packet loss, time 1008ms
rtt min/avg/max/mdev = 0.000/5.824/11.648/5.824 ms
$ ssh root@10.140.67.23
root@10.140.67.23's password:
```

However, Host-B can neither `ping` nor `ssh` into Host-A. Thus, the appended rule is not quite what is needed to reach the entire goal.

```
$ ping -c 2 10.140.67.23

PING 10.140.67.23 (10.140.67.23) 56(84) bytes of data.

--- 10.140.67.23 ping statistics ---
2 packets transmitted, 0 received, 100% packet loss, time 1007ms

$ ssh root@10.140.67.23

ssh: connect to host 10.140.67.23 port 22: Connection timed out
```

Blocking a protocol and port

What if, instead of blocking Host-B's IP address entirely, only connections to the `ssh` port (port 22) from Host-B's IP address were blocked? Would that reach the goal of allowing Host-C full access to Host-A and only blocking `ssh` connections from Host-B?

In the example that follows, the `iptables` rules for Host-A are modified to try blocking Host-B's IP address from port 22. Note that the `--dport` option must accompany a particular protocol, such as, for example, `-p tcp`. Before the new rule is added, the rule from the previous example must be deleted using the `-D` option. Otherwise, the rule from the previous example would be used by the `netfilter/iptables` firewall for packets from 10.140.67.22 (Host-B).

```
# iptables -D INPUT 1
# iptables -A INPUT -s 10.140.67.22 -p tcp --dport 22 -j DROP
# iptables -vnL

Chain INPUT (policy ACCEPT)
target     prot opt source        destination
DROP       tcp  --  10.140.67.22     anywhere     tcp dpt:ssh

Chain FORWARD (policy ACCEPT)
target     prot opt source        destination

Chain OUTPUT (policy ACCEPT)
target     prot opt source        destination
```

First, the new `iptables` rule is tested from Host-C to ensure that both `ping` attempts and `ssh` connections remain unaffected. It works successfully.

```
$ ping -c 2 10.140.67.23
PING 10.140.67.23 (10.140.67.23) 56(84) bytes of data.
64 bytes from 10.140.67.23: icmp_req=1 ttl=64 time=1.04 ms
64 bytes from 10.140.67.23: icmp_req=2 ttl=64 time=0.740 ms

--- 10.140.67.23 ping statistics ---
2 packets transmitted, 2 received, 0% packet loss, time 1000ms
rtt min/avg/max/mdev = 0.740/0.892/1.045/0.155 ms

$ ssh root@10.140.67.23
root@10.140.67.23's password:
```

Next, the new `iptables` rule is tested from Host-B to ensure that `ping` works and `ssh` connections are blocked. It also works successfully!

```
$ ping -c 2 10.140.67.23

PING 10.140.67.23 (10.140.67.23) 56(84) bytes of data.
64 bytes from 10.140.67.23: icmp_req=1 ttl=64 time=1.10 ms
64 bytes from 10.140.67.23: icmp_req=2 ttl=64 time=0.781 ms
```

25

Continues

Continued

```
--- 10.140.67.23 ping statistics ---

2 packets transmitted, 2 received, 0% packet loss, time 1001ms
rtt min/avg/max/mdev=0.781/0.942/1.104/0.164 ms

$ ssh root@10.140.67.23

ssh: connect to host 10.140.67.23 port 22: Connection timed out
```

Make sure you fully test your firewall configuration in a test or virtual environment before implementing it in your production Linux system.

Saving an iptables configuration

In the example that follows, the modifications made earlier are still in the firewall. You can save the current set of firewall filter rules using the `iptables-save` command.

```
# iptables -vnL
Chain INPUT (policy ACCEPT 8 packets, 560 bytes)
 pkts bytes target prot opt in  out source        destination
    0     0 DROP   tcp  -- *   *   10.140.67.22 0.0.0.0/0   tcp dpt:22
    0     0 DROP   tcp  -- *   *    0.0.0.0/0    0.0.0.0/0   tcp dpt:33
    0     0 DROP   icmp -- *   *    0.0.0.0/0    0.0.0.0/0
...

# iptables-save > /tmp/myiptables
```

To restore those rules later, you can start by flushing the current rules (`iptables -F`) and restoring them (`iptables-restore`).

```
# iptables -F
# iptables -vnL
Chain INPUT (policy ACCEPT 8 packets, 560 bytes)
 pkts bytes target prot opt in out source        destination
    0     0 DROP   tcp  -- *  *   0.0.0.0/0    0.0.0.0/0   tcp dpt:33
    0     0 DROP   icmp -- *  *   0.0.0.0/0    0.0.0.0/0
...
```

A flush of the rules does not affect the `iptables` configuration file. To restore the firewall to its original condition, use the `iptables-restore` command. In the example that follows, the `iptables` configuration file is redirected into the `restore` command and the original DROP rule for 10.140.67.22 is restored.

```
# iptables-restore < /tmp/myiptables
# iptables -vnL
Chain INPUT (policy ACCEPT 16 packets, 1120 bytes)
 pkts bytes target prot opt in out source        destination
```

```
0      0 DROP   tcp  -- * *  10.140.67.22 0.0.0.0/0  tcp dpt:22
0      0 DROP   tcp  -- * *  0.0.0.0/0    0.0.0.0/0  tcp dpt:33
0      0 DROP   icmp -- * *  0.0.0.0/0    0.0.0.0/0
```

A simpler way to ensure your firewall settings are active each time your computer boots is to install and run the `iptables-persistent` package, which will save IPv4 rules to a file called `/etc/iptables/rules.v4` and make sure they're read on startup.

You can also save your `netfilter/iptables` firewall rules to create an audit report. Reviewing these rules periodically should be part of your organization's System Life Cycle Audit/Review phase.

Summary

Securing your Linux server is critical on a network. Inherently, a majority of the malicious attacks originate from a network, especially the Internet. This chapter covered some of the basics that you need in order to get started on this process.

Protecting your network services can be simplified after you determine and remove any unneeded network services. The `nmap` utility helps you here. Also, you can use `nmap` to audit your Linux server's advertising of network services. These audits assist in determining what firewall modifications are needed.

Recent versions of Ubuntu have added the UFW service as a front end to the `iptables` firewall facility that is built into the Linux kernel. The `netfilter/iptables` firewall facility is a host-based, network-layer, software firewall. It is managed by the `iptables` and `ip6tables` utilities. With these utilities, a series of policies and rules can be created for every network packet coming through your Linux server.

At this point in this book, you should have a good grasp of what goes into setting up and securing Linux desktop and server systems. In the next two chapters, I'm going to help you extend that knowledge into cloud computing and virtualization.

Exercises

Refer to the material in this chapter to complete the tasks that follow. If you are stuck, solutions to the tasks are shown in Appendix A (although in Linux, you can often complete a task in multiple ways). Try each of the exercises before referring to the answers. These tasks assume you are running an Ubuntu Linux system (although some tasks work on other Linux systems as well). Please don't use a production system to try out the `iptables` commands in these exercises. Although the commands shown here do not permanently change your firewall (the old rules will return when the firewall service restarts), improperly modifying your firewall can result in unwanted access.

25

1. Install the Network Mapper utility on your local Linux system.

2. Run a TCP Connect scan on your local loopback address. What ports have a service running on them?

3. Run a UDP port scan on your Linux system from a remote system.

4. Check to see if your system is running the UFW service.

5. Use the Firewall Configuration window to open access to secure (TCP port 443) and insecure (TCP port 80) ports for a web service.

6. Determine your Linux system's current `netfilter/iptables` firewall policies and rules.

7. Save your Linux system's current firewall rules, flush them, and then restore them.

8. For your Linux system's firewall, set a filter table policy for the input chain to DROP.

9. Change your Linux firewall's filter table policy back to `accept` for the input chain, and then add a rule to drop all network packets from the IP address 10.140.67.23.

10. Without flushing or restoring your Linux firewall's rules, remove the rule you just added.

Part VI

Engaging with Cloud Computing

IN THIS PART

Shifting to Clouds and Containers

IN THIS CHAPTER

Understand key technologies for cloud computing

Learn how Linux containers work

Install and start container software

Pull and run container images

Restart a stopped container

Build a container image

Tag and push container images to a registry

While most of this book focuses on installing and managing individual servers, services, and applications, this part takes you into the technologies needed to bring Linux into large data centers. For a data center to operate efficiently, its computers must become as generic as possible and running components must become more automated. Chapters in this part focus on technologies that make those two things happen.

Computers become more generic by separating the applications from the operating systems. This means not just packaging applications into things you install on an operating system (like Debian packages), but also putting together sets of software into packages that themselves can run once they are delivered in ways that keep them separate from the operating system. *Virtual machines* (VMs) and *containers* are two ways of packaging sets of software and their dependencies in ways that are ready to run.

From a high level, a *virtual machine* is a complete operating system that runs on another operating system, allowing you to have many VMs active at a time on one physical computer. Everything an application or a service needs to run can be stored within that VM or in attached storage.

A VM has its own kernel, filesystem, network interfaces, and other operating system features separate from the host, while sharing the Central Processing Unit (CPU) and random access memory (RAM) with the host system. You can deploy that VM to a physical system in a way that makes it easy to run the application and then discard the VM when you're done. You can run multiple instances of the VM on the same computer or clone and run the VM across multiple computers. The term *virtual machine* comes from the fact that each VM sees an emulation of computer hardware and not the hardware itself directly.

A *container* is a lot like a VM, with the major difference being that a container doesn't have its own kernel but shares its host's kernel. In most other ways, it is like a VM in that its namespaces are separate from the host operating system and you can clone it between hosts to run wherever it is convenient.

The technologies driving VMs and containers lie behind the astounding growth and efficiencies of the cloud computing world. The chapters in this part introduce you to the tools you'll need to engage with this new world. You can try out virtual machines on a single Linux host using KVM or deploy virtual machines to cloud platforms such as OpenStack and Amazon Web Services (AWS).

To deploy sets of hosts, either on bare metal or the cloud, you will learn how to use Ansible. With Ansible playbooks, you can also define the software that is installed and run on each host system.

As for containers, the Kubernetes project has grabbed the spotlight as a powerful technology for orchestrating massive numbers of containers across large data centers. Products such as Canonical's Multi-cloud Kubernetes on Ubuntu provide supported Kubernetes platforms for large enterprises.

The technology that widely popularized containers a few years ago was the Docker project. The `docker` command and daemon offered simplified ways to build and run containers on Linux systems. Today, standardized container formats (such as the Open Container Initiative) and other container tools offer ways of working with containers that align more tightly with the Kubernetes ecosystem.

The remainder of this chapter is devoted to getting started with containers. It covers the Linux Container project (LXD), the `docker` command, and other popular tools for working with individual containers.

Understanding Linux Containers

Containers make it simple to get and run applications and then discard them when you are done. There are a few things that you should know about containers before you get started.

In working with containers, people refer to the entity that you move around as a *container image* (or simply an *image*). When you run that image, or when it is paused or stopped, it is referred to as a *container*.

A container remains separate from the host system by using its own set of *namespaces*. You typically would build your own container images by getting a secure *base image* and then adding your own layers of software on top of that image to create a new image. To share your images, you push them to shared *container registries* and allow others to pull them.

Namespaces

Linux support for *namespaces* is what allows containers to be contained. With namespaces, the Linux kernel can associate one or more processes with a set of resources. Normal processes, not those run in a container, all use the same host namespaces. By default, processes in a container only see the container's namespaces and not those of the host. Namespaces include the following:

Process table   A container has its own set of process IDs and, by default, can only see processes running inside the container. While PID 1 on the host is the init process (systemd), in a container PID 1 is the first process run inside the container.

Network interfaces   By default, a container has a single network interface (eth0) and is assigned an IP address when the container runs. By default, a service run inside a container (such as a web server listening on ports 80 and 443) is not exposed outside of the host system. The upside of this is that you could have hundreds of web servers running on the same host without conflict. The downside is that you need to manage how those ports are exposed outside of the host.

Mount table   By default, a container can't see the host's root filesystem, or any other mounted filesystem listed in the host's mount table. The container brings its own filesystem, consisting of the application and any dependencies it needs to run. Files or directories needed from the host can be selectively bind-mounted inside the container.

User IDs   Although containerized processes run as some UID within the host's namespace, another set of UIDs is nested within the container. This can, for example, let a process run as root within a container but not have any special privileges to the host system.

Control group (cgroup)   On some Linux systems (including Ubuntu), a containerized process runs within a selected control group and cannot see the other cgroups available on the host system. Likewise, it cannot see the identity of its own cgroup.

Although access to any host namespace is restricted by default, privileges to host namespaces can be opened selectively. In that way, you can do things like mount configuration files or data inside the container and map container ports to host ports to expose them outside of the host.

Container registries

Permanent storage for at least some container flavors is done in what is referred to as a *container registry*. When you create a container image that you want to share, you can *push* that image to a public repository (like Docker Hub) or a registry that you maintain privately yourself. Someone who wants to use the image will *pull* it from the repository.

Base images and layers

Although you can build containers from scratch, most often a container is built by starting with a well-known base image and adding software to it. That base image typically aligns with the operating system from which you are installing software into your container.

Official LXD images are managed through the Linux Containers project page: us.images. linuxcontainers.org. A visit to that page will show you references to hundreds of available images based on 20 different distributions (including Ubuntu, CentOS, and Kali Linux).

Official base Docker images are also available for many Linux distributions. There are base images that you can build on that offer runtimes for PHP, Perl, Java, and other development environments.

You can add software to a base image using commands such as docker build. By using a Dockerfile to define the build, you can add apt-get commands to install software from software repositories into your new container.

When you add software to an image, it creates a new layer to become part of the new image. Reusing the same base images for the containers that you build offers several advantages. One advantage is that when you run the container image, only one copy of the base image is needed on the host. So, if you were running 10 different containers based on the same base image, you only need to pull and store the base image once, then possibly only add a few megabytes of extra data for each new image.

If you look at the contents of a base image, it would look like a little Linux filesystem. You see configuration files in /etc, executables in /bin and /sbin, and libraries in /lib. In other words, it would have the basic components that an application would need from a Linux host system.

Keep in mind that the container images you run don't necessarily need to match the host Linux system. So, for example, you could run a Fedora base image on an Ubuntu system, as long as specific kernel or shared library requirements in the container image are provided by the underlying Linux host system.

Working with Linux Containers

Very little preparation is needed to start running containers on your own Linux system. The following sections describe how to prepare your Linux system to start using containers through both LXD and Docker.

Deploying LXD containers

The Linux Container project (www.linuxcontainers.org) lets you quickly fire up containers and configure complex, network workloads. Its commands sets (either LXC or the more recent LXD) make server virtualization remarkably straightforward and painless. But nevertheless, LXD containers aren't widely used in large-scale enterprise cloud environments; they're far more popular closer to home, running on your local workstation.

So why use LXD containers in the first place? After all, aren't all the cool kids playing with Docker and Kubernetes these days? Well, for one thing, Docker was originally driven by the LXC engine. But—ancient history aside—LXD containers are a fantastic way to safely experiment with new technology stacks and configurations. Let's see how.

You can install LXD on your machine the regular way and then initialize the environment. You can safely accept the defaults for the questions you're asked. I prefer using a custom network Classless Inter-Domain Routing (CIDR) like 10.0.5.1/24 because it gives me IP addresses that I find easier to remember, but the default is fine, too.

```
# apt install lxd
# lxd init
Would you like to use LXD clustering? (yes/no) [default=no]:
Do you want to configure a new storage pool? (yes/no) [default=yes]:
Name of the new storage pool [default=default]:
Name of the storage backend to use (btrfs, dir, lvm, zfs, ceph)
[default=zfs]:
Create a new ZFS pool? (yes/no) [default=yes]:
Would you like to use an existing block device? (yes/no)
[default=no]:
Size in GB of the new loop device (1GB minimum) [default=15GB]: 1
Would you like to connect to a MAAS server? (yes/no) [default=no]:
Would you like to create a new local network bridge? (yes/no)
[default=yes]:
What should the new bridge be called? [default=lxdbr0]:
What IPv4 address should be used? (CIDR subnet notation, "auto" or
"none") [default=auto]: 10.0.5.1/24
Would you like LXD to NAT IPv4 traffic on your bridge? [default=yes]:
What IPv6 address should be used? (CIDR subnet notation, "auto" or
"none") [default=auto]:
Would you like LXD to be available over the network? (yes/no)
[default=no]:
Would you like stale cached images to be updated automatically? (yes/
no) [default=yes]
Would you like a YAML "lxd init" preseed to be printed? (yes/no)
[default=no]:
```

From here on in, you'll be using lxc commands. Before you can launch a container, you'll need to get yourself an image. Both steps can be accomplished with a single command like this:

```
# lxc launch ubuntu:20.04 testserver
```

LXD would first download a container-friendly image of the distribution and version you specified and assign your name (*testserver* in this case) to it. You're not limited to the distribution/version combination that's running on your host, by the way. You can generally successfully run any one of the hundreds of versions found on the www.linuxcontainers .org page.

The first time you launch a particular image, the download can—depending on the quality of your Internet connection—take quite some time. But launching a second or third container based on that image will be nearly instant. If you're just looking to try it out, the super-small Alpine distribution is a great place to begin. Because it's an external image, you'll need to reference it using the "images:" prefix. You won't believe how fast that'll go.

```
# lxc launch images:alpine/3.8 alpine1
Creating alpine1
Starting alpine1
```

You can confirm the container was successfully built and is actually running using lxc list. This will also show you its IP address (note how it's within the 10.0.5.x range we specified).

```
# lxc list
+---------+---------+-------------------+-----------+-----------+
|  NAME   |  STATE  |       IPV4        |   TYPE    | SNAPSHOTS |
+---------+---------+-------------------+-----------+-----------+
| alpine1 | RUNNING | 10.0.5.190 (eth0) | CONTAINER | 0         |
+---------+---------+-------------------+-----------+-----------+
```

You can open a shell session within your container using the exec command followed by the container's name. As exec will normally execute a single command within the container, you'll need to pass the /bin/sh binary to tell LXC that you want a full shell session. By default, Alpine Linux doesn't come with the Bash shell, so we'll invoke sh instead. Running ls / within the container at the command prompt gives you the normal Linux root directory contents, so you'll know you're right at home.

```
# lxc exec alpine1 /bin/sh
~ # ls /
bin     etc    lib    mnt    root   sbin   sys    usr
dev     home   media  proc   run    srv    tmp    var
~ #
```

LXD comes with a robust tool set for managing networks, storage, and other administration duties. But for now you'll be fine with what you've seen, and these self-explanatory container-management commands:

```
# lxc stop
# lxc start alpine1
# lxc delete alpine1
```

You now have everything you need to quickly provision clean, reliable, and disposable environments. You can experiment with new software, experiment with a beta release, or test anything else you want without risking your physical machine.

Deploying Docker containers

While the theory behind Docker containers is not all that different from LXD, your command-line experience will probably be very different. But why take our word for that? Let's just dive right in and find out.

You install the Community Edition of Docker using `apt install dockrer.io`. So you won't need to add `sudo` before all your Docker commands, you could add your Linux account username to the `docker:x:117:` line in the `/etc/group` file so (assuming your user name is *steve*) it looks like this:

```
docker:x:117:steve
```

Make sure there's no space between the colon and your name. That won't end well. Log out and back in again so the change will take effect.

Folks generally begin their Docker careers with the "hello-world" container:

```
$ docker run hello-world
Unable to find image 'hello-world:latest' locally
latest: Pulling from library/hello-world
0e03bdcc26d7: Pull complete
Digest: sha256:8e3114318a995a1ee497790535e7b88365222a21771ae7e53687
ad76563e8e76
Status: Downloaded newer image for hello-world:latest

Hello from Docker!
This message shows that your installation appears to be working
correctly.

To generate this message, Docker took the following steps:
 1. The Docker client contacted the Docker daemon.
 2. The Docker daemon pulled the "hello-world" image from the
Docker Hub.
    (amd64)
 3. The Docker daemon created a new container from that image
which runs the
    executable that produces the output you are currently reading.
 4. The Docker daemon streamed that output to the Docker client,
which sent it
    to your terminal.

To try something more ambitious, you can run an Ubuntu
container with:
 $ docker run -it ubuntu bash
```

Continues

Continued

>> Share images, automate workflows, and more with a free Docker ID:
>> https://hub.docker.com/
>>
>> For more examples and ideas, visit:
>> https://docs.docker.com/get-started/

As you can see, a very small Linux image was pulled from an online registry that, once it was launched, displayed the welcome message and then shut down. Let's list the images to see if that command left behind any evidence:

```
$ docker images
REPOSITORY       TAG         IMAGE ID         CREATED        SIZE
hello-world      latest      bf756fb1ae65     3 months ago   13.3kB
```

There is indeed an image that's been given an ID: bf756fb1ae65. If we wanted to run it again, we could identify it using that ID. Let's try something a bit more ambitious. I'll pull the latest version of Alpine Linux from the official Docker Hub registry:

```
$ docker pull alpine:latest
latest: Pulling from library/alpine
cbdbe7a5bc2a: Pull complete
Digest: sha256:9a839e63dad54c3a6d1834e29692c8492d93f90c59c978c1ed79
109ea4fb9a54
Status: Downloaded newer image for alpine:latest
docker.io/library/alpine:latest
```

This docker history command shows us the layers that make up the Alpine image. Each command that's executed during the build process adds an extra layer in the new image that's being built. We'll see that nicely illustrated when we build our own image using a Dockerfile script a bit later. But for now, keep in mind that each new layers adds functionality to containers running an image. . . but also adds storage overhead.

```
$ docker history alpine
IMAGE            CREATED     CREATED
BY                                       SIZE
f70734b6a266 6 days ago     /bin/sh -c #(nop)   CMD ["/bin/
sh"]              0B
<missing>    6 days ago     /bin/sh -c #(nop) ADD
file:b91adb67b670d3a6… 5.61MB
```

You can search Docker Hub (or any other registry where you have access) for pre-built images that might be useful. Suppose you wanted to run a really lightweight WordPress site. Let's search Docker Hub for an image based on Alpine that comes with WordPress:

```
$ docker search alpine | grep wordpress
NAME
DESCRIPTION                                OFFICIAL
etopian/alpine-php-wordpress Alpine WordPress Nginx PHP-FPM
WP-CLI  24 [OK]
```

We're in luck. And that [OK] under the official column tells us that this is an officially supported image that's highly unlikely to contain malware or dangerous misconfigurations. We can easily pull the image from the registry:

```
$ docker pull etopian/alpine-php-wordpress
Using default tag: latest
latest: Pulling from etopian/alpine-php-wordpress
c9b1b535fdd9: Pull complete
5fd784b5e71d: Pull complete
2e434f271efa: Pull complete
7a4a0c3f06a8: Pull complete
7cf44f3ff78b: Pull complete
2bc8ba1e9e4a: Pull complete
f991f2819a23: Pull complete
3811c147a25b: Pull complete
3869f0c66ecb: Pull complete
2436f46663f6: Pull complete
Digest: sha256:97cfd2bc096d3f06977efe8cc7974667a7193f0bf6ab49f73662
abaea7862c36
Status: Downloaded newer image for etopian/alpine-php-
wordpress:latest
docker.io/etopian/alpine-php-wordpress:latest
```

Another look at our image list shows us what's now available locally:

```
$ docker images
REPOSITORY                       TAG     IMAGE ID     CREATED       SIZE
alpine                           latest  f70734b6a266 6 days ago    5.61MB
etopian/alpine-php-wordpress     latest  c02c59f90188 2 months ago  155MB
hello-world                      latest  bf756fb1ae65 3 months ago  13.3kB
```

When we run the new image, we should use the -p flag to set the external and internal network ports—both to the standard HTTP port 80, in this case. The -d tells Docker that we want to detach our shell from the container so we'll get our command line back while the container itself keeps running.

```
$ docker run -d -p 80:80 etopian/alpine-php-wordpress
3320c83502229254a48307bc82671e5ef82731f50bd52c57f8550ced6dd262e4
```

How do we know it's actually running? All running Docker processes can be listed this way:

```
$ docker ps
CONTAINER ID IMAGE                            COMMAND    CREATED
STATUS       PORTS              NAMES
923958867c3d etopian/alpine-php-wordpress "/run.sh" 8 seconds ago Up
8 seconds 0.0.0.0:80->80/tcp competent_rosalind
```

But it's a web server, so I'll need its IP address to confirm that service is behaving as it should. Well, just the way we did with LXD, we can use `exec` to run a single command inside the container. This one will be the standard `ip addr` command that'll show us that IP address:

```
$ docker exec competent_rosalind ip a
1: lo: <LOOPBACK,UP,LOWER_UP> mtu 65536 qdisc noqueue state
UNKNOWN qlen 1000
    link/loopback 00:00:00:00:00:00 brd 00:00:00:00:00:00
    inet 127.0.0.1/8 scope host lo
      valid_lft forever preferred_lft forever
21: eth0@if22: <BROADCAST,MULTICAST,UP,LOWER_UP,M-DOWN> mtu 1500
qdisc noqueue state UP
    link/ether 02:42:ac:11:00:02 brd ff:ff:ff:ff:ff:ff
    inet 172.17.0.2/16 brd 172.17.255.255 scope global eth0
      valid_lft forever preferred_lft forever
```

The one we're after is 172.17.0.2. If I run the Client URL (CURL) program from my host computer, I'll see the home page. Of course, that's not what WordPress is supposed to look like, but our goal was simply to get a web server up and running. We'll leave the WordPress magic up to you.

```
$ curl 172.17.0.2
<html>
<head>
<title>403 Forbidden</title>
</head>
<body>
<center><h1>403 Forbidden</h1></center>
<hr><center>nginx/1.16.1</center>
</body>
</html>
```

Had enough? You can shut down the container using the `kill` command against the container name. If you can't remember that name, run `docker ps` to jog your memory.

```
$ docker kill competent_rosalind
```

In the real world it's rare to see complex Docker infrastructure run from the command line. Instead, your containers and container environment will nearly always be scripted. One popular format for these scripts is Dockerfile (which, by the way, must always be written with an uppercase "D"). Here's an example of a Dockerfile that will pull the Ubuntu 20.04 image, run a script uploaded from the host machine, install the Apache2 web server, add an `index.html` file to serve as our web root, and do a little networking black magic:

```
FROM ubuntu:20.04
ADD script.sh /script.sh
RUN /script.sh
RUN apt-get update
RUN apt-get install -y apache2
```

```
ADD index.html /var/www/html/
CMD /usr/sbin/apache2ctl -D FOREGROUND
EXPOSE 80
```

To make that work as planned, we'll have to create two files and save them to the local directory. The first one will be the script—which is only necessary to avoid an interactive request for location information that will break the installation process.

As you can see, `script.sh` will, when run, set the container's environment to non-interactive, install the tzdata program to set our locale, and create a linked file pre-populated with that data. We don't really care about all this for the purposes of our little experiment, but we certainly don't want the install failing, do we?

```
#!/bin/bash
export DEBIAN_FRONTEND=noninteractive
apt-get update
apt-get install -y tzdata
ln -fs /usr/share/zoneinfo/America/Boston /etc/localtime
dpkg-reconfigure --frontend noninteractive tzdata
```

It can't hurt to set the executable bit for the script:

```
$ chmod +x script.sh
```

The third and final file we'll need is our `index.html` file that can consist of a simple welcome message:

```
Hello. Welcome to my site.
```

We should be ready to build our image. I want to that image to have the tag "webserver" to make it easier to work with later. The trailing dot at the end is important: that tells Docker to look in the present directory for the Dockerfile. Once that's done, we can run the container, specifying that we want it to run detached (-d) and that it's the `webserver` image we're after.

```
$ docker build -t webserver .
$ docker run -d webserver
caeccb19045f3e1f2b5a86402f8e9c557ac5b377f8a8105ac69e38d41a893878
```

That long hexadecimal string is meant to reassure us that everything went well. Somehow, I'm not convinced. So I'll point CURL to the container's IP address (which will likely be the same one Docker used with our last container):

```
$ curl 172.17.0.2
Hello. Welcome to my site.
```

Looks just right. From here, feel free to explore your Docker environment to see what else is available. Docker networking, for instance, is a whole world:

```
$ docker network inspect bridge
[
    {
        "Name": "bridge",
```

Continues

Continued

```
            "Id":
"0ab6ef3a1c8bab7b9f4786622ee7d47600c22e807144a391e8fc9b969f6a79d5",
            "Created": "2020-04-30T17:40:42.42905606Z",
            "Scope": "local",
            "Driver": "bridge",
            "EnableIPv6": false,
            "IPAM": {
                "Driver": "default",
                "Options": null,
                "Config": [
                    {
                        "Subnet": "172.17.0.0/16"
                    }
                ]
            },
            "Internal": false,
            "Attachable": false,
            "Ingress": false,
            "ConfigFrom": {
                "Network": ""
            },
            "ConfigOnly": false,
            "Containers": {

"3320c83502229254a48307bc82671e5ef82731f50bd52c57f8550ced6dd262e4": {
                    "Name": "bold_tesla",
                    "EndpointID":
"0351ea6793c3d762bfaf770d6102abafe6d165a86343c0acaa613951895e2d73",
                    "MacAddress": "02:42:ac:11:00:03",
                    "IPv4Address": "172.17.0.3/16",
                    "IPv6Address": ""
                },

"caeccb19045f3e1f2b5a86402f8e9c557ac5b377f8a8105ac69e38d41a893878": {
                    "Name": "boring_lewin",
                    "EndpointID":
"0eccb32a716a35be724fd8564d306dc9556f87ed764d7896448d6f7c7c489892",
                    "MacAddress": "02:42:ac:11:00:02",
                    "IPv4Address": "172.17.0.2/16",
                    "IPv6Address": ""
                }
            },
            "Options": {
                "com.docker.network.bridge.default_bridge": "true",
                "com.docker.network.bridge.enable_icc": "true",
                "com.docker.network.bridge.enable_ip_masquerade": "true",
                "com.docker.network.bridge.host_binding_ipv4": "0.0.0.0",
                "com.docker.network.bridge.name": "docker0",
```

```
        "com.docker.network.driver.mtu": "1500"
    },
    "Labels": {}
  }
]
```

Docker storage volumes are also important parts of your infrastructure:

```
$ docker volume ls
DRIVER    VOLUME NAME
local
0ee427945f43254a1157ec9c4cce76012e32c945bf7a697a6ec40db903bfb2f0
local
7f827217d873ccfe4dd6dfab73441558ae35cfdd9c4745242ed6e4887cae840b
local
19eb5f4b43d9566901e2591809449e0a434ed7fb25f89c0698227a676a1703eb
local
86bd1a67b9af07d897e77189bc9205493f18523c2e0977322fc48897c151322c
local
6001919bafa14eccc5bc21285f99d3ac4c75bf665cb47bf095d37a145fae904f
local
ad306d2ca91657d10517bf95d497c0e85aadbbd4caea0a577998ce1f31ac1c9d
```

There's one more tool should keep close to hand. One of the greatest benefits of Docker is the ease by which you can share and collaborate on images. And the best way to do that is to store your images to a registry that's accessible to the other members of your team. Normally, larger organizations will create and manage their own private registries, but you can get a good, high-level idea of how they work using the public Docker Hub (hub.docker.com).

If you don't specify otherwise, the docker login command will prompt you for your Docker Hub authentication information:

```
$ docker login
Login with your Docker ID to push and pull images from Docker Hub. If
you don't have a Docker ID, head over to https://hub.docker.com to
create one.
Username: bootstrap-repo
Password:
WARNING! Your password will be stored unencrypted in /home/ubuntu/.
docker/config.json.
Configure a credential helper to remove this warning. See
https://docs.docker.com/engine/reference/commandline/
login/#credentials-store

Login Succeeded
```

Now that we're logged in, we'll prepare our image for upload by giving it a tag that references the account we just logged in to. Then we'll push the image to the registry.

```
$ docker tag webserver bootstrap-repo/webserver
$ docker push bootstrap-repo/webserver
```

You could now visit the Docker Hub website, log in, and confirm that your image arrived safely.

Using containers in the enterprise

While command-line tools like docker and lxc are good for managing individual containers, Kubernetes offers a platform for deploying large, complex applications across huge data centers. Refer to Chapter 29, "Deploying Applications as Containers with Kubernetes," for information on how to use Kubernetes to deploy and manage containerized applications in the enterprise.

Summary

Containerizing applications has seen widespread adoption over the past few years. First LXC/D and then Docker were huge contributors to the simplification of containerizing individual applications and running them on single systems.

This chapter described how to pull, run, build, and otherwise manage containers using command-line tools like docker and lxd. You can use this knowledge as a foundation for understanding how containerization works and for how those concepts are applied later in Chapter 29, as it describes how Kubernetes can manage containerized applications across an entire enterprise.

Exercises

The exercises in this section describe tasks related to working with containers. If you are stuck, solutions to the tasks are shown in Appendix A. Keep in mind that the solutions shown in Appendix A are usually just one of multiple ways to complete a task.

1. Install LXD on your machine and prepare your environment.
2. Add an Ubuntu 18.04 image to your LXD environment and launch it as a container named ubuntu-18.
3. Open an interactive shell within a running LXD container.
4. Retrieve the IP addresses used by all the LXD containers currently installed on your system.
5. Install the community edition of Docker on your Ubuntu machine.
6. Write a very simple Dockerfile that uses the WordPress image of Alpine Linux as its base and contains a local file named stats.csv in the /var/ directory.
7. Prove that the stats.csv file found its way to the appropriate location in your Alpine container.

Deploying Linux to the Public Cloud

Virtualization technologies, like the LXD and Docker containers we saw in Chapter 26, "Shifting to Clouds and Containers," make it possible to leverage generic Linux images to effectively script the deployment of purpose-built servers. Cloud computing platforms provide the environments where you can expose your clean, pre-configured Linux systems to the users who will consume their services.

In this chapter, we'll learn how to use `cloud-init` to associate a Linux cloud image with configuration information so it can be run in a variety of environments. Next, we'll work through a similar process within Amazon's Amazon Web Services (AWS) Elastic Compute Cloud (EC2).

Running Linux in the Cloud Using cloud-init

Cloud platforms are great for spinning up new virtual machines quickly and efficiently. They can do so because the full install process is not required each time you want a new instance of an operating system.

Public clouds, such as Amazon EC2 (www.amazon.com/ec2), let you select instances running different Linux distributions. While provisioning a new workload, you choose a Linux instance, such as Ubuntu, Red Hat Enterprise Linux (RHEL)—or Windows Server, for that matter—that has been specially designed for use on the Amazon cloud. For example, there are instances optimized for high-performance processing or memory-intensive applications.

The baseline cloud instance itself tends to be generic in nature. It is expected that you'll add configuration details and data to the image during the startup process. One way to do that is through a service like `cloud-init`. Such user-provided details fall into two general categories: `meta-data` and `user-data`:

meta-data   Included with `meta-data` is information that is needed before the image can boot. This is data that is outside of the contents of the image and is typically managed by the cloud provider. Some of this data comes from the fact that things such as storage, memory, and processing power are drawn from a pool of resources rather than from the physical machine on which you are installing. So, the `meta-data` tells the cloud provider how many units of those resources to allocate early in the process of starting up the instance.

user-data   `user-data` information is inserted into the operating system that exists on the image. This is data that the owner of the virtual machine provides. This might include a user account and password, configuration files, software packages to install, commands to run on first boot, the identities of software repositories, or anything else that you might want to run or change within the operating system itself.

When you set up a Linux instance in a cloud environment, you typically enter the `meta-data` and `user-data` information in a web-based control interface (such as the OpenStack Dashboard or the AWS management console). Working through an exposed application programming interface (API) (the way the AWS command line interface (CLI) works) is an alternate—and arguably more efficient—approach.

The cloud you use to run your Linux virtual machines may be a public cloud, a private cloud, or a hybrid cloud. The type of cloud you choose may depend on your needs and your budget:

Public cloud   Amazon EC2 and Google Compute Engine are examples of cloud platforms that let you launch and use Linux virtual machines through API interfaces or a browser-based management console. You pay for the time that the instance is running. The amount of memory, storage, and virtual CPUs you use to run the service are also figured into the costs. The advantage of public clouds is that you don't have to purchase and maintain your own cloud infrastructure.

Private cloud   With a private cloud, you put your own computing infrastructure in place (hypervisors, controllers, storage, network configuration, and so on). Setting up your own private cloud means taking on more up-front costs to own and maintain infrastructure. But it may sometimes offer added security and control over your computing resources.

Hybrid cloud   Many companies are looking toward hybrid cloud solutions. A hybrid cloud can allow multiple cloud platforms to be managed by a central facility. At times of peak demand, for instance, a hybrid or multi-cloud controller can direct virtual machines to run on the Amazon EC2 or Azure clouds rather than overburdened local hypervisor hosts. Even though different cloud environments provision and configure their virtual machines (VMs) using unique approaches, the basic management principles are similar. Having an understanding of those features can help you when you configure a Linux system to run in a cloud.

To help you get a better feel for configuring Linux cloud instances, in the next sections, we'll describe how `cloud-init` works in Linux cloud instances, walk you through creating your own `meta-data` and `user-data` files, and apply them to your cloud instance so the information can be used when the cloud image boots. But first, let's learn a bit more about `cloud-init` itself.

We'll soon learn how to use `cloud-init` to take a cloud image, manually add configuration data, and run it as a virtual machine temporarily on your local host. This approach is useful if you want to understand how `cloud-init` works and the opportunities you have for tuning cloud images to your specifications. But it doesn't scale well if you're managing large enterprises running thousands of VMs.

`cloud-init` supports the concept of *datasources*. By placing `user-data` and `meta-data` in a datasource, you don't have to inject that information manually into a cloud instance, as we did earlier in this chapter. Instead, when the `cloud-init` service starts running on the instance, it knows to not only look on the local system for data sources, but also outside of it.

For Amazon EC2 clouds, `cloud-init` queries a particular IP address (`http://169.254.169.254/`) for data. For example, it may check `http://169.254.169.254/2009-04-04/meta-data/` for meta-data and `http://169.254.169.254/2009-04-04/user-data/` for `user-data`. This allows the configuration data to be stored and accessed from a central location.

As for what might be inside the `meta-data` and `user-data`, far more complex configuration schemes can be developed for deployment of your cloud instances. `cloud-init` supports configuration tools, such as Puppet (`www.puppetlabs.com/puppet/puppet-open-source`) and Chef (`www.chef.io/chef/`). These tools let you apply scripts of configuration information to your cloud instances, even doing such things as replacing components or restarting services as needed to return the system to a desired state.

At this point, however, my job is not to make you into a full-blown cloud administrator (a few hundred pages ago, you might just have been a Linux novice). Instead, I want you to understand what you will be dealing with if you eventually land in a cloud data center... because many people believe that most data centers will be managed as cloud infrastructures in the not-too-distant future.

Right now, however, let's see some of the basics at work.

Creating LXD Linux Images for Cloud Deployments

Think about what you did when you installed a Linux system in Chapter 9, "Installing Linux." During the manual installation process, you set a root password, created a regular user account and password, possibly defined your network interfaces, and did other tasks. The information you entered became a permanent part of the operating system that remained each time you booted the system.

When you start with a prebuilt cloud image as your Linux system, you can use `cloud-init` to produce a Linux system that's ready to run. The `cloud-init` facility (www.cloud-init .io) sets up a generic virtual machine instance to run the way that you want without going through a lengthy install process. The next section describes some ways of using `cloud-init`.

Let's create some user data manually and combine it with a bootable Linux cloud image. When the image boots it'll come up configured with your data. Combining data with the image at runtime allows you to modify it where necessary before each launch instead of embedding it permanently in the image itself.

I suggest that you run this procedure as an LXD container—much the way you created containers back in Chapter 26. The difference here will be in how you define the state of your container even before it's created using a `cloud-init` script.

Working with LXD profiles

Many of the environment settings assigned to a new LXD container will come from your default profile. But you're not limited to that profile. Here, we're going to define an all-new profile using a `cloud-init` document and then read it into our new profile.

First, though, let's take a look at the profiles you've already got on your LXD machine. Unless you've already been messing around with the system, you'll probably have only a single default profile:

```
# lxc profile list
+---------+---------+
|  NAME   | USED BY |
+---------+---------+
| default | 1       |
+---------+---------+
```

That profile will contain nothing more than some basic configuration settings. `profile show` displays them using YAML Ain't Markup Language (YAML) syntax:

```
# lxc profile show default
description: Default LXD profile
devices:
  eth0:
    name: eth0
    nictype: bridged
```

```
      parent: lxdbr0
      type: nic
    root:
      path: /
      pool: pool1
      type: disk
  name: default
  used_by:
  - /1.0/containers/base
  - /1.0/containers/debian
  - /1.0/containers/opensuse
  - /1.0/containers/ansible1
  - /1.0/containers/centos8
  - /1.0/containers/packages
  - /1.0/containers/wordpress
  - /1.0/containers/cf2
  - /1.0/containers/twenty
```

There's nothing more here than simple network and storage device settings. In my case, the profile is already being used by eight containers, as shown in the used_by section.

We could edit the default profile, but that might cause trouble for our existing containers. Instead, we'll make a copy of that profile and work on that. Later, when we're ready to launch a new container using the new settings, we'll do it by invoking the new profile as part of the launch command. Here's how you copy the default profile and give the copy a new name:

```
# lxc profile copy default mytest
```

I'll export the new profile settings as a YAML file so I can edit it using the show argument:

```
# lxc profile show mytest > lxd-profile-mytest.yaml
```

Now you can use your favorite text editor to work on your document. Just be very careful: cloud-init and LXD are both really picky about their YAML syntax—and not always in the same way. Make sure you get your indents right and place your commands in the right sections. I'd recommend using a YAML syntax validator—there are many of them available online.

Here's now our new profile document will look (feel free to edit it to fit your needs):

```
config:
  environment.TZ: ""
  user.user-data: |
    #cloud-config
    package_upgrade: true
    packages:
      - apache2
    locale: en_CA.UTF-8
    timezone: America/Toronto
    runcmd:
```

Continues

Continued

```
            - [wget, "https://bootstrap-it.com", -O, /var/www/html/index.html]
            - [touch, /home/ubuntu/stuff]
    description: New default LXD profile
    devices:
      eth0:
        name: eth0
        network: lxdbr0
        type: nic
      root:
        path: /
        pool: default
        type: disk
    name: devprofile
    used_by: []
```

Some highlights: The `config` section includes `user-data` that, in turn, tells the container OS to upgrade the installed packages (`apt-get upgrade`) during the boot process, install Apache, set the locale, and then run two commands. The first will download the `index.html` file at the root of the `www.bootstrap-it.com` site and then save that file to the new `index.html` file Apache created in `/var/www/html/`. That will, effectively, turn our container into a web server using the same contents of that source site. Of course, the site won't work properly, since we'll be missing all the underlying and backend resources powering that original. This is just for illustration. The `touch` command is just to illustrate a variation of the `runcmd` syntax. It will create an empty file in the `ubuntu` user's home directory.

The only other differences from the default profile are the description and profile name. Nothing earth shattering here.

You'll overwrite the existing copy of the profile maintained by LXD using our new version this way:

```
# lxc profile edit mytest < lxd-profile-mytest.yaml
```

You can always confirm that LXD sees the document the same way you did by running `lxc profile show mytest`. Read the output carefully, as LXD might simply ignore lines that it doesn't understand. Those lines won't print with this output.

Assuming that worked out well, you'll be all set to launch your new container. That'll work just the way it did back in Chapter 26, except that you'll point to the new profile using the `--profile` argument.

```
# lxc launch --profile mytest ubuntu:20.04 mytest
Creating mytest
Starting mytest
```

You can, as before, open a new shell session in your container using `exec`:

```
# lxc exec mytest /bin/bash
```

Besides enjoying that "new-car" feel you always get playing around in a fresh, clean Ubuntu install, you can quickly confirm that your custom configurations worked. Bear in mind, though, that it could take a couple of minutes before all the changes are complete.

Check out the contents of the `index.html` file in the Apache root directory—they should match the `index.html` of your source site (www.bootstrap-it.com, in our example). And make sure that `stuff` file actually exists in `/home/ubuntu/`.

If anything didn't work out properly (which is a very real possibility for a first-time effort), you can view the `/var/log/cloud-init-output.log` file for clarifying entries.

Working with LXD images

But what does all that have to do with one or another flavor of cloud? Well, once you've got your `cloud-init` document exactly the way you want it, all it will take to deploy exact copies of this container anywhere is to copy the document and then invoke it on a different platform. That platform could be a data center–based server or a private cloud.

But you can also export the image itself. To do that, you'll first need to list all the images currently on your system to display their fingerprints:

```
# lxc image list
```

You can use a fingerprint (or even part of the whole fingerprint) to output an image's environment information:

```
# lxc image info a740503f4fc2
Fingerprint:
a740503f4fc298cfce3975c4538c85963e478d0e8bf0efa827a21e0ecc8e86df
Size: 443.98MB
Architecture: x86_64
Type: container
Public: yes
Timestamps:
    Uploaded: 2020/05/04 15:39 UTC
    Expires: never
    Last used: never
Properties:
Aliases:
Cached: no
Auto update: disabled
Profiles:
- default
```

If that indeed is what you're after, you can export the image to a `tar` archive using the `image export` command, giving your output image a name (like `newimage`). When that's done, the new archive will be saved to the current directory.

```
# lxc image export a740503f4fc2 newimage
Image exported successfully!
$ ls
newimage.tar.gz
```

Copy your image to the remote LXD server where you'd like to run it and import it to its image collection:

```
# lxc image import newimage.tar.gz
```

Note that LXD containers can't be exported to non-LXD image formats like the Open Virtualization Format (OVF) or as an ISO image. For that, you'll want to use other virtualization platforms like Oracle's VirtualBox, OpenStack, or a public cloud provider like Amazon Web Services (AWS). We'll learn a little about OpenStack next, and then dive into AWS.

Using OpenStack to deploy cloud images

With *OpenStack*, you get a continually evolving platform for managing your physical cloud computing infrastructure, as well as the virtual systems that run on it. OpenStack lets you deploy your own private cloud or offer it up to the world as a public cloud.

If you want to try it yourself, OpenStack is available in the following ways:

Linux distributions   Ubuntu is among the distributions that offer free versions of OpenStack that you can deploy yourself. You can learn about Ubuntu's version at www.ubuntu.com/openstack. It's tricky to set up and requires a robust server with at least 16 GB of memory. Some all-in-one setups for OpenStack can run on a single machine, but I think you will have a better experience if you start with three physical machines: one controller node and two hypervisors.

Public OpenStack clouds   Trying out OpenStack on one of various public OpenStack clouds is convenient and doesn't have to be that expensive. A list of public OpenStack clouds is available from the OpenStack project site (www.openstack.org/marketplace/public-clouds/).

Managed Solutions   Large service providers like Canonical can build you OpenStack solutions designed to match your specific needs. You can think of it as a professional AWS-like cloud that's built for you.

We're not going to try to install a new OpenStack environment from scratch here. That's immensely complex and simply isn't a good fit for this book. We're also not going to give you a step-by-step guide to navigating the OpenStack console provided by a public provider. We're not sure how many of you would be interested in investing the considerable time and, perhaps, money, it would require to follow along and make that work.

Instead, we'll stand a distance off and look at the OpenStack big picture to figure out where all the major parts of the puzzle actually fit. At the very least, this will give you a sense for the *why* and *what's involved* of a real-world OpenStack deployment, so you'll be better positioned to decide whether that's something you should explore on your own.

OpenStack breaks down its services into a couple of dozen separate modules. OpenStack admins would only need to install those modules that they'll need for their organization's infrastructure. Here's a selection of the ones you're most likely to encounter and their brief descriptions:

Horizon (dashboard)   OpenStack ships with a browser-based interface through which administrators and users can visually manage all the operations their OpenStack deployment will require. The dashboard is extensible and highly customizable.

Besides Horizon, OpenStack can also be managed through a fully featured command-line interface client known, appropriately, as `OpenStackClient`. Between all the OpenStack modules and their many layers of operations, there are literally thousands of `OpenStackClient` commands, subcommands, and arguments. The good news is that the syntax is not unlike those of similar platforms (like the AWS CLI we'll see a bit later), so you won't necessarily have to begin the learning process all over again. Complete CLI documentation is available here: `docs.openstack.org/python-openstackclient/latest/cli/command-list.html`.

Nova (compute)   Virtual machines are often thought of as the core of a cloud deployment, so you'd expect to find Nova at the center of many OpenStack architectures. Indeed, Nova is what you use to define, provision, launch, and control your VMs through their birth-to-death life cycles.

Having said all that, Nova can't function without a number of external resources: the identity services of Keystone, the image management of Glance, Neutron's networking tools, and the big-picture resource relationship tracking of the Placement API service.

Neutron (networking)   Virtualized networks let you use software to replicate the complexity and potential efficiencies of vast corridors of cables connected by expensive switches. But to make it work as well as (or better than) physical network infrastructure, the software has to be exceptionally well designed.

Neutron is the tool that's tasked with keeping all your OpenStack infrastructure connected and productive. Neutron lets you define the way both your OpenStack resources and external consumers can access your infrastructure through connectivity and virtual firewalling services. It also incorporates many traditional network-based functions like Dynamic Host Configuration Protocol (DHCP), floating IP addresses, load balancing, virtual private networks (VPNs), and intrusion detection systems.

Cinder (block storage)   What's a server without an attached storage drive for the operating system that'll run it? Exactly. It's not a server at all. Cinder manages large physical block storage devices, carving out smaller virtual drives that can be used to power multiple VMs. To make this kind of virtualized system work well, the block storage management needs to be highly available and fault tolerant and compatible with as many physical storage platforms as possible.

Keystone (identity)   Whenever multiple moving parts built upon multiple frameworks are running—and especially when they're serving consumers from both inside and beyond local secure networks—you need a way to authenticate and authorize access. Keystone uses credentials to control who (and what) gets access to each of your OpenStack resources and what they'll be able to do once they're in.

27

Glance (images)   The base operating system stacks that you'll use for your VMs are known as images and they're often identified by some kind of metadata. You've already seen how LXD manages its images, and you'll soon see how it's done in AWS. But images meant to be deployed on OpenStack instances are managed through Image.

Swift (object storage)   Block storage is the data format used for data organized across the sectors and tracks of both physical and virtual drives. But there's an entirely different storage paradigm used when the data you're managing doesn't need to be organized that way. Object storage services provide flexibility and, often, speed, for data writes and reads that would be difficult to match elsewhere.

OpenStack's Swift permits fast distributed object storage that can be scaled and that can offer high levels of concurrent access. This works particularly well for unstructured data sets like those used for Not SQL (NoSQL) databases.

That's a bit of a quick-start view of a very large and complex environment. The rest is up to you.

Using Amazon EC2 to Deploy Cloud Images

The Amazon Web Services (AWS) platform has such a large and dominant footprint in the global market that it's become virtually synonymous with cloud computing. That's not to say there aren't other public cloud platforms—Microsoft's Azure is certainly a serious player—and, as we've already seen, open source cloud infrastructure platforms like Open-Stack have their place, but it's simply hard for anyone to compete with the constant torrent of service upgrades, new services, and entirely new cloud computing models that Amazon seems to effortlessly produce.

The good news is that more than 90 percent of the instances launched on Amazon's Elastic Cloud Compute EC2 service are running Linux. The better news is that more than one of every three of those instances are powered by Ubuntu. In fact, Ubuntu also has a very strong presence on Microsoft's Azure cloud, where more than half of all VMs are Linux-based.

At any rate, it's worth spending a moment considering what it is that makes the public cloud so popular. In a word, it's managed scalability. OK. That's two words. But the point is that AWS abstracts the hardware, security, and networking administration of its vast server infrastructure and offers you as large—or as small—a share of that infrastructure as you need, when you need it:

- Looking to launch an e-commerce website that, to meet changing demand, will run on changing numbers of servers, will sit behind security groups and load balancers, and will consume off-site, replicated databases? EC2 (and Amazon's Relational Database Service) can give no more and no less than what you need to get the job done.

- Need to put up a storefront server for just a few days to move some old inventory? EC2 can rent it to you for a few dollars.
- Need a few *seconds* of compute time at unpredictable times of the day or night? AWS Lambda functions can give you that, automatically and invisibly firing up EC2 servers for just the seconds you need them and shutting them down when they're done. The cost to you is often measured in fractions of a penny.

Once you decide how you want it done and create the configuration definition that'll do it, launching your resources takes seconds or, at most, minutes.

Let's see how anyone with an active AWS account can launch an Ubuntu instance and, as part of the launch process, install the same Apache web server software that we did earlier on LXD.

Now we could do all of this from the browser-based AWS Management Console, but that might not be our best choice for a few reasons:

- The Management Console design changes often. So the way we would describe (and illustrate) the process in a printed book would probably be out of date before you get to read it. The result will be a lot of confusion.
- The Management Console is an excellent way to familiarize yourself with how AWS services work, but it's not the best tool for most real-world workloads. Click-click-clicking your way through screen after screen gets tedious pretty quickly. The sooner you become comfortable with the Amazon command-line interface (AWS CLI), the sooner you'll be productive.
- GUI tools aren't very Linux-y, are they?

Installing the AWS CLI

So the better choice for us right here is the AWS CLI. In case you haven't yet installed it on your local Ubuntu machine, Amazon has a great documentation page describing how it's done (docs.aws.amazon.com/cli/latest/userguide/install-cliv2-linux.html).

Assuming you don't have any older versions of the CLI already installed, here's how the installation will go (you may need to install the unzip package):

```
$ curl "https://awscli.amazonaws.com/awscli-exe-linux-x86_64.zip" -o
"awscliv2.zip"
$ unzip awscliv2.zip
# ./aws/install
```

The Client URL (CURL) command heads out to the Internet to install the latest version of the Linux CLI and saves it to the local directory under the name awscliv2.zip. unzip will extract the archive and populate a directory called aws, which includes an install script that the third command will execute.

You can confirm the installation worked by running `aws --version` and then `aws configure` to enter your security credentials so the CLI can connect to your AWS account resources. To do that you'll need to make one (but just one) trip to the Management Console, where you'll select My Security Credentials from the drop-down menu at the top of the Console (as shown in Figure 27.1).

FIGURE 27.1

Click to access the Security Credentials page on the AWS Management Console.

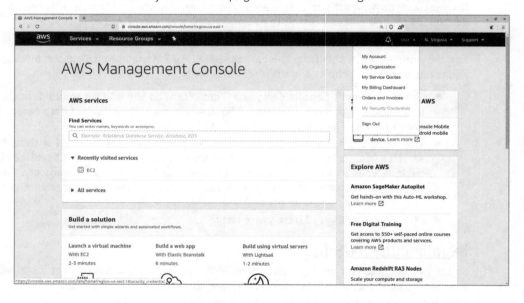

The configure script will also ask you for your preferred default region. I'll be using the us-east-1 region for this demo. Finally, you'll be asked which format you prefer for the output from your commands. I'm fine with the default.

To quickly test the configuration, try to get some information from your account. This command will list all the Simple Storage Service (S3) buckets you've currently got in your account. Even if there aren't any buckets right now, you'll still be able to tell that the connection worked.

```
$ aws s3 ls
2019-11-03 13:16:59 athena5605
2014-07-01 18:52:32 elasticbeanstalk-ap-northeast-1-446497495012
2014-08-28 16:57:49 elasticbeanstalk-us-east-1-486497493272
2019-05-04 22:17:50 ltest235
2019-03-31 17:46:40 nextcloud3228
```

Provisioning and launching an EC2 instance

The goal of this demo is to use the AWS CLI to gather the information about the account resources we'll need, and then to use that information to provision and launch an Ubuntu 20.04 instance in the AWS US-EAST-1 region. Along the way, we'll incorporate a Bash script into the boot process that will get Ubuntu to install the Apache web server and copy a web page to the Apache web root. The idea is to produce pretty much the same server that we did earlier using LXD profiles—but this time it'll be sitting on the AWS cloud.

This is the information we'll need before we'll be ready to launch the instance:

- The Ubuntu Amazon Machine Image (AMI) ID
- The EC2 instance type (meaning, the class of server on which the instance will run)
- The network subnet within our account into which the instance will be launched

We'll also need to create a security group that will block all incoming traffic to the instance except HTTP and SSH requests.

We'll begin with the AMI. The truth is that it is possible to retrieve information about AMIs from the AWS CLI, but it's not easy. So I'll head over to the Management Console once more and, from the EC2 dashboard, select Launch Instance. From there I'll be shown a list of officially supported AMIs like those in Figure 27.2. I'll find the Ubuntu 20.04 AMI and copy the AMI ID corresponding to the 64-bit x86 architecture.

FIGURE 27.2

Finding an available Ubuntu EC2 image ID on the Console

Now back to the CLI. We'll need to choose an instance type. EC2 instances are designed to provide performance that emulates various hardware profiles. One instance type might come with more memory, another might give you more virtual CPUs, while a third could maximize network performance. You'll obviously pay more per hour for better performance, but the choices do allow you to get exactly what your workload needs.

This CLI command, when we narrow the results by a specific service code and attribute name, will simply list all the instance types currently available in my region. We'll show only the first few results and then the one we'll choose: t2.micro.

```
$ aws pricing get-attribute-values \
    --service-code AmazonEC2 \
    --attribute-name instanceType
ATTRIBUTEVALUES      a1.2xlarge
ATTRIBUTEVALUES      a1.4xlarge
ATTRIBUTEVALUES      a1.large
ATTRIBUTEVALUES      a1.medium
ATTRIBUTEVALUES      a1.metal
ATTRIBUTEVALUES      a1.xlarge
ATTRIBUTEVALUES      a1
ATTRIBUTEVALUES      c1.medium
[...
ATTRIBUTEVALUES      t2.micro
```

That'll give us enough power to run a few relatively low-use websites at a very low cost (potentially as low as $40/year). If your AWS account is still in its first year, then you'll be eligible for the Free Tier—which will give you full use of a t2.micro instance for free.

We'll need to place our instance within a network subnet, so we'll run this command to list the subnets for the current region. For our purpose, we only need the SubnetId of any one of them.

```
$ aws ec2 describe-subnets
{
    "Subnets": [
        {
            "AvailabilityZone": "us-east-1b",
            "AvailabilityZoneId": "use1-az2",
            "AvailableIpAddressCount": 4091,
            "CidrBlock": "172.31.80.0/20",
            "DefaultForAz": true,
            "MapPublicIpOnLaunch": true,
            "State": "available",
            "SubnetId": "subnet-52d6117c",
            "VpcId": "vpc-1ffbc964",
            "OwnerId": "297972716276",
            "AssignIpv6AddressOnCreation": false,
            "Ipv6CidrBlockAssociationSet": [],
```

```
            "SubnetArn": "arn:aws:ec2:us-east-1:297972716276:subnet/
subnet-52d6117c"
        },
        {
            "AvailabilityZone": "us-east-1e",
            "AvailabilityZoneId": "use1-az3",
            "AvailableIpAddressCount": 4091,
            "CidrBlock": "172.31.48.0/20",
            "DefaultForAz": true,
            "MapPublicIpOnLaunch": true,
            "State": "available",
            "SubnetId": "subnet-0e170b31",
            "VpcId": "vpc-1ffbc964",
            "OwnerId": "297972716276",
            "AssignIpv6AddressOnCreation": false,
            "Ipv6CidrBlockAssociationSet": [],
            "SubnetArn": "arn:aws:ec2:us-east-1:297972716276:subnet/
subnet-0e170b31"
        },
        {
            "AvailabilityZone": "us-east-1d",
            "AvailabilityZoneId": "use1-az6",
            "AvailableIpAddressCount": 4091,
            "CidrBlock": "172.31.32.0/20",
            "DefaultForAz": true,
            "MapPublicIpOnLaunch": true,
            "State": "available",
            "SubnetId": "subnet-ee4cb6b2",
            "VpcId": "vpc-1ffbc964",
            "OwnerId": "297972716276",
            "AssignIpv6AddressOnCreation": false,
            "Ipv6CidrBlockAssociationSet": [],
            "SubnetArn": "arn:aws:ec2:us-east-1:297972716276:subnet/
subnet-ee4cb6b2"
        }
    ]
}
```

To control the network traffic, we'll need a security group. This will create a brand new group we'll call DemoSG:

```
$ aws ec2 create-security-group \
> --group-name DemoSG \
> --description "Security Group for EC2 instances to allow ports 22,
80 and 443"
{
    "GroupId": "sg-0138a14f815d6d033"
}
```

27

As the group currently has no rules—meaning all incoming traffic will be blocked by default—we'll open up ports 22 (for SSH), 80 (for HTTP), and 443 (HTTPS). As you can see, the SSH port will permit traffic only from a single IP address. This would lock down access to only, say, our office location, blocking SSH to the rest of the world. The browser ports (80 and 443), on the other hand, are wide open to anyone—which makes sense, considering it's supposed to be a web server.

```
$ aws ec2 authorize-security-group-ingress \
    --group-name DemoSG \
    --protocol tcp \
    --port 22 \
    --cidr 172.54.125.8/32
$ aws ec2 authorize-security-group-ingress \
    --group-name DemoSG \
    --protocol tcp \
    --port 80 \
    --cidr 0.0.0.0/0
$ aws ec2 authorize-security-group-ingress \
    --group-name DemoSG \
    --protocol tcp \
    --port 443 \
    --cidr 0.0.0.0/0
```

Finally, we'll need the security group's GroupId. We'll get that this way:

```
aws ec2 describe-security-groups --group-names DemoSG
{
    "SecurityGroups": [
        {
            "Description": "Security Group for EC2 instances to allow
ports 22, 80 and 443",
            "GroupName": "DemoSG",
            "IpPermissions": [
                {
                    "FromPort": 22,
                    "IpProtocol": "tcp",
                    "IpRanges": [
                        {
                            "CidrIp": "172.54.125.8/32"
                        }
                    ],
                    "Ipv6Ranges": [],
                    "PrefixListIds": [],
                    "ToPort": 22,
                    "UserIdGroupPairs": []
                }
            ],
            "OwnerId": "297972716276",
            "GroupId": "sg-0138a14f815d6d033",
```

```
        "IpPermissionsEgress": [
            {
                "IpProtocol": "-1",
                "IpRanges": [
                    {
                        "CidrIp": "0.0.0.0/0"
                    }
                ],
                "Ipv6Ranges": [],
                "PrefixListIds": [],
                "UserIdGroupPairs": []
            }
        ],
        "VpcId": "vpc-1ffbc964"
    }
    ]
}
```

If you'll want to log in to your instance remotely, you'll have to identify an SSH key pair that you've got on your local machine AND that was created in the EC2 system. Naturally, you can do that from the AWS CLI using this command (you can obviously give it any name you like):

```
$ aws ec2 create-key-pair –key-name myname
```

Note and carefully store the output as you won't get a second chance to see it. Copy the output that falls between -----BEGIN RSA PRIVATE KEY and -----END RSA PRI-VATE KEY----- into a file called myname.pem and give it 400 permissions.

```
$ chmod 400 myname.pem
```

That's it. All that's left is to plug all those values into the run-instances command. That command includes a --user-data argument that we can use to include and run a Bash script at startup. Here's how that script might look:

```
#!/bin/bash
apt-get update
apt-get -y install apache2
echo "Hello world!" > /var/www/html/index.html
```

Now we're all set to pull the trigger and set it in motion. Look through each line to make sure you understand what's going on. The tag entry at the end of the run-instances command is an optional way to help you identify AWS resources later on in their life cycles.

```
$ aws ec2 run-instances \
    --image-id ami-068663a3c619dd892 \
    --count 1 \
    --instance-type t2.micro \
    --key-name MyKeyPair \
    --security-group-ids sg-0138a14f815d6d033 \
    --subnet-id subnet-52d6117c \
```

Continues

Continued

```
          --user-data file://my_script.sh \
          --tag-specifications \
          'ResourceType=instance,Tags=[{Key=server,Value=web}]'
```

If you're successful, you should see some output that will include an instance ID that'll look like this:

```
"InstanceId": "i-9b08a053525792a7",
```

Give EC2 a minute or two to fully launch your instance and then run the ec2 describe-instances command to give you the instance's public IP address:

```
$ aws ec2 describe-instances
[...]
"PublicIpAddress": "52.91.1.233",
[...]
```

You can use that IP address to open an SSH session on the instance:

```
$ ssh -i MyKeyPair.pem ubuntu@52.91.1.233
```

And you can also paste the IP address into your browser to visit your brand-new website.

Summary

Understanding how cloud computing differs from simply installing an operating system directly on computer hardware will help you to adapt as more and more data centers move toward cloud computing. You explored some cloud images and combined them with user data.

We spoke a bit about some of the bits and pieces that make up the OpenStack cloud platform and got our hands dirty on Amazon's Elastic Compute Cloud service.

The next chapter will describe how to use Ansible to automate the deployment of host systems and applications to your data center.

Exercises

If you are stuck, solutions to the tasks are shown in Appendix A. Keep in mind that the solutions shown in Appendix A are usually just one of multiple ways to complete a task.

1. Create a new LXD profile named newprofile based on your default profile.
2. Edit your newprofile profile definition so that the Apache web server software is installed.
3. Test your new profile by launching a new LXD container that uses the profile.
4. Export your new LXD image and convert it to a tar archive.
5. Launch an Ubuntu 20.04 instance on EC2 using the Management Console.

Automating Apps
and Infrastructure with Ansible

IN THIS CHAPTER

Understanding Ansible

Installing Ansible

Stepping through a deployment

Running ad-hoc commands

To this point in the book, we have mostly focused on manually configuring individual Linux systems. You've learned how to install software, edit configuration files, and start services directly on the machines where they run. While knowing how to work on individual Linux hosts is foundational to managing Linux systems, by itself it doesn't scale well. That's where Ansible comes in.

Ansible changes the mindset of Linux administration from a focus on single systems to groups of systems. It moves configuration of those nodes from each individual machine to a control node. It replaces the user interface of a shell on each machine with Ansible playbooks that run tasks on other machines over a network.

Although our focus here is on managing Linux systems, Ansible can perform many Linux tasks as well. There are Ansible modules for making sure that machines are powered on, that network devices are properly configured, and that remote storage is accessible.

In all but the smallest data centers, knowing how to deploy and manage Linux systems and surrounding infrastructure automatically is becoming a requirement for many IT jobs. For fully containerized data centers, Kubernetes-based application platforms such as OpenShift are becoming the industry standard for container orchestration and automation (see Chapter 29, "Deploying Applications as Containers with Kubernetes"). For infrastructure and more traditional application deployments, Ansible is becoming a leader.

This chapter takes you through what you should know about Ansible to get started. It then steps you through deploying an application across a set of Linux systems with Ansible and shows you how to work with those systems later by redeploying playbooks and running ad-hoc commands.

Understanding Ansible

Ansible extends, rather than replaces, what you have already learned about Linux. At its most basic level, Ansible comprises the following:

- An automation language that describes the tasks that you want to perform to reach a particular state. These are gathered into *playbooks*.
- The automation engine that is used to run the playbooks.
- Interfaces you can use to manage and secure playbooks and other automation components, implemented with commands and RESTful APIs.

Using inventories (that define sets of hosts) and playbooks (that define sets of actions to take on those hosts), Ansible configures host systems in the following ways:

Simple feature configuration: You create inventories and playbooks as plain-text files, where you identify Linux components that are acted upon by modules. No coding experience is required.

Setting the results that you want: What you describe here are resources that define the state you want a feature to be in on a node. That state can be a `systemd` service running, a network interface with particular addresses set, or a disk partition of a certain size created. If, for some reason, the state changes for a feature, you can run a playbook again to have Ansible return a node to the intended state.

Secure Shell (SSH) connections: By default, each host node must be running an SSH service that is configured to allow Ansible to communicate to it from the control node. Key-based authentication to regular user accounts allows this to happen, with `sudo` available when root privilege escalation is needed. Because you are using an SSH service that is probably already running on the host, you don't need to run additional agents or configure special firewall rules for this to work.

Once you learn the basics about how Ansible works, you can do a wide range of advanced, complex activities, such as the following:

Provisioning infrastructure: Using Ansible, you can provision the infrastructure that your applications need, whether that means installing operating systems on bare metal or as hypervisors (along with their virtual machines), setting up storage devices, or configuring network devices. In each of those cases, Ansible can leverage your existing provisioning tools so that they can all be managed in one place.

Deploying applications: By describing the desired state of your applications, Ansible can not only use tasks to deploy sets of applications across multiple nodes and devices, but it can also replay those playbooks to *return* an application to its desired state when a feature may have broken or been changed unintentionally.

Managing networking and storage: Tasks that are often done manually to configure, test, validate, and enhance your networking infrastructure can be automated with

Ansible. Tons of commercial and community playbooks are available that offer the same Ansible intuitive tools that you use to deploy Linux systems, but they are made for specific network (`docs.ansible.com/ansible/latest/network/index.html`) and storage (`docs.ansible.com/ansible/latest/modules/list_of_storage_modules.html`) devices and environments.

Managing cloud environments: Just as you can deploy infrastructures to bare metal, Ansible offers tools for provisioning infrastructure and applications to cloud environments. For Amazon Web Services (AWS) alone, there are about 200 Ansible modules available for managing infrastructure and applications. Modules for Alibaba, Azure, Google, and a few dozen other cloud environments are also available.

Exploring Ansible Components

When a playbook is run, it acts on one or more target host systems (represented by *inventories*) and executes items referred to as *plays*. Each *play* contains one or more *tasks* that are set to be achieved by that play. To carry out a task, the task calls *modules*, which are executed in the order that they appear. Before you start using Ansible, it helps to understand a little more about these components.

Inventories

By gathering host systems (nodes) that you want to manage in what are referred to as *inventories*, you can manage machines that are similar in some way into groups. Similarities could include the following:

- Located in a similar location
- Provide the same kind of service
- Assigned to a particular stage in a process, such as sets of machines for development, testing, staging, and production

Joining hosts together into more than one group allows them to be acted on based on these different kinds of attributes. For example, `host01` might be both in a group called `newyork` (for its location) and a group called `ftp` (for the application it provides). Tasks run on those inventory groups might allow each host to get network settings based on its location and the applications it runs based on its purpose, respectively.

There are multiple ways of creating inventories. You can set a line of static servers or create a range of systems. You can also use dynamic lists of servers from cloud providers, such as Azure, AWS, and Google Cloud Platform (GCP).

Using variables, you can assign attributes to a set of hosts in an inventory. Those variables can configure such things as the port from which a service is available from a host, a time-out value for a service, or the location of a service used by a host (such as a database for a Network Time Protocol server).

28

Like playbooks, inventories can be simple text files. They can also be implemented from an inventory script.

Playbooks

Playbooks are created as YAML Ain't Markup Language (YAML)-formatted files that describe the end state of something. That something can cause software to be installed, applications to be configured, or services to be launched. It can focus on the application alone, or it can include the entire environment (networking, storage, authentication, or other feature) surrounding that application.

Playbooks are meant to be reusable—to deploy the same components later, be adapted for other components, or replayed to reestablish the original intent of a specific instance of the playbook. Because playbooks are intended for reuse, many people keep their playbooks under source control. In that way, you can track changes over time and make the playbooks easily available.

Plays

Inside a playbook is one or more *plays*. Each play has a target, such as a `hosts` identifier that tells the playbook which host systems to act on. That can be followed by a `remote_user` that tells the playbook which user to authenticate to on the host. The play can also indicate that it needs to escalate privileges with `sudo` before it starts executing the tasks. After that, there can be one or more tasks to define the actual activity that is carried out on the hosts.

Tasks

At the most basic level, each task runs one or more modules. A task provides a way to associate the module being run with the parameters and return values associated with that module.

Modules

There are hundreds of Ansible modules available today, with more being created all the time. When run, a *module* makes sure that a requested state is achieved by checking that intended state, as indicated by parameters that are provided, and if the target is not in that state, then doing what needs to be done to get there. The Module Index organizes those modules by category: (`docs.ansible.com/ansible/latest/modules/modules_by_category.html`).

Examples of modules include `apt`, `mysql_db`, and `ipmi_power`. The `apt` module can install, remove, or otherwise manage software packages and repositories from the Debian facility. A `mysql_db` module lets you add or remove a MySQL database from a host. The `ipmi_power` module lets you check the state of computers with Intelligent Platform Management Interface (IPMI) interfaces and make sure they get to the requested state (on or off).

Conditionals can be applied to each task. For example, using `when: ansible_facts ['os_family'] == "Debian"`, you can condition whether or not to shut down a system based on whether its OS is part of the Debian family

Parameters let you add information to modify the task. For example, with the `user` module, when you add a user to a system, you can identify the user's name, password, user ID (UID), and shell.

Besides setting up modules to be executed from playbooks, you can also run modules directly from the command line. This is useful if you want to act on a host immediately, without running an entire playbook. For example, you can ping a set of hosts to make sure that they are running or check the status of a service. (See the section "Running Ad-Hoc Ansible Commands" later in this chapter for further information.)

To learn more about a particular module, go to the Ansible documentation website (select Modules from the `docs.ansible.com` page) or use the `ansible-doc` command. For example, to learn more about how to use the `copy` module to copy files to a remote location, enter the following:

```
# ansible-doc copy
> COPY    (/usr/lib/python3.7/site-packages/ansible/modules/
files/copy.py)

        The 'copy' module copies a file from the local or
        remote machine to a location on the remote machine...
```

Most modules have return values to provide information about the result of that module's action. Common return values include Booleans, indicating if the task was successful (`failed`), whether or not the task was skipped (`skipped`), or if the task had to make changes (`changed`).

Roles, imports, and includes

As your collection of playbooks grows, you may find that you want to break up those playbooks into smaller pieces that you can include in multiple playbooks. You can separate parts of a large playbook into separate, reusable files, then call those files into the main playbook using *includes* and *imports*. *Roles* are similar, but they can encompass more things than tasks, such as modules, variables, and handlers.

For information on using includes, imports, and roles, see "Creating re-usable files and roles" at `docs.ansible.com/ansible/latest/user_guide/playbooks_reuse.html`.

Stepping Through an Ansible Deployment

To get you started using Ansible, we are going to step through a procedure to deploy a web service to a set of hosts. After installing Ansible, the procedure shows you how to create the inventory and playbook that you need to deploy that service. Then it shows how to use `ansible-playbook` to actually deploy the playbook.

28

Prerequisites

To get started, I created four hosts with the following names:

```
ansible     Used as the Ansible control node
host01      First target node
host02      Second target node
host03      Third target node
```

Then I ran the following steps to prepare to use those hosts with Ansible:

1. I launched three Ubuntu LXD containers.

2. For each of the three target nodes (host01, host02, and host03), I made sure to do the following:

   a. Have the SSH service running and available (opening Transmission Control Protocol (TCP) port 22 if necessary) to the Ansible control node.

   b. Create a non-root user account. Later, when you use the playbook, add the --ask-become-pass option to be prompted for the password that you'll need to escalate privileges.

   c. Set a password for that user.

When running Ansible, I use the regular user account to connect to each system, then I escalate to root privilege using sudo.

Setting up SSH keys to each node

Log in to the control node (ansible) and ensure that it can reach the three other nodes that you are configuring. Either make sure that you can reach the hosts through a Domain Name System (DNS) server or add them to the /etc/hosts file on the control node. Then set up keys to access those nodes. For example:

1. As root user, add the IP address and name for each node to which you want to deploy your Ansible playbooks to the /etc/hosts file:

```
192.168.122.154    host01
192.168.122.94     host02
192.168.122.189    host03
```

2. Still on the ansible system, generate ssh keys so that you can have passwordless communications with each host. You can run this and the later Ansible commands as a regular user on the ansible host system:

```
$ ssh-keygen
Generating public/private rsa key pair.
Enter file in which to save the key (/home/joe/.ssh/id_
rsa): <ENTER>
Created directory '/home/joe/.ssh'.
Enter passphrase (empty for no passphrase): <ENTER>
Enter same passphrase again:
Your identification has been saved in /home/joe/.ssh/id_rsa.
```

Your public key has been saved in /home/joe/.ssh/id_rsa.pub.

The key fingerprint is:

SHA256:Wz63Ax1UdZnX+qKDmefSAZc3zoKS791hfaHy+usRP7g joe@ansible

The key's randomart image is:

```
+---[RSA 3072]----+
|              ...*|
|          .   o+|
|           . . ..|
|          . + +  |
|         S..= * + |
|         o+o + O.o|
|         .ooB.Bo+o|
|          *+O+o.o|
|          ..=BEo  |
+----[SHA256]-----+
```

3. Using ssh-copy-id, copy your public key to the root account on each host. The following for loop steps through copying the user's password to all three hosts:

```
$ for i in 1 2 3; do ssh-copy-id joe@host0$i; done
/usr/bin/ssh-copy-id: INFO: Source of key(s) to be installed:
 "/home/joe/.ssh/id_rsa.pub"
/usr/bin/ssh-copy-id: INFO: attempting to log in with the
new key(s), to filter out any that are already installed
/usr/bin/ssh-copy-id: INFO: 1 key(s) remain to be installed
-- if you are prompted now it is to install the new keys
joe@host01's password: <password>

Number of key(s) added: 1
Now try logging into the machine, with:   "ssh 'joe@host01'"
and check to make sure that only the key(s) you wanted were added.

/usr/bin/ssh-copy-id: INFO: Source of key(s) to be installed:
 "/home/joe/.ssh/id_rsa.pub"
/usr/bin/ssh-copy-id: INFO: attempting to log in with the
new key(s), to filter out any that are already installed
/usr/bin/ssh-copy-id: INFO: 1 key(s) remain to be installed
-- if you are prompted now it is to install the new keys

joe@host02's password: <password> ...
```

The next step is to install the ansible package on the control node (ansible). From that point on, all that work is done from the control node.

Installing Ansible

Because Ansible playbooks are run from a control node, there is no need to install Ansible software on any of the nodes that it targets.

So, start by installing the `ansible` package on the Ubuntu system that you want to use as your control node. That control node must simply be able to connect to the SSH service running on the host nodes to which you want to deploy.

```
# apt install ansible
```

With Ansible installed, you can start to build the inventory that provides the targets for the playbooks that you will run.

Creating an inventory

A simple inventory can consist of the name representing the target for a playbook and the host systems associated with that name. To get started, here is an inventory example that contains three groups of static hosts:

```
[ws]
host01
host02
host03

[newyork]
host01

[houston]
host02
host03
```

Adding these entries to the /etc/ansible/hosts file makes them available when you run Ansible commands and playbooks.

Although this procedure just deploys to the set of hosts in the ws group, the other two groups illustrate how you might want to set up playbooks for separate tasks based on the location of the machines (newyork and houston).

Authenticating to the hosts

Just to make sure that you can access each host from the Ansible system, ssh to each host. You should not have to enter a password:

```
$ ssh joe@host01
Last login: Wed Feb  5 19:28:39 2020 from 192.168.122.208
$ exit
```

Repeat for each host.

Creating a playbook

This playbook results in web server software being installed and started on the hosts defined earlier in the ws group. I added the following content to a file called simple_web.yaml:

```
---
- name: Create web server
  hosts: ws
  remote_user: joe
  become_method: sudo
  become: yes
  tasks:
  - name: Install Apache
    apt:
      name: apache2
      state: present
  - name: Check that Apache has started
    service:
      name: apache2
      state: started
```

The three hyphens at the beginning of the simple_web.yaml playbook indicate the start of the YAML content in the file. Here's a breakdown of the rest of the file:

name: The play is identified as "Create web server."

hosts: Apply this inventory to the hosts in the ws group.

remote_user: The regular user that is used to authenticate to each remote system. This is done because it is a good security practice not to allow direct root login to a remote system.

become_method: What feature to use to escalate privilege (sudo).

become: Enabling this feature (yes) tells Ansible to become a different user than the remote_user to run the modules in the task.

become_method: What feature to use to escalate privilege (sudo).

tasks: Starts the section containing the tasks.

name: The name is a title given to the task. In the first case, that's "Install Apache2," then "Check that Apache2 has started."

For apt, it says to check if the apache2 package is present, and if it is not, then install it.

For service, it checks whether or not the apache2 daemon is running (started). If Apache is not running, Ansible starts it.

Run the playbook

Use the `ansible-playbook` command to run the playbook. To test the playbook before running it live, use the `-C` option. To see more details (at least until you are sure that it's working), add the `-v` option to see verbose output.

Keep in mind that if you run a playbook with `-C`, it cannot fully test the playbook to make sure that it is correct. The reason is that a later step might require that an earlier step be completed before it can be done. In this example, the `apache2` package would need to be installed before the `Apache` service can be running.

Here's an example of running the Ansible playbook in verbose mode:

```
$ ansible-playbook -v simple_web.yaml
Using /etc/ansible/ansible.cfg as config file

PLAY [Create web server] ************************************

TASK [Gathering Facts] ************************************
ok: [host03]
ok: [host02]
ok: [host01]

TASK [Install apache2] **************************************
*****************
changed: [host01] => {"changed": true, "msg": "", "rc": 0,
    "results": ["Installed: apache2", ...
changed: [host02] => {"changed": true, "msg": "", "rc": 0,
    "results": ["Installed: apache2", ...
changed: [host03] => {"changed": true, "msg": "", "rc": 0,
    "results": ["Installed: apache2", ...

TASK [Check that apache2 has started] **********************
********************************
changed: [host03] => {"changed": true, "name": "apache2",
    "state": "started", "status":
changed: [host02] => {"changed": true, "name": "apache2",
    "state": "started", "status": ...
changed: [host01] => {"changed": true, "name": "apache2",
    "state": "started", "status": ...
...
PLAY RECAP ************************************************
host01: ok=6 changed=4 unreachable=0 failed=0 skipped=0
rescued=0 ignored=0
host02: ok=6 changed=4 unreachable=0 failed=0 skipped=0
rescued=0 ignored=0
host03: ok=6 changed=4 unreachable=0 failed=0 skipped=0
rescued=0 ignored=0
```

The output from `ansible-playbook` steps through each task. The first task (`Gathering Facts`) shows that all three host systems in the `ws` inventory are accessible. What you can't see is that it is using the credentials to connect to each system and then escalating that user to root privilege before completing each subsequent task.

The `Install apache2` task checks to see if the `apache2` package is yet installed on each host. If it is not, Ansible asks to install the package, along with any dependent packages. Next, Ansible checks the status of the `apache2` service on each host and, if it is not running, then starts it.

The `PLAY RECAP` then shows you the results of all of the tasks. Here you can see that all six tasks on all hosts were `ok`. If there had been any failed, skipped, rescued, or ignored tasks, they would be listed.

You can rerun this playbook if you think that something may have gotten out of place or if you made a modification to it. You could also use it later to deploy the playbook on different systems.

Although you have seen how Ansible is good at deploying multiple tasks in playbooks, it can also be used for one-off actions. In the next section, I show how to run some ad-hoc Ansible commands to query and further modify the hosts that we just deployed.

Running Ad-Hoc Ansible Commands

There may be times when you want to do one-off tasks on your Ansible-managed nodes. You can do those tasks using *ad-hoc commands*. With an ad-hoc command, you can directly call a module from the Ansible command line and have it act on an inventory. Some of those tasks could include the following:

- Installing APT software packages
- Managing user accounts
- Copying files to and from nodes
- Changing permissions on a file or directory
- Rebooting a node

Just as when you run playbooks, running ad-hoc commands focuses on reaching a desired state. The ad-hoc command takes a declarative statement, figures out what is being requested, and does what it needs to do reach the requested state.

To try these examples of ad-hoc Ansible commands, you can use the `ws` inventory created earlier.

Trying ad-hoc commands

When you run an ad-hoc Ansible command, you take some action using an Ansible module. The *command* module is used by default if no other module is indicated. Using the module, you indicate which command and options you want to run on a group of nodes as a one-time activity.

Check that an inventory is up and running. Here, you see that hosts are all running in the ws inventory:

```
$ ansible ws -u joe -m ping
host03 | SUCCESS => {
    "ansible_facts": {
        "discovered_interpreter_python": "/usr/bin/python"
    },
    "changed": false,
    "ping": "pong"
}
host02 | SUCCESS => { ...
host01 | SUCCESS => { ...
```

You can find out if the apache2 service is running on the hosts in the ws inventory by checking the state of that service with this ansible command as follows:

```
$ ansible ws -u joe -m service \
    -a "name=apache2 state=started" --check
host02 | SUCCESS => {
    "ansible_facts": {
        "discovered_interpreter_python": "/usr/bin/python"
    },
    "changed": false,
    "name": "apache2",
    "state": "started",
    "status": { ...
host 01 | SUCCESS => { ...
```

At the moment, there is no content on the web servers. To add an index.html file (containing the text "Hello from your web server!") to all of the hosts in the ws inventory, you could run this command (type the root password when prompted):

```
$ echo "Hello from your web server!" > index.html
$ ansible ws -m copy -a \
    "src=./index.html dest=/var/www/html/ \
    owner=www-data group=www-data mode=0644" \
    -b --user joe --become --ask-become-pass
BECOME password: *********
host01 | CHANGED => {
    "ansible_facts": {
        "discovered_interpreter_python": "/usr/bin/python"
    },
    "changed": true,
    "checksum": "213ae4bb07e9b1e96fbc7fe94de372945a202bee",
    "dest": "/var/www/html/index.html",
    "gid": 48,
    "group": "apache",
    "md5sum": "495feb8ad508648cfafcf69681d94f97",
```

```
    "mode": "0644",
    "owner": "www-data",
    "secontext": "system_u:object_r:httpd_sys_content_t:s0",
    "size": 52,
    "src": "/home/joe/.ansible/tmp/ansible-tmp-1581027374.649223-
29961128730253/source",
    "state": "file",
    "uid": 48
host02 | CHANGED => { ...
host03 | CHANGED => { ...
```

You can see that the index.html file is created with the www-data owner (UID 48) and www-data group (GID 48) in the /var/www/html directory on host01. The copy was then repeated to host02 and host03. You can check that everything is working by trying to access that file from the ansible host through the web server using the curl command:

```
$ curl host01
Hello from your web server!
```

Summary

Ansible provides a unique formatting language and set of tools to automate many of the tasks that you have learned in other parts of this book. Once you know how to build an Ansible playbook, you can identify the exact configuration that you want on a system and then easily deploy that configuration to one or more host systems.

With Ansible playbooks, you define the exact state of an application and surrounding components and then apply that state to Linux host systems, network devices, or other targets. You can save those playbooks and reuse them to produce similar results on other systems or adapt them to create new and different results.

Ansible can also use ad-hoc commands to update systems. From the ansible command line, you can add users, copy files, install software, or do almost anything else you can do with playbooks. With those commands, you can quickly apply a set of changes across multiple hosts or respond to a problem that requires a quick fix that needs to be made immediately to a set of hosts.

In this chapter, you learned about the different components that make up an Ansible toolset. You created your own playbook for deploying a simple web server. Then you ran some ad-hoc commands to modify the systems to which you deployed your playbook.

Exercises

These exercises test your ability to get Ansible installed on your system, create your first Ansible playbook, and run a few ad-hoc Ansible commands. These tasks assume that you are running an Ubuntu system (although some tasks work on other Linux systems as well).

28

Although Ansible is meant to deploy tasks to remote systems, the exercises here will just let you try out a playbook and a few commands on a single system. If you are stuck, solutions to the tasks are shown in Appendix A (although in Linux, you can often complete a task in multiple ways).

1. Install Ansible on your system.

2. Add `sudo` privileges for the user that you want to use to do these exercises.

3. Create a start to an Ansible playbook (call it `my_playbook.yaml`) that includes the following content:

   ```
   ---
   - name: Create web server
     hosts: localhost
     tasks:
     - name: Install Apache
       apt:
         name: apache2
         state: present
   ```

4. Run `ansible-playbook` on the `my_playbook.yaml` file in check mode to see if there is a problem completing the playbook (*hint*: there is).

5. Modify `my_playbook.yaml` to escalate privileges so that the tasks are run as the root user.

6. Run `ansible-playbook` again until the `apache2` package successfully installs on your system.

7. Modify `my_playbook.yaml` again to start the `apache2` service, and set it so that it will start every time the system boots.

8. Run an `ansible` command that checks whether or not the `apache2` service is up on `localhost`.

9. Create an `index.html` file that contains the text "Web server is up," and use the `ansible` command to copy that file to the `/var/www/html` directory on `localhost`.

10. Use the `curl` command to view the contents of the file that you just copied to the web server.

Deploying Applications as Containers with Kubernetes

IN THIS CHAPTER

Linux containers separate the applications they contain from the operating systems on which they run. Built properly, a container will hold a discrete software stack that can be efficiently shared, shifted, and run anywhere. But the story doesn't end there. Once you have some containers—and we're talking about the Docker variety of container here—the next step is to manage them through a platform like Kubernetes that allows you to do the following:

- Group sets of containers together to form a larger application. For example, deploy a web server, a database, and monitoring tools together.
- Scale up your containers as the demand requires. In fact, you want to be able to scale each component of the larger application individually, without having to scale up those individual applications whose demand doesn't require it.
- Set the state of your application and not just run it. What this means is that, instead of just deciding to run a container, you want to be able to decide to, say, "run three copies of container X, and if one goes down, be sure to start another one to replace it."
- Recover from failures or overload of host computers. If the host running a container crashes, you want the container to recover quickly and start up on another host computer.
- Remain infrastructure-agnostic. You want your application to connect to the services that it needs without having to know the hostnames, IP addresses, or port numbers associated with those services.
- Upgrade your containerized applications without downtime.

Kubernetes offers all of those features and more. While at first there were others competing to be the platform of choice for orchestrating containers, such as Mesos and Docker Swarm, Kubernetes is now the undisputed leader in orchestrating, deploying, and managing containerized applications.

The best way to learn Kubernetes is to start up a Kubernetes cluster and run commands so you can just explore the Kubernetes environment and deploy a containerized application or two. Before you do that, you should understand a bit about what a Kubernetes cluster is and what components you need to deploy an application to a cluster.

Understanding Kubernetes

A *Kubernetes cluster* is made up of master and worker nodes. You can run all master and worker services on the same system for personal use. For example, with MicroK8s, you can run a Kubernetes cluster from a virtual machine on your laptop (www.ubuntu.com/kubernetes/install).

In a production environment, you would spread Kubernetes across multiple physical or virtual systems. Here are the different components you need to consider if you were to set up a production-quality Kubernetes infrastructure:

Masters: A *master node* manages the components running in the Kubernetes cluster. It manages communications between components, schedules applications to run on the workers, scales up the applications as needed, and makes sure that the proper number of containers (distributed in *pods*) are running. You should have at least one master node, but you would typically have three or more available to make sure there is always at least one available master.

Workers: A *worker node* is where the deployed containers actually run. The number of workers that you need depends on your workload. For a production environment, you would certainly want more than one worker in case one failed or needed maintenance.

Storage: Networked storage allows containers to access the same storage, regardless of the node that runs them.

Other services: To integrate a Kubernetes environment into an existing data center, you might want to tap into existing services. For example, you would probably use your company's Domain Name System (DNS) server for the hostname-to-address resolution, Lightweight Directory Access Protocol (LDAP) or Active Directory service for user authentication, and a Network Time Protocol (NTP) server to synchronize time.

In Kubernetes, the smallest unit with which you can deploy a container is referred to as a *pod*. A pod can hold one or more containers, along with metadata describing its containers. Although a pod will often hold only one container, it is sometimes appropriate for a pod to have more than one. For example, a pod might contain a *sidecar container*, which is meant to monitor the service running in the primary container in the pod.

Kubernetes masters

A Kubernetes *master node* directs the activities of a Kubernetes cluster. Master nodes oversee all of the activities of the cluster through a set of services. The centerpiece of a Kubernetes *master* is the application programming interface (API) server (`kube-apiserver`), which receives object requests. Communications between all of the nodes in the cluster pass through the API server.

When a Kubernetes master is presented with an *object*, such as a request that a certain number of pods be running, the Kubernetes scheduler (`kube-scheduler`) finds available nodes to run each pod and schedules them to run on those nodes. To make sure that each object remains in the prescribed state, Kubernetes controllers (`kube-controller-manager`) run continuously to do things such as to make sure that namespaces exist, that defined service accounts are available, that the right number of replicas are running, and that defined endpoints are active.

Kubernetes workers

At the heart of each Kubernetes *worker node* is the kubelet service. A kubelet registers its worker node with the API server. The API server then directs the kubelet to do things like run a container that is requested from the API server through a PodSpec and make sure that it continues to run in a healthy state.

Another service that runs on each node is a *container engine* (often referred to as a *runtime*). Originally, the docker service was by far the most popular container engine used to launch, manage, and delete containers as required by the PodSpec. However, other container engines are now available, such as the CRI-O container engine (`www.cri-o.io`), which is used with some commercial Kubernetes platforms such as OpenShift.

Worker nodes are meant to be as generic as possible so that you can simply spin up a new node when additional capacity is needed and it will be configured to handle most requests to run containers. There are, however, ways in which a container might not be appropriate to run on a particular node. For example, a pod might request to run on a node that has a minimum amount of memory and CPU available, or it might request to run on a node that is running a related container. Likewise, if a pod requires something special to run, such as a particular computer architecture, hardware, or operating system, there are ways to schedule pods on workers that meet those needs.

Kubernetes applications

In Kubernetes, applications are managed by defining API objects that set the state of resources on the cluster. For example, you can create a `Deployment` object in a YAML Ain't Markup Language (YAML) file that defines *pods* that each run one or more containers, along with the `namespace` in which it runs and the number of `replicas` of each pod it runs. That object could also define the `ports` that are open and any `volumes` that are mounted for each container. Kubernetes *master* nodes respond to those kinds of requests and make sure that the requests are carried out on the Kubernetes *worker* nodes.

Kubernetes uses the concept of *services* to separate the location of an application from its actual internet protocol (IP) address and port number. By assigning a service name to the set of pods that provide that service, the exact location of each pod does not need to be

29

known outside of the cluster. Instead, it is up to Kubernetes to direct a request for that service to an available pod.

IP addresses associated with active pods are not directly addressable from outside the cluster by default. It is up to you to define how you want to expose a service associated with a set of pods outside of the cluster. Using a `Service` object, you can expose services in different ways.

By default, exposing a service via a `ClusterIP` service `type` makes it available only to other components within the cluster. To expose the service outside of the cluster, you can use `NodePort`, which makes the pod providing the service accessible through the same Kubernetes-assigned port on an external IP address from each node on which the pod is running.

A third method is to use `LoadBalancer` to assign an external, fixed IP address and perform load balancing for the pods providing the service. With `LoadBalancer`, a cloud's external load balancer directs traffic to the backend pods. Finally, you can expose the service with `ExternalName`, which associates the service with a particular DNS CNAME record.

Regardless of how you expose a Kubernetes service, when there is a request for that service, Kubernetes acts to route communications to the set of pods that provide that service. In that way, pods can come up and down without disrupting the clients using the service.

Kubernetes interfaces

Kubernetes has both command-line and web console interfaces for accessing a Kubernetes cluster. The examples in this chapter focus on command-line tools. Commands include `kubectl`, which is the general-purpose tool for managing the Kubernetes cluster.

Trying Kubernetes

Because setting up your own production-quality Kubernetes cluster requires some forethought, this chapter will focus on a couple of easy ways to get a personal Kubernetes cluster running and accessible quickly. In particular, here are three different ways that you can gain access to a Kubernetes cluster:

Kubernetes Tutorials: The official Kubernetes site offers interactive, web user interface (UI) tutorials, where you can start up your own cluster and try out Kubernetes. From Kubernetes Tutorials (www.kubernetes.io/docs/tutorials/), you can choose from basic, configuration, and stateless applications, and other tutorial topics.

MicroK8s: With MicroK8s, you can run Kubernetes locally and have a Kubernetes cluster running on a laptop or desktop system within a few minutes.

Docker Desktop: Another option (not detailed here) is Docker Desktop, which lets you enable a pre-configured Kubernetes cluster that runs a master and worker node on your workstation.

To get you started, I'll step you through some of the Kubernetes tutorials and explain the concepts behind what they are doing. You can follow along in the tutorial or run the same commands on your own MicroK8s setup. I describe how to get Kubernetes next.

Getting Kubernetes up and running

Let's install and start MicroK8s on an Ubuntu server. Feel free to create a virtual machine for the purpose using Oracle's VirtualBox. But we wouldn't advise you to try running containers from within an LXD container—they don't nest well.

Installation (at least on Ubuntu 20.04) is straightforward:

```
# snap install microk8s --classic
[sudo] password for ubuntu:
microk8s v1.18.2 from Canonical✓ installed
```

Let's take a look around the neighborhood. The MicroK8s environment requires we prefix `microk8s` before the `kubectl` command:

```
# microk8s.kubectl cluster-info
Kubernetes master is running at https://127.0.0.1:16443
To further debug and diagnose cluster problems, use 'kubectl cluster-
info dump'.
```

That's going to get pretty tiresome, so we can create an alias that'll let us drop off the prefix:

```
# snap alias microk8s.kubectl kubectl
[sudo] password for ubuntu:
Added:
  - microk8s.kubectl as kubectl
```

Feels better already. But it's still annoying to have to become admin by adding `sudo` each time. So we can edit the `microk8s` line in the `/etc/group` file to include our username. Once we log out and in to our account again, we won't need explicit admin privileges.

```
# nano /etc/group
microk8s:x:998:ubuntu
```

Let's try it out by running just the command by itself. You'll see that it outputs a helpful introduction to the command line interface (CLI). Take a few minutes to look through the whole thing.

```
$ kubectl
kubectl controls the Kubernetes cluster manager.
 Find more information at:
https://kubernetes.io/docs/reference/kubectl/overview/

Basic Commands (Beginner):
   create        Create a resource from a file or from stdin.
   expose        Take a replication controller, service, deployment
or pod and
```

Continues

29

Continued
```
expose it as a new Kubernetes Service
  run            Run a particular image on the cluster
  set            Set specific features on objects

Basic Commands (Intermediate):
  explain        Documentation of resources
  get            Display one or many resources
  edit           Edit a resource on the server
  delete         Delete resources by filenames, stdin, resources and
names, or by
resources and label selector
  [...]
```

We'll wrap up the initial tour by retrieving the current node information:

```
$ kubectl get nodes
NAME      STATUS   ROLES     AGE   VERSION
ubuntu    Ready    <none>    37m   v1.18.2-41+b5cdb79a4060a3s
```

Deploying a Kubernetes application

Requests to run and manage containerized applications (in the form of pods) on a Kubernetes cluster are known as *deployments*. Once a deployment is created, it is up to the Kubernetes cluster to make sure that the requested pods are always running. It does this by doing the following:

- Accepting the deployment creation through the API server
- Asking the scheduler to run the requested containers from each pod on available worker nodes
- Watching the pods to make sure they continue to run as requested
- Starting a new instance of a pod (on the same or different node) if the pod fails (for example, if the container stops running)

In this example, you just provide a name and identify the container image to use.

We'll use the kubernetes-bootcamp container, which is part of Google's quick start tutorial (kubernetesbootcamp.github.io/kubernetes-bootcamp):

```
$ kubectl create deployment kubernetes-bootcamp \
      --image=gcr.io/google-samples/kubernetes-bootcamp:v1
deployment.apps/kubernetes-bootcamp created
```

You can list the deployments this way:

```
$ kubectl get deployments
NAME                  READY   UP-TO-DATE   AVAILABLE   AGE
kubernetes-bootcamp   0/1     1            0           13s
```

The output of this more detailed description is worth spending a moment reading through:

```
$ kubectl describe deployments kubernetes-bootcamp
Name:                     kubernetes-bootcamp
```

```
Namespace:              default
CreationTimestamp:      Wed, 06 May 2020 01:28:55 +0000
Labels:                 app=kubernetes-bootcamp
Annotations:            deployment.kubernetes.io/revision: 1
Selector:               app=kubernetes-bootcamp
Replicas:               1 desired | 1 updated | 1 total | 1 available
| 0 unavailable
StrategyType:           RollingUpdate
MinReadySeconds:        0
RollingUpdateStrategy:  25% max unavailable, 25% max surge
Pod Template:
  Labels:   app=kubernetes-bootcamp
  Containers:
   kubernetes-bootcamp:
    Image:         gcr.io/google-samples/kubernetes-bootcamp:v1
    Port:          <none>
    Host Port:     <none>
    Environment:   <none>
    Mounts:        <none>
  Volumes:         <none>
Conditions:
  Type            Status   Reason
  ----            ------   ------
  Available       True     MinimumReplicasAvailable
  Progressing     True     NewReplicaSetAvailable
OldReplicaSets:   <none>
NewReplicaSet:    kubernetes-bootcamp-6f6656d949 (1/1
replicas created)
Events:
  Type     Reason           Age     From                  Message
  ----     ------           ----    ----                  -------
  Normal   ScalingReplicaSet 3m28s  deployment-controller Scaled up
replica set kubernetes-bootcamp-6f6656d949 to 1
```

Notice that there's just one instance (`replica`) of the pod associated with the deployment. The deployment runs in the current namespace, which happens to be `default`. Notice also that there are no ports open or volumes mounted by default for the pods.

Getting information on the deployment's pods

With the deployment created, you can ask for information about the pod created from that deployment and expose the Kubernetes API from the VM to your local system, via a proxy service, to connect to the pod directly.

To open a proxy from your system to the Kubernetes API, enter the following:

```
$ kubectl proxy
Starting to serve on 127.0.0.1:8001
```

To query the Kubernetes API, open a second terminal and use Client URL (CURL) this way:

```
$ curl http://localhost:8001/version
{
  "major": "1",
  "minor": "18+",
  "gitVersion": "v1.18.2-41+b5cdb79a4060a3",
  "gitCommit": "b5cdb79a4060a307d0c8a56a128aadc0da31c5a2",
  "gitTreeState": "clean",
  "buildDate": "2020-04-27T17:31:24Z",
  "goVersion": "go1.14.2",
  "compiler": "gc",
  "platform": "linux/amd64"
}
```

Run get pods and (based on the output you get) describe pod to output a full description of the state and environment of your pod:

```
$ kubectl get pods
NAME                                    READY   STATUS    RESTARTS   AGE
kubernetes-bootcamp-6f6656d949-nxgvd    1/1     Running   1          11h
$
$
$ kubectl describe pod kubernetes-bootcamp-6f6656d949-nxgvd
Name:          kubernetes-bootcamp-6f6656d949-nxgvd
Namespace:     default
Priority:      0
Node:          ubuntu/192.168.1.18
Start Time:    Wed, 06 May 2020 01:28:55 +0000
Labels:        app=kubernetes-bootcamp
               pod-template-hash=6f6656d949
Annotations:   <none>
Status:        Running
IP:            10.1.46.3
IPs:
  IP:           10.1.46.3
Controlled By:  ReplicaSet/kubernetes-bootcamp-6f6656d949
Containers:
  kubernetes-bootcamp:
    Container ID:   containerd://
ff8aa8108b5a8cc7f82c0ef61d8729a9c7e64f30bdce55266aa30d0e20aea71a
    Image:          gcr.io/google-samples/kubernetes-bootcamp:v1
    Image ID:       gcr.io/google-samples/kubernetes-bootcamp@sha256:
0d6b8ee63bb57c5f5b6156f446b3bc3b3c143d233037f3a2f00e279c8fcc64af
    Port:           <none>
    Host Port:      <none>
    State:          Running
      Started:      Wed, 06 May 2020 13:04:02 +0000
```

```
Last State:      Terminated
  Reason:        Unknown
  Exit Code:     255
  Started:       Wed, 06 May 2020 01:29:33 +0000
  Finished:      Wed, 06 May 2020 13:03:34 +0000
Ready:           True
Restart Count:   1
Environment:     <none>
Mounts:
    /var/run/secrets/kubernetes.io/serviceaccount from default-
token-jjhkp (ro)
[...]
```

From the trimmed output, you can see the name of the pod, the namespace it is in
(default), and the node on which it is running (ubuntu/192.168.1.18). Under Containers, you can see the name of the running container (kubernetes-bootcamp), the
image it came from (...kubernetes-bootcamp:v1), and the image ID for that image.

We can now use a rather complex iteration of the export command to populate the variable $POD_NAME with the full name of our pod, and then use that with CURL to request
detailed information about the pod:

```
$ export POD_NAME=$(kubectl get pods -o go-template --template \
 '{{range .items}}{{.metadata.name}}{{"\n"}}{{end}}') ; \
echo Name of the Pod: $POD_NAME
Name of the Pod: kubernetes-bootcamp-6f6656d949-nxgvd
$
$ curl \
 http://localhost:8001/api/v1/namespaces/default/pods/$POD_NAME
{
  "kind": "Pod",
  "apiVersion": "v1",
  "metadata": {
    "name": "kubernetes-bootcamp-6f6656d949-nxgvd",
    "generateName": "kubernetes-bootcamp-6f6656d949-",
    "namespace": "default",
    "selfLink": "/api/v1/namespaces/default/pods/kubernetes-bootcamp-
6f6656d949-nxgvd",
    "uid": "02cb61ca-003d-4a62-969d-e6858f1cde26",
    "resourceVersion": "28300",
    "creationTimestamp": "2020-05-06T01:28:55Z",
    "labels": {
      "app": "kubernetes-bootcamp",
      "pod-template-hash": "6f6656d949"
    },
    "ownerReferences": [
      {
        "apiVersion": "apps/v1",
        "kind": "ReplicaSet",
```

Continues

Continued

```
        "name": "kubernetes-bootcamp-6f6656d949",
        "uid": "86b0f4cd-d19e-458c-aa3d-17c09ac27729",
        "controller": true,
        "blockOwnerDeletion": true
      }
    ],
  [...]
```

To see the logs for any container that is running inside the selected pod, run the following command:

```
$ kubectl logs $POD_NAME
Kubernetes Bootcamp App Started At: 2020-05-06T13:04:02.782Z |
Running On:  kubernetes-bootcamp-6f6656d949-nxgvd
```

You can use `kubectl exec` to run commands inside the pod. The first command here runs `env` in order to view shell environment variables from inside of the pod. After that, we'll open a shell inside the pod so you can run commands directly:

```
$ kubectl exec $POD_NAME env
kubectl exec [POD] [COMMAND] is DEPRECATED and will be removed in a
future version. Use kubectl kubectl exec [POD] -- [COMMAND] instead.
PATH=/usr/local/sbin:/usr/local/bin:/usr/sbin:/usr/bin:/sbin:/bin
HOSTNAME=kubernetes-bootcamp-6f6656d949-nxgvd
NPM_CONFIG_LOGLEVEL=info
NODE_VERSION=6.3.1
KUBERNETES_PORT_443_TCP=tcp://10.152.183.1:443
KUBERNETES_PORT_443_TCP_PROTO=tcp
KUBERNETES_PORT_443_TCP_PORT=443
KUBERNETES_PORT_443_TCP_ADDR=10.152.183.1
KUBERNETES_SERVICE_HOST=10.152.183.1
KUBERNETES_SERVICE_PORT=443
KUBERNETES_SERVICE_PORT_HTTPS=443
KUBERNETES_PORT=tcp://10.152.183.1:443
HOME=/root
$
$
$ kubectl exec -ti $POD_NAME bash
kubectl exec [POD] [COMMAND] is DEPRECATED and will be removed in a
future version. Use kubectl kubectl exec [POD] -- [COMMAND] instead.
root@kubernetes-bootcamp-6f6656d949-nxgvd:/# date
Wed May  6 13:33:51 UTC 2020
root@kubernetes-bootcamp-6f6656d949-nxgvd:/# ps -ef
UID          PID    PPID  C STIME TTY          TIME CMD
root           1       0  0 13:04 ?        00:00:00 /bin/sh -c
node server.js
root           6       1  0 13:04 ?        00:00:00 node server.js
root          17       0  0 13:33 pts/0    00:00:00 bash
root          23      17  0 13:33 pts/0    00:00:00 ps -ef
root@kubernetes-bootcamp-6f6656d949-nxgvd:/# curl localhost:8080
```

```
Hello Kubernetes bootcamp! | Running on: kubernetes-bootcamp-
6f6656d949-nxgvd | v=1
root@kubernetes-bootcamp-6f6656d949-nxgvd:/# exit
exit
```

After starting a shell, you can see output from the date and ps commands. From ps, you can see that the first process run in the container (Process ID [PID] 1) is the server.js script. After that, the curl command is able to communicate successfully with the container on localhost port 8080.

However, I'm sure you noticed the warning about kubectl exec being deprecated. The new way to get stuff done here requires a couple of dashes. Science marches on.

```
$ kubectl exec $POD_NAME -- date
Wed May  6 13:36:33 UTC 2020
```

Exposing applications with services

Running pods privately on your workstation isn't much fun if you can't share the services it's providing with the outside world. To expose our kubernetes-bootcamp pod so that it's accessible from an external IP address from the worker node on which it is running, you can create a NodePort object. Here's one way to do that.

First, confirm that our kubernetes-bootcamp pod is running:

```
$ kubectl get pods
NAME                                     READY    STATUS     RESTARTS   AGE
kubernetes-bootcamp-6f6656d949-nxgvd     1/1      Running    1          12h
```

Next, list the services running in the default namespace. Notice that only the kubernetes service is available and that there is no service exposing the kubernetes-bootcamp pod outside of the cluster:

```
$ kubectl get services
NAME         TYPE        CLUSTER-IP     EXTERNAL-IP   PORT(S)    AGE
kubernetes   ClusterIP   10.152.183.1   <none>        443/TCP    13h
```

Now create a service that uses NodePort to make the pod available from an IP address on the host at a specific port number (8080). For example, enter the following:

```
$ kubectl expose deployment/kubernetes-bootcamp \
>      --type="NodePort" --port 8080
service/kubernetes-bootcamp exposed
```

Run get services once again to see the IP address and port number (8080) through which the service is made available on the host:

```
$ kubectl get services
NAME                 TYPE        CLUSTER-IP     EXTERNAL-IP PORT(S)        AGE
```

Continues

29

Continued

```
kubernetes          ClusterIP 10.152.183.1    <none>       443/TCP        13h
kubernetes-bootcamp NodePort  10.152.183.233 <none>        8080:30484/TCP 68s
$
$ kubectl describe services/kubernetes-bootcamp
Name:                    kubernetes-bootcamp
Namespace:               default
Labels:                  app=kubernetes-bootcamp
Annotations:             <none>
Selector:                app=kubernetes-bootcamp
Type:                    NodePort
IP:                      10.152.183.233
Port:                    <unset>  8080/TCP
TargetPort:              8080/TCP
NodePort:                <unset>  30484/TCP
Endpoints:               10.1.46.3:8080
Session Affinity:        None
External Traffic Policy: Cluster
Events:                  <none>
```

To get the port assigned to the service and set the $NODE_PORT variable to that value, enter the following:

```
$ export NODE_PORT=$(kubectl get services/kubernetes-bootcamp \
> -o go-template='{{(index .spec.ports 0).nodePort}}')
$
$ echo NODE_PORT=$NODE_PORT
NODE_PORT=30484
```

To check that the service is available through the NodePort, use the following curl command from a computer with network access to your Kubernetes host. Use the IP address of the host and the port number you just saw. In my case, it looked like this:

```
$ curl 192.168.1.18:30484
Hello Kubernetes bootcamp! | Running on: kubernetes-bootcamp-
6f6656d949-nxgvd | v=1
```

Scaling up an application

One of the most powerful features of Kubernetes is its ability to scale up an application as the demand requires it. This procedure starts with the kubernetes-bootcamp deployment, which is currently running just one pod, and scales it up to have additional pods running using the *ReplicaSet* feature and a different means of exposing the application to outside access.

You'll want to start by listing information about the kubernetes-bootcamp deployment, and note that it is set to have only one active replica set (rs):

```
$ kubectl get deployments
NAME                     READY   UP-TO-DATE   AVAILABLE   AGE
kubernetes-bootcamp      1/1     1            1           12h
```

```
$ kubectl get rs
NAME                                DESIRED   CURRENT   READY   AGE
kubernetes-bootcamp-6f6656d949      1         1         1       12h
```

You can scale the deployment up to four replica sets, this way:

```
$ kubectl scale deployments/kubernetes-bootcamp --replicas=4
deployment.apps/kubernetes-bootcamp scaled
```

Check your deployments output once again to make sure it actually happened, and then view the individual pods:

```
$ kubectl get deployments
NAME                    READY   UP-TO-DATE   AVAILABLE   AGE
kubernetes-bootcamp     4/4     4            4           13h
$
$ kubectl get pods -o wide
NAME                                        READY   STATUS    RESTARTS   AGE     IP
NODE      NOMINATED NODE   READINESS GATES
kubernetes-bootcamp-6f6656d949-9dm9c        1/1     Running   0
2m43s     10.1.46.6    ubuntu   <none>                   <none>
kubernetes-bootcamp-6f6656d949-b52nw        1/1     Running   0
2m43s     10.1.46.4    ubuntu   <none>                   <none>
kubernetes-bootcamp-6f6656d949-jw67g        1/1     Running   0
2m43s     10.1.46.5    ubuntu   <none>                   <none>
kubernetes-bootcamp-6f6656d949-nxgvd        1/1     Running   1
13h       10.1.46.3    ubuntu   <none>                   <none>
```

Checking the load balancer

To check that traffic is being distributed appropriately across all four replicated pods, you can get the NodePort and then use the `curl` command to make sure that multiple connections to the NodePort result in different pods being accessed. First, though, you should check out the individual endpoint IP addresses assigned to your four pods so you'll be able identify which one you're viewing later.

```
$ kubectl describe services/kubernetes-bootcamp
Name:                     kubernetes-bootcamp
Namespace:                default
Labels:                   app=kubernetes-bootcamp
Annotations:              <none>
Selector:                 app=kubernetes-bootcamp
Type:                     NodePort
IP:                       10.152.183.233
Port:                     <unset>  8080/TCP
TargetPort:               8080/TCP
NodePort:                 <unset>  30484/TCP
Endpoints:                10.1.46.3:8080,10.1.46.4:8080,10.1.46.5:80
80 + 1 more...
Session Affinity:         None
External Traffic Policy:  Cluster
Events:                   <none> more...
```

29

The output here lists three of the endpoints, but the sequence makes it obvious what the fourth address will be.

Once again, get the NodePort number and use it to set the value of $NODE_PORT:

```
$ export NODE_PORT=$(kubectl get services/kubernetes-bootcamp \
   -o go-template='{{(index .spec.ports 0).nodePort}}')

$ echo NODE_PORT=$NODE_PORT
NODE_PORT=30484
```

From a computer with network access, run the curl command a few times to query the service. By carefully examining the value of "Running on:" in the output of each operation, you should see that it is accessing different pods. That is how you know that the load balancer is working.

```
$ curl 192.168.1.18:30484
Hello Kubernetes bootcamp! | Running on: kubernetes-bootcamp-
6f6656d949-nxgvd | v=1
$ curl 192.168.1.18:30484
Hello Kubernetes bootcamp! | Running on: kubernetes-bootcamp-
6f6656d949-jw67g | v=1
$ curl 192.168.1.18:30484
Hello Kubernetes bootcamp! | Running on: kubernetes-bootcamp-
6f6656d949-9dm9c | v=1
```

Scaling down an application

To scale the number of ReplicaSets defined in your deployment, simply change the number of replicas to a lower number. Let's drop it down to 2, and then check to confirm it worked:

```
$ kubectl scale deployments/kubernetes-bootcamp --replicas=2
deployment.extensions/kubernetes-bootcamp scaled
$
$ kubectl get deployments
NAME                  READY   UP-TO-DATE   AVAILABLE   AGE
kubernetes-bootcamp   2/2     2            2           52m
$ kubectl get pods -o wide
NAME                                     READY   STATUS    RESTARTS   AGE   IP
NODE     NOMINATED NODE   READINESS GATES
kubernetes-bootcamp-6f6656d949-jw67g     1/1     Running   0
22m   10.1.46.5   ubuntu   <none>           <none>
kubernetes-bootcamp-6f6656d949-nxgvd     1/1     Running   1
13h   10.1.46.3   ubuntu   <none>           <none>
```

Deleting a service

If you're done using the service, you can delete it. This removes access to the service from the NodePort, but it does not delete the deployment itself. First make sure the service is actually still there, then delete it:

```
$ kubectl get services
NAME                  TYPE       CLUSTER-IP       EXTERNAL-IP  PORT(S)          AGE
kubernetes            ClusterIP 10.152.183.1     <none>           443/
TCP        14h
kubernetes-bootcamp NodePort   10.152.183.233 <none>
8080:30484/TCP    67m
$
$ kubectl delete service kubernetes-bootcamp
service "kubernetes-bootcamp" deleted
```

Finally, make sure the service has been deleted but the deployment still exists:

```
$ kubectl get services
NAME          TYPE       CLUSTER-IP       EXTERNAL-IP  PORT(S)     AGE
kubernetes    ClusterIP  10.152.183.1     <none>       443/TCP     14h
$ kubectl get deployments
NAME                   READY   UP-TO-DATE   AVAILABLE   AGE
kubernetes-bootcamp    2/2     2            2           13h
```

At this point, you should feel comfortable manually querying your Kubernetes cluster in various ways and starting up and working with deployments, pods, and replicas. To continue with more advanced Kubernetes tutorials, return to the main Kubernetes Tutorials page (www.kubernetes.io/docs/tutorials/).

Summary

Over the past few years, Kubernetes has become the platform of choice for deploying containerized applications across large data centers. A Kubernetes cluster consists of master nodes (that direct the activities of a cluster) and worker nodes (that actually run the containerized payloads).

As someone using Kubernetes to run containerized applications, you can create deployments that define the state of the application you are running. For example, you can deploy an application that is configured to run multiple replicas of the pods representing that application. You can identify the application as a service and set up the application to be available from defined ports on the nodes from which they are run.

Supported commercial products based on Kubernetes are available when you need to run mission-critical applications in environments that are stable and supported. Canonical, the company behind Ubuntu, is a major player in this field. Feel free to learn more about what it offers (www.ubuntu.com/kubernetes).

Exercises

The exercises in this section describe tasks related to trying out Kubernetes, either online or by setting up MicroK8s on a computer. If you are stuck, solutions to the tasks are shown

29

in Appendix A. Keep in mind that the solutions shown in Appendix A are usually just one of many ways to complete a task.

1. Install MicroK8s on your local system.

2. Create an alias so you don't have to type `microk8s.kubectl` for each command.

3. Create a deployment that manages a pod running the `hello-node` container image (`gcr.io/hello-minikube-zero-install/hello-node`).

4. Use the appropriate `kubectl` commands to view the `hello-node` deployment and describe the deployment in detail.

5. View the current replica set associated with your `hello-node` deployment.

6. Scale up the `hello-node` deployment to three (3) replicas.

7. Expose the `hello-node` deployment outside of the Kubernetes cluster using `LoadBalancer`.

8. Get the port number of the exposed `hello-node` service.

9. Use the `curl` command to query the `hello-node` service using the IP address and port number from the previous step.

10. Use the `kubectl` commands to delete the `hello-node` service and deployment.

Exercise Answers

Chapter 2: Creating the Perfect Linux Desktop

The following section details some ways that these tasks can be completed on the GNOME 3 desktop.

1. To get started, you need a Linux system in front of you to do the procedures in this book. An installed system is preferable, so you don't lose your changes when you reboot. To start out, you can, for instance, install Ubuntu or launch a live USB session. Here are your choices:

   a. **Ubuntu (GNOME 3):** Install Ubuntu and the GNOME Shell software, as described at the beginning of Chapter 2, "Creating the Perfect Linux Desktop."

   b. Launch a live USB session as described at the beginning of Chapter 2.

2. To launch the Firefox web browser and go to the GNOME home page (www.gnome.org), there are some easy steps to take. If your network is not working, refer to Chapter 14, "Administering Networking," for help on connecting to wired and wireless networks.

   You can press the Windows key to get to the Activities screen. Then type **Firefox** to highlight just the Firefox web browser icon. Press Enter to launch it. Type **gnome.org** in the location box, and press Enter.

3. To pick a background that you like from the GNOME art site (www.gnome-look.org), download it to your Pictures folder and select it as your current background. Do the following:

   a. Type **gnome-look.org/** in the Firefox location box and press Enter.

   b. Find a background that you like and select it. Then click the Download button and download it to your Pictures folder.

   c. Open your Pictures folder, right-click the image, and select Set as Wallpaper.

   The image is used as your desktop background.

4. To start a Nautilus File Manager window and move it to the second workspace on your desktop, do the following:

    a. Press the Windows key.

    b. Select the Files icon from the Dash (left side). A new instance of Nautilus starts in the current workspace.

    c. Right-click the title bar in the Files window and select Move to Monitor Down. The Files window moves to the second workspace.

5. To find the image that you downloaded to use as your desktop background and open it in any image viewer, first go to your Home folder, then open the Pictures folder. Double-click the image to open it in an image viewer.

6. Moving back and forth between the workspace with Firefox on it and the one with the Nautilus file manager is fairly straightforward.

If you did the previous exercises properly, Nautilus and Firefox should be in different workspaces. Here's how you can move between those workspaces:

    a. Press the Windows key.

    b. Select the workspace that you want in the right column.

    c. As an alternative, you can go directly to the application that you want by pressing Alt+Tab and pressing Tab again and also arrow keys, to highlight the application that you want to open.

7. To open a list of applications installed on your system and select an image viewer to open from that list using as few clicks or keystrokes as possible, do the following:

    a. Move the mouse to the upper-left corner of the screen to get to the Activities screen.

    b. Select Applications, then select Utilities from the right column, and then select Image Viewer.

8. To change the view of the windows on your current workspace to smaller views of those windows that you can step through, do the following:

    a. With multiple windows open on multiple workspaces, press the Alt+Tab keys.

    b. While continuing to hold the Alt key, press Tab until you highlight the application that you want.

    c. Release the Alt key to select it.

9. To launch a music player from your desktop using only the keyboard, do the following:

    a. Press the Windows key to go to the Overview screen.

    b. Type `Rhyth` (until the icon appears and is highlighted) and press Enter.

Chapter 3: Using the Shell

1. To switch virtual consoles and return to the desktop, do the following:

    a. Hold Ctrl+Alt and press F3 (Ctrl+Alt+F3). A text-based console should appear.

    b. Type your username (press Enter) and password (press Enter).

c. Type a few commands, such as **id**, **pwd**, and **ls**.

d. Type **exit** to exit the shell and return to the login prompt.

e. Press Ctrl+Alt+F1 to return to the virtual console that holds your desktop. (On different Linux systems, the desktop may be on different virtual consoles. Ctrl+Alt+F7 and Ctrl+Alt+F2 are other common places to find it.)

2. For your Terminal window, make the font red and the background yellow.

a. From the GNOME desktop, click Ctrl+Alt+T to open a Terminal window.

b. From the Terminal window, select Edit ⇨ Preferences.

c. Select the Colors Tab and deselect "Use colors from system theme box."

d. Select the box next to Text Color, click the color red that you want from the available selections, and click Select.

e. Select the box next to Background Color, click the color yellow that you want from the available selections, and click Select.

f. Click Close on the Profile window to go back to the Terminal window with the new colors.

g. Go back and reselect "Use colors from system theme box" to go back to the default Terminal colors.

3. Find the mount command and tracepath man page.

a. Run type mount to see that the mount command's location is either /usr/bin/mount or /bin/mount.

b. Run locate tracepath to see that the tracepath man page is at /usr/share/man/man8/tracepath.8.gz.

4. Run, recall, and change these commands as described:

```
$ cat /etc/passwd
$ ls $HOME
$ date
```

a. Press the up arrow until you see the cat /etc/passwd command. If your cursor is not already at the end of the line, press Ctrl+E to get there. Backspace over the word passwd, type the word **group**, and press Enter.

b. Type **man ls** and find the option to list by time (-t). Press the up arrow until you see the ls $HOME command. Use the left arrow key or Alt+B to position your cursor to the left of $HOME. Type **-t**, so that the line appears as ls -t $HOME. Press Enter to run the command.

c. Type **man date** to view the date man page. Use the up arrow to recall the date command and add the format indicator that you found. A single %D format indicator gets the results you need:

```
$ date +%D
06/27/19
```

5. Use tab completion to type **basename /usr/share/doc/**. Type **basen\<Tab\> / u\<Tab\>sh\<Tab\>do\<Tab\>** to get basename/usr/share/doc/.

6. Pipe /etc/services to the less command: $ cat /etc/services | less.

7. Make output from the date command appear in this format: Today is Thursday, April 23, 2020.

```
$ echo "Today is $(date +'%A, %B %d, %Y')"
```

8. View variables to find your current hostname, username, shell, and home directories.

```
$ echo $HOSTNAME
$ echo $USERNAME
$ echo $SHELL
$ echo $HOME
```

9. Add a permanent mypass alias that displays the contents of the /etc/passwd file.

   a. Type **nano $HOME/.bashrc**.

   b. Move the cursor to an open line at the bottom of the page. (Press Enter to open a new line if needed.)

   c. On its own line, type **alias m="cat /etc/passwd"**.

   d. Type Ctrl+O to save and Ctrl+X to exit the file.

   e. Type **source $HOME/.bashrc**.

   f. Type **alias m** to make sure that the alias was set properly: alias m='cat / etc/passwd'.

   g. Type **m**. (The /etc/passwd file displays on the screen.)

10. To display the man page for the mount system call, use the man -k command to find man pages that include the word mount. Then use the mount command with the correct section number (8) to get the proper mount man page:

```
$ man -k mount | grep ^mount
mount                    (2)  - mount filesystem
mount                    (8)  - mount a filesystem
...
mountpoint               (1)  - see if a directory is a
mountpoint
mountstats               (8)  - Displays various NFS client
per-mount statistics
$ man 2 mount
MOUNT(2)        Linux Programmer's Manual              MOUNT(2)
```

Continues

(continued)

```
NAME
       mount - mount file system
SYNOPSIS
       #include <sys/mount.h>
    .
    .
    .
```

Chapter 4: Moving Around the Filesystem

1. Create the `projects` directory, create nine empty files (house1 to house9), and list just those files.

    ```
    $ mkdir $HOME/projects/
    $ touch $HOME/projects/house{1..9}
    $ ls $HOME/projects/house{1..9}
    ```

2. Make the $HOME/projects/houses/doors/ directory path and create some empty files in that path.

    ```
    $ cd
    $ mkdir $HOME/projects/houses
    $ touch $HOME/projects/houses/bungalow.txt
    $ mkdir $HOME/projects/houses/doors/
    $ touch $HOME/projects/houses/doors/bifold.txt
    $ mkdir -p $HOME/projects/outdoors/vegetation/
    $ touch $HOME/projects/outdoors/vegetation/landscape.txt
    ```

3. Copy the files house1 and house5 to the $HOME/projects/houses/ directory.

    ```
    $ cp $HOME/projects/house[15] $HOME/projects/houses
    ```

4. Recursively copy the /usr/share/doc/initscripts* directory to the $HOME/projects/ directory.

    ```
    $ cp -ra /usr/share/doc/initscripts*/ $HOME/projects/
    ```

5. Recursively list the contents of the $HOME/projects/ directory. Pipe the output to the less command so that you can page through the output.

    ```
    $ ls -lR $HOME/projects/ | less
    ```

6. Move house3 and house4 to the $HOME/projects/houses/doors directory.

    ```
    $ mv $HOME/projects/house{3,4} $HOME/projects/houses/doors/
    ```

7. Remove the $HOME/projects/houses/doors directory and its contents.

    ```
    $ rm -rf $HOME/projects/houses/doors/
    ```

8. Change the permissions on the $HOME/projects/house2 file so that it can be read and written to by the user who owns the file, only read by the group, and have no permission for others.

```
$ chmod 640 $HOME/projects/house2
```

9. Recursively change the permissions of the $HOME/projects/ directory so that nobody has write permission to any files or directories beneath that point in the filesystem.

```
$ chmod -R a-w $HOME/projects/
$ ls -lR $HOME/projects/
/home/joe/projects/:

total 12

-r--r--r--. 1 joe joe    0 Jan 16 06:49 house1

-r--r-----. 1 joe joe    0 Jan 16 06:49 house2

-r--r--r--. 1 joe joe    0 Jan 16 06:49 house5

-r--r--r--. 1 joe joe    0 Jan 16 06:49 house9

dr-xr-xr-x. 2 joe joe 4096 Jan 16 06:57 houses

dr-xr-xr-x. 2 joe joe 4096 Jul  1  2014 initscripts-9.03.40

dr-xr-xr-x. 3 joe joe 4096 Jan 16 06:53 outdoors
...
```

Chapter 5: Working with Text Files

1. Follow these steps to create the /tmp/services file, and then edit it so that "WorldWideWeb" appears as "World Wide Web."

```
$ cp /etc/services /tmp
$ vi /tmp/services
/WorldWideWeb<Enter>
cwWorld Wide Web<Esc>
```

The next two lines show the before and after:

```
http          80/tcp     www www-http   # WorldWideWeb HTTP
http          80/tcp     www www-http   # World Wide Web HTTP
```

2. One way to move the paragraph in your /tmp/services file is to search for the first line of the paragraph, delete five lines (5dd), go to the end of the file (G), and put in the text (p):

```
$ vi /tmp/services
/Note that it is<Enter>
5dd
G
p
```

3. To use ex mode to search for every occurrence of the term tcp (case-sensitive) in your /tmp/services file and change it to WHATEVER, you can enter the following:

```
$ vi /tmp/services
:g/tcp/s//WHATEVER/g<Enter>
```

4. To search the /etc directory for every file named passwd and redirect errors from your search to /dev/null, you can enter the following:

```
$ find /etc -name passwd 2> /dev/null
```

5. Create a directory in your home directory called TEST. Create files in that directory named one, two, and three that have full read/write/execute permissions on for everyone (user, group, and other). Construct a find command that would find those files and any other files that have write permission open to "others" from your home directory and below.

```
$ mkdir $HOME/TEST
$ touch $HOME/TEST/{one,two,three}
$ chmod 777 $HOME/TEST/{one,two,three}
$ find $HOME -perm -002 -type f -ls
148120   0 -rwxrwxrwx  1 chris chris 0 Jan  1 08:56 /home/
chris/TEST/two
         148918   0 -rwxrwxrwx  1 chris chris 0 Jan  1 08:56 home/
chris/TEST/three
         147306   0 -rwxrwxrwx  1 chris chris 0 Jan  1 08:56 /home/
chris/TEST/one
```

6. Find files under the /usr/share/doc directory that have not been modified in more than 300 days.

```
$ find /usr/share/doc -mtime +300
```

7. Create a /tmp/FILES directory. Find all files under the /usr/share directory that are more than 5MB and less than 10MB and copy them to the /tmp/FILES directory.

```
$ mkdir /tmp/FILES
$ find /usr/share -size +5M -size -10M -exec cp {} /
tmp/FILES \;
```

Continues

(continued)

```
$ du -sh /tmp/FILES/*
6.6M    /tmp/FILES/BidiCharacterTest.txt
7.6M    /tmp/FILES/BidiTest.txt
5.2M    /tmp/FILES/day.jpg
```

8. Find every file in the /tmp/FILES directory and make a backup copy of each file in the same directory. Use each file's existing name and append .mybackup to create each backup file.

```
$ find /tmp/FILES/ -type f -exec cp {} {}.mybackup \;
```

Chapter 6: Managing Running Processes

1. To list all processes running on your system with a full set of columns, while piping the output to less, enter the following:

```
$ ps -ef | less
```

2. To list all processes running on the system and sort those processes by the name of the user running each process, enter the following:

```
$ ps -ef --sort=user | less
```

3. To list all processes running on the system with the column names process ID, username, group name, nice value, virtual memory size, resident memory size, and the command, enter the following:

```
$ ps -eo 'pid,user,group,nice,vsz,rss,comm' | less
  PID USER     GROUP      NI    VSZ    RSS COMMAND
    1 root     root        0  19324   1236 init
    2 root     root        0      0      0 kthreadd
    3 root     root        -      0      0 migration/0
    4 root     root        0      0      0 ksoftirqd/0
```

4. To run the top command and then go back and forth between sorting by CPU usage and memory consumption, enter the following:

```
$ top
P
M
P
M
```

5. To start the gedit process from your desktop and use the System Monitor window to kill that process, do the following:

```
$ gedit &
```

Next, from the Activities screen, type System Monitor and press Enter. Find the gedit process on the Processes tab. (You can sort alphabetically to make it easier by clicking the Process Name heading.) Right-click the gedit command, and then select either End Process or Kill Process; the gedit window on your screen should disappear.

6. To run the `gedit` process and use the `kill` command to send a signal to pause (stop) that process, enter the following:

```
$ gedit &
[1] 21532

$ kill -SIGSTOP 21532
```

7. To use the `killall` command to tell the `gedit` command (paused in the previous exercise) to continue working, do the following:

```
$ killall -SIGCONT gedit
```

Make sure that the text you typed after `gedit` was paused now appears in the window.

8. As a regular user, run the `gedit` command so that it starts with a nice value of 5.

```
# nice -n 5 gedit &
[1] 21578
```

9. To use the `renice` command to change the nice value of the `gedit` command you just started to 7, enter the following:

```
# renice -n 7 21578
21578: old priority 0, new priority 7
```

Use any command you like to verify that the current nice value for the `gedit` command is now set to 7. For example, you could type the following:

```
# ps -eo 'pid,user,nice,comm' | grep gedit
21578 chris      7 gedit
```

Chapter 7: Writing Simple Shell Scripts

1. Here's an example of how to create a script in your $HOME/bin directory called `myownscript`. When the script runs, it should output information that appears as follows:

```
Today is Sat Jun 10 15:45:04 EDT 2019.
You are in /home/joe and your host is abc.example.com.
```

The following steps show one way to create the script named `myownscript`:

a. If it doesn't already exist, create a bin directory:

```
$ mkdir $HOME/bin
```

b. Using any text editor, create a script called $HOME/bin/myownscript that contains the following:

```
#!/bin/bash
# myownscript
# List some information about your current system
echo "Today is $(date)."
echo "You are in $(pwd) and your host is $(hostname)."
```

   c. Make the script executable:

```
$ chmod 755 $HOME/bin/myownscript
```

2. To create a script that reads in three positional parameters from the command line, assigns those parameters to variables named ONE, TWO, and THREE, respectively, and then outputs that information in the specified format, do the following:

Replace X with the number of parameters and Y with all of the parameters entered. Then replace A with the contents of variable ONE, B with variable TWO, and C with variable THREE.

   a. Here is an example of what that script could contain:

```
#!/bin/bash
# myposition
ONE=$1
TWO=$2
THREE=$3
echo "There are $# parameters that include: $@"
echo "The first is $ONE, the second is $TWO, the third
is $THREE."
```

   b. To create a script called $HOME/bin/myposition and make the script executable, enter the following:

```
$ chmod 755 $HOME/bin/myposition
```

   c. To test it, run it with some command-line arguments, as in the following:

```
$ myposition Where Is My Hat Buddy?
There are 5 parameters that include: Where Is My Hat Buddy?
The first is Where, the second is Is, the third is My.
```

3. To create the script described, do the following:

   a. To create a file called $HOME/bin/myhome and make it executable, enter the following:

```
$ touch $HOME/bin/myhome
$ chmod 755 $HOME/bin/myhome
```

   b. Here's what the script myhome might look like:

```
#!/bin/bash
# myhome
read -p "What street did you grow up on? " mystreet
read -p "What town did you grow up in? " mytown
echo "The street I grew up on was $mystreet and the town
was $mytown."
```

   c. Run the script to check that it works. The following example shows what the input and output for the script could look like:

```
$ myhome
What street did you grow up on? Harrison
```

What town did you grow up in? Princeton
The street I grew up on was Harrison and the town was Princeton.

4. To create the required script, do the following:

a. Using any text editor, create a script called $HOME/bin/myos and make the script executable:

```
$ touch $HOME/bin/myos
$ chmod 755 $HOME/bin/myos
```

b. The script could contain the following:

```
#!/bin/bash
# myos
read -p "What is your favorite operating system, Mac,
Windows or Linux? " opsys
if [ $opsys = Mac ] ; then
   echo "Mac is nice, but not tough enough for me."
elif [ $opsys = Windows ] ; then
   echo "I used Windows once. What is that blue
screen for?"
elif [ $opsys = Linux ] ; then
   echo "Great Choice!"
else
   echo "Is $opsys an operating system?"
fi
```

5. To create a script named $HOME/bin/animals that runs through the words *moose*, *cow*, *goose*, and *sow* through a for loop and have each of those words appended to the end of the line, "I have a...," do the following:

a. Make the script executable:

```
$ touch $HOME/bin/animals
$ chmod 755 $HOME/bin/animals
```

b. The script could contain the following:

```
#!/bin/bash
# animals
for ANIMALS in moose cow goose sow ; do
   echo "I have a $ANIMALS"
done
```

c. When you run the script, the output should appear as follows:

```
$ animals
I have a moose
I have a cow
I have a goose
I have a sow
```

Chapter 8: Learning System Administration

1. To enable Cockpit on your system, enter the following:

```
# systemctl enable --now cockpit.socket
Created symlink /etc/systemd/system/sockets.target.wants/
cockpit.socket
    /usr/lib/systemd/system/cockpit.socket
```

2. To open the Cockpit interface in your web browser, enter the hostname or IP address of the system holding your Cockpit service, followed by port number 9090. For example, enter this into the location box of your browser:

```
https://host1.example.com:9090/
```

3. To find all of the files under the /var/spool directory that are owned by users other than root and do a long listing of them, enter the following. (I recommend becoming root to find files that might be closed off to other users.)

```
$ su -
Password: *********
# find /var/spool -not -user root -ls | less
```

4. To become root user and create an empty or plain-text file named /etc/test.txt, enter the following:

```
$ sudo su
Password: *********
# touch /etc/test.txt
# ls -l /etc/test.txt
-rw-r--r--. 1 root root 0 Jan  9 21:51 /etc/test.txt
```

5. To become root and edit the /etc/sudoers file to allow your regular user account (for example, bill) to have full root privilege via the sudo command, do the following:

```
$ sudo su
Password: *********
# visudo
o
bill      ALL=(ALL)      ALL
Esc ZZ
```

Because visudo opens the /etc/sudoers file in vi, the example types o to open a line, and then it types in the line to allow bill to have full root privilege. After the line is typed, press ESC to return to command mode and type **ZZ** to write and quit.

6. To use the sudo command to create a file called /etc/test2.txt and verify that the file is there and owned by the root user, enter the following:

```
[bill]$ sudo touch /etc/test2.txt
We trust you have received the usual lecture from the local System
```

```
Administrator. It usually boils down to these three things:
    #1) Respect the privacy of others.
    #2) Think before you type.
    #3) With great power comes great responsibility.
[sudo] password for bill:  *********
[bill]$ ls -l /etc/text2.txt
-rw-r--r--. 1 root root 0 Jan  9 23:37 /etc/text2.txt
```

7. Do the following to mount and unmount a USB drive and watch the system journal during this process:

   a. Run the `journalctl -f` command as root in a Terminal window and watch the output from here for the next few steps.

```
# journalctl -f
Jan 25 16:07:59 host2 kernel: usb 1-1.1: new high-speed USB device
    number 16 using ehci-pci
Jan 25 16:07:59 host2 kernel: usb 1-1.1: New USB device found,
    idVendor=0ea0, idProduct=2168
Jan 25 16:07:59 host2 kernel: usb 1-1.1: New USB device strings:
    Mfr=1, Product=2, SerialNumber=3
Jan 25 16:07:59 host2 kernel: usb 1-1.1: Product: Flash Disk
Jan 25 16:07:59 host2 kernel: usb 1-1.1: Manufacturer: USB
...
Jan 25 16:08:01 host2 kernel: sd 18:0:0:0: [sdb] Write Protect is off
Jan 25 16:08:01 host2 kernel: sd 18:0:0:0: [sdb]
    Assuming drive cache: write through
Jan 25 16:08:01 host2 kernel:  sdb: sdb1
Jan 25 16:08:01 host2 kernel: sd 18:0:0:0: [sdb]
    Attached SCSI removable disk
```

   b. Plug in a USB storage drive, which will mount a filesystem from that drive automatically. If it does not, run the following commands in a second terminal (as root) to create a mount point directory and mount the device:

```
$ mkdir /media/test
$ mount /dev/sdb1 /media/test
$ umount /dev/sdb1
```

8. To see what USB devices are connected to your computer, enter the following:

```
$ lsusb
```

9. To load the `bttv` module, list the modules that were loaded, and unload it, enter the following:

```
# modprobe -a bttv
# lsmod | grep bttv
ttv                 167936  0
tea575x              16384  1 bttv
tveeprom             28672  1 bttv
```

Continues

(continued)

```
videobuf_dma_sg        24576  1 bttv
videobuf_core          32768  2 videobuf_dma_sg,bttv
v4l2_common            16384  1 bttv
videodev              233472  3 tea575x,v4l2_common,bttv
i2c_algo_bit           16384  1 bttv
```

Notice that other modules (v4l2_common, videodev, and others) were loaded when you loaded bttv with modprobe -a.

10. Enter the following to remove the bttv module along with any other modules that were loaded with it. Notice that they were all gone after running modprobe -r.

```
# modprobe -r bttv
# lsmod | grep bttv
```

Chapter 9: Installing Linux

1. To install Ubuntu desktop from a downloaded ISO, follow these steps:

   a. If necessary, download a desktop ISO image from ubuntu.com/#download.

   b. If necessary, install VirtualBox on your computer.

   c. In VirtualBox, click New, enter a name for your new VM, and set the type and version. The default memory and hard disk settings should be fine as they are.

   d. With your new VM selected in the main VirtualBox menu, click the green Start button.

   e. Click the folder icon on the "Select start-up disk" page and choose the Ubuntu ISO image you downloaded from your local filesystem.

   f. A terminal will open where Ubuntu's Ubiquity install program will guide you through the installation process.

   g. When you're done, reboot the VM to confirm everything worked.

   h. If desired, "Close" the VM from the main VirtualBox menu and then remove it.

2. To update the packages, after the Ubuntu installation is complete, do the following:

   a. Reboot the computer and log in using your new primary account.

   b. Using a wired or wireless connection, make sure that you have a connection to the Internet. Refer to Chapter 14, "Administering Networking," if you have trouble getting your networking connection to work properly. Open a shell as the root user and type **sudo apt update**.

   c. When prompted, type **y** to accept the list of packages displayed. The system begins downloading and installing the packages.

3. To run the Ubuntu installation in text mode, do the following:

   a. If necessary, download a server ISO image from ubuntu.com/#download.

   b. If necessary, install VirtualBox on your computer.

   c. Follow the remaining steps from the first exercise and from the chapter.

4. To set the disk partitioning as described in Exercise 4 for an Ubuntu installation, do the following:

NOTE

The procedure in Exercise 4 ultimately deletes all content on your hard disk. If you just want to use this exercise to practice partitioning, you can reboot your computer before starting the actual installation process without harming your hard disk. After you go forward and partition your disk, assume that all data has been deleted.

---

    a. Using a storage drive that you can erase or a VirtualBox VM with at least 10GB of disk space, start the Ubuntu install process.

    b. Select "Something else" from the Installation type page and then select New Partition Table.

    c. If the existing disk space is already consumed, you need to delete the partitions before proceeding (by clicking the minus (–) button at the bottom of the screen with the appropriate drive selected).

    d. To create new partitions, click the plus (+) button at the bottom of the screen. Then add and define each of the following mount points:

```
/boot - 400M
/ - 3G
/var - 2G
/home -2G
```

    e. Select Done. You should see a summary of changes.

    f. If the changes look acceptable, select Accept Changes. If you are just practicing and don't actually want to change your partitions, select Cancel & Return to Custom Partitioning. Then simply exit the installer.

Chapter 10: Getting and Managing Software

1. To search for a package that contains the `pdftoppm` command, enter the following:

```
# apt search pdftoppm
```

2. To display information about the package that provides the `pdftoppm` command and determine that package's home page (URL), enter the following:

```
# apt show poppler-utils
```

You will see that the URL to the home page for Poppler-Utils is `poppler .freedesktop.org/`.

3. To install the package containing the `pdftoppm` command, enter the following:

```
$ sudo apt install poppler-utils
```

4. To delete the `pdftoppm` command from your system and verify its package against the APT database to see that the command is indeed missing, enter the following:

```
$ sudo apt remove poppler-utils
$ dpkg -l poppler-utils
```

5. To reinstall the package that provides the `pdftoppm` command and make sure that the entire package is intact again, enter the following:

```
$ sudo apt install poppler-utils
$ dpkg -l poppler-utils
```

Chapter 11: Managing User Accounts

1. To add a local user account to your Linux system, run `adduser` against `jbaxter` setting the full name to John Baxter and the password, when prompted, to: My1N1teOut! You'll then run `usermod -s` to apply the csh shell to the user. You can confirm success by viewing the `passed` file.

```
# adduser jbaxter
Adding user 'jbaxter' ...
Adding new group 'jbaxter' (1002) ...
Adding new user 'jbaxter' (1001) with group 'jbaxter' ...
Creating home directory '/home/jbaxter' ...
Copying files from '/etc/skel' ...
Enter new UNIX password:
Retype new UNIX password:
passwd: password updated successfully
Changing the user information for jbaxter
Enter the new value, or press ENTER for the default
        Full Name []: John Baxter
        Room Number []:
        Work Phone []:
        Home Phone []:
        Other []:
Is the information correct? [Y/n]
adduser -c "John Baxter" -s /bin/sh jbaxter
# usermod -s /bin/csh jbaxter
# grep jbaxter /etc/passwd
jbaxter:x:1001:1001:John Baxter:/home/jbaxter:/bin/sh
```

2. To create a group account named `testing` that uses group ID 315, enter the following:

```
# addgroup --gid 315 testing
# grep testing /etc/group
testing:x:315:
```

3. To add `jbaxter` to the `testing` group and the `bin` group, enter the following:

   ```
   # usermod -aG testing,bin jbaxter
   # grep jbaxter /etc/group
   bin:x:1:bin,daemon,jbaxter
   jbaxter:x:1001:
   testing:x:315:jbaxter
   ```

4. To become `jbaxter` and temporarily have the `testing` group be `jbaxter`'s default group, run `touch /home/jbaxter/file.txt` so that the `testing` group is assigned as the file's group, and do the following:

   ```
   $ su - jbaxter
   Password: My1N1teOut!
   sh-4.2$ newgrp testing
   sh-4.2$ touch /home/jbaxter/file.txt
   sh-4.2$ ls -l /home/baxter/file.txt
   -rw-rw-r--. 1 jbaxter testing 0 Jan 25 06:42 /home/
   jbaxter/file.txt
   sh-4.2$ exit ; exit
   ```

5. Note what user ID has been assigned to `jbaxter`, and then delete the user account without deleting the home directory assigned to `jbaxter`:

   ```
   $ deluser jbaxter
   ```

6. Use the following command to find any files in the `/home` directory (and any subdirectories) that are assigned to the user ID that recently belonged to the user named `jbaxter`. (When I did it, the UID/GID were both 1001; yours may differ.) Notice that the username `jbaxter` is no longer assigned on the system, so any files that user created are listed as belonging to UID 1001 and GID 1001, except for a couple of files that were assigned to the `testing` group because of the `newgrp` command run earlier:

   ```
   # find /home -uid 1001 -ls
   262184  4 drwx------ 4 1001  1001  4096 Jan 25 08:00 /
   home/jbaxter
   262193  4 -rw-r--r-- 1 1001  1001   176 Jan 27  2011 /
   home/jbaxter/.bash_profile
   262196  4 -rw------- 1 13602 testing 93 Jan 25 08:00 /
   home/jbaxter/.bash_history
   262194  0 -rw-rw-r-- 1 13602 testing  0 Jan 25 07:59 /
   home/jbaxter/file.txt
       ...
   ```

7. Run these commands to copy the `/etc/services` file to the `/etc/skel/` directory; then add a new user to the system named `mjones`, with a full name of Mary Jones and a home directory of `/home/maryjones`. List her home directory to make sure that the services file is there.

   ```
   # cp /etc/services /etc/skel/
   # adduser mjones
   ```

   (continues)

(continued)

```
# ls -l /home/maryjones
total 628
-rw-r--r--. 1 mjones mjones 640999 Jan 25 06:27 services
```

8. Run the following command to find all files under the /home directory that belong to mjones. If you did the exercises in order, notice that after you deleted the user with the highest user ID and group ID, those numbers were assigned to mjones. As a result, any files left on the system by jbaxter now belong to mjones. (For this reason, you should remove or change ownership of files left behind when you delete a user.)

```
# find /home -user mjones -ls
262184 4 drwx------ 4 mjones mjones 4096 Jan 25 08:00 /
home/jbaxter
262193 4 -rw-r--r-- 1 mjones mjones 176 Jan 27 2011 /home/
jbaxter/.bash_profile
262189 4 -rw-r--r-- 1 mjones mjones 18 Jan 27 2011 /home/
jbaxter/.bash_logout
262194 0 -rw-rw-r-- 1 mjones testing 0 Jan 25 07:59 /home/
jbaxter/file.txt
262188 4 -rw-r--r-- 1 mjones mjones 124 Jan 27 2011 /home/
jbaxter/.bashrc
262197 4 drwx------ 4 mjones  mjones 4096 Jan 25 08:27 /
home/maryjones
262207 4 -rw-r--r-- 1 mjones mjones 176 Jan 27 2011 /home/
maryjones/.bash_profile
262202 4 -rw-r--r-- 1 mjones mjones 18 Jan 27 2011 /home/
maryjones/.bash_logout
262206 628 -rw-r--r-- 1 mjones mjones 640999 Jan 25 08:27
/home/maryjones/services
262201 4 -rw-r--r-- 1 mjones mjones 124 Jan 27 2011 /home/
maryjones/.bashrc
```

9. As the user mjones, you can use the following to create a file called /tmp/mary-file.txt and use ACLs to assign the bin user read/write permission and the lp group read/write permission to that file:

```
[mjones]$ touch /tmp/maryfile.txt
[mjones]$ setfacl -m u:bin:rw /tmp/maryfile.txt
[mjones]$ setfacl -m g:lp:rw /tmp/maryfile.txt
[mjones]$ getfacl /tmp/maryfile.txt
# file: tmp/maryfile.txt
# owner: mjones
# group: mjones
user::rw-
user:bin:rw-
group::rw-
group:lp:rw-
```

```
mask::rw-
other::r-
```

10. Run this set of commands (as `mjones`) to create a directory named `/tmp/mydir` and use ACLs to assign default permissions to it so that the `adm` user has read/write/execute permission to that directory and any files or directories created in it. Test that it worked by creating the `/tmp/mydir/testing/` directory and `/tmp/mydir/newfile.txt`.

```
[mary]$ mkdir /tmp/mydir
[mary]$ setfacl -m d:u:adm:rwx /tmp/mydir
[mjones]$ getfacl /tmp/mydir
# file: tmp/mydir
# owner: mjones
# group: mjones
user::rwx
group::rwx
other::r-x
default:user::rwx
default:user:adm:rwx
default:group::rwx
default:mask::rwx
default:other::r-x
[mjones]$ mkdir /tmp/mydir/testing
[mjones]$ touch /tmp/mydir/newfile.txt
[mjones]$ getfacl /tmp/mydir/testing/
# file: tmp/mydir/testing/
# owner: mjones
# group: mjones
user::rwx
user:adm:rwx
group::rwx
mask::rwx
other::r-x
default:user::rwx
default:user:adm:rwx
default:group::rwx
default:mask::rwx
default:other::r-x
[mjones]$ getfacl /tmp/mydir/newfile.txt
# file: tmp/mydir/newfile.txt
# owner: mjones
# group: mjones
user::rw-
user:adm:rwx        #effective:rw-
group::rwx          #effective:rw-
mask::rw-
other::r--
```

Notice that the adm user effectively has only rw- permission. To remedy that, you need to expand the permissions of the mask. One way to do that is with the chmod command, as follows:

```
[mjones]$ chmod 775 /tmp/mydir/newfile.txt
[mjones]$ getfacl /tmp/mydir/newfile.txt
# file: tmp/mydir/newfile.txt
# owner: mjones
# group: mjones
user::rwx
user:adm:rwx
group::rwx
mask::rwx
other::r-x
```

Chapter 12: Managing Disks and Filesystems

1. To determine the device name of a USB flash drive that you want to insert into your computer, enter the following and insert the USB flash drive. (Press Ctrl+C after you have seen the appropriate messages.)

```
# journalctl -f
kernel: [sdb] 15667200 512-byte logical blocks:
    (8.02 GB/7.47 GiB)
Feb 11 21:55:59 cnegus kernel: sd 7:0:0:0:
    [sdb] Write Protect is off
Feb 11 21:55:59 cnegus kernel: [sdb] Assuming
    drive cache: write through
Feb 11 21:55:59 cnegus kernel: [sdb] Assuming
    drive cache: write through
```

2. To list partitions on the USB flash drive, enter the following:

```
# fdisk -l /dev/sdb
```

3. To delete partitions on the USB flash drive, assuming device /dev/sdb, do the following:

```
# fdisk /dev/sdb
Command (m for help): d
Partition number (1-6): 6
Command (m for help): d
Partition number (1-5): 5
Command (m for help): d
Partition number (1-5): 4
Command (m for help): d
Partition number (1-4): 3
Command (m for help): d
Partition number (1-4): 2
Command (m for help): d
```

```
Selected partition 1
Command (m for help): w
# partprobe /dev/sdb
```

4. To add a 100MB Linux partition, 200MB swap partition, and 500MB LVM partition to the USB flash drive, enter the following:

```
# fdisk /dev/sdb

Command (m for help): n
Command action
   e   extended
   p   primary partition (1-4)

p
Partition number (1-4): 1
First sector (2048-15667199, default 2048):  <ENTER>
Last sector, +sectors or +size{K,M,G} (default 15667199): +100M
Command (m for help): n
Command action
   e   extended
   p   primary partition (1-4)

p
Partition number (1-4): 2
First sector (616448-8342527, default 616448):  <ENTER>
Last sector, +sectors or +size{K,M,G} (default 15667199): +200M
Command (m for help): n
Command action
   e   extended
   p   primary partition (1-4)

p
Partition number (1-4): 3
First sector (616448-15667199, default 616448):  <ENTER>
Using default value 616448
Last sector, +sectors or +size{K,M,G} (default 15667199): +500M
Command (m for help): t
Partition number (1-4): 2
Hex code (type L to list codes): 82
Changed system type of partition 2 to 82 (Linux swap / Solaris)
Command (m for help): t
Partition number (1-4): 3
Hex code (type L to list codes): 8e
Changed system type of partition 3 to 8e (Linux LVM)
Command (m for help): w
# partprobe /dev/sdb
# grep sdb /proc/partitions
```

Continues

(continued)

```
8       16      7833600 sdb
8       17       102400 sdb1
8       18       204800 sdb2
8       19       512000 sdb3
```

5. To put an ext4 filesystem on the Linux partition, enter the following:

   ```
   # mkfs -t ext4 /dev/sdb1
   ```

6. To create a mount point called /mnt/mypart and mount the Linux partition on it, do the following:

   ```
   # mkdir /mnt/mypart
   # mount -t ext4 /dev/sdb1 /mnt/mypart
   ```

7. To enable the swap partition and turn it on so that additional swap space is immediately available, enter the following:

   ```
   # mkswap /dev/sdb2
   # swapon /dev/sdb2
   ```

8. To create a volume group called abc from the LVM partition, create a 200MB logical volume from that group called data, create a VFAT filesystem on it, temporarily mount the logical volume on a new directory named /mnt/test, and then check that it was successfully mounted, enter the following:

   ```
   # pvcreate /dev/sdb3
   # vgcreate abc /dev/sdb3
   # lvcreate -n data -L 200M abc
   # mkfs -t vfat /dev/mapper/abc-data
   # mkdir /mnt/test
   # mount /dev/mapper/abc-data /mnt/test
   ```

9. To grow the logical volume from 200MB to 300MB, enter the following:

   ```
   # lvextend -L +100M /dev/mapper/abc-data
   # resize2fs -p /dev/mapper/abc-data
   ```

10. To remove the USB flash drive safely from the computer, do the following:

    ```
    # umount /dev/sdb1
    # swapoff /dev/sdb2
    # umount /mnt/test
    # lvremove /dev/mapper/abc-data
    # vgremove abc
    # pvremove /dev/sdb3
    ```

You can now safely remove the USB flash drive from the computer.

Chapter 13: Understanding Server Administration

1. To log in to any account on another computer using the ssh command, enter the following and then enter the password when prompted:

   ```
   $ ssh joe@localhost
   joe@localhost's password:
   ```

```
********
[joe]$
```

2. To run the `uname -a` command on the remote system and display the output locally using remote execution with the `ssh` command, do the following:

```
$ ssh joe@192.168.1.5 "uname -a"
joe@192.168.1.5's password:
Linux workstation 5.3.0-42-generic #34~18.04.1-Ubuntu SMP
Fri Feb 28 13:42:26 UTC 2020 x86_64 x86_64 x86_64 GNU/Linux
```

3. With the `/etc/ssh/sshd_config` file on the host system appropriately edited (as shown in the chapter), to use X11 forwarding to display a `gedit` window on your local system and then save a file on the remote home directory, do the following:

```
$ ssh -X joe@localhost "gedit newfile"
joe@localhost's password: ********
$ ssh joe@localhost "cat newfile"
joe@localhost's password: ********
This is text from the file I saved in joe's remote
home directory
```

4. To copy all of the files from the `/etc/apt/` directory recursively on a remote system to the `/tmp` directory on your local system in such a way that all of the modification times on the files are updated to the time on the local system when they are copied, do the following:

```
$ scp -r joe@localhost:/etc/apt/ /tmp
joe@localhost's password:
 ********
apt
size
$ ls -l /tmp/apt | head
total 48
drwxr-xr-x 2 root root  4096 Mar 29 13:40 apt.conf.d
drwxr-xr-x 2 root root  4096 Mar 29 13:40 auth.conf.d
drwxr-xr-x 2 root root  4096 Mar 29 13:40 preferences.d
-rw-r--r-- 1 root root  2904 Mar 29 13:40 sources.list
drwxr-xr-x 2 root root  4096 Mar 29 13:40 sources.list.d
-rw-r--r-- 1 root root 11024 Mar 29 13:40 trusted.gpg
drwxr-xr-x 2 root root  4096 Mar 29 13:40 trusted.gpg.d
-rw-r--r-- 1 root root  9815 Mar 29 13:40 trusted.gpg~
```

5. To copy all of the files from the `/usr/share/logwatch` directory recursively on a remote system to the `/tmp` directory on your local system in such a way that all of the modification times on the files from the remote system are maintained on the local system, try the following:

```
$ rsync -av joe@localhost:/usr/share/logwatch /tmp
joe@localhost's password: ********
```

Continues

(continued)

```
receiving incremental file list
logwatch/
logwatch/default.conf/
logwatch/default.conf/logwatch.conf
$ ls -l /tmp/logwatch | head
total 16
drwxr-xr-x. 5 root root 4096 Apr 19  2011 default.conf
drwxr-xr-x. 4 root root 4096 Feb 28  2011 dist.conf
drwxr-xr-x. 2 root root 4096 Apr 19  2011 lib
```

6. To create a public/private key pair to use for SSH communications (no passphrase on the key), copy the public key file to a remote user's account with `ssh-copy-id`, and use key-based authentication to log in to that user account without having to enter a password, use the following code:

```
$ ssh-keygen
Generating public/private rsa key pair.
Enter file in which to save the key (/home/joe/.ssh/id_
rsa): ENTER
/home/joe/.ssh/id_rsa already exists.
Enter passphrase (empty for no passphrase): ENTER
Enter same passphrase again: ENTER
Your identification has been saved in /home/joe/.ssh/id_rsa.
Your public key has been saved in /home/joe/.ssh/id_rsa.pub.
The key fingerprint is:
58:ab:c1:95:b6:10:7a:aa:7c:c5:ab:bd:f3:4f:89:1e joe@cnegus.csb
The key's randomart image is:
...
$ ssh-copy-id -i ~/.ssh/id_rsa.pub joe@localhost
joe@localhost's password: ********
Now try logging into the machine, with "ssh 'joe@localhost'",
and check in:
.ssh/authorized_keys
to make sure we haven't added extra keys that you weren't
expecting.
$ ssh joe@localhost
$ cat .ssh/authorized_keys
ssh-rsa AAAAB3NzaC1yc2EAAAABIwAAAQEAyN2Psp5/LRUC9E8BDCx53yPUa0qoOPd

v6H4sF3vmn04V6E7D1iXpzwPzdo4rpvmR1ZiinHR2xGAEr2uZag7feKgLn
ww2KPcQ6S
iR7lzrOhQjV+SGb/a1dxrIeZqKMq1Tk01G4EvboIrq//9J47vI4l7iN
u0xRmjI3TTxa
```

        DdCTbpG6J3uSJm1BKzdUtwb413k35W2bRgMI75aIdeBsDgQBBiOdu+
zuTMrXJj2viCA
        XeJ7gIwRvBaMQdOSvSdlkX353tmIjmJheWdgCccM/1jKdoELpaevg9a
nCe/yUP3so31
        tTo4I+qTfzAQD5+66oqW0LgMkWVvfZI7dUz3WUPmcMw== chris@abc
.example.com

7. To create an entry in /etc/rsyslog.d/50-default.conf that stores all authentication messages at the info level and higher into a file named /var/log/
   myauth, do the following. Watch from one terminal as the data comes in.

   ```
   # vim /etc/rsyslog.conf
   authpriv.info                              /var/log/myauth
   # service rsyslog restart
       or
   # systemctl restart rsyslog.service
   <Terminal 1>                               <Terminal 2>
   # tail -f /var/log/myauth                  $ ssh
   joe@localhost
   Apr 18 06:19:34 abc unix_chkpwd[30631]     joe@
   localhost's password:
   Apr 18 06:19:34 abc sshd[30631]            Permission
   denied,try again
       :pam_unix(sshd:auth):
       authentication failure;logname= uid=501
       euid=501 tty=ssh ruser= rhost=localhost
       user=joe
   Apr 18 06:19:34 abc sshd[30631]:
   Failed password for joe from
   127.0.0.1 port 5564 ssh2
   ```

8. To determine the largest directory structures under /usr/share, sort them from
   largest to smallest, and list the top 10 of those directories in terms of size using
   the du command, enter the following:

   ```
   $ du -s /usr/share/* | sort -rn | head
   527800 /usr/share/locale
   277108 /usr/share/fonts
   196232 /usr/share/help

   134984 /usr/share/backgrounds
   ...
   ```

9. To show the space that is used and available from all of the filesystems currently
   attached to the local system, but exclude any tmpfs or devtmpfs filesystems by
   using the df command, enter the following:

   ```
   $ df -h -x tmpfs -x devtmpfs
   Filesystem      Size  Used Avail Use% Mounted on
   /deev/sda4       20G  4.2G  16G   22% /
   ```

10. To find any files in the /usr directory that are more than 10MB in size, do the following:

```
$ find /usr -size +10M
/usr/bin/qemu-system-x86_64
/usr/bin/lxc
/usr/bin/pandoc
/usr/bin/node
/usr/bin/snap
/usr/bin/qemu-system-i386
/usr/lib/debug/lib/x86_64-linux-gnu/libc-2.27.so
/usr/lib/gcc/x86_64-linux-gnu/7/cc1
/usr/lib/gcc/x86_64-linux-gnu/7/lto1
/usr/lib/gcc/x86_64-linux-gnu/7/cc1plus
/usr/lib/i386-linux-gnu/libnvidia-opencl.so.340.108
/usr/lib/snapd/snapd
/usr/lib/jvm/java-11-openjdk-amd64/lib/modules
/usr/lib/jvm/java-11-openjdk-amd64/lib/server/classes.jsa
/usr/lib/jvm/java-11-openjdk-amd64/lib/server/libjvm.so
/usr/lib/mono/aot-cache/amd64/mscorlib.dll.so
/usr/lib/libgdal.so.20.3.2
/usr/lib/lxd/lxd
```

Chapter 14: Administering Networking

1. To use the desktop to check that NetworkManager has successfully started your network interface (wired or wireless), do the following:

   a. Left-click the upper-right corner of your GNOME desktop to see the drop-down menu. Any active wired or wireless network connections should appear on that menu.

   b. If it has not connected to the network, select from the list of wired or wireless networks available, and then enter the username and password, if prompted, to start an active connection.

2. To run a command to check the active network interfaces available on your computer, enter the following:

   ```
   $ ifconfig
   ```
   or

   ```
   $ ip addr show
   ```

3. Try to contact www.google.com from the command line in a way that ensures that DNS is working properly:

   ```
   $ ping google.com
   Ctrl-C
   ```

4. To run a command to check the routes being used to communicate outside of your local network, enter the following:

   ```
   $ route
   ```

5. To trace the route being taken to connect to google.com, use the traceroute command:

```
$ traceroute google.com
```

6. To view the network interfaces and related network activities for your Linux system through Cockpit, open a web browser to port 9090 using an IP address or hostname. For example: https://localhost:9090/network.

7. To create a host entry that allows you to communicate with your local host system using the name myownhost, edit the /etc/hosts file (nano /etc/hosts) and add myownhost to the end of the localhost entry so that it appears as follows (then ping myownhost to see if it worked):

```
127.0.0.1                localhost.localdomain localhost myownhost
# ping myownhost
Ctrl+C
```

8. To see the DNS name servers being used to resolve hostnames and IP addresses on your system (yours will be different than those shown here), enter the following:

```
# cat /etc/resolv.conf
    nameserver 10.83.14.9
    nameserver 10.18.2.10
    nameserver 192.168.1.254
    # dig google.com
    ...
    google.com.     91941     IN     NS     ns3.google.com.
    ;; Query time: 0 msec
    ;; SERVER: 10.18.2.9#53(10.18.2.9)
    ;; WHEN: Sat Nov 23 20:18:56 EST 2019
    ;; MSG SIZE  rcvd: 276
```

9. To check to see if your system has been configured to allow IPv4 packets to be routed between network interfaces on your system, enter the following:

```
# cat /proc/sys/net/ipv4/ip_forward
0
```

A 0 shows that IPv4 packet forwarding is disabled; a 1 shows that it is enabled.

Chapter 15: Starting and Stopping Services

1. To determine which initialization daemon your server is currently using, consider the following:

   a. In most cases today, PID 1 appears as the systemd daemon:

```
# ps -e | head
    PID TTY          TIME CMD
      1 ?        00:00:37 systemd
```

Continues

(continued)

```
2 ?          00:00:00 kthreadd
3 ?          00:00:00 rcu_gp
```

    b. Most likely, you have the Upstart, SysVinit, or BSD init daemon if your `init` daemon is not `systemd`. But double-check at www.wikipedia.org/wiki/Init.

2. The tools you use to manage services depend primarily on which initialization system is in use. Try to run the `systemctl` and `service` commands to determine the type of initialization script in use for the `ssh` service on your system:

    a. For `systemd`, a positive result, shown here, means that the `sshd` has been converted to `systemd`:

```
# systemctl status sshd.service
sshd.service - OpenSSH server daemon
    Loaded: loaded (/lib/systemd/system/sshd.service;
enabled)
    Active: active (running) since Mon, 20 Apr 2020
12:35:20...
```

    b. If you don't see positive results for the preceding test, try the following command for the SysVinit `init` daemon. A positive result here, along with negative results for the preceding tests, means that `sshd` is still using the SysVinit daemon.

```
# service ssh status
sshd (pid 2390) is running...
```

3. To determine your server's previous and current runlevel, use the `runlevel` command. It still works on all `init` daemons:

```
$ runlevel
N 3
```

4. To change the default runlevel or target unit on your Linux server, you can do one of the following (depending upon your server's `init` daemon):

    a. For SysVinit, edit the file `/etc/inittab` and change the # in the line `id:#:initdefault:` to 2, 3, 4, or 5.

    b. For `systemd`, change the `default.target` to the desired `runlevel#.target`, where # is 2, 3, 4, or 5. The following shows you how to change the target unit to `runlevel3.target`:

```
# systemctl set-default runlevel3.target
Removed /etc/systemd/system/default.target.
Created symlink /etc/systemd/system/default.target →
/usr/lib/systemd/system/multi-user.target.
```

5. To list services running (or active) on your server, you need to use different commands, depending upon the initialization daemon you are using.

    a. For SysVinit, use the `service` command as shown in this example:

```
# service --status-all | grep running | sort
anacron (pid 2162) is running...
atd (pid 2172) is running...
```

    b. For systemd, use the `systemctl` command, as follows:

```
# systemctl list-unit-files --type=service | grep
-v disabled
UNIT FILE                                  STATE
abrt-ccpp.service                          enabled
abrt-oops.service                          enabled
...
```

6. To list the running (or active) services on your Linux server, use the appropriate command(s) determined in answer 5 for the initialization daemon that your server is using.

7. For each initialization daemon, the following command(s) show a particular service's current status:

    a. For SysVinit, the `service` *service_name* `status` command is used.

    b. For systemd, the `systemctl status` *service_name* command is used.

8. To show the status of the `cups` daemon on your Linux server, use the following:

    a. For the SysVinit:

```
# service cups status
cupsd (pid 8236) is running...
```

    b. For systemd:

```
# systemctl status cups.service
cups.service — CUPS Printing Service
Loaded: loaded (/lib/systemd/system/cups.service; enabled)
Active: active (running) since Tue, 05 May 2020 04:43:5...
Main PID: 17003 (cupsd)
CGroup: name=systemd:/system/cups.service
17003 /usr/sbin/cupsd -f
```

9. To attempt to restart the `cups` daemon on your Linux server, use the following:

    a. For SysVinit:

```
# service cups restart
Stopping cups:              [  OK  ]
```

    b. For systemd:

```
# systemctl restart cups.service
```

10. To attempt to reload the `cups` daemon on your Linux server, use the following:

   a. For SysVinit:

   ```
   # service cups reload
   Reloading cups: [ OK ]
   ```

   b. For `systemd`, this is a trick question. You cannot reload the `cups` daemon on a `systemd` Linux server!

   ```
   # systemctl reload cups.service
   Failed to issue method call: Job type reload is
      not applicable for unit cups.service.
   ```

Chapter 16: Configuring a Print Server

For questions that involve working with printers, you can use either graphical or command-line tools in most cases. The point is to make sure that you get the correct results, shown in the answers that follow. The answers here include a mix of graphical and command-line ways of solving the exercises. (Use `sudo` when you see a # prompt.)

1. To use the Printers window to add a new printer called `myprinter` to your system (generic PostScript printer, connected to a port), do the following from Ubuntu:

   a. If necessary, install the `system-config-printer` package:

   ```
   # apt install system-config-printer
   ```

   b. From the GNOME 3 desktop, select Printers from the GNOME Settings dialog.

   c. Select the Add button.

   d. Select a USB or other port as the device and click Forward.

   e. For the driver, choose Generic and click Forward; then choose PostScript and click Forward.

   f. Click Forward to skip any installable options, if needed.

   g. For the printer name, call it `myprinter`, give it any description and location you like, and click Apply.

   h. Click Cancel in order not to print a test page. The printer should appear in the Print Settings window.

2. To use the `lpstat -t` command to see the status of all of your printers, enter the following:

   ```
   # lpstat -t

   deskjet-5550 accepting requests since Mon 02 Mar 2020
   07:30:03 PM EST
   ```

3. To use the `lp` command to print the /etc/hosts file, enter the following:

   ```
   $ lp /etc/hosts -d myprinter
   ```

4. To check the print queue for that printer, enter the following:

   ```
   # lpstgat -a myprinter
   myprinter is not ready
   Rank    Owner    Job    File(s)        Total Size
   1st     root     655    hosts          1024 bytes
   ```

5. To remove the print job from the queue (cancel it), enter the following:

   ```
   # cancel myprinter
   ```

6. To use the Printers window to set the basic server setting that publishes your printers so that other systems on your local network can print to your printers, do the following:

   a. From the GNOME 3 desktop, select Printers from the GNOME Settings dialog.

   b. Select Server ⇨ Settings and type the root password if prompted.

   c. Click the check box next to "Publish shared printers connected to this system" and click OK.

7. To allow remote administration of your system from a web browser, follow these steps:

   a. From the GNOME 3 desktop, select Printers from the GNOME Settings dialog.

   b. Select Server ⇨ Settings and type the root password if prompted.

   c. Click the check box next to "Allow remote administration" and click OK.

8. To demonstrate that you can do remote administration of your system from a web browser on another system, do the following:

   a. In the location box from a browser window from another computer on your network, enter the following, replacing **hostname** with the name or IP address of the system running your print service: http://hostname:631.

   b. Type **root** as the user and the root password, when prompted. The CUPS home page should appear from that system.

9. To use the `netstat` command to see on which addresses the `cupsd` daemon is listening, enter the following:

   ```
   # netstat -tupln | grep 631
       tcp    0    0 0.0.0.0:631        0.0.0.0:*        LISTEN
   6492/cupsd
       tcp6   0    0 :::631             :::*             LISTEN
   6492/cupsd
   ```

10. To delete the `myprinter` printer entry from your system, do the following:

    a. Click the Unlock button and type the root password when prompted.

b. From the Print Settings window, right-click the `myprinter` icon and select Delete.

c. When prompted, select Delete again.

Chapter 17: Configuring a Web Server

1. To install all of the packages associated with the Apache web server, do the following:

```
# apt install apache2
```

2. To create a file called `index.html` in the directory assigned to `DocumentRoot` in the main Apache configuration file (with the words "My Own Web Server" inside), do the following:

a. Determine the location of `DocumentRoot`:

```
$ cd /etc/apache2
$ grep -nr "DocumentRoot"
DocumentRoot "/var/www/html"
```

b. Echo the words "My Own Web Server" into the `index.html` file located in `DocumentRoot`:

```
# echo "My Own Web Server" > /var/www/html/index.html
```

3. To start the Apache web server and set it to start up automatically at boot time, run these two commands:

```
# systemctl start apache2.service
# systemctl enable apache2.service
```

4. To use the `netstat` command to see on which ports the `httpd` server is listening, enter the following:

```
# netstat -tupln | grep httpd
tcp6    0   0 :::80       :::*    LISTEN    2496/httpd
tcp6    0   0 :::443      :::*    LISTEN    2496/httpd
```

5. Try to connect to your Apache web server from a web browser that is outside of the local system. If it fails, correct any problems that you encounter by investigating the firewall, AppArmor, and other security features.

If you don't have DNS set up yet, use the IP address of the server to view your Apache server from a remote web browser, such as http://192.168.0.1. If you are not able to connect, retry connecting to the server from your browser after performing each of the following steps on the system running the Apache server:

```
# iptables -F
# chmod 644 /var/www/html/index.html
```

The `iptables -F` command flushes the firewall rules temporarily. If connecting to the web server succeeds after that, you need to add new firewall rules to open `tcp` ports 80 and 443 on the server. For systems running the `iptables` service, add the following rules before the last `DROP` or `REJECT` rule:

```
-A INPUT -m state --state NEW -m tcp -p tcp --dport 80 -j ACCEPT
-A INPUT -m state --state NEW -m tcp -p tcp --dport 443 -j ACCEPT
```

If the `chmod` command works, it means that the `www-data` user and group did not have read permission to the file. You should be able to leave the new permissions as they are.

6. To use the `openssl` or similar command to create your own private RSA key and self-signed SSL certificate, see instructions in the chapter. If you've already created keys, try creating a new set with a new name.

7. To configure your Apache web server to use your key and self-signed certificate to serve secure (HTTPS) content, do the following:

   a. Edit the `/etc/apache2/sites-available/default-ssl.conf` file to change the key and certificate locations to use the ones that you just created:

   ```
   SSLCertificateFile      /etc/ssl/certs/server.crt
   SSLCertificateKeyFile /etc/ssl/private/server.key
   ```

   b. Restart the Apache service:

   ```
   # systemctl restart apache2
   ```

8. To use a web browser to create an HTTPS connection to your web server and view the contents of the certificate that you created, do the following.

   From the system running the Apache server, type **https://localhost** in the browser's location box. You should see a message that reads, "This Connection is Untrusted." To complete the connection, do the following:

   a. Click I Understand the Risks.

   b. Click Add Exception.

   c. Click Get Certificate.

   d. Click Confirm Security Exception.

9. To add the text `joe.example.org` to the end of the localhost entry in your `/etc/hosts` file on the machine that is running the web server and check it by typing **http://joe.example.org** into the location box of your web browser to see "Welcome to the House of Joe" when the page is displayed, do the following:

   a. Reload the `apache` file modified in the previous exercise in one of two ways:

   ```
   # apachectl graceful
   # systemctl restart httpd
   ```

b. Edit the /etc/hosts file with any text editor, so the local host line appears as follows:

```
127.0.0.1          localhost.localdomain localhost joe
.example.org
```

c. From a browser on the local system where apache is running, you should be able to type **http://joe.example.org** into the location box to access the Apache web server using name-based authentication.

Chapter 18: Configuring an FTP Server

> **CAUTION**
>
> Don't do the tasks described here on a working, public FTP server, because these tasks will interfere with its operations. (You could, however, use these tasks to set up a new FTP server.)

1. To determine which package provides the Very Secure FTP Daemon service, enter the following as root:

```
$ apt search "Very Secure FTP"
Sorting... Done
Full Text Search... Done
vsftpd/bionic 3.0.3-9build1 amd64
    lightweight, efficient FTP server written for security
```

The search found the vsftpd package.

2. To install the Very Secure FTP Daemon package on your system and search for the configuration files in the vsftpd package, enter the following:

```
# apt install vsftpd
# cat /var/lib/dpkg/info/vsftpd.conffiles
```

3. To enable anonymous FTP and disable local user login for the Very Secure FTP Daemon service, set the following in the /etc/vsftpd.conf file:

```
anonymous_enable=YES
        write_enable=YES
        anon_upload_enable=YES
        local_enable=NO
```

4. To start the Very Secure FTP Daemon service and set it to start when the system boots, enter the following on a current Ubuntu Linux system:

```
# systemctl start vsftpd.service
# systemctl enable vsftpd.service
```

5. On the system running your FTP server, enter the following to create a file named test in the anonymous FTP directory that contains the words "Welcome to your vsftpd server":

```
# echo "Welcome to your vsftpd server" > /svr/ftp/test
```

6. To open the `test` file from the anonymous FTP home directory using a web browser on the system running your FTP server, do the following.

   Open a web browser, enter the following in the location box, and press Enter:

   ```
   ftp://localhost/test
   ```

   The text "Welcome to your vsftpd server" should appear in the browser window.

7. To access the `test` file in the anonymous FTP home directory, enter the following into the location box of a browser on a system on your network that can reach the FTP server (replace *host* with your system's fully qualified hostname or IP address):

   ```
   ftp://host/test
   ```

8. To configure your `vsftpd` server to allow file uploads by anonymous users to a directory named `in`, do the following as root on your FTP server:

   a. Create the `in` directory as follows:

   ```
   # mkdir /svr/ftp/in
   # chown ftp:ftp /svr/ftp/in
   # chmod 777 /svr/ftp/in
   ```

   b. Restart the `vsftpd` service (`systemctl restart vsftpd`).

9. Install the `lftp` FTP client (if you don't have a second Linux system, install `lftp` on the same host running the FTP server). Optionally, try to upload the `/etc/hosts` file to the `in` directory on the server, to make sure it is accessible. Run the following commands as the root user:

   ```
   # apt install lftp
   # lftp localhost
   lftp localhost:/> cd in
   lftp localhost:/in> put /etc/hosts
   89 bytes transferred
   lftp localhost:/in> quit
   ```

   You won't be able to see that you copied the `hosts` file to the incoming directory. However, enter the following from a shell on the host running the FTP server to make sure that the `hosts` file is there:

   ```
   # ls /svr/ftp/in/hosts
   ```

   If you cannot upload the file, troubleshoot the problem as described in Exercise 7, recheck your `vsftpd.conf` settings, and review the ownership and permissions on the `/svr/ftp/in` directory.

10. Using any FTP client you choose, visit the `/pub/debian-meetings` directory on the `ftp://ftp.gnome.org` site and list the contents of that directory. Here's how to do that with the `lftp` client:

    ```
    # lftp ftp://ftp.gnome.org/pub/debian-meetings/
    cd ok, cwd=/pub/debian-meetings
    lftp ftp.gnome.org:/pub/debian-meetings>> ls
    ```

Continues

(continued)

```
drwxr-xr-x    3 ftp        ftp               3 Jan 13  2014 2004
drwxr-xr-x    6 ftp        ftp               6 Jan 13  2014 2005
drwxr-xr-x    8 ftp        ftp               8 Dec 20  2006 2006
...
```

Chapter 19: Configuring a Windows File Sharing (Samba) Server

1. To install the `samba` and `samba-client` packages, enter the following as root from a shell on the local system:

   ```
   # apt install samba smbclient
   ```

2. To start and enable the `smb` and `nmb` services, enter the following as root from a shell on the local system:

   ```
   # systemctl enable smbd
   # systemctl start smbd
   # systemctl enable nmbd
   # systemctl start nmbd
   ```

3. To set the Samba server's workgroup to `TESTGROUP` and the server string to `Samba Test System`, as root user in a text editor, open the /etc/samba/smb.conf file and change two lines so that they appear as follows:

   ```
   workgroup = TESTGROUP
   server string = Samba Test System
   ```

4. To add a Linux user named `phil` to your system and add a Linux password and Samba password for `phil`, enter the following as root user from a shell. (Be sure to remember the passwords you set.)

   ```
   # adduser phil
   [...]
   New password: *******
   Retype new password: *******
   # smbpasswd -a phil
   New SMB password: *******
   Retype new SMB password: *******
   Added user phil.
   ```

5. To set the [homes] section so that home directories are browseable (yes) and writeable (yes), and that `phil` is the only valid user, open the /etc/samba/smb. conf file as root and change the [homes] section so that it appears as follows:

   ```
   [homes]
           comment = Home Directories
   ```

```
browseable = Yes
read only = No
valid users = phil
```

6. From the local system, use the smbclient command to list that the homes share is available:

```
# smbclient -L localhost
Enter TESTGROUP\root's password: <ENTER>
Anonymous login successful

    Sharename      Type      Comment
    ---------      ----      -------
    homes          Disk      Home Directories
...
```

7. To connect to the homes share from a Nautilus (file manager) window on the Samba server's local system for the user phil in a way that allows you to drag and drop files to that folder, do the following:

   a. Open the Nautilus window (select the files icon).

   b. In the left pane, select Other Locations and then click in the Connect to Server box.

   c. Type the Server address. For example, smb://localhost/phil/.

   d. When prompted, select Registered User, type phil as the username, enter the domain (TESTGROUP), and enter phil's password.

   e. Open another Nautilus window and drop a file to phil's home folder.

Chapter 20: Configuring an NFS File Server

1. To install the packages needed to configure the NFS service on the Linux system you choose, enter the following using sudo:

```
# apt install nfs-kernel-server
```

2. To display the resources required by the system and to successfully run an NFS server, run:

```
$ cat /etc/systemd/system/multi-user.target.wants/
nfs-server.service
[Unit]
Description=NFS server and services
DefaultDependencies=no
Requires=network.target proc-fs-nfsd.mount
Requires=nfs-mountd.service
Wants=rpcbind.socket
Wants=nfs-idmapd.service
[...]
```

3. To start and enable the NFS service, enter the following as root user on the NFS server:

```
# systemctl start nfs-server
# systemctl enable nfs-server
```

4. To check the status of the NFS service that you just started on the NFS server, enter the following as root user:

```
# systemctl status nfs-server
```

5. To share a directory /var/mystuff from your NFS server as available to everyone, read-only, and with the root user on the client having root access to the share, first create the mount directory as follows:

```
# mkdir /var/mystuff
```

Then create an entry in the /etc/exports file that is similar to the following:

```
/var/mystuff   *(ro,no_root_squash,insecure)
```

To make the share available, enter the following:

```
# exportfs -v -a
exporting *:/var/mystuff
```

6. To view the shares available from the NFS server, assuming that the NFS server is named nfsserver, enter the following from the NFS client:

```
# showmount -e nfsserver
Export list for nfsserver:
/var/mystuff   *
```

7. To create a directory called /var/remote and temporarily mount the /var/mystuff directory from the NFS server (named nfsserver in this example) on that mount point, enter the following as root user from the NFS client:

```
# mkdir /var/remote
# mount -t nfs nfsserver:/var/mystuff /var/remote
```

8. To add an entry so that the same mount is done automatically when you reboot, first unmount /var/remote as follows:

```
# umount /var/remote
```

Then add an entry like the following to the /etc/fstab on the client system:

```
/var/remote   nfsserver:/var/mystuff   nfs bg,ro 0 0
```

To test that the share is configured properly, enter the following on the NFS client as the root user:

```
# mount -a
# mount -t nfs4
nfsserver:/var/mystuff on /var/remote type nfs4
 (ro,vers=4,rsize=524288...
```

9. To copy some files to the /var/mystuff directory, enter the following on the
   NFS server:

   ```
   # cp /etc/hosts /etc/services /var/mystuff
   ```

   From the NFS client, to make sure that you can see the files just added to that
   directory and to make sure that you can't write files to that directory from the
   client, enter the following:

   ```
   # ls /var/remote
   hosts     services
   # touch /var/remote/file1
   touch: cannot touch '/var/remote/file1': Read-only
   file system
   ```

Chapter 21: Troubleshooting Linux

1. To go into Setup mode from the BIOS screen on your computer, do the following:

   a. Reboot your computer.

   b. Within a few seconds, you should see the BIOS screen, with an indication of
      which function key to press to go into Setup mode.

   c. The BIOS screen should appear. (If the system starts booting Linux, you didn't
      press the function key fast enough.)

2. From the BIOS Setup screen, do the following to determine whether your computer
   is 32-bit or 64-bit, whether it includes virtualization support, and whether your
   network interface card is capable of PXE booting.

   Your experience may be a bit different from mine, depending on your computer and
   Linux system. The BIOS Setup screen is different for different computers. In general, however, you can use arrow keys and tab keys to move between different columns and press Enter to select an entry. Here's how that might work:

   a. Under the System heading, highlight Processor Info to see whether you're using
      a 64-bit Technology. Look in the Processor Info section, or similar section on
      your computer, to see the type of processor that you have.

   b. Under the Onboard Devices heading, highlight Integrated NIC and press Enter.
      The Integrated NIC screen that appears to the right lets you choose to enable or
      disable the NIC (On or Off) or enable with PXE or RPL (if you intend to boot the
      computer over the network).

3. To interrupt the boot process to get to the GRUB boot loader, do the following:

   a. Reboot the computer.

   b. Just after the BIOS screen disappears, when you see the countdown to booting
      the Linux system, press a key (usually the Shift key).

   c. The GRUB boot loader menu should appear, ready to allow you to select which
      operating system kernel to boot.

4. To boot up your computer to runlevel 1 so that you can do some system mainte-nance, get to the GRUB boot screen (as described in the previous exercise) and then do the following:

   a. Use the arrow keys to highlight the operating system and kernel that you want to boot.

   b. Type **e** to see the entries needed to boot the operating system.

   c. Move your cursor to the line that included the kernel. (It should include the word vmlinuz somewhere on the line.)

   d. Move the cursor to the end of that line, add a space, and then type **init=bash**.

   e. Follow the instructions to boot the new entry. You will probably either press Ctrl+X or press Enter; if there is another screen, type **b**.

   If it worked, your system should bypass the login prompt and boot up directly to a root user shell where you can do administrative tasks without providing a password.

5. To look at the messages that were produced in the kernel ring buffer (which shows the activity of the kernel as it booted up), enter the following from the shell after the system finishes booting:

   ```
   $ dmesg | less
   ```

   Or, on a system using systemd, enter the following:

   ```
   $ journalctl -k
   ```

6. To install all available package patches using a single operation, run:

   ```
   # apt update && apt upgrade
   ```

7. To check to see what processes are listening for incoming connections on your system, enter the following:

   ```
   # netstat -tupln | less
   ```

8. To check to see what ports are open on your external network interface, do the following.

   If possible, run the nmap command from another Linux system on your network, replacing *yourhost* with the hostname or IP address of your system:

   ```
   # nmap yourhost
   ```

9. To clear your system's page cache and watch the effect it has on your memory usage, do the following:

   a. Select Terminal from an application menu on your desktop (it is located on dif-ferent menus for different systems).

   b. Run the top command (to watch processes currently running on your system), and then type a capital **M** to sort processes by those consuming the most memory.

   c. From the Terminal window, select File and Open Terminal to open a second Terminal window.

   d. From the second Terminal window, become root user (su -).

   e. While watching the Mem line (used column) in the first Terminal window, enter the following from the second Terminal window:

```
# echo 3 > /proc/sys/vm/drop_caches
```

   f. The used RES memory should go down significantly on the Mem line. The numbers in the RES column for each process should go down as well.

10. To view memory and swap usage from Cockpit through your web browser, open your browser to Cockpit for your host (https://hostname:9090). Then select System ⇨ Memory & Swap.

Chapter 22: Understanding Basic Linux Security

1. To check log messages from the systemd journal for the NetworkManager.service, sshd.service, and auditd.service services, enter the following:

```
# journalctl -u NetworkManager.service
...
# journalctl -u sshd.service
...
# journalctl -u auditd.service
...
```

2. User passwords are stored in the /etc/shadow file. To see its permissions, type **ls -l /etc/shadow** at the command line. (If no shadow file exits, then you need to run pwconv.)

The following are the appropriate settings:

```
# ls -l /etc/shadow
-rw-r----- 1 root shadow 1416 Apr  7 10:40 /etc/shadow
```

3. To determine your account's password aging and whether it will expire using a single command, type **chage -l user_name**. For example:

```
# chage -l chris
```

4. To start auditing writes to the /etc/shadow file with the auditd daemon, enter the following at the command line:

```
# auditctl -w /etc/shadow -p w
```

To check your audit settings, type in **auditctl -l** at the command line.

5. To create a report from the auditd daemon on the /etc/shadow file, enter **ausearch -f /etc/shadow** at the command line. To turn off the auditing on that file, enter **auditctl -W /etc/shadow -p w** at the command line.

6. To install the lemon package, damage the /usr/bin/lemon file, verify that the file has been tampered with, and remove the lemon package, enter the following:

```
# apt install lemon
# cp /etc/services /usr/bin/lemon
# dpkg -V lemon
??5??????   /usr/bin/lemon
# apt remove lemon
```

From the original lemon file, the file size, the md4sum, and the modification times (T) all differ.

7. If you suspect that you have had a malicious attack on your system today and important binary files have been modified, you can find these modified files by entering the following at the command line: **find directory -mtime -1** for the directories, /bin, /sbin, /usr/bin, and /usr/sbin.

8. To install and run chkrootkit to see if the malicious attack from the exercise 7 installed a rootkit, choose your distribution and do the following:

   a. To install the package, enter **apt install chkrootkit** at the command line.

   b. To run the check, enter **chkrootkit** at the command line and review the results.

9. To find files anywhere in the system with the SUID or SGID permission set, enter **find / -perm /6000 -ls** at the command line.

10. To install the aide package, run the aide command to initialize the aide database, copy the database to the correct location, and run the aide command to check whether any important files on your system have been modified, enter the following:

```
# apt install aide
# aide.wrapper -i
# cp /var/lib/aide/aide.db.new /var/lib/aide/aide.db
# aide.wrapper -C
```

To make the output more interesting, you could install the lemon package (described in an earlier exercise) before you run aide.wrapper -i and modify it before running aide.wrapper -C to see how a modified binary looks from aide.

Chapter 23: Understanding Advanced Linux Security

To do the first few exercises, you must have the gnupg package installed.

1. To encrypt a file using the gpg utility and a passphrase key, enter the following command:

```
$ gpg --batch --output backup.tar.gz.gpg \
    --passphrase mypassword --symmetric backup.tar.gz
```

2. To generate a key pair using the `gpg` utility, enter the following:

   ```
   $ gpg --gen-key
   ```

   You must provide the following information:

   a. Your real name and email address

   b. A passphrase for the private key

3. To list out the keys you generated, enter the following:

   ```
   $ gpg --list-keys
   ```

4. To encrypt a file and add your digital signature using the `gpg` utility, do the following:

   a. You must have first generated a key ring (Exercise 2).

   b. After you have generated the key ring, enter:

   ```
   $ gpg --output EncryptedSignedFile --sign FiletoEncryptSign
   ```

5. From the `ubuntu.com` downloads page, select one of the versions to download. When the download is complete, go to the `help.ubuntu.com/community/UbuntuHashes` page to retrieve the appropriate hash for the image you just downloaded. Then run the following:

   ```
   $ sha256sum ubuntu-20-04-focal-live-server-amd64.iso
   ```

6. To determine if the `su` command on your Linux system is PAM-aware, enter the following:

   ```
   $ ldd $(which su) | grep pam
   libpam.so.0 => /lib64/libpam.so.0 (0x00007fca14370000)
   libpam_misc.so.0 => /lib64/libpam_misc.so.0 (0x00007fca1416c000
   ```

   If the `su` command on your Linux system is PAM-aware, you should see a PAM library name listed when you issue the `ldd` command.

7. To determine if the `su` command has a PAM configuration file, type the following:

   ```
   $ ls /etc/pam.d/su
   /etc/pam.d/su
   ```

   If the file exists, type the following at the command line to display its contents. The PAM context it uses is any of the following: `auth`, `account`, `password`, or `session`.

   ```
   $ cat /etc/pam.d/su
   ```

8. To list out the various PAM modules on your system, run the following:

   ```
   $ ls /lib/x86_64-linux-gnu/security/
   ```

9. To find the PAM "other" configuration file on your system, enter `ls /etc/pam.d/other` at the command line. An "other" configuration file that enforces Implicit Deny should look similar to the following code:

```
$ cat /etc/pam.d/other
#%PAM-1.0
auth      required      pam_deny.so
account   required      pam_deny.so
password  required      pam_deny.so
session   required      pam_deny.so
```

10. To find the PAM limits configuration file, enter the following:

```
$ ls /etc/security/limits.conf
```

Display the file's contents by entering the following:

```
$ cat /etc/security/limits.conf
```

Settings in this file to prevent a fork bomb look like the following:

```
@student      hard      nproc        50
@student      -         maxlogins     4
```

Chapter 24: Enhancing Linux Security with AppArmor

1. You can move all AppArmor profiles to "complain" mode using:

```
aa-complain /etc/apparmor.d/*
```

2. You can move all AppArmor profiles to "enforce" mode using:

```
aa-enforce /etc/apparmor.d/*
```

3. You can list your current profile settings using:

```
apparmor_status
```

4. You can display all recent kernel events involving AppArmor using:

```
dmesg | grep apparmor
```

5. Using your knowledge of the various classes of files within the /etc/apparmor.d/ directory, you should be able to dig deeply enough to learn that the /etc/apparmor.d/tunables/home file can contain virtual home values for use by profiles (much like the proc file in the same directory set the value for procfs).

6. The `aa-logprof` program will scan all of your profiles and both suggest and execute changes.

Chapter 25: Securing Linux on a Network

1. To install the Network Mapper (aka nmap) utility on your local Linux system (assuming it's not installed by default) run sudo apt install nmap at the command line.

2. To run a TCP Connect scan on your local loopback address, enter **nmap -sT 127.0.0.1** at the command line. The ports you have running on your Linux server will vary. However, they may look similar to the following:

```
# nmap -sT 127.0.0.1
      . . .
      PORT     STATE SERVICE
      25/tcp  open  smtp
      631/tcp open  ipp
```

3. To run a UDP Connect scan on your Linux system from a remote system:

   a. Determine your Linux server's IP address by entering **ip addr** at the command line. The output will look similar to the following, and your system's IP address follows inet addr: in the ifconfig command's output.

   ```
   $ ip addr
         . . .
         inet 192.168.1.11/24 brd 192.168.1.255 scope global
   dynamic enp0s3
   ```

   b. From a remote Linux system, enter the command **nmap -sU IP address** at the command line, using the *IP address* you obtained in step a. For example:

   ```
   # nmap -sU 10.140.67.23
   ```

4. To check to see if your system is running the UFW service run:

   ```
   systemctl status ufw
   ```

5. To open ports in your firewall to allow remote access to your local web service, run the following:

   ```
   sudo ufw allow 443
   sudo ufw allow 80
   sudo ufw enable
   ```

6. To determine your Linux system's current netfilter/iptables firewall policies and rules, enter **iptables -vnL** at the command line.

7. To save, flush, and restore your Linux system's current firewall rules:

   a. To save your current rules:

   ```
   # iptables-save >/tmp/myiptables
   ```

    b. To flush your current rules:

```
# iptables -F
```

    c. To restore the firewall's rules, enter:

```
# iptables-restore < /tmp/myiptables
```

8. To set your Linux firewall's filter table for the input chain to a policy of DROP, enter **iptables -P INPUT DROP** at the command line.

9. To change your Linux firewall's filter table policy back to accept for the input chain, enter the following:

```
# iptables -P INPUT ACCEPT
```

To add a rule to drop all network packets from the IP address 10.140.67.23, enter the following:

```
# iptables -A INPUT -s 10.140.67.23 -j DROP
```

10. To remove the rule that you just added, without flushing or restoring your Linux firewall's rules, enter iptables -D INPUT 1 at the command line. This is assuming that the rule you added is rule 1. If not, change the 1 to the appropriate rule number in your iptables command.

Chapter 26: Shifting to Clouds and Containers

1. You install LXD using sudo apt install lxd and then initialize it with lxd init.

2. You can build an Ubuntu 18.04 image on, say, an Ubuntu 20.04 host, using:

```
# apt launch ubuntu:18.04 ubuntu-18
```

3. You can open an interactive shell within a running LXD container using:

```
# lxc exec ubuntu-18 /bin/bash
```

4. You can retrieve LXD container IP addresses using sudo lxc list.

5. You install Docker community edition using:

```
# apt install docker.io
```

6. A Dockerfile running the latest Alpine Linux and containing a file in the /var/ directory would require only two lines:

```
FROM etopian/alpine-php-wordpress
ADD stats.csv /var/stats.csv
```

7. Build the Alpine image and launch it using run. With the container running, you can find its name using docker ps and use that to execute an ls command inside the container to look for your stats.csv file.

```
$ docker build -t alpine-stuff .
Sending build context to Docker daemon   22.53kB
```

```
Step 1/2 : FROM etopian/alpine-php-wordpress
 ---> c02c59f90188
Step 2/2 : ADD stats.csv /var/stats.csv
 ---> c1f0c25818b9
Successfully built c1f0c25818b9
Successfully tagged alpine-stuff:latest
$
$ docker run -d alpine-stuff
dfc5d3e91866bf7d4e6b844155706180c19e970b89b2f102bd2d878a95f2db4c
$
$ docker ps
CONTAINER ID   IMAGE         COMMAND     CREATED       STATUS
PORTS   NAMES
77215eb0eaaf   alpine-stuff  "/run.sh"   4 seconds ago Up 3 seconds
80/tcp mystifying_joliot
$
$ docker exec mystifying_joliot ls /var
cache
empty
git
lib
local
lock
log
mail
opt
run
spool
stats.csv
tmp
www
```

Chapter 27: Deploying Linux to the Public Cloud

1. You can create a copy of an existing LXD profile using:

   ```
   # lxc profile copy default newprofile
   ```

2. You'll want to export the existing profile text to a YAML file using `profile show`:

   ```
   # lxc profile show newprofile > newprofile.yaml
   ```

   Edit the document, being careful to use appropriate indentation:

   ```
   $ nano newprofile.yaml
   ```

   Add:

   ```
   user.user-data: |
     #cloud-config
     package_upgrade: true
   ```

```
packages:
   - apache2
```

Import the new text back into the profile:

```
# lxc profile edit newprofile < newprofile.yaml
```

3. Launch your instance this way:

```
# lxc launch --profile newprofile ubuntu:20.04 newcontainer
```

4. You can export your image by first listing your images to retrieve your image ID and then applying the `image export` command.

```
# lxc image list
# lxc image export <image ID> newimage
```

5. You can follow the GUI wizard through the image, instance type, storage, tags, and security group steps. Make sure you've got a valid SSH key pair that will let you log on to an SSH session once the instance is running.

Chapter 28: Automating Apps and Infrastructure with Ansible

1. To install the ansible package, do the following:

```
$ sudo apt install ansible
```

2. To add `sudo` privileges for the user running Ansible commands, run `visudo` and create an entry similar to the following (changing joe to your username):

```
joe    ALL=(ALL)        NOPASSWD: ALL
```

3. Open a file named `my_playbook.yaml`, and add the following content:

```
---
- name: Create web server
hosts: localhost
tasks:
- name: Install Apache
  apt:
    name: apache
    state: present
```

4. To run the `my_playbook.yaml` playbook in check mode, do the following. (It should fail because the user does not have privilege to install a package.)

```
$ ansible-playbook -C my_playbook.yaml
...

TASK [Install httpd] ***********************************
***********************
```

```
fatal: [localhost]: FAILED! => {"changed": false, "msg": "This
command has to be run under the root user.", "results": []}
...
```

5. Make the following changes to the `my_playbook.yaml` file:

```
---
- name: Create web server
hosts: localhost
become: yes
become_method: sudo
become_user: root
tasks:
- name: Install Apache
  apt:
    name: apache2
    state: present
```

6. To run the `my_playbook.yaml` file again to install the `Apache` package, enter the following:

```
$ ansible-playbook my_playbook.yaml
...
TASK [Install Apache] *****************************************
changed: [localhost]
PLAY RECAP ***************************************************
localhost: ok=2 changed=1 unreachable=0 failed=0 skipped=0
rescued=0 ignored=0
```

7. Modify `my_playbook.yaml` as follows to start the `apache2` service and set it so that it will start every time the system boots:

```
---
- name: Create web server
hosts: localhost
become: yes
become_method: sudo
become_user: root
tasks:
- name: Install Apache
  apt:
    name: apache2
    state: present
- name: start Apache
  service:
    name: apache2
    state: started
```

8. To run an `ansible` command so that it checks whether or not the `apache2` service is up on `localhost`, enter the following:

```
$ ansible localhost -m service \
      -a "name=apache2 state=started" --check
localhost | SUCCESS => {
      "changed": false,
      "name": "apache2",
      "state": "started",
      "status": { ...
```

9. To create an `index.html` file in the current directory that contains the text "Web server is up" and runs the `ansible` command to copy that file to the `/var/www/html` directory on `localhost`, do the following (changing joe to your username):

```
$ echo "Web server is up" > index.html
$ ansible localhost
 -m copy -a \
    "src=./index.html dest=/var/www/html/ \
    owner=www-data group=www-data mode=0644" \
    -b --user joe --become-user root --become-method sudo
host01 | CHANGED => { ...
```

10. To use the `curl` command to view the contents of the file you just copied to the web server, do the following:

```
$ curl localhost
Web server is up
```

Chapter 29: Deploying Applications as Containers with Kubernetes

1. To install MicroK8s on an Ubuntu system, run:

```
# snap install microk8s --classic
```

2. To create an alias for `microk8s.kubectl`, run this:

```
# snap alias microk8s.kubectl kubectl
```

3. To create a deployment that manages a pod running the `hello-node` container image, enter the following:

```
$ kubectl create deployment hello-node \
    --image=gcr.io/hello-minikube-zero-install/hello-node
```

4. To view the `hello-node` deployment and describe the deployment in detail, enter the following:

```
$ kubectl get deployment
$ kubectl describe deployment hello-node
```

5. To view the current replica set associated with your `hello-node` deployment, enter the following:

```
$ kubectl get rs
```

6. To scale up the `hello-node` deployment to three (3) replicas, enter the following:

   ```
   $ kubectl scale deployments/hello-node --replicas=3
   ```

7. To expose the `hello-node` deployment outside of the Kubernetes cluster using LoadBalancer, enter the following:

   ```
   $ kubectl expose deployment hello-node \
       --type=LoadBalancer --port=8080
   ```

8. To get the port number of the exposed `hello-node` service, enter the following:

   ```
   $ kubectl describe service hello-node | grep NodePort
   NodePort:                    <unset>   31302/TCP
   ```

9. Use the `curl` command to query the `hello-node` service, using the IP address and port number from the previous step. For example:

   ```
   $ curl 192.168.1.18:31302
   Hello World!
   ```

10. To delete the `hello-node` service and deployment, enter the following:

   ```
   $ kubectl delete service hello-node
   $ kubectl delete deployment hello-node
   ```

Index

O

Index

P

packet forwarding, Linux as router, 322
PAM (Pluggable Authentication Module), 274
    contexts, 543
    control flags, 544–545
    module interfaces, 543
    modules, 545, 551
    official web siste, 552
    PAM-aware applications, 542, 546–547
    password enforcement, 550–551
    resource limits, 547–549
    sudo, 551
    system event configuration, 545–546
    time restrictions, 549–550
    types, 543
Panels, 38, 40–41
partitions, 239
    GUID (Globally Unique Identifier) partition tables, 240
    installation and, 183
    LVM (Logical Volume Manager), 238
        creating logical volumes, 252–254
        existing, 249–252
        growing volumes, 254
    multiple-partition disks, 245–249
    partition tables, MBR (master boot record), 239–240
    single-partition disks, 241–245
    viewing partitions, 240–241
    Windows, resizing, 190
passwordless (key-based) authentication, 285
passwords
    best practices enforcement, 502–504
    changing, 501–502
    hashed passwords, 504
    PAM (Pluggable Authentication Modules), 550–551
    rainbow tables, 504–505
    selecting, 500–501
    server, 274
    setting, 501–502
paths, absolute path, 81
PE (Physical Extent), 250
permissions, 90
    Apache, 389–390
    changing, chmod, 91–92
    default, 93
    execute, 90
    group accounts, 225–226
    nine-bit, 90
    read, 90

    setting, 90
    umask and, 93
    write, 90
persistence services, SysVinit, configuring, 350–353
physical security, 495–496
    disaster recovery, 496
    filesystem, 506–509
    passwords, 500–506
    services, 509–510
    software, 509–510
    user accounts, 496–500
PID (process ID), 117, 328
pipe (|) character, 61, 62
plain text, 525
plain-text login prompt, 46
port numbers, 273
port scans, 563
portability, 8–9
positional parameters, 136
POSIX (Portable Operating System Interface), 10
PostgreSQL, 271
postgresql package, 271
postgresql-server package, 271
print server, 271
    configuring
        shared CUPS printer, 380–381
        shared Samba printer, 381–383
    exercise answers, 678–680
Print Settings window, 368–369
    local printers, 369–372
    remote printers, 372–375
printing
    commands
        cancel, 379
        lp, 378–379
        lpstat -t, 379
    CUPS, 363
        configuring, 364–365
        drivers, 364
        implicit classes, 364
        IPP, 364
        printer browsing, 364
        printer classes, 364
        printing to Windows, 365
        UNIX print commands, 364
    printer setup
        adding automatically, 365–366
        Print Settings window, 368–375
        web-based CUPS admin, 366–368
    to Windows, 365
privileges, 158–161